Nonprofit Management

ALL-IN-ONE

Dr. Beverly A. Browning, MPA, DBA; Sharon Farris; Maire Loughran; Alyson Connolly, BFA, MFA; Shiv Singh; and Stephanie Diamond

for dummies®
A Wiley Brand

Nonprofit Management All-in-One For Dummies®

Published by: **John Wiley & Sons, Inc.**, 111 River Street, Hoboken, NJ 07030-5774, www.wiley.com

Published simultaneously in Canada

For general information on our other products and services, please contact our Customer Care Department within the U.S. at 877-762-2974, outside the U.S. at 317-572-3993, or fax 317-572-4002. For technical support, please visit https://hub.wiley.com/community/support/dummies.

Wiley publishes in a variety of print and electronic formats and by print-on-demand. Some material included with standard print versions of this book may not be included in e-books or in print-on-demand. If this book refers to media such as a CD or DVD that is not included in the version you purchased, you may download this material at http://booksupport.wiley.com. For more information about Wiley products, visit www.wiley.com.

Library of Congress Control Number: 2023933818

ISBN 978-1-394-17243-6 (pbk); ISBN 978-1-394-17244-3 (ebk); ISBN 978-1-394-17245-0 (ebk)

SKY10078833_070224

Contents at a Glance

Table of Contents

Introduction

It may sound corny, but we feel a certain sense of mission when it comes to nonprofits. We've started them, directed them, raised funds for them, consulted for them, volunteered for them, given money to them, and written about them. We've worked with nonprofits in one way or another for more years than we care to remember.

Why have we continued to work for nonprofit organizations? Yes, we care about others and want to see the world become a better place — our values are important to us. But, to be honest, that's not the only reason we've worked for nonprofit organizations for so many years. We believe the reason is that we can't think of anything more interesting or more challenging to do.

Starting a new program is exciting. Securing your first grant is thrilling. Working with the multifaceted personalities that come together on a board of directors is fascinating. Learning a new skill because no one else is there to do it (even bookkeeping!) is fun. Seeing the faces of satisfied clients, walking along a restored lakeshore, hearing the applause of audiences — all are gratifying.

That's why we do it.

About This Book

This book is a generous conglomeration of material from a number of *For Dummies* books, carefully selected to cover the gamut of nonprofit management — everything you need to know to start and manage a charitable organization, from applying for your tax exemption to raising money to pay for your programs to handling the accounting to feeling comfortable speaking publicly or posting on social media about the cause.

To make the content more accessible, we've divided it into six minibooks:

- **Book 1:** Bringing Your A-Game to Nonprofit Management
- **Book 2:** Fundraising for Your Good Cause

- **Book 3:** Applying for and Winning Grants
- **Book 4:** Being Smart about Nonprofit Bookkeeping and Accounting
- **Book 5:** Speaking on Behalf of Your Nonprofit
- **Book 6:** Spreading the Word through Social Media Marketing

We try to be honest about the difficulties you'll sometimes face. You probably won't be able to achieve everything you set out to accomplish, and you'll always wish you had more resources to do more things. Still, we can't imagine doing anything else. Maybe you'll feel the same way after you jump into the nonprofit world.

Note: When we refer to nonprofit organizations, unless we say otherwise, we're talking about organizations that have been recognized as 501(c)(3) nonprofits and are considered public charities by the IRS.

As you're reading, you may note that some web addresses break across two lines of text. If you're reading this book in print and want to visit one of these web pages, simply key in the web address exactly as it's noted in the text, pretending the line break doesn't exist. If you're reading this as an e-book, you've got it easy — just click (or tap) the web address to be taken directly to the web page.

Foolish Assumptions

When writing this book, we made some assumptions about who may be interested in reading it. Here are some of the readers we imagined:

- You have an idea that will help solve a problem in your community, and you believe that starting a nonprofit organization is the best way to put your idea into action.
- You serve on a board of directors and wonder what you're supposed to be doing.
- You may be anyone from a full-time staff member to a volunteer charged with fundraising tasks.
- You care about the mission you're raising funds to support and want to make a positive difference.
- You're seeking research and education on grant-writing sources and approaches.

- You direct or manage a midsize nonprofit and want to understand a little more about how to manage day-to-day operations and take care of your own books.
- You're interested in keeping the books of a nonprofit organization.
- You may be required to speak publicly about your nonprofit.
- You're using social media sites (such as Facebook or Twitter) to promote your nonprofit.
- You don't have time to waste; you need to get to work right away with ideas and tools that can help you succeed.

If any (or all!) of these describe you, we're confident this book will answer your questions and give you the information you're seeking.

Icons Used in This Book

We use the following icons throughout the book to flag particularly important or helpful information.

REMEMBER

The Remember icon emphasizes important information that you should be ready to put into practice.

TECHNICAL STUFF

You may not need this technical stuff today (and can skip over it), but — who knows? It may be invaluable tomorrow.

TIP

This icon is posted next to little hints and suggestions gleaned from our experience over the years. Put these ideas to good use to save yourself some time, energy, or money.

WARNING

Warnings are just what you think they may be. We alert you to information that can help you avoid problematic situations.

Beyond the Book

In addition to the material in the print or e-book you're reading right now, this product comes with some access-anywhere goodies on the web. Check out the free Cheat Sheet for fundraising resources for new nonprofits, e-grant tips, ways to make keeping the books a little easier, and a list of top tools for your social media marketing efforts. To get this Cheat Sheet, simply go to `www.dummies.com` and type **Nonprofit Management All-in-One For Dummies Cheat Sheet** in the Search box.

Where to Go from Here

One of many handy features about this book is that it's modular, which means you can start reading anywhere you like! If you're new to the nonprofit world, we suggest beginning with Book 1, where you find fundamental information to get you moving in the right direction. If you're familiar with nonprofits already but want to better understand the responsibilities and activities associated with fundraising, grant writing, or bookkeeping and accounting, you can find the answers you need in Books 2, 3, and 4, respectively. Book 5 provides valuable information on becoming a more effective public speaker — skills that can help you no matter what level your involvement is with a nonprofit organization. If you need help to publicize and market your programs via social media, we offer some suggestions in Book 6.

Whether you're new to the nonprofit world or a seasoned professional, we think you'll find helpful and valuable information in this book to get you started or continue your good work.

1

Bringing Your A-Game to Nonprofit Management

Contents at a Glance

IN THIS CHAPTER

» Defining the nonprofit sector

» Getting started with a nonprofit

» Encouraging volunteerism

» Identifying the key components of a strong mission statement

» Creating an effective mission statement with the help of your board

» Acquiring the resources your nonprofit needs

Chapter 1
Journeying into the World of Nonprofit Organizations

It's a typical day in your hometown. Your alarm wakes you from a restful sleep and you switch on your radio to hear the latest news from your local public radio station. You hear that a research institute's study reports that economic indicators are on the rise and that a health clinic across town is testing a new regimen for arthritis. Plato, your golden retriever/Labrador mix, adopted from the animal shelter when he was 5 months old, bounds onto your bed to let you know it's time for breakfast and a walk. Plato is followed by Cynthia, your 4-year-old daughter, who wants to help you walk Plato before she's dropped off at her preschool housed in the community center. You remember that you promised to bring canned goods to the food bank that's next-door to Cynthia's school. You haven't even had coffee yet, but already your morning is filled with news and services provided by nonprofit organizations.

You know that your public radio station is a nonprofit because you hear its pledge drives three or four times a year and you volunteer a few hours each month for the food bank, so clearly that's a nonprofit, too. But you may not know that the research institute is probably a nonprofit organization, just like the health clinic where the arthritis research is being tested and the animal shelter where you found Plato. Cynthia's preschool and the community center where the preschool rents its space are likely nonprofit organizations. Whether you realize it or not, all of us — rich, poor, or somewhere in between — benefit from the work of nonprofit organizations every day.

Nonprofits find revenue from a variety of sources in order to provide services. Because most nonprofits serve a need in the community, tax-deductible donations are an important revenue source. Sometimes nonprofits charge a fee for the service they provide or the work they do. Other nonprofits may sign contracts with your city or county to provide services to residents. Usually, nonprofit organizations scrounge up their income from a combination of all these revenue sources.

The nonprofit sector isn't a distinct place — it isn't some plaza or district that you come upon suddenly as you weave your way through the day. It's more like a thread of a common color that's laced throughout the economy and people's lives. No matter where people live or what they do, it's not easy to reach the end of a day without being affected by the work of a nonprofit organization.

Perhaps your lifelong goal is to find a way to help others in your community, your state, your country, or the world. (If this statement is true of you, thank you, kind citizen.) You think about your options every day, but you haven't the foggiest notion about the next steps to take to help you reach this admirable goal. You have so many topics to research and tasks to determine how to complete — and so much necessary funding to nail down to help you get started. Think of this chapter as the beginning of the journey. Here we help you understand exactly what a nonprofit organization is and how to start and manage one.

TIP

Check out File 1-1 at `https://www.wiley.com/en-us/Nonprofit+Kit+For+Dummies%2C+6th+Edition-p-9781119835745#downloads-section` for a list of web resources related to the topics we cover in this chapter.

What Is a Nonprofit Organization?

People hear the term *nonprofit* and picture a different type of business where the owner isn't allowed, by tax law, to make a profit or draw a paycheck. But, in fact, some nonprofit organizations end their fiscal year with a profit, and that's good because surplus cash (also referred to as *reserves*) keeps a nonprofit operating in the black versus the red.

Comparing for-profits to nonprofits

REMEMBER

The main difference between a for-profit corporation and a nonprofit corporation is what happens to the profit. In a for-profit company like Amazon, Google, United Parcel Service, or your favorite fast-food chain, profits are distributed to the owners (or shareholders). But a nonprofit can't do that. Any profit remaining after the bills are paid has to be invested into the organization, whether into its service programs, infrastructure, and so on, or stored in reserve for a rainy day. Profit can't be distributed to individuals, such as the organization's board of directors.

What about shareholders — do nonprofits have any shareholders to pay off? Not in terms of a monetary payoff, like a stock dividend. Rather than shareholders, nonprofit organizations have *stakeholders* — they're the people who benefit from the nonprofit's mission and services to their target population (those in need, from animals to humans). These people are often called stakeholders because by being committed to the success of the nonprofit, they have a stake in it; stakeholders include board members, volunteers, community partners, and the people whom the nonprofit serves directly and indirectly.

Introducing the coveted 501(c)(3) status for nonprofits

When we use the term *nonprofit organization* in this book, for the most part we're talking about an organization that has been *incorporated* (or organized formally) under the laws of its state and that the Internal Revenue Service (IRS) has classified as a 501(c)(3) and determined to be a public charity. If the term *501(c)(3)* is new to you, add it to your vocabulary with pride. In no time, "five-oh-one-see-three" will roll off your tongue as if you're a nonprofit expert.

REMEMBER

Private foundations also have the 501(c)(3) classification, but they aren't *public charities*. They operate under different regulations, and we don't cover them in this book.

Other kinds of nonprofit organizations *do* exist; they're formed to benefit their members, to influence legislation, or to fulfill other purposes. They receive exemption from federal income taxes and sometimes relief from property taxes at the local level. (These types of organizations aren't discussed in this book.)

Nonprofit organizations classified as 501(c)(3) receive extra privileges under the law. They are, with minor exceptions, the only group of tax-exempt organizations that can receive contributions that are tax-deductible for their donors.

The Internal Revenue Code describes the allowable purposes of 501(c)(3) nonprofit organizations, which include serving religious, educational, charitable, scientific, and literary ends.

TIP

Check out File 1-2 at `https://www.wiley.com/en-us/Nonprofit+Kit+For+Dummies%2C+6th+Edition-p-9781119835745#downloads-section` for a more detailed list of the activities that 501(c)(3) nonprofits take on.

A SECTOR BY ANY OTHER NAME

Not everyone thinks that *nonprofit sector* is the best name. That's because of the array of organizations with different types of nonprofit status. Some of these organizations are formed to benefit their members — such as fraternities and labor unions — and don't share a broad public-serving intent. Another reason *nonprofit sector* may not be the best choice of terms is its negative connotation. After all, what's worse than not making a profit? But, as we point out earlier, and we remind you again in later chapters, not making a profit isn't the determining factor. Here are some alternative terms you may hear:

- **Voluntary sector:** This term emphasizes the presence of volunteer board members and the significance of voluntary contributions and services to the work of 501(c)(3) organizations. In this definition, the organizations alone don't represent the meaning of *nonprofit;* the definition includes the vast web of supporters who participate as volunteers and donors.
- **Independent sector:** This term emphasizes the public-serving mission of these organizations and their volunteers and their independence from government. (Independent Sector is also the name of a nonprofit organization that provides research, advocacy, and public programs for and about the nonprofit sector.)
- **Charitable sector:** This term emphasizes the charitable donations these organizations receive from individuals and institutions.
- **Third sector:** This term emphasizes the sector's important role alongside government and the for-profit business economy.

We use the term *nonprofit sector* throughout this book, but we want you to understand its limitations and be familiar with other commonly used terms.

REMEMBER

Being a nonprofit organization doesn't mean that an entity is exempt from paying all taxes. Nonprofit organizations pay employment taxes, employee salaries, and wages just like for-profit businesses do. In some states, but not all, nonprofits are exempt from paying sales tax and property tax, so be sure that you're familiar with your jurisdiction's laws and nonprofit reporting requirements. Also, check with the appropriate office in your state to see whether you're required to apply for a state tax exemption or a license to solicit funds.

Embracing and Sharing Your Inspiration

The nonprofit sector is exciting. It encourages individuals with ideas about solving social problems or enhancing arts, culture, the environment, or education to act on those ideas. It creates a viable place within our society and economy for worthy activities that have little chance of commercial success. Nonprofit organizations combine the best of the business world with the best of government social-service programs, bringing together the creativity, zeal, and problem solving from the business side with the call to public service from the government side.

Speaking from experience, volunteerism is inspiring. Everyone has heard stories of tightly knit communities where neighbors gather to rebuild a home that was lost to a fire or a hurricane. That spirit of pitching in to help is the best part of living in a community in which people share values and ideas.

Communities have become more diverse and are populated with neighbors who come from a wide variety of places and cultures. The nonprofit sector provides institutions and opportunities where everyone can come together to work toward the common good. Volunteerism gives everyone the chance to pitch in to rebuild "the house and make it a home again."

Applying the term *voluntary sector* to nonprofit organizations came about for a good reason. The U.S. Census Bureau reported that 77.3 million people volunteered at least once in 2020.

When you're working in a nonprofit, you'll likely be supervising volunteers — and they'll likely supervise you. What we mean is that (with few exceptions) nonprofit boards of directors serve as unpaid volunteers. And if you're the executive director, your supervisors are the trustees or board members of the organization. At the same time, you likely depend on volunteers to carry out some or all of the activities of the organization. You may serve as a volunteer yourself.

REMEMBER

The word *supervision* sounds harsh, and we don't mean to suggest that nonprofits are or should be run with an iron hand. The board of directors does have ultimate responsibility, however, for the finances and actions of a nonprofit organization, and, therefore, people serving in that capacity have a real duty to make sure that the organization has sufficient resources to carry out its activities and that it's doing what it's supposed to be doing.

We prefer to think of nonprofits as organized group activities. You need to depend on others to reach your goals, and they need to depend on you. We talk about boards of directors in Chapter 2 of this minibook and working with volunteers in Chapter 5. If your nonprofit employs paid staff or hopes to someday, Chapter 6 provides some guidance in hiring and managing employees.

Honing Your Mission Statement

The mission statement is an organization's heartbeat (see Figure 1-1). In anatomy, your heart is the engine that fuels your entire body. For your nonprofit, the mission conveys the passion in your existence. Your mission statement impacts every stakeholder and is the reason your staff shows up at work. It's the reason your board members work hard to support the nonprofit's work in the community. The mission statement is the driving mantra for your volunteers who show up day after day to roll up their sleeves and carry out their job descriptions. Finally, your mission statement is the living, breathing, *actionable* reason that other organizations in the community want to be partners and step up, when needed, to fill gaps in services. Most importantly, a succinct and compassion-filled mission statement speaks to the hearts (and wallets) of potential donors.

REMEMBER

A mission statement should state what the organization's reason for existence is, how the mission will be achieved, and who will benefit from the organization's activities. The mission should be

- **Memorable:** You want to carry the statement around in your mind — at all times. Stakeholders should be able to remember it with ease and help your organization live it in their daily contributions.
- **Focused:** You want the statement to be narrow enough to focus on the reason your organization exists but broad enough to support organizational growth and expansion.
- **Compelling:** You want to communicate the need your organization addresses and the importance of doing something about it. (Bonus points if it also attracts potential board members to want to join your board and be a part of ongoing inspiration and change.)

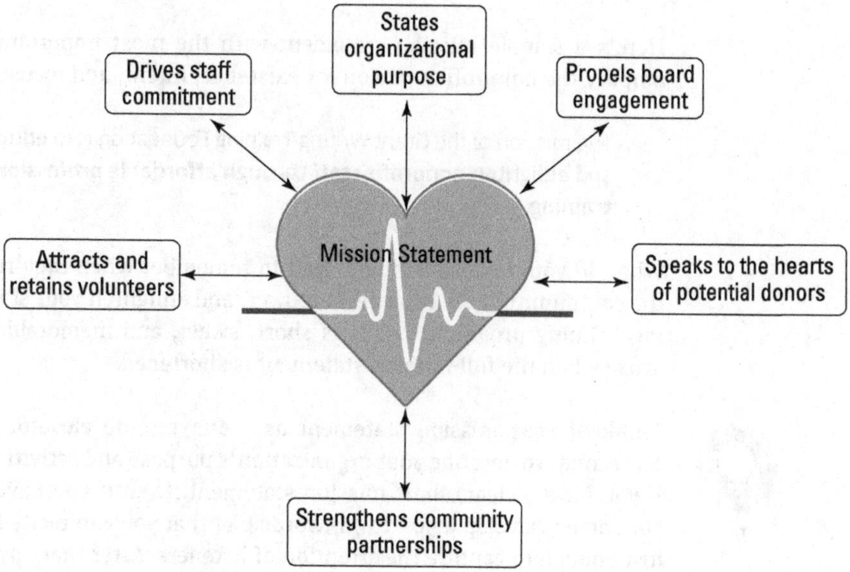

FIGURE 1-1: A strong mission statement is an organization's heartbeat.

» **Easy to read:** Your statement should be written in plain language so that folks don't need a set of footnotes to decipher it. Be sure to limit your use of adjectives, and try to avoid jargon.

After you decide on your organization's mission statement, you can use it as your go-to reference when making decisions about your nonprofit's activities. Add your mission statement to your Form 990 tax report to the IRS, in brochures, and in grant proposals. You may even print it on business cards for your board members and staff.

TIP

For more about drafting your mission statement, see Book 2, Chapter 1.

Keeping your mission statement short and sweet

Times have changed from when nonprofit organizations had long, drawn-out mission statements that spanned pages and read like a rambling fact sheet. Instead, we suggest keeping your mission statement short and succinct — aim for one or two memorable sentences that speak about the present and can be easily remembered by your board members, staff, volunteers, and community stakeholders. That way, everyone can remember why your nonprofit organization exists, what it does for the community, and how they can help it stay on focus daily. Save your lengthy writing for the vision statement.

Here's a sample mission statement with the most important words bolded to amplify the nonprofit's reason for existence, intent, and focus:

> The mission of the Grant Writing Training Foundation is to **educate, empower,** and **enlighten nonprofit staff through affordable professional development training.**

What do your board members need to remember when they're out and about in the community? "We educate, empower, and enlighten your staff through affording training programs." This is short, sweet, and memorable — and it makes sense when the full mission statement is shortened.

TIP

Think of your mission statement as a one-minute elevator speech. You have 60 seconds to describe your organization's purpose and activities. Doing so is easy if you have a clear, short mission statement. Even if you have a longer mission statement, develop a 50- to 75-word spiel that you can recite from memory. Say just enough to capture the attention of listeners. After that, give them a business card with the nonprofit's contact information (on the front) and the full mission statement (on the back).

Stating your mission — the goal for services

When thinking of your organization's reason for existing, think of your desired end result. What would you like to see happen? What would the world (or your community) be like if your organization were to succeed?

To say that you have to have a mission to change lives seems almost too basic. Maybe you're thinking, "*Of course* I have a reason for forming my nonprofit. Why do you think I bought this book? I want to start a nonprofit to [fill in the blank]." We bring up this point because clarifying the reason for your nonprofit's existence is basic to creating your mission statement. Why should your nonprofit exist?

For example, you may know that you love cats and dogs and have always wanted to work with them, but that isn't the same thing as identifying a nonprofit organization's reason for existing. The mission statement for a fictitious humane society might be written this way:

> Friends of Animals provides temporary shelter and medical care for homeless puppies, dogs, kittens, and cats until responsible, loving homes can be found.

This sentence doesn't describe the shelter's facilities or how it recruits and trains volunteers, but it does clearly state which animals it serves and that it doesn't intend to foster them as long as they live but rather to place them in good homes.

And if someone visited Friends of Animals with a ferret, a pony, or a tarantula, its staff would know to refer that person to another shelter.

REMEMBER

Knowing and understanding your organization's purpose is essential to making important organizational decisions. It's also a fundamental tool to use when asking for money, recruiting additional board members, hiring and motivating staff, and publicizing your activities. Also, remember that your governing board's input in developing the mission statement is not an option. Buy-in begins with inclusion!

Specifying who will be served by the nonprofit

After you and the governing board have determined the nonprofit's purpose, the primary beneficiaries of its services are documented and included in the mission statement. Their needs — whether they're kittens or refugees — make your mission compelling and achievable. Defining who will benefit from your nonprofit helps to focus your organizational activities and is an essential ingredient in the mission statement.

Some organizations have a more general audience than others. If your nonprofit's focus is preserving historic buildings, the beneficiary of this activity may be current and future residents of a city, a county, or even a state. It may also be the workers you train in the crafts needed to complete the building restorations.

Explaining how you'll accomplish your mission

After you know your organization's mission and its beneficiaries, the next step is deciding how to make it happen. Mission statements usually highlight a phrase describing the methods your nonprofit will use to accomplish its purpose. Think about the activities and programs you'll provide to fulfill your mission. Take a look at these examples:

- To indicate how it will accomplish its mission, the Friends of Animals' mission statement may say, "Our mission will be accomplished by veterinary professionals and dedicated volunteers who provide temporary shelter for homeless animals."
- The mission of a human-services nonprofit organization may state, "Our mission will be accomplished by providing juvenile offender reentry recidivism counseling-and-support services for minority probationers exiting the Nassau County Juvenile Detention Center."

REMEMBER

When describing how your organization addresses its purpose, you don't want to be so specific that you have to rewrite its mission statement every time you add a new program. At the same time, you want the mission statement to be concrete enough that people reading it (or hearing you recite it) can picture what your organization does.

Incorporating diversity, equity, and inclusion (DEI) into your mission statement

What does it mean to incorporate *diversity, equity,* and *inclusion* (or *DEI*) into your mission statement? Let's look at who's involved and how to add language that is direct and memorable.

- It takes a village! Involve the founder and/or executive director and the governing board in articulating a brief but striking DEI statement.
- Remember that adding DEI to your mission statement is core to the organization's values and the way it will conduct business (programs and services).
- Use positive words like *inclusive, celebrate, grow, freedom, experience,* and *commitment* or *committed.*

Now let's revisit this mission statement and start adding the DEI language:

> Our mission is to provide juvenile offender reentry recidivism counseling-and-support services for minority probationers exiting the Nassau County Juvenile Detention Center by ensuring that our programs are inclusive to all and committed to celebrating diversity, equity, and inclusion for youth and their families during detention and post-detention.

As you can see, not all the parts of DEI have to be included. However, the parts you do include must have an impact on your service population.

Imagining Your Future with a Vision Statement

Simply put, a *vision statement* is your dream — your broadly described aspiration for what your organization can do. Vision statements can describe a future desired condition as a result of the organization's activities, but they're more typically applied to the organization itself. Usually, the statement includes phrases like "the best" or "recognized as a leader."

Table 1-1 provides an example of this future-visioning process.

TABLE 1-1 **Visioning the Future while Looking at the Present**

Who We Are Now	Where We See Ourselves in Five Years
New nonprofit	One of the best social enterprise nonprofits
Limited financial resources	Endowed
Small footprint in our neighborhood	Recognized statewide as a leader
Hoping to move chronically homeless single mothers with children into Alternative Dwelling Units (ADUs)	Pioneer in changing zoning policies to permit ADUs in multiple residential neighborhoods enabling single-parent homeless families to live in permanent safe housing

Capturing your vision statement

A *vision statement* can be long or short. We recommend that you assemble a group of internal stakeholders (founder, board members, staff, and volunteers). Start by spelling out the basic components in a vision statement. Here are the most important aspects a vision statement should convey (or communicate) to the public at-large, including your stakeholders:

- » Project what your nonprofit organization will do over the next five years.
- » Write in future tense.
- » Provide directional language.
- » Be descriptive.
- » Dare to be audacious or bold in your prediction!

Here's an example of a vision statement from a fictitious nonprofit organization serving a Tribal nation in the Pacific Northwest region of the United States:

> By 2026, the Native Cultural Food Preservation Institute will encourage Native youth to adapt and embrace the food preservation techniques of their ancestors. Over time, fishing, hunting, and foraging for berries and herbs will result in the restoration of Tribal health-and-wellness practices to reduce obesity, hunger, and debilitating health. The Institute's Native herbal research projects and position statements on American Indian Cultural Food Preservation will be widely circulated to our sister Tribes across the nation and Canada. We will be a conduit for

improving Native health. The future of Native health and wellness will be managed via robust education programs, cultural food preservation reclamation initiatives, and an embrace of the ways of our ancestors.

Notice how this vision statement reflects the cultural essence of the organization's purpose and direction.

Asking "Where are we going?" and "Why?"

If your nonprofit organization is small and at this point has only a founder and two or three board members, you can simply convene that small group and ask, "Where are we going and why?" Here are three statements you're likely to hear in this first round of asking the same question over and over:

"We're going to change the world!"

"We're going to become the largest nonprofit in our state!"

"We're going to be debt-free!"

Don't criticize or belittle your stakeholders. Do you know how many people live for today, and think for today, and never set goals or create a vision for the future? We would have to say that, likely, millions have fallen short of seeing themselves or their nonprofit organizations as sustainable for many years to come. This fear is a common one for new nonprofit founders. Their dreams start out with huge, grandiose ideas — only to have each one of them fizzle at the starting gate. Why? Lack of money, lack of planning, lack of foresight, and lack of appropriate stakeholders at the table on day one of forming their nonprofit organizations. This is why it's important to invite the right people to join your board and lead the organization from a flatline status to a soaring status.

Finding the Resources to Do the Job

One distinctive feature of the nonprofit sector is its dependency on contributions. We devote Book 2 to advice about getting contributions from fundraising.

Gifts from individuals of money, goods, services, time, and property make up the largest portion of that voluntary support. This portion, which is also the oldest of the voluntary traditions in the United States, dates back to colonial times. Since the late 19th century, private philanthropic foundations have emerged as another source of support, and more recently — particularly after World War II — the federal government and corporations have become important income sources. Earned income from fees for service, ticket sales, and tuition charges also is an important revenue source for many nonprofits; in fact, in 2013 nearly three-quarters of the revenues for public charities was earned.

Who is giving to nonprofit organizations?

Among private, nongovernmental sources of support, gifts from living individuals — as opposed to bequests from people who have died — have always represented a large portion of total giving, but philanthropic giving by foundations and corporations has been growing. According to the Giving USA Foundation, in 2019 corporations represented the largest portion of total giving and the COVID-19 pandemic is furthering this trend. This resulted in corporations giving the largest share of nonprofit sponsorships and grants. For new nonprofit organizations, the best fundraising strategy is to take a balanced approach that includes multiple forms of contributions.

Supporting your mission with fundraising

Nearly every nonprofit organization depends on generous donors for the cash it needs to pay its bills and provide its services. Even if you have income from ticket sales, admission charges, or contracted services, you'll find that raising additional money is necessary to keep your organization alive and thriving.

Corporate contributions are the largest source of contributed income to nonprofit organizations. But you can't just sit and wait by the mailbox for the donations to begin arriving. How will contributors even know that your new nonprofit is up and running, providing services? Two basic rules of fundraising are that potential funders need to be asked for donations and thanked after giving one. Book 2 covers fundraising.

Grants from foundations and corporations make up a smaller percentage of giving to nonprofits, but their support can be invaluable for start-up project costs, equipment, technical support, and sometimes general operating costs. Some organizations get most of their income from foundation grants; others get very little. Book 3 covers grants and how to win them.

Fundraising works better if people know you exist. That knowledge also helps draw people to your theater or to sign up for your programs. Here's where marketing and public relations enter the picture. Book 3, Chapter 9 helps you figure out what your message should be and how to circulate it to the world.

REMEMBER

Make no mistake about it: Fundraising is hard work. But if you approach the task with a positive attitude and make your case well, you can find the resources you need.

IN THIS CHAPTER

» Understanding the board's control and liability

» Distinguishing between the role of founder and executive director

» Creating an advisory board

Chapter 2

From the Top: Examining the Nonprofit Management Structure

If you're the nonprofit founder, you might be thinking: "I am the visionary. I started this nonprofit. I have ownership, and leverage, and I get to tell the board yes or no regarding their decisions. I recruited these members. They're not going to take over my dream of helping this community."

However, there is no owner of a nonprofit. Instead, a governing board guides and oversees the organization, like an owner might. Understanding the governing board's role in your management structure, processes, and decision making should be a top priority for nonprofit founders, executive directors, and volunteers alike.

Founders, don't worry — while it may seem like you're turning over the reins to the board of directors, you still can determine your role within the nonprofit organization. You are the founder and you have the vision for moving forward.

In this chapter, we take a closer look at the top-down structure of most nonprofit organizations and explain who wields the most authority and how that impacts the rest of the organization's structure.

REMEMBER

Nonprofit organizations don't belong to any single person or group of founders or governing board. They belong to their stakeholders and the public at-large for the greater good of their mission.

TIP

Check out File 7-1 at `https://www.wiley.com/en-us/Nonprofit+Kit+For+Dummies%2C+6th+Edition-p-9781119835745#downloads-section` for a list of web resources related to the topics we cover in this chapter.

Managing a Nonprofit: A Bird's-Eye View

Exactly what is the management structure for a nonprofit organization? Take a look at Figure 2-1 for an example.

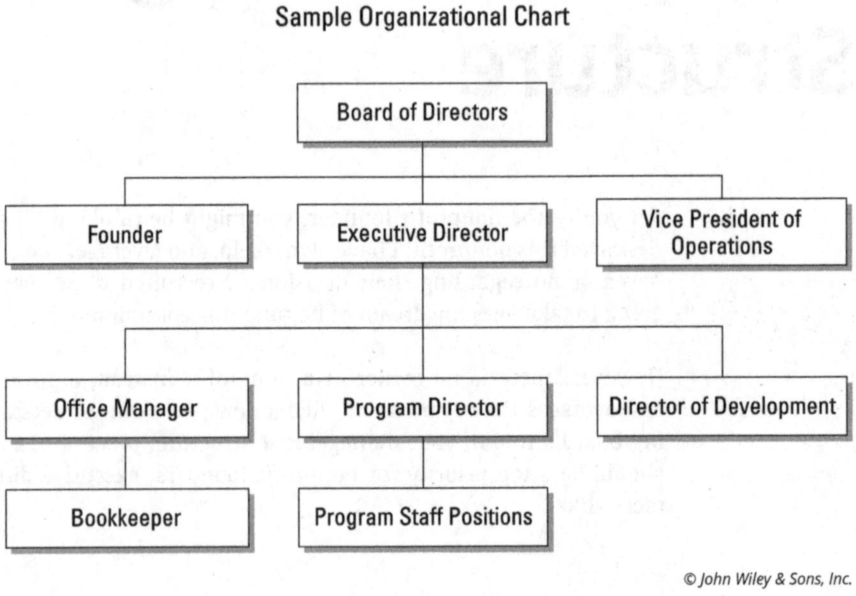

FIGURE 2-1: Organizational chart of a typical larger nonprofit agency.

Your board of directors is the governing body. They're at the top of your organizational chart. The board has authority over the founder as well as the executive director and advisory board as the nonprofit grows and those positions are added. Though communications are two-way, your board has the final say. The board decides what will be implemented, how much will be spent, and even who will be nominated when the time comes for board elections or expansion.

Appreciating the Governing Board's Role and Responsibilities

As the saying goes, with great power comes great responsibility. Every member of your governing board is responsible for the organization's financial management, operational decision-making process, risk management, and more. In other words, your governing board members are the foundation for a solid and successfully managed nonprofit organization.

Understanding the board's management oversight duties

A nonprofit's board of directors has the legal responsibility to provide oversight and accountability for the organization. The board must ensure that your nonprofit organization is carefully handling the funding entrusted to it. The board must also follow all legal and ethical standards. Recommended governance practices include carrying out the duties behind these three types of responsibilities:

- **Governance**
  - Making policy and strategy decisions.
  - Overseeing and monitoring organizational performance.
  - Ensuring overall accountability.
- **Legal**
  - Holding at least one annual meeting of the board of directors.
  - Creating policies related to disclosing and managing conflicts of interest.

» **Financial**

- Formalizing the process of setting compensation for the executive director, including approving the compensation package.
- Reviewing IRS Form 990 and ensuring its accuracy before it's filed with the IRS.
- Ensuring that an annual financial audit is conducted.
- Approving financial policies that ensure checks and balances with regard to the income and expenses. This includes determining who signs the checks and deposits the money as well as monitoring the income statements on a regular basis. The board can even authorize who can sign grant applications and contracts over a specific amount (typically, the signee is the board president).

The buck stops at the board of directors. As such, the board is in a position of liability. If someone is unhappy with your services, if a passerby falls and is injured on the nonprofit's property, or if program staff has overstepped their position with a client, volunteer, or community partner, a lawsuit can even be filed. All eyes will be on the board for taking action, making decisions, and being accountable on behalf of the nonprofit.

TIP

For a list of resources of the areas that a new and/or small nonprofit board needs to know about, turn to Book 3, Chapter 2.

Protecting your board from liability

Did you know that fear of personal liability stops many people from joining a board of directors? Some state laws offer protection to people affiliated with public charities. However, this is not the case in every state. So, when you're recruiting board members, ask for their contributions to purchase directors-and-officers (D&O) insurance.

D&O insurance protects the personal assets of nonprofit directors (including board officers) and their spouses in the event that employees personally sue them, vendors, competitors, funders, clients, or other parties for actual or alleged wrongful acts in managing the nonprofit. D&O insurance covers legal fees, settlements, and judgments arising out of lawsuits and wrongful-act allegations brought against your nonprofit organization. Costs vary among insurance companies; make sure to get several quotes before you settle on a D&O insurance provider.

A SAD CASE OF NO D&O

Consider, for example, a new nonprofit, without D&O insurance coverage on their board members, that applied for a grant from a major community-based funding source. The nonprofit won a $95,000 grant award to create a rural community outreach program to provide case management, workforce-entry skills, transportation for clients to job interviews, and job placement. When the check arrived, the board treasurer endorsed and deposited the check into the bank. The program had been heavily promoted throughout the rural community. If you don't yet see any red flags in this story, you should! Here are some questions to ask yourself:

- Did the board treasurer have full board approval to accept the grant award on behalf of the nonprofit organization?
- Was there a board resolution to validate the authority to accept the funding? The board must make a resolution to accept grant funds and record it in the board meeting minutes. This establishes a record of funds received.
- Did the board treasurer have approval from the rest of the board's executive committee to deposit the check on their own? The resolution covers the authorization to deposit the funds.
- Did the board treasurer make a copy of the check to add to the next board meeting's agenda? This risk management task creates a record of when the check was dated, which is a signal that the grant-funded program is ready to start its implementation. The copy of the check also provides a clear audit trail for your nonprofit's accountant. A separate accounting record should be created to track expenditures from the grant funding.

Well, here's the rest of the sad story for this rural nonprofit organization. The grant writer who was hired to write the grant application that won a $95,000 award for the nonprofit was also the new program's evaluator. The grant writer started to see evidence of improper record keeping and forged case management files. As the contracted evaluator, the grant writer started to ask questions about the case management files and why the client documentation was written in the same ink pen color and in the same handwriting when the grant allowed two part-time contracted social workers. Was only one social worker hired? Where were the receipts for transportation vouchers, job interview clothing, an invisible computer lab, and a training program to help unemployed low-income rural residents?

What do you think happened next? Six months into the 12-month funding cycle, the grant writer felt an ethical duty to speak with the funder and ask them to make an unannounced site visit to the nonprofit's training facility (operating in a large community

(continued)

(continued)

room of a community-based church). The program director and pastor of the church (who were both partners in the soon-to-be discovered crime), did not expect the site visit. The outcome of the site visit by the funder resulted in a legal letter demanding 100 percent of the grant-award monies ($75,000) back from the nonprofit organization.

A lawsuit was filed as well when the nonprofit did not respond. Oh, did we forget to say that the board had no D&O insurance coverage? When the nonprofit could not come up with the $75,000 from the organization's coffers, the burden shifted to the board of directors. They were clueless, had never heard of D&O insurance, and did not ask the program director or the pastor any questions because they trusted them. And did we mention yet that the board treasurer (the holder of the nonprofit's checkbook) was the program director's wife?

The board of directors became personally liable for repaying the $75,000. Some lost their homes; others had liens put on their homes, preventing them from selling to come up with the monies. Others had their paychecks garnished via small claims court. The court's judgment against the nine board members was harsh but certainly deserved. Why? No candidate for joining a board of directors should be eager to say yes without first asking many questions about protection from financial liability. Fast-forward: The nonprofit has closed. The church board fired the pastor. Sadly, the community lost its trust in everyone associated with the nonprofit.

Redefining the Nonprofit Founder's Role

Every founder needs to determine their role within the nonprofit organization. Probably the most difficult thing to realize is that you won't be the owner of the nonprofit organization. As a tax-exempt nonprofit organization, your nonprofit will be accountable to the people it serves, to its funders, to the attorney general in your state or territory, and to the general public. Naturally, a founder is an important figure in the nonprofit organization that was founded on their vision. Even though founders deserve respect and gratitude, ultimately, there is no such position as founder — however, every founder has a choice to be part of the staff or part of the board.

Suppose that you're most interested in being part of the daily activities in the nonprofit organization. In that case, you could request that the board of directors appoint you as vice president of operations. This means you'd be responsible for overseeing the nonprofit's operations on a day-to-day basis; however, you'd still report directly to the board who would be responsible for giving you strategic direction and assessing your performance.

The chief executive usually serves as an *ex officio* nonvoting member of the board, which provides a shield against conflict of interest and questions about accountability while forming a necessary and constructive partnership with the board.

If you want to ensure that you have a direct say in the nonprofit organization's future, you may want to become a board member and decide to be the first chair. Still, remember that every board member has only one vote — including the chair — and the full board must always speak with one voice to the outside world. However, as the founder, you can form the initial board with members who believe in the organization's mission, share your strategic goals, and devote their time and energy to help you.

Suppose that the nonprofit organization cannot hire staff right away. In that case, you will have a working board where each member has individual fiduciary and governing duties as a board member and individual tasks and responsibilities to carry on the daily affairs. The important issue is remembering which hat each member is wearing at different times to keep accountability intact.

If the governing board decides to create an advisory board, this may be the perfect place to plant yourself as the visionary behind the nonprofit organization. An *advisory board* is a body that provides nonbinding strategic advice to the management of a nonprofit organization. The informal nature of an advisory board gives greater flexibility in structure and management compared to the board of directors.

Adding an Advisory Board

Advisory boards are typically composed of an informal group of accomplished experts and advisors hand-picked by the board of directors. Advisory boards expand the nonprofit organization's capacity, reach, and impact. This list describes the typical types of advisory boards:

- **Fundraising:** Donors who want a larger role with your nonprofit organization can be asked to join your advisory board.
- **Programmatic:** Members with your nonprofit's service-area experience can help provide advice on program improvements. Programmatic members can also be asked to serve on an internal stakeholder's evaluation team for grant-funded projects and existing programs that require annual performance evaluations. Advisory board members can spot broken links in program services, incorrect data collection processes, and other red flags that are spotted only when examining the evaluation findings for each program.

If you're the founder, you can always opt to join the advisory board instead of taking a more laborious position such as vice president of operations. However, keep in mind that you're one of many members. Each advisory board member may have differing viewpoints and ideas for how to help the nonprofit organization build its capacity. You're a member, not the leader. Advisory boards have no designated leaders — every member has the same input ability. It takes a consensus of the advisory board members to move a recommendation up to the board of directors for review and possible adoption into a resolution.

The advisory board reports directly to the board of directors. It makes recommendations to the board of directors and takes direction from the board of directors. The advisory board cannot be influenced or swayed by the executive director, program staff, volunteers, or even the nonprofit organization's community partners. Again, the founder may opt to join the advisory board if the board of directors is not a comfortable fit. The advisory board is more relaxed but highly informed in their respective professional fields. Advisory board members come with high levels of education, experience, and expertise, and each member freely offers what they know to help the board of directors on all advisory board assignments. Members work seamlessly, cooperatively, and without subjective motives.

Expanding to Take on an Executive Director

The executive director of a nonprofit organization oversees the heads of each department, such as marketing, human resources, program development, and funding development. After you can start hiring or contracting for staff positions, your most important role is to bring in people from diverse backgrounds. Your hiring or contracting practices must embrace diversity, equity, and inclusion.

Successful executive directors are goal-driven and possess a high degree of motivation and energy. They are *doers*. They have a record of productivity and embracing the importance of the organization's mission.

As executive director, you report to your board of directors, and the chief liaison is the board's chair or president, or CEO. This is the body that hires executive directors, monitors and evaluates their performances, and directs the search for a new executive director if that task becomes necessary. The board's directive becomes your marching order for managing the nonprofit organization.

To be effective in leadership, as the executive director, you must be an excellent communicator and a marathon-like fund-raiser, and you must have the vision to put the mission into a long-term view. Your entire staff looks to you for an example of dedication, commitment, and approachability. Your office door should be open unless you're discussing confidential matters. In other words, you must be a hands-on executive director.

Typically, when you see a job posting for a nonprofit executive director, here are some of the typical duties and responsibilities:

- Collaborate with the board of directors to identify, create, and implement the strategic plan.
- Identify, recruit, train, and develop a talented team of employees who can lead critical departments and manage subordinates.
- Develop the organizational culture and promote transparency and collaboration throughout the nonprofit and with community stakeholders.
- Approve and monitor all fundraising efforts.
- Represent the nonprofit at community events and with funders in ways that strengthen and oversee the mission and financial stability for future operations, and ultimately, sustainability.

As the executive director, your line of accountability is directly to the board of directors. As your governing board, they approve, monitor, and guide your duties and responsibilities to the nonprofit organization. Often you are directed by the board to downsize staff because the board is carrying out their fiduciary role to keep the nonprofit in operation. The board may see red flags in the monthly and annual expenditures that must be addressed. Reducing staff size is typically the first step in stopping the bleed of expenses that may eventually be more than the revenues coming into the nonprofit. As much as you may want to defend not laying off key staff members, the board's decision must be followed swiftly and with explanations to staff about what is happening and why such difficult decisions must be made.

REMEMBER

You must respect your line of accountability to the board of directors. When the board directs you to do something that you may not agree with, keep in mind that *they* are responsible for the governance of the nonprofit organization. Every action that occurs in the day-to-day operation of the nonprofit comes under the jurisdiction and scrutiny of the board of directors. Their volunteer (unpaid) role is selfless. The board's focus should always be on the nonprofit's mission, vision, and legacy in the community.

IN THIS CHAPTER

» Finding out why nonprofits plan

» Wading into the planning process

» Converting plans into action

» Creating program plans

» Planning for facilities

Chapter 3

Strategic Planning: Embracing the Ongoing Process

The word *planning* can be intimidating. It conjures up images of daylong meetings in stuffy conference rooms with consultants wielding dry erase markers. Of course, not all planning takes that sort of effort. People make plans all the time, from organizing vacations to deciding how to complete all their errands on a Saturday afternoon.

Strategic planning is a group project that calls for research, brainstorming, discussion, and, in the end, agreement on a goal and the strategies and tactics needed to reach that goal. Simply put, *strategic planning* is deciding where to go and how to get there. The planning process helps ensure that your stakeholders are headed in the same direction.

In this chapter, we cover planning for nonprofits in all its forms, from organizational planning to work planning to program planning to facility planning. Plan to join us!

TIP

Check out File 8-1 at https://www.wiley.com/en-us/Nonprofit+Kit+For+Dummies%2C+6th+Edition-p-9781119835745#downloads-section for a list of web resources related to the topics we cover in this chapter.

Understanding the Importance of Planning

No nonprofit organization has unlimited funds. Even the largest, wealthiest nonprofit needs to decide how to allocate its resources effectively. Planning helps you make decisions about how to align your organization's mission with its resources by answering questions such as these: "Is now the best time to invest in a new program?" "Is our safe house program still filling a community need?" "Is our resilience training center convenient to the people we're trying to serve?"

A nonprofit organization undertakes planning for several reasons:

- » To build a structure that guides its activities in pursuit of its mission
- » To allocate organizational resources in the most effective ways
- » To create a framework against which the organization's performance can be evaluated
- » To adapt to changes in the external environment
- » To reach agreement among board, staff, and community stakeholders on desirable goals for the organization and well-considered ways to meet those goals

Think of a plan as a blueprint or scheme describing what needs to be done to accomplish an end. In an ideal world, if your organization completes every step of its plan, you achieve your goals. However, not all plans are written as recipes that — if followed closely — will serve up a perfect meal. Scenario plans, for example, help an organization think through alternatives it may choose among; other planning approaches invite organizations to assess and revisit their strategies frequently.

REMEMBER

The *act* of planning has value apart from the document that's ultimately created. That's because, in theory, the strategic planning group comes to a shared understanding of your nonprofit organization's mission, and the decision-making process ensures that everyone understands what needs to be done and agrees that it's worth doing.

Making Your Organization's Strategic Plan

Strategic planning is what people usually think about when they consider planning — and previously a strategic plan covered a period from three to five years of nonprofit operations; however, today, in this changing and often volatile global economy, we advise creating a short-term strategic plan. Let's focus on one year (your founding year). The strategic plan is the guiding document where you set goals for the organization and describe the objectives that must be accomplished to achieve those goals. The plan also includes action steps, timelines for achieving the objectives in order to achieve your goals by the end of the plan year, and designations for who will carry out each action step.

Soon after your board of directors approves your mission statement and vision statement, use those statements to begin drafting your strategic plan. Follow these steps for successful planning:

1. **Hear from stakeholders.**
2. **Research and make decisions about goals and the strategies to meet them.**
3. **Draft the plan.**
4. **Submit the final draft to the full board for discussion and adoption.**
5. **Act on the plan.**
6. **Routinely evaluate your progress.**

REMEMBER

Planning is an ongoing activity. Planning for the purposes of refining objectives, creating a budget, and developing fundraising programs goes on all the time. This means that the strategic plan needs to be revisited routinely (we recommend monthly) to determine your progress in meeting the plan's goals, objectives, and overall organizational performance. In the last quarter of your current year's strategic plan, determine goals that weren't met and why, and then start working on the strategic plan for the upcoming year.

TIP

See Book 3, Chapter 10 for a discussion of goals in the context of grant writing.

Getting ready

Make no mistake: An all-out strategic planning effort requires considerable time, energy, and commitment from everyone involved. Some nonprofits spend a year or more developing a strategic plan.

Don't jump into the strategic planning process without understanding that it will add to your workload and complicate your life for a while. Keep in mind that you can't plan by yourself. If you're the executive director of a nonprofit organization who thinks that a full-bore planning effort is needed but the board of directors doesn't agree, don't try to start the process on your own. Take a couple of steps backward and begin the work of persuading board members that planning is worth the effort.

WARNING

Don't start the strategic planning process if your nonprofit is in crisis mode. It's tempting, for example, to launch a strategic planning effort if you just lost a major source of funding. But you have more immediate concerns to deal with in that situation. Delay strategic planning until you see a period of smooth sailing.

If you have the support, and if foreclosure isn't hanging over your agency's head, the best way to get started is to form a *strategic planning committee.* This small group of board members, staff, and one or two outside people can take on the role of guiding the strategic planning process and, in the beginning, pull together the questions, facts, and observations that you need in order to make your strategic planning decisions.

Working with your nonprofit's mission and vision statements

Reviewing the organization's mission and vision statements is one of the first tasks facing a new nonprofit that's developing a plan. (Chapter 1 of this minibook covers mission and vision statements.) Ask yourself these questions:

- Is the problem the nonprofit set out to solve still a problem?
- Do the organization's current programs and activities address the mission in a meaningful way?
- Is the mission statement clear yet flexible enough to allow the organization to grow and adapt?
- Does the vision statement still reflect where we want to be as an organization five years down the road?

REMEMBER

Keep your mission statement in mind throughout the strategic planning process. At every turn, ask yourself: "If we do this, will we be true to our mission?"

Hearing from all your stakeholders

Unless you have a very small organization, you probably can't include every single person in the planning process. You do need to include all stakeholder groups, however. A *stakeholder* is someone who has a reason for wanting the organization to succeed. Paid employees and members of the board certainly qualify. But these two groups, who are the most closely connected to the nonprofit, are by no means the only people who have a stake in the organization's success.

In our view, you also should include a representative from each of the following groups in planning:

- Users of services
- Community leaders
- Donors
- Volunteers

REMEMBER

One purpose of strategic planning is to bring together stakeholders in pursuit of a common goal. People work harder to achieve the goals when they're asked to help set the goals.

WARNING

Guard against bias. Sometimes people get so close to the situation they're evaluating that they can't see the true picture with an objective eye. Include outside people who gain no personal benefit from the outcome.

Also, don't assume that all your stakeholders know what they're talking about in every instance. For example, if someone says that receiving a grant to pay the costs of a program start-up is a piece of cake, check with potential funders before you agree that it's an easy task.

Yes, honesty can create conflict. Be prepared for it. Set some rules for attending strategic planning meetings. Make sure that all participants have a chance to state their cases. Arguments can be productive if they exchange ideas about what is best for the organization and don't disintegrate into shouting matches.

Surveying the external situation

Early in the strategic planning process, you need to collect information about external (outside) factors that influence your nonprofit's operation. Someone, or a subcommittee of the strategic planning committee, should find the answers to the following questions and distribute them to everyone on the committee before the formal planning meetings begin:

- What are the demographic and other trends in our area and in our organization? Will these trends have an impact on the number of people or animals who may need or use our services in the future?
- What are the trends in the professional arena in which our nonprofit operates? Are new methods being developed? Are we complying with current laws regulating our field? Does the future show a shortage of professionally trained staff? Is technology changing the way people acquire knowledge or services?
- Are other nonprofits providing similar services in the community? If so, how are our services different? Should we be working together? How are we distinctive?
- How stable are the funding sources on which we depend? What about changes in government funding? Changes in our earned revenue? Can we find new potential sources of funding?

The decisions you make are only as good as the information on which you base them. Therefore, it's important to find the best and most up-to-date data available that may have an impact on your organization and its programs, and it's important not to overlook unfavorable trends.

You may want to collect information from the general public or the constituents served by your nonprofit. We also recommend conferring with major donors, foundation representatives, and other nonprofits or government agencies that work closely with you. Surveys, interviews, and focus groups are ways to gather input from the public. Before you undertake any of these techniques, however, spend some time thinking about what you want to learn. Write a list of questions for which you want answers.

TIP

If possible, consult with someone experienced in preparing surveys or interview protocols, because the phrasing of questions and the way you distribute your surveys affect the answers you get. Look for expertise in this area from consulting firms that work with nonprofits, at local colleges and universities, or from marketing or market research firms.

REMEMBER

Bad information leads to bad decisions. Or, put another way, garbage in, garbage out. When gathering background information to guide planning decisions, take the time to seek out the most accurate, up-to-date facts available.

PLANNING FOR UNCERTAINTY

No matter how well you plan, circumstances can, and probably will, change. So, of course, creating a strategic plan requires that you make assumptions about the future; sometimes these assumptions turn out to be wrong. Maybe, for example, a dependable funding source drops out of the picture; maybe a major industry in your city closes its doors; or maybe new government regulations affect your programs. Unexpected events within your nonprofit or in your community can dump cold water on your carefully designed plans.

But this doesn't mean that your nonprofit should abandon planning. Fundamentally, planning is about making decisions that are based on the best available information and the most careful thought you can muster. If conditions change or a new opportunity arises, the analytical muscles that your organization has developed through that thoughtful decision making should prepare it to respond quickly and appropriately to apply new strategies. Remember that all plans are living, breathing documents and can be adjusted as conditions change.

Looking at the internal situation

In addition to surveying the environment in which the organization operates, you need to expend some effort assessing the organization itself. Consider the following factors when doing an internal analysis:

- What are the organization's major accomplishments? What are its milestones?
- Whom does it serve and what does it offer them? If we're a new nonprofit organization, whom will we serve and what can we offer them with limited start-up funding?
- Is the board of directors fully engaged with the organization? Should any weaknesses on the board be filled? Is the board engaged in aggressive fundraising?
- What are the staff's capabilities? Does the organization have enough staff — and the right staff that is sufficiently trained and licensed? If we can't hire staff yet, how can our volunteers help us in delivering services?
- Do our governing documents — such as our articles of incorporation — allow for our current and planned activities?

- Is the organization's office and program space in the right location and of the right size? If we're working out of a personal residence until we can afford to lease office space, how can we appear to be more established? Can we use a personal mailbox address for correspondence? How do we explain this to potential funders?
- Does the organization have adequate technology? Are its technology systems integrated with one another? Do employees and/or volunteers need additional training in using technological tools? Are equipment needs anticipated?
- Has the organization operated within its budget? Is financial reporting adequate? Are appropriate financial controls in place? If we're not ready yet because we don't have a large budget, how can we put these controls in place?
- What does the organization's program cost and how does it pay for it? If we're a new nonprofit, how can we identify funding for our programs? Can we charge a fee for services? How will the community react if we charge a fee for our services?
- Does the organization have a variety of funding sources? Are those funding sources stable? If we're a new nonprofit, where do we start with introducing ourselves to potential funders and donors? What is the board of director's role in securing early funding and contributions?

THE ARTICLES OF INCORPORATION

Articles of incorporation are documents detailing key elements of your nonprofit organization. You will need to get the papers you need from the appropriate state office. Your state office may even have provided sample articles of incorporation and instructions about how to prepare your own. Pay close attention to the instructions, and follow them step-by-step. The whole process may be as simple as filling in the blanks. Although you can amend articles of incorporation, it requires filing additional forms and paying more fees, so you may as well spend time getting them right the first time.

IRS Publication 557 contains information about the language needed in the articles of incorporation, along with some sample articles. You can download this publication from the IRS website at `www.irs.gov/pub/irs-pdf/p557.pdf`.

SCENARIOS FOR THE FUTURE

Scenario planning is an approach that involves imagining several futures in which your organization may find itself and then using those imagined futures to determine the strategies that your nonprofit needs in order to thrive in the years to come. The practitioners of scenario planning don't pretend that they're prophets or seers, but this planning method provides a framework for thoughtful conversations among the leaders of the nonprofits, corporations, and government agencies that engage in it.

Scenario planning pushes you to define the most pressing issue facing your organization. For example, if your organization works to provide equal access to information technology for everyone, you may want to ask which aspect limits some people's access now — whether it's equipment, service costs, training, or available Internet access — and which conditions are changing that might solve or exacerbate the problem. After you've figured out the question you want to address — often the most difficult thing to do — you need to collect as much information as possible about trends that may impact access to technology. That may include future cost projections for computers; projected family-income figures; trends affecting libraries, adult education, and after-school programs that have provided free access to technology; business trends in the technology industry; and efforts by local governments to provide wireless access to their communities, to name only a few.

Then you can begin thinking about how the future may play out by creating several descriptions — some would say *stories* — of possible future conditions. After you arrive at this point, you begin to talk about the roles your organization might play in each of those stories that would enable it to fulfill its mission.

Calling in the SWOT team

One common way to analyze the information you've collected is to perform a *SWOT* analysis, which is the acronym for *s*trengths, *w*eaknesses, *o*pportunities, and *t*hreats. A SWOT analysis is usually done in a facilitated meeting in which the participants have agreed-on ground rules. If you prefer, stakeholders can complete their individual versions of the analysis and then come together to discuss the results as a group.

TIP

We recommend using a professional meeting facilitator. A facilitator brings experience and a neutral viewpoint to the proceedings and can be effective in helping a group arrive at a consensus about organizational goals — even goals that may be unpopular with some staff or board members.

Be honest when looking at your organization's strengths and weaknesses. It's tempting, for example, to put the best face on the activities of the board of directors. They're volunteers, after all. How much time do they *really* have to give to the organization? But if you avoid identifying important deficiencies because you don't want to hurt someone's feelings, your planning efforts will be handicapped by bad information.

For example, the results of a SWOT analysis for an organization providing counseling services to unemployed adults may look something like this:

Strengths

- The program staff is highly qualified and committed.
- Clients give program services a high-quality rating.
- The organization has an accumulated budget surplus equal to approximately five months of operating expenses.
- Program costs are funded largely by local government grants.

Weaknesses

- The cost per client is higher than in similar programs.
- Contributed income from individuals is low.
- The programs aren't well known to the general public.
- The organization has no community partnerships with other nonprofit organizations, government agencies, or large-scale corporations.

Opportunities

- The closure and shrinking of nearby industries indicate that more members of the client base will be working as part-time independent contractors without employee benefits.
- The organization's marketing campaign has attracted additional visitors to its website.
- The organization has modest cash reserves to invest in growth.
- No one in the organization has discussed how the board of directors can help start an endowment fund for the organization.

Threats

» Local government (the primary funding source) has announced plans to open its own job training and placement programs in three years.

» Over the past five years, program costs have increased at a rate of 3 percent per year.

As this example shows, one or more items often can be listed as both strengths and weaknesses. Here, the fact that the nonprofit organization is largely funded by the government is a strength, but it's also a weakness because it creates a situation in which the organization relies on a single source of funding.

A review of this SWOT analysis reveals a nonprofit organization that has been successful in providing quality services and getting those services funded by government contracts. It has been financially prudent and developed modest cash reserves. However, the working conditions are changing for its clients, and the program's future may be in jeopardy if it continues to rely heavily on government resources. A major new competitor is entering its field.

This nonprofit organization has limited time and resources to diversify revenues. If its government funding is cut completely, it may have to close, spending its cash reserve on connecting its clients to other services, meeting with its donors to thank them, telling stories of its clients' successes on its website, providing modest severance packages to loyal employees, and taking necessary accounting and legal steps to close.

In the meantime, because its clients need new entrepreneurial and planning skills to manage their changed employment status, it has the opportunity to develop distinctive programs responding to current needs. It also has opportunities to develop an individual donor campaign led by the board of directors; meet with other nonprofits, local colleges, and business leaders about sharing counseling and training services; and seek coverage of its programs in the local media.

REMEMBER

A SWOT analysis can be a powerful guide to developing a plan because it looks at both your nonprofit organization's inner workings and external environment. As your committee moves on to the next planning step, where you decide together on goals and strategies for coming years, it can refer to the SWOT analysis as a reminder to celebrate and further develop strengths, tackle weaknesses, and prepare for change.

Putting the plan in writing

After the research, analysis, and discussion, it's time to determine future directions and put the results into a final plan. Ideally, the plans of your nonprofit organization become apparent after sifting through and discussing the material that's assembled. If the strategic planning group can't reach a consensus, it may want to test its ideas on the board of directors or a few trusted peers to help it come to an agreement.

TIP

It can be easy to come up with a long laundry list of goals and then skim lightly over the strategies you'll use to achieve them. We recommend limiting your goals to a half dozen or fewer and paying full attention to the related strategies.

Ensuring that your goals make sense

Organizational goals need to be specific; measurable when they're attached to time-bound objectives; and attainable within one year. The easy way to get started with writing your goals is to start them with verbs. By using verbs to write your strategic planning goals, you're indicating that action will occur to enable the goals to be achieved within each year's strategic plan.

Here are some examples of well-written strategic planning goals:

- Provide the Village of Hempstead's families in need of funding to adopt a child with the needed resources to enable their family to become complete.
- Empower homeless women in San Diego County to change their lives via our new social services street outreach and safe-shelter program.
- Educate high school students enrolled in the Biloxi school district about the importance of diversity, equity, and inclusion in the school setting, future workplaces, higher education, and life.
- Create a farm-based shelter-and-adoption program for the lower desert's feral cats.

Itemizing the parts that form your strategic plan

When you reach a consensus about your organization's goals, assemble a written strategic plan. The components of the plan should include the following items, in the order shown:

- An executive summary
- A statement of the organizational mission and vision

- A description of the strategic planning process
- Organizational goals
- Strategies to achieve those goals (measurable objectives and implementation plans for programs and services)
- Appendixes that contain summaries of the background material used to determine the strategic plan, including a list of the people who participated in creating the strategic plan

Assign the task of drafting the document to your best writer. When the draft is finished, the strategic planning committee should review it to ensure that everything in the plan is stated clearly. Submit the final draft to the full board for discussion and adoption.

WARNING

A common failing of strategic planning documents is the use of jargon and vague language. A strategic plan that uses such wording and lacks clarity is a poor guide and does nothing to increase your credibility with your constituents or your funders. You don't want readers to finish reading it and ask, "What is it that they're going to do?"

Adjusting your strategic plan when necessary

Although having a strategic plan is important, flexibility in its implementation is just as important. Things change. Reviewing your strategic plan is an ongoing activity — preferably monthly but at least quarterly, your board, executive director, and program staff should revisit it to check on the progress you've made and identify whether assumptions and predictions were correct. You may find that you need to employ new strategies to achieve your carefully developed goals.

Putting Plans into Action

Unfortunately, too many well-crafted strategic plans end up in a drawer or on a bookshelf. Participants may have expended great effort to create the document, and board and staff may have formed close bonds during the strategic planning process. But if the decisions made during that board/staff retreat at the charming lakeside inn aren't translated into tasks, what's the point — other than camaraderie?

REMEMBER

No matter what sort of strategic plan you create — organizational, fundraising, marketing, program, or facility-related — you need to break the larger, all-encompassing strategies into a sequence of steps that enables you to chart your progress over time. The following sections help you do that.

Defining and setting goals, objectives, strategies, and outcomes

Getting lost in all the terminology of strategic planning is easy. Here are brief definitions of four common terms — goals, objectives, strategies, and outcomes — using a simple example of traveling from Chicago to New York to attend a professional conference:

- *Goals* are your organization's aspirations. Goals can be set at the organizational level, the program or department level, or the individual employee level. Using a road trip as an analogy, a goal is to arrive in New York, having left from Chicago.
- *Objectives* are smaller steps that one must accomplish to reach a goal, and they're always stated in a way that can be measured. So, on a trip from Chicago to New York, an objective may be to drive 325 miles on the first day. When you pull into the motel parking lot, you can check the odometer to see whether you've achieved your objective.
- *Strategies* are approaches or ways to achieve goals. Usually, more than one option exists. You can travel to New York by several methods: plane, train, automobile, bicycle, or on foot. After considering the costs, your schedule, and your hiking ability, you decide to travel by car.
- *Outcomes* describe the results of reaching a goal. In this example, you reach the goal — New York — and learn useful information at your conference. Outcomes are written in past tense.

To see how all four terms come into play, look at the example of a development plan in Table 3-1. Reading from top to bottom, you have the whole plan, from organizational goal to outcome.

REMEMBER

Don't get bogged down in terms. How you label the different steps in your plan is less important than clarifying what you need to accomplish and the steps you'll take to succeed.

TABLE 3-1 Organizational Goal to Outcome

What We Call It	Example
Organizational goal	Diversify income.
Strategic goal	Develop a reliable annual campaign.
Objective 1	By the end of Year 1, retain 80% or more of current annual fund donors.
Objective 2	By the end of Year 1, increase new prospects by 100% (the baseline is zero), by way of board and advisory committee contacts.
Objective 3	By the end of the first quarter in Year 1, increase the number of new prospects responding to the January fundraising campaign by 10% or more.
Strategy	Increase individual contributed income.
Outcome	Increase organizational finances from new funders who have committed to contributing to the next three annual fundraising campaigns.

Creating a work plan

You can see in Table 3-1 that the objectives are measurable results. Achieving each objective in the table requires several steps. Here's where *work plans* (also referred to as action plans) come into play. Work plans break tasks into small steps so that they can be easily managed.

Work plans — the nuts-and-bolts of strategic planning — contain strategies for achieving specific objectives, identify deadlines for completion, and note who's responsible for completing the task. A work plan answers the following questions for each objective:

- What is the end result?
- How long will it take to do the job?
- Who will be responsible for doing the job?
- What resources are needed?

A typical work plan may look like Table 3-2.

Work plans require that a job be broken down into smaller tasks. In Table 3-2, for example, the three objectives can be split into even smaller tasks.

WARNING

Be aware that you can take the creation of a work plan to the point of absurdity. Don't make work plans so detailed and specific that writing the plan takes more time than doing the work that the plan specifies.

TABLE 3-2 Sample Work Plan: Create an Appeal Letter

Objective	By When	By Whom	Resources Needed	Date Completed
Attend workshop on fundraising letters	February 28	Allen	Find workshop via the Foundation Center	February 26
Draft letter and seek feedback	March 15	Allen and board committee	Committee meeting for feedback	March 15
Revise and copyedit letter	March 20	Ashley and Gina	Experienced editor	March 25

Planning for Programs

Program planning is such an important part of nonprofit work that we think it needs its own section. Nearly all nonprofit organizations provide a service of one sort or another. The organization provides services by way of programs. A small nonprofit may have only one. Larger nonprofits may have dozens. No matter how many programs you have, you may be thinking of adding a new one or changing the ones you have. We walk you through the process in the following sections.

Working as a team

When you're developing programs for the first time, it's important to create a team that includes the executive director, program staff, volunteers, and community partner representatives. Your team members will all have insight on how to plan successful programs. Each team member brings a different viewpoint to the program planning process, so it's important to listen and capture their input.

As with strategic planning, program planning should be done as a group exercise. It doesn't have to be as extensive as the strategic planning process, but you gain more acceptance of the new program and guard against omitting important details when you work with others to develop new programs.

The best and most productive way to facilitate a program planning team session is to guide the discussion using a theory of change worksheet. A *theory of change* is a description of why a particular way of working will be effective, showing how change happens in the short, medium, and long terms to achieve the intended results. A theory of change can be developed at the beginning of the program planning process or to describe an existing program (so that you can evaluate it). It's particularly helpful if you're planning or evaluating a complex program, but it can also be used for almost every decision-making process.

TO EXPLAIN YOUR PROGRAM, TAKE A TIP FROM THE BUSINESS SECTOR

If you were starting a new business and looking for investors, one of the first things you'd do is create a business plan. Nonprofits are wise to follow this model when developing a new program. A business model is useful in explaining the program and can form the basics of grant proposals when you seek funding.

Business plans should include the following information:

- An executive summary that covers the main points of the plan
- An explanation of the need for the program and who will use it (This information is comparable to the market analysis in a for-profit business plan.)
- A description of the program and your strategies for implementing it
- Why your organization is best poised to implement the program
- Résumés and background information about the people who will provide and manage the program services
- Three-year projections of income and expenses for the project, including an organizational budget for the current year

A theory of change worksheet includes questions like these to ask your program planning team members:

- » What type of program is needed to create change in our target population?
- » What should the intervention components of the program be, and for how long?
- » What are some best practice examples of how programs similar to the one we're planning have been successful and produced desirable outcomes?
- » What are the current demographics of our target population?
- » How can we prove that the need for our programming exists?
- » Are we proposing unique or innovative programming, or are we duplicating programming already offered by other nonprofit organizations and public agencies in our region?
- » What are the goals for our program?
- » What resources do we already have in place to support this new program?

» What resources do we need from the community and potential funders to support this new program?
» What outcomes should we project for our target population when the program is implemented?
» How can we measure the achievements of our target population as they progress through our program?
» What will it cost to implement our program?
» What are some potential sources of funding for this new program?
» What in-kind support can we expect from our regional partners?

Think ahead with all planning efforts about how you are going to evaluate the program and the data you will be collecting.

TIP

The Global Partnership for Sustainable Development Data created a useful theory of change document. Check out `https://media.wiley.com/product_ancillary/20/11198357/DOWNLOAD/Nonprofit-Kit-For-Dummies-6th-Edition-File-8-7-9781119835721.pdf` to view this example.

Most theories of change also include *outputs* (the quantifiable results the program will produce) — for example, ten partnerships established and supported or five in-kind contributions from new partners. You're projecting the results or outcome of your program implementation's impact.

Assessing needs

A *needs assessment* is an important part of program planning. If you're thinking of starting a new program, for example, a needs assessment to determine whether the program is necessary should be the first step you take.

A needs assessment is more or less a research project. You don't necessarily need to hold to the strict requirements of scientific inquiry, but just as you do when collecting information to help guide strategic planning, you should do everything possible to ensure that the information is accurate and free of bias.

Determining the questions to be answered

Your needs assessment should evaluate the answers to the following questions:

» **Are other organizations providing the same service?** Obviously, you don't want to duplicate services if another organization is already doing the job. If you believe that your competition isn't doing a good job, that's another question. Jump to the second point.

- **How many people might use the service?** Making a good estimate of the number of people the new program will serve is important. Doing so helps you justify establishing the program and helps you plan for staff needs.
- **Can and will people pay for the service?** If so, how much? How many of the people you hope to serve will need discounted tuition or scholarships, for example?
- **Do we need to meet any special requirements for providing the program?** Does the program need to be near good public transportation? Is parking important? Will people come to the neighborhood where you're providing the services? Will the program require you to register your services, obtain licenses, or obtain operating permits?
- **What are the trends?** Will the number of people using the service increase or decrease in the future? Is the population in your community increasing, decreasing, or staying the same?

Researching the best solutions

Just as when you collect information for strategic planning, your goal in program planning is to find the most accurate, unbiased data available. Don't depend on only one source. Here are some ways to get the information you need:

- **Talk to colleagues in your community.** Ideally, you have relationships with the people and organizations that provide similar services. Ask their opinions about your ideas for new programming.
- **Look at census data.** The best sources for population information are the numbers collected by way of a census (www.census.gov). Some municipal and regional planning groups also publish population-growth projections. These projections are estimates, but census data doesn't represent an absolutely accurate count of the people in your community, either. Gather all the numbers you can get.
- **Visit a funding information network or the Candid website.** By looking at funding trends, you can piece together a picture of which services are available and who is supporting them. You can find a funding information network library near you at `https://candid.org/find-us` or subscribe to its services online at the Foundation Directory Online by Candid. In addition to guiding you to potential funding sources, this website's *Philanthropy News Digest* (PND by Candid) shares research and articles produced by foundations.

- **Get information from current or potential users of the service by distributing questionnaires and hosting focus groups.** The questions you ask determine, in large part, the answers you receive. If possible, find someone who has experience in preparing survey questions to guide you.
- **Look at similar programs in other communities.** Although you can't always depend on the experience of others fitting exactly with your particular situation, examining what others have done is always wise.

TIP

Check out File 8-8 at `https://www.wiley.com/en-us/Nonprofit+Kit+For+Dummies%2C+6th+Edition-p-9781119835745#downloads-section` for a sample needs assessment questionnaire.

REMEMBER

Some people say they don't want to share an idea with others because they're afraid someone may steal it. Although you can't rule out the chances of this happening, we believe that it's a rare occurrence. In almost all cases, being open about your plans is a good idea.

Brainstorming the resources needed to implement new programs

Just because a new program is needed doesn't necessarily mean that your organization should be the one to start it. You need to take other factors into account. Work with the program planning team and invite your board treasurer or financial director or accountant to join in the program planning session. Look at *all* aspects of what it takes to fund, implement, evaluate, and continue a new program after the first round of start-up funding.

Consider the factors in the following sections when assessing your ability to start a new program.

Estimating the cost of programs

A new program almost always adds expenses to your organizational budget. To be sure that you don't get yourself into a financial hole, carefully project the extra costs you'll have from additional staff and increased space, equipment, and insurance. After you have solid expense projections, you have to project where you'll find the added revenue needed to pay these costs.

Evaluating organizational and staff capability

Does your nonprofit organization have the knowledge and expertise to provide the program services? This question may not be a concern if the proposed program is merely an extension of what you've been doing. If your organization is branching out into new areas, however, be sure that you or someone else in the organization has the credentials to provide a quality program.

Also, pay attention to hidden staff costs. For example, consider whether your current program director will have sufficient time to provide adequate supervision for the new program. Will you need to hire a new staff person or consultant to implement the program? Is this a one-time cost or a recurring cost to continue the program? Will this person require a computer, cellphone, insurance, or office space?

Remembering special requirements

Check whether you need additional licensing, accreditation, or permits to provide the program. This is especially important for human-services programs. For example, if you've been working with teenagers and want to expand to elementary and preschool children, find out whether your program space must meet additional building-code requirements in order to serve a younger client group.

Fitting it into the mission

From time to time, we're all tempted by the idea of doing something new. Gee, wouldn't it be nice if we could sell goldfish in the front lobby? But you have to ask yourself what selling goldfish has to do with your organization's mission. If you go too far afield, you can detract from the hard work of addressing your organizational purpose. Also, if you go beyond what is permitted by your purpose statement in your articles and bylaws, you may be acting unlawfully beyond your organization's authority and perhaps outside of its tax-exempt status.

Thinking long term

An idea that looks good today may not look good next year or the year after. Don't forget that costs rise year after year. Your staff appreciates occasional raises. Try to imagine where the program will be five and ten years into the future.

REMEMBER

Funding sources may be available to launch a new program or expand services. But it's wise to have a plan for sustaining the program after it's launched, by identifying funding sources for its ongoing support after the initial funding source is gone.

IN THIS CHAPTER

» Recognizing the need for evaluation

» Orienting yourself to what the evaluation process involves

» Analyzing the results and implementing them

Chapter 4
Evaluating Your Work: Are You Meeting Your Goals?

How do you know whether your nonprofit organization is meeting its goals? How do you know whether your approach is valid, your staff is qualified, and your clients benefit from what you do? When your nonprofit's resources are scarce, you may want to put all of them into providing direct benefits to the people you serve. But, wait. When resources are scarce, they must be used in the best possible way. That's why you have to set aside some of the organization's time, money, and attention for evaluation.

Most organizations gather information during the normal course of doing their work. A good evaluation can be one in which you collect information in a consistent, systematic way and ask the right questions so that you learn from its patterns and particulars. This chapter outlines what goes into a meaningful evaluation and explains how to interpret the results and implement any necessary changes. Book 4, Chapter 5 has information about setting and prioritizing goals in the context of budget planning.

TIP

Check out File 9-1 at https://www.wiley.com/en-us/Nonprofit+Kit+For+Dummies%2C+6th+Edition-p-9781119835745#downloads-section for a list of web resources related to the topics we cover in this chapter.

REMEMBER

We use the word *evaluation* as a general term in this chapter to mean any act of reflecting on the quality and success of your nonprofit's work. Some professionals differentiate between an assessment and an evaluation, however. An *assessment* is the ongoing use of measures or tools (such as exams or surveys) to indicate progress being made, and an *evaluation* is a systematic, rigorous comparison of one's results to defined expectations or standards or another program. Check out the nearby sidebar for more definitions of evaluation terms.

EVALUATION: SOME DEFINITIONS OF TERMS

- **assessment:** An ongoing activity of measuring progress. Often the term is used in the context of education to mean gauging what someone has learned. Tests are a common form of assessment, but other forms of measurement — such as notes from observations, and the quality of student papers and presentations as demonstrations of learning — are valid and appropriate.
- **evaluation:** A process for gauging the quality, effectiveness, or results of a project or program. The term is often used interchangeably with *assessment,* but they are not the same. An evaluation should be rigorous and systemic. It may be based on an analysis of multiple assessments. If you think of these terms in the context of grade school, an assessment is a weekly spelling test, and an evaluation is an analysis of a student's strengths, weaknesses, patterns, and progress as a speller.
- **formative evaluation:** A formative evaluation looks at a project's policies and procedures, questioning whether that project is running smoothly and efficiently. Its audience often is intended to be an agency's staff; a formative evaluation helps them improve their practices. Often a formative evaluation is enacted in the early stages of a program, testing and refining how the work is to be done.
- **summative evaluation:** As is suggested by the word *sum,* a summative evaluation often is based on the collection and analysis of data and always focuses on the ultimate outcome or results of a project. Its meaning is similar to *impact evaluation.*
- **impact evaluation:** An impact evaluation — sometimes called a summative or outcomes evaluation — asks not just what your project accomplished and whether it ran smoothly but also whether it effected change. It asks who was served and whether the work had value. If we were to look at the example of the student speller, an impact evaluation might analyze the advancing difficulty of words mastered

and/or progress in the student's writing and reading abilities. Did the student's comprehension improve? If spelling ability is tested in classroom spelling bees, such an evaluation might also look at changes in a student's public speaking ability and confidence.

- **context evaluation:** A context evaluation takes place during the preliminary stages of a project and seeks to measure how well the project's design suits the setting in which it will take place. The acronym *CIPP* sometimes is used for this kind of evaluation; it stands for *c*ontext, *i*mpact, *p*rocess, and *p*roduct. Why spend time on such a complex inquiry before a project is fully launched? The point is to thoughtfully consider alternative approaches before it gets fully under way — potentially saving time and resources that might be wasted on an unsuccessful approach.
- **antecedent evaluation:** An antecedent evaluation asks what factors in the environment affect the project's implementation and results. For example, what if a large number of students transfer into the school where the project is taking place — changing the ratio of teachers to students in the classroom being studied? That contextual change might slow the student's progress and self-confidence.

Knowing the Importance of Evaluation

Unlike for-profit businesses, nonprofits can't evaluate their performance solely by showing a profit at the end of the year or by increasing the value of their stock. Indeed, they may generate a budget surplus to invest in their future work, but that isn't their primary purpose. Some people say that nonprofits have to achieve a *double* bottom line, one in which their finances are healthy and their activities are meeting their goals — or what a friend of ours calls "an appropriate balance of mission and resources." That's where evaluation comes in: It can measure how successful you've been at focusing on your purpose and achieving your challenging goals and objectives.

Evaluating your work goes hand in hand with every aspect of leading and managing your organization. An evaluation can

- Tell you whether your planning strategies are working and whether you need to adjust them
- Guide you in hiring the right staff for the work to be done and in making good use of volunteers' time and energies
- Help you draft your annual budget by pointing out where resources are most needed

- Convey the information you need to market your work to the constituents you want to serve
- Strengthen your fundraising by arming you with information for reports on your work to foundations and donors
- Alert you if a program is having the effect that you want to achieve with your clients

In short, to know where you're going, you need to know where you've been. Evaluation can tell you whether you're on the right road or need to recalibrate your route.

Working Through the Evaluation Process

You've probably been part of an evaluation before, whether a personal performance evaluation or a program evaluation, but maybe you've never been in charge of the entire process. Not to worry: This section provides an outline of the process, gives you some pointers about what to evaluate, and helps you select who will perform the evaluation.

Evaluations have three main components:

- **Set up an evaluation.** This step involves determining the type of evaluation you need to perform, asking the right questions, assigning someone the responsibility to gather and analyze the information you need in order to answer those questions, and deciding where and how you'll find that information.
- **Conduct the evaluation.** During this step, you gather the information you need consistently and measure what you're learning in an honest (and perhaps even self-critical) way. You may find that you need to devise tools to gather that information — such as surveys of constituents, focus groups, formal observations, or one-on-one interviews. Pre- and post-tests are an easy way to ascertain if learning or other desired outcomes have taken place.
- **Interpret the data.** In almost all cases, your understanding is deeper (and your findings more valid) if you compare the information you compile to something else. That "something else" may be results for the people you serve before they participated in your program. It may be results for people who didn't participate in any comparable program (a placebo). Or, it may be results for people who participated in a different kind of program. We address this stage in the later section, "Analyzing Results and Putting Them to Work."

Selecting the right kind of evaluation

Evaluations come in many varieties. The type you choose depends on whether a program is brand-new or has been refined, how much is known about what works in the field in which you're operating, whether you want to prove that your approach is a model that can influence others, and how much money you have to invest in evaluation.

Your organization may consider these two basic types of evaluation:

- **Formative:** You analyze the progress of your nonprofit's work while your work is in process.
- **Summative:** You reach the end of a phase or a project and reflect on its accomplishments.

Now that you can drop these terms easily into conversations, let us introduce three other kinds of evaluation you want to know:

- **Process:** Did the project do what it was supposed to do and on schedule? Did you acquire an office, hire three key staff, promote programs, or sign up participants? Very good. In your process evaluation, tell your readers about the steps you took — the story of your program activities.
- **Goal-based:** In a goal-based evaluation, you measure what took place and compare it to the original intentions. Did the project reach its goals? For example, your goal may be to "establish a tuberculosis awareness program in the southeastern quadrant of the city that reaches 500 individuals during its first year." Determining whether a program was established is simple; figuring out how many people the program reached is a little more difficult. This answer depends, of course, on the method the project is using to reach people. In other words, you must define what you mean by *reach* before you start measuring the program's results.
- **Impact or outcomes evaluation:** In an impact evaluation, you ask whether you met your objectives and outcomes. Did the project achieve the desired results and make a meaningful difference? Although it requires time and attention, this type of evaluation is relatively straightforward. For example, if you oversee a tuberculosis awareness program, a desired outcome may be increased numbers of people being tested for TB and, if they have contracted it, taking their medication consistently to improve their health and reduce the likelihood they will infect others. Evaluating such an outcome requires an in-depth study of the population in that section of the city to determine whether they acted on the knowledge they gained and — if they were infected — continued to follow a strict regimen for taking their medication. Public health department data about rates of tuberculosis infections can be tracked yearly for the neighborhoods served.

One of the hardest and most important things to ascertain in an outcomes evaluation is whether your organization has set the most meaningful objectives and outcomes.

SHAPING AN OUTCOMES EVALUATION

As an example of shaping an outcomes evaluation, let's say your organization provides shelter to people who have no home. You may have identified the following aspirations:

- **Measurable Objective 1:** By the end of the funding cycle, increase temporary housing availability by 25 percent for chronically homeless adolescent males.
- **Measurable Objective 2:** By the end of the funding cycle, increase by 40 percent the number of clients completing self-assessment competencies to identify barriers to their finding and maintaining secure housing.
- **Measurable Objective 3:** By the end of the first quarter, increase by 10 percent the number of people per month who enroll with local and federal subsidized housing programs.
- **Outcome 1:** An increased number of chronically homeless adolescent males have taken advantage of nightly shelter beds, counseling, and connections to subsidy programs to secure long-term, affordable housing.

Suppose this were your organization and your evaluation to devise. In that case, you could measure whether you met the first three objectives by keeping intake records for people staying at your organization and taking advantage of its counseling and referral services. It would be harder to measure the outcome, but possible if you had good working relationships with the local and federal housing program staff or if part of your organization's work involved sending out caseworkers to check on former clients to see how they're doing, which would have a major impact on your program budget.

If you want to consider whether you've established the right objectives and outcomes or whether there may be a better way to serve your constituents, you can

- **Survey your constituents** to find out how they lost their housing and ask what they think they most need to maintain a stable place to live.
- **Talk to colleagues** (perhaps partners at the local and federal programs with which you're working) about gaps in services available to people who lack stable housing.
- **Invest in research into your region's job and housing markets,** and investigate the types of leases or mortgages that were common to people who lost their apartments or homes. You may find that your best goal is to address some of the root causes of your constituents' situations.

Planning for evaluation

Before you jump into launching a new organization or program, we strongly recommend that you decide how you'll evaluate it. That way, from the beginning, you can set up methods for collecting information, identify who will be responsible, and budget for the costs. By establishing an evaluation plan at a program's inception, you can collect initial information about the people or places you plan to serve. Hence, you have baseline data to which you can compare your results.

A logic model provides a visual outline of your program or project's resources, goals, and intended outcomes. Your logic model can guide you in understanding what you need to know about your nonprofit's work and its results. A sample logic model is shown in Figure 4-1.

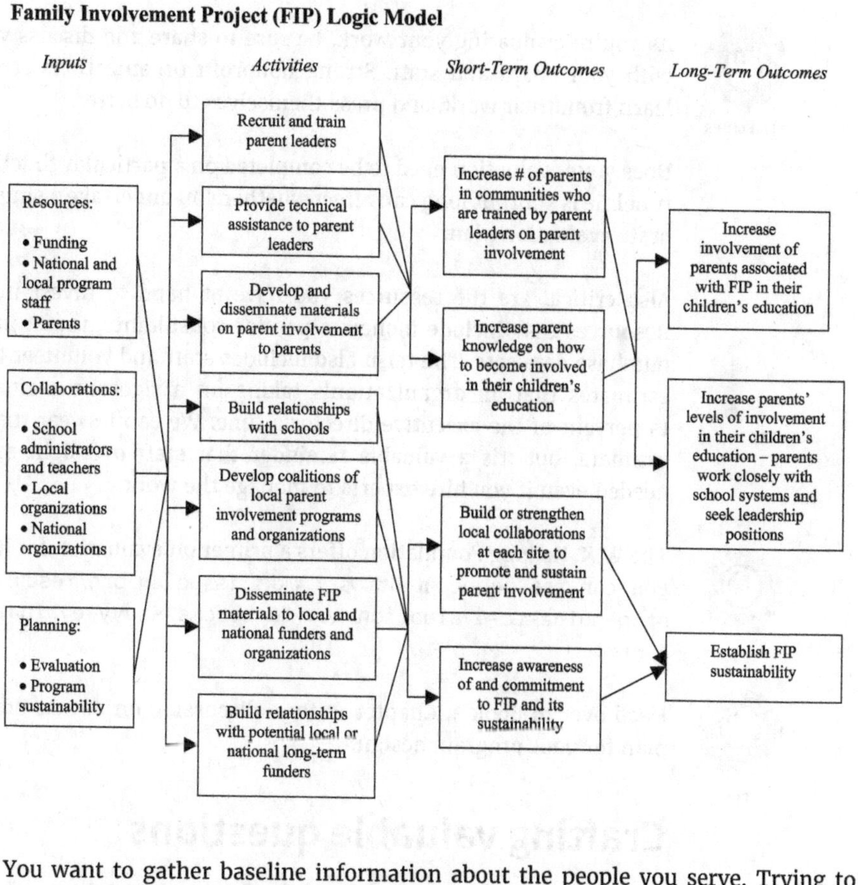

FIGURE 4-1: Sample logic model.

REMEMBER

You want to gather baseline information about the people you serve. Trying to backtrack later to re-create such information is profoundly difficult.

Evaluating Your Work: Are You Meeting Your Goals?

As you set up your evaluation, first identify the purpose and audience. Are you trying a risky new approach to offering a program? Do you need to fulfill the requirements of a government contract? Are you expected by a foundation to share your results with peer organizations doing similar work? Should your evaluation follow standard practices or protocols in your field? Are you hoping to publish your results to be read by a general audience? Or, do you just want to share what you learn with your board and staff to make program adjustments and strengthen your work?

Before you design detailed surveys and interview plans, ask yourself what information your nonprofit already has at hand. It may include attendance records, referrals from other nonprofits, unique visitors to your website, instructors' progress reports, numbers of trees planted, and many other data points that can illustrate your program's progress and reputation.

REMEMBER

As you're evaluating your work, be sure to share and discuss what you discover with your board and staff. Strong nonprofit organizations remain self-critical, learn from their work, and press themselves to do better.

Does your evaluation need to be completed on a particular timeline? Whether that timeline is short or long can affect whether you undertake a simpler or more elaborate evaluation plan.

Also critical are the resources you have at hand to invest in your evaluation. Resources may include money to pay for consultants, invest in focus groups, or purchase data sets. The term also includes staff and volunteer time. We've heard estimates that an organization's taking on a rigorous evaluation will require 15 percent of the executive director's time. We can't swear that it's an accurate estimate, but it's a valuable reminder that staff oversight and leadership are needed even if you hire experts to manage the work.

TIP

The W.K. Kellogg Foundation offers a primer on evaluation for its grantees, which you can see online at `https://wkkf.issuelab.org/resource/the-step-by-step-guide-to-evaluation-how-to-become-savvy-evaluation-consumers-4.html`.

TIP

Head over to Book 3, Chapter 10 for a discussion on how to create an evaluation plan for your program design.

Crafting valuable questions

The most important (and often the hardest) step to take in evaluating your nonprofit organization's work is to ask the right questions. What do you need to know to understand whether you've been successful?

If your organization has written a long-range plan, an obvious place to begin is by looking at the measurable objectives defined in that plan and asking how you will know whether you've met them. You may want to push yourself harder and ask whether you met your outcomes, which describe the longer-term, significant change you intend to achieve.

Here are some other topics nonprofits often ask about when evaluating their work:

- **Cost-benefit:** What does it cost per person to provide the service? Is that more or less than an industry standard? If you have multiple programs, does the one being studied cost more or less per person than others?
- **Sustainability:** Have you been able to raise the funds needed to continue the program? Have you been able to retain qualified staff?
- **Staff and board reflection:** What are you learning from your work? What have you done well, and what has surprised you?
- **Participation:** Are you attracting the people you intended to serve?
- **Client satisfaction:** What do your constituents say about the program? Do they refer others to it? Do they believe their suggestions and criticisms are taken seriously?
- **Volunteer engagement:** Are you attracting and retaining volunteers? How do they rate their satisfaction with their participation? Do they refer others to your volunteer opportunities?
- **Best practices:** If you work in a field in which studies have identified the traits of effective programs, does your program have those traits?
- **Context:** Has the context in which you offer your services changed? How has that affected the people you serve? Have their needs changed?
- **Critical feedback:** What do experts (theater critics, researchers, and so on) have to say about your work and how it compares to the work of others?
- **Model program:** Do others recognize you for the quality of the program? Are you called upon to share your approach and advise others?

TIP

Don't be afraid to ask yourself, "What needs to happen for our nonprofit to no longer be needed?" Maybe it's that streams and creeks are running free, a healthy marsh system is in place, and your town's low-lying areas are no longer flooding. This answer may seem far away from what you can achieve in three or five years. Still, it's valuable to ask the question and remind yourself that your nonprofit wasn't created to operate forever, but rather to work toward achieving a meaningful outcome.

Choosing evaluators: Inside or outside?

One key decision you must make about your program evaluation is who will be responsible for conducting it. The work may involve gathering information from several staff members and clients, and after that, information is compiled, analyzing what it means. You need one or more people to

» Design the evaluation plan and clarify the questions to be asked.

» Create the evaluation tools (surveys and interview protocols, for example), if needed.

» Collect the information to be analyzed (or train others to collect it).

» Organize and analyze the findings and write a report.

If you're undertaking a simple process evaluation, a well-organized and fair-minded staff member can be put in charge. Who else can better understand the purpose of the organization and the nuances of what it's trying to do than someone directly involved in the work? To institute some checks and balances in the process, one person may be responsible for compiling the information. Then a team of staff or board members may discuss its interpretation before a report is written.

"Inside" evaluation offers several advantages. It's usually less costly than hiring an outsider, and the insider doesn't need to be briefed on the work of the nonprofit. On the other hand, the selected person may not be trained in the evaluation process, and some staff members may resent having their work judged by a fellow staff member. Also, those steeped in the day-to-day work of a nonprofit may find it difficult to step back and cast a critical eye over it. Their closeness to the work may bias the findings. Clients and staff may be more forthcoming with an outside person or one they don't know.

REMEMBER

A person who works inside your organization may do a good job of reporting whether programs meet their goals. It can be harder for that person to recommend other approaches that may be more effective.

If you're undertaking a more complex evaluation, you may want to hire a professional evaluator who knows your field and writes well. In hiring such a person, you gain the advantages of their expertise in research methods, knowledge of the work of comparable organizations, and lack of bias in interpreting the information collected. An assessment made by an independent evaluator may be taken more seriously by your funders and peers. Of course, we can't claim that anyone who is paid a fee by your nonprofit to work for you is 100 percent unbiased: That person may hope to be hired again in the future.

What if you have a modest budget and still want good consulting practices to be worked into your evaluation? Three approaches we've used in the past have been to

- » Contact local colleges and universities to see whether a graduate student or faculty member is interested in evaluating your work for academic credit, a dissertation, or a publication.
- » Hire an evaluation firm to design your tools and protocols, train your staff to implement them, and then write an independent analysis of your findings after your staff has compiled them. Your staff will do the more time-consuming part of the project, but the professional adds design expertise and an outside perspective.
- » Compile information to be evaluated internally, share it with an evaluator, and hire that person to analyze and write about the findings.

Conducting Your Evaluation

After you have thought through the planning steps, refined the questions to be asked, chosen your tools for measuring results, and put the right person in charge of your evaluation, doing the work to study your program or nonprofit is relatively easy. You'll want to decide on a time frame (either a single discrete period or a defined number of days or hours per month) for conducting your study and stick to it. If someone on your staff is responsible for the evaluation, be careful that the individual isn't pulled away by other tasks.

If you're using a survey, an exam, or a checklist for making observations, make sure it's designed by someone who knows how to word and structure such a tool. How that tool is used is just as important as its design: If several staff members or volunteers are helping collect data, be sure to brief them as a group before they begin so that everyone is recording the information in the same manner. Of course, you should check for and insist on accuracy and thoroughness. Data is meaningless if it's gathered inconsistently.

Analyzing Results and Putting Them to Work

Imagine that you've collected and organized the information to tell you what you want to know about your organization. It's at hand in lists and charts and graphs. Now you know whether your programs are outstanding and whether your work enhances your clients' lives.

Wait! Not so fast. Just as you must decide on the right questions to investigate as you set out on your evaluation, you need to ask questions about the data you've compiled. Having data and descriptive information isn't the same thing as having knowledge and understanding. Now you must interpret the information and decide how to apply it.

TIP

Evaluation software can help you organize and review your findings. Several websites review nonprofit program evaluation software. One is SourceForge, at `https://sourceforge.net/software/job-evaluation/for-nonprofit`.

Interpreting results

Although it may seem unscientific, we suggest that you ask yourself what your hunches are before you look closely at the information compiled. Be honest with yourself: What do you think the findings will show, and what do you wish they would show?

Often a moment of insight comes when the pattern revealed in the data isn't what you expected to find. As you identify any such surprises, you can probe more deeply to ask why and how those results didn't meet expectations.

After you've read the data against your assumptions, it's time to look at it anew as though you had no expectations. What general picture does it present? What stands out? Is the information consistent over the year, or does it vary — perhaps according to the season, age of participants, or changes in your staff?

We recommend that you include others in this exercise — ask a few key staff and board members and maybe even a few of your constituents. What do they see? What is surprising to them? Of course, if you hired an evaluation consultant, let that person's experience guide you at this phase.

REMEMBER

Although you don't want to confuse people with ambivalent or anything-goes interpretations, seeking more than one point of view can be valuable. Bring a balanced perspective to the findings: Don't embrace all the praise and discount all the criticism (or vice versa). You can learn from both.

ASKING MORE OF THE DATA

Any finding, whether it's positive or negative, is worth probing more deeply. Let's take the case of an education policy and advocacy group as an example. The group invested in a communications manager and an improved website and data systems to expand its reach. When it wanted parents and other community members to know about legislation under review in the state senate or assembly, it sent alerts by email and social media posts.

Because the group was using the web and social media as its programmatic tools, it made sense for the group to look at its online analytics, many of which looked good:

- Its email list was growing steadily, and the click-through rate to its website was higher than the industry average.
- The number of unique visitors to its website grew from month to month, and, on average, visitors read three pages when they went there.
- The number of people who "liked" the group on Facebook grew steadily, and many of them shared its posts with others.
- A small but gradually expanding number of people followed its tweets.

These are good signs of a growing online presence, but it's still worth asking whether the people who like the group on Facebook also take action and contact their representatives or talk to their school boards about the subjects raised. Social media friends and followers are good, but do they include people with influence in local or state government or education policy?

As is true in many cases, the depth and quality of involvement of people in this organization were more important to its success than the total number of passive fans.

Using your evaluation to strengthen your work

You've looked at your evaluation findings with trusted colleagues; you've turned them inside out and upside down to see them from every angle. Now it's time to interpret them, to tell their story. Likely what you've discovered is not all positive and not all negative. Perhaps you've noticed that some services are rated more highly than others, and some short-term objectives have been met, but others remain elusive. It's time to step back from your organization and programs, and acknowledge any disappointing results, and set short-term and long-term goals to improve upon them.

A program may be flawed in its design, in how it's executed, or in who is leading it; and its effectiveness can be smothered by external circumstances that are beyond its control — a shift in the economy or demographics, a change in public policy, or even a natural disaster, like the COVID-19 pandemic, can derail it.

Some changes will be obvious and easy to make. Maybe a different program schedule would be more convenient for working parents, or better training for volunteers would make them feel more involved and successful. When your findings suggest no easy responses, turn to ideas from others — best practices in your field, model programs, or scholarly research. Don't forget to ask the clients you serve.

Evaluation findings also should be shared with your board, which is ultimately responsible for your nonprofit's fulfilling its mission and purpose. It may decide that some programs aren't a good investment of the nonprofit's hard-won resources and recommend cutting them.

Telling the truth

If your evaluation results are disappointing, face them honestly and share what you've discovered. You may share them discreetly with your board or with the funders who know you well, but doctoring your data or analyzing the findings in a disingenuous way can hurt your organization's reputation and that of your evaluation consultant if you hired one. And all that time and effort you put into your evaluation is lost if you allow it to sit on a shelf collecting dust.

Sharing the evaluation results with your stakeholders

Every person at the program planning meeting represents your stakeholder's group. The term *stakeholder* refers to any individual or group interested in your nonprofit organization. Stakeholders include people directly involved, such as board members, people you serve, donors, community partners, or foundations that give you grants (past, current, and future). This group is entitled to see the outcome of the grant-funded program's planning, implementation, and evaluation processes. When you share how well your program did (qualitatively and quantitatively), you engage in *dissemination,* which means to spread something, especially information, widely. As a transparent public tax-exempt charity, you need to determine how you want to share your evaluation findings.

These days, the public deeply values transparency. Unless your evaluation report contains confidential information, we recommend that you create an executive summary of your findings and publish them as a brochure or PDF available from your website or shared in a meeting with your stakeholders.

TIP

You may find that a poor evaluation lowers staff morale, but if those staff members are invited to participate in creative problem solving, improving customer service, and other goal-setting activities, working with the evaluation can contribute to building their teamwork and resolve.

Ultimately, you must embrace and attempt to understand the evaluation findings. Many people start nonprofits based on their ideals, and many of them work long hours with limited resources to achieve quite ambitious results. Achieving those results depends on collecting good information and interpreting that information with integrity and resolve.

At the end of the day, the purpose of your evaluation is to benefit your nonprofit organization and the stakeholders it serves.

IN THIS CHAPTER

» Recognizing what motivates volunteers

» Setting up your volunteer program

» Recruiting volunteers

» Making sure a volunteer is right for your nonprofit

» Helping volunteers do their work

» Showing your appreciation and thanks

Chapter 5
You Can Count on Me! Working with Volunteers

Millions of potential volunteers are just waiting for the right nonprofit organization to invite them to volunteer. Just about every nonprofit charitable organization uses volunteers in some capacity. For example, in most cases, board members serve without compensation. And, for many nonprofit organizations in the United States, volunteers do all the work, from planting the trees to paying the bills. Even if your organization employs paid staff, volunteers still provide valuable services. Organizations depend on volunteers to staff telephone hotlines, lead scout troops, tutor students, coach youth sports teams, serve hot meals, organize fundraising events, and stuff envelopes. If you're going to manage a nonprofit organization, you need to know how to work with volunteers.

Of course, you may be sitting alone in your office and asking, "Where are these millions of volunteers?" This chapter offers suggestions to help you determine what kind of volunteers you need, how to find them, and how to keep them happy after they arrive.

TIP

Check out File 10-1 at `https://www.wiley.com/en-us/Nonprofit+Kit+For+Dummies%2C+6th+Edition-p-9781119835745#downloads-section` for a list of web resources related to the topics we cover in this chapter.

Knowing Why People Volunteer

The classic stereotype of a volunteer is someone who has lots of time to spare and is looking for something to do. Although this perception may have been true in the past, when many women stayed out of the workforce and gave their free time to charity, that stereotype no longer fits; however, even today women still represent the largest majority of volunteers. It's still true that more women volunteer than men, but people between the ages of 35 and 54 are the likeliest to volunteer. This is the age range when both men and women are likely balancing careers with raising families, not to mention taking care of aging parents, going to the gym, and keeping up with email and social media.

Why is it that people, even very busy ones, volunteer their time? We think it's because they've recognized the benefits of volunteering time to a favorite organization and because nonprofit organizations have become smarter about asking them.

REMEMBER

Understanding why people volunteer makes it easier for you to find volunteers, organize their work, and recognize their contributions. However, not everyone is motivated by the same factors. People volunteer for a variety of reasons, including their desire to

- **Help the community and others.** Helping others usually comes to mind first when people think of the reasons that people volunteer. But as you see when you read deeper into this list, volunteers' motives aren't always this simple.

  TIP

  What appeals to retired volunteers? Being able to give back to their communities on their own terms and when they're available and healthy enough to volunteer.

- **Express their values.** Believing in an organization's mission is an important motivator for volunteers. A person who believes it's important for all children to have access to a quality education is more likely to volunteer at a local school or tutoring program.
- **Increase self-esteem.** Volunteering makes people feel better about themselves. Giving a few hours a week, or even a month, to an organization creates good feelings.

» **Help out their friends.** Friends are often the first people we turn to when we need help. Volunteering is also a helpful way to get together with friends regularly.

» **Make new friends.** Volunteering is usually a social activity. People often use this opportunity to meet interesting people who share their interests and values.

» **Try out a job.** People considering a job in the nonprofit sector often discover that volunteering is a good way to take a peek at what happens on the inside.

» **Polish their résumés.** Adding volunteer experience to a résumé shows a commitment to helping others or to working in a particular field.

TIP

What appeals to young volunteers? Being able to earn community-service credit hours for their high school or college community-service requirements.

» **Develop new skills.** A volunteer job often gives people an opportunity to learn how to do something they didn't already know how to do.

» **Enjoy doing something they love.** Many volunteer jobs come with intrinsic benefits for their participants. Ushers at the symphony get to hear the music. Gardeners removing invasive plants from a native plant preserve get to spend a day in a beautiful natural setting.

Keep this list in mind and you'll realize that you don't have to focus your recruitment efforts exclusively on retired people or others who have a lot of leisure time. If you provide an environment in which volunteers can bring their friends, meet others who share their interests, and learn new skills, you can attract even the busiest people to volunteer. Remember that you have no reason to be apologetic about asking for help: Volunteering benefits the people who step forward to assist you.

Designing a Volunteer Program

Most start-up organizations depend on volunteers because money to pay staff is unavailable. But the lack of resources isn't the only thing that drives a nonprofit to operate with an all-volunteer staff. Some nonprofits make a deliberate decision to operate solely with volunteers to contain their costs and to achieve results with a collective effort among people who care deeply enough to contribute their time and energy.

REMEMBER

Many nonprofit organizations struggle to engage volunteers who reflect the racial and ethnic diversity of the communities they serve. Creating a more inclusive volunteer program will send a message to your funders (we represent the entire community), your board members (we are practicing diversity, equality, and inclusion organization-wide), and to potentially interested volunteers (we want everyone to consider volunteering for our organization).

Here are some ways you can cultivate a successful volunteer program:

- » **Shift your language.** You're not selling used cars — you're tapping into the core of humanity's existence by asking people to contribute their time to help other people or animals. Your goal is to touch their hearts and minds when asking someone to give up their time to help others. When you're seeking volunteers to care for rescue animals, for example, talk about the animals you've had throughout your life. Strike a chord of familiarity, soften their hearts, open the way for a conversation about your organization, its mission, and why it needs dedicated volunteers to help it reach full capacity in delivering services to others.
- » **Build relationships.** When someone finally agrees to volunteer with your nonprofit organization, *acknowledge their contributions.* Ask about their health. Make small talk to build a friendship relationship versus a formal boss/volunteer relationship. Take the time to get to know your volunteers — each and every one of them. Remember their names and know what they like to do when it comes to volunteer assignments.
- » **Understand socioeconomic differences.** You must understand what motivates every volunteer and how you can personalize your relationship with that person. Even an effort as small as using a volunteer's first name versus Mr. or Mrs. Smith makes a difference. Take the time to listen to volunteers when they have recommendations for improvement or are concerned about your location or the type of people you serve. Be grateful that they're giving their time to your organization.
- » **Be observant.** What does the volunteer who is homeless like to do? What are the undiscovered skills you see in their attempts to carry out their volunteer work? Maybe someone is bilingual and can help with translating for a client who doesn't speak English. Or the volunteer might have insight into the behavior of another homeless person that is critical for you to know in order to understand irregular behaviors, such as always being late, eating everyone else's leftovers in the kitchen, or standing by the heater during winter.
- » **Strive for inclusive representation.** If all the people who are homeless stand around in the backyard to eat their lunch while everyone else eats in the volunteer lunchroom or board meeting room, you aren't practicing inclusiveness. How can that hurt your organization? It can damage its reputation, goodwill, and mission in the community you serve.

Considering a volunteer coordinator

Although volunteers don't expect to be paid every two weeks, that doesn't mean they come without costs. Recruiting, training, managing, retaining, and thanking volunteers require effort from someone in the organization. We recommend assigning someone the job of *volunteer coordinator*, a person responsible for overseeing or performing the following duties:

- **Recruiting:** Volunteers don't grow on trees. Depending on how many volunteers you need and the turnover rate of current volunteers, recruiting may be a continuous process.
- **Training:** Volunteers don't come to work knowing everything they need to know. They can do any job for which they're qualified, but don't expect them to know the ropes until they're told what to do and how to do it.
- **Scheduling:** Volunteers need a schedule. Scheduling is even more important if your organization uses volunteers to staff an office or manage other tasks that require regular hours.
- **Appreciating:** Although it's last on this list, it may be the most important. Volunteers need to know that their work is valuable to the organization. You don't have to pass out plaques, but we do recommend heartfelt acknowledgment. Saying thank you and regularly acknowledging the impact made by volunteers is essential to retaining your volunteers.

TIP

If your organization depends heavily on, or is staffed exclusively by, volunteers, consider recruiting your volunteer coordinator from among board members or more experienced volunteers. You can create committees to take responsibility for many jobs, but some detail-oriented tasks — such as scheduling or bill-paying — are better managed by a single responsible person.

Determining your need for volunteers

Look around your nonprofit organization and decide how many volunteers you need and what functions they can perform. We recommend creating (or helping your volunteer coordinator create) a schedule of tasks to be completed — planning what needs to be done and how many people it will take to do the work. Table 5-1 lists the kinds of volunteer assignments you may jot down. By having such a list and prioritizing the tasks, you know what to do when an unexpected volunteer walks in the door.

TABLE 5-1 **Sample Volunteer Task List**

Task	Number of People	Time
Data entry — donor list	1 person	3 hours per week
Social media posting and monitoring	2 people	5 hours per month
Answering the telephone	8 people	36 hours per week
Childcare	2 people	3 hours on Saturdays
Filing	1 person	2 hours per week

WARNING

You can have too many volunteers — almost nothing is worse than asking people to help and then finding that you have nothing for them to do. You may want to have both your chart of immediate tasks (such as shown in Table 5-1) and a few back-burner projects — such as sorting team uniforms by size or taking inventory in the supply cabinet — in case you end up with more people than you need on a given day.

In the beginning, you may have to experiment before you know exactly how many volunteers you need for a particular job. For example, you may eventually discover that a 2,000-piece mailing takes about five hours for four people to complete. You also may find that preparing the soil and planting 200 seedlings takes two volunteers a full day.

TIP

Don't overlook one of your largest resources for volunteers. Many corporations want their employees to have volunteer days where a group of their employees go out and volunteer together. This can often lead to the company donating to your nonprofit organization as a result of their employee community engagement policies and perks.

Writing volunteer job descriptions

Volunteers perform better if they know what they're supposed to do. Preparing job descriptions for volunteer positions also helps you supervise better and know what skills you're looking for in volunteers. (Take a look at Chapter 6 of this minibook for detailed information on writing a job description.)

Volunteer job descriptions should be even more complete than paid-employee job descriptions. If you can break jobs into small tasks, all the better, because volunteers often share the same job. For example, a different person may answer the office telephone each day of the week. In that case, to bring consistency to the job, you should store by the telephone a job description that includes a list of telephone procedures, staff extensions, frequently used telephone numbers, and other important information.

Also, part of your job descriptions should include what background checks your organization will conduct, and that all references listed by the volunteers will be checked.

Organizing volunteers

Many nonprofits invite their volunteers to join a committee. Committees enable volunteers to step forward, offer their best skills, and learn how to do new things. An advantage of forming committees is that it reinforces the social benefits of volunteering. As committee members get to know one another and figure out how to manage their tasks successfully, you or your volunteer coordinator can step back and let them take full responsibility. Using this approach, you find out if the person is reliable, will show up on time, follow through on tasks, and has a good disposition.

Here's a fictitious example that gives you an idea of how to organize committees. The Senior Health and Wellness Program provides telephone referral and information sources for seniors seeking help with weight loss. It was started by three people who had lost weight and decided to help others do the same. A ten-member board of directors provides governance for the Senior Health and Wellness Program and assumes key volunteer roles in the organization. The nonprofit has five committees, each of which is chaired by a board member but made up of individuals who provide volunteer services:

- **Telephone committee:** The Senior Health and Wellness Program provides most of its services via telephone. The office receives about 100 calls each day from people seeking information about weight loss and referrals to health clinics and counselors. The telephones are answered 12 hours a day, from 9am to 9pm, Monday through Friday. Two volunteers share responsibility for the phones in three-hour shifts. The nonprofit needs 40 volunteers each week to answer phones and provide information. The Senior Health and Wellness Program also needs backup volunteers in case someone is ill or can't make their shift for any reason.
- **Program committee:** This committee researches programs to which callers can be referred, maintains the database containing referral information, and provides training to telephone volunteers. Committee members include one physician, two registered nurses, two dieticians, and one physiotherapist who provide professional oversight.
- **Publicity committee:** The Senior Health and Wellness Program uses several methods to tell the public that its services are available. The publicity committee prepares and sends news releases and creates and distributes public service announcements to radio stations. In addition, the committee operates a speakers' bureau of people who have benefited from the program's

services. The committee has also developed a website, a Twitter feed connected to any news that's posted on the website, and a Facebook page; each of these outlets offers basic information about weight loss and invites readers to sign up for a monthly email newsletter. The website maintains links to recommended programs in cities across the United States and Canada.

» **Fundraising committee:** The Senior Health and Wellness Program raises funds in several different ways, including annual senior-oriented walkathons, email appeal letters sent to people who have joined its contact list by way of its website, and gifts from businesses promoting a healthy lifestyle. Committee members plan and coordinate the fundraising events, write and transmit the appeal letters, and make personal calls on the business sponsors. They also call on all volunteers to make personal gifts, identify possible donors, and provide lists of contacts.

» **Administration committee:** The Senior Health and Wellness Program receives individual donations from people who use its services, grants from foundations, and limited support from the regional area agency on aging in the city in which it's based. The fundraising and community outreach committees are responsible for maintaining the organization's financial books, writing thank-you letters to donors, and maintaining a database of past donors.

REMEMBER

You may discover other tasks that can be assigned to additional volunteer committees. The kinds of jobs that need to be done vary, depending on the type of service your organization provides. The point to remember is that volunteer work needs to be organized (and supervised) in much the same way as paid work.

In an all-volunteer organization, the responsibility for ensuring that the work is done in a timely and effective manner resides with the board of directors. The board must be committed to finding new volunteers and supervising their work. And board members must be ready to step in to do a job if no volunteers can be found.

REMEMBER

Board members who also serve as program volunteers must remember to keep their roles as board members (governance and fiduciary) separate from their roles as program volunteers. In the latter case, the volunteers are operating like staff, not board members. Yes, there's a difference.

Searching for Volunteers

Most organizations are always on the lookout for volunteers. After all, volunteers move away, grow tired, lose interest, or take new jobs with new hours. If your organization depends on volunteers, you probably need to maintain an ongoing recruitment process. This section shows you how.

Getting the word out

To cast a wide net, you need to use more than one method to find volunteers — and you don't want to spend much money on those methods. After all, you're looking for free help. Persistence matters: Good volunteer recruitment is like a healthy habit that you want to repeat. Here are some of the most common and most successful methods for recruiting volunteers:

- **Placing announcements in the media:** Newspapers and radio and television stations sometimes publish or air short public service announcements for nonprofit organizations.
- **Posting fliers:** Grocery stores, churches, coffee shops, college campuses, laundromats, schools, and civic buildings often have bulletin boards where you can post announcements. For best results, place them thoughtfully. For example, put your call for foster homes for kittens at the pet food store and your community garden poster at the plant nursery.
- **Taking advantage of word of mouth:** Encourage your current volunteers to recruit others. Have a bring-a-friend day with time for socializing. Ask volunteers to post your posters in their places of business, and don't forget to invite your own friends and associates.
- **Contacting schools and churches:** Both of these institutions look for ways for students and members to become involved in community service. *Service learning* — by which students learn about a topic by volunteering in their communities — is a growing practice. In fact, many high schools and colleges maintain centers for community relations and student volunteering.

  REMEMBER

  Reach out to the young people in your area. By doing so, you benefit from their skills and ideas, and you also contribute to training the next generation of volunteers!
- **Relying on clubs and fraternal groups:** Many professional and social clubs include serving the community in their missions. From Kiwanis International and local Elks Lodges to the Junior League, chamber of commerce, and campus-based sororities and fraternities, clubs and membership groups can be excellent volunteer resources.
- **Approaching corporations and businesses:** In some communities, businesses look for community involvement opportunities for their employees. If a company has a community relations, community affairs, or corporate giving department, it's likely to be a good place to begin asking about employee volunteers.
- **Going online:** Finding volunteers may be as easy as booting up your computer. Besides posting volunteer listings on your organization's website, you also can post on other sites. Several organizations maintain databases where your organization can list its volunteer needs. Prospective volunteers can

search the databases by ZIP code and the type of volunteer work available. Check out the following sites:

- *VolunteerMatch* (www.volunteermatch.org) invites nonprofits to set up accounts identifying the kinds of volunteers they need.
- *Points of Light* (www.pointsoflight.org) manages several projects linking volunteer centers to one another. Its HandsOn Network links volunteers at 250 centers in 30 countries to meaningful projects. It also operates networks for youth volunteers, alums of AmeriCorps who want to continue volunteering, and corporate volunteers.
- *Idealist* (www.idealist.org) and Craigslist (www.craigslist.org) are other widely used tools for finding volunteers.
- *United Way* (www.unitedway.org) may have a volunteer tutoring or mentoring program in your area.
- *Youth Service America* (www.ysa.org) helps you involve young volunteers in your work. It organizes an annual global youth-service day and other opportunities for volunteers between the ages of 5 and 25.

Nonprofit organizations also recruit volunteers from their pages on social networking sites, such as Facebook, Twitter, and LinkedIn. To get your name out there, create a page for your organization. These platforms work particularly well when you describe specific activities that your contacts can do to assist your nonprofit, and when people who know your organization well post photographs and news for their friends to read. Their networks extend your nonprofit's reach. Book 6 provides more information about using social media to make friends and influence people.

REMEMBER

Opportunities to do things with friends motivate many people to volunteer.

Looking for volunteers at other organizations

No, we don't suggest that you steal volunteers from other nonprofits, but some organizations do exist to provide volunteer help. Many communities have volunteer centers that participate in a national network of organizations that recruit and place volunteers in nonprofits.

Similarly, the Corporation for National and Community Service (www.grants.gov) was established by Congress in 1993 to operate AmeriCorps, Senior Corps, the Social Innovation Fund, and the Volunteer Generation Fund. This agency is charged with encouraging national service via volunteering and helping nonprofits and public agencies make the best use of this resource. The corporation awards grants that help organizations strengthen their community by the use of volunteers.

LOOKING TO THE WEB FOR INSPIRATION

Take tips from other nonprofits about ways to reach out to and invite volunteers by way of your website. Remember that you can do much more than describe your nonprofit on your website or social media pages: You can even put people to work for you who don't even step inside your nonprofit's doors. Among many fine examples, here are four sites that inspire involvement:

- DoSomething.org (`www.dosomething.org`): This social networking site invites people to identify causes they care about and then volunteer. Its use of strong visual imagery, surveys, and clearly described activities is a good model for a social media site that succeeds at engaging volunteers.
- Humane Society of the United States (`www.humanesociety.org`): The homepage offers clear, prominent instructions on actions you can take to advance the well-being of animals.
- Surfrider Foundation (`www.surfrider.org`): This site has a Take Action menu, which invites visitors to advocate for legislation and activities that protect shores and the ocean.
- Water.org (`www.water.org`): This site makes excellent use of photographs and graphics that illustrate the effectiveness of its work.

REMEMBER

If your organization wants to take advantage of a program offered by the Corporation for National and Community Service, you may need to apply for a federal or state grant, which usually requires sound accounting procedures and extensive reporting of program activities. Turn to Book 3, chapters 4 and 6, for information about government grants. Book 4 covers bookkeeping and accounting considerations for nonprofit organizations.

Finding volunteers with special skills

If you're looking for volunteers with special training or experience, spend some time thinking about where you can find them. Limit your recruitment efforts to places where you're most likely to identify the people with the talents you need.

Suppose that your organization is seeking someone with accounting experience to help maintain your books. Local accounting firms, corporate offices, and professional accounting societies may be good recruiting grounds for someone who can assist with bookkeeping. If your organization needs help with a legal matter, some bar associations link nonprofits to attorneys who are willing to volunteer. Most importantly, don't forget about the Service Corps of Retired Executives (SCORE). Their website is `https://www.score.org`.

TIP

Sometimes your nonprofit competition won't mind sharing contacts who are loyal to a particular kind of volunteer activity. In our city, for example, several organizations host film festivals once each year, and volunteers who love to see the films volunteer to sell tickets, greet the media, and manage other tasks, migrating from one festival to the next. Rather than detract from their contributions to one organization, their "migrant" style of volunteering makes these volunteers more knowledgeable and strengthens their skills. When recruiting for short-term volunteer assignments, don't be afraid to ask your "competition" if you can invite some of their great bird watchers, marathon runners, brownie bakers, or scarecrow makers.

Hiring interns

Interns are specialized volunteers who come to you as part of an education or training program. In most cases, a student intern's goal is to develop practical, hands-on work experience.

Sometimes internship programs require your organization to pay a fee or provide the intern with a modest stipend. If you pay a stipend, be aware that you may be creating an employer-employee relationship that is subject to federal, state, and local laws, including minimum wage requirements, employment taxes, and other obligations. If you're working with an established internship program in your community, these potential liabilities are likely covered. If you're recruiting interns on your own, refer to fact sheet 71, Internship Programs Under the Fair Labor Standards Act, available from the Department of Labor website (`www.dol.gov/whd/regs/compliance/whdfs71.htm`). You may also want to consider adding interns to your liability insurance policy. (Refer to the later section, "Insuring your volunteers," for more details.)

As with employees and volunteers, you should provide the intern with clear expectations about duties, attendance, and other aspects of the job. If you decide to go this route, be ready to spend time supervising and evaluating the intern's job performance. Don't forget that the intern's experience is part of their grade.

Interviewing and Screening Volunteers

Require potential volunteers to fill out job applications just as though they were applying for paid work. Ask for references and check them. Review résumés and conduct formal interviews. (See Chapter 6 of this minibook for information about job interviews.) Avoid paranoia, but don't discount your gut feelings, either.

If you're using volunteers in professional roles, such as accounting, check their qualifications just as you would check the qualifications of an applicant for a paid position. This process may offend potential volunteers, but it's far better to make sure that the person can do the job, even if they're doing it for free.

A CHEAT SHEET FOR THE FAQs

Be prepared to answer questions when people call to volunteer. If you're already using volunteers to answer the telephone, prepare a list of common questions and answers and place that list near the telephone. Here are some sample FAQs that the Senior Health and Wellness Program, a fictional nonprofit discussed in the earlier section, "Organizing volunteers," may need:

- **What are the hours I would be needed?** We answer the phones five days a week, from 9 in the morning until 9 at night. We ask people to work a three-hour shift once a week.
- **How will I know what to say?** All volunteers receive one day of training. Training is offered once a month, and almost always on Saturdays.
- **What kind of advice can I give?** Our volunteers can't give medical advice or advice on specific diets. Volunteers refer callers to existing services and professionals. We ask volunteers to be positive and to offer general support to all callers.
- **How do I know where to refer people?** We have an extensive database of weight-loss-related counseling services, physical therapists, and senior exercise programs at local community centers. It's a simple matter of looking through our computer database to find the appropriate phone numbers.
- **What if I get sick and can't cover my shift?** We have volunteers on standby to cover unexpected absences. If you aren't able to volunteer on a regular, weekly basis, you may consider being a backup volunteer.
- **Are we asked to do any other work?** Sometimes we ask volunteers to help with mailings between phone calls.
- **Will you pay my auto (or public transportation) expenses?** We're sorry, but our budget doesn't cover reimbursing volunteers for expenses. Some expenses may be deductible on your income tax, however. You should check with your tax specialist.
- **Can I deduct the value of my time from my income taxes?** No, the IRS doesn't allow tax deductions for volunteer time.

These questions and answers also can be printed in a brochure and mailed to potential volunteers who request more information. Be sure to include background information about your organization in the mailing.

If you're placing volunteers in sensitive jobs, such as working with children or providing peer counseling, screen your applicants carefully. Criminal background screening, including a fingerprint check, is sometimes required by law, by licensing requirements, or by your insurance carrier. Some states and counties also require a test for tuberculosis. Check with local authorities about the requirements in your area.

REMEMBER

We realize that screening can be a delicate issue. You're walking a tightrope between the right to privacy and the right of the organization to be sure that no harm befalls its clients. The failure to undertake a background check potentially can result in liability problems for the individual who "hires" the volunteer. Some potential volunteers may be offended by background checks. Explain that the procedures aren't directed at them personally but are in place to ensure that clients are protected. Also, treat all volunteer applicants the same. In other words, don't pass up screening someone just because they're a personal friend.

Managing Your Volunteers

Just like managing paid employees, working with volunteers requires attention to management tasks. Volunteers need training and orientation as well as clear, written lists of responsibilities and expectations. Basic expectations for volunteers are easily outlined in a *volunteer agreement form.* You also want to maintain records of the time and tasks volunteers contribute to your organization and consider whether to include volunteers in your insurance coverage.

Providing adequate training

The degree and extent of volunteer training depends on the type of job you're asking them to do. Volunteers who answer telephones, for example, may need more training than those who stuff envelopes for the publicity committee. To successfully answer phones, these volunteers need to know background information about the program or service, information about the types of services available, proper telephone etiquette, and emergency procedures, among other details.

TIP

If you need to provide a full day's training or training over a longer period, we suggest consulting with a professional trainer to either provide the training or help you design the curriculum. Although you may be concerned about investing too much of volunteers' valuable time in training, remember that key motivations for volunteering include meeting people and enjoying time with friends. Trainings can be great opportunities to introduce volunteers to one another and build camaraderie among them. It's a good idea to schedule refresher training sessions for ongoing volunteers, too.

In addition to offering on-site training, give volunteers written materials that restate the information covered in the training. Include with these materials attendance requirements, details about whom to contact in case of illness, and other necessary information that volunteers may need to know when carrying out their tasks.

Larger organizations that use many volunteers sometimes publish a *volunteer handbook*. This type of handbook doesn't need to be an elaborately printed document — it can be several typed pages stapled together, a simple loose-leaf notebook, or a PDF posted on the organization's website. The more information you provide, the better your volunteers can perform.

Keeping good records

Keep records of your volunteers and how much time they spend doing work for your organization. Potential donors and funders may be impressed by the number of volunteers and the time they donate to your nonprofit organization. Or you may be asked to provide a reference for a volunteer who's working to develop job skills or providing a service in an organized volunteer program. You also may need to dismiss a volunteer who's unreliable, and having clear, written records of hours and tasks can justify that difficult act.

If you use professional volunteers to perform tasks that you'd otherwise have to pay for, you can include the value of the volunteer time as an in-kind contribution on your financial statement. Book 4 explains more about financial statements.

Insuring your volunteers

Typically, nonprofit organizations carry liability and property insurance. Almost all states require that workers compensation insurance be in place to cover on-the-job injuries to employees (but not necessarily to volunteers). Beyond this basic insurance, coverage depends on the type of services provided and the degree of risk involved.

Keep in mind that volunteers usually aren't liable for their actions as long as they work within the scope of the volunteer activity to which they've been assigned, perform as any reasonable person would perform, and avoid engaging in criminal activity. Unfortunately, people these days have become more eager to file lawsuits. If someone sues you or one of your volunteers, you have to legally defend the case even if it's without merit. One advantage of having liability insurance is that your insurance carrier takes on the responsibility of defending the suit.

Workers compensation may or may not be available to volunteers in your state. If you can include volunteers under your state law, consider doing so, because a workers comp claim usually precludes the volunteer from filing a suit for damages against your organization. Plus, you want a volunteer who suffers an injury to be covered.

Insuring volunteers is a subject of debate in the nonprofit sector. Some people take the position that insurance agents and brokers try to persuade you to insure anything and everything. Others believe that liability insurance and, in some cases, workers compensation insurance should be provided. As is the case with all insurance questions, evaluate your risks and decide whether the cost of insuring against risks is a good investment. For example, if you fail to provide protection to a volunteer who is seriously injured, the reputation and future success of your organization can be harmed. This process is called *risk management*. To find information about risk management for nonprofit organizations, contact the Nonprofit Risk Management Center (`www.nonprofitrisk.org`).

Saying farewell to bad volunteers

If you work with lots of volunteers, especially volunteers who perform complex and sensitive jobs, you may discover one or more volunteers who lack the skills or personalities to perform at an acceptable level. We hope you never face this situation, but if you do — for example, maybe someone is giving out inaccurate information or acting rudely — do *not* ignore the situation.

Discussing the problem behavior with the volunteer is the first step. Treat this meeting as if you're counseling a paid employee whose job performance is below par. Written job descriptions, written standards for performance, and records of volunteer time and contributed tasks are important when discussing problem behavior.

WARNING

Exercise caution when meeting with a volunteer about their unacceptable behavior, especially if you have no clearly written performance guidelines. Volunteers who are released have been known to sue nonprofit agencies. If you have concerns about this possibility, consult an attorney before you do anything. Also, ask another member of your paid staff to sit in on your meeting with volunteers when you're disciplining them or letting them go. Witnesses are critical when you get sued. The he-says-she-says rationale doesn't stand up in a court of law. Witnesses are gold. You can also record the meeting as well as document the reasons for dismissal in the volunteer's personnel file.

REMEMBER

Talking to someone, volunteer or not, about poor work is never pleasant. However, if someone working for your organization is being disruptive, giving out inaccurate information, or otherwise causing potential harm to your program or the people you serve, you have a responsibility to correct the problem. Plus, the other volunteers probably know that this volunteer isn't pulling their weight and will appreciate that poor performance is not acceptable.

Showing Appreciation for Your Volunteers

Volunteers give their time and, in many cases, expertise to help your organization succeed. It's only right that you thank them, and thank them often. Thank them in the hallway after they've completed their work for the day, and also formally recognize their contributions. Here are some standard ways of recognizing volunteers:

TIP

- **Annual recognition event:** This kind of event is the most formal (and probably the most expensive) way of thanking volunteers. Some organizations have a sit-down dinner or wine-and-cheese reception once a year to say thanks and give awards to volunteers who've made extraordinary contributions.
- **Gifts:** Although tokens of appreciation may be much deserved, we recommend caution when giving gifts to volunteers. Don't spend lots of money buying presents, because you can bet that some volunteers will ask why you're spending scarce nonprofit money on something that isn't necessary. Getting a local business to donate gift certificates or other items is a better way to go.
- **Admission to performances or events:** If your organization presents plays, musical performances, lectures, or readings, consider offering free admission to some events.
- **Public acknowledgment:** You can identify your volunteers in your newsletter or on your website. An alternative is an annual newspaper ad that lists the names of your volunteers.
- **Thank-you letters:** Don't underestimate the power of a simple thank-you note. Unless you have hundreds of volunteers, make sure you write the notes by hand. Most people appreciate a handwritten note more than a form letter or email. Try to let volunteers know how their work has made a difference.

In addition to thank-you letters and recognition events, you can increase volunteer satisfaction (and retention) by treating volunteers well on a day-to-day basis. Here are some easy tips to keep volunteer satisfaction high:

- **Don't make volunteers work in isolation if you can avoid it.** Many volunteers give their time because they enjoy socializing with others.
- **Vary the job to avoid boredom.** You may need help cleaning the storeroom or hand-addressing 1,000 envelopes, but try to assign jobs that offer more mental stimulation as well.
- **Pay attention to the work done by your volunteers.** Your interest in what they're doing adds value to their work and recognizes that many of them are volunteering to develop new skills.
- **Help volunteers understand your nonprofit's work.** If they've been answering the telephones in the front office, give them a behind-the-scenes tour or a chance to observe or participate in other activities of the organization.
- **Bring in pizza or cookies once in a while as an impromptu thank-you.** Food can provide a great break from a monotonous job or a celebration of a major task's completion.
- **Talk to your volunteers.** Get to know them as friends of your organization who are committed to its work.

IN THIS CHAPTER

» Preparing your organization for paid employees

» Taking care of the groundwork

» Interviewing and hiring potential staff

» Getting a new hire started

» Handling the day-to-day management

» Working with contracted consultants

Chapter 6

Working with Paid Staff and Contractors

Some nonprofits have paid staff from the beginning. For example, nonprofits that start out with grant funding to operate a program may have paid staff. Other nonprofits may start more slowly, with the board of directors and other volunteers initially doing all the work and hiring paid employees later. And many nonprofits never have any paid staff. These organizations may use consultants or rely on volunteers.

No rules exist about when a nonprofit organization should start employing paid staff. The organization must determine whether it has enough work to justify employees and whether it has the resources to pay salaries and associated expenses. Hiring your first employee should be cause for celebration. It means that your nonprofit has reached a milestone in its development. But it also means that the organization (and the board of directors) will have more responsibilities to raise funds and ensure that proper personnel policies are put in place and followed. This chapter covers the details.

TIP

Check out File 11-1 at `https://www.wiley.com/en-us/Nonprofit+Kit+For+Dummies%2C+6th+Edition-p-9781119835745#downloads-section` for a list of web resources related to the topics we cover in this chapter.

Determining Your Staffing Needs

Knowing when to take the leap from being an all-volunteer group to being a boss of a paid employee isn't easy, and it's not a leap to take without looking at where you're about to land. Hiring employees creates responsibilities for the board, not the least of which is making the payroll every two weeks or every month. You also need to pay payroll taxes and provide a workplace, equipment, and — don't forget — guidance and supervision. Expect to take on more bookkeeping duties and more complex financial reports because you need to keep track of payroll records, vacation time, and sick days — and choose which holidays your organization will observe. (The last one should be a snap, right?)

To ease into the transition, a nonprofit may begin by hiring an independent contractor to handle a specific task, such as bookkeeping or grant writing, and then go from there. (We discuss working with independent contractors and consultants later in this chapter.)

REMEMBER

A variety of situations, such as these examples, may signal that it's time to hire your first employee:

- **A staff that's pushed to the limit:** Volunteers are growing tired, and the work isn't getting done as well or as quickly as it should.
- **Increased demand for services:** Your organization's services have increased to the point that someone needs to focus consistently on administrative details.
- **Increased resources:** Resources have increased to the point that you can now pay a regular salary.
- **The need for specialized skills:** The organization is starting a new activity that requires someone with a specific professional license or degree, and no volunteer is appropriately qualified.
- **Increased responsibility after receipt of a grant:** The nonprofit receives a major grant that provides more resources *and* requires significant record keeping and program management.

Hiring salaried employees should be a long-term commitment. For this reason, you need to have sufficient cash flow to ensure regular payment of salaries, benefits, and payroll taxes.

TIP

A crisis can sometimes take place when a volunteer-run organization hires its first staff member. Knowing that they're now paying someone to be responsible, board members may decide to "sit on their hands" and let others do the work. The hiring of your first staff member is a good time to honor board and volunteer contributions to the organization (to maintain motivation) and to invest in a board retreat or training event that reminds everyone of the work ahead and the board's important role in it.

WARNING

When you add paid employees to your organization, you assume legal responsibilities that begin with the recruitment process. We recommend that you consult *Human Resources Kit For Dummies*, 4th Edition, by Andrea Butcher (Wiley), to be sure you cover all the bases.

Getting Your Nonprofit Ready for Paid Employees

Before you write a job description or place an ad online, you need to invest time in some up-front prep work, readying your nonprofit organization to take on paid employees. This preparation, which we cover in the following sections, includes writing personnel policies, setting up payroll systems, and choosing benefits.

Developing your personnel policies

Personnel policies and procedures outline how an organization relates to its employees. These policies are essential for both supervisors and employees because they provide guidelines for what's expected in the workplace and on the job. The guidelines lay out expectations for employees, ensure that all employees receive equal treatment, and provide the steps necessary for disciplinary action when needed (see the later section, "Following the reprimand-and-dismissal process," for more info about disciplinary action).

Many start-up and small organizations that have only one or two full-time employees give personnel policies a low priority. We suggest, however, that you begin early to formalize your rules by spelling them out in an employee handbook. Doing so doesn't take *that* much time, and it can save you headaches down the road.

WARNING

You must follow federal and state, and (sometimes) local labor laws when establishing personnel policies. The U.S. Department of Labor website (`www.dol.gov`) contains the latest information on federal laws. If you're uncertain about whether you can require certain behavior or work hours from your employees, consult an attorney.

When forming policies, begin with the easy stuff: Decide on your organization's office hours, holidays, vacation policy, sick pay, and other basic necessities.

Determining work time and off time

Most organizations follow the lead of others when setting holiday and vacation policies: Although you find a lot of variation, many nonprofits in the United States grant two weeks' vacation per year to new employees. Employees typically receive more vacation time after a longer period of service, such as three weeks after three years, and four weeks after five to eight years. The most common sick leave policy is ten days per year. While you're at it, you want to give some thought to bereavement and maternity/paternity-leave policies.

Paid vacation time is a benefit to both employees and employers. Employees return from vacation rested and ready to give their best efforts to the organization. For this reason, you should encourage people to take vacations during the year in which they earn the vacation. Most organizations and businesses don't allow employees to accrue vacation time beyond a certain amount. This policy ensures that employees use vacations for the purpose for which they're intended. Such a policy also limits the need to make large cash payments for unused vacation time when employees resign or are terminated.

When it comes to choosing on which holidays your organization will close, follow the U.S. federal holiday schedule — banks and government offices are closed for business because many of these holidays fall on weekdays. Also, because many of these holidays fall on Monday, some of them will result in your staff and volunteers having a three-day weekend. Check the U.S. Office of Personnel Management at `www.opm.gov/policy-data-oversight/pay-leave/federal-holidays/#url=Overview` for the dates of federal holidays by year.

January: New Year's Day, Martin Luther King Jr. Day

February: Washington's Birthday

May: Memorial Day

July: Independence Day

September: Labor Day

October: Columbus Day, Indigenous Peoples' Day

November: Veterans Day, Thanksgiving Day

December: Christmas Day

REMEMBER

If you ask your employees to work on a federal holiday, you will undoubtedly have to pay them overtime in compliance with federal wage and labor laws.

TIP

Consider reviewing the personnel policies of other nonprofit organizations in your area. A few telephone calls to other executive directors may help answer questions that arise as you refine your policies. Community Resource Exchange has sample personnel policies in its Sample Personnel Manual section at `www.crenyc.org/resources/tools-publications`.

Covering other important items

In addition to vacations and holidays, which are discussed in the earlier section, you should add statements that cover the following basic areas in your personnel policies:

- The ability of the board of directors to change the policies
- Nondiscrimination in employment, usually presented as a policy established by the board of directors — especially important if your organization is seeking government grants or contracts — and other policies established by the board
- Procedures to encourage and protect employees and volunteers if they report wrongdoing — a whistleblower policy, in other words

  The National Council of Nonprofits provides guidance in this area at `www.councilofnonprofits.org`.
- Policies regarding parental leave and long-term disability
- Hiring procedures and the probationary period (described in the later section, "Evaluating your new hire's progress.")
- A statement of the employment termination policy, including a grievance procedure

Many organizations also include a statement of the organization's mission and vision statements, its values, and a brief outline of its history.

Exploring payroll setup options

When an organization begins employing workers, it first must establish a payroll system. The organization needs to decide how often to distribute paychecks, for example. Some states specify how frequently employees must be paid. Check with your state's department of labor about possible rules governing payment frequency. If your state doesn't specify payment periods, you can disburse paychecks on any schedule you choose — weekly, biweekly, semimonthly, or monthly. In our experience, semimonthly is the most common schedule for payment.

REMEMBER

Biweekly means every two weeks and results in 26 paychecks per year; *semimonthly* means twice a month and results in 24 paychecks per year.

TIP

Although in-house staff can handle payroll, contracting with a payroll service is a better option. Most banks either provide payroll services or can recommend a service. Payroll services are inexpensive — they're almost always cheaper than assigning a staff person the job of handling payroll. They make the proper withholding deductions based on income level, number of dependents, and state laws; make tax deposits; and maintain a record of vacation and sick leave. Usually when you contract with such a service, it requires that you keep enough funds on deposit with the company to cover two or three months of salaries and benefits.

WARNING

If you decide to handle your own payroll, be sure to make tax deposits on time. Failure to pay federal and state payroll taxes can get your organization in serious trouble and can even result in personal liability for board members. Check the Internal Revenue Service (IRS) website (`www.irs.gov`) for the latest information.

Here's a list of typical types of deductions, although state tax laws vary:

- Federal income tax
- Social Security and Medicare (must be matched by the organization)
- State income tax
- State unemployment and disability insurance

Providing benefits and perquisites

Health insurance is a benefit that your organization may or may not be able to provide to its paid employees. The cost of health insurance decreases based on the size of the group to which you belong. If your organization has only a single employee, purchasing health insurance may be costly unless you can join a larger group. Check with your state association for nonprofit organizations to see whether it has a health insurance program that covers your employees. The National Council of Nonprofits (`www.councilofnonprofits.org`) has information and links to other helpful websites, including your state's nonprofit associations.

After your nonprofit organization is thriving, you may want to consider offering more benefits, such as retirement plans and long-term disability insurance.

Preparing to Hire

After you write your personnel policies, put your payroll system in place, and choose your benefits, you're finished with the groundwork needed to hire one employee or a hundred employees. You're probably just hiring one person for now. To set off on that path, you need to clearly describe what the job entails, set salary levels, and announce the position. This section walks you through those important steps.

Composing a job description

One of the first things you should do when looking to hire a paid employee is to write a job description for the position you want to fill. Completing this exercise helps you clarify the skills needed for the job and guides you in selecting among applicants. The final description serves as a job blueprint for the new employee.

A job description usually includes

- A short paragraph describing the job and the work environment
- A list of duties and responsibilities
- A list of skills and abilities needed for the job
- Experience and education required
- Special qualifications required or desired

When writing a job description, keep in mind that work in nonprofit organizations can be split into these three broad areas:

- **Services:** Services are the reason the organization exists in the first place. They may, for example, develop protected open space on a coastal bluff, provide home visits and hot meals to seniors, or organize after-school activities for children. This list is almost unlimited.
- **Administrative functions:** These functions include bookkeeping and accounting, office management, property or building management, marketing, website design, clerical services, benefits administration, and contract management. You can add to this list as needed.
- **Fundraising:** This area falls under various names, including *resource development* and *advancement*. Depending on the size of your organization, one person may be in charge of all aspects of raising money, or different people may specialize in writing grants to foundations and government agencies, creating sponsorships with corporations, or raising money from individual donors.

The larger these areas (or departments) are, the greater the specialization within them. But when you're looking to hire your first staff member, that first person may have job responsibilities in more than one area, and perhaps even in all three areas. It may seem to be too much to describe in a single document, but that complexity and the high level of responsibility this person will have make it particularly important to create a job description that's crystal clear.

Considering necessary qualifications

Some nonprofit jobs require various levels of formal education and special training. If you're hiring someone to provide counseling services, for example, that employee probably needs to meet certain education and licensing requirements to provide the services legally. If you're hiring someone to work with children, the applicant may need to pass various background checks or drug testing, depending on the laws of your state.

TIP

Professional and business associations can provide helpful information about job qualifications. In addition to any degrees and certifications, you may want to specify that applicants have a certain amount of experience doing the work you'll ask them to do. However, if you do so, be prepared to pay a higher salary to fill the position.

WARNING

You can't, of course, require that an applicant be of a particular ethnic background, race, age, creed, gender, or sexual orientation. You can't deny employment to someone who is expecting a child. Neither can you refuse employment to a person with a disability as long as that person can perform the job with reasonable accommodations.

Establishing nonprofit salary levels

Deciding on a fair salary for your employees isn't easy. Compensation levels in nonprofits range from hardly anything to six-figure salaries at large-budget organizations. (Keep in mind, however, that large nonprofits represent only a small percentage of active nonprofits.) We guide you through the process in the next two sections.

Considering factors that affect salary

Although exceptions always exist, the following factors may determine salary levels:

- **Geographic location:** Salary levels differ from place to place because of the cost of living. If your nonprofit is in a major metropolitan area, expect to pay more to attract qualified staff than if you're located in a rural area.

» **Experience and education:** Someone with ten years of experience can command higher compensation than someone just beginning a career. Education levels also affect salary, as does having specialized knowledge or skills.

» **Job duties and responsibilities:** Employees who direct programs and supervise others typically earn more than employees who have fewer responsibilities.

» **Nonprofit type:** Compensation levels vary from one nonprofit to the next. Organizations providing health services, for example, typically have higher salary levels than arts organizations.

» **Union membership:** Labor unions set standards for salaries and benefits in many fields, from musicians to nurses and educators.

» **Organizational culture:** This category, which is more difficult to define, is connected to the organization's traditions and values. For example, nonprofits with boards of directors filled with business and corporate members often offer higher salary levels than organizations with boards that have no corporate perspective.

Scoping out salaries of comparable positions

A salary survey, which you can conduct by phone or mail, is a good way to assess the current salary levels in your area and for your nonprofit type. Telephone surveys probably should be done from board president to board president because most people are reluctant to reveal their own salaries. Mail surveys can be constructed so that respondents remain anonymous.

The simplest method of finding salaries of comparable positions is to look at other job listings. Not all ads give a salary level, but those ads that do can give you a general idea of what others are paying for similar work.

Some nonprofit management organizations conduct annual or biannual surveys of salary levels in the areas in which they work. More often than not, access to the surveys requires payment, but it's probably a good investment because these surveys tend to be the most complete and up to date. A good place to inquire about salary surveys is at your state association of nonprofits (see the National Council of Nonprofits website at `www.councilofnonprofits.org`). Idealist Careers also has links to nonprofit salary survey information at `www.idealistcareers.org/salary-surveys`. Local community foundations also may be a good resource of salary data in your geographic area and for the budget size of your organization.

TIP

Using a search firm can be helpful in hiring, especially if the position requires a national search. Be prepared to pay a hefty fee, however. Fees are often based on a percentage of the first year's salary.

Announcing the position

After you decide on the qualifications and skills needed for the job you want to fill, advertise its availability. Here's a list of places to publicize your job opening:

- **Professional journals:** If you're hiring for a professional position, professional journals are the place to advertise the job. Search the web to track down the addresses of appropriate trade-specific journals.
- **Websites:** The web has become a valuable marketplace for job seekers. Many websites charge a fee for posting a job opening. Work for Good (`www.workforgood.org`) and Idealist Careers (`www.idealistcareers.org`) are popular sites. Also consider Craigslist (`www.craigslist.org/about/sites#US`), Monster (`www.monster.com`), CareerBuilder (`www.careerbuilder.com`), and LinkedIn (`www.linkedin.com`).
- **Word of mouth:** Spread the word to other nonprofits — especially those in your field — places of worship, and anywhere else people congregate. Place a job description on your website and announce it on your Facebook page and Twitter feed. Don't forget to email the announcement to colleagues.

Making the Hire

When it comes time to make the big decision, sifting through résumés, conducting interviews, and deciding on an employee can be a daunting task. Sometimes, the right choice jumps out at you; at other times, you have to choose between two or three (or two dozen!) candidates who have equal qualifications. That's when making up your mind becomes difficult.

Looking at résumés

Résumés and cover letters give you the first opportunity to evaluate candidates for a position. Respond quickly with a postcard or an email to tell applicants that you have received their materials. If possible, give a date by which they can expect to hear from you again. Doing so reduces the number of phone calls asking whether you've received the résumé and when you plan to make a decision. It's also the polite thing to do.

REMEMBER

Résumés come in various formats, and we offer no strong opinion about which one is best. Regardless of how the résumé is organized and whether it's on paper or online, here are the questions we ask ourselves when reviewing a résumé:

- **Is it free of typographical errors and misspellings?** A typo may be excused if everything else appears to be in order, but more than a couple of errors implies that the candidate may be careless on the job.
- **Is the information laid out in a logical, easy-to-follow manner?** The relative clarity of the résumé can give you insight into the applicant's communication skills.
- **Does the applicant have the proper job experience, education, and licenses, if needed?** We like to give a little slack on experience because sometimes highly motivated and effective employees are people who have to grow into the job. Also, nonprofit organizations often receive résumés from people who are changing careers. They may not have the exact experience you're looking for, but the knowledge they gained in their previous jobs might easily transfer to the position you're trying to fill.
- **How often has the applicant changed jobs?** You can never be guaranteed that an employee will stay as long as you want, but you have to ask yourself, "If I hire this person, will they pack up and move on even before finishing job training?" At the same time, don't automatically let higher-than-average job-switching turn you off to an excellent candidate. Maybe the person has an explanation. Ask.

Cover letters can also be good clues to an individual's future job performance. For one thing, you get an idea of the applicant's writing abilities, and you may even gain some insight into their personality. Some job announcements state that a cover letter should accompany the résumé, and some even go so far as to ask the applicant to respond to questions such as, "Why are you well suited to this job?" or "What do you think are the major issues facing so-and-so?" It's up to you to decide whether asking a list of questions enables you to more easily compare applicants to one another.

TIP

If good writing skills are required for a job you're posting, ask applicants to include writing samples with their cover letters and résumés.

You'll probably reject at least half the résumés out of hand. We never cease to be amazed by how many people apply for jobs for which they lack even the minimal qualifications. We realize that searching for a job is difficult and frustrating, but we also wonder whether applicants read our Position Available ads as closely as they should.

Separate your résumés into two groups — one for rejected applications and one for applications that need closer scrutiny. Send the rejected candidates a letter or an email thanking them for their interest. From the other pile, decide how many candidates you want to interview. Reviewing the résumés with a couple of other board members to bring several perspectives to the choice is often helpful.

One technique is to select the top three applicants for interviews. Reserve the other applicants for backup interviews if the first three are unsuitable or if they've already accepted other jobs.

Interviewing candidates

After you've chosen the top three to eight résumés, invite the applicants in for an interview. Interviewing job candidates is a formidable task. Big companies have human resources departments with trained interviewers who spend their days asking questions of prospective employees. We're neither human resources specialists nor trained interviewers, but here are some tricks we've learned over the years:

- **Prepared lists of three or four standard questions that you ask all applicants enable you to compare answers across applicants.** The interview shouldn't be so formal that it makes both the candidate and you uncomfortable, but standardizing it to some degree is beneficial. Here's a short list of typical questions:
  - Why are you interested in this position?
  - What do you see as your strengths? As your weaknesses?
  - How would you use your previous work experience in this job?
  - What are your long-term goals?
- **Team interviews with three or more people can give interviewers good insight into how the applicant will perform in board and community meetings.** You can test communication and teamwork skills between candidates and existing staff and volunteers. Also, different people notice different aspects of each applicant's responses or behaviors.

  TIP

  Avoid making the candidate face a large group, which might make any reasonable person unnecessarily nervous.
- **If an employee isn't your first hire and the job to be filled is for a director or supervisor position, have each finalist meet at least some of the staff they'll supervise.** Giving staff members a chance to meet their potential new boss is courteous, and their impressions are helpful in making the final selection.

WARNING

You can't ask applicants personal questions about their age, religious practices, medical history, marital status, sexual orientation, or racial background. You can't ask about arrests or felony convictions without proof of the necessity to ask. Nor can you ask whether someone has children or about any physical or mental conditions that are unrelated to performing the job. Workforce has a useful article about interview questions at `www.workforce.com/news/interview-questions-legal-or-illegal-2`.

Taking notes during the interview is acceptable, and you may also find that preparing a checklist on which you can rate the applicant in different areas is a helpful exercise. If you do, try to rate applicants discreetly. A job interview is stressful enough without letting the applicant know that you rated them a 3 on a scale of 1 to 10.

Digging deeper with references

Letters of recommendation can be helpful starting points in evaluating candidates, but we assume that no one would include a negative recommendation in an application packet. Therefore, we do think it's necessary to check references by telephone or even in a personal meeting, if possible.

But sometimes, even talking to references provides little useful information. A job applicant wants to put their best face forward, so naturally they choose people with favorable opinions as references. Also, employment laws are such that speaking to a former employer often yields little more than a confirmation that your applicant was employed between certain dates.

If you do have the opportunity to have an exploratory conversation with the candidate's former employer, pay close attention to what the person is *not* saying, and attend to the description of the candidate's abilities. For example, if you need someone who is attentive to financial details but the former employer talks only about the applicant's friendliness and phone manner, you may not have found the right person for your position. Some typical questions ask what duties the applicant handled in previous jobs, what their strengths and weaknesses were on the job, whether they had a positive attitude toward work, and whether the reference would rehire the candidate.

If the applicant is working for another organization, don't contact the current employer. You don't want to breach the person's confidentiality.

You can conduct formal background checks of education credentials, criminal history, and other information as long as you receive the applicant's permission. In addition, a sex offender check should be completed on any person that you might hire. If you feel that this type of research is necessary, we suggest hiring a reputable company that specializes in this sort of work. However, you can conduct informal Internet searches about the applicant.

REMEMBER

The lengths to which you go to collect information about an applicant depend on the magnitude of the position. If you're hiring someone to lead a large and complex organization, you likely want to dig deeper into a candidate's background than if you're hiring a data entry clerk. But for any position, you want to know as much as possible about an individual's previous job performance before making an offer.

Making your decision

We can't tell you how to make the final decision about whom to hire. You have to weigh qualifications, experience, poise, and desire. These decisions can be difficult, and, frankly, you may not be certain that you've made the right choice until the new employee performs on the job. If possible, gather more than one opinion.

If qualifications and experience are equal, intangible factors come more into play. Will the candidate fit well into the organizational culture? Will the candidate's style of work fit with the organization's management style? Do the applicant's professional goals fit with the organization's goals? If this employee is your first, is the candidate a self-starter type, or do they need active supervision to do a good job?

WARNING

Document your reasons for making a personnel decision: Base those reasons primarily on the candidate's performance in previous jobs and experience that's relevant to your position. Be cautious when making a personnel decision based on intangible factors. A candidate who's charming may be a treat to have around the office, but that doesn't always mean the person will do the job well.

Onboarding a New Hire

Much hard work is behind you after you've made a hiring decision. But keep in mind that any employee's first days and months are challenging, and you want to give careful attention to helping your new staff member make a good start.

Confirming employment terms in writing

After a new employee accepts a position orally, we recommend that you send a letter to cement the details in writing. Enclose a copy of the personnel policies (see the section "Developing your personnel policies," earlier in this chapter) and place a signature line near the lower right corner of the letter so that the new hire can acknowledge receipt of the letter and the personnel policies. Ask the employee to return a copy of the signed letter to you, and keep the letter in the employee's personnel file.

The letter should specify the employee's starting date, job title, and salary as well as other information that you agreed to in the pre-hire discussions held between the organization and the employee. For example, you may include a brief statement about the employee's responsibilities and agreed-on work schedule.

Getting your new hire started on the job

REMEMBER

In the United States, one of the first things a new employee must do is complete a W-4 form (for income tax withholding) and an I-9 form (to show proof of the employee's legal right to work in the country). These forms are required by law and are available on the IRS website (www.irs.gov).

After all the necessary paperwork is out of the way, you need to spend some time acclimating your new hire to the working environment. New employees don't begin producing at top form on the first day of work. Absorbing the details of the organization and discovering the ins and outs of new job duties take time. This fact is particularly true when the person hired is the organization's first employee and has no model to follow.

Whether you're a board member for an organization that's hired its first employee or the director of an organization bringing someone new onto the staff, here are some ways to ease an employee's transition to a new job:

- **Provide good working conditions.** You may think that a reminder to purchase the basic furniture and tools someone needs to perform their work is too basic, but we've heard about new employees who faced not even having a desk on their first day.
- **Show the new person around.** Provide a tour of the office and programs and introduce the new hire to volunteers and board members. Review office emergency procedures on day one. Oh yeah, and don't forget to show the new employee where the restroom is!
- **Give the employee information about the organization.** Make available the organization's files and records, including any policies and guidelines that affect the employee's duties and the performance of their work. Reading board minutes, newsletters, solicitation letters, donor records, and grant proposals will steep the person in the organization's work.
- **Answer questions.** Encourage new employees to ask questions, and provide the answers as soon as possible. Particularly if the person is the organization's one-and-only employee, board members should check in regularly, making themselves available as resources. Being a one-person staff can be lonely and overwhelming.
- **Offer special training.** A new employee may need special training — for example, about a software program or laws and regulations specific to your nonprofit — to perform the job. Sometimes you may have to send the employee to a workshop; at other times, they can be trained by a board member, a volunteer, or another staff member.

Evaluating your new hire's progress

REMEMBER

Conduct a performance evaluation within the first six months of employment. The evaluation should be written (and added to the employee's personnel file) and discussed in a meeting with the employee. Rating employees on a number scale on various aspects of the job was once the common format. Today, a narrative evaluation that addresses performance in achieving previously agreed-on goals and objectives is much more helpful.

TIP

Many employees are happier in their jobs if they have ongoing opportunities to learn about new areas and develop new skills. An annual employee review is an excellent opportunity to review professional development goals with the employee. It's also a good time to review ways — via workshops, training, or trying on new roles — that the person may continue to grow in the job.

Looking to the future: Creating a professional development plan

You should establish professional development goals for new employees as soon as they come on board to work for your nonprofit organization. Even if you're not budgeted for employee travel to trainings, workshops, and employment-related conferences, everything you need for training is offered virtually, on the Internet. Many professional development courses online are free or low-cost. Investing in a new employee's future is critical to their employment retention in your nonprofit organization.

When you're thinking about the types of professional development needed, consider looking at your strategic plan's goals. How will those goals be achieved if new staff aren't trained in the goal's areas of implementation? For example, if one of your strategic plan goals is to create a community lending library for children at the level of elementary school, you might have your new employee take an online course in offering appropriate reading materials for young children or starting a lending library. Or, if you've just hired a grant-management assistant who needs to be trained in all aspects of using a spreadsheet and grant-management software, get that person started on their professional development track on day one on the job.

Look at other online training options that will enable your new employee to complete at least one type of training every month. Have the employee report back to you to describe what they learned and how they will apply it in the workplace. Encourage self-directed learning as well. Some of the following websites offer free or low-cost professional development training:

- **Shaw Academy:** A low-cost, online Microsoft Excel training course (www.shawacademy.com/courses/business/online-excel-course/)
- **Intuit QuickBooks:** Free online QuickBooks accounting product training (https://quickbooks.intuit.com/accountants/training-certification/)
- **Nonprofit Ready:** Free online grant-writing classes (www.nonprofitready.org/grant-writing-classes)
- **Alison:** Free online human resources course (https://alison.com/courses/human-resources)
- **Grants Learning Center:** Free online federal grant-management training (www.grants.gov/learn-grants.html)
- **Nonprofit Learning Lab:** Free online fundraising, grants, volunteer management, and marketing training (www.nonprofitlearninglab.org/webinars)

Managing Employees

Much of this chapter focuses on small organizations that are hiring their first staff members. In these organizations, the board oversees the staff member, and someone taking on the coordinator role — either board or staff — oversees the volunteers.

What if your organization has grown more complex? Everyone needs a boss. In nonprofit organizations, the board assumes that role for the executive director, who in turn provides supervision to other employees, either directly or by way of a management team. The common way to visualize these relationships is in an *organizational chart*, a schematic drawing showing the hierarchical management relationships in an organization.

A chart such as the one shown in Chapter 2 of this minibook (refer to Figure 2-1 there) may be overkill for your nonprofit, especially if you're the only employee, but for larger organizations, charts help delineate management responsibilities and clarify who reports to whom.

Recognizing what a manager or supervisor does

This list describes the various aspects of responsibility in managing employees:

- **Planning:** Planning occurs at all levels, beginning with the board of directors, which carries out organization planning, and ending with the custodian, who plans how best to complete cleaning and maintenance tasks. Managers should work closely with the employees they're supervising to develop department and individual goals.
- **Leading and motivating:** You may want to add *inspiring* to this category. Good management grows out of respect and cooperation. Be sure that staff members are familiar with the organization's goals and that they know how their work helps foster those goals.
- **Gathering tools and resources:** Don't ask someone to dig a hole without giving them a spade. In other words, you can't expect employees to do a good job if they don't have the means to do it. Time, equipment, proper training, and access to information are necessary.
- **Problem solving:** This is one of the most important aspects of good management. You can bet that problems will arise as you manage your organization and employees. Be understanding and creative in solving these problems. Ask for help in the form of ideas and suggestions from the employees you supervise.
- **Evaluating:** Employees should receive formal evaluations once each year. Effective evaluation begins with goal setting, and you want to help subordinates set clear goals and objectives.

Clarifying the lines of communication

We can't say enough about the importance of good communication. If your nonprofit has only a staff member or two, your job is easier than if you need to communicate with several dozen employees. Either way, good communication is essential. You also must clarify the lines of communication. In other words, staff below the level of executive director shouldn't be able to communicate directly with the board of directors.

REMEMBER

One person, and one person only, is the direct communicator with the board: the executive director.

Of course, confidentiality is important in certain matters. For example, if the organization is contemplating a major change, such as a merger with another organization, certain information needs to be withheld from the staff by the executive director and the board. On the other hand, letting rumors circulate about changes that may affect staff can create worse problems than being forthcoming about the details of a potential change. Give people as much information as you can, and be sure they have a chance to tell you how they feel. However, in sharing critical information, be sure to get the board's approval first.

REMEMBER

Communication is a two-way street. A good manager or supervisor keeps an open ear and devises ways to ensure that all employees have a way to voice complaints, offer suggestions, and participate in setting goals and objectives.

Holding regular staff meetings

Too many meetings can be a waste of time, but having regularly scheduled staff meetings is a good way to transmit information to employees, give them an opportunity to offer input and feedback, and keep everyone working toward the same goal. Tend to these tasks when arranging staff meetings:

- **Schedule regularly occurring meetings in a standard time slot.** Hold meetings no more often than once a week and no less often than once a month, depending on the needs of the organization.
- **Provide an agenda for every meeting.** Nothing is worse than attending a meeting that has no purpose and no direction.
- **Keep to a schedule.** Unless you have big issues to talk about, one hour is usually long enough to cover everything you need to discuss.
- **Provide time on the agenda for feedback.** Be sure that everyone has a chance to speak.

Writing emails to staff

Use emails to introduce new policies and other important information so that you eliminate misunderstandings. By putting the information in writing, you can clearly explain the situation. If the policy is controversial, distribute the email shortly before a scheduled staff meeting so that employees have an opportunity to respond.

Some larger organizations create staff e-newsletters that cover organizational programs and achievements. People work better if they receive recognition for their work. Stories about client successes, gains made by the organization, and announcements about staff comings-and-goings help instill feelings of accomplishment and organizational loyalty.

For very large organizations, a dedicated website or intranet that's accessible only to employees can transmit information and offer staff the opportunity to provide feedback and communicate with one another.

Chatting around the water cooler

Although formal written communication is important, nonprofit leaders also need to communicate informally by being accessible to staff in the hallways and around the water cooler. Some people communicate concerns better in an informal setting than in a staff meeting. Managers or supervisors who sit behind closed doors all the time often have a difficult time relating with their staff. However, don't force the camaraderie. Let it develop naturally.

Following the reprimand-and-dismissal process

Having personnel policies in place that specify the steps for reprimanding an employee, as well as ending employment when necessary, is critically important. Be sure to follow such policies to the letter.

Firing should never be the first step when an employee is falling short of your employment expectations. If someone you've hired is doing less than a stellar job, follow these general steps:

1. **Identify and document the issues.**
2. **Coach the employee to rectify the issue.**
3. **Create a performance improvement plan — that is, lay out in writing the steps for the person's improvement.**

   REMEMBER

   Many people deserve an opportunity to improve. Speak candidly and firmly with the employee about the level of improvement or change in behavior you expect. Set written goals for an improved performance, and specify a date for a follow-up consultation.
4. **Terminate the employee if they show no significant improvement after the improvement plan.**
5. **Conduct an exit interview.**

   Even in a tiny nonprofit organization, the key to not being sued is to document, document, and then document even more. Always have a board member sit in on an exit interview. Let the employee have their say and vent their frustration. In today's world of people who make a living from filing and winning lawsuits, a witness is needed for all dismissals.
6. **Respect the employee's privacy.**

   REMEMBER

   Don't share your complaints with others; discuss the matter only with the board chair.

7. **Encourage the employee to leave as soon as the termination meeting ends, watch as they collect their personal items, and then walk them to the exit.**

   You have to make this effort because a single disgruntled former employee can damage your organization's records and documents in a few days, hours, or even minutes.

Check out this excellent article from Entrepreneur.com for additional guidance on how to discipline and fire employees: `www.entrepreneur.com/article/79928`.

WARNING

Wrongful discharge lawsuits are common and can be *expensive*. As a precaution, you may want to investigate the possibility of employment liability coverage. If you need to terminate an employee and are unsure how to proceed, consult with a human resources specialist, your insurance carrier, or an attorney. The up-front investment may save you much time, expense, and trouble later.

Sometimes, organizations have to let employees go because they no longer have sufficient money to pay the employees' salaries. If you're a boss in this situation, try out these suggestions:

- **Give the employee as much warning as possible about the date of termination.** Don't keep it quiet while pulling out all the stops to raise money to save the position. Surprising employees with the bad news is inconsiderate.
- **Try to plan ahead and provide some severance pay to help out while the employee seeks a new job.** Although you may want to keep the person on the job until the last possible minute, good employees deserve good treatment. If someone leaves your agency with good feelings, you're in a better position to hire them back later.
- **Offer to serve as a reference or write letters of recommendation.** If the money isn't coming in and you can't find a way to keep the employee on, this gesture is one of the best things you can do.

Working with Independent Contractors

Maybe your organization isn't quite ready to take the leap into the employment waters. However, if you have work that needs to be done that volunteers can't do, working with an *independent contractor* may be a way to accomplish some organizational goals.

According to employment and tax laws in the United States, you can hire people in two ways: as salaried employees or as independent contractors. Rarely do you say to yourself, "I need an independent contractor to design my web page" or

"I need an independent contractor to write more grants for us." More commonly used terms are *consultant* and *freelancer*. For example, a small organization may contract with an accountant or a bookkeeper to maintain financial records and prepare financial reports.

Independent contractors aren't just a resource for small organizations: Large-scale, well-heeled nonprofits also use them. A good organizational consultant, hired as an independent contractor, can bring a fresh perspective to assessing an organization's work, a depth and breadth of experience that the organization hasn't yet developed, and focused attention to a project — say, the writing of a new strategic plan — that staff can't give while managing day-to-day operations.

Differentiating an independent contractor from an employee

Technical differences between employees and independent contractors are reflected in how you hire, pay, and manage them. Independent contractors are almost always paid a flat fee or hourly rate for their work — ideally, on a schedule that's set out in a contract that specifies the work to be done and the fee. Although you don't have to withhold federal and state payroll taxes, you need to file IRS Form 1099, which records the amount paid over a full year (usually, a calendar year) and the contractor's social security number or their business's federal tax ID number (EIN).

REMEMBER

Proceed with caution because a thin line often exists between an independent contractor and an employee. Just because someone works a limited number of hours each week doesn't mean that the person should be considered an independent contractor. The IRS doesn't look kindly on trying to pass off employees as independent contractors. Here's a short list of factors that differentiate an independent contractor from an employee:

- **Independent contractors are just that — independent.** Although setting time parameters for the job is fine, contractors typically are free to set their own schedules and work with little direction from the organization. They typically provide their own offices and equipment.
- **Duties should be written into a contract, and the contractor should provide invoices for services provided.** The contract should be limited to a specific period, and no vacation time or sick leave should be provided.
- **If you have to provide extensive training for the contractor to do the job, chances increase that the contractor may be considered an employee.** In hiring an independent contractor, you're supposed to be engaging someone with specific expertise.

» **A contractor who is working only for your organization and is putting in many hours each week may be considered an employee.** If you hire a contractor with the idea that the relationship will continue indefinitely rather than for a specific project or period, or if that contractor provides services that are a key part of your regular business activity, such as executive director, the IRS believes that you likely have the right to direct and control that worker's activities. To the IRS, this association looks like an employer-employee relationship.

WARNING

If you think you may be pushing the envelope on the question of contractor vs. employee, consult an attorney or a tax specialist who can give you proper advice. Authorities are increasingly scrutinizing the distinction between regular employees and independent contractors. The IRS may require employers who pay individuals as contractors, when they're really employees, to pay back payroll taxes and penalties. Board members and responsible managers can be held personally liable for these taxes.

The IRS has defined *common-law rules* for determining whether someone is an employee or an independent contractor. Check IRS Publication 15A, *Employer's Supplemental Tax Guide*, for a definition of these rules. The publication is available on the IRS website at `www.irs.gov`.

TIP

If you want to hire someone for a short-term assignment or a limited number of hours and the work is taking place in your offices, using your equipment, and requiring your regular supervision, consider using a temporary employment agency. The agency handles the employee's benefits, including employment taxes, and reassigns them if they're a poor fit for the job. Although using a temp agency may cost more than hiring the person directly, the agency can help you find someone who's qualified.

Establishing the roles for independent contractors

Independent contractors can help you with just about any aspect of your organization, from managing personnel matters to hooking up a computer network. But nonprofits most commonly bring them in to help with

» **Fundraising:** Fundraising consultants help with grant writing, planning for fundraising, special events, direct mail, and major gift-and-capital campaigns, among other methods of raising funds.

» **Organizational development:** Organizational development consultants may guide your board and staff through a planning process or help you develop the tools needed to evaluate your organization's work, to name just two examples.

» **Marketing and public relations:** Consultants can help you spread the word about your organization's good work by handling a public relations campaign directed at the media, developing your website, creating compelling brochures and newsletters, creating short promotional films, and many other strategies.

» **Evaluation and assessment:** Evaluators can take an in-depth look at an organization's programs, bringing specialized skills to that assessment and the value of an unbiased point of view.

Have a clear idea of what you want to accomplish before you seek help. Sometimes you don't know exactly what you're aiming to accomplish, but you should still try to articulate as clearly as possible what your aim is in hiring a consultant before you go looking for one.

Finding a consultant: Ask around

We have no single best way to find consultants. You can certainly search the web for nonprofit consultants who work in your area, but we think one of the better ways is to make a few calls to other nearby nonprofits or funding agencies. You may also be able to find a consultant by inquiring at a nonprofit support organization.

TIP

We prefer consultants who have more than one way of doing things. Not all nonprofits are alike, and what works for one may not work for another. Also, as your project evolves, you may find that you need a different kind of help than you originally imagined. Believe us: Changes happen all the time. Ask the consultant whether they're willing to consider revisiting the project goals along the way and adjusting the approach if the need arises.

Some consultants work as sole practitioners; others work in consulting companies. Working with a company or consulting group may give you access to more varied expertise. On the other hand, consultants working alone tend to have lower overhead expenses, so their fees may (and we stress *may*) be lower.

Interviewing consultants

Interviewing a consultant is similar to interviewing a regular job applicant. You want to review the résumé carefully to see whether the candidate's experience and expertise match your needs. Don't be intimidated just because the person sitting across the table from you has more experience than you do. That person is working for you. Ask any questions that you feel are necessary so that you can be sure you've chosen the right person.

Interview more than one person before you make your decision. As with interviewing for staff positions, having more than one person present at the interview is important because it lets you see how the prospective consultant interacts with a small group and gives you multiple perspectives on the consultant.

TIP

You may have the opportunity to use a volunteer consultant supplied by a program that provides free or low-cost assistance to nonprofits — interview these individuals just as you would paid consultants. Remember that you'll invest time in working with this person, so you need to be certain that they're right for your organization.

Ask interviewees to describe their method or approach to the problem or project that you're seeking to solve or complete. You shouldn't expect them to give you a full-blown plan in the interview, but you should expect a good picture of the initial steps they'll take. Also, if your project culminates in a written report, ask the applicant for writing samples.

Developing and executing the contract

You need to have a signed contract with every consultant with whom you work. These points should be clearly stated in the contract:

- **The scope of work and expected results:** You can include more or less detail here, depending on the type of project. If you're hiring the consultant to facilitate a one-day retreat for your board of directors, be sure that the contract includes the preparation time needed. Also, will the consultant be writing a report after the retreat? Try to touch on as many details as possible. The more specific, the better. Sometimes, if the scope of work is detailed, that detail is included as an attachment to the main part of the contract.
- **Fees, of course:** Some consultants charge an hourly rate plus expenses; others charge a flat rate that may or may not include expenses per project. The contract should state that you must approve expenses over a certain amount. Or you can write into the agreement that expenses are limited to a certain sum each month. Consultant fees vary, just like salaries, from one geographic area to another and depend on the type of work to be done and the consultant's experience.

WARNING

Don't pay fundraising consultants a percentage of money raised. Although some consultants, grant writers, and, in particular, telemarketers work under this arrangement, percentage payment isn't considered good practice by most fund-raisers and nonprofit managers. See the Association of Fundraising Professionals' code of ethics (`https://afpglobal.org`) for more information about this issue.

- **The schedule of when you'll pay the fees:** Some consultants who work on an hourly basis may send you an invoice at the end of the month. Consultants working on a flat-fee basis may require advance payment on a portion of the fee. This is fine. It's protection for the consultant, who probably has as many cash flow issues as you do. Don't make the final payment before the project is completed, however. Be sure to ask the consultant for an estimate of out-of-pocket expenses and the plan for billing you for such costs.
- **Special contingencies:** What if the consultant gets sick? What if your organization faces an unforeseen crisis and you have no time to work with the consultant? What if you've chosen the wrong consultant? You should include a mutually agreed-on way to end the contract before the project is completed. A 30-day cancellation notice is common.
- **A timetable for completing the work:** You and the consultant need to negotiate the timetable. Have you ever had remodeling work done on your house? You know that contractors can get distracted by other work, right? That's why having a schedule is vital.
- **The organization's role in the project:** If the consultant needs access to background materials, records, volunteers, board members, or staff, you must provide this access in a timely manner so that the consultant can complete the job on schedule.
- **Required insurance:** What if your consultant injures someone in the course of working on your project? If the person is uninsured, the liability can become your organization's responsibility. Just to be on the safe side, many consultant contracts include standard language about the consultant's responsibility to carry liability insurance and pay workers compensation insurance and other legally required benefits if the consulting company has employees who will be working on your project.
- **Ownership of the finished product:** This point doesn't apply to every consulting project, but if yours focuses on developing a study or report, specify in the contract whether your organization or the consultant has (or both have) the rights to distribute, quote, and otherwise make use of the results. Often, the organization has the right to publish and produce the report if it properly credits the author and if the consultant owns the copyright and has permission to make use of lessons learned in articles or future studies. Sometimes, you agree to seek approval from one another before using the work.

TIP

We think that having the consultant prepare the contract is a good idea. It's the final chance to make sure the person understands what you want done. You may suggest changes when you see the first draft.

2 Fundraising for Your Good Cause

Contents at a Glance

IN THIS CHAPTER

» Getting familiar with the case statement and its main purpose

» Writing a compelling case statement step by step

» Beefing up an outdated case statement

» Sharing your case statement in print and electronic format

Chapter 1

Developing Your Case Statement: Winning with Words

If you're new to fundraising, chances are that you're also new to the case statement. Your organization's case statement is an all-important vision document that spells out the major aspects of your organization's story, from your mission to your program goals and objectives, to board members, staff, and key volunteer leaders. Think of your case statement as the fabric you use to create all your other messages — promotional pieces, letters to donors, grant proposals, and more.

You may not be — or have any intention of becoming — an attorney, but there's something to be said for being able to make your case. And when the economy is pitching and swaying around you and you're trying to stay afloat (or, in better financial times, trying to navigate the squalls of abundance pouring your way), a well-developed, clear case statement is your map and guide. Your ability to describe your organization's mission, goals, objectives, programs, staff, and plans in one cohesive, well-thought-out document — your case statement — will impress your donors. It'll also impress the people working with you and others in the fundraising community. And, even more important than impressing your donors and partners, your case statement will help them understand why you exist, why you do what you do, and why they want to join you in doing it. This chapter shows you how to put together a top-notch case statement and what to do with it.

Stating Your Case

Before you can write your case statement, you need to understand what your case is and how you use the case statement after you've written it. You also need to know how to get started. (See the later section, "Developing a Case Statement: A Step-by-Step Guide," for details on how to write your statement.) This section lays the groundwork so you're prepared to state your case effectively.

Understanding what the case statement is and how you use it

REMEMBER

A *case statement* is a clear statement of the need your organization addresses, how you address it, what makes you unique, and how others can help. Done well, the case statement provides the basis for all your other published materials as well. The message you generate in the case statement speaks for itself through presentations, brochures, newsletters, annual reports, and more. The tone, flavor, style, and focus of this information, carried from one piece to the next, help build the overall identity of your organization. Your potential donors will notice the fact that your message is the same across different brochures. Consistency carries a message of dependability, clarity, and honesty.

Another use of the case statement — especially a good-looking one — is the effect it leaves behind. You can't be everywhere at once, and you can't always be the one to represent your organization, so it helps to have a document that gives a potential donor the facts of your organization — in more detail than you can or would offer in a face-to-face meeting. In putting together a case statement, your board and staff have to come together to communicate with each other about the central vision of the organization, which helps everyone see eye to eye.

Getting started with your case statement

Unfamiliar with case statements? Don't worry. Here are some questions people often ask as they begin to draft case statements for the first time. These inquiries give you a quick glance of what goes into a case statement:

- **How long should the case statement be?** The answer: As long as it needs to be. Now, before you start groaning, check out the later section, "Developing a Case Statement: A Step-by-Step Guide," for a list of the items you need to include in your case statement. The length has everything to do with how much you have to say for each item.
- **How often should you write a case statement?** Theoretically, you write a case statement one time from scratch, and then you update it as needed. Because you have sections for programs, budget, and more, some parts of your case may need revising every year. Other parts, such as the staffing section or the history section, need revisions only as changes warrant them. (See the later section, "Giving Life to an Outdated Case Statement," for more advice.)
- **Who should write the case statement?** Ideally, a person who has a clear sense of the vision of your organization — someone with spark — should write the case statement. But this type of writing can be difficult, and the drier the text, the less likely donors and evaluators are to make it all the way to the end. If you have someone on your board or your staff who's a talented, lively writer, solicit that person's services; otherwise, have the person most likely to get the job done write a draft of the statement and then have a committee of reviewers go through the draft and offer opinions, make suggestions, and add information as needed.
- **Should you include pictures and charts in a case statement?** Your board or leadership group should decide the way in which you publish your case statement, but, in general, it never hurts to look good. Don't overwhelm your readers by providing too many charts, using too many or conflicting fonts, or shouting at them with headlines that are too big. Simple and understated are best. But a few photos — especially of a program in progress, your new facility, or your cheerful staff — can help hold the reader's interest and build a bit more recognition for your organization. (Check out the later section, "Formatting your case," for more pointers on making your document look good.)
- **Should you make your case statement into a video?** These days you can use videos for all kinds of storytelling, and your case is no exception. You can show the spark you want to communicate to your viewers by linking images — emotional, hopeful, or heart-wrenching — with your cause in your donor's mind. Telling your case visually can be helpful when you're filling out corporate and foundation grant applications, as well as when you're introducing your organization to potential donors in another state or country or on another continent. You can post your video on your website so that it plays whenever somebody lands on your homepage, or you can post your video case statement on YouTube or Facebook. (See the later section, "Putting the case statement to work: From paper to online posts," for ideas about what to include in the video.)

» **Should you make your case statement available as a PDF file on the web?** Absolutely! The more information about your organization you provide, the better — for both your donors and your organization. One suggestion, however: Hold back any sensitive financial data from the general public eye. Provide a link so that any visitors who want to see your financial data can send you an email request.

Making the Case Compelling

The case statement does more than provide the basis for the message you use in your grant proposals, PR materials, and other documents. The case statement gives you the opportunity to think through all the aspects of your organization, from mission to governance to program delivery, and to make sure you connect all the dots along the way.

REMEMBER

Times of economic challenge and change — whether the financial landscape is improving or worsening — provide a great opportunity for you to revisit your case statement and assess whether it really speaks to the current needs of your community or constituents.

What makes a case compelling for one group may leave another cold, so knowing what your donors care about — and explaining clearly how your organization gives them the opportunity to help in that particular area — is key to writing a compelling case. This helps donors make the connection between the cost of the unmet need and their ability to make a difference. For example, a healthcare organization might include in their case statement something like this: "Nearly 70 percent of patients admitted to our medical facility are indigent or covered by Medicaid. Together, we can work on systemic change in the Medicaid system as well as create a private healthcare foundation to raise supplemental funds to supplement the reimbursement caps in Medicaid payments."

The following list offers suggestions for the types of information you can include in your case to demonstrate the need and set the context for your services:

» **Animal welfare:** Tell today's story of issues that connect with what's on your readers' minds. Include national statistics, such as the number of dogs and cats euthanized each year, the number of abandoned animals, or the number of kittens that would be born without your spay and neuter clinic. Share stories of specific animals and families your organization has helped, and be sure to include stories of care, advocacy, and passion when you introduce your staff and volunteer corps.

- **Art organizations:** Explain how the current economic climate is affecting art organizations as a whole. Find recent statistics on the number of closings or program suspensions in your area of specialty. List how many other nonprofit art centers are closing; describe how the symphonies of neighboring cities are faring; tell the stories of theaters under siege. Find out whether art programs are being cut in your local schools. Connect the local need for arts advocacy to the very real benefit your art organization brings to your community, and tell compelling stories to fan the fire of advocacy in the hearts of your readers.
- **Education:** It's no secret that governments change how much money they spend on education in times of economic change. Everyone knows the importance of education, but people often think funding comes from elsewhere, and that can lead your potential donors to ask, "Why should I give? You get money from the government." To tell your story compellingly, you need to have both facts and figures — national statistics about funding cutbacks, teacher layoffs, and program suspensions, as well as data that demonstrates the needs of the people you serve. Connect the facts with stories of the difference your organization has made in the lives of real people that the services you offer touch, and invite the readers to see how your organization is an important part of the broader education landscape.
- **Environment:** Today you can find all sorts of statistics on global warming, climate change, conservation measures, and domestic and international efforts to make positive changes for the environment. When you're considering what story to tell in relation to your organization, choose your facts and figures carefully, and be sure to begin and end with the facts. Know where your organization stands in terms of key issues, and take the extra effort to make your stance clear for your potential donors. Understanding your story in the context of developing science helps your donors find their connections to your cause.
- **Healthcare and social service:** In times of economic downturn, the need for services in all human services organizations — from healthcare groups to advocacy of all kinds — increases while funding decreases. Whatever your focus may be, know the national and international statistics in your area. Be able to share stories of real people impacted by the cause you address, and show — with compassion and care — how your organization has helped families meet their challenges. Make sure your stories are current and real; help readers get to know and identify with the real people you're asking them to help.

TIP

If your organization mobilizes to respond to a crisis — for example, a shortage at your food pantry, the emptying of your supply of flu vaccines, or the impact of a devastating storm — tell those stories in your case statement. The crisis may be temporary, but the story will capture the reader's imagination and demonstrate your ability to fulfill your mission.

» **International organizations:** People have been saying "It's a small world" for decades, but perhaps at least in part because of the advent of the web, this mantra seems to have become true. Today people from all over the globe can get involved in advocating for those in countries they've never visited. They can feel drawn to make a difference for children in Africa; they can be inspired by art in Paris; they can want to support an ecovillage in the United Kingdom or the resettlement of Ukrainian refugees in countries with open borders.

  If your organization has international appeal, include both big-picture and person-to-person stories in your case statement. The international donor cares about initiatives in which people and organizations work together in peace to reach a common goal, so be able to share the vision and collaboration of your organization while you tell powerful stories of individual lives and communities that have been impacted for the better by what you do.

» **Religious organizations:** Faith is an ever-important — but often unseen — component in the lives of individuals, groups, and nations. Fundraising for a faith-based organization, beyond any national affiliation or tithing program, is still a challenge for congregations of all types. Although your programs provide the channel for the good you accomplish in the world, be sure to tell the human story — who's impacted by what you do, how many people you've helped, and what your community would look like if you weren't present to meet the need you see. Connect these facts with the story of your faith and tell how your specific response to the need is providing a much-needed ministry. Communicating the story of how you meet the universal need to alleviate suffering and help others move forward can provide a compelling invitation for others to support you whether they're part of your tradition or not.

TIP

When you're brainstorming ways to tell your story in the case statement, invite others in your organization — from board members to staff to your favorite donors — to share their favorite stories about your organization. You may wind up with a few great stories to include, and at the very least, you'll have some great content for your web page or PR materials.

Developing a Case Statement: A Step-by-Step Guide

Okay, it's time to get started with the case statement. Here, assume you're the person responsible for writing the tell-all compelling document — the first draft, anyway — and that your board, your focus group, and any staff members you've selected to help with the review process will then review your draft, making revisions and suggestions as they go. Of course, if your organization does everything by a committee and you're drafting the document as a team, take the steps described in this section, multiply them by the number of people on the team, and pad whatever schedule you set for your tasks (which varies depending on your goal and the size of your organization) to provide extra time for each additional team member.

The following sections walk you through the process of writing a case statement using a fictional young nonprofit that serves teenagers who are experiencing homelessness as an example.

Step 1: Mission: Why are you here?

The first step is to draft your *mission statement.* The best mission statements, as we describe in Book 1, Chapter 1, share the following characteristics:

- They're clear, concise, and easy to understand. The shorter, the better — fine-tune your mission message so you can deliver it in the time it takes an elevator to move from one floor to the next.
- They capture and hold the reader's interest.
- They include a call to action that gives the reader a reason to respond now.

REMEMBER

Your mission statement should draw readers in and hold their attention. Start out strong. Describe the issue you're addressing; explain your solution; and then specifically describe your organization and show how it uniquely addresses the problem you opened with. The process looks like this:

- Big picture (problem)
- Zooming in (solution)
- Close up (the specific ways in which your organization addresses the problem)

Imagine that you're a part of the nonprofit organization called Angels on the Street. Because you're a fund-raiser for the organization, you know that Angels on the Street's mission is "to identify and reach out to disenfranchised teenagers in the community, offering fun, educational, and safe activities that help them build better relationships with peers and parents." But when potential donors and others ask your board members about the mission of your organization, here are some examples of how the board members respond:

"We're here to serve the needs of youth."

"We help teens in trouble."

"We get kids off the street."

WARNING

Although none of the board members is dead wrong in the summary of your mission, none of them hit the nail on the head, either. They all have different ideas of what the organization is all about. When people have different ideas about what the organization does, they may be pulled in different directions, which can mean wasted effort, money, time, or worse. When you define and stick to a clear, specific mission for your organization, you make sure everyone's efforts are spent directing the organization down the same path.

To improve Angels on the Street's fundraising efforts, the organization hires Jessica as its first full-time *development director* (who's in charge of fundraising for an organization) and asks her to draft a case statement. Consider how Jessica handles each of the elements described earlier in the Angels on the Street's mission statement:

- **Big picture:** Homeless teens are living under bridges, in abandoned tenements, and in boxes and doorways in every major city nationwide. Homeless teens often run away as young as 12 years old, learn the prostitution trade weeks later, and eat only every other day, surviving on the scraps left by those who have homes, families, and futures.
- **Zooming in:** You may want to think a rural community doesn't have homeless teenagers living on the streets. You may want to think the best about our community, but you'd be closing your eyes to a real problem facing us today. Last year more than 350 teenagers lived under bridges, in abandoned buildings, and in the doorways of our community. Homeless adolescents lived on the streets along with the shadows of drug addiction, horrendous poverty, illness, depression, and the haunting nightmares of sexual abuse and exploitation.
- **Close up:** Angels on the Street is a 501(c)(3) organization that began with the simple mission of getting help for these kids — whether that help is connecting them with their families, giving them bus fare home, finding sufficient counseling services, providing occupational training, or moving them into transitional housing. Angels on the Street reaches out and offers a hand and a heart to hurting teens, giving them a home, a chance, and the skills they need to create a life free from the horrors of homelessness.

The resulting mission statement that Jessica draws up looks something like this:

> Homeless teens. Not a problem here? Better look again. Come join us and help us get these kids back home to their beds, their rooms, and their families. And for those kids who don't have a home to go back to, you can provide a means for them to complete their education and pick up the tools they need to enter the workforce, which gives them a real chance to succeed in the adult world.

Step 2: Goals: What do you want to accomplish?

After you've established the *why* of your organization — the mission — you need to think about the *what*. What are you trying to accomplish? Your organization's response to the need you focused on in the mission statement makes up the *goals* section of the mission statement. Book 1, Chapter 3 has a deeper discussion on goal setting in the context of your organization's overall strategic plan; here, we discuss goals (and objectives, in Step 3) as they pertain to the overarching process of creating your case statement.

TIP

When writing about your goals, try to paint pictures in your reader's mind. Images last longer than abstract figures, so for example, describe the hope when homeless teens see the Angels on the Street van drive slowing down the street. Don't focus on their plight of precarious living situations.

Jessica, the development director of Angels on the Street (see the mission statement in the preceding section), came up with the following goals:

- Goal 1: Provide emergency shelter and supportive services for homeless teens.
- Goal 2: Reunite teens with their families whenever possible.
- Goal 3: Enable teens who can't return home to become self-sufficient.

TIP

Make sure to think about *organizational* goals here. For example, instead of describing the new programs you want to offer, focus on the larger challenges you seek to address through your organization, such as helping to preserve the natural waterways in your area, improving the reading skills of recovering addicts, or taking arts education into private schools by the year 2025.

Step 3: SMART objectives: How will you reach your goals?

SMART objectives give you a way to tell the people who read your case statement how you'll accomplish the goals you define in the preceding section. While the goal for Angels on the Street may be to get homeless teens off the street, the objective may be to work with local agencies to find housing for 75 teens a year.

REMEMBER

Make your objectives specific, measurable, achievable, realistic, and time-bound (in other words, SMART).

The objectives Jessica comes up with for Angels on the Street show specifically how the organization plans to work toward each of its goals. For example, the first goal is to get teens off the street by providing emergency shelter and supportive services, so the SMART objective for Goal 1 is this:

> By the end of 2023, increase the number of homeless teens who are living in emergency shelters and receiving supportive services by 30 percent.

The second goal is to reunite teens with their families whenever possible, so the SMART objective for Goal 2 is this:

> By the end of 2023, increase the number of homeless teens reuniting with their families by 50 percent.

The third goal is to enable teens who can't return home to become self-sufficient, so the SMART objective for Goal 3 is this:

> By the end of 2023, increase self-sufficiency for teens who can't return home by 75 percent.

TIP

Here are some questions you should be able to answer "yes" to as you write your objectives:

- Are your objectives specific?
- Are your objectives measurable?
- Did you set achievable objectives?
- Are the measurements in the objectives realistic?
- Did you include a date by which the objectives will be achieved or attained?

REMEMBER

If your organization is using an existing case statement, find out when the objectives were last updated. Because objectives are measurable and tied to programmatic responses to your organization's goals, they will — and should — be revised every year.

Step 4: Programs: What exactly do you provide?

In the *programs* section of your case statement, you get to pull out the stops a bit and toot the horn of your organization. What are your most effective programs? What are you most proud of? This section enables you to talk about what your organization does and how it helps the people it serves.

In the case statement for Angels on the Street, Jessica writes about the TLC program that her organization currently offers, taking medical supplies and basic food and clothing items to kids living on the street. The major parts of this program, which include creating links to area agencies, reuniting teens with families, and providing residential training for kids who can't return home, are all projects Angels on the Street plans to launch this year to further its mission.

TIP

Be sure to include a paragraph about each of the programs your organization offers. Then when you need to use selected paragraphs in a grant proposal, for example, you can simply remove the paragraphs that don't apply and leave those that do. (Book 3 covers how to write — and win — grants.) Thus, you have a minimum of effort and an economy of work. The case statement helps you say what you need once — powerfully and succinctly.

Step 5: Governance: What's the anatomy of your board?

Not all prospective donors are board-savvy, but you can be sure that any donor considering giving you a large gift or any foundation reviewing your grant proposal will want to know how your organization is governed. Who comprises your board? What different areas and interests do they represent? You answer these questions in the *governance* section of your case statement.

Be sure to include the following elements in your governance section:

- The legal status of your organization — 501(c)(3) status if you have it
- An overall picture of your board, including the number of members, member selection process, terms of service, and committee structure
- Specific information about key people on your board
- Information about the administrator, or executive director, of your organization

In the governance section of the Angels on the Street statement, Jessica lists the executive director and all board members, their board titles, and their current professional affiliations. She also lists key volunteer leaders who have been part of special events and fundraising campaigns or who have served in an advisory capacity.

Step 6: Staff: Who are the people behind your services?

The next important step is to include information on who actually provides the services to the people you serve — in other words, your *staff*. In the staff section of the case statement, you need to include both general information about how your staffing system is set up and specific information on the duties of key roles. You may want to include summarized job descriptions to give readers an idea of which tasks go with which roles.

In addition to describing the different hats your staff members wear, you need to talk about the staff members themselves. Stick to the key staff members in your organization — people in roles unlikely to change often, such as the executive director, the director of development, and so on. Also introduce key volunteers and people who have been ready, willing, and able to take on leadership roles for your organization's cause.

In the staff section of Angels on the Street's case statement, Jessica shares brief bios of each of the key staff members, including the program directors and staff members directly involved in program delivery. This section shows the range of talent and experience that staff members bring to the organization.

TIP

You may want to request copies of your staff members' résumés as you create your case statement so that you have them when you need them later. After all, staff will be an important part of all the grant proposals you submit, too, and you want to attach the résumés of key people in your programs along with your grant proposals.

TIP

If you're a start-up nonprofit organization, you may not have staff yet. That's okay. In your staff section, mention that you're a start-up organization, describe any current staffing conditions, and mention where you envision your staffing to be a year from now.

Step 7: Location: Where do you live and work?

The *location* section of your case statement describes where you provide the services you offer. You may have a traditional office in a traditional part of town, or you may be an Internet-based 501(c)(3) that does its work in the home offices and computers of various board and staff members. Or you may even work out of a museum or out of a delivery van.

Wherever your location is, describe it. Explain how the location is right for the services you provide and how many people you can serve there. Show how it helps you meet your goals. Include any plans for improvement or enhancement you have for the facility, and be sure to illustrate how these improvements will help you better meet your service goals.

The location section in the Angels on the Street case statement details the physical location of the organization's main office, as well as three small satellite offices that are hosted on local college campuses and run by volunteers.

Step 8: Finances: Is your organization financially responsible?

Although the *finance* section certainly includes your current financial statements, one of the most important things a donor looks for is an explanation — a summary — of your financial picture. As part of this summary, you want to include information about your current income and expenses, the overall financial picture today, and your projections for tomorrow.

TIP

Most importantly, make sure you write your finance section in understandable terms. Not everybody is an accountant, but everybody knows that 1 + 1 = 2.

REMEMBER

It pays to keep your books in tip-top shape. Book 4 covers the ins and outs of bookkeeping and accounting for nonprofit organizations.

Step 9: Development: What will you do in the future?

Anyone thinking of contributing to your cause wants to know that you'll be around tomorrow. If they donate $1,000 to your symphony today, they want to know that they'll be able to come hear Mozart in the summer series. The *development* section of your case statement is where you show your prospective donor that you'll be here tomorrow, and you do so by explaining that

- Your organization has a vision for the future.
- You have a specific plan for carrying out that vision.
- You have checks and balances in place to ensure accountability.
- You have credible people monitoring programs, finances, and growth.
- You have the means for evaluating your own progress and revising goals as needed.

For the development section of the Angels on the Street case statement, Jessica includes a new program currently in the planning stage, as well as a write-up of an expanded web effort and plans for a new special event.

TIP

This section requires big-time board input. If you're the lone development person or a volunteer putting together a case statement for the first time, you may not be able to address these issues for your particular organization. Not all organizations have a system of self-evaluation, although everyone seems to agree it's a much-needed facet of nonprofit management. If you're in the dark about the details of your organization's development plan, request a meeting with your executive director or board chairperson. Asking and answering questions about the way your programs get evaluated may just start a domino effect that causes your board to think about these development issues seriously for the first time.

Step 10: History: What successes are you building on?

Many charitable organizations — especially the ones that have been around for a long time — want to tell you all about their histories. They can keep you rooted in your seat for hours, describing great people, events, and influences that came about because of their existence in your community. They're glad to show you photos of past volunteers and produce a timeline of significant achievements.

The only thing wrong with this approach is that it puts your donors to sleep. Today's donors want to know the highlights that show you have momentum and accomplishments to build on, but their focus is all about *today's* issues. History is all well and good and is important as a means for gauging how your organization has lived up to its promises in the past, but people giving money today want to know where the money will go *today.* They want to join with you in solving a need *today.* They're interested in doing something *today* that will help make things better for tomorrow. For this reason, the *history* section comes at the end of the case statement; however, don't let its position in the case statement fool you into thinking that your organization's history is unimportant.

REMEMBER

History gives your organization a power that new organizations don't have — a reconnecting energy that summons the best of the past with the hope for tomorrow. Your past successes are essential for convincing donors that their money will actually accomplish something. The people involved with your organization catch the spark first ignited by your organization's founders when they relive the history of the need, the mission, and the people. But the viability of your current request doesn't lie in your organization's past. You're raising money today because there's a need for what you do today. Speak to that need. Put real faces on the need, describing people whose lives improve because of your mission. See Book 3, Chapter 9, for more about developing a compelling narrative for your organization.

GETTING INPUT FROM YOUR STAKEHOLDERS

A *stakeholder* is someone who has an interest in your organization — whether that person is a donor, a volunteer, a staff member, or a board member. One way to find out what your stakeholders think is to create a *focus group*. In essence, a focus group is any group of people you bring together to concentrate on a particular task, document, program, or problem. Although focus groups can help you get a feel for issues you need to address in more depth, don't mistake them for a representative sampling of public opinion. If four out of six people in your focus group think that your idea is a great one, for example, you can't take that to mean that the same percentage of the general public will feel the same way. Test your ideas, throw them out in a focus group, and listen carefully to the ideas and suggestions offered. Then use the preliminary information you've gathered to target and launch a more in-depth investigation, if needed.

The history section of the Angels on the Street case statement includes the story of the organization's beginning — the compassionate wish of an individual to do something for teenagers in trouble. Jessica writes a compelling section sharing how the organization has grown thanks to a dedicated and passionate volunteer corps.

Giving Life to an Outdated Case Statement

Maybe you already have a case statement, but you're looking for ways to breathe new life into the old document and hopefully attract more funding at the same time. Put on your reviewer's hat (you may want to invite input from colleagues as well) and consider the following questions:

- Is the need you address in your case statement compelling? Does it connect with today's real need?
- Are your programs described fully, with measurable outcomes?
- Do your objectives seem realistic?
- Does the description of your board sound like it has a lot of energy, as though your organization is ready for growth?
- Is your staff section current, spotlighting talents and abilities that meet today's need?

» Is your financial section up to date and written in understandable terms? Have you demonstrated support from major donors and foundations?

» Does your history section connect with today's lively story of your organization?

If you hesitate in answering any of these questions, consider overhauling your case statement. Bring in fresh new stories, and include developments in technology. (Do you use Twitter? Are you blogging now?) Add phrases or stories that show that your organization really does address a real need in your community today. An hour or two spent reworking an old case statement can go a long way toward helping your donors recognize why they want to support your efforts.

TIP

Always keep a primary copy of your case statement updated with changes, revisions, and ideas that others suggest. You may find that as the years go by, some ideas work better than others, some programs are explained better than others, and some foundations request more information in certain areas because your case isn't quite detailed enough on some points. You can make those adjustments over time, improving the case as you go along. Your case statement, like your organization, is an evolving, growing entity. Be sure to keep it up to date as your organization evolves.

Sharing Your Case Statement

After your board reviews the case statement and you make any last-minute changes, you're ready to begin sharing it with the world. How you go about sharing your case depends on who your potential donors are. Today's donors are more technologically savvy than donors in years past, so they may prefer to receive your case statement electronically, either by email or via a link to a file you've posted online in document, video, or presentation format. Of course, your older donors may not be too keen on all the newfangled Internet stuff, so being prepared to provide good, old-fashioned print versions of the case statement is important, too.

Formatting your case

Whether you decide to offer the case as a print or electronic document, you need to put some time and effort into making the format of the document as pleasing as possible. A well-formatted document is easy to read and helps the reader understand the main points quickly through the use of headings and bullet points. Here are a few suggestions for formatting the case statement:

- **Use a readable font.** The people reading your case may be young, old, or anywhere in between, so don't make the typeface (or *font*) too small. Generally setting your word processor to 12-point Times New Roman is a good choice.
- **Make your headlines stand out — but not too far out.** You need to have headings for each of the major categories, and you need to choose a type size and style that lets readers know you're changing tracks. A larger font, like Arial 16 bold, accomplishes this task. Consider using built-in styles for consistency.
- **Avoid using too many fonts.** The flexibility of word processing gives you so many different fonts and formatting choices to play with that you can drive yourself — and your readers — batty by using too many bells and whistles in a single document.
- **Include charts if necessary.** Charts are a great way to show complex information at a glance in the finance section, but don't include them elsewhere if you don't need them. Including visual effects gratuitously may seem like a good idea in the name of holding people's attention, but unneeded information in a case statement is just a waste of space.

Putting the case statement to work: From paper to online posts

As organizations become more comfortable with the variety of communication methods available — from traditional reports and brochures to online videos and tweets — they get more and more creative about the ways they tell their stories and provide information to donors.

After you have the case statement in its final form, you can reuse what you've created in several ways. Not only is reusing your case statement's content a smart use of your time, but it helps build the credibility of your organization because all your messages are consistent. You can use the information you created in your case statement in virtually everything you produce for your organization, including brochures, newsletters, grant proposals, campaign plans, appeal letters, speeches, press releases, public service announcements, videos, and your website's content.

TIP

After you have a finished case statement, you can use the full document in the following ways:

- Save an electronic version of the document as a PDF (Portable Document Format) file and post a link to it on your website. A PDF file preserves the format of the document and enables readers to print it no matter what kind of computer they're using.

» Use the text as a basis for slides and bullet points in a PowerPoint presentation you can give to donors or make available on your website.

» Print copies of the case statement and include them in informational folders you take with you when visiting potential donors or foundations.

TIP

You can also use specific sections of your case statement to create fun and effective identity pieces. For example:

» Use the text from the governance section to do a five-minute video introducing your board members to the general public.

» Use the basics from your program section to tell the story of your programs by filming a day in the life of one of the families who receives your services. In addition to posting the edited video on your website, YouTube, or any number of other video-posting sites, you can include a link that users can click to download a copy of PR materials, which you can also create using the information from your case statement.

See how easy it is to put your case statement to work for your organization? Oh, and it's so efficient. Create your case once, and use it many times.

IN THIS CHAPTER

- » Crafting a well-thought-out fundraising plan
- » Monitoring for red flags
- » Leveraging your money to make money
- » Knowing where to find help

Chapter 2
Creating a Fundraising Plan

What exactly do you need to have in place before you can start raising funds? No organization can exist for very long on good intentions alone. To be a successful fund-raiser, you need to be able to demonstrate to your donors (1) what you have, (2) what you need, (3) how you plan to get it, and (4) how you plan to account for it after you receive it.

This chapter discusses the fundraising plan — your roadmap, and the strategic document for your short- and long-term fundraising strategies. Not only will a good plan help you attract support from stakeholders inside and outside your organization, but it will also provide a chart for you to steer by as you navigate through uncertain economic times.

Drafting the Perfect Fundraising Plan

When the economy is pitching and swaying and you aren't sure how long you can even keep the doors open, putting time and energy into envisioning the future of your organization a year or more down the road may seem like a waste of time. But creating a well-thought-out fundraising plan is more than an empty exercise of wishful thinking. The time and energy you invest in creating a well-ordered, thoughtful plan can pay great dividends toward assessing all the potential revenue streams you have and figuring out how you can develop each of those channels more fully.

REMEMBER

Your fundraising plan needs to include the following items:

- **Clear statement of your mission:** Your case statement.
- **Fundraising goal:** What program or other goals you're raising money for.
- **Needs statement:** Description of your fundraising market and resources.
- **Financial target:** Fundraising goals you want to reach. You may want to set targets at different intervals, such as six months, one year, two years, and five years.
- **Selected fundraising method(s):** What types of fundraising campaigns you plan to use to reach your goals.
- **Targeted markets:** The different donor groups that campaigns may appeal to and how you plan to reach them.

When you write up your fundraising plan, you need to include specific information, such as the overall time frame, the benchmark goals you want to make during that period, the resources you plan to use, some information on campaign leadership, and the fundraising budget for the campaign. Don't have a budget yet? No worries. You'll get the scoop on creating a budget in the later section, "Budgeting Your Fundraising Efforts." The following sections get you started with your fundraising plan.

TIP

Make sure the people who will carry out your fundraising plan are part of the creation process. Nobody wants to hear, "We just decided that our goal is to raise $1 million this year. Do you think you can do that?"

Starting with the case statement

The first step in building your fundraising plan is to write your organization's case statement — your carefully expressed reason for being — which is discussed in detail in Chapter 1 of this minibook. If you don't have a copy of your organization's case statement in front of you, get one.

REMEMBER

Starting with the case statement is a must because it includes the goals and objectives you set for your organization, which are essential parts of your fundraising plan.

Identifying your goals

After you've identified your organization's mission, it's time to describe what your organization wants to fund. In other words, it's time to draft your *goals*, which we also discuss in Book 1, Chapter 3, where we cover putting together your organization's strategic plan. You may need to generate money for programs, raise funds for operating costs, cover the costs of expanding your offices, or build an endowment. Or you may want to do all of the above.

Most nonprofit organizations have four primary fundraising goals. They need funding for

- **Programs:** These enable you to fulfill your mission.
- **Everyday operations:** These include all the costs involved in running your organization day to day.
- **Capital enhancements:** These include building renovations and other facility improvements.
- **Building an endowment:** An endowment enables you to provide for your organization's long-term future.

REMEMBER

In precarious times of economic turbulence, you probably have a fifth fundraising goal: survival, which is otherwise known as keeping the doors open and the lights on. Achieving this goal may mean looking for creative partnerships or putting your general operating fund front and center.

TIP

Identifying your specific fundraising goals is key to setting up your plan. Just saying, "We have to raise money — for everything!" isn't going to get you very far. Whatever your fundraising goals are, apply these three questions to each goal:

- Why do we want to achieve this particular goal?
- What benchmarks are involved in achieving this goal?
- How much will this goal cost to achieve?

Your answers to these questions need to be focused and specific. What you come up with eventually becomes your goals statement.

Building a needs statement

After you're clear on your mission and identify your specific fundraising goals, you're ready to consider how you plan to reach those goals. Keep the following five questions in mind as you define the big picture of your fundraising plan:

- » What resources do you have?
- » What resources do you need?
- » Where have you come up short recently?
- » Which fundraising method is the right one for you?
- » Which *market* (the people or groups you turn to for money) do you want to approach?

Armed with the answers to these questions, you can create your *needs statement*, which summarizes how you'll go about raising funds. This statement presents a clearer picture of what you have and what you need.

Assessing your existing resources

So far, you've been laying out your overall fundraising approach. The next step is to gather specific information for your fundraising plan and identify the people who will drive it. If you already have a lot of information about your organization's previous plan and the people available to make it work, you may not need to start your fundraising plan from scratch. Either way, here are the essential items you need to include as you consider your organization's existing resources:

- » The donor lists
- » Histories of the amounts your donors have contributed in the past
- » Fundraising strategies that your organization's previous fund-raisers used — and how much money they raised
- » Any market studies done by your organization gauging public awareness of your organization
- » Public relations materials used in the past (membership brochures, annual reports, copies of press releases, and so on)
- » A list of potential donors
- » A list of the volunteers or staff who participated in past fundraising efforts
- » A list of the board members experienced in fundraising

- A detailed description of a specific program or campaign that directly addresses your needs statement

TIP

If your organization has done fundraising previously in any sort of organized way, you may already have some of this information available to you. If you're new to the organization or the fundraising role, ask someone who's been with the non-profit for a few years to help you round up this data.

Before you start writing your fundraising plan, you may need to do some research. Taking some time now to investigate what's been done before can save you valuable time later and help you focus your efforts and resources. If you discover, for example, that a program appeal fell flat two years ago, you can carefully investigate the whys behind that bomb before you launch a similar program. The economic climate may have been much different two years ago, but you can still benefit from looking carefully at a campaign postmortem. Also, remember that you aren't limited to financial statements and donor reports; you can engage long-time volunteers and board members to get some great stories and insights about previous fundraising efforts and their results.

Determining what you need

After you have a sense of the resources you already have, you can determine what you still need as you get organized for fundraising. The following list provides some possibilities:

- **Updated mission statement and goals:** If your organization already has a mission statement and a list of fundraising goals, you still need to look at them carefully to update them to fit your organization's current situation.
- **Development committee:** This committee isn't a must, but it's useful if you have the people power.
- **Complete slate of board members:** This list includes all your board members, not just those with fundraising experience. And don't forget to incorporate training for the members who are inexperienced in fundraising.
- **Donor list:** This all-important list is the database of all donors who have ever given to your organization in any capacity.
- **Assessment of public opinion regarding your organization:** You might think of this as your "brand." What do people think of when someone mentions your organization?
- **Clients or previous clients:** Your clients are the people who need what you offer or who have benefitted from your programs in the past.

Setting your financial targets

The leaders of your organization — the board, the executive director, and the program director — are responsible for telling you exactly how much money you need to raise as your organization's fund-raiser. You may be in on the discussions, of course, especially when they get to the "Do you think it's doable?" part, but the financial targets are really up to them to decide.

REMEMBER

If you've seen a big decline in revenues or you've recently seen your investment values plummet, you may be understandably wary about setting specific financial targets. When the economy goes topsy-turvy, gauging when things will stabilize is anybody's guess. Even when times are tough, however, the best approach is to keep your eyes on your goal and keep moving forward. This is no time to lessen your expectations for fundraising. You can create the targets with the best information and insight you and your board can pull together, knowing that some factors, like the economy, may be outside your control.

Plan your fundraising targets for

- **The present:** Funding for current expenses, such as a summer academic tutoring program, the acquisition of a 15-passenger van, or the salary of a special speaker for a volunteer appreciation event.
- **The short term:** Funding for upcoming expenses, such as for the next semester, the next year, or until a specific program ends.
- **The long term:** Funding for a three-year plan or an endowment plan.
- **A cash reserve:** Funding to help you navigate through uncertain financial waters. Plan to tuck away six to nine months' worth of operating funds for a potentially rainy day.

Putting the all-powerful giving pyramid to work

One tool that's extremely valuable in planning for the realization of your financial goal is the *giving pyramid.* The giving pyramid is useful for visualizing (and communicating) how you make your revenue. It can also help you determine how many large gifts you need to obtain to reach different benchmarks in your target amount. For example, suppose that the first benchmark of your three-year fundraising plan is to raise $250,000 the first year. With the giving pyramid, you can figure out how many gifts at various levels you need to reach that goal. Figure 2-1 shows you what the giving pyramid looks like.

GOAL-SETTING TIPS

Goal setting in tough times isn't easy because you may not know what the financial landscape will look like 6 or 12 months down the road. Here are some tips for setting workable goals for your organization no matter what the economy looks like:

- Make sure the people involved in the fundraising are involved in the goal setting as well.
- Be specific about how much you want to raise. Don't use vague phrases such as "as much as we can get."
- Consider setting two goals — a lower one that the staff realizes is what you need to bring in to keep operating, and a higher goal you share with the public. That way you cover your bases in a shifting economy, and if you reach your higher goal, great — but if not, you still have what you need to keep the doors open.
- Set benchmarks for the campaign to motivate you and your fellow fund-raisers. Know how many $1,000, $5,000, and $10,000 gifts you want to obtain by a certain date, for example.

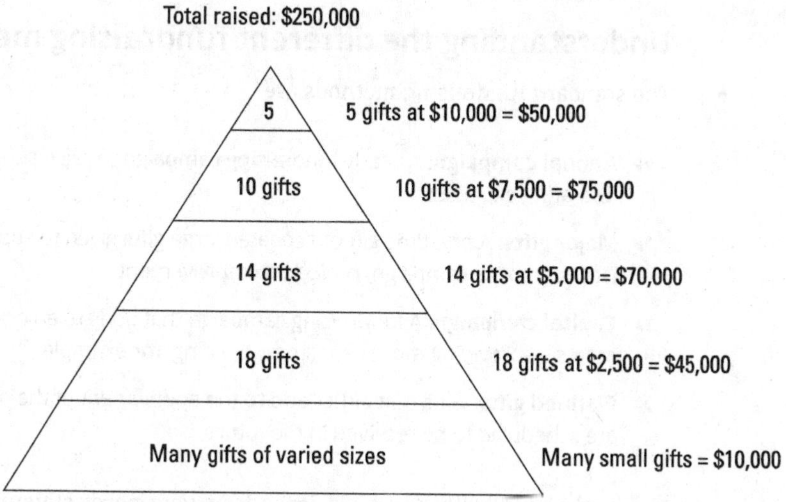

FIGURE 2-1: Use a giving pyramid to plan how many gifts in different sizes you need to reach your goal.

© John Wiley & Sons, Inc.

Not long ago, while some fund-raisers were working on an annual campaign for a major nonprofit organization, they were aiming for a goal of $300,000, which was made up mostly of small gifts. But twice during that campaign, people walked into the office, took out their checkbooks, and said something like, "You know,

I've been coming here for more than five years and just love it. Here's a check for $25,000." The fund-raisers were floored both times. The moral of the story? Count on the smaller gifts, but don't forget to cultivate major gifts along the way. (See chapters 5 and 6 of this minibook for more about major gifts.)

REMEMBER

An old fundraising joke goes like this: "It's easy to raise a million dollars! Just find a willing millionaire to write you that one big check." In reality, though, it's the multitude of smaller gifts, along with those well-cultivated major gifts, which bring you to your goal.

Getting started with the right methods

Your fundraising plan includes all the campaigns, events, grants, and so on that you use for your overall fundraising strategy. When you begin a fundraising campaign, you first have to decide what your fundraising goals are. Then you must choose which fundraising *method,* or means, you want to use to reach your goals. If you know you want to increase your donor base by 20 percent and reach a fundraising goal of $500,000 by year's end, for example, you've already established the endpoint. What you need to do next is choose the right fundraising method that'll get you there.

Understanding the different fundraising methods

The standard fundraising methods are

- **Annual campaign:** A yearly fundraising campaign to raise support for operating expenses
- **Major gifts:** A one-time gift or repeated large gifts given to support a particular program or campaign, project, or improvement
- **Capital campaign:** A fundraising campaign that adds to an organization's assets — providing money for a new building, for example
- **Planned gifts:** Gifts that either add to the endowment of the organization or are scheduled to be received in the future

The fundraising method you use depends on your needs statement. If you're raising funds for day-to-day operations, you want to create an annual fund campaign to reach that end. If you're focusing on building an endowment for your organization, think more along the lines of planned giving.

What about special events? Don't forget the black tie and tails or long gown you have hanging in the back of your closet. Special events can be great fundraisers when you do them right. Unless you've publicized that your organization will use the proceeds of your special event for a particular purpose, the money you raise at your event can go wherever you need it to: the operating fund, the capital campaign, a special project, a particular program, or the endowment fund.

Creating a method comparison worksheet

If you have a track record to use, look back through your fundraising budget for past campaigns. How much did you raise for your annual fund? How much did you spend raising that amount? Compare and contrast similar numbers for your direct mail campaign, your donor renewal program, your special events, and so on. Where did you break even? Where did you make significant money? Where did you take a loss? Use Table 2-1 to compare the effectiveness (or lack thereof) of the fundraising methods your organization has used in the past. Doing so can help you choose which methods to use in the future.

TABLE 2-1 Method Comparison Worksheet

Method	Income	Expenses*	Percentage (Income Divided by Expense)
________	________	________	________
________	________	________	________
________	________	________	________
________	________	________	________
________	________	________	________
________	________	________	________

** Include staff time in the expenses*

TIP

When you calculate the expense of putting a particular method into action, don't forget to include the staff time. You may need to estimate the number of hours staff members dedicated to working on a specific campaign or method and then use the hours multiplied by their wages to calculate the cost. Having even ballpark figures related to cost per hour can be useful in evaluating the method's effectiveness.

Discovering fundraising markets

The next step in creating your fundraising plan is to identify your *markets*. From where do you raise the majority of your funds? Again, if you're an existing organization, you have data that gives you the answer pretty quickly. Look through the data carefully, but don't get stuck in the past. If you're just starting out, you need to put some thought and planning into where you should begin. Think about current economic trends, community issues, and the cultural climate before deciding on the right market and the right method for your effort.

The best fundraising plans don't focus too heavily on any one market; instead, they mix and match constituencies to make sure they're continually raising both short- and long-term funds. Consider the markets in Table 2-2 and think about the amount of time it takes to receive a gift from each.

TABLE 2-2 Markets and More

Market	Short-Term	Long-Term	Description
Individual donors	✓	✓	Funded by Salesforce.org and based on surveys, data from multiple sources, and interviews, the report "Understanding Philanthropy in Times of Crisis: The Role of Giving Back During COVID-19" found that the share of individuals reporting that they gave to charitable organizations, individuals, or businesses increased between 4 percentage points and 6 percentage points between May and September 2020. Individual donors were most likely to support human services and health organizations in response to the pandemic, with 81 percent of respondents in May and 87 percent in September indicating they maintained or increased their giving in that area. (See `https://scholarworks.iupui.edu/bitstream/handle/1805/26934/philanthropy-crisis-nov21.pdf`.)
Affinity groups	✓		Affinity groups, such as professional associations or special interest groups, are usually a source of short-term, programmatic funding; they typically apply a specific time period to their donations.
Churches	✓	✓	Depending on your relationships with sponsoring churches, you may receive specific program support or ongoing operational support. Although you may receive small to medium gifts from many churches consistently, the likelihood that you'll get a major gift from a church is small. Even so, the best market for major gifts — individual donors — may come to you through a church contact.

Market	Short-Term	Long-Term	Description
Corporations	✓	✓	Corporations are often more interested in funding a specific program — something they can see their name on or something that aligns with their product or service — than in providing for operational expenses or endowment concerns. According to data from Candid, $6.2 billion in corporate giving in 2020 was related to COVID-19 relief, while Giving USA 2021's conservative estimate for COVID-19 relief provided by U.S. corporations and corporate foundations to U.S.-based nonprofits was $1.1 billion, excluding pledges. For a short-term relationship, corporations may supply program or equipment grants. Over the long term, expect to cultivate a partnering relationship. In times of economic upheaval, corporations may pare down philanthropic giving substantially while they work to shore up and stabilize their own operations.
Foundations	✓		Foundations, by and large, are interested in offering solutions, which means programs, programs, and more programs. Most notably, foundation gifts went up 15.6 percent, increasing from $76.61 billion in 2019 to $88.55 billion in 2020. That's $11.94 billion more — over half the total rise in giving of $22.78 billion. (The 2019 total was $448.66 billion.) Generally, foundations don't want to fund either annual fund campaigns or the "bricks and mortar" of capital drives. In thinking about your funding needs, coming up with a grant proposal for a specific program that fits the mission of a particular foundation is a great way to meet short-term funding goals.
Government	✓	✓	Similar to corporations (but with a lot more red tape), the government may be able to provide your organization with program-related moneys, staff salaries, and perhaps even ongoing operational support. Long-term involvement is possible, although you won't build a sizeable endowment from the support of government grants.

TECHNICAL STUFF

A decade ago, low-income working families were the most generous givers in the United States. However, today the largest givers are billionaires. Have you heard of Warren Buffett, Melinda French Gates, MacKenzie Scott, and Jeff Bezos?

GIVING CIRCLES: A NEW AND PROMISING APPROACH

In the past two decades, a new kind of citizen philanthropy has brought a hopeful new opportunity for fund-raisers. *Giving circles* are groups of individuals who pool their money and other resources (like time) and decide collectively where to donate their funds. What do we know about the characteristics of giving circles? These groups

- Give more than average donors because they're aware of the impact their collective gift makes and because members inspire each other to give more
- Think more strategically about where they give because the group as a whole makes the decision
- Tend to be more engaged than average donors in the communities where they live
- Are more likely to talk about the causes they support with others in their lives
- Are likely to give to organizations that support women, the arts, and ethnic and minority groups

Giving circles often have their own processes that they use to determine what they'll fund and how you can get your organization on their radar screens. Do some research to find out about giving circles in your area that may be open to receiving new proposals, hearing your presentation, or just having a conversation. You can use the United Philanthropy Forum membership tab to get started (`www.unitedphilforum.org/directory`), scrolling through the list of international members.

Avoiding Plan-Busters like the Plague

WARNING

This chapter talks about what you can do to put together your fundraising plan and begin working toward its success. One of the challenges of fundraising in tough times is that even the best plan may take a while to come to fruition depending on the economic climate and other variables outside your control. In the meantime, here are some red flags that you can — and should — watch out for along the way:

» **Choosing the wrong leadership:** The leadership for your fundraising effort greatly affects the way others perceive their roles in your campaigns. Make sure you have positive, can-do people with willing attitudes and strong connections in your leadership roles; they can make a huge difference in the effectiveness of your fundraising campaigns.

» **Not knowing your mission:** Knowing your mission seems pretty basic, doesn't it? Well, it's not only basic; it's essential. You aren't going to be able to raise any money for your organization unless you know why your organization exists and whom you serve. Make sure you have a strong, clear case before you even think about fundraising.

» **Having unrealistic expectations:** Be realistic in your needs statement and in the goals you set as a result. If you raised $200,000 last year, you may be shooting too high to aim for $500,000 this year.

» **Dealing with bad timing:** If your organization has recently suffered a setback in the news — a board member resigned in anger; a legal suit is pending; a large funder just denied a gift — now may not be the best time to launch a fundraising campaign, but that doesn't mean you should just drop out of the market. Think through your messaging, focus your campaign, and tell your story honestly and clearly to call attention to what really matters — getting your programs or services to the people who need them.

Budgeting Your Fundraising Efforts

You've no doubt heard the phrase "it takes money to make money." Well, this phrase holds true for fundraising just like any business endeavor. Essentially, you have to spend fundraising dollars to raise funds — a fact that may concern some donors if your fundraising efforts seem too extravagant. And because you're in the business of raising money, you'd better go about it in a businesslike way. To meet your goals most effectively, you need to carefully plan, budget, and account for all the money you bring in and spend.

A *budget* is a financial plan that shows how you intend to use your resources to pay the expenses you incur to fulfill your mission. Your fundraising budget, which your board approves as part of your organization's overall budget, is an important planning instrument for you, as well as a great way to show your potential funders — whether those funders are individuals, corporations, or foundations — the black-and-white details of your fiscal responsibility.

Making sure you include everything in your budget . . . but don't overbudget

The categories in your fundraising budget vary depending on the type of work your organization does, but a few basic ideas take effect across the board. First, make sure fundraising has its own section in the overall operating budget of your organization. In that budget, be ready to put down numbers for the following items:

- How much time you're allocating for fundraising
- How much staff time will be spent in support of fundraising
- What the real expenses are for running your fundraising program

Second, when you're planning out the expenses of your fundraising program, be sure to consider costs in all the following areas. (The top four are likely to apply only to larger organizations; smaller organizations or community groups may have only one or two paid staff, if any. See Book 3, Chapter 12 for more details about creating a budget that accounts for your funding needs; Book 4, Chapter 5 has information about creating your operating budget.)

- Salaries and wages
- Pension plan contributions

WHEN OPPORTUNITY STRIKES . . .

Out of the blue, a bolt of awareness may electrify your cause. For example, take the ongoing heated conversation in the United States about healthcare. This issue has stirred up (and rightfully so) discussion on issues that touch all levels of family life, from the youngest to the oldest members of society. If your organization's mission relates to healthcare or social services, the current debate may call attention to your cause.

Although you can't prepare for such occurrences when you're setting up your fundraising plan, be aware of the pulse of your environment. Identify issues that are related to you and keep your eye on them. Take advantage of stories in the news — when the link is genuine — so potential donors can understand better than ever how your organization can address the topic they're concerned about.

If taking advantage of current events sounds distasteful to you — as though it's in some way exploiting a big need in your society — think again. With a topic as seemingly basic as good, universal healthcare, opinions get polarized, views grow stronger, and a wave of frustration — both personal and cultural — ripples through the culture. At times like these, society has a natural need for balance and action, and stories showing that good work is still being done, that people care, and that the people most in need are being cared for are more important than ever. If your organization can be a legitimate part of that healing and provide some of the answers, you're not exploiting anyone. You're simply taking advantage of a real opportunity to further your mission.

- Employee benefits
- Payroll taxes
- Supplies
- Telephone and Internet access
- Website design and maintenance
- Utilities
- Postage and shipping
- Rent
- Equipment costs
- Printing and publications
- Travel

In times of economic transition, it can be a challenge to gauge how much you need to allocate for the various expenses your organization incurs. Two rules of thumb to keep in mind:

- First, include in your budget everything you're likely to need for the year (including a cash reserve fund for emergencies), and project what you need, considering the current rate of inflation.
- Second, go over your budget carefully — with the assistance of your board and key staff members — to weed out all unnecessary expenses and qualify the costs you project.

A lean, effective budget based on your real needs and best-educated projections is much easier to track and manage in the long run than a budget that is woefully underfunded or one that includes amounts earmarked for nonessential extras that tie up funds that could be used to reach more people.

TIP

You may be familiar with Form 990, the IRS form that nonprofits use to provide full disclosure of their activities and finances. While you're putting together your budget, think about the data you need to complete your 990 and plan your budget categories accordingly. Book 4, Chapter 8 discusses Form 990 in detail. (You can get a copy of the form online at `www.irs.gov`.)

Figuring out the cost of raising money

So how much money does it take to make money? Different types of fundraising methods require different investments, but the range can run anywhere from a few cents on the dollar for major gifts, planned giving, and capital campaigns to upwards of 50 cents per dollar raised for special events. This wide range of costs is another reason you need to make sure you select the right fundraising method for your campaign.

Using Affordable and Functional Fundraising Software

Fundraising software can help you organize your fundraising plan and donor lists and supply valuable reports and analyses of your results. Should you make the investment not only to buy the software, but also to transfer all your data into it? The answer is yes, yes, yes!

First, the odds are you don't have to reinvent the wheel here. You can import the donor lists you now keep in a spreadsheet or word processing program into most mainstream fundraising software programs. After you transfer your current data into such a program, here are the areas in which you can expect to reap benefits:

- Donor management, including cross-references among family members and coworkers
- Volunteer management, including scheduling and tracking of hours worked
- Membership management, including keeping track of renewal notices, membership cards, and more
- Pledge processing with cash flow projections and delinquent notices
- Major-gift management, including tracking memorial gifts and generating automatic acknowledgments
- Direct mail, email, and other campaigns, including helping you organize your lists, personalize communications, and weed out duplicates sent to the same address

Yes, you may have to spend some time inputting data into the software, you may have to spend some money purchasing the software, and you may have to spend some more time training volunteers and staff to use it. But in the end, fundraising software helps your organization track all the details more efficiently. And because your organization profits from keeping a record of its activities, the software, in turn, allows you to develop and grow.

TIP

Here are some fundraising software products worth a look:

- **Network for Good:** This software is built for small and growing nonprofits. It brings all of the tools, features, and guidance needed to raise funds and build strong donor relationships. You can check this out online at www.networkforgood.com/all-in-one-platform/.
- **Bloomerang:** This software is designed to assist small and medium-sized nonprofits in delivering a better giving experience. Check it out online at https://bloomerang.co/product/.
- **DonorPerfect:** This program has a robust set of features for small to midsize organizations; you can purchase the software or buy a monthly subscription online at www.donorperfect.com.
- **FundRaiser Software:** This simple-to-use donor management program is useful for managing your donor lists, tracking all communications, and creating reports based on activity in donor accounts. Check it out online at www.fundraisersoftware.com.
- **Blackbaud eTapestry:** This web-based fundraising software makes it easy for your donors to give online and easy for you to update your records from anywhere — not just from a single office location. In addition, eTapestry helps you create and send email campaigns. Check it out online at www.blackbaud.com/products/blackbaud-etapestry.

TIP

Many companies offer free trial versions of their software that you can download and try out to see whether they're right for you.

IN THIS CHAPTER

» Identifying donors among your stakeholders

» Getting your board on board to find potential donors

» Investigating prospective donors

» Creating an up-to-date donor information system

» Keeping donor research confidential

Chapter 3
Mining for Donors

This chapter is all about the "who" in your fundraising plan. Your organization's donors — whether they're individual givers, couples, affinity groups, foundations, or corporations — all believe in the work you do and contribute to your cause. Cultivating relationships with your organization's donors and starting new relationships with people who are likely to catch the spark of your mission and involve themselves in your cause require a dedicated effort and a well-thought-out plan. Rest assured that your work — in good times and bad — is likely to be rewarded.

Finding Your Stakeholders

A *stakeholder*, as we've explained elsewhere in this book, is anybody who has a stake in what you do. In other words, your work affects your stakeholders in some positive way; the existence of your organization makes a difference to them. Your stakeholders are the people you want to research as possible donors (if they aren't already); they may be board members, staff, volunteers, clients your organization serves, vendors, or contributors to your cause.

REMEMBER

Agencies have different types of stakeholders, including the ones in the following list. You may recognize some of your own donors in this list:

- **Clients:** Your clients are the beneficiaries of your services. Who can better understand how worthwhile your mission is than those who have experienced it first hand? For example, the family of an Alzheimer's patient who found a daytime caregiver and developed better coping skills through your organization is a potential contributor to your organization. The patient's family members believe in your cause because they've had a personal connection with it, and so they may be more than willing to give back to your cause in some way.
- **Current and past donors:** Current donors believe enough in what you do to donate their money and possibly their time, energy, and talents to your cause. Past donors have given to you before but, for whatever reason, may not be giving now. At some point, your cause inspired them to give, so it's reasonable to expect that they'll give again.
- **Major donors:** Your major donors give at a high level and are already aligned with your mission and your message. They've made the connection between spark and action and already support you, perhaps with their time and effort as well as with their dollars. See Chapter 5 of this minibook for more about major donors.
- **Staff and volunteers:** Your staff members and volunteers are the champions of your cause. You know they believe in the work they do because they commit a significant amount of time and energy to fulfilling your mission. Staff members and volunteers are in the unique position of being able to see the results of what you do and have a sense of the continuing and far-reaching possibilities of your organization.

  For example, staff members of a research think tank see the research being done, the people benefiting from that knowledge, and the possibilities for the future. Volunteers in an arts organization see increasing support for the arts, productions of exciting programs, and strong and growing arts education programs. Your staff and volunteers, who believe so strongly in the mission, make for a potential donor pool for your organization.
- **Board members:** Your board members steer the course for your organization. So who should believe in the work you do more than they do? Your board members care enough to commit their time, their effort, their vision, and often their professional and personal resources; they should also be giving financially.

  You must have a board committed to the cause, and the need to get every board member to give. Foundations look for 100 percent board giving as one of the criteria for funding. But beyond that, having a board that includes all-giving members is a good example for all the other stakeholders, from staff to volunteers to clients.

- **Vendors:** Your vendors supply your paper products, your payroll services, your software support, and many other products and services you need to keep your organization running. These businesses and individuals know something about what you do, the people you serve, and the people who work with you.

  For example, perhaps you buy used vans for a meal-delivery service from a particular van dealership. The dealership is probably glad to get your business and may make a potential donor. The link your vendors have to your organization is a closer one than the link you're trying to form with a new business you're considering approaching, so put your vendors on your stakeholder list.

- **Neighboring organizations:** These organizations are people or groups in your community that benefit from the services you offer. Certainly, you have agencies in your area that are glad you exist. For example, if a local community theater occasionally works in tandem with a larger theater arts organization, the organization may be a good source of money, costume, or prop donations.

Recognizing Your Bread and Butter: Individual Donors

The following sections help you understand the relationships that different potential donors have with your organization and how to use that knowledge to cultivate them as real donors.

Understanding donor levels

Donors come in all shapes and sizes, as well as all giving levels. Your organization's fundraising environment is composed of the following four distinct levels of involvement:

- **Level One:** People closest to the heart — and hopefully the passion — of your organization, including members of the board, managers, and major givers
- **Level Two:** People who work with or are served by your organization, including volunteers, staff, current donors, members, patrons, and clients

- **Level Three:** People who may have given to your organization in the past but who aren't active donors
- **Level Four:** People in the general population who have interests compatible with your mission but who as yet don't know you exist

Identifying potential donors

When you identify potential donors, make a list of specific people who fit into each of the top three donor levels described in the preceding section. The following steps show you how:

1. **Identify by name those people involved with your organization at Level One.**
2. **List the names of your potential Level Two donors.**
3. **List your Level Three prospective donors.**

After you have a list of possible donors, plug the names into your donor tracking system so you can follow up on them later. (See the later section, "Keeping Track of Your Organization's Donors and Their Contributions," for more information about this tracking system.)

Doing Business with Corporate Donors

Corporations normally give for one or more of the following four reasons:

- They think giving is part of being a good corporate citizen.
- They want to support and align with the mission of their business.
- Your organization's mission resonates with an individual in the company who champions your cause.
- Companies that are known for giving are considered better places to work by employees. (For example, Airbnb employees are proud of the way their employer provides temporary housing to people who have been displaced by conflict, illness, or natural disasters in their home countries.)

That being said, however, corporate donations aren't likely to be a major portion of your overall fundraising campaign — especially in challenging economic times. According to *Giving USA 2021*, corporate giving in the United States totaled $16.88 billion in 2020, which was a decline of 6.1 percent over 2019.

Finding Foundations That Care

Foundation giving can be a great boon to your organization, but winning a major foundation grant is often a time-consuming and lengthy process. Do your homework so you don't waste your time or the foundation's by submitting a grant that doesn't have a chance of succeeding. In other words, find good research sources that help you understand which foundation is likely to be a good match to your mission.

TIP

The first step in your search for the right foundation is to get your hands on different foundations' giving guidelines to see what types of organizations and programs they tend to fund. Find out whether your organization fits their guidelines. Community foundations are another useful resource for you as you begin exploring fundraising channels. Not only is your local community foundation a place to find funds, but it's also a repository of information about all the nonprofit organizations in your community. For more details on finding foundations and applying for grants, head to Book 3.

Asking Your Board All the Right Questions

Luckily, all the work of identifying potential donors doesn't fall on your shoulders. Your board is instrumental in helping to identify the people and resources that can make your organization grow. One way to help your board advance funding is to get them away from the daily tasks they do so they can brainstorm about donor research and support. You can hold an inexpensive off-site meeting to enable board members to let go of the operating expense hassles and focus on the long-term picture.

So what questions do you put to the board when you get their attention? You may have a list of your own, but as you explore areas in which you can find donors to give to your cause, don't forget to address the two overarching questions posed in the following sections.

Where did you forget to expand your donor base?

As you think through your strategic plan, you'll probably discover some unmet needs you want to address. And if you choose to explore ways to address those newly discovered needs, your exploration of a new area may lead you to some more potential donors, which is one way to expand your general donor base.

REMEMBER

The following questions can help you explore donor areas that your organization may not have thought about yet:

- Do you have new members or subscribers coming in regularly?
- Is your group growing or stagnating?
- What areas of activity can your organization consider?
- Are any of your programs outdated or unnecessary?
- Have you identified new programs that would reach new populations?
- What's the average age of your members? Do you need to implement strategies to reach a broader group of people?

Whom did you forget to ask?

While adding new programs to bring new donors to your door is an excellent way to expand your donor base, you may be (and probably are) overlooking potentially valuable donors who are as close as your boardroom table. To find these donors, remind your board members to think of friends, colleagues, and other contacts they have who may be interested in donating to your organization.

TIP

If your board is lukewarm about using its collective contacts, try a little experiment. At the next board meeting, take a set of note cards, and five minutes before the meeting adjourns, say, "I'm working on donor prospecting this week, and I'd appreciate it if before you left today, you'd list three peers or companies you think could be potential donors to our organization. And while you're at it, put a check mark beside the people you'd like to suggest we interview as possible board members for the future."

Using Table 3-1, list the potential donors your board members come up with and add a few of your own. You can then find out more about the potential donors by talking to the board members who recommended them or doing your own sleuthing. Write the donor's or company's name in the Potential Donor column. In the Individual/Corporate column, write *Individual* or *Corporate* to indicate which one the donor represents. Write the contact's name or how the potential donor is linked to your organization in the Link/Contact column. In the Ability to Give column, write *Y* (Yes) or *N* (No) to indicate whether the potential donor has the financial means to give. Finally, write *Y* or *N* in the Links to Major Donors column to indicate whether the donor may be able to open the door to other people in positions of power or affluence.

TABLE 3-1 Data on Level-Four Donors

Potential Donor	Individual/Corporate	Link/Contact	Ability to Give	Links to Major Donors
Mary Brown	Individual	Third cousin of our largest contributor	Y	Y

REMEMBER

The key here is that you have at your disposal a number of people — in your organization or on your board — who are likely to know the answers to your questions about potential donors. You just need to ask the questions.

TIP

Take a look at the donor recognition list published in the annual report of an organization in your community that serves an audience similar to the one you serve. Notice the individual donors and giving levels as well as corporate sponsors and foundation gifts, and add any names to the lists you're compiling in the different donor levels.

Checking Out Potential Donors

Say your board comes up with some great names of potential donors for you to follow up on. What do you do next? Or maybe your board comes up with a list of unlikely prospects. No one seems to have the type of resources you're looking for. Now what? Because these two situations are very different from each other, the following sections look at each one individually.

Pursuing promising prospects

You have a list in front of you of 15 of the top givers in your city, with links through the board members who know them personally. Before you get too excited and march up to their front doors asking for major donations, you need to do some homework.

Your homework involves exploring personal, financial, and professional information about the donors before you meet them so you can strategize the relationships you hope to develop. Your strategy includes finding out what types of contributions the donors may be able to make to your organization, what types of investments may appeal to them based on commitments they've made to other causes, and how you plan to approach the prospective donors when you meet them and when you ask for their commitments.

The most effective fundraising takes place between peers, which means that for the best results, the board member who identified Ms. Van Halen as a good prospect should be the one to call on her. The board member is her link to the organization. The board member knows her and can say, "You know, Marilyn, I'm on the board of this organization, and I'm really proud of what's going on here. Would you like to come over for a tour of our facility? I'd like to show you around myself. And maybe we can have lunch together afterward if you have the time."

Clearly, Ms. Van Halen's relationship with the board member is a key component in furthering her interest in your cause and in your organization. See Chapter 6 of this minibook for more information about perfectly executing "the Ask."

Finding the silver lining with unlikely prospects

Even if your board survey comes up dry — which may mean you don't have the best mix of people on your board — you still have plenty of places to start to build your donor list and look for those high-level donors. And in the meantime, you can work on improving your board.

TIP

As you build your donor list with little or no help from your board, start by doing the following:

- **Examine lists (public lists, that is) that similar organizations keep of their donors.** For example, an art museum looks at the patron list published by the symphony and vice versa.
- **Keep an eye on your community.** Take a look at your local paper and note the names of local philanthropists who crop up repeatedly in print. Likewise, keep an eye on national, international, and online news if your mission reaches farther than a local constituency. Watching, listening, and taking notes can help you discover potential resources you may miss if you don't keep your fundraising eyes and ears open.
- **Review the list of political donors.** Political donations are a matter of public record; every political campaign committee must file its list of donors with the commission in their state. Somebody who gives $2,500 to a political campaign may be willing to give to you, too — and you may be able to determine what a particular donor cares most about by understanding the key issues of the candidate's platform they support.
- **Visit the places where people go to be seen.** Certain places in your community equate to a certain status. Perhaps one of the gathering places is a historical home, a symphony hall, or a science center. Visit these places and

read the plaques on the walls; look at the named statues in the garden; pore over the portraits on the walls. This type of sleuthing can show you which families in your area have wealth — and are using it to further causes that capture their imaginations and their passions.

Researching on the Internet

When it comes to trying to find new potential donors, one of your best research tools today is the Internet. It provides a wealth of information that is easily searchable, and you can use it 24 hours a day, 7 days a week, whereas your local library or chamber of commerce likely closes its doors every evening.

TIP

Bookmark your favorite sites, display history lists of sites you've visited recently, and use research tools to make your browsing experience easier. Here are some of the most useful tools and approaches to use when researching online:

- **Browse websites.** Countless websites are available to help you build your donor list. For example, if you're researching a potential corporate giver, you definitely need to visit the corporation's website. You can also visit the site of your local community foundation to find the latest nonprofit news in your area, read about funding opportunities, and learn about other nonprofit organizations. Check out industry standards like Candid (`candid.org`) to find data, links, and articles to help you gather information and resources on fundraising. Visit discussion boards, foundation sites, and social networking sites like LinkedIn to uncover more about potential donors.
- **Use search engines.** Search engines abound online, and they're useful tools. But not all search engines are equal. Most are capable of providing quick, targeted results in response to search words, phrases, or questions; others include the best results from a variety of search engine results in addition to custom vetted information; and still others offer related material like product reviews, mapping features, and more. When you search for information on specific donors, you may be able to discover what the donors' giving interests are, which organizations they support, and what roles they serve on corporate or nonprofit boards. These pieces of information will be helpful to you as you determine whether your mission is a likely fit for these particular donors.
- **Locate people online.** Donor research means uncovering information about people, and lucky for you, the Internet has great resources for doing just that. You can browse white pages for just about every town online. You can also browse corporate sites that list board members or senior managers by name or search for news about potential donors to find their current organizational affiliations.

- **Explore government websites.** Government sites offer free information about trends in the economy that may influence future giving and regulations, tax benefits of giving, and more — all of which are important to know as you approach potential donors. As you plan your fundraising strategy, you may find the following government sites useful:
  - IRS (`irs.gov`)
  - Catalog of Federal Domestic Assistance (`sam.gov/content/assistance-listings`)
  - Combined Federal Campaign (`opm.gov/cfc`)

  Also check out specific agencies related to your mission, such as the Administration on Aging and the Administration for Children and Families.

Keeping Track of Your Organization's Donors and Their Contributions

After you identify and research new donors, how do you keep track of all the information you accumulate? You need a system that's comprehensive enough to store all kinds of data from multiple meetings — because you're going to be meeting with potential high-level givers more than once or twice — and to essentially track an entire relationship. Such a system requires a lot of time and planning. The following sections walk you through the how-to's.

Creating an effective donor information form

A *donor information form*, whether on paper or in the computer, gives you a place to keep all of a donor's data as you research and find out more about the donor. The following list outlines the most important categories of information you need to include on your forms and in your database records:

- **Administrative data:** The date the form or record is created, the name of the person who created it, and the way in which the donor was referred to you (board member, another donor, friend, mailing, event, and so on).
- **Name and contact information:** The first, middle, and last name of the donor; the donor's title; and the donor's contact information, including residential and business addresses, phone numbers, and email addresses.

If your donor is a business or foundation, include pertinent information about the organization in general and the name of and information for your contact within the company.

- **Interests and business affiliations:** The donor's professional position and memberships, foundation or philanthropic interests, awards and honors, key relationships, special interests, and political, religious, and military affiliations.
- **Education:** The individual donor's educational background, details of any continuing relationship the donor has with an educational institution, and social or business activities that tie the individual or organization to education.
- **Family:** The name of the individual donor's spouse, children, parents, and pets, including any significant or relevant information such as birthdays, anniversaries, or hobbies.
- **Resources:** The names of the donor's bank, financial planner, tax advisor, and attorney.
- **Finances:** Information on the donor's income, assets, past contributions made, and so on.
- **Gift record:** A listing of all gifts the donor has pledged and made to your organization.
- **Visitation record:** A listing of all contacts made to the donor by you or a member of your development staff or board.
- **Opt-in/Opt-out:** Give your organization's donors the option of opting in or opting out of your email communications and note their preferences. When donors opt out of your online communications, be sure to honor their requests and remove them from your send lists for messages and newsletters.
- **Comments:** Any comments you have about interactions you've had with the donor or mailings the donor has received.

TIP

Make your donor form simple and effective. Plan for multiple pages, with the first page collecting quick-look items, like the donor's most recent gift (date and amount) or the program they most like to support. Make the form easy to follow and understand, and organize the categories of information logically. Leave plenty of space for comments so you — or board members who contact the donor — can make notes about the visit or call. Include columns for totaling gifts and pledges so you can see donation totals and dates at a glance.

TIP

In time and with some effort, you'll have hundreds of donor information forms, and you'll want to have easy access to them. Create a good storage system of binders (or folders on your computer) labeled clearly so you know which records are kept there (A–D, Corporate Donors, or whatever). Of course, in the long term you'll want all of this data captured in your donor management software as well so you can use it in later searches. Try to stay on top of your data by entering information soon after you gather it. That way it won't get buried on your desk.

Keeping good donor records

Keeping your donor records up to date and accurate is a vital part of a good fundraising system. Whether you use an online donor management system or keep track of your data in a custom database or an Excel worksheet, be sure to track your data consistently. In general, note all the interactions you have with your organization's donors, summarizing what you talked about and did, what pledges and gifts were submitted, and what your next steps will be in cultivation.

Maintaining Confidence: The Issues and Ethics of Handling Personal Data

When you accumulate information on a person of high status in your community, you have something other people want. People at dinner parties would love to hear about the net worth of Ms. Van Halen. A con artist would be interested in knowing that you're doing research on wealthy older women in your region.

REMEMBER

Fight the temptation to disclose what you're working on — and certainly respect the privacy of the people you're preparing to approach. The information you gather is meant to assist you in finding the right match — both for the donors and for your organization — nothing more. When you find donors who share your interest in an issue, who have the ability to give and the motivation to do so, it's an equitable, honorable relationship. You help the donors make a difference in an area they care about, and they help you further your work. Everybody wins.

WARNING

Divulging information about the person you're researching is bad business, bad fundraising, and bad news. Revealing personal information destroys the respectful relationship that should be at the heart of any fundraising effort. It makes the donor nothing more than a mark you're approaching to "hit up" for cash. And you certainly won't keep that person as a donor; in fact, you may get a reputation for lack of discretion that scares away other donors.

REMEMBER

Here are a few other ethical reminders you need to remember during every fundraising effort you take part in:

- Make sure your board knows and approves of your methods of donor research.
- Review the Donor Bill of Rights and Code of Ethics from the Association of Fundraising Professionals (`afpglobal.org`) to make sure your approach is ethical from the start.
- Carefully consider whether a donor would consent to the type of research you're doing or would be outraged to find that such research was being done.
- Keep your computer (and all the information stored on it) secure. Don't post lists on your website, and don't give access to your records to sharp computer hackers via the Internet. Protect your computer with a firewall or other security software.
- If you're in doubt about a research practice, check it out with your executive director or attorney.

REMEMBER

If you leave your position at your current organization and go to work for a similar agency, can you take your donor information with you? The answer is simple. Whether or not you're legally bound by a confidentiality or noncompete clause in your employment contract, donor information stays with your current organization — no question.

IN THIS CHAPTER

» Experiencing the impact of a personal visit

» Getting acquainted with donors before and during your first meeting

» Understanding the donor-organization relationship

» Knowing your donor's context

» Cultivating the donor-organization relationship

Chapter 4
Meeting Your Donor with Grace and Grit

Fundraising isn't for the fainthearted, no matter what the economic climate may be. And you may never be more aware of the need for courage on the job than when you sit down with your donors for the first time. What should you do at your initial meetings with donors? Imagine the successful outcomes of your meetings? Be careful to present just the right image? All of the above?

Smart fundraising isn't a hit-'em-fast endeavor. It's about relationship building, which enables donors to grow continually closer to your mission and to help increasingly through their time, efforts, and gifts. This chapter shows you how to think about the motivations and potential hot buttons of the donors you meet face to face. Keep in mind that you won't visit every donor personally, of course. For example, the low-hanging fruit donors who send you a $50 check every year for your annual fund don't expect you to appear on their doorsteps to take each of them to lunch. But Mr. Benefactor, who gave a special gift to a program fund last year, makes a good prospect for your endowment campaign this year. As part of building a relationship with him, visits are expected and, hopefully, welcome. This chapter helps you focus on the quest of building positive, long-lasting relationships with your donors.

Evaluating the Importance of a Visit

Attentiveness and respect are two keys to building relationships in the world of donor cultivation. Mailings are fine, but you don't draw donors closer to the mission of your organization or higher up on your giving chart by sending them mailing after mailing. Phone calls are more personal than mailings as long as you don't construe them as telemarketing ploys — at least donors hear a warm voice and know they're getting your personal attention. However, for a potentially major, long-term donor, plan to make regular face-to-face visits. After all, you have a shared interest — your organization and the work it does. Take your donors to lunch or visit them at their homes; bank on the fact that you're nurturing far-reaching and, hopefully, continuously rewarding relationships.

So, when is the appropriate time to begin planning regular visits to a donor? Donors need special, personalized treatment at the special gifts level of giving and above. Your goal is to secure the commitment of donors whose philanthropic goals match those of your organization. The special gifts level of giving is the first indication that the donor is willing to make a serious commitment to your organization. When the donor gives you this first hint, it's up to you to take the ball and run with it. To nurture this important relationship, you need to do more research, make a greater effort, spend more time, and create more opportunities for interaction with the donor.

REMEMBER

Visits — and the time they take — let donors know that they're important, their contributions matter, and you want them to be happy. Not to mention, they keep the door open so your relationship can grow.

Preparing to Meet Potential Donors

Some of your donors have probably been giving to your organization for years. Some likely started out as volunteers helping with your big annual event; others may have served on your board for a term or two. Over the years, you may have sent these long-term donors your quarterly newsletter and a few mail appeals — one for your annual fund and another for a special program fund. In general, you can observe the following characteristics about these long-term donors:

- They're engaged with the mission of your organization.
- They've had enough of a good experience to keep coming back.
- They may have increased both their giving and their involvement over the past few years.

TIP

These long-term donors are your first candidates as you begin your research for major gift donors. Chances are that you came up with a number of donors' names during this part of the process. As you evaluate the donor files, consider several key points:

- » How many times has your organization already contacted these donors?
- » What donations have these donors already given to your organization?
- » What affiliations do they have with other nonprofits in your community?
- » What's their potential for giving? (That is, what can you deduce about their financial status?)

Fully armed with the answers to these important questions, you're ready to contact each potential donor for a meeting.

To begin your personal contact with a potential major gift donor, you dial their number. After they answer, you say what you've rehearsed many times:

> "Hi, Ms. Donor," you say. "This is Jamie from New Beginnings. I was going over our volunteer records, and I see that you've been giving both time and money to our organization for three years now."
>
> Ms. Donor takes a minute to process the information.
>
> "Well, we're glad to help," she says. "We've really enjoyed our time there."

As the call continues, you tell Ms. Donor that you'd like to invite her and her spouse to be your guests at lunch, so you can thank them for their involvement and introduce them to new happenings at your organization. Ms. Donor says she'll talk to her spouse about it and asks you to call back Monday. When you call back as requested, you and Ms. Donor schedule the luncheon.

To make sure your first face-to-face meeting with Ms. Donor (and all other prospective donors) goes as smoothly as possible, you need to think about the following:

- » What you offer a donor who gives to your organization
- » How charitable giving is really a win-win proposition
- » What motivates a donor to give

The following section explores each of these issues in detail to help you prepare for your initial donor meetings.

Examining the Giving Relationship between the Donor and the Organization

In exchange for everything your donors give to you, you and your organization offer something in return. The relationship between you and your donors isn't a one-sided one in which the only dynamic is that the donors give and the non-profit takes. Both sides have tangibles and intangibles to offer and receive, with the intangibles probably being the more important. These important intangibles include the following:

- » The donor feels like an appreciated, valued part of a select group.
- » The organization feels the security of being able to count on the donor's involvement and contribution year after year.

This equal exchange not only helps the organization grow, but also enables the donor to benefit from the relationship. The following sections show what both your organization and the donor get out of the relationship.

Showing potential donors the value of their gifts

When donors give to your organization, what do they get in return? Hopefully, they see the effectiveness of their gifts and feel assured that their money is going where you said it would (through stories in your newsletters, websites, or other communications about the programs and services they support). You show your donors that you value them and their gifts by

- » **Providing financial information:** When you explain planned giving options, you educate donors about the various estate and tax-planning opportunities available. By working with the donors' financial advisors or tax attorneys, you can assist in designing the right giving plan to meet the donors' financial needs.
- » **Evaluating options:** Your donors' time is valuable. When you clearly and simply communicate the mission of your organization — in print, in person, or on the web — your donors can make informed choices about the charitable organizations they want to support. You inform your donors about all their giving options and assist them in getting involved with an issue close to their heart.

» **Interacting and corresponding regularly:** You need to regularly show donors where their money is going by inviting them in for a visit and enlisting their help, care, and vision in building the organization. As donors get involved in and gain an appreciation for your organization, they become part of a bigger system working to solve the problems of the world at large.

» **Being accountable:** After you receive that first fundraising gift, you owe your donor accountability. Report on what effect the gift has had on your clients, what good has come of it, and how you plan to continue the growth in the future.

» **Demonstrating the good that's being done:** When a donation leads to a positive outcome — a person finds a good job, or a family moves into an affordable home because of a particular donation — don't miss out on the opportunity to enable the people who received the services to thank the donors in their own words. Ask the recipients of your services to write personalized notes to the donors, sharing what happened because of their generous gifts. These personal notes enable donors to hear directly from recipients how their donations changed their lives — and that's powerful stuff.

Getting more than money from your donors

What do donors offer your organization? You're probably thinking, "Money!" But that's only partially right, and it's not even the important part. Although your donors do show their involvement through financial contributions, the most important donation they make is the donation of their belief.

If donors didn't believe in what you do or in your ability to carry out what you promise, they wouldn't spend their time — much less their money — on you. The strength of the belief your donors have in you and your organization may vary over time and circumstances, but it's your job to keep that belief strong and the interest growing. In tough economic times, even though donations may dip for a period of time, you can keep the belief and connection strong. So don't make the mistake of thinking your donors offer you only money. Some of the critical intangibles your donors provide are

» **Time in voluntary services:** Volunteers deliver all types of service in nonprofit organizations all over the globe. The dedication and sweat equity they offer is a testament to their belief in your mission and their partnership in your cause.

- **Material goods donated:** Some donors may prefer to give your organization supplies, tickets to community events, or materials instead of monetary gifts; these material goods can be a great help for donations ranging from computer equipment to classroom supplies to vehicles and buildings.
- **Donations of services and resources:** Other donors may want to provide in-kind donations that offer professional services or resources for free. You may be able to secure high-quality legal help, investment consultation, or human resources services through these kinds of donations.
- **Goodwill in conversations with friends:** Don't underestimate the value of a respected member of your community having a positive experience with your organization. Your donor may then share the story with friends, who suddenly see your organization in a whole new light. This kind of trusted referral — from someone people look up to and trust — makes all the difference in how open they may be to developing a relationship with an organization they don't know.

REMEMBER

The tax benefit for your donors is something important to keep in mind as you talk about the upsides of giving — for you and for them. In 2022, donors who skip itemizing on their tax return can deduct up to $300 if filing single and up to $600 for couples. Donors who itemize can take a tax deduction of up to 50 percent of their adjusted gross income. For those donors who make major gifts, that percentage can add up to a sizable deduction.

Checking out what motivates giving consistency

Why do people give — and why *don't* they? Table 4-1 has some interesting responses.

These reasons aren't listed in any particular order. It's important to note that — although you may hope people give to your organization because they believe in your mission — tax deductions, marketing, or image may play a bigger role in why a particular donor decides to give or not give.

One of the reasons people don't give is compassion fatigue, as you can see in Table 4-1. So what is that? In recent years, the term *compassion fatigue* has described the situation in which the donor is bombarded and overloaded with calls for help. They've been asked by too many different causes, which spread them too thin, especially when they're concerned about finances themselves.

TABLE 4-1 Reasons for Giving . . . and Not Giving

Reasons to Give	Reasons to Not Give
They have an emotional response to a cause.	They weren't asked.
They like the tax deductions.	They're unhappy with the way the organization is handling finances.
They share a belief in the cause.	Their interests and priorities have changed.
The nonprofit's image appeals to them.	Nobody said thank you the last time they gave.
The nonprofit's marketing materials attract their attention.	They no longer have the resources to give.
They want a sense of belonging — joining something bigger than themselves.	They didn't like the manner in which they were approached.
They want to give back to a cause that helped them or someone they care about.	They're insecure about the organization.
They get good seats at a basketball game in return for their donation (personal gain).	The organization doesn't have long-term plans.
Their peers influence them.	They weren't asked for the right amount.
They enjoy donating.	The cause doesn't motivate them.
They have personal experience with the cause.	They haven't been part of a culture of giving.
They want to give in memory of someone.	They have compassion fatigue.
They want to set an example.	They don't care what others think about them.
They hope to pass on a legacy.	They want to spend everything now and not worry about leaving a legacy because no one left a legacy for them to inherit.
They like the honor that accompanies donating one's time and treasures.	They're likely selfish and self-centered.
They have spiritual reasons (tithing) for giving.	They already tithe to their church and don't feel obligated to give beyond their 10 percent commitment.
They want to have a voice in the larger discourse.	They've given up on trying to change the world one act at a time.
They feel empathy for the cause and its benefactors.	They struggle with helping nonprofits that should be getting by on grants.
They want to make a difference.	Making a difference doesn't matter if the right people don't know about their contributions.
The right person asked them.	The person who asked them was so vastly different from what they expected that they were hesitant to give.

TIP

As a fund-raiser, be sensitive to any messages your donors give you that indicate changes in their relationships with your organization. Be candid with your observations and ask them whether you can do anything to alleviate any concerns they have about supporting your organization. By inviting the donors to share their ideas and opinions, you may wind up strengthening the bond they have to your cause.

Considering Your Donor's Context

Knowing how your donors may be feeling and thinking can help you communicate — in a way they can understand — why giving to your organization is a good idea, even in tough times. The following sections offer some insights into how your donors may be feeling during a slow economy.

TIP

Involve your board as you consider how your donors are responding to your current economy. What do your board members feel is realistic? Are some groups affected more than others? Brainstorm ways to keep the mission of your organization moving forward while considering your donors' realities, and be sure to incorporate these ideas in your communications with donors.

Engaging potential donors with limited means (for now)

During times of economic uncertainty, people who live paycheck to paycheck struggle to make ends meet, so they're unlikely to feel comfortable giving a major gift to your organization, no matter how much they want to. A large portion of your giving population may fall in this group, and your younger givers may comprise a large percentage. Similarly, people on a fixed income, who may include baby boomers and senior citizens (see the later section for more about these folks), may be cautious about giving right now. How can you reach out to this group of donors with limited means and encourage them to give, letting them know you value their involvement with your organization — whether they can give $5, $50, or $500?

TIP

In the short term, providing flexible, easy ways for donors to give — and feel good about what they give no matter the amount — is key. You can stress your own need to raise funds for daily operations by translating what the donor's small donation can provide (something a donor can readily identify with). For example, say something like "Your $20 donation buys three back-to-school kits for second-graders in your neighborhood."

In the long term, tell donors that you know the economy will improve and that people will feel comfortable giving once again at higher levels. Including this idea in your messaging not only lets your donors know that you're adjusting to meet them where they are right now, but also sends a message that things will get better soon (and lets donors know you're counting on them to increase their giving when they're able to do so).

Connecting with affluent donors

Whenever the stock market drops, everyone goes on edge — including your more affluent donors. The major givers in your group may not experience the same level of impact that other donors do during economic downturns, but all people with investments, homes, and futures watch the churning markets with trepidation and worry. The good news is that eventually a sense of solid recovery will spread throughout the economy, and even the investments that suffered a major drop will begin to climb again.

Meeting reluctant retirees on their level

Of all the groups in your donor list, the reluctant retiree is likely feeling the impact of the economic downturn most of all. Unlike younger donors who are just starting out, retirees have often worked their whole lives to arrive at retirement, ready to relax and live on what may be limited means. They may have planned carefully, saved religiously, and invested wisely — only to see their retirement funds drain away over a few nightmarish months of a recession.

The long-term good news for the retiree is that their portfolios will recover, but chances are they'll never feel as buoyant as they did before the recession hit. Because of the shock of the drop and the shifting of their expectations, the retiree becomes a cautious donor.

TIP

You may be able to meet baby boomers and seniors where they are by bargaining down, suggesting that they choose to give $50 a month instead of a larger lump sum. You can offer additional options to help secure the income your organization needs while affording the donor control by offering automatic deductions from the donor's bank account. It's easy and efficient, and both your donor and your organization can budget for it.

REMEMBER

Don't underestimate the intrinsic need people have to help make the world a better place, no matter what their finances may say. Giving — even if it's only a fraction of what they used to give — still makes people feel good and demonstrates the reality that no matter how tight things may be financially, good is still getting done.

Cultivating the Initial Donor-Organization Relationship

As you continue to talk and get to know your potential donors both personally and financially, you build trust and discover where your shared ideals lie. If the situation is right, by the end of your first meeting with a donor, you should communicate the following ideas:

- You value the donor's involvement with your organization.
- You want to involve the donor on a deeper level.
- You have ideas for helping the donor meet estate goals and avoid excessive taxation.
- You want to write up a few ideas and meet with the donor to discuss them in the coming weeks.

At this point in your blossoming relationship with the donor, it's important to keep the trust building. At the end of your first meeting, you want the donor to leave with a good feeling about you and their relationship with your organization. So, avoid the following when you're in this initial relationship-building stage:

- **Being vague about how the donor's money is going to be used:** Today's donor, having grown up in an age of media exposés, is somewhat leery about how nonprofit organizations spend their contributions. Be forthcoming with your organization's financial information because it speaks volumes about your credibility. And even if you don't want to reveal information about the sources of your income and how it's used, you have to make this info (which appears on IRS Form 990; see Book 4, Chapter 8) available to the general public whenever it's requested.

  TIP

  Speak candidly about the value of contributions for the general support of your organization. Say something simple like "We have to turn on the lights every day and put gasoline in the truck." Most people understand that general support — the money that goes to keeping your doors open — may be the most important money you raise in tough times.

- **Making assumptions:** Making assumptions can lead to missed opportunities, especially during down economies. For example, if you assume that donors in their 30s aren't interested in an estate-planning option, you may lose a major donor because you failed to give them a convincing reason to donate. For example, if your donor's father died at age 35, the donor is likely to be sensitive to the issues involved with caring for one's family in the long term in the event of an untimely death. The key here is to *listen* to your donors. They'll lead you to the gift area that's right for them.

TIP

- **Being afraid to bargain down:** When you're at a point when you're ready to ask for a specific gift, don't be afraid to ask for a lesser amount if the donor rejects your initial amount. Generally speaking, most people are flattered that you considered them part of a group that could give the amount you requested, so no harm is done. If your donor says no to $50,000, don't be afraid to say, "Would you be more comfortable with $25,000, given over three years?"
- **Promising more than you can deliver:** Some fund-raisers get so focused on the goal that they promise the moon to a donor to secure a gift. If you're one of those people, fight the temptation. Every interaction with your donor either builds credibility or detracts from it, and making promises you can't possibly keep only hurts your organization in the long run.

REMEMBER

- **Forgetting to say thank you:** How can you overlook something so simple? Easily. Organizations often focus on receiving and not on giving. Recognizing your donors by saying thank you, sending cards, making phone calls, or planning a luncheon needs to comprise about 20 percent of your fundraising time. Seems like too much time? Well, it isn't if you recognize that your primary goal is building relationships with your donors, not raising money. *Thank you* are two of the best friendship-building words in the English language. Don't forget to use them.

One way to continue to cultivate your relationship with donors is to recognize your donors for their contributions. A great way to do so is to get your donors together at a dinner or other social gathering. This type of event not only recognizes your donors' contributions, but also strengthens their relationships with your organization.

TIP

If you decide to hold a donor recognition dinner, try getting a sponsor to underwrite the meal for you. You can have a box lunch or a formal fete brought in, rewarding your donors and giving visibility to your sponsor — and it won't come out of your budget. Everybody wins!

IN THIS CHAPTER

- » Thinking about major gifts with tomorrow in mind
- » Turning new and existing donors into major givers
- » Recognizing your major donors in a big way

Chapter 5 Cultivating Major Givers

Every donor who has given to your organization in the past, who gives today, or who will give tomorrow is important to the continuation of your mission. The donor who gives in a big way to your organization — in terms of time, talent, or treasure — is one of your primary stakeholders and is close enough to your cause to care greatly. This chapter takes a look at the special relationship you nurture with new and existing major givers, whether they're already giving at a top level or you hope to help them increase their gifts over the years to come.

Cultivating relationships with major givers is both an art and a science — and doing so successfully requires honesty, respect, and an ongoing commitment to long-term benefits for both the giver and the receiver. This chapter helps you think through the process of cultivating major givers and acknowledging their gifts and commitment appropriately.

Seeking a Major Gift Today for Tomorrow

Asking for a major gift when the economy is pitching and swaying is completely unrealistic, right?

Wrong.

In fact, no matter what the financial landscape looks like, major givers are a breed apart from all others. These demonstrated givers have a history of contributing to your organization, they believe in what you're doing, and they have experience with the work you do and the people you serve. People you identify as potentially able to make major gifts have demonstrated an interest level high enough to give a significant contribution. It's up to you to determine whether they also have the financial ability to do so. If they do, you need to use the data you gather to come up with the right amount to ask for.

According to the *2021 Bank of America Study of Philanthropy: Charitable Giving by Affluent Households*, the wealthiest Americans give from a high sense of commitment to their local communities and tend to be very loyal to the organizations they support. Thus, even in challenging financial times, organizations can expect major givers to continue to support their favorite causes in terms of both finances and volunteer hours.

Working with major gifts and planned-giving programs requires long-term cultivation because donors who eventually make a major gift or bequest do so only after establishing a trusting relationship with your organization. They get to know you over time, during which you answer all their questions, demonstrate your mission, model good follow-through and ethical behavior, and show that you care. Gradually, the relationship moves closer to the point at which you can confidently — and comfortably — ask for a major gift.

TIP

When you encounter people who aren't ready to give a major gift at a particular time, one way to encourage them to give something is to invite them to put your cause in their wills. The idea here is that even though the donors aren't ready to write a big check at the moment, putting your organization in their wills gives them a way to contribute to your organization in the future. Many organizations that develop major endowments and big gifts do so in this way, over a period of years. Gradually, over time, these major gifts build a pipeline of giving.

Your donors, both new and existing, can put your organization in their wills easily thanks to the *codicil*, a legal document that's an amendment to a will, spelling out that a specific grant of money will be subtracted from the corpus of the estate. You can draft a codicil for interested donors to use, and your donor can then provide you with a letter saying that the codicil has been completed. The letter enables you to count the contribution toward your organization's funding without needing to have a copy of the donor's will in hand.

Finding the Holy Grail of Fundraising: The Major Gift

After you're fired up to begin cultivating major gifts no matter what the financial climate looks like, you may be wondering what qualifies as a *major gift*. Well, no matter how hard you look, you won't find a hard-and-fast rule about what constitutes a major gift; a major gift in your organization may be completely different from a major gift in another organization. The following sections show you how to plan for major gifts and build a relationship with those new and existing donors who may be willing to donate the big gifts you're seeking.

TIP

Does your organization have a gift program that enables donors' gifts to keep on giving? People want their money to be used for something good, something that creates change for the better. For this reason, scholarship programs, research for cures, and programs that battle the recognized ills of society (like poverty, drug abuse, and illiteracy) are good candidates for major gifts. Who wouldn't want to be able to say, "I gave the money that led to a cure for multiple sclerosis?"

Planning your way to major gifts

Although you may think — and logically so — that the best (and perhaps only) time to receive major gifts is when donors feel like giving them, realize that a lot of planning on the part of the fund-raiser goes into acquiring major gifts. For example, fund-raisers often plan to secure major gifts when they gear up for specific fundraising campaigns. And they begin cultivating the relationship with the donor months, if not years, before they're ready to ask for the donation. In fact, a major gift often serves as the very foundation of a campaign, ensuring the success of the campaign before the organization launches it completely. For example:

- You're planning a capital campaign and you need to determine how many major gifts you need in each of several ranges to meet your goal. (Creating a giving pyramid can help you determine what you need to know. See Chapter 2 of this minibook to find out how to create a giving pyramid.)
- You're starting a new scholarship program, and you ask a board member to donate a major gift as a challenge grant to encourage other members to give.
- You're building an endowment fund, and you plan to use major gift strategies and planned-giving opportunities to bring in the funds you need.

REMEMBER

You can have a major giving program even if you're a small organization just starting out because you need to cultivate low-level donors over time and grow them into major donors. The normal progression of fundraising is to bring the donor closer and closer to your cause through the years, which also means increasing the amount of giving along the way. If you haven't thought about your current giving program as leading to major gifts, get ready to explore a new and profitable area!

Reviving your pool of current donors

Before you begin targeting major gifts, make sure your donor list is current and active. Your organization already has a record of who has given major gifts to your organization in the past. Find this record and scour its content. Who has given in the past and is still active in the organization today? Who has given before but disappeared in recent years? Follow up with any currently inactive donors, and try to find out why they stopped being active in your organization. Maybe personal contact from you is just what the donor needs to get reinvolved in your organization.

After you find the information on gifts made to your organization, list all the major gifts your organization has received in the past three years. Then for each major gift, include information on the program the money was targeted for (if any), the amount given, the terms of the gift (paid in one year, over three years, and so on), and of course, the donor who gave the gift. How has your organization used these gifts? What activity have these donors had since they gave their gifts? With the proper attention, you can get these donors to continue to be active in your organization. Research shows that if your donors have given before — especially within the past 18 months — they'll be likely to give again. Cygnus Applied Research reports that most major donors are interested in ensuring the sustainability of organizations they already support as opposed to supporting organizations that are unfamiliar to them.

TIP

Of course, unforeseen events and situations happen, and sometimes organizations fall out of favor with a donor for one reason or another. But being new to the fundraising position in your organization gives you a great excuse to reinitiate contact with all your donors. When you call a currently inactive donor, say something like "Mrs. Williams, I'm the new development person at New Beginnings. I can see that you were very active in 2016 and 2017, and your involvement really helped our organization. I'm calling to introduce myself, thank you for what you did with us in the past, and invite you back."

Targeting your major gifts

As discussed in Chapter 2 of this minibook, one of the first steps of effective fundraising is knowing what your dollar goal is. Are you trying to raise $50,000 or $5 million this year? If you plan to renovate your building, calculate the renovation cost. If you need money for a certain music outreach program, determine exactly how much you need. Before you make a solid plan for the how, when, where, and why of major gifts, you need to know the how much — as in *how much* money you need to raise to reach your program goals.

After you know your dollar goal, you can create a giving pyramid to help you determine the kind of major gifts you're looking for and how many of them you need. (Check out Chapter 2 of this minibook for how to create a giving pyramid.)

REMEMBER

Keep in mind that your fundraising plan — and the giving pyramid — doesn't include only major gifts. You need to have several different major gift levels, such as $25,000, $50,000, and $75,000, as well as categories for lesser gifts. Not every donor gives the same level of gift, of course, and some, given a choice and gentle encouragement, may give a much higher amount than you expected.

Cultivating new and existing donors who have a lot to give

After you determine how many major gifts you need to receive to reach your fundraising goal, you need to begin thinking about which donors can help get you there. Where can you find major donors? The possibilities are endless. Here are just a few of the places where you can begin your search:

- On your board
- In the ranks of your volunteer corps
- On your donor list
- On the boards of other similar organizations
- In the community — people making waves
- In the community — people making headlines
- In the community — people making money

TIP

By far, your best tool for finding major donors is your donor list, which is why maintaining an up-to-date list and using it regularly is so important.

Cultivating major donors in seven steps

The folks who are most likely to give major gifts are those who are closest to your organization — stakeholders, clients, and board members who obviously share the mission of your organization. (Read more about donor levels in Chapter 3 of this minibook.) They care deeply about the cause and the furthering of your mission, and because their passion is in line with your own, they're going to be your highest-level donors.

THE MAJOR DONOR PROFILE

If you're not sure what your major donors will look like, consider the following common characteristics. Major donors

- Are usually already involved with your organization.
- Are involved in a number of community activities in both the for-profit and the nonprofit worlds. (The best donor to solicit is one who has already given to something else.)
- Often have high profiles in a community and feel they have a responsibility to give back.
- Often have already raised their families (in other words, they're in their 50s and up) or haven't had children.
- Often have at least some college education.
- May have volunteered when they were young.
- Typically itemize their tax returns.
- Are often involved in religious organizations.

But most major donors don't start out being major donors. Often, they grow closer to your organization over time, perhaps starting out by making a $100 donation to your annual fund and then gradually moving closer to the heart of your organization, where they may give larger gifts to specific programs.

REMEMBER

The donors who give at a low level today are your major givers of tomorrow, which means that *cultivation* — the art of enhancing and building the donor-organization relationship — is not only good practice, but also good business. Today's $100 donor may be tomorrow's $25,000 donor.

The process of involving a donor at ever-increasing levels of giving is a logical one and consists of the following steps:

1. **Identify the donors you feel are good prospects for major gifts.**
   - Review your donor list and giving records.
   - Talk to board members.
   - Research *Marquis Who's Who in America* (`marquiswhoswho.com`) in your area of involvement.

- Use other research methods as needed. (See Chapter 3 of this minibook for more about donor research.)

Make a sublist of your main list, showing only those prospects you want to follow up on as potential major givers. For example, you might use your donor management software to create a sublist of donors who have given to a specific program in the past or who have given at a particular giving level.

2. **Research the prospective donors.**

   As you do your homework on the individuals on your sublist, verify that their interests do, in fact, support the type of work your organization does. Get a sense of their giving interests, other philanthropic activities, likes and dislikes, preferences, and commitments.

3. **Based on what you know about the donor, design a strategy for cultivating the relationship with them.**

   What type of program or sponsorship opportunity may the donor be interested in? Would it be best to visit the donor in person, invite the donor out for a visit, or something else? How could a board member, volunteer, or supporter with a strong relationship to the donor support the cultivation strategy? The strategy you develop for each donor needs to be custom-tailored to the donor's needs, interests, and priorities.

4. **Build, or cultivate, the relationship with the donor.**

   Depending on the prospect, you may meet the donor several times over a period of months or contact them via a number of means, such as a phone call, letter, or personal visit. Regardless of how you cultivate your donor-organization relationships, schedule true solicitation calls only when you feel your donors are receptive. Be sure to acknowledge the donor's past giving history and involvement through the process.

5. **Ask the prospective donor for the gift (a process called "the Ask," which is explained in Chapter 6 of this minibook).**

   After you've cultivated the relationship with the prospective donor, you're in a position to ask for the major gift. Keep in mind that you can't just jump from Step 1 to Step 5. Even if your donor gives major gifts hand over fist, you need to build your relationship with that donor before the donor offers the gift and continue to do so afterward.

REMEMBER

A delayed gift doesn't necessarily mean no gift. In shifting economic times, your major givers are likely to be paying close attention to the stock market as they consider the gifts they plan to make. A delay may mean that your donor is waiting for a better time to donate stock, which may appreciate in the future.

6. **Express your thanks for the gift.**

After you receive the major gift (assuming your solicitation is successful), expressing your thanks paves the way for a repeat gift at some point. Saying thank you graciously and remembering — and honoring — any promises you make to the donor allow you to cultivate the donor-organization relationship even further. But if you neglect to express your thanks or otherwise overlook the generosity of the gift, the donor may feel unappreciated, or worse, taken advantage of — and you won't see repeat gifts from that donor in the months and years to come.

TIP

Recognize every gift in a unique way that's appropriate. You need to honor each donor so they know you truly appreciate the gift and the patronage. This equal recognition is especially important when your donors know each other and are likely to compare your recognition efforts. Note, though, that people in the major giver category don't need another plaque. Something more personal, like a photo of the donor with a client or at the front door of the building they contributed to, will have more meaning and create a lasting memory.

7. **Account for how the gift is used.**

What you do with the gift is as important to the donor as what you do to get the gift. After you secure any gift — but especially a major gift — it's important that you do with it what you said you would. Donors want to see where their money goes, and you need to be willing to provide that information as soon as the donor requests it, if not before. Doing so goes a long way toward building the donor-organization relationship and may ensure that you get another gift.

Building a giving club

TIP

Although you may initially solicit major gifts for a particular program or campaign you want to fund, you eventually need to incorporate a major giving program as part of your regular fundraising strategy. Colleges and universities have perfected the art of major giving programs by creating *giving clubs*, which serve a number of fundraising-related purposes:

- They inform your donors about the benefits they receive at each of the different giving levels.
- They help donors feel like a part of something while building a sense of identity for your organization.
- They make it easy for you to show donors how they can "upgrade" to a higher level of giving in subsequent years.

For example, as part of your alma mater's giving club, when you give a large gift, your school may affix your name to the new library, to the endowed chair of a particular department, to a scholarship fund, or to any number of other long-lasting recognition opportunities. While every donor won't be a legacy donor, each one deserves recognition even in the smallest way to show your appreciation.

As a member of your organization's fundraising team, you can begin a giving club by identifying the club levels you want to create, the names you want to assign to each level, and the benefits you want to offer the donors who give. Table 5-1 lists four different giving club levels for a garden club association.

TABLE 5-1 An Example of a Giving Club

Level I: $500–$999, The Crocus Club Benefits	Level II: $1,000–$2,499, The Lily Club Benefits	Level III: $2,500–$4,999, The Iris Club Benefits	Level IV: $5,000 and above, The Rose Society Benefits
Garden membership	All of the Crocus Club benefits, plus . . .	All of the Lily Club benefits, plus . . .	All of the Iris Club benefits, plus . . .
Tickets for two to an evening premiere	Dinner with the chamber orchestra at the garden	Two tickets for a tour of the Boardwalk Garden Home	Breakfast with a Master Gardener
Free subscription to the *GardenWalk* newsletter	Six gardening classes with a Master Gardener	An evening for two in the garden with a horse-drawn carriage ride	A special birding event for Rose Society members
		Free admission to all garden events	An all-expenses-paid trip for two to our sister garden in Bulgaria, the land of roses

Recognizing Major Donors for Their Contributions

It's so important to remember that giving isn't just an "I give, you get" transaction; it's an equitable trade that benefits everyone involved. Your organization receives something, to be sure, but you give something as well. What you give your donors may be intangible — the good feeling that comes from helping a cause they believe in, for example. Or the recognition you offer them may include a thank-you note, call, or visit to say, "Your gift was very important to us." The following sections offer ideas for acknowledging your donors' contributions.

Meeting your donors' expectations

What do major givers want to receive in return for their gifts? For one thing, they want personal contact with your organization. Personal relationships are especially important at the major giving level. Donors want to be sure you know who they are. They want to be recognized as higher-level participants than the donors who send in the $100 check once a year to your annual fund. The following list details some of the things major givers expect when they give a major gift:

- **Confidence in the board:** Your major givers are more interested in the makeup of your board than people who give at a lower level. They feel better about making sizeable contributions when they have confidence in the leadership and fiduciary responsibility of your organization, the chairman, the executive director, and other board members.
- **The efficiency of the management:** In addition to confidence in the board, major givers want some assurances that the organization is well run, efficient, and dedicated to fulfilling its mission. No one wants to donate a large sum of hard-earned money to an organization that may dry up and blow away next year.
- **The credibility of your advisory board:** Some organizations cultivate an honorary or advisory board to offer insight, perspective, and credibility to the board. Though these individuals don't do much in the way of legwork, having their names on your letterhead can be impressive.
- **Recognition:** Some major givers — although not all — want recognition from your organization, from the community, and from their peers for their support of your organization. Part of your job as the fund-raiser is finding the appropriate recognition that will be meaningful to your donors.
- **Personal contact:** This can't be stressed enough — your major givers want to hear from you. Notes, calls, and visits all say to a donor, "You're important to us, and we want to keep you informed about what's going on." By giving at high levels, major givers make a significant commitment to you, and they most likely expect an equal commitment from your organization.
- **Financial advice:** Some major givers may want professional assistance before their gifts are complete — from their lawyers, financial planners, or a foundation executive. Have someone on your staff or board who can speak knowledgeably about planned-giving instruments and tax issues who complements, not replaces, your major giver's own financial counsel.

Providing donor recognition

Imagine that you're about to receive a major gift. Mr. Jonas listened to your presentation, liked your ideas, and is receptive to your suggestion that he donate $200,000 over the next three years. Now you're back at your desk, soaking up your success. Enjoy the moment — for a moment. But then take the time to ask yourself, "Now what?" When you receive a major gift or the promise of one, you need to acknowledge the donor right away.

REMEMBER

Recognizing your major giver is as important as all the steps you've taken leading up to the point of receiving the major gift. Note that getting major gifts is about building relationships. So by receiving Mr. Jonas's $200,000 gift, you've agreed to accept and be accountable for that gift — and his involvement — over the next three years. In effect, you've said the following:

- "We value *you* — not just your money."
- "We'll use this donation wisely, as promised."
- "We'll be good stewards of this gift and be accountable to you for it."

TIP

In addition to keeping the promises you make to your donor, you need to recognize a major giver in other ways, such as the following:

- Write a handwritten thank-you note on nice stationery.
- Follow up by calling your donor.
- Make visits or have lunch with your donor periodically.
- Get your donor involved in high-level donor affairs, such as preview parties, soirees, grand openings, open houses, and so on.
- Assign the donor to a board position or a committee seat.
- Name a program, a building, a garden, or an evening after the donor.
- Invite your donor to focus groups where you discuss the future of the organization.
- Invite your donor to special events, such as seeing the birth of a baby cheetah at the zoo, going backstage to meet a national speaker, or being a dinner guest with a high-profile actor who's in town for a guest appearance in the local production of *Our Town*.

IN THIS CHAPTER

» Getting over the fear of asking for the big bucks

» Selecting the best person to do the asking

» Understanding how to ask for money

» Knowing what to do after you get a response — yes or no

» Continuing to build your relationship with donors

Chapter 6 Making the Major Gift Ask

Does the title of this chapter put your stomach in knots and raise your blood pressure? If so, you're not alone. It's not unusual for people in fundraising, both experienced and new, to dread that oh-so-frightening one-on-one conversation with the donor when it's time for "the Ask." When you're going after a major gift, you eventually have to face the terrifying moment when you actually ask the donor for money. The stage is set. The spotlight is on you. Your tongue feels like it's the size of Texas, and you hope the donor doesn't notice that your hands are shaking. What's worse is that you're highly aware of the tumultuous economy and the impact it's had on almost everyone you know. Where on earth will you find the chutzpah to ask your donor for what your organization needs?

This chapter gives you a look at that terrifying moment and puts it in perspective with some basic management techniques for recognizing and responding to the challenges of asking for a major gift.

Pushing through the Fear by Focusing on the Greater Goal

The bad news is that sooner or later you have to push through your fear of asking people for money. The good news is that eventually "the Ask" gets easier, you get somewhat used to it, and being prepared, relaxed, and tuned in to your organization's mission really helps. This section addresses some common qualms and explores ways to make you more at ease as you do "the Ask."

Accepting that you have to talk about money

The fear of asking for money has numerous roots, many of which are completely understandable. First, money is still considered one of the big taboo subjects in society. You don't just start asking personal questions about money in polite company. It's none of your business how much one person makes as VP of their company or how much another has in their savings account ... unless you happen to be raising funds for an organization that you (and potentially those two potential donors) care deeply about.

No matter how you feel about asking for money, keep in mind that developing a fundraising system typically takes the work of many people many months — it's not a one-man or one-woman show — which means you're not the only one who has to face "the Ask." By the time you get to the point when you're ready to ask a potential donor for a major gift, you'll have done considerable legwork and research on that donor and their relationship with your organization, which means you'll feel more comfortable and determined than you think when you finally reach the "Ask." (See Chapter 3 of this minibook for more about researching your donors.)

TIP

As you get ready to ask a donor for a major gift, keep in mind your organization's main goal: to further its mission in your community, not to get big bucks from rich folks. Note also that you've laid the groundwork in your relationship with the donor up to this point, so chances are that the donor is anticipating the ask. Here are two tips to help you stay focused on the work at hand instead of getting blindsided by the money issue:

- **Remember what's real.** Money is an exchange mechanism, and you're helping your donor participate in a charitable effort they care about. Both your organization and the donor get something out of the donor's major gift.

» **Think about the other person.** Devote yourself to helping the other person give, not to taking their money. If the donor is concerned about something, try to allay those concerns. If the donor doesn't think it's the right time to give, help explore why and find out whether other giving options are possible. If you focus on the giving rather than the getting, you can focus on the donor instead of just money.

Understanding that "no" doesn't equal failure

Another reason some people dread "the Ask" is because they have a fear of hearing "no." For these people, perhaps "no" feels like a personal rejection or the end of the line. Maybe "no" is one more nail in a fundraising campaign coffin.

TIP

Well, it's time to turn all those ideas on their heads. "No" only means what you make it mean — and when and if you do hear a "no," think of it as *not yet* instead. If you continue respecting your donor, honoring your relationship, and listening to what your donor *does* want to do for your organization, that "no" can bring you one step closer to an eventual "yes." Keep these tips in mind:

» **Go for a "yes," but realize that you can live with a "no."** Expect that the donor wants to make the donation, but remind yourself that a "no" isn't personal and has more to do with the circumstances and mindset of the donor than with anything you say or do.

» **Turn a "no" into a "not yet."** The donor-organization relationship doesn't end with a single "no." The relationship you've taken the time to build will continue whether or not the donor makes this particular gift. Keeping this idea in mind can help you remember what's important about what you're doing — building relationships and matching the right people with the right causes at the right time.

Throughout this chapter, you find out how to listen to a "no" with a different ear and to recognize new possible outcomes of hearing "no." You also find out when to bargain down and when to regroup. It's a matter of changing your attitude that "no" is a word to be feared to considering how a "no" can lead to a "yes."

CAN'T ASK RIGHT NOW?

Even though you've been working up to it for weeks, if you're tempted to delay asking a major donor for a gift because of the volatile economy, reconsider. As mentioned in Chapter 5 of this minibook, major donors are feeling the pinch like everybody else, but they also have plans in place to help them weather the economic flows successfully. Good times or bad, the major donor still has a giving plan in place and is still looking for organizations to support — your organization may as well be one of them.

Listen to your donor's signals, of course, but don't scrap your plan just because of the doomsayers on television or talk radio shows. Go ahead and keep the appointment, work on your plan, and hope for the best. Your donor will let you know if your request is outside the realm of possibility right now, and then you always have the option of bargaining down.

Remembering that you're a donor, too

A cardinal rule of fundraising is this: You must be a giver yourself if you're going to ask others for major gifts for your organization. Before awarding grants, foundations want to know that the board is a 100 percent giving board. Being a fellow donor carries a lot of weight for you and your organization, and even if donors never know whether you give (few people actually ask), you'll be more comfortable knowing that you're asking another person to do something you're willing to do yourself.

Spending some time thinking about your own giving patterns can be a helpful way to prepare for meeting a major donor. One fund-raiser remembers their father coming home for dinner after volunteering at United Way. Their father said, "I spent the whole day looking at budgets for nonprofit organizations. I never knew what all these different organizations did. And I decided maybe I ought to be a giver." Having had that experience in their early childhood, the fund-raiser recognized from their father the value of giving, and that experience became one that built their own habit of giving throughout their life.

Keep in mind that your giving doesn't have to be on the same level as the gift you're asking for, although it helps enormously with major gifts. For example, if one CEO approaches another and says, "I'd like you to join me in being a member of the Chamber Society," the message is that the asking CEO already gives at that high level and that the other CEO is being asked to donate at the same level. This comparison serves as a kind of endorsement for the prospective donor, and if the peer-to-peer relationship is such that the donor respects the asker, this endorsement sets up a natural "yes."

TIP

So, you can see that being a giver is an important part of requesting donations from a major giver, but should you ever divulge how much you give? Although the answer may vary from donor to donor, one subtle way to handle this issue is to have your organization's giving levels ready to show the donor. You can say, "My husband and I give at this level, and I was hoping you would do the same," while pointing out the appropriate category. That way no dollar amounts are named, and the donor is invited to consider a specific amount. And of course, you can always bargain down if you need to.

Choosing the Right People to Make the Ask

Long before you go on that donor visit during which you intend to solicit a donation, you need to figure out who does the asking for your organization. Few things look more unprofessional than a fundraising team, standing on that proverbial doorstep, unsure about who's doing what, which is why finding and preparing the right person to do the asking is key in securing major gifts. The right person ideally

- Has a peer-to-peer relationship with the prospective donor
- Is also a giver
- Is comfortable with fundraising
- Understands that the donor expects to be asked to give
- Is a people person, able and willing to focus on building relationships with donors over time
- Is forthcoming, honest, and willing to help donors resolve any questions or concerns that may be keeping them from giving
- Is confident and secure, unshaken by a "no" that could be a "yes" down the road

TIP

Perhaps the single biggest consideration in choosing the person who does "the Ask" is the peer-to-peer relationship. If you're approaching the CEO of a corporation for a major gift, have your organization's CEO or a person on your board who's a peer in terms of social, economic, and professional status do "the Ask." Similarly, if you're approaching someone who has volunteered for the organization for a long time, send another volunteer — not a paid staff member — to do the asking. The similarity of the roles — whether those roles are professional, social, experiential, or professional — helps build a sense of trust between the donor and the fund-raiser. People in unequal positions of power — a CEO and a paid staff member, for example — often have trouble reaching the comfort zone that people of like means or status share. And of course, whether the donor is asked by a peer or a staff member, an established relationship should already exist, so the donor anticipates the coming question.

The following sections explain how two people can work together to ask for a major gift, as well as what you should keep in mind if you're doing "the Ask" on your own.

Teaming up for dollars

Some people prefer to work in fundraising teams, which are often made up of a paid staff member and a board member. The board member is traditionally the one doing "the Ask," and the staff member goes along for support and encouragement.

The problem with the two-person approach is that some donors may feel "ganged up on" if they're put in the minority. For this reason, you need to be explicit about your intention to visit as a team: "Michelle has a brief presentation she'd like to show you about our new waterworks. Would 2:30 this afternoon be a convenient time for us to come by?"

On the flip side, two people can be helpful in fundraising calls because

- They represent two different views of your organization.
- They give the donor a feeling that many people support the work.
- They're more likely to cover all the key points, omitting nothing important.
- If one person is having trouble establishing rapport with the donor, the other person may hit it off.
- The second person may bring additional ideas to the conversation.
- With two people listening to the donor, they're more likely to hear the donor's perspective and respond appropriately.

TIP

Practice makes perfect. Even though your board members may be CEOs and top-level community members, they can still use a brush-up on fundraising skills. Before you begin an active campaign in which your board members are soliciting gifts (or accompanying you on donor visits), reserve time to do some role-playing. Be sure to reverse the role-play so the asker also gets to play the role of the donor. Have one member act as the potential donor and one member act as the fund-raiser and then switch. Don't make it too easy, and have fun! Also, don't forget about using Zoom to do the role-play. Having a recording of the scenario allows the party on the learning side to see their facial expressions, tone of voice, and overall ability to deliver a smooth ask.

In the real world, all kinds of interruptions and roadblocks happen during fundraising calls, and the better prepared you and your board members are for them, the better the outcomes will be. With this idea in mind, in one role-playing session, a fundraising team had the "donor" keep answering an invisible phone on their invisible desk during the meeting. The "fund-raiser" could barely get a sentence out without an interruption. In the meeting, the team laughed, watching the "donor" frazzle the "fund-raiser," but the team knew how helpful this practice could be for their fund-raisers.

Flying solo

If you choose to go on your fundraising calls alone, you have a number of factors working in your favor:

- You're the only one responsible for doing the preparation, which means nothing (hopefully) will fall through the cracks.
- You have a good chance (assuming a peer-to-peer relationship) of reaching a comfort zone with the donor on a one-to-one basis.
- You won't feel that anyone is looking over your shoulder.
- You can go with your instincts to direct the flow of the conversation.

WARNING

On the other hand, the amount of responsibility you carry on a solo visit may be a bit heftier. For example:

- You have to be careful what you promise — no one checks and balances you but you.
- You can't ask an informed third party how well you did in the call.
- You rely on your own facts and figures, with no one to back you up. (You'd better know your stuff!)
- If the donor call doesn't go well, nobody can help you out of it but you.

Developing the Mechanics of Asking

After you investigate some of your attitudes about money and consider who's the best person in your organization to do the asking, you're ready to get down to the nuts and bolts of "the Ask." This section takes you through the actual process and gives you tools to use along the way.

Recognizing the equitable exchange

Picture this: You have a pair of concert tickets you can't use. You decide to call a few friends to see whether anyone else can use the tickets. You dial the phone happily, feeling that special "I have something great for you!" feeling. The first two friends you call say they have other plans for the night, but they're pleased that you thought of them; the third is thrilled and accepts the tickets gratefully. After the concert, they call and tell you all about it (it was great, apparently), and want to take you to lunch to thank you for thinking of them. You didn't get to go to the concert, but you did get to be part of an exchange that made another person happy, which can leave you with a pretty good feeling.

Why does your role in fundraising have to be any different than the situation with the concert tickets? Granted, you aren't giving away concert tickets (unless, of course, you work for a symphony and are giving them to your high-level donors), but what you're offering your donor is as important and as valued as a nice gift.

REMEMBER

Fundraising isn't just about getting money from people who have a surplus of it. It's about matching caring people with the organizations that support the areas they care about, whether those areas are music, art, human services, education, civic affairs, or health.

Using the tools of the trade

Until the advent of the Internet and digital everything, the standard tools of the trade in fundraising involved a lot of costly, slick, four-color print brochures and annual reports. You may still have some professional leave-behinds to give to your donor, but you may also take along a laptop with a PowerPoint presentation.

TIP

At the very least, you need to take the following items with you to any visit during which you plan to do "the Ask":

- A card or brochure showing your giving levels
- A presentation (if you're using your laptop), brochure, or report that tells the story of the difference you make
- Pledge cards

REMEMBER

Taking a laptop or tablet to a presentation may be a hip and low-cost way to tell the story of your organization, but not all donors will like it. If you use the laptop or tablet to display the presentation, be sure to close the laptop or tablet and place it on the floor after you finish the presentation so that it isn't an obstacle or a distraction between you and the donor while you're chatting afterward. Also, be sure to rehearse your presentation in the office before you show it to your donor. Recovering from technical glitches and then moving to a successful ask is a huge challenge.

Knowing the donor

By the time you reach "the Ask," you should know the donor well. Consider the answers to the following questions as part of the preparation for your donor visit:

- How long has the donor been giving to your organization?
- Why does the donor care about your cause?
- How much has the donor given in the past?
- How did the donor's past gifts help the clients who receive your services?
- What are the donor's key interests?
- Which of your programs are aligned with the donor's key interests?
- Have you prepared to ask for a donation in one of those key areas?
- How much are you asking the donor to contribute?
- What do you expect the donor's concerns to be?
- How will you address those concerns?
- What recognition opportunity will be meaningful for the donor?

REMEMBER

It bears repeating: The more you know before you ask, the better experience both you and your prospects will have, and the more likely your prospects will be to see the match between your mission and their interests. Check out chapters 3 and 4 of this minibook for more about getting to know your donors.

Checking out each step of "the Ask"

You can break down almost every process — including the process of asking for a major gift — into a simple step-by-step procedure. The following steps can help you navigate the safe areas for conversation and comfort-building as you ask a potential donor for a major gift:

1. **Open:** 3–5 minutes

   You know about the introductions bit. As you're walking into the meeting, you and the donor both talk about the weather. You also mention how great the irises looked outside the conservatory this spring, which provides a segue into the next section of your conversation.

2. **Engage:** 5–20 minutes

"Have you ever been out to see the gardens in full bloom?" you say.

"No," the donor replies.

"Oh, this year we included 14 new varieties of hybrids," you continue, which enables you to spotlight a few of the things you did with the donor's contributions to the Flower Fund last year.

The point of this step is to truly engage the donor, understand where they're coming from, and find out a bit more about their specific interests right now. The engage step enables you to see where the donor's "hot buttons" are currently, even though you may already know what they cared about last year. For example, you know the donor isn't interested in funding renovations if you hear, "I'll never give to that group again if they're going to remodel their offices with my money!" You also uncover any new key interests that may help you see further how your organization's mission and the donor's interests match.

TIP

The most important three words to remember during this stage of the visit are "Ask and listen!" Know what questions you want to ask ahead of time so you can get a good sense of what the donor wants to know more about, what their concerns may be, and how you can resolve those concerns. Be aware of your history with this donor, but also keep your mind — and ears — open to hear new connections that may arise. Most importantly, use this step to listen carefully. Watch the donor's face; read their body language; wait for the signs that they are really excited about what they're talking about. From that sensitive listening, you can begin to get a sense of which type of gift would most engage this particular donor's imagination and interest.

3. **Tell your story:** 10–15 minutes

Now you're in the groove. You've set the stage, found out about the donor's primary interests, and discovered the angle that gives you the best chance of appealing to their philanthropic interests. You now explain the program or campaign you're here to talk about. You talk compellingly about the need (which the donor should empathize with) and explain how your program or organization serves that need in such a way that gets the donor interested in being involved. During this step, you rely on the information you brought with you, perhaps handing the donor brochures as you talk or showing the donor slides of the possibilities or programs you're discussing.

TIP

During this step, don't do all the talking; it's important to stay alert to clues from your donor about any concerns or questions. Stop and answer the questions. Be forthcoming and consider each answer you give as a step toward bringing the donor into a better understanding of your organization.

4. **Ask for involvement:** 5–?? minutes

In sales terms, this last stage is called *the close.* Fund-raisers are often reluctant to use sales terminology (it isn't a sales job, after all), but the result is the same: You need to ask the donor for a donation. Sooner or later, it comes down to that important question.

You move right from your presentation to the close. "I can see that you're interested in our visiting horticulturist program. I thought that you'd be one of the people most excited about this idea. We were hoping you'd make a lead gift of $25,000 to start out this new program. And with your permission, we would like to name the program after you and your partner, for all the important contributions you've made to the garden and to the community in the past 40 years. Is this amount something you're comfortable with?"

You've brought it to a yes or no response. If you get a "no," don't panic; you still have some things to do to try to turn that "no" into a "yes." (See the next section for more details.) If you do get a "yes," hand the donor an elegant pen for writing the check, or bring out that pledge card.

REMEMBER

As hard as it may be to remember, this donor visit isn't about you or your organization. It's about your donor and how you can provide them the service of contributing to a cause they care about, which means you need to fight the temptation to monopolize the conversation (something that's very easy to do, especially if you're feeling nervous). Instead, sit back and listen attentively. What's the donor really saying? What are their interests? How can you best serve the donor? You best represent your organization when you truly have the donor's best interests at heart.

Moving Beyond "No"

Suppose that the worst happens, and the donor says "no." Chances are your donor isn't going to say, "No! And get out!" but rather something a little less harsh, such as

- "Not right now."
- "I'll think about it."
- "I need to talk to my financial advisor about it."
- "I don't think that's something I'm prepared to do right now."

DEALING WITH THE LESS-THAN-PERFECT CALL

Not all your calls will go the way you want them to. You'll have an occasional meeting when somebody is put off by what you're doing. Remember one important rule: "Don't worry about it!" Move on to your other prospects. With the number of people you're going to see and calls you're going to make, a few of the calls may not go well.

If you remember the big picture — what your goals are — and know that a certain percentage of calls aren't going to be perfect, you can deal with the ups and downs that come with the territory. You can continue to build the relationship with the donor and get closer to that eventual "yes" even with a flopped call.

The most important thing to remember at this point in "the Ask" is that in fundraising, you'll get all kinds of "no's" and partial "no's," but you can't just give up at this point and say, "Oh, okay. Well, thanks for your time."

WARNING

Is it ethical to mention other people in the donor's social group who have given to your organization? Doing so may be ethical, but whether or not it's a smart thing to do depends on the donor. Some people are put off by what they hear as "name dropping." Others are encouraged when they hear that people they respect have given to your programs; those names serve as a kind of endorsement for your organization. Listen carefully to your donor, and if you gauge interest in knowing who else has given, mention someone the donor may recognize and notice their response.

Rating Your Yes-Ability

After you finish the call, do a quick assessment to see how you did. If you did "the Ask" on your own, think about your comfort level — and that of your donor — during the conversation. Take a look at your results. Where do things stand now? Did you get the gift? Did you get one step closer to the gift? Replay the conversation and notice where you did well and where you want to improve for next time.

If you have a partner for your fundraising call, you have a built-in evaluator. After you leave the donor, ask your partner, "How do you think we did?" Hopefully your partner will feel comfortable talking about the good — and not-so-good — parts of the visit. You can find out valuable information from the insights of another person who's at least partially objective. You may want to ask your partner the following questions:

- "Did we seem well prepared?"
- "Do you think we handled the question about last year's shortage the right way?"
- "Do you think the donor felt comfortable with spreading the gift over three years?"
- "Did you notice anything you think we should work on?"
- "What aspect of the visit do you think we did best?"

After you complete the call, you need to document the information in the donor's file. Write down the answers to the previous questions, as well as pertinent facts you need for fundraising calls in the future. Even if you received the Big Gift, you need to continue to build your relationship with that donor, as you see in the following section.

TIP

If the meeting didn't go as planned, continue building the relationship with the donor over the coming months. You may want to change the venue — meet for coffee instead of going to the house, for example — or, if necessary, consider sending somebody else to call on the donor. You don't want to leave a bad taste in the donor's mouth about you or your organization, and replacing the difficult meeting with a better experience afterward creates a better memory all around.

Following Up after "the Ask"

Finally, the call is over. You're driving back to your office with the nice feeling of having a $25,000 check for your organization in your briefcase. Your donor was gracious and pleased that you approached them to give the lead gift for your new program. The donor likes the idea of having naming rights for the new program and wants to serve on the committee to help organize the kickoff event.

What are your responsibilities toward the new donor now that you're taking a check back to your office? You'll be faced with this ethical question over and over again in fundraising.

REMEMBER

Donors aren't just money sources. They're people with interests and passions and troubles and fears. It's not unusual to meet a major donor late in their life who has lost a spouse and wants to spend time talking, remembering, and visiting. When that donor writes you a major check, you have an obligation to show the donor that your relationship isn't just about money. Here are some ways you can follow up with a donor after you receive a major gift:

- Send the all-important thank-you note.
- Make a follow-up phone call.
- Provide information on the new program as it develops.
- Send your organization's newsletter or e-newsletter.
- Send invitations to all high-level social events.
- Set up occasional lunches or visits.
- Send invitations to participate in focus groups or special engagements.
- Send invitations to get involved in other organizational events that the donor may be interested in.

REMEMBER

"The Ask" doesn't have to be a panic-inducing event. Even if you don't get the answer you want, you can make this process a positive contribution to building the relationship between you and the donor, which is likely to lead to a "yes" down the road.

3

Applying for and Winning Grants

Contents at a Glance

IN THIS CHAPTER

» Diving into grant-writing basics

» Creating a funding development plan

» Finding foundation and government grants

» Meeting submission requirements

» Preparing for acceptance or rejection

Chapter 1

Grant-Writing Basics for Beginners

This chapter gives you an overview of everything grant-related and encourages you to read on through each chapter in this minibook to get the full picture of every aspect of the grant-writing journey. If you have always wanted to learn more about grant writing, want to build relationships with potential funders, learn how to connect with your elected officials to stay in the know about federal grant-funding opportunities, and secure funding, this and the following chapters in this minibook put you in the driver's seat on your journey. So get out your highlighters and sticky notes, and let's get started!

Orienting Yourself on Grant-Seeking Basics

In order to hone your "find a grant now" skill set, you need a lot of basic information. First things first: what a grant is *not*. A grant is *not* a way to pay off your debts, like mortgages, student loans, government loans, or utility bills. It's *not* a way to fund your first trip abroad. A grant also is *not* a way to get out of jail free. You won't find a grant funder that will give you free money for personal needs.

This section covers common terms and lays out the basic information you need to know to jump on the grant-seeking boat without a life preserver.

Learning common grant-writing terminology

Basically speaking, a *grant* (sometimes labeled a *cooperative agreement* by government funding agencies) is a monetary award of financial assistance to eligible grant applicants. The principal purpose of the grant is to transfer dollars from a funding agency or entity (*grantor*) to a recipient (*grantee*), who undertakes to carry out the proposed objectives (the written implementation plans in the grant application narrative) that they committed to when they submitted the grant application. Here are some common grant-writing terms and their definitions:

- **Grant/cooperative agreement:** The distinguishing factor between a grant and a cooperative agreement is the degree of government (state, federal, or local) participation or involvement during the grantee's actual start-up and implementation of the proposed activities.

  REMEMBER

  A grant award is made via a contract or agreement between the funding agency (the *grantor*) and the recipient (the *grantee*), with the grant supporting the activities and deliverables (implementation strategies and measurable time-bound objectives or benchmarks) detailed in the proposal/application (and finalized during the process of confirming the grant award). Reading the grant application's guidelines thoroughly (and multiple times) is critical to being funded. (Refer to chapters 3–5 of this minibook for tips on finding grant-funding opportunities.)

- **Grantor:** A grantor (also known as a *grant maker* or *funder*) is the organization or agency that receives your funding request and decides to fund it or reject it. Grantors include the grant-making agencies of the federal government, many state and local government agencies (including in the U.S. territories), and more than 100,000 foundations and corporate grant makers. Two categories of grantors exist:
  - **Public-sector funder:** Any government grant maker (federal, state, county, or local unit of government) that awards grants with money that comes from congressional allocations, federal pass-through dollars to states and municipalities, or taxpayer dollars — the public-sector. See Chapter 3 of this minibook for more about these funders.
  - **Private-sector funder:** A foundation or corporate grant maker (independent of private foundation, operating foundations, corporate foundations, and community foundations) that uses funds from private sources — investments, contributions, donations, or grants — to fund eligible grant applicants. Chapter 5 of this minibook has more information on these funders.

» **Grantee:** The grantee is the eligible grant applicant designated to receive a grant award. All grants require the grantee to use the funds as written (and as promised) in the grant application. The required grant award paperwork is considered a contract between the grantor and the grantee. Up until you're awarded the grant, you're a *grant applicant;* you become a grantee only if you are approved for funding and agree to accept the award.

REMEMBER

Be certain you are an eligible grant applicant before applying for the grant.

So, how do you get a grantor to give you a grant and make you a grantee? After you've reviewed the guidelines (at least three times) for submitting an application and made initial contact with the potential funder, you're ready to research, write, and submit your *grant application* or *proposal* (also known as a *funding request*). To find out more about the pieces or sections of a grant application/proposal, check out the later section, "Looking at the components of a grant application."

Checking out different types of grants

Almost every grant-funding agency publishes specific types of funding it awards to prospective grant seekers. When you know what you want to use grant monies for, you can evaluate whether your request fits with the type of funding the grantor has available. For example, if you want money for architectural fees related to a historical preservation project, you can skip applying to a grantor that's only accepting grant requests for small technology-related equipment.

Look long and hard at the different categories of funding offered:

» **Annual campaigns:** Grants to support annual operating expenses, infrastructure improvements, program expansion, and, in some cases, one-time-only expenses (such as a cooling-system replacement).

» **Building/renovation funds:** Grants to build a new facility or renovate an existing facility. These projects are often referred to as *bricks-and-mortar projects.* Building funds are the most difficult to secure; only a small percentage of foundations and corporations award grants for this type of project.

» **Capital support:** Grants for equipment, buildings, construction, and endowments. This type of request is a major undertaking by the applicant organization because this type of large-scale project isn't quickly funded. An organization often needs two to three years to secure total funding for such a project.

- **Challenge monies:** Grants that act as leverage to secure additional grants from foundations and corporations. They're awarded by grant makers that specifically include *challenge grants* or *challenge funds* in their grant-making priorities. These grants are contingent on you raising additional funds from other sources. Typically, a challenge grant award letter directs you to raise the remaining funding from other grantors; however, that typically excludes government grants.
- **Conferences/seminars:** Grants to cover the cost of attending, planning, and/or hosting conferences and seminars. You can use the funding to pay for all the conference expenses, including securing a keynote speaker, traveling, printing, advertising, and taking care of facility expenses such as meals.
- **Consulting services:** Grants to strengthen an organization's capacity can be used to retain the services of a consultant or consulting firm. For example, if you bring in a consultant to do a long-range strategic plan or an architect to develop plans for a historical preservation project, you can apply for a grant to cover these types of expenses.
- **Continuing support/continuation:** Grants additional funds to your organization after you've already received an initial grant award from that same grantor. These monies are intended to continue the program or project initially funded.
- **Endowments:** Grants to develop long-term, permanent investment income to ensure the continuing presence and financial stability of your nonprofit organization. If your organization is always operating in crisis-management mode, one of your goals should be to develop an endowment fund for long-term viability.
- **Fellowships:** Grants to support graduate and postgraduate students in specific fields. These funds are typically awarded to institutions and not directly to individuals, with the exception of some international fellowship funders.
- **General/operating expenses:** Grants for general line-item budget expenses. You may use these funds for salaries, fringe benefits, travel, consultants, utilities, equipment, and other expenses necessary to support agency operations.
- **Matching funds:** Grants awarded with the requirement that you must match the grant award with your own monies or with in-kind contributions.
- **Program development:** Grants to pay for expenses related to the expansion of existing programs or the development of new programs.
- **Research:** Grants to support medical and educational research. Monies are usually awarded to the institutions that employ the individuals conducting the research.

- **Scholarship funds:** Grants to eligible organizations seeking to award scholarships to eligible individuals. Remember that when funds are awarded directly to an individual, they're considered taxable income (that is, the recipient owes taxes on them).
- **Seed money:** Grants awarded for a pilot program not yet in full-scale operation. Seed money gets a program underway, but other monies are necessary to continue the program in its expansion phase.
- **Technical (consulting) assistance:** Grants to improve your internal program operations as a whole (versus consulting on one specific program). Often, this type of grant is awarded to hire an individual or firm that can provide the needed technical assistance.

Understanding your eligibility for grants

The types of organizations or entities eligible to apply for a grant vary from grantor to grantor. Each type of grantor — government (public) or foundation (private) — always includes clear, published grant-making guidelines that indicate who or what type of entity is eligible to apply for those specific grant funds. To access these grant-making guidelines, simply visit the grantor's website.

Funders typically include one or more of the following types of grant applicants in their *eligible applicant* language:

- State government
- County government
- City or township government
- Federally recognized Native American tribal governments
- Independent school districts
- Nonprofits with and without Internal Revenue Service (IRS) 501(c)(3) (nonprofit) status
- Private, public, and state-controlled institutions of higher education
- Public and Native American housing authorities
- For-profit businesses
- For-profit organizations other than businesses
- International nonprofits (called *nongovernmental organizations* or NGOs)
- Individuals

TIP

Always check with the funder in advance to make sure that the entity that you're applying for is an eligible grant applicant. For example, funders view a nonprofit as an IRS-approved 501(c)(3) designated tax-exempt organization. Just being incorporated as a nonprofit in your state (for United States-based grant makers) is not going to qualify you to apply for funds. You definitely need IRS approval in writing.

REMEMBER

Familiarize yourself with Grants.gov before you actually plan on applying for funding. All federal grant applicants have to do a lot of up-front work before they can submit an application for funding consideration.

Grants are awarded to organizations that have applied to the IRS for nonprofit status and have received the 501(c)(3) designation as well as to units of government (state agencies, counties, cities, towns, and villages) and government agencies, including state colleges and universities. Foundation and corporate grantors focus predominantly on nonprofit organizations and aren't inclined to fund for-profits. However, a few grants are given to individuals.

In some instances, government agencies have set up separate 501(c)(3) nonprofit structures in order to scoop up more private-sector (foundation and corporate) grant awards.

Recognizing the Purpose of a Funding Development Plan

REMEMBER

If you're searching for funding to support an entire organization or a specific program, the first rule in grant seeking is that you don't write a grant request without first completing a comprehensive planning process that involves the grant applicant organization's key stakeholders. These are the *target population* members (the people your organization serves), administrative staff, and the board of directors.

Without key stakeholder input on what your target population needs and the plan for closing the gap on these needs, you're jumping off the cliff without a parachute. You must have an organized *funding development plan* to guide your organization in adopting priority programs and services and then identifying all potential grantors you plan to approach with grant requests. A funding development plan answers questions such as the following:

- What programs are strong and already have regular funding to keep them going? Are they likely to be refunded?

- What community needs aren't being addressed by your organization or other organizations providing similar services?
- What new programs need funding and is there evidence of the needs?
- What opportunities exist to find new funding partners and who will be responsible for making the initial contact with each funder?
- What existing grants expire soon and can you reapply or do you have to find new funding?

When the stakeholders answer these questions, you can begin to look at the plethora of areas where grants are awarded and start prioritizing the type of funding you need. (For more information on funding development plans, see Chapter 2 of this minibook.)

Sleuthing Out Funding Sources

Everyone wants grants; that is, everyone wants money! If you're feeling clueless about how to find potential funding for your organization, you simply need to use your favorite search engine. You can search for potential sources that are interested in what your organization needs in the way of goods and services. Get your fingers moving on the keyboard and start searching for the monies that may be waiting for your organization. While you're at it, why not start with the nation's wealthiest relative, Uncle Sam?

TIP

Did you know that the U.S. government is one of the largest grant-making entities? That's correct, Uncle Sam doles out approximately $500 billion in grant awards annually. If you want to score big in grant awards, you may want to consider targeting federal grant-making agencies and researching their daily grant announcements. After all, there are 26 grant-making agencies giving away boatloads of money to eligible grant applicants who have mastered writing highly competitive grant applications.

REMEMBER

Public government grants come in two types:

- A *competitive grant* is one where applicants compete against each other for a limited amount of funding.
- A *formula grant* is awarded based on a predetermined formula (a set amount of money per person) established by the funding agency. Formula grants aren't considered competitive. For example, community action agencies are funded formula grants, in part, through the Community Services Block Grant

(CSBG) program. These grants are awarded on a service-population-based formula. The agencies receive these funds year after year by merely updating the previous year's application and resubmitting.

The following sections explain what type of public-sector grant money (or grantor) will pay you to implement your idea, project, or program.

Federal funding: Raiding Uncle Sam's stash

The first place to look for big pots of money is in Uncle Sam's closet of federal funding agencies. Chapters 3 and 4 of this minibook explain public-sector grants and wade through the main federal e-grant portal, Grants.gov.

TIP

Many newly established nonprofit organizations think that they should apply for government grants before raising seed funding from local foundations and corporations. Your organization needs an established, credible track record for implementing, evaluating, and prudently managing funding from smaller fish in the sea before jumping into the federal grant application process.

TIP

To find active or current grant-funding opportunities from Uncle Sam, go to `www.grants.gov`, which gives you daily funding announcements on money you can apply for *now*, provided your organization is an eligible grant applicant.

State and local government funding: Seeking public dollars closer to home

Each state receives grant monies from the feds and from tax revenues that are funneled into and out of the state's general funds. After taking their fair (or unfair) share for administrative overhead, states re-grant the money to eligible agencies and organizations in the form of competitive grants or formula grants.

You can search the Internet to find state agencies that award grants. Examples of some of the state agencies that re-grant federal monies are agriculture, commerce, education, health, housing development, natural resources, and transportation. You can also contact your state legislator's local office for assistance in identifying grant opportunities in your state.

TIP

There's a wide variation in state grant making. It's always best to meet with your state-level elected officials and funding agency representatives to pave the way for successful grant seeking.

Identifying foundations that award grants

Private foundations typically get their monies from a single-donor source, such as an individual, a family, or a corporation. Others raise funds from a variety of donor sources. You can find hundreds of private foundations in the *Foundation Directory Online* by Candid or by typing "list of private foundations" or "private foundations" plus your state's name into your favorite search engine.

Public foundations, on the other hand, are supported primarily through donations from the general public. That's a no-brainer, right? Public foundations also receive funding from foundation and corporate grants, as well as individual donors. Again, the *Foundation Directory Online* by Candid website can give you loads of information on these types of foundations. Visit `https://learning.candid.org/resources/knowledge-base/what-is-a-foundation`.

REMEMBER

The grant-seeking and grant-making processes may differ for public and private foundations. Always contact potential foundation funders to introduce your organization, start to build a communications bridge, and inquire about their grant-making processes.

Getting Acquainted with Grant Submission Requirements

One of the biggest keys in grant writing is recognizing the different application formats that funders require you to submit. Some grantors require more information than others. Today, at least 90 percent of funders with websites require online e-grant applications. Others require traditional paper-written narratives, forms, budgets, and mandatory attachments.

REMEMBER

Determine the writing format for each funding source you identify. Carefully view each private-sector funder's website, and if you're still not sure about what to write or how to write it, make a quick call or send an email to the listed contact person. Governmental agencies have their own application kits, and you can submit applications to these agencies only at certain times in the year when there is a specific funding deadline published.

Looking at the components of a grant application

A *government grant* or *cooperative agreement application* is a written funding request you use to ask for money from a government agency. Government grant applications are specific to each of the federal grant-making agencies. Even state agency grant applications that are funded with federal pass-through dollars closely mirror federal grant application guidelines and grantee requirements.

Each federal agency has dozens of agencies under its wing that release Notices of Funding Availability (NOFAs), Notices of Funding Opportunity (NOFOs), Requests for Applications (RFAs), Funding Opportunity Announcements (FOAs), or Requests for Proposals (RFPs). Each NOFA, NOFO, RFA, FOA, and RFP has different funding priorities and guidelines for what you need to write in order to submit a responsive and reviewable grant application.

Government and other types of grant applications generally require that you write narrative responses for the following sections (each of which are covered in more depth in chapters 8–12 of this minibook):

- Executive summary or abstract
- Statement of need
- Program design or methodology
- Adequacy of resources or key personnel
- Evaluation plan
- Organization background/history or organization capability
- Sustainability statement
- Budget

A foundation or corporate grant application typically takes the form of a proposal. A *proposal* is a structured document that must follow each grant maker's specific guidelines. Writing a proposal to a foundation or corporation requires the same adherence to the guidelines and incorporation of relevant information as completing government grant applications.

Perusing government grant application guidelines

Although government grant application formats vary from agency to agency and department to department, some common threads exist in the highly detailed, structured, military-like regimen that's commonly referred to as an *application package*. These common threads include a standard cover form, certification and assurances forms, narrative sections, and the budget narratives and related forms. And of course, all government grant applications require mandatory attachments or appendixes, such as résumés of project staff and copies of your nonprofit status determination letter from the IRS. (Head to Chapter 4 of this minibook for more about the application package.)

REMEMBER

Always follow the pagination, order of information, and review or evaluation criteria guidelines. All government grants are awarded on the basis of your meeting point-weighted review criteria, which are written and published in each funding agency's grant application guidelines. (Most grants use a 100-point system.) The review criteria tell you what the peer reviewers will base their ratings on in the application package. With the competition being so hot and heavy for all government grants, you want to carefully craft an award-winning narrative that scores a minimum of 95 points. The grant applications recommended for funding typically score between 95 and 100 points.

Several federal grant-making agencies issue grant applications guidelines where their scoring rubrics often have up to 1,000 points. While this is rare, expect anything and everything when it comes to federal grant-seeking and award processes.

TIP

As you read through the application guidelines, highlight all narrative writing requirements and look for sections that tell you how the grant reviewers rate or evaluate each section of the narrative. By formatting and writing your narrative sections to meet the review criteria, you can edge out the competition and increase your funding success rate. (Find out how to prepare and write for the review criteria in Chapter 7 of this minibook.)

Getting your request in the door at foundations and corporations

Before you even consider approaching a foundation or corporation with a grant request, you absolutely must research each and every potential foundation and corporate funding source. Don't rely solely on online grant-research databases. Let your fingers do the typing to find each potential funder's website. Read every link and become highly familiar with each source. Find out the organization's funding priorities, the number of grants it awards annually, and the grant request range. Become very fluent in who they are, what they fund, when they fund, and their mission statement.

REMEMBER

Whenever contract information is available, be sure to go out of your way to introduce your organization to the grantor before applying. It's critical that you get a green light before submitting your grant application. Building a relationship before asking for a grant is the first step in this introductory process.

TIP

As a new grant seeker of a particular funder, make sure your grant request is near the low end of the grantor's grant range. Private-sector funders don't want to award mid- to high-funding award range amounts until after they test the waters with a small grant award. After you've demonstrated ethics, cost-effective grants management, and accountability to the funder, you can then ask for larger grants in future requests.

In the past, some private-sector funders have been swamped daily with large volumes of unsolicited grant proposals. To circumvent this influx of steady reading and decision making, more and more private-sector funders have moved toward requiring an initial *letter of inquiry* (see Chapter 2 of this minibook), which is a brief letter asking about the foundation's interest in your project. If the organization is interested, it then asks you to submit a full grant proposal. If you fail to submit the letter of inquiry, you may find the door closed to your unsolicited grant proposal.

Whether the private-sector funder is large or small, the attachments are a major portion of what counts with this group of grantors. The private-sector funder may ask for a copy of your organization's IRS letter of tax-exemption, a board of directors roster, organizational and project budgets, a copy of the nonprofit's tax return, Form-990, an organizational chart, and an audited financial statement.

Your organization's executive director or a member of your governing board's executive committee should build a relationship with any potential private-sector funder before you start begging for a grant. Courtesy and protocol mean everything in the private-sector funding environment, so always establish communications via email, a letter of inquiry, or a face-to-face meeting before sticking your hand out.

TIP

If a board member at your organization happens to know a board member at the foundation or corporation you're targeting for funding, board-member-to-board-member contact can help a lot. Foundations and corporations make decisions based on specific funding priorities, which change periodically, sometimes even annually, based on the direction that the board of directors wants to take the foundation or corporation. Although the program staff initially reviews your grant proposal and makes recommendations to the board of directors, the board has the final approval or veto. Remember, board members can override staff decisions.

Making a List and Checking It Twice

REMEMBER

Whether you're submitting a hard copy of your grant application or a digital (e-grant) version, always follow the funder's instructions! Here are some additional must-do's when preparing a grant application:

- Read the guidelines three times: one time to understand the general instructions, a second time to focus on the technical formatting requirements, and a third time to note the narrative content requirements.
- Highlight all technical and content requirements.
- Call the funder (if permissible) to clarify any conflicting instructions and ask questions in general.
- Write the grant in chronological order (the same order that the funder asks for the information in its guidelines).
- Get a second and third set of eyes to read the guidelines and check your application document line for line. Your readers should be looking at grammar, punctuation, formatting, content, clarity, connection between the narrative sections, budget accuracy, and inclusion of all mandatory attachments.

TIP

Don't forget to keep a copy of your proposal documents for your own files! For easy access, consider moving your grant-related backup files from your computer's hard drive to cloud-based storage.

Tracking Your Submission Status

After you submit all your funding requests, you need to develop a tracking system that helps you keep up with their progress and cues you when the period of silence from grantors has been too long. Most public-and private-sector grantors specify a time frame for when they will announce grant awards somewhere in the application packet or in the published description of their application process. At the federal and state levels, you can even enlist tracking support from your legislative team. To do this, you can directly call or write. However, at the corporate and foundation levels, you're on your own (unless, of course, members of your board of directors have friends and associates on the grantor's board of trustees).

The old-school approach is to develop a manual or electronic tracking system to monitor what you've written, who received it, and the status of your funding request (pending, funded, or rejected). However, the new and easier way to keep track of submitted requests is to purchase grant management or tracking software. There are many cloud-based grant management options that may meet your needs. You can find out what's available by typing "grant management systems" into your favorite web browser. These systems can cost thousands of dollars. However, many offer a free trial or demonstration, so you can see whether the program suits your needs before you buy. See Book 1, Chapter 6 for a list of websites that offer free or low-cost professional development training, including grant management training.

TIP

Keeping track of how many grant requests you submit on an annual basis is a best practice. You also want to know how many of those requests were funded. For example, if you wrote 20 grant applications and 10 were funded (at any level), one-half or 50 percent of your requests were successful. Your success percentage is interpreted as your *funding success rate*. When you're looking for a raise or promotion, or simply trying to start your own grant-writing consulting business, everyone who has control over your future will ask you for your funding success rate. Track it; know it!

Jumping for Joy or Starting All Over?

When you win, you celebrate, right? Well, yes, you celebrate, but you also notify your stakeholders of your success in winning a grant award. And you prepare for the implementation phase now that monies are on the way. When you win a grant award, it's important to remember to thank the funder (by a letter, a resolution, an invitation to your board meeting to acknowledge their monetary gift, and so on) and determine whether you can issue a press release or whether their contribution is confidential.

REMEMBER

If your grant request wasn't awarded, you have some critical steps to take to determine why your funding request was denied and when you can resubmit it:

1. **Contact the funding agency and ask why your grant application wasn't recommended for funding.** Ask for a review of your application or for the reviewer's remarks. You may have to ask for this feedback in writing so the grantors have a paper trail of whom they release information to and why.
2. **When you know where the weakness is in your grant application, develop a plan for rewriting.** You want to rewrite the weak sections of your narrative and ready it for submission to other grantors and even for future resubmission to the same grant-making agency that rejected the first request. Grantors usually allow you to reapply in the next funding cycle (the next year).

IN THIS CHAPTER

- » Assessing your organization's grant readiness
- » Determining your governing board's grant readiness
- » Creating a grant-funding plan
- » Increasing your chances for success
- » Managing your plan on an ongoing basis

Chapter 2
Preparing for Successful Grant Seeking

Typically, new and/or small nonprofit organizations that want to apply for grants are not always grant-ready. Grant readiness is the foundation or framework for successful grant seeking. This chapter shows you how to determine whether your organization is grant-ready. In addition, it shows you how to ascertain your governing board's capacity, assess your organization's capacity, create a grant-funding plan, and most importantly, how to increase your chances for successful grant seeking.

Grant-Seeking Readiness Priorities for Nonprofits

These are the questions to ask. If you answer no to any of them, you need to work with the board of directors to help turn any no's into yes's. Don't panic at the number of no's you may have; just focus on one no at a time. It's important to estimate a timeline for your anticipated grant readiness. Okay, let's get started with the questions:

- **Does your organization have a staff member or volunteer assigned to grant writing?** Having at least one person trained in how to research grants and write grant proposals is necessary for grant-seeking continuity.
- **Does your organization subscribe to grant-funding alerts about public- and private-sector grant-funding opportunities?** If you are truly serious about scoring grant awards, you absolutely need to keep updated on the type of available funding, what you need to write, and the deadlines for each application.
- **Do you have all of your organizational documents in a cloud folder so they are easily accessible from any technology device at work, home, and elsewhere?** When you find a grant-funding opportunity that has a close deadline (such as 48 hours from your discovery of the availability of new money), can you quickly prepare a funding request and attach the mandatory documents from your cabin in the mountains?

  Oh, by the way, did you know that grant professionals (grant writers with experience, grit, and speed-reading skills) never leave their homes without their laptops or tablets in the event they will have to prepare a grant application from the seating area of an airport gate, a hotel room, or the beach? Yep, grant writers are in high demand, and if they want to keep their jobs and clients, they must be able to be attentive, responsive, and ready to write anytime, anywhere.

Before you apply for grant funding (the pre-award phase)

Here are the documents that you should upload to a cloud folder (such as Dropbox, OneDrive, Google Drive, or another one of your choice):

- Updated mission, vision, and value statements
- Current strategic plan
- Current organizational chart
- Current fact sheets and flowcharts for all programs (how services are or will be delivered)

- Memoranda of Understanding (MOUs) or Memoranda of Agreement (MOAs) from a minimum of five community or regional collaborative agencies that are committed to providing matching funding or in-kind (soft cash) contributions
- Accurate and thorough job descriptions for all program staff (filled as well as unfilled positions)
- Updated résumés and bios for current staff (limit to maximum of two pages each)
- Organizational budgets for current and next fiscal year
- Current financial statements
- Current financial audit report
- Articles of incorporations and bylaws
- Certificate of good standing from the state agency where the articles of incorporation were filed
- Most recent IRS Form-990 (nonprofit tax return form) or 990-N (for newer nonprofits with minimal revenues during their most recent fiscal year)
- Current data about your volunteers: number of volunteers, total hours per volunteer per year, and value of their contribution (for more, see `https://independentsector.org/value-of-volunteer-time-2021/`)
- Current board of directors' policies and procedures
- Current board of directors' roster/list (member names, officers identified, terms, professional titles, affiliations, contact information, gender, and ethnicity)
- Current boilerplate document that contains organizational history, including year founded, number and qualifications of staff, list of programs, mission, vision, values, awards, stories and testimonials, accreditations, certifications, and recent accomplishments
- Current map of target area(s) for service delivery and demographics about the target population (those you will serve with grant funding)
- Recent evaluation reports with program service-related outcomes and/or performance measures collected
- Current logic model for every program
- Current sustainability statement (must be created by the board of directors)
- Evidence of capability to manage grant awards (accounting practices and evidence of a clear audit trail for expenses paid for with grant funding)

After you receive your first grant award (the post-award phase)

You wanted to bring more money into your organization, and that's a great goal. However, is your organization ready to manage grant awards from small to mega-amounts? Here's a checklist for evaluating your post-award grant-management capabilities:

- Thorough understanding of grant-funding reporting and accounting requirements
- Ability to track and report cash-match commitments by budget expense line items
- Ability to understand how to track and report in-kind (soft cash) contributions by budget expense line items

Procedures required for grant award risk management

At this point, you're likely wondering why risk management is even necessary. The answer is to ensure that organizational ethics are in place in the event of a funder's audit or a lawsuit filed by a disgruntled client, participant, partner agency, staff member, or volunteer. It's better to be safe than sorry!

- Liability insurance coverage for the board of directors
- Sexual molestation insurance rider if you are providing services to youth
- Drug and criminal background screening policies and practices
- Policy for check writing and the number of authorized signatures needed (who can sign and countersign)
- Board of directors composition reflects the population you serve with grant funding

Building your governing board's capacity

If your board of directors has not been trained in nonprofit organizational capacity building, get them trained fast. What do they need to know? Let's take a look at all of the areas that a new and/or small nonprofit board needs to know about:

- Boardsmanship (Robert's Rules of Order) (www.rulesonline.com)
- Board member roles and responsibilities (https://boardable.com/blog/board-member-responsibilities/)
- Teamwork and consensus building (www.forbes.com/sites/forbesnonprofitcouncil/2020/03/16/13-tips-for-facilitating-teamwork-with-a-nonprofit-board-of-directors/?sh=17cd0527786e)
- Responsibilities of board committees (https://boardsource.org/resources/board-responsibilities-structures-faqs/)
- Strategic planning for sustainability (https://nonprofitinformation.com/nonprofit-sustainability/)
- How to raise funds for your nonprofit organization (https://boardable.com/blog/nonprofit-board-fundraising/)

Assessing your nonprofit organization's capacity to seek grants

Conducting an annual organizational self-assessment is important; the assessment's findings help you identify capacity strengths and challenges so that your organization can create capacity-building goals. Here are the most important areas to assess:

- **Leadership capacity:** Your leadership's ability to inspire, prioritize, make decisions, provide direction, and know how to innovate existing static programs into promising fundable programs.
- **Adaptive capacity:** Your board and leaders' ability to monitor, assess, and respond to internal and external changes related to grant seeking and managing grant awards.
- **Management capacity:** Your leadership's ability to ensure the effective and efficient use of organizational resources, such as in-kind soft cash match for grant awards.
- **Operational capacity:** Your leadership's ability to implement key organizational and programmatic functions to fulfill the written promise of a funded grant request.

Creating a Grant-Funding Plan

Your grant-funding plan is really a guide and a roadmap for where the dollars will come from for two years to support your programs. Just a few years ago, the trend was to create three- to five-year long-range funding plans. Today, if an organization wants to be on the cutting edge and able to roll with the economic punches, as well as the shifts in priorities by existing funding sources, its strategy needs to focus on two fiscal years. Yes, that's it — 24 months.

If you have current funders that traditionally fund your organization year after year, their decision-making processes will be shorter. For example, if you have a track record for implementation success (carrying out the program's goals and activities that you committed to in writing), then there is likely a turnaround time of six months or less from the time your organization requests funding until you get the check in the mail.

On the other hand, if you're planning to approach new funders, which means building a relationship before asking, the time between the grant application's submission and the funding decision could be longer than 12 months. What you thought would be awarded in this fiscal year won't be coming into your bank account until the *next* fiscal year. This means you need to track funding priorities and decision-making time frames so you don't build your annual organizational operating budget on dollars that won't come in for 12 to 24 months.

REMEMBER

This is a grant-funding plan for your *grant-seeking* goals. But there are also funding plans for securing dollars from individual contributions, special events, and miscellaneous sources. This minibook is focused solely on grant writing, however, which means you need to focus on developing a plan for going after grants from all types of grantors.

The following sections acquaint you with the components of a typical grant-funding plan, show you an example of one, and give you a checklist of how to keep your plan in tiptop shape.

Looking at the funding plan components

The grant-funding plan (created in table format) that we use the most for grant seeking captures eight fields in this order (see Figure 2-1):

- **Program, Service, or Activity:** This is where you list the program, service, or activity priorities that are written in your organization's strategic plan.

» **Funding Source:** In this column, you identify the funding source(s) that you plan to approach to support your programs, services, or activities in the current and next fiscal years.

TIP

You can have multiple funding sources that you contact for one program. Putting all your eggs in one basket (applying to only one funder) and then receiving a rejection letter nine months later is not your goal. If you did that, you would have to start all over with only three months left in the year. Approach multiple funders for every program, service, or activity in need of funding.

» **Address, Telephone, Email, and Website:** By incorporating this column into your funding plan, you have clickable links to quickly email or review the websites of current and potential funders. Adding the mailing address reduces your time-on-task when sending out a letter of inquiry. And, most important, the phone number is handy when you need to speak with the designated contact person for the funder.

» **Contact Person/Title:** Research the funder's website and even call their office to make sure that you have the correct name of the contact person and their title. Make sure to ask how the contact person gender-identifies, if there's any chance of confusion. Names like Chris and Pat can belong to men and women.

» **Request:** The amount of grant funding that you plan to request goes in this column. Make sure to review the funder's profile for their grant-making range. Stay below the top of the range if you're a first-time grant applicant with the funder.

» **Application Deadline/Giving Cycle:** This column captures the grant application's deadline(s) and when grants are awarded by the funder. Some funders only accept and award grants once a year, while others may have multiple grant application submission deadlines and giving cycles.

» **Assigned To:** In this column, you add the name(s) of the board member(s) or administrative-level staff that are assigned to making contact with the funder to continue previous funding conversations or begin initial conversations with new funders.

» **Status/Results:** This is where you insert the status of the funding request for example: "Contacting in September," "First contact meeting went well on September 5, 2022," "Grant application submitted on September 5, 2022," or "Funding declined for September 2022 giving cycle; letter indicated to apply again next year (2023); follow-up meeting requested to discuss problems with grant application."

Funding Plan: ABC Nonprofit Organization January 2, 2022–December 31, 2023							
Most recent modification date:							
Program, Service or Activity	**Funding Source**	**Address, Telephone, Email, and Website**	**Contact Person/Title**	**Request**	**Application Deadline/Giving Cycle**	**Assigned To**	**Status/Results**
Nonprofit Capacity Building Services	Mt. Morris Community Foundation	7777 S. 77th Rd., Branson, MI 85341 No website published info@mtmorris@gmail.com	Dr. Bev Browning, Program Officer for Community Capacity Building Initiatives	$50,000	February 3 Notification letters will be sent out September 1.	New funder contact team: Board President and Grant Writer	Face-to-face meeting scheduled for November 4, 2016.
	Miracle Bank Corporate Giving Program	555 W. Wonderland Dr., Browning, AR 55555 jbrowning@mb.com www.mb.com	Mr. John Browning, Corporate Giving Director	$10,000	February 10 Award letters will be sent within six weeks of submission date; rejected requests will not be notified.	Board Treasurer and Executive Director	Conference call scheduled for January 10 (Board Treasurer's wife works at this bank).
After School Academic Enhancement	Specifica Department of Education Services – 21st Century Community Learnings Centers grant program	4243 S. State Funding Ave., Specifica, MO 87878 sjones@specificadoe.mo.gov www.spedificadoe.mo.ogv	Dr. Sydney Jones, Director 21st Century Community Learning Centers Program	$150,000 per year for three years	March 5 Notification emails will be sent by July 15.	Grant writing consultant specializing in writing this specific grant application	Grant writer attending new applicant orientation meeting on January 28. She will report back to the Executive Director before starting work on the application.
	Grant Writing Training Foundation	P.O. Box 9999, Goodyear, AZ 77777 ascott@gwtf.org www.gwtf.org	Ms. Aaliyah Scott, Executive Director	$25,000	Continuation application due April 4. This money is already committed to our organization and a request for Year 2 of 4 funding. Check will be issued within four weeks of continuation application submission date.	Grant writing consultant	Annual funding supporter. Needs to receive a letter of appreciation from the Board of Directors and be included in our annual partnership luncheon. Board will take action at next meeting.

FIGURE 2-1: An example of a funding plan.

Updating critical funding plan information

The Status/Results column of your funding plan (refer to Figure 2-1) must be updated continuously. After you meet with the funder and can assess their level of interest in supporting your organization, you'll need to change the meeting status note to the feedback received and add the next step (for example, "Apply this cycle," "Wait until next year," or "Not interested in this project"). Here are some essential activities needed on your part to keep the funding plan a working document:

- **Write it down.** You need to officially document your funding plan ideas. Create funding plan templates and hand one to everyone at the meeting. This way, all parties are on board and writing/talking about the same things in the same sequence.
- **Use it.** The funding plan must become a daily guide to help your organization decide what programs or services have funding priority and how to fund them most logically.
- **Keep it up to date.** Update your funding plan's Status/Results column every time you apply for grant funding or receive the results of your efforts. Record whether you're being funded, and if so, the funding amount. If you don't secure the money, find out why your efforts failed.
- **Review and revise it annually.** Why? Both your needs and funders' priorities change, sometimes as often as annually. For example, just because a lot of money is available for programs for after-school academic programs this year doesn't mean that this funding area will still be the focus next year.

  Your plan must change to reflect what funders want to fund. In other words, your funding plan isn't just about what your organization wants or needs; it's about what funders want to fund within the parameters of your organization's mission.

REMEMBER

REMEMBER

Involve both your board of directors and your administrative staff in fleshing out the funding plan and updating it. Sit down and have a brainstorming session to determine your funding priorities. Ask administrative staff about unmet needs, waiting lists, or any feedback from frontline employees. Ask board members to assess programmatic weaknesses from their viewpoint as well. When the Status/Results column changes, update it immediately and get a copy of the modified plan document out to all who need it as their roadmap for assignments.

TIP

Keep your funding plan flexible. Funders change their priorities often, and your target population's needs are likely to change as well. So be willing to review previous evaluation reports or results from funded programs and stay on top of newly released community needs assessments. Update the funding plan by removing and adding programs and services, and then incorporate these changes into your revised document.

Increasing Your Chances for Grant-Seeking Success

When you're ready to start your grant-funding research, keep your funding plan template close at hand. You're likely to find a lot of potential funding opportunities, so reading the opportunity and then perusing the plan to make sure the opportunity fits is a smart move. You're searching for perfect fits between what you need and what the funder wants to fund.

REMEMBER

The best way to sustain a high funding success rate is to identify multiple funding sources for each project initiative in your funding plan. Then submit your grant proposals to all of them.

TIP

Sending out multiple proposals is standard practice as long as you tell all the funders that you plan to approach other sources. Providing each proposal with a simple one-page attachment labeled "Funding Sources Receiving This Request" is the most ethical way to inform all funders of your strategy. (See an example of such a document in Chapter 13 of this minibook.) Or you can list other sources you've approached on the actual grant application, if such a section exists.

The following sections explain what you need to know to find a broad range of potential funding sources.

Looking for needles in a haystack

To identify as many potential grant-funding sources as possible for your organization, you need to carefully research the primary sources of funding: the public sector (federal, state, and local government) and the private sector (foundations and corporations).

As you read information on each funder, you see few, if any, funders want to receive a grant proposal without any warning from the applicant. For many, you need to, in a sense, be invited to submit a full grant request after you've met each funder's initial contact requirements. That's why your *initial approach* (your first contact with the funder) is so important.

Review each funder's initial approach preference using their website or funding database subscription to find what *initial contact* or *approach document* they require. Chapter 5 of this minibook covers how to find private-sector funders and mine the right information. You can find more information regarding these documents in the later section, "Using a letter of inquiry intent to comply with pre-application guidelines."

REMEMBER

Focus on finding open or current grant-funding opportunities first. Then you can print out expired notices and contact the grant-making agency to see whether the funding will be available again in the future.

TIP

Create a day-to-day work plan to monitor a project that will require multiple funding requests. When you're juggling multiple funders, stay organized by using a table or spreadsheet format to develop a work plan and also plot this information, as shown in Figure 2-2. Your work plan is an extension of all the details plotted out in your funding plan. The work plan is an ancillary document to track all potential funders for one program. Make sure the funder number listed on your table matches up with the correct grant proposal. Also, as you move through the application process, fill in the last two columns on the right-hand side. In the status column, you can enter: writing scheduled, writing in progress, submitted, and pending decision. For the outcome column, you can fill in funded or rejected when you know.

Tracking Multiple Potential Funders

Funder	Initial Approach	Deadline	Average Range of Funding	Anticipated Notification Date	Date Submitted	Status	Outcome
1	E-grant application	Rolling annually	Up to $5,000	90 days from submission			
2	Letter proposal	June 15 & December 15 annually	Up to $15,000	60 days following deadline			
3	Common Grant Application	April 1 annually	Up to $12,000	60 days following deadline			
4	Letter of inquiry	1st of each month annually	Up to $15,000	30 days from submission			
5	Online letter of inquiry	Rolling annually	Up to $25,000	90 days from submission			
6	E-grant application	December 31	Up to $10,000	90 days following deadline			
7	E-grant application	April & October	Up to $25,000	60 days from submission			
8	E-grant application	Quarterly	Up to $1,000	45 days from submission			
9	Letter of inquiry	May 15 annually	Up to $2,500	45 days following deadline			
10	Letter of inquiry	Rolling annually	Up to $5,000	60 days from submission			

Illustration by Ryan Sneed

FIGURE 2-2: Make a chart to track multiple potential funders for one program.

Conducting a federal funding search

Thankfully, the federal government aids your federal funding search with its one-stop grant opportunity information website, Grants.gov (www.grants.gov). Visiting this site is the quickest way to conduct a federal funding search.

After you log on to Grants.gov, choose Grant Opportunities from the Search drop-down. Then type your search terms in the Keyword(s) Search field. Sample keywords include "after school," "capacity building," "rural telecommunications," and "prevention." Your search should produce a list of federal grant opportunity announcements that contain your keyword(s). Simply click each one to read the announcement and determine whether it fits your specific funding needs.

TIP

You may want to search Grants.gov on a weekly or monthly basis because the federal government releases new grant opportunity announcements daily (except for federal holidays). Or simply sign up for Grants.gov alerts under Manage Subscriptions (in the upper-right corner of the homepage) to get free alerts by email.

Performing a foundation or corporate funding search

When you're ready to conduct a foundation or corporate funding search, the place to turn to is Candid (`https://candid.org`). This center's resources and online grant-research database (*Foundation Directory Online* by Candid) provide grant seekers, grant makers, researchers, policy-makers, the media, and the general public with up-to-date information on grant funding and other nonprofit-related issues.

Through the *Foundation Directory Online* by Candid, you can download profiles of foundations whose interests, priorities, and types of funding support match your funding needs. These profiles include the foundation's address, website, contact person, funding priorities, award range, preferred method of initial approach, and much more. To conduct your search, you can either subscribe to the directory (varying levels of subscriptions are available), or use Candid's website to locate a Funding Information Network (FIN) near you that has a subscription to the directory.

TIP

When you start using the Candid's resources, you see several information fields for entering your keywords. Keep it simple. If you're looking for money to provide housing for the homeless, first search for "housing" and screen the results. For the second search, type in "homeless" and again screen the results, eliminating duplicate funders found in the first search. This search approach yields far more potential grant sources than typing in a search string made of two or more words. Be sure to check the box to exclude foundations that don't accept unsolicited grant proposals to save yourself considerable time and disappointment. (Refer to Chapter 5 of this minibook for more about foundation and corporate grants.)

TIP

To find out more about researching foundation or corporate funding sources located outside the United States, visit the Fundsnet Services website (`https://fundsnetservices.com`). It's accessible, free of charge, and has pages of international funders listed.

Talking to potential funders

Some funders indicate in their grant database profiles or on their websites that a potential grant seeker should call and speak to one of their program officers before submitting a letter of inquiry or attempting to submit an online e-grant application request. The purpose of this request is to circumvent any applicants that have funding requests that do not align with their mission, values, funding priorities, or preferred geographic areas.

In other words, funders do not want to be bothered with unnecessary paperwork from organizations they do not intend to fund. This saves time on their part and on your part. Don't chase lost leaders; that is, funders not interested in receiving any form of written information from you or your organization.

If you do have an opportunity to email, call, Zoom, or meet in-person with a potential funder, you might wonder what you should say. Here are a few short lists of guiding scripts for every possible form of contact with potential funders:

Contact via email:

- » Introduce yourself and your organization to the funder.
- » Tell the funder why you are contacting them (shared mission, previous funding from them, Board of Director connection, attendance at one of their technical assistance meetings or webinars, or some attention-grabbing connection).
- » State your problem.
- » Give the solution.
- » Share the amount of funding needed.
- » Ask for permission to submit a full funding request based on their guidelines.
- » Thank them for their time.
- » Proofread and send the email.
- » Follow up in five days.

Video meeting or telephone contact:

- » Be ready.
- » Have a written script.
- » Have a timer (or a three-minute hourglass).

- Keep it simple.
- Speak with a smile.
- Take copious notes.

In-person meeting:

- Prepare a folder with relevant information on your organization.
- If you are going to work with a fiscal agent, make sure to include at least one fact sheet about the fiscal agent.
- Take a copy of your IRS 501(c)(3) tax-exempt approval letter.
- Listen to the funder and take notes, if needed.
- Do not be overzealous! Do not talk for more than three minutes at a time.

Using a letter of inquiry to comply with pre-application guidelines

Many foundations state in their published guidelines that they prefer the initial approach to be a *letter of inquiry*, which is a one- to three-page letter in which you ask about their interest in receiving a full grant proposal from your organization. This letter allows the funder to make sure that what you're requesting is within its area of interest and funding award range. Nowadays, some foundation funders require a brief letter of inquiry because they're overwhelmed with requests for funding and the letter is a way to weed out applicants.

Candid is one source for linking to foundation websites to view their funding guidelines. Another way is to use your favorite Internet search engine to locate the funder's website. Checking a funder's website provides you with the most current guidelines. You may also find that some foundation funders have online inquiry forms; others request a letter of inquiry. However, not all foundations, particularly smaller local foundations, have websites. If the foundation doesn't have a website, be sure to get in touch with the contact person identified in the Foundation Center's foundation profile.

Use the following suggestions to practice crafting your own letter of inquiry:

- **All requests for funding must be on grant applicant letterhead, unless otherwise specified by the grantor, which can often be the case in electronic LOI forms and those with upload options.** This introductory format gives the funding agency a clear visual affirmation of the applicant organization, its location, and how to contact the applicant in writing, by telephone, or by email.

- **Call the funder to verify the gender, name, title, and address of the contact person.** After all, to make a professional impression with the letter of inquiry, the contact person's information must be correct.

  REMEMBER

  Verifying contact information is especially important when you're contacting a funder whose first name is gender-ambiguous, such as Terry, Pat, or Kim. Find out whether that person is a Ms., Mrs., Mr., or Dr. Respect titles and use them to reach the right person the first time.

- **In the first two sentences, introduce your organization.** Tell the funding agency who's sending the letter, your nonprofit status, and why you're reaching out. For example:
  - *The Grant Writing Training Foundation is a 501(c)(3) private operating foundation located in Arizona. As director, I am writing to invite your organization to be a financial stakeholder in the foundation's mission to provide affordable training programs.*

- **In the next two to four sentences, plant the seeds for your needs.** Share startling facts and statistics about the problem your organization seeks to address with grant funds:
  - *Annually, the foundation is approached by approximately 40 small- to mid-size nonprofit organizations that want to host a Grant Writing Boot Camp at their location. The typical potential site host is an intermediary agency like the United Way or the state-level association of nonprofits. Given this discouraging economy, board members, volunteers, and inexperienced staff members at many organizations are all given the task of grant writing; few, if any, have experience and most don't know how to begin this massive technical process.*

- **In one sentence, note how you want the recipient to be involved.** Ask for the funding agency's investment or partnership in your efforts to provide specific programs and services to the target population:
  - *Our board realizes that the foundation cannot financially afford to accept all invitations for training partnerships; however, with your assistance, we can at least develop a productive training schedule to meet the demand for our programs.*

- **In no more than three sentences, show the funder your plans by writing futuristic global goals.** For the example here, write something like "The foundation's goals are to" and then add the goals.

- **In no more than seven sentences, sell, tell, and ask directly for help.** For example, sell the funder on the problem or need that the grant funds will address, tell the story in plain language, and ask for grant-funding support, including the amount of funding needed:
  - *Other nationally accredited grant-seeking and proposal-writing training programs are often three to five days in length and charge $2,000+ per registrant. Feedback from previous attendees at these types of workshops (survey conducted annually for the past five years by the Foundation) shows that the trainer is reading from a script and unable to answer critical questions on the spot. In addition, the elongated training time frame is not appealing for anyone who has to take a full week off from work at their employer's expense. The Grant Writing Training Foundation's two-day Grant Writing Boot Camp is comprehensive, compressed, and internationally accredited by several national grants industry associations. Registrants receive 14 continuing education units, a* Grant Writing For Dummies *reference book, and a notebook full of writing exercises and resources. Our board is asking you to consider underwriting at least 10 Boot Camps next year at a cost of $20,000 each (20 registrants will attend each of the ten two-day sessions free of charge).*
- **In one sentence, ask for technical assistance if the funder can't fund your project.** Some needs your organization identifies may be instructional rather than monetary. For example, you may ask the funder to show you how to do a specific task, and then you can combine that knowledge with the resources that you have:
  - *If you cannot consider awarding grant funds at this time, the board is asking for technical assistance in connecting with state-level nonprofit associations, councils, and foundations that may be potential site hosts.*
- **In one sentence, show hope in your closing.** Sign off with "Waiting to hear from you," "Hopefully," or some other impactful closing.
- **In one line of type, make sure the CEO signs the letter of inquiry.** This step shows that the top administrator for your organization is aware of your request for grant funding.
- **Remember to proofread the letter yourself, as well as have someone else provide input on the content and character of the letter.**

TIP

You can find a template for a letter of inquiry at `https://www.dummies.com/book-companion/grant-writing-for-dummies-7th-edition-companion-site-290757/`.

Using a letter of intent

Some government grant-making agencies and a handful of foundations request a *letter of intent* (a document that states you intend to apply for a grant in an open/active funding cycle). Just about all the funders that request a letter of intent have their own specific online format.

You can find an example of the letter of intent format (predominantly requested from federal grant-making agencies) at the U.S. Department of Justice website (`www.justice.gov/ovw/page/file/1107796/download`). It is one of 26 federal grant-making agencies. This file is a PDF download of a one-page letter of intent's suggested content.

Waiting Patiently for Next Steps

After you have communicated with a potential funder, if the foundation's director or program officer does not invite you to submit a letter of inquiry or grant application on behalf of your nonprofit organization, wait at least 3-4 weeks after the encounter. At that time, you can pick up the telephone and call to inquire if it's okay to submit a letter of inquiry or a grant application and ask for the suggested grant request range. Make sure to confirm which one of your programs they are most interested in reading more about.

If the potential funder says they are not able to support your nonprofit organization at this time, politely thank them and ask if it's okay to circle back to them in the next funding cycle or the next fiscal year. Count to ten and start the initial contact process with the next funder in your funding plan. This is a rinse-and-repeat process until you hit the jackpot and are invited to submit a request for funding.

IN THIS CHAPTER

» Taking a close look at nearby public funding

» Stepping into the world of federal grant-making agencies

» Understanding the different types of grants

Chapter 3
Venturing into Public-Sector Grants

This chapter takes you on a journey down the government's grant-making highway, which starts in Congress and ends in your state, county, town, village, or city. Before we get started, though, let's set the record straight when it comes to government money: There is no such thing as a "free" grant or "free money." Every grant award comes with strings attached. Either you have to spend your own money first (reimbursement grant) and submit receipts to get grant funds, or you have to file reams of electronic paperwork to generate an electronic funds transfer into your organization's bank account.

Looking for Local Funding First

Washington, D.C., is a funding epicenter for U.S. government grant-making agencies. Congress creates legislation and then votes to allocate funding to hundreds of grant-making programs annually. This funding then trickles down to your state capital. (Note that there are plentiful opportunities for nonprofits and units of local government to apply directly to a federal funding agency for a grant, providing they are eligible grant applicants.)

Federal dollars trickle down in three forms:

- **Formula:** This money is paid based on a preset head-count (enrollments and population) formula.
- **Entitlement:** State agencies get these monies because federal legislation entitles them to receive it every fiscal year. An entitlement grant is one in which funds are provided to specific grantees on the basis of a formula, prescribed in legislation or regulation, rather than on the basis of an individual project. The formula is usually based on such factors as population, enrollment, per-capita income, or a specific need. Entitlement grants often result in pass-through grants to municipalities and nonprofits.
- **Competitive grant or cooperative agreement awards:** The state, municipality, nonprofit, or other grant applicant with the best grant application wins this money.

Some states and U.S. territories post all their federal pass-through funding and re-granting opportunities on one website. (*Re-granting* and *pass-through* refer to grants made from the monies a state or territory has received from the federal government.) In addition, some states and territories develop their own grant programs funded entirely through state dollars. If you're fortunate enough to live in a state or territory that does so, check out their website for a mailing list. You may be able to sign up for email grant notice alerts from their Capitol-based agencies.

However, most states or territories don't post these announcements where they are easy to find, so you have to be a really great Internet detective to find the monies in your state or territory (not to mention in Washington, D.C.). You need to surf a bit each day to catch all the new postings for grant-funding opportunities. When we're searching for state grants in Washington state, we use Google and type in "grants, state of Washington agencies." The results are a list of state agencies in Washington state that have grant-funding opportunities posted on their websites.

REMEMBER

Most state and territory grants usually award less money and require just as much paperwork as federal grants. But the odds of winning a grant are better at the state level than at the federal level. It's a no-brainer: The main reason you face better odds is that fewer grant applicants are competing for the state-level monies.

The next sections reveal how to find grant monies available at the state and local government levels.

Finding out where the money is in your state or territory

To find grant opportunities at the state level:

- **Visit your state government or territory website.** If you search the state site and can't find a listing of all the state's grant opportunities, call the governor's office and ask to be directed to the various agencies that give grants. Only track grant-funding opportunities from the agency that administers the federal programming for the type of funding that your organization is seeking. For example, a charter school will track state Department of Education grant alerts. A substance abuse prevention agency will track state Department of Health and/or Human Services grant alerts.
- **Email or call each appropriate state agency.** Contact the agencies responsible for carrying out legislative funding mandates relevant to your own funding needs and be sure to get on their mailing lists for grant-funding opportunity alerts.

When you receive an alert about a state or territory grant-funding opportunity you're interested in applying for, look for the link that connects you to the grant application summary and download the complete grant application (including guidelines). Look for the following information:

- **Type of application:** Is it an electronic or a print application? For example, the majority of grant applications are submitted electronically via online e-grant portals; some state agencies can still only accept hard copies.
- **Due date:** Make sure the due date is manageable and gives you enough time to collect topic-related information and write the application. A reasonable amount of time is 30 days from the date the grant-funding announcement is published or issued via email and the actual due date of the application.
- **Who's eligible to apply:** Every grant competition has a section listing the types of grant applicants eligible to apply for funds (see Chapter 1 of this minibook for more about eligibility). If your organization's forming structure (local education agency, nonprofit, and so forth) isn't listed, consider partnering with an eligible applicant. (Head to chapters 6 and 7 of this minibook for more on finding the right grant-seeking partners.) You may also want to contact the funding agency to clarify any non-published eligible applicants because your organization may be eligible to apply after all.
- **The number of grants to be awarded:** You may have to call the funding agency's contact person to find out the number of available grants; this information often isn't included in state grant application guidelines.

TIP

Unless you're the only organization delivering highly specialized services/programs and have no competitors, don't apply for competitive grant funds where fewer than three awards will be made statewide. The fewer the number of grant awards, the worse the odds are for winning an award.

All grant applicants have a fair chance of winning a state or territory agency grant award if a sufficient number of awards are available. Always ask how many grants will be awarded so you know how many ways the money will be divided. This information can help you develop a more competitive project budget — staying conservative and on the low end of the average grant range. (Browse Chapter 12 of this minibook for pointers on putting together a winning budget section in your grant or cooperative agreement proposal.)

Looking for pass-through funding

At the local government level (county, town, village, township, hamlet, and city), look for public monies at the County Board of Commissioners, local Area Agencies on Aging, the Mayor's Office on Neighborhoods (or a similar Federal Community Development Block Grant administrator), regional housing authorities (they sub-grant for neighborhood-based services), your county-based department of social services, and more. All these agencies receive direct funding from state agencies and federal pass-through funding for re-granting purposes at the local level (more on pass-through funding in the following section).

TIP

Because not all funding opportunities are posted on websites that are easy to find, you want to develop connections with agency representatives to find out the inside scoop. Also, ask questions of local elected officials and track down these publicly available grant funds. Be aggressive in asking questions about what funds are available, who can apply, and who the contract person is for the agency re-granting the monies.

Analyzing the Types of Federal Funding Available

Federal government grant monies come in two forms:

- **Direct grants:** You apply directly to the federal government. There is no intermediary agency.

» **Pass-through grants:** Your state applies to the federal government for a grant. After receiving the grant, the state then passes the federal monies on to applicants.

REMEMBER

Pass-through monies are still considered federal monies even though they're distributed by state agencies.

Whether in the form of direct or pass-through grants, federal monies are also classified as either *competitive* or *formula.*

This section provides you with the scoop on the pros and cons of direct and pass-through grants, and some details you need to know about competitive and formula grants. *Note:* Some of the terms in this section may seem to overlap with the kinds of allocations listed earlier in the chapter, but that's just because the government ran out of unique names to use (that's our theory, anyway). The grants in this section are different entities from those earlier terms.

Discovering direct grants

The advantages to applying for a direct grant award or *cooperative agreement,* which comes straight from the federal government, include the following:

» **Direct grants have no middlemen and none of the extra layers of red tape added by intermediary grant-making agencies.** You apply directly to the federal government for a grant in response to an announcement of the availability of funds.

» **When you compete for a direct grant, you communicate directly with a program officer in a division of a federal agency.** This interaction means one-on-one attention, so be sure to review the application guidelines thoroughly and then compile all your questions. You can email or call the grant-making agency's contact person for clarification and answers. Doing so up front clears the way for the topic research and the grant-writing process.

REMEMBER

Avoid being a nuisance! Don't call and make small talk. Have your questions ready before approaching the agency contact and ask if the individual prefers to have questions emailed. Be prepared to take copious notes. If you feel you still lack a clear answer about how to proceed, ask again.

Some federal agencies have a deadline for submitting questions via email or by phone; read the grant application guidelines to make sure you can still make the call or email contact. If the window has passed, look at the agency's website for a link to frequently asked questions (FAQs). Others have probably asked the same questions you have, and the agency may have posted the answer for the general public to review. Also, remember to check daily for modifications to the initially posted grant applications guidelines.

TIP

Once you identify funding opportunities that you want to track, you can sign up for Grants.gov grants and receive email notifications when the application cycle opens for forecasted funding. To subscribe to those notifications, you need to register for an individual account (login and password required). Then just click Subscribe in the upper-right corner of the funding opportunities Synopsis tab.

TIP

Many federal agencies host a technical assistance call or webcast in which potential applicants can participate. In this forum, program staff members responsible for the grant application typically provide an overview of the application notice, highlighting key points of information, and then open the call to questions from potential applicants. These discussions provide a great opportunity to hear from program officers, ask questions, and learn from the questions of other applicants. You can find the date, time, and access information for any webinar in the full Notice of Funding Availability (NOFA) announcement, Request for Proposal (RFP), Funding Opportunity Announcement (FOA), or Request for Application (RFA), as well as on the funding agency's program-specific website. It's important to participate in these webinars to hear the full scope of what's expected in a grant application recommended for funding.

Look for a link to the Full Announcement on the Related Documents tab in the View Grant Opportunity page (the same link you clicked to view the Synopsis). Figure 3-1 shows you what to expect when you're on the Grants.gov site (`www.grants.gov`), perusing a NOFA, RFP, FOA, or RFA.

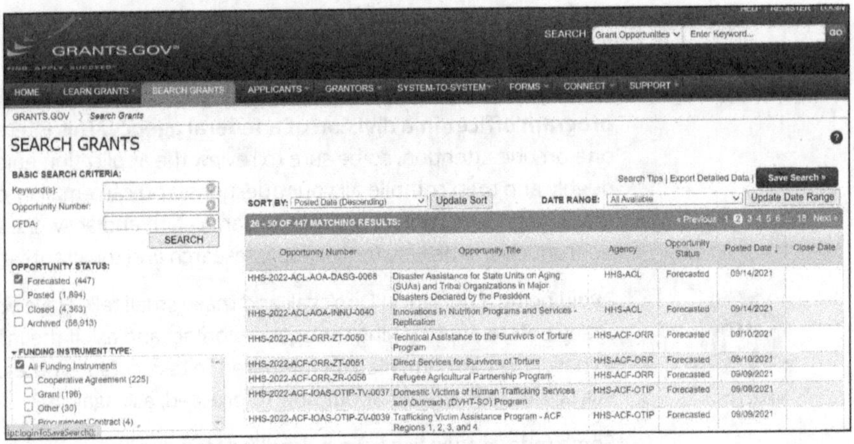

FIGURE 3-1: Figuring out differences among types of federal grants.

Source: `https://www.dummies.com/business/nonprofits/grants/how-to-figure-out-differences-among-types-of-federal-grants/`

WARNING

The one major disadvantage to applying for a direct grant award is that they're tough to win. You compete with other grant applicants from all 50 states and U.S. territories. If the feds are only planning to award money to ten grant applicants, your chances are slim — even with a stellar funding request. You may even be competing with state agencies, which further narrows your chances. Urban and rural poverty pockets receive first priority for most social-services-related program funding (such as housing, education, and health and human services) and other grant-making areas earmarked for social-issue hot spots. If you aren't proposing services in one of these high-needs geographic funding areas, your chances of winning a federal grant from a competition that gives 5 to 25 extra review points to high-needs, census-data-supported geographic areas are reduced to almost nothing. Not all funding programs have these types of service priorities.

Using the eligible applicant criteria to track the funding stream

Pass-through grants have two advantages:

- **When you apply for pass-through grant funds at the state level, you compete against other grant applicants in your state only.** As a result, you encounter considerably less competition than at the federal, direct grant-seeking level.
- **When you're making an appearance before the state agency program staff, you can get info on previously funded grants.** Under the Freedom of Information Act (FOIA), all government agencies must provide requested public information to the requestor (you, the public), so don't feel like you're being a bother. Make sure the list contains the grant recipients and award amounts. And ask for a copy of a successful grant application from a previous competition. Knowing how winners write can boost your chances.

TIP

You can use the FOIA to obtain information about all types of grants funded by any government agency.

The only disadvantage to applying for pass-through grants is that the grant awards are often smaller than those for a direct grant. The legislation determines the award allocation. So, it's a trade-off: Pass-through awards are smaller, but they're also easier to win.

Pass-through grant awards can be significantly smaller than direct grant awards because the state takes money off the top of each federal grant to cover administrative costs. Then the amount that's left must be divided geographically and politically. For example, grants may go to certain areas of a state or territory because those areas haven't won many grant awards recently. The money may go to other areas because that district's state senator or representative has a lot of power and influence with a state agency. Like it or not, politics can have a major influence over grant making.

Knowing the difference between competitive and formula grants

To win a *competitive grant* or cooperative agreement, you must compete with other grant applicants for a limited amount of money. A team of *peer reviewers* (experts and laypeople who apply to read and score grant applications) looks at your application and decides how many points you receive for each narrative section in the body of the grant request. The applications with the highest scores are recommended for funding. (See Chapter 7 of this minibook for details on the peer review process for grant applications.)

A *formula grant* (a fill-in-the-blanks, no-brainer form), on the other hand, is money disbursed by a state agency or municipality to a grant applicant based on a preset standard or formula.

A great example of formula monies is a grant program administered by the U.S. Department of Justice. The Justice Assistance Grant (JAG) Program (not to be confused with the military's Judge Advocate General Program) is the leading source of federal justice funding to state and local jurisdictions. The program provides monies to states, territories, tribes, and local governments, which they in turn use to support program areas including law enforcement, prosecution and courts, prevention and education, corrections and community corrections, drug treatment and enforcement, planning, evaluation, technology improvement, and crime victim and witness programs. All JAG allocations are calculated by the Bureau of Justice Statistics (BJS) based on the statutory JAG formula and displayed on the JAG website each fiscal year.

Learning your way around Grants.gov

Every day you can receive a free email alert from Grants.gov announcing grant-funding opportunities from any of the federal grant-making agencies. Just log on and subscribe. Simply choose one or more agencies and wait 24 hours to start cruising through the daily list of federal grant announcements.

Here's how Grants.gov can help you find federal grant monies for your organization:

- **You can search for current and past grant-funding opportunities.** Log on daily and check for postings in your area of interest. A subject search (for example, "housing," "legal services," or "after-school programs") is the easiest way to narrow down specific grant competitions in your project or program area. Using the Newest Opportunities tab on the homepage allows you to double-check for federal funding availability alerts you may have missed.

- **You can register for notification of grant opportunities.** Subscribe to a daily email alert. Look for the Manage Subscriptions link at the upper right of the homepage.
- **You can browse through the Applicants tab (at the top of the homepage) to look at all sorts of materials.** For example, you can learn about the Grants.gov workspace, apply for grants, track your application, or click one of the resource links for grant eligibility, individual and organization registrations, applicant tools and tips, applicant FAQs, submitting UTF-8 special characters in your upload filenames, Adobe software compatibility, and encountering error messages.

You can also apply for grants directly through Grants.gov after you've reviewed the Apply for Grants link under the Applicants tab and completed the registration process.

REMEMBER

You must be registered in order to upload your grant application documents to Grants.gov.

After registering, you can do the following:

- **Prepare to apply for grants.** Click the link provided for a grant and read the full announcement. If it fits your organization, you can download the grant application package.
- **Access active grant application packages.** In addition to the required forms, you can access lists of FAQs regarding each grant. Usually, these questions originate at the funding agency's technical assistance call or webcast (see the earlier section, "Discovering direct grants," for more on these discussions).
- **Download, complete, and submit grant application packages online through the e-grant system portal.** Grants.gov gives you links to download the grant application forms or complete the forms online. You can also submit your entire grant application online, including uploading your narrative and attachments in the requested formats.
- **Check the status of an application submitted via Grants.gov.** After you submit your grant application package, you can check back frequently to see whether your request has been accepted or rejected.

For more on federal grant application packages, turn to Chapter 4 of this minibook.

Understanding forecasted funding announcements

When you're searching for grant-funding opportunities on Grants.gov, you will see that there are four types of Opportunity Status listings:

- **Forecasted:** A forecasted grant-funding opportunity is a planned or projected funding opportunity from a federal agency. The agency is giving you advance notice that a funding opportunity is on the way. There is no guarantee that the forecasted funding opportunity will materialize into a posted funding opportunity. You can track forecasted opportunities by subscribing to any changes made to a specific opportunity. Figure 3-2 shows what a grant search screen looks like for forecasted funding opportunities.
- **Posted**: A published funding opportunity seeking eligible grant applicants to apply for federal funding.
- **Closed:** A published funding opportunity that has ended. No more grant applications will be accepted until the opportunity opens again (typically, annually around the same time).
- **Archived:** Once a funding opportunity is closed or deleted, the Grants.gov workspace continues to be available to allow applicants to reuse their form data to populate forms in other workspaces.

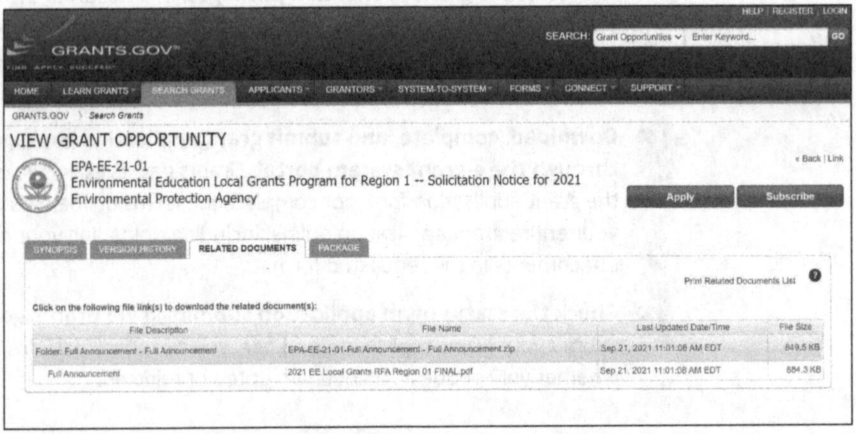

FIGURE 3-2: Search for grants.

Source: `https://www.grants.gov/web/grants/search-grants.html`

IN THIS CHAPTER

» Getting familiar with Grants.gov

» Applying for federal grants

» Registering your organization on Grants.gov

» Perusing standard federal grant application forms

Chapter 4
Navigating the Federal Grant Submission Portals

Established in 2002, Grants.gov is the federal government's e-government initiative operating under the governance of the Office of Management and Budget. It provides a centralized location for grant seekers to find and apply for federal funding opportunities. Through it you can find information on the more than 1,000 grant programs available through the federal grant-making agencies.

This chapter takes you on a guided tour of the Grants.gov homepage and gives you some pointers on getting your organization registered to apply for federal grants and cooperative agreements. We also lead you through those confusing grant application forms and the downloading and uploading processes for the entire grant application.

REMEMBER

Grants.gov has ongoing maintenance days that may coincide with the day you plan to submit your grant application. Monitor all alerts for maintenance starting ten days prior to your application's submission deadline. When you're ready to submit your application, follow the online directions, and don't procrastinate until the last minute to upload your application. You'll breeze through the once-stormy waters of federal e-grant applications.

Navigating the Grants.gov Website

The Grants.gov homepage at `www.grants.gov` is your gateway to everything you need to know to find federal grants, apply for federal grants, and follow up on submitted federal grant applications. The page looks simple on first glance, but in reality it can be a bit confusing. So even though the information in this section may seem somewhat repetitive after you actually visit the Grants.gov website, going on a guided tour can still be helpful.

Here's a breakdown of each tab on Grants.gov and what you can expect to find when you click them:

- **HOME:** On this tab, you find a link to download the Grants.gov mobile application for searching and submitting on the go. Other clickable icons include Search Grants, Get Started, Grant Policies, Grant-Making Agencies, Prevent Scams, Community Blog, Twitter Feed, YouTube Videos, User Guide, and Support Center. ***Note:*** Grants.gov changes its homepage icon lineup frequently, so you may have to search for these links or icons.
- **LEARN GRANTS:** On this tab, you find the Grants Learning Center where you see links for Grants 101, Grant Policies, Grant Eligibility, Grant Terms, Grant Agencies, Grant Systems, Grant Programs, Grant Careers, Grant Reporting, Grant Fraud, and Grant Events.
- **SEARCH GRANTS:** This tab takes you to a new Grants.gov web page where you can not only view snippets of current grant-funding opportunities, but also type in basic search criteria: keyword, opportunity number, or the Catalog of Federal Domestic Assistance (CFDA) number (now housed at `https://sam.gov/content/home` in their homepage directory under Assistance Listings). You can also search grant-funding opportunities that are forecasted (might not have reach posted status), posted (currently available to apply for), closed (no longer accepting grant applications), and archived (very old grant-funding announcements). The other search boxes are for the type of grant, by eligible applicant, by category, and by funding agency.
- **APPLICANTS:** On this tab, there are eight categories of information: Check Your Eligibility, Get Registered, Apply for Grants, Track Your Application, Adobe Compatibility, Applicant Training, Applicant FAQs, and Manage Subscriptions.
- **GRANTORS:** This tab and its links allow staff at the federal grant-making agencies to register and post opportunities on Grants.gov, access training materials to assist the agencies in navigating Grants.gov, find FAQs, and get help.

- **SYSTEM-TO-SYSTEM:** This tab provides applicants and agencies with the information necessary to link Grants.gov functionality with existing systems within their own organizations.
- **FORMS:** Here you can access a variety of federal forms — including government-wide and agency-specific forms — currently used for creating grant application packages at Grants.gov. (For information about federal grant application forms, head to the related section later in this chapter.)
- **CONNECT:** On this tab, you can manage your Grants.gov subscriptions, join the system's social media pages, get help with the Grants.gov mobile application, and peruse the Grants.gov newsletter archive.
- **SUPPORT:** This tab takes you to Support, FAQs, Report Fraud, Find Help and Learn, About the Program, Grants.gov Releases, and Feedback.

Understanding Grant Applicant Eligibility

Many types of organizations are eligible to apply for government funding opportunities. Typically, most grant applicant organizations fall into the following categories:

- **Government organizations:** State, territory, local, city or township, special districts, and Native American tribes (federally and non-federally recognized).
- **Education organizations:** Independent school districts, public and state-controlled institutions of higher education, and private institutions of higher education.
- **Public housing organizations:** Public housing authorities and Native American housing authorities.
- **Nonprofit organizations:** Nonprofit organizations with or without 501(c)(3) status.
- **For-profit organizations:** Any for-profit group other than small businesses.
- **Small businesses:** The U.S. Small Business Administration (SBA) has established size standards for small businesses. Check out the standards at Grants.gov or the SBA's website, www.sba.gov.
- **Individuals:** Individuals can submit grant applications on their own behalf, and not on behalf of a company, organization, institution, or government. If you're registered as an individual, you're allowed to apply only to funding opportunities that are open to individuals.

» **Foreign applicants:** The authorizing legislation for each grant-making program determines whether foreign applicants can apply for funding. Before applying, foreign applicants should thoroughly review the IRS website (`www.irs.gov`) and search for their most recent guidance for Aliens and International Taxpayers.

Registering as an Organization on Grants.gov

To apply for a grant, you and/or your organization have to register on Grants.gov. This registration process can take three to five business days, or as long as two weeks if you don't complete all the steps in a timely manner. The following sections explain how to register as an organization (which is most common) and as an individual.

An *organization registration* is for an individual who is responsible for submitting a grant on behalf of a company; state, local, or tribal government; academic or research institution; nonprofit; or any other institution.

To get your nonprofit organization registered to submit grant applications on the Grants.gov system, follow these steps:

1. **Obtain a D-U-N-S number.** D-U-N-S stands for Data Universal Number System; a *D-U-N-S number* is a common tracking number for doing business with the government (federal, state, and local). All D-U-N-S numbers are provided by Dun & Bradstreet. Call 866-705-5711 or access the Dun & Bradstreet website at `https://www.dnb.com`.

   TIP

   Before you apply for a D-U-N-S number, ask your grant administrator or CFO whether your organization already has one. Select your country or territory from the pull-down menu, click Continue, then choose Continue to Government Update to start your search.

2. **Register with the System for Award Management (SAM) at `www.sam.gov`.** Grants.gov uses SAM.gov to establish roles and IDs for electronic grant applicants. SAM registration is not completed on the Grants.gov website. Once the SAM registration is complete, you need to return to Grants.gov to continue your registration process. If your organization already has an Employer Identification Number (EIN), your SAM registration will take seven to ten

business days to process. If you're just applying for your EIN, you can get an EIN *immediately* by applying online at `www.irs.gov/Businesses/Small-Businesses-&-Self-Employed/Apply-for-an-Employer-Identification-Number-(EIN)-Online`.

The information requested at SAM.gov is similar to what your organization submits in its annual IRS tax return, such as name of organization, address, contact person, and contact person's information. You also have to upload the organization's banking information (the bank's tracking number and the organization's bank account number) to facilitate electronic banking between the government and your organization. (You didn't think they still sent the check in the mail, did you?)

3. **Create a username and password with the Grants.gov credential provider.** You can create your own username and set a password on the Grants.gov and SAM.gov websites. After you complete all your SAM.gov information, you get directed back to Grants.gov to complete your registration with the access-point information. This is a same-day process.

TIP

On SAM.gov, you'll find some new terms, namely MPIN and TPIN. An MPIN, or Marketing Partner ID Number, is a personal code consisting of nine characters; it's mandatory if you want to use SAM.gov. TPIN stands for Trading Partner Identification Number; it's a confidential number assigned to organizations that currently are or intend to become federal contractors. Check out this online user guide for how to register with SAM.gov: (`www.grants.gov/help/html/help/Register/RegisterWithSAM.htm`).

4. **Obtain AOR Authorization.** If you're not the E-Business Point of Contact (E-Biz POC) at your organization, have that person log in to Grants.gov to confirm you as an *Authorized Organization Representative* (AOR). Only an AOR can log on and conduct business or grant-related transactions with the federal government. Your organization may have more than one AOR, or the AOR and E-Biz POC may be one and the same.

TIP

An AOR can log in using the username and password obtained in Step 3 to track their AOR status and see whether they have been approved by the E-Biz POC.

Logging in as an applicant is instantaneous, but you have to wait to become an AOR until your organization's E-Biz POC logs in and approves you as an AOR. Watch your email from SAM.gov and Grants.gov!

Viewing Tutorials in the Grants.gov Workspace

The Grants.gov workspace is the standard way for organizations or individuals to apply for federal grants in Grants.gov. The workspace allows a grant team to simultaneously access and edit different forms within an application. Plus, the forms can be filled out online or offline — your choice.

The Grants.gov workspace also allows applicants and organizations to tailor their application workflow. Learn more about how to start working in the workspace under the Applicants tab on the Grants.gov homepage. Figure 4-1 shows the first view of the workspace overview.

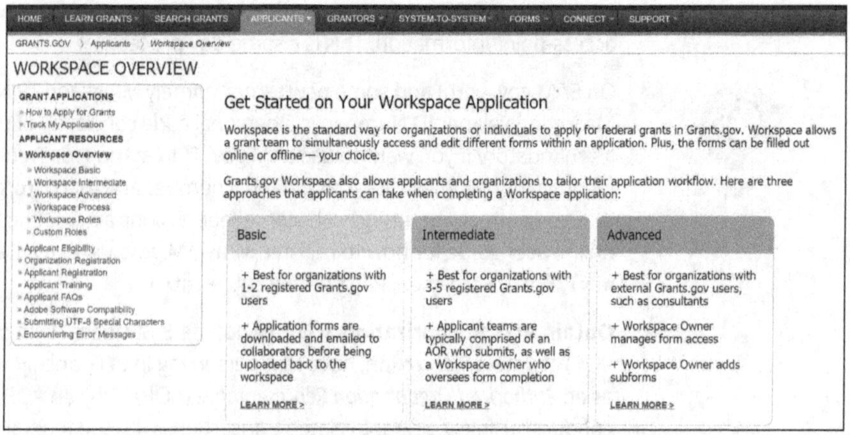

FIGURE 4-1: Get started on your workspace application.

Source: `https://www.grants.gov/web/grants/applicants/workspace-overview.html`

Accessing Application Package Instructions

All the federal grant application forms you need are available through the Grants.gov website. These easy steps help you find and submit an application:

1. **Preview and download your grant application package.** To download this package, log on to the Grants.gov homepage and click the Applicants tab. At the Apply for Grants link, you need the FON or the Catalog of Federal Domestic Assistance (CFDA) number to download your grant application package. Once

you are on the Synopsis tab in the NOFO, click Related Documents to see any files available for downloading. There will be a ZIP file and a separate PDF file. You can access the grant application package forms from the Package tab in the synopsis.

2. **Review, fill in, and complete the online application package forms.** The mandatory forms can be previewed before you download them from the Package tab. While the forms for each federal funding agency may differ, these are the standard mandatory forms: Application for Federal Assistance (SF-424), Project Abstract Summary, Disclosure of Lobbying Activities (SF-LLL), Budget Information for Non-Construction Programs (SF-424A), Budget Narrative Attachment Form, Project Narrative Attachment Form, and Key Contacts.

   REMEMBER

   The application package consists of front-and-back forms required by the grant-funding agency. This *package,* as Grants.gov labels it, doesn't refer to your grant application narrative or mandatory internal attachments or appendixes, but instead, to a series of federal forms to be filled out in the Grants.gov online workspace.

3. **Submit the completed grant application.** After you enter all the necessary information online *and* upload all your mandatory internal attachments and narrative documents in the PDF format, you're ready to submit your grant-funding request to the Grants.gov workspace.

   TIP

   After the submission is complete, a confirmation screen appears with a Grants.gov tracking number (at the bottom of the screen) as well as the official date and time of the submission. Record this tracking number so you can refer to it if you need to contact Grants.gov or give it to your congressional officials for tracking your grant application after submission.

4. **Track the status of your submitted grant application package.** After submitting your grant application, you can check the status by clicking the Track My Application link under the Applicants tab on the Grants.gov homepage. From there, enter your application's tracking number.

   Your application status can be marked as any of the following:

   - **Received:** Grants.gov has received the application but not yet validated it.
   - **Validated:** Grants.gov has validated the application, which is now available for the agency to download.
   - **Received by the agency:** The funding agency has confirmed receipt of the application package.
   - **Agency tracking number assigned:** The funding agency has assigned the application an internal tracking number. (However, keep in mind that not all agencies assign tracking numbers.)

- **Rejected with errors:** Because of errors, Grants.gov can't process your application. You'll receive information by email on how to address the errors and resubmit the application.

TIP

You also get email updates from Grants.gov as the status of your application changes.

Reviewing Some of the Mandatory Government Grant Application Forms

Each federal agency has its own standard grant application forms and its own guidelines for filling out the forms. Some agencies have fewer than 10 forms; others have more than 20. Underestimating the importance of the mandatory forms and the importance of filling them out properly may result in your grant application being disqualified on a technical error.

When filling in any form, always read the instructions that come with the online grant application guidelines first. Look for the checklist provided in every grant application announcement. This checklist tells you what to provide in your application, including mandatory forms, narrative sections, and attachments or appendixes.

TIP

Most federal grant-making agencies make exceptions to the standard Grants.gov application upload requirement and allow grant applicants to submit a paper application instead, although the agency may require that you request and receive approval to submit a paper application before the submission deadline. The checklist becomes even more important for hard-copy submissions, however, because you must assemble the forms, narrative, attachments, and appendixes in a specific order. Otherwise, your application may be rejected on receipt. If you can submit digitally, it is, by far, the best way to know it's over and done with. The paper submission process is cumbersome and a lot more stressful.

The *cover form* is the top page of all federal grant applications. It's what the feds see when they open your application package. For years, the application cover form has been known as the Application for Federal Assistance Cover Form. The current cover form — SF-424 — is five pages when printed out. It has 21 sections that cover the basic who, what, when, where, and why of your project and organization, with instructions for responding to each field, and ends with a federal debt delinquency explanation page. See Chapter 8 of this minibook for more information about filling out the SF-424.

The following sections provide an overview of the rest of the most common federal grant application forms: budget forms, assurance forms, and lobbying disclosure forms. Many state funding agencies use similar forms; the required forms are listed in the grant guidelines for each funding competition. These forms are listed in the order in which you're most likely to see them in grant application guidelines.

Budget information forms

One form you have to fill out is a three-page, six-section set of federal budget forms often referred to as SF-424A (non-constructions programs) and SF-424C (constructions programs). You can download these forms at `www.grants.gov/web/grants/forms.html`. The six sections of this Non-Constructions Programs Budget Information form set are labeled Sections A through F:

- **Section A** is where you lay out your budget summary (your federal grant request and your nonfederal matching monies).

  TIP

  Make sure the totals in your budget worksheet and budget narrative match the total in your SF-424A or C.

- **Section B** is for detailing the budget categories line item by line item.

  WARNING

  When you get to Section B, you especially want to have read the instructions for these forms, because each agency differs in how it wants you to fill in the columns for multiyear federal funding requests.

- **Section C** is where you list the source of your nonfederal monies (called *nonfederal resources*).
- **Section D** asks you to forecast your first-year grant-funding needs (referred to as *forecasted cash needs*).
- **Section E** is where you tell the federal government the total amount of grant funds needed in the second through fifth years of your project. However, fill in this section only if the grant award is for multiple years.
- **Section F** is where you explain any amounts requested in the federal portion of your budget that are unusual or unclear to someone (such as a federal grant reader/peer reviewer) outside your agency. In this section, you also explain your already-negotiated indirect cost rate (contact the Office of Management and Budget, `www.whitehouse.gov/omb`, to start this lengthy process well before you plan to apply for federal grant funding). Finally, Section F is also where you can add any other explanations or comments to explain your rather large or mysterious budget.

Chapter 12 of this minibook gives you greater insight into the budget line-item preparation process.

Assurances forms

The federal government wants assurances that your organization — the grant applicant — can meet all governmental funding expectations. And it gets these assurances from SF-424B (non-construction programs) and SF-424C (construction programs). This online form lets you add your electronic signature and submit.

TIP

If you have questions regarding this form, contact the awarding agency. Also, note that some federal awarding agencies may require you to certify to additional assurances; if that's the case, they'll let you know how to proceed.

The assurances cover your legal authority to (among other things)

- Apply for grants
- Address your commitment to record keeping
- Provide safeguards for conflict of interest
- Protect the meeting time frame established in your grant application
- Comply with multiple federal laws regarding fairness and equity for program staff and participants

REMEMBER

By signing the assurances and other required forms, you are conveying to the government funding agency that your organization will comply with all applicable requirements of all other federal laws, executive orders, regulations, and policies governing this program.

Disclosure of lobbying activity form: SF-LLL

If you hired a lobbyist to make sure more federal or state dollars come your way, you must fill out the Disclosure of Lobbying Activities form, or *SF-LLL*. (This form is often optional, so be sure to read the funding agency's guidelines.)

A *lobbyist* is an individual or a firm that spends a lot of time on Capitol Hill or at your state capitol schmoozing with elected officials. Lobbyists work for both for-profit and nonprofit agencies. They're on a (paid) mission to convince legislators to vote one way or another to benefit their client agencies. Lobbyists apply a lot of pressure, and a lot of money flows as a result.

CHECKING OUT OTHER E-GRANT PORTALS FOR FEDERAL GRANT-MAKING AGENCIES

Some federal agencies have their own e-grant upload portals separate from Grants.gov. The process varies from agency to agency, so read the grant application guidelines carefully to look for the submission process. Here are a few examples:

- **Department of Justice (DOJ):** Although you generally submit competitive/discretionary grant applications through Grants.gov, you must submit formula grants, congressional earmarks, and continuation grants through DOJ's Office of Justice Program's Grants Management System (GMS), called JustGrants. For detailed instructions and tips on applying through GMS, refer to the GMS online training tool at `https://justicegrants.usdoj.gov/about`.
- **National Science Foundation (NSF):** To apply for a grant from the NSF, you must register with FastLane, a portal that allows individuals and organizations to interact directly with the NSF regarding proposals, funding awards, and more. FastLane is available from the NSF homepage at `www.nsf.gov` or directly at `www.fastlane.nsf.gov`. FastLane can be tricky for new users. Make sure to spend time learning how to use the system before your grant application is due.
- **Department of Health and Human Services:** The Office of Extramural Research requires grant applicants to register with the eRA Systems in their ASSIST system. This system can facilitate preparing and submitting grant applications to this agency. To learn more about the eRA Systems, visit their portal at `https://era.nih.gov/applicants`.

TIP

If you're looking for any other federal grant application forms, this is the website to find them: `www.grants.gov/web/grants/forms/sf-424-mandatory-family.html`.

IN THIS CHAPTER

» Opening the door to finding private-sector funding opportunities

» Utilizing grant-research databases

» Adhering to the funder's criteria

» Prioritizing your potential funder's list

Chapter 5 Researching Potential Private-Sector Funders

The earlier chapters in this part focus on grant-making agencies in the public sector. This chapter takes a look at the other segment of funding possibilities: private-sector grant makers. *Private-sector funding* comes from foundations and corporations. This philanthropic well represents corporate and foundation grant makers whose *endowments* (the funds that start each giving entity) came from individuals, families, other foundations, and for-profit corporations or businesses.

These funders are plentiful at the local, state, national, and international levels. How do you find foundation and corporate funders and determine what they like to fund? Jump into this chapter to find out.

Finding Foundations and Corporations with Grant-Making Programs

REMEMBER

Conducting a thorough Internet search is the best way to find private-sector grant-funding opportunities. We can't stress strongly enough the importance of reading grant-research database funder profiles (which provide an overview of what they fund, how to make the initial contact, and whom to contact) and then searching the Internet for every bit of information you can find on each funder before emailing, writing, or calling to ask questions or introduce your organization. If you don't do this homework, you're never going to access the road that leads to building an initial and lasting relationship with potential funders. Don't be a time-waster by trying to skip protocol — unless of course you actually *want* to commit grant-seeking suicide (this means never receiving a grant award from funders that typically do fund projects or programs like the one you're planning to propose to them)!

Understanding the time and effort required

How do you set up your search? Start by writing down every possible descriptor of your project and its target population (who will benefit or be served). Then begin researching those keywords and fishing for clues in the resulting links. Sometimes the links returned by the search engine can be misleading, so you have to click through to see whether your hit is a relevant funding lead for your project.

Some grant-research databases require time-consuming profile inspections; many of the search returns will not be a good match for your project or program. Other databases with different algorithms have higher levels of matching profiles. You need to decide, based on cost and your available time, which database works best for you. Finding the right funders can take from a couple of hours to 30 days working on one profile per day.

TIP

It's also a good idea to start fleshing out your program description and objectives even before having a specific grant-funding opportunity available. This also helps you to further hone your keyword search skills when you've got a document that you can extract keywords from.

TIP

More is more! Not all potential funders become actual funders, and you don't want to spend 9 to 12 months counting on yeses from only one or two funders only to have them respond with a no. If you need up to $25,000, you must search for at least 5 potential funders. For up to $50,000, search for at least 10 possible funders, and for needs of up to $100,000, search for 20 potential funders. For amounts of more than $100,000, be sure to have at least 25 to 30 names on your list of possible funders.

Subscribing to helpful funding alert resources

After doing Internet searches, the next-best tactic is to subscribe to e-newsletters that contain private-sector funding alerts. These give you the inside scoop on what private-sector funders are currently funding. A couple of useful e-newsletters are the *Philanthropy News Digest* (http://philanthropynewsdigest.org) and the *RFP Bulletin* (http://philanthropynewsdigest.org/rfps), both of which are produced by Candid.

Here are some additional ways to set yourself apart from the grant-seeking pack:

- **Review each funder's online resource materials to help you tailor your grant application to the funder's current interest area.** This means grant application guidelines and an annual report (which contains financial information on the funder and usually a section on previous grants funded).
- **Look for lists of previous grantees on the funder's website.** This list can tell you how much the funder funds, whether grants have been awarded in your geographic area, and whom the funder has invested grant monies in (look for grantees similar to your own grant applicant organization).
- **Email each funder to inquire about grant-writing guideline updates that may not be posted on the funder's website yet.** It's always possible they exist; asking never hurts. Be sure to keep your email focused on guideline updates, though. Don't ask for money or write endless paragraphs about your organization.
- **Follow to a T all the directions provided by the funding source on how to apply for grants.** If you get one item wrong, your proposal can be disqualified, even if everything else is golden.

WARNING

This list highlights some pitfalls to avoid when grant seeking:

- **Don't rely on outdated websites for current contact information.** Don't use anything older than one year (scroll down to the bottom of a website's homepage to see the date it was last updated). Current information is crucial because funders don't forward snail mail or email when a key contact person is no longer working for them. With snail mail, if you address your funding request to the wrong person, you simply get it back stamped *return to sender.* With email, you may get a message that this person is no longer with the funder, or you may not get any notice. So, although you think you've initiated the first step to build a relationship with a program officer or foundation director, your email is hanging out unread in some dormant email system.

  Save embarrassment by calling for the current contact person, the correct spelling of the person's name, and the correct position title. Most importantly, ask how the person prefers to be addressed: Mr., Mrs., or Ms. Double-checking the email address doesn't hurt, either.
- **Don't look for national funders before you start to contact local funders.** Look for money at home first. Check sources in your own community and

county. You have a better chance of getting your first grant award from a funder that already knows about your organization.

- **Don't call the funding source with a dozen questions before you read their grant application guidelines.** Be sure you know a bit more about the funder. If you have new questions about instructions or information not found in the grant application guidelines, feel free to call. However, don't call repeatedly with questions that the guidelines answer.

  If you decide to call, make sure to jot down some notes about the call and the person you speak with. Write down their name and title, the date and time of the call, and what you discussed. Having a contact at the funder's office can help if your grant application is rejected and you want the inside scoop on why.
- **Don't write a grant application or proposal without having completed extensive research about the funder's grant-making priorities.** Know what your targeted funders fund — their grant-making priorities — and only submit requests that meet their current interests.
- **Don't broadcast your funding sources to colleagues working for other nonprofits.** Keep in mind that you're competing for funding. Learn to treasure, or keep quiet about, your findings, lest others apply as well and lessen your chances of winning.

Scouring GuideStar for Foundation Funders

Did you know that 90 percent of U.S. foundations don't have websites? Candid's GuideStar (`www.guidestar.org`) is a multifunctional nonprofit profile digital warehouse that provides limited free access as well as subscription-based access to a multitude of information on all nonprofits that file Form-990s and Form-990-N tax returns with the Internal Revenue Service.

GuideStar is a nonprofit warehousing website that collects the tax returns of nonprofits and creates skeleton profiles within its nonprofit research directory. Every nonprofit with an active 501(c)(3) is housed in the GuideStar database. Be sure to claim your profile in GuideStar. Anyone can review the most recent tax returns, employer identification numbers (EINs), and a bit of financial information to learn more about nonprofits.

Another way you can use GuideStar is to search for foundation and corporate grant makers that have filed their 501(c)(3) tax returns with the IRS. What information can you glean by looking at a potential funder's tax return? Well, for one, when a potential funder does not have a website and you can't locate any way to contact the funder, GuideStar has the key to scouring for this information. Type the name of the foundation; if more than one foundation exists with the same name, use the drop-down search box on the left to select the state for the potential funder (your state). This will narrow down any duplicate names across the states. Scroll down the screen and look for the annual Form-990 links and click the most current year's tax return filed by the foundation. You are mining for gold nuggets that will lead you to local family foundations that award grants but are not visible in any grant-research database. This is also known as *backdoor research.*

Using Candid's Online Grant-Research Database

In the United States, the largest database for corporate and foundation funding sources is that of the *Foundation Directory Online* by Candid at `https://fconline.foundationcenter.org`. The Foundation Center became part of Candid in 2019 and made some operational changes to enable Candid to take the lead in the partnership.

The *Foundation Directory Online* by Candid has three subscription levels:

- » Essential (110,000+ grant-maker profiles)
- » Professional (240,000+ expanded grant-maker profiles, key decision makers, keyword search including 990s and 990-PFs, and a lot more)
- » Enterprise (for foundations, academic institutions, and large organizations that require unlimited access for staff and the public)

If you decide to pay for a subscription, you get access to detailed information on foundation and corporate funders at your fingertips when you need it — at home or at work. The pages of info you pull up on these funders are referred to as *grant-maker profiles.* Subscriptions to the *Foundation Directory Online* start at about $32 and go as high as nearly $200 a month. These subscription rates are for one licensed user. Adding more users will increase your monthly rate. Call them if your organization is interested in an Enterprise-level subscription.

After you become a paid subscriber to the *Foundation Directory Online*, you can start your funder research in three different ways, depending on your subscription level:

- **Grant makers (available at all subscription levels):** This type of search, at a minimum, allows you to search by the following:
  - Grant-maker name
  - Grant-maker location (state, county, city, metro area, and ZIP code)
  - Fields of interest
  - Types of support
  - Geographic focus
  - Trustees, officers, and donors
  - Type of grant maker
  - Total giving
  - Keyword

TIP

Searching by grant maker is easy and productive. With this search, you can usually find at least 10 to 20 potential private-sector funding sources for each project.

- **Companies (available at subscription levels higher than Essential):** This search option allows you to search *corporate grant makers* (businesses that have developed corporate giving programs). When you can't find funders in the Foundation-Only section, searching for grant opportunities in the Companies section is a good idea.
- **Grants (available at all subscription levels):** This option allows you to search by the following:
  - Grant-maker name
  - Grant-maker state
  - Recipient name
  - Recipient state/county
  - Recipient city
  - Recipient type
  - Subjects
  - Types of support
  - Keyword

Scoring a Match to the Funder's Grant-Making Criteria

After you locate information on a foundation or corporate funding source, you need to quickly scan its profile to determine whether you have a perfect match. A *perfect match* means that you fit the funder's organizational, geographic, and programming criteria and that the funder provides the kind of funding you need in an amount to make an approach worthwhile.

REMEMBER

You can't persuade a funder to change its award guidelines or funding priorities; you're the one who has to do the changing to fit the funder's funding criteria. If you can't change your program or project, that particular funding source isn't the best one for you. In that case, simply keep looking for a better match.

Every resource that lists funding sources presents the information on the funder in a generalized profile format. When you look at a funder's profile, you can scan some specific information fields to determine whether reading about this particular funding source is worth your time. Focus on the following fields:

- **Limitations:** Look at the limitations field first. Your organization may be eliminated before it can even get to the starting gate. Does the wording in this section eliminate your program or project? If so, move on to the next funder's profile. If not, move on to the next critical information field.

  Typical limitations you may see listed in the grant maker's online profile include

  - Specific geographic giving area (countries, states, and counties)
  - Restrictions on whom it funds and what it funds

  WARNING

  Most mainstream foundation funders don't award grants for religious purposes, to individuals, or for *capital projects* (building construction, renovation, or major equipment purchases).

- **Purpose and activities:** Every foundation and corporate giver has a purpose statement, located at the beginning of the funding profile. Does the funding source's purpose statement reflect your organization's values? Do any of the activities that the funder prefers to fund match activities that your organization is or will be undertaking? If not, read no further. Move on to another funder's information profile. If you can identify with this funder's purpose, move on to the next critical information field.

» **Fields of interest:** Does the program area that you're seeking grant funds for match with any of the funding source's fields of interest?

REMEMBER

Keep in mind that the language you use to describe your program may not be the language the funder uses to list its fields of interest. Think of your program area in broad terms and generic categories. For example, say you need grant funding for a program that will tutor and mentor at-risk elementary school students after school and on the weekends. You probably won't find terms/phrases such as *tutoring, mentoring, at-risk*, or *after-school* in the funder's fields of interest entry. Rather, you may find terms such as *education (K–12), elementary education, public education, private education*, and *youth programs and services*. The second list is broader than the first.

» **Types of support:** What types of activities does this funder pay for? If you're trying to erect a new building and the funder lists only *general operating support, conferences*, and *seed money* under types of support, this funding source isn't the one you want to approach with a construction project.

TIP

Even if this funder isn't willing to support the type of activity you're currently seeking funds for, save the funder's information if you think it may be willing to support some other aspect of your organization.

» **Previous grants or grantees:** Have any previous grants been funded in your state? Have any previous grants been for projects similar to yours or in your project area? Getting a funder to award grant monies in a state where it hasn't previously awarded grants is difficult. If a funder has a track record for previous grants in your state or previous grants for projects similar to yours, the door is open to receive your funding request. (You can search by location of foundation or geographic limitations to help narrow your search.) However, if these aren't the circumstances you face, you may have to email or call the funder to determine whether proceeding with a funding request is worth your time.

» **Amounts of grants previously funded:** Does your guesstimated project budget fit into the range of prior grant awards? Use the funder's prior grant-making amounts to gauge where your request should fall.

REMEMBER

You never want to request a grant amount that exceeds the top grant awarded by the funder — that strategy is a bit too risky. If you're looking for $100,000 and the largest grant awarded was $5,000, you need to find multiple funders for your project. Also, if you are a first-time grant applicant, it's best to ask at the low end of the funder's giving range.

Knowing Whom to Contact First

After you identify the potential private funders that are the best fit for your program, follow these steps:

1. **Contact each funding source (via email, letter, or phone call) and ask to be included in the funder's mailing list.** Doing so normally means that you get annual reports, grant-making guidelines, research, and other information that keeps you up to date. Armed with this information, you're ready to take the next step.

   TIP

   You can also use this contact point to inquire whether the funding-request guidelines listed on the organization's website are current.

2. **Organize your potential foundation and corporate sources by the application due dates.** This step is critical because some private-sector funders have only once-yearly competitions. You may be a few weeks or many months away from the annual date for grant submissions. After all your hard work, you don't want to miss an opportunity to get a grant funded because you submitted your application late.

   Sorting by due date helps you anticipate how much work you'll have in any given month. Be as organized as possible to maximize your chances of getting the grants you want. Grant management software can be extremely helpful for organizing (see the nearby sidebar for advice on what to look for in this type of software).

   TIP

   Subscribe to a cloud-based file storage service. You can create electronic folders for each funder. You should have massive amounts of information at this point and keeping everything in order is crucial. If something that you want to keep is not in a downloadable file format, consider copying the information from web pages and pasting them into a word-processing program. This way, you can save them into the folder in readable and manageable formats.

3. **When you're ready to write, focus first on the proposals and applications that have due dates in 60 days or less.** Get busy! Check out chapters 8–12 of this minibook for details on completing an outstanding application.

MAKING WRITING AND TRACKING EASIER WITH SOFTWARE

A grant-writing management software program allows you to keep track of the entire grant application process, including preplanning steps, partner information, funder information, due dates for fiscal and evaluation reports, and grant closeout. Commercial software programs are available to capture any and all segments of the grant-seeking process.

You can search for "grant-writing management software" using your favorite search engine to get links to everything on the current market. The best characteristics to look for in any grant-writing management software are the ability to

- Write grant proposals and track proposal submissions in the same software. Using one software or cloud-based grants management system (subscription-based) helps you keep track of the information you're collecting on potential funders, as well as set up alerts to grant application due dates and other critical to-do's.
- Set alerts for reports due or funding source decision-making dates so you can call or email the funder to see whether it has a decision on your request yet.
- Manage grant-related reports, including tracking financial expenditures.

IN THIS CHAPTER

» Recognizing red flags in NOFAs

» Writing to meet the peer reviewers' expectations

» Convincing other agencies to take a stakeholder's seat in your grant application

Chapter 6

Finding Federal Grant Opportunities That Fit Your Needs

Most grant writers start their grant-writing endeavors by writing proposals for foundation and corporate grants. This is definitely the easier route for most grant writers, new or veteran. However, sooner or later you'll need to start exploring bigger pots of money. These bigger pots are typically found in grant-funding opportunities at the federal level, which means you need to get comfortable reading federal grant application guidelines. This includes reading every word in a Notice of Funding Availability (NOFA), searching for and highlighting the technical requirements for your grant application, and asking the right crew of potential partners to support your grant applications submission.

All federal funding agencies publish guidelines that spell out the type of grant or cooperative agreement application that they expect grant applicants to submit (called the NOFA language). The guidelines and the review points assigned to each section of the narrative guide you in what to write. Your content will be scored by peer reviewers. The higher your score, the higher your chances of winning.

REMEMBER

You must read and reread every sentence of a NOFA *before* you start researching the topic and writing your federal grant application. Then highlight the mandatory requirements throughout the document so that you can easily refer to them and make sure you've covered them all.

This chapter covers everything you need to know to decide whether your organization should apply for a federal grant-funding opportunity once you scrutinize the NOFA details and determine your organization's capability to manage a grant-funded program.

Dissecting the Notice of Funding Availability (Over and Over Again)

Suppose you receive an email alert about a grant or cooperative agreement opportunity from a federal grant-funding agency, and you think that you have a chance to win the grant. But you don't know where to start or whether the grant's really worth pursuing. This section walks you through the essentials of determining whether this competition is right for your organization. You'll also get a quick lesson in *Grantlish* — the art of talking about grants — so you have a better understanding of the review criteria language and terms.

REMEMBER

Winning a coveted government grant award means you must understand the importance of reading and following directions with no deviation from the funding agency's guidelines. When you download and open a NOFA from Grants.gov, read the entire notice a minimum of four times to ensure that you don't miss any crucial points:

1. **The first time, look for the list of eligible applicants who can apply for the funding.**
2. **On the second pass, skim the basics, such as the name of the funding agency, the deadlines, the number of grants to be awarded, and the range of the grant awards.**
3. **The third time, zero in on the application's formatting requirements, such as page limits, margins, and font types and sizes.**
4. **On the fourth and final pass, seek out the peer review criteria.**

   The *peer review criteria* is the point-based rating system a government agency uses to decide — section by section — whether your grant or cooperative agreement application cuts the mustard and is recommended for funding. (For more about the peer review point-based system, see Chapter 7 of this minibook.)

Figuring out who can apply

Before you look at the details of the funding announcement to see what's being offered, you must determine whether your organization is eligible for the competition and, if so, whether it's ready to start competing. The following sections help you do both of these things.

Verifying your eligibility

Are you eligible for that NOFA you just came across? Before you conclude that the grant or cooperative agreement matches your needs, check out the eligibility paragraph in the funding synopsis or full announcement to make sure your organization is eligible to apply for these federal funds. Otherwise, you'll waste a lot of time working on an application that will no doubt be rejected.

Here's a sampling of what you see when you look under the Eligible Applicants section of the synopsis or full announcement:

- Nonprofits having a 501(c)(3) status with the IRS, other than institutions of higher education
- Nonprofits that don't have a 501(c)(3) status with the IRS, other than institutions of higher education
- For-profit organizations other than small businesses
- Small businesses
- Native American tribal governments (federally recognized)
- Native American tribal organizations (other than federally recognized tribal governments)
- Public housing authorities/Native American housing authorities
- Independent school districts
- Private institutions of higher education
- Public and state-controlled institutions of higher education
- State governments
- County governments
- Special district governments
- City or township governments

TIP

If your organization's structure is listed under the eligible applicant section, great! If not, don't give up; look for a potential partnering organization that's eligible to apply and then contact that organization as soon as possible to see whether it's interested in being the grant applicant and fiscal agent. What's your role in this situation? You're considered a subcontracted and funded partner agency. Remember, you don't have to be the grant applicant to secure a portion of the grant funds. Partnering with another organization as a subcontractor can be an excellent strategy for building financial sustainability.

WARNING

If your organization has not won previous federal grant awards and has no experience in managing large amounts of electronic reporting processes, then applying for Uncle Sam's money — at this time — may not be the best move on your part. Why? All staff must be on board and willing to assist with any new programs. In addition, you may have to hire new staff on Day 1 of the proposed program start date; however, the feds won't be transferring any money from the big bank account in Washington, D.C., to your local bank account up front. If your organization's finances are limited, you need money in the bank to support early-on program start-up expenses until your reimbursement or other type of payment arrangement comes in.

Making sure you're ready to take on a massive research and writing project

After you're sure of your eligibility, ask yourself whether your organization is ready to start competing for a specific grant award opportunity. You also need to decide whether you're able to fulfill the grant program's purpose after the organization is funded. When you click the full grant-funding announcement link (found in the synopsis), look for the *purpose of funding* or *description of funding* statement (usually a paragraph in length), which tells you exactly what the funding agency plans to fund.

Here are some examples of funding statement purposes:

- **National Endowment for the Humanities:** This notice solicits applications for the National Digital Newspaper Program (NDNP). NDNP is a partnership between NEH and the Library of Congress (LC) to create a national digital resource of historically significant newspapers published between 1690 and 1963, from all 56 states and U.S. jurisdictions. This searchable database will be permanently maintained by LC and will be freely accessible online (see Chronicling America: Historic American Newspapers). An accompanying national newspaper directory of bibliographic and holdings information on the website directs users to newspaper titles available in all types of formats.

During the course of its partnership with NEH, LC will also digitize and contribute a significant number of newspaper pages drawn from its own collections to the NDNP database.

- **Environmental Protection Agency:** Applications will be evaluated based on the extent to which the applicant demonstrates: a vision for the cleanup, reuse, and redevelopment of brownfield sites and a strategy for leveraging resources to help accomplish the vision; the environmental, social, health, and economic needs and benefits of the target area; strong community engagement; reasonable costs and eligible tasks and appropriate use of grant funding; the capacity for managing and successfully implementing the cooperative agreement; and other factors.
- **Department of Education:** The Project SAFE grant program is intended to improve students' safety and well-being by providing resources to local educational agencies (LEAs) that adopt and implement strategies to prevent the spread of the Novel Coronavirus Disease 2019 (COVID-19) consistent with guidance from the Centers for Disease Control and Prevention (CDC) and that are financially penalized for doing so by their state educational agency (SEA) or other state entity.
- **Department of Agriculture:** The USDA SBIR program focuses on transforming scientific discovery into products and services with commercial potential and/or societal benefit. Unlike fundamental research, the USDA SBIR program supports small businesses in the creation of innovative, disruptive technologies and enables the application of research advancements from conception into the market. Different from most other investors, the USDA SBIR program funds early or "seed" stage research and development that has commercial potential. The program provides equity-free funding and entrepreneurial support at the earliest stages of company and technology development.

If, after reading through your selected federal funding opportunity's purpose of funding statement, you find that one or more of its purposes fits your organization's long-range plan for program development or expansion, you have a green flag. (Head to the next section for more on identifying go and no-go points.)

WARNING

If your organization has no experience in any of the mentioned programming areas and you just want to apply for easy money, be aware that your capacity to fulfill the purpose on receipt of funding may be limited. This situation definitely signals a red flag.

Using a checklist to determine whether you should apply for a grant

Grants.gov is the go-to resource for finding the most current federal grant-funding opportunities. (Refer to Chapter 4 of this minibook for more information on Grants.gov.) To start receiving free email alerts:

1. **Go to the Grants.gov homepage (`www.grants.gov`).**
2. **Click the Connect tab (top right).**
3. **Select Manage Subscriptions.**
4. **Scroll down to Custom Email Notifications.**
5. **Choose what you want to subscribe to (News, Grant Opportunities, and so on) and enter your email.**

If you think you have a lot of email now, just wait until you start receiving the Grants.gov daily "here's the money" list. It's detailed and filled with clickable web addresses where you can go to read full funding announcements — not just a few lines of detail. This site is the beginning of your journey to read about each grant program's application guidelines and the peer review criteria that determine whether you win or lose.

When you receive the email from Grants.gov, you see a listing of potential grant-funding announcements. Here's an example of an entry:

> Notice of Funding Opportunity (NOFO) for the Department's Fiscal Year 2021 Comprehensive Housing Counseling Grant Program
>
> Department of Housing and Urban Development

The email listing also includes a link to the web address where you can click through to read the synopsis (summary) of the NOFA and click through again to read the full application document. In the synopsis, you can quickly cruise through the summary of the announcement to look for information that can best be called *red stop flags* and *green go flags.* A red flag means "Warning, do not apply!" Take these steps when you're cruising through the summary:

1. **Look for the number of grants to be awarded.** The number of awards is one of the first flags. You have virtually no chance at winning a highly competitive grant award when the number of grants awarded is in the single digits (meaning only one to nine awards will be made). How can you stand a chance of winning one of these limited awards when you're competing with grant

applicants from 50 states, several U.S. territories, and possibly any one of nearly 600 federally recognized tribal organizations?

What number of awards can you consider to be a green "get ready to apply" flag? If the funder is awarding at least 40 grants for general competitions (open to a very large list of potential grant applicants) and at least 10 grants for a limited competition (open to a small number of industry-specific grant applicants, such as museums or libraries), then you're good to go.

Here's an example of how this information will look in a federal agency's NOFA:

Expected Number of Awards: 25

2. **Determine the grant application deadline.** For example, you may see application deadline information that looks like this:

   Original Closing Date for Applications: February 7, 2022

   Current Closing Date for Applications: February 7, 2022

   If the original closing date and current closing date are different, it's because some aspects of this NOFA have likely been changed based on funding agency updates. This would be a red flag because it means you would need to read the updated set of grant application guidelines to see the specific changes. Any change may affect your grant application narrative, due date, required attachments, or state agency sign-offs. (Sometimes a federal funding agency requires you to submit your grant application package to a state agency for review and sign-off before it'll accept your application.)

   TIP

   Most competitive NOFAs give the grant writer at least 30 days — often more — from the date of publication on Grants.gov. If this announcement were published on February 1 and marked as due February 7, that's a sign the feds already know whom they want to award this grant to, which is why the turnaround time for the grant application due date is so short.

   The following NOFA example is a luxury timeline for any grant writer because there are more than 30 days between the NOFA's first publication and the closing (due) date. If your organization is eligible and you're planning to apply for these grant monies, such a timeline is a definite green flag.

   Posted Date: January 14, 2021

   Creation Date: December 8, 2021

   Original Closing Date for Applications: February 7, 2022

   Current Closing Date for Applications: February 7, 2022

WARNING

Many times, funding agency staff find errors in the first publication of the NOFA or interested grant applicants start emailing and calling the funding agency's program officer with questions because there is a bit of confusion or lack of clarity in the first NOFA release. When this happens, the funding agency publishes modifications or addendums. This is labeled as an update in the synopsis and usually all the changes within the guidelines document are highlighted to reduce confusion. If you miss modifications made midway through the grant-writing process, your application will not score high peer review points because it won't match the most recent updates. Check Grants.gov daily for these unexpected changes and be ready to redirect your writing or modify your project budget well before the grant application deadline. You can also sign up to be alerted for modification updates.

TIP

If you're going to research and write a winning government grant application, you need time on your side. Any deadline that's 30 or more days from the date of the grant-funding opportunity announcement is definitely appealing. Fewer than 30 days is not so appealing.

REMEMBER

If you're making your first attempt at applying for a government grant, look for a closing date that allows you at least 30 days for researching and writing. Having less than three weeks to write your first federal grant may be overwhelming unless you can devote 100 percent of your work time to the grant. Normal writing time for a federal grant is 40 to 100 hours, and research can add another 20 to 40 hours. So give yourself ample time — even if you're a veteran grant writer.

3. **Find out the total estimated funding available for grant awards.** Say the estimated total program funding noted in a funding announcement is $9,750,000 million. The NOFA further states the *award ceiling* (maximum grant award for one grant applicant) and *award floor* (minimum grant award for one grant applicant). Here's a green-flag example:

   Estimated Total Program Funding: $9,750,000 million

   Award Ceiling: $400,000

   Award Floor: $0 (zero dollars)

Ready to put the preceding steps into practice? Take a look at Figure 6-1, which shows a Grants.gov NOFA. If you follow Step 1, you notice that there will be 25 grant awards. So far, this NOFA is a go!

When you have no obvious red flags and several green flags (meaning you have at least 30 days to research and write your federal grant application and at least ten grants will be awarded), you can start eyeballing the full application document.

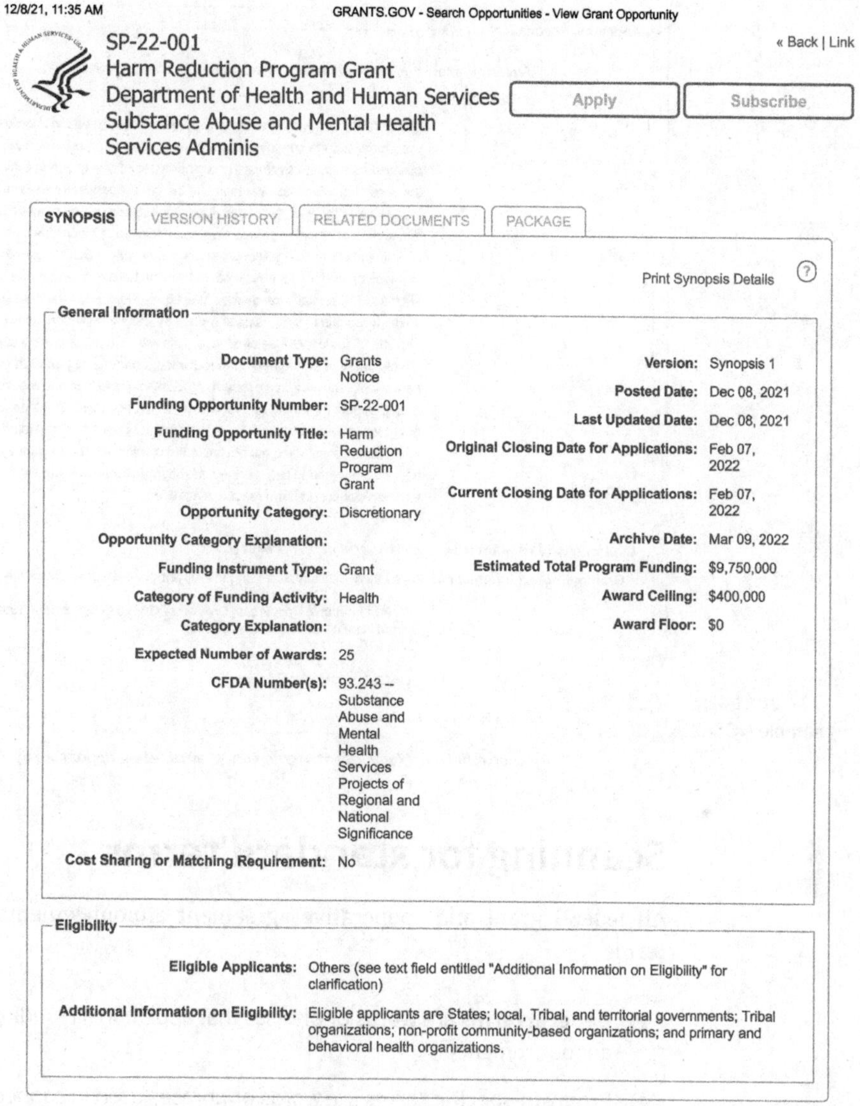

12/8/21, 11:35 AM GRANTS.GOV - Search Opportunities - View Grant Opportunity

SP-22-001
Harm Reduction Program Grant
Department of Health and Human Services
Substance Abuse and Mental Health Services Adminis

« Back | Link

Apply | Subscribe

SYNOPSIS | VERSION HISTORY | RELATED DOCUMENTS | PACKAGE

Print Synopsis Details

General Information

Document Type:	Grants Notice
Funding Opportunity Number:	SP-22-001
Funding Opportunity Title:	Harm Reduction Program Grant
Opportunity Category:	Discretionary
Opportunity Category Explanation:	
Funding Instrument Type:	Grant
Category of Funding Activity:	Health
Category Explanation:	
Expected Number of Awards:	25
CFDA Number(s):	93.243 -- Substance Abuse and Mental Health Services Projects of Regional and National Significance
Cost Sharing or Matching Requirement:	No
Version:	Synopsis 1
Posted Date:	Dec 08, 2021
Last Updated Date:	Dec 08, 2021
Original Closing Date for Applications:	Feb 07, 2022
Current Closing Date for Applications:	Feb 07, 2022
Archive Date:	Mar 09, 2022
Estimated Total Program Funding:	$9,750,000
Award Ceiling:	$400,000
Award Floor:	$0

Eligibility

Eligible Applicants:	Others (see text field entitled "Additional Information on Eligibility" for clarification)
Additional Information on Eligibility:	Eligible applicants are States; local, Tribal, and territorial governments; Tribal organizations; non-profit community-based organizations; and primary and behavioral health organizations.

FIGURE 6-1:
(continued)

Additional Information

Agency Name: Substance Abuse and Mental Health Services Adminis

Description:

The purpose of the program is to support community-based overdose prevention programs, syringe services programs, and other harm reduction services. Funding will be used to enhance overdose and other types of prevention activities to help control the spread of infectious diseases and the consequences of such diseases for individuals with, or at risk of developing substance use disorders (SUD), support distribution of opioid overdose reversal medication to individuals at risk of overdose, build connections for individuals at risk for, or with, a SUD to overdose education, counseling, and health education, refer individuals to treatment for infectious diseases, such as HIV, sexually transmitted infections (STIs), and viral hepatitis, and encourage such individuals to take steps to reduce the negative personal and public health impacts of substance use or misuse. This will include supporting capacity development to strengthen harm reduction programs as part of the continuum of care. Recipients will also establish processes, protocols, and mechanisms for referral to appropriate treatment and recovery support services. Grantees will also provide overdose prevention education to their target populations regarding the consumption of substances including but not limited to opioids and their synthetic analogs. Funds may also be used to help address the stigma often associated with risky behaviors and participation in harm reduction activities.

Link to Additional Information: samhsa.gov/grants/harm-reduction

Grantor Contact Information: If you have difficulty accessing the full announcement electronically, please contact:

Office of Financial Resources, Division of Grants Management Substance Abuse and Mental Health Services Administration
(240) 276-1400

FOACSAP@samhsa.hhs.gov

FIGURE 6-1: A sample NOFA.

Source: `https://www.grants.gov/web/grants/view-opportunity.html?oppId=334991`

Scanning for standard terms

All federal grant and cooperative agreement announcements use two types of terms:

- **General terms** are words or phrases that appear in all funding announcements.
- **Program-specific terms** are words or phrases used in connection with a particular program.

Knowing both types of terms and using them correctly throughout your grant application increases your review criteria points and therefore the likelihood that your application will be recommended for funding.

Getting the gist of general terms

Knowing general terms can help you understand what any funding agency is talking about in the grant or cooperative agreement announcement. If you've only been schooled in oranges, and the funding agency writes its entire announcement in apples, you'll be lost if you don't understand the key terms used.

REMEMBER

Some key general terms you may encounter in grant announcements include the following:

- **Budget period:** The interval of time by which a grant program defines its funding cycle. The cycle can range from one year to multiple years. For example, a large percentage of federal grants start on the first day of the federal fiscal year, October 1; the budget period for grants awarded on October 1 ends on September 30 of the following year.
- **Nonprofit organization:** Typically defined according to what the tax code classifies as a "charitable" or 501(c)(3) organization.
- **Project period:** The total time a project is approved for support, including any extensions. This time period can range from 12 months to 60 months (or longer).

UNDERSTANDING HOW THIRD-PARTY ARRANGEMENTS WORK

Check out this example of a third-party arrangement: Say you find a competition that fits your organization, which is a zoological society located in an urban area. However, under the eligibility section of this grant opportunity, only zoological society consortiums that jointly cover more than three states can apply for these funds.

Using your regional and national zoological society networking list, you contact several similar organizations in your region to ask whether they're aware of the available funding and whether they want to form a consortium with your society. Depending on which society has the strongest credentials (years in operation, size of property, annual visitor count, number of exotic animals, and so on), your society or another society with more impressive credentials may take the lead as the grant applicant.

When one of your collaborative partners indicates that they will commit to supporting your proposed projects, it's critical that you create a Memorandum of Understanding (MOU) or Memorandum of Agreement (MOA) to capture their proposed contributions. MOUs and MOAs are formal written documents describing a cooperative relationship between two or more parties wishing to work together on a project. What is the difference between an MOU and MOA? An MOU is a legal document, and an MOA is a cooperative agreement. Federal grant makers require MOUs, while foundations request MOAs.

When you have a working MOU or MOA, you're ready to start negotiating your piece of the financial pie — a place in the contractual section of the budget summary and detail. In other words, your society is on its way to becoming a third-party contractor.

» **Third party:** Any individual, organization, or business entity (different from your partners) that isn't the direct recipient of grant funds but will subcontract with the grantee to act as its fiscal agent and carry out specified activities in the plan of operation.

» **Third-party arrangement:** An arrangement in which the fiscal agent is the third party in the grant or cooperative agreement application. (See the nearby sidebar, "Understanding how third-party arrangements work.")

Seeking out program-specific terms

Every government program, both federal and state, has its own terms and definitions. These program-specific terms appear in the full grant application guidelines.

TIP

Each government agency provides its own definitions of the terms in the grant-funding opportunity announcement (see the earlier section "Figuring out who can apply"). Use the same terms as those published in the announcement when you write your grant application. By using each agency's terms and its definitions, you meet the basic requirement of the review criteria — showing that you understand the fed's language.

Scrutinizing the Review Criteria

When you click the link to access the full announcement in a grant-funding opportunity announcement (the synopsis), you see the full-blown grant application guidelines document, usually as a PDF file. Scroll down in the document to look for the *Review Criteria* section. (This section is also often called the *Evaluation Criteria* section.)

Understanding the review criteria can help you determine whether the grant-funding opportunity is one you should invest time and effort in pursuing. After all, if you can't fully meet key criteria, you have no reason to go after the grant or cooperative agreement. Likewise, if you can meet all the criteria, following the guidelines closely gives you a much better chance of receiving the points needed for recommendation.

REMEMBER

The Review Criteria section of the document cuts to the chase by showing you how each section of the grant application narrative is rated. This section tells you — to the letter — exactly what the peer reviewers expect to read in a winning grant application. It also tells you the total number of possible points a winning narrative section can earn during the peer review process. (For more details about peer reviews and the points they award, see Chapter 7 of this minibook.)

IN THIS CHAPTER

» Getting your grant application past the technical review

» Understanding the peer review process

» Writing to score higher peer review points

» Exploring evaluation assistance options

» Deciding whether to use a third-party evaluator

Chapter 7
Winning with Peer Review Scoring Factors

Consider the grant-writing process: You open your email to find the daily alert from Grants.gov or another funding alert subscription database. As you scroll through the alerts, you find a notice that looks perfect for your organization. You quickly click the handy link to read the Notice of Funding Availability (NOFA) synopsis. Wow, you may be on to something here. Now you click through again to read the full grant application announcement. Yes, your organization qualifies to apply for this funding. Yes, your organization is ready (capable) to take on this challenge with the intent of finishing first. And finally, you see that 55 grants will be awarded. Jackpot! Go! Green flag!

The competition will be stiff, but at least your organization has a chance at winning some of Uncle Sam's money. You even have all your collaborative partners on board, and a third-party evaluator has stepped up to write the evaluation plan section of the grant application's narrative. (See the later section, "Using Third-Party Evaluators.") The stars are aligning for this grant application to really happen.

Now that everything's falling into place, you're ready to start writing your grant application narrative. This chapter provides an overview of what's required based on standard government agency review criteria (see specifics for each part of the application in chapters 8–12 of this minibook). Remember that writing to meet a grant application's review criteria is as important as identifying the right funding source and preparing your response.

REMEMBER

In general, the basics of review criteria apply to all types of grant guidelines. Government guidelines are the most rigid, so use the example throughout this chapter. If you can write government grant applications, you can write anything!

Complying with the Technical Review Requirements

When you first submit a grant application to a federal agency for funding consideration, your application goes through a *technical review process* (or simply, a *pre-review*). This pre-review includes checking to see whether you've completed and signed all the required forms. The pre-review process also verifies your compliance with formatting instructions and checks the page length of your narrative and all other documents. Many government grant and cooperative agreement applications have narrative length restrictions, such as no more than 20 double-spaced pages. A couple of the federal grant-making agencies have even reduced their page limits to 10 pages. We can collectively celebrate when all of the 26 grant-making agencies replicate this *less is more* approach.

REMEMBER

The *narrative* is the body or main event in your grant application. It's where you write about your organization's history and capability as a grant applicant, the statement of need for grant funding, and the program design (plan of action) for planning and implementing the grant-funded program. In addition, the narrative of a grant application contains writing sections for the program's management plan (key personnel responsibilities and task descriptions), the evaluation plan, the sustainability statement, and the budget details and summary.

WARNING

If you fail to pass one of the pre-review mandatory checks, your application doesn't move from the pre-review phase to the peer review phase.

When you first read a grant or cooperative agreement opportunity announcement (refer to Chapter 6 of this minibook for more on these announcements), some basic information points can give you clues about how to set up your word-processing software to correctly format the narrative. As you read through the formatting instructions, pay attention to the following information. The quicker you find this often-buried information in the Notice of Funding Availability (NOFA), the sooner you can get started with the writing process.

- **The line spacing required:** This can be single or double. Either way, it matters. Search the announcement for the word "single" or "double" to quickly find the line-spacing requirements. This approach is the easiest way to find and note line-spacing requirements.
- **The font type and size you must use:** Search the announcement for the word "font" to quickly find the font type and size requirements. Not all grants require a specified font, but many do.
- **How page limits and page numbers are handled:** Most grant application narratives have page limits. The limitations may apply only to the narrative or they may apply to the narrative plus all the mandatory or required attachments. Typically, extra narrative-supporting charts, résumés, letters of commitment, and other documents are considered a part of the attachments. When they're included in the page count, it can be stressful for the grant writer. Page numbering can also present due diligence moments. The pagination requirements can begin with the first form and end with the last page in the appendixes or can apply only to the narrative section of the request. Some funding agencies also require that you write an abstract (read more about how to create an abstract in Chapter 8 of this minibook). Keep in mind that e-grant applications (where the entire grant application is filled out online) have character limits as opposed to pagination requirements found in a hard-copy grant application.

REMEMBER

In addition to the formatting requirements, the instructions may include specific program requirements. To be sure of the requirements, check the funding announcement before preparing your application.

REMEMBER

Always read the grant application guidelines and then be sure to follow the instructions for forms and formatting to the letter.

TIP

For the roughly 10 percent of government funding agency announcements that *don't* specify font type and size requirements for writing the grant application's narrative, call the program officer and ask about the preferred formatting. This way, you can't go wrong and you eliminate guessing and stressing.

Understanding the Peer Review Process

After you pass the technical review process, your application goes to a peer review panel to begin the peer review process. A *peer review panel* usually includes at least three experts from around the country who work in the field that the grant competition is directed to. It's called a *peer review* because you're accepted or rejected by your peers, not by a government program officer. Each reviewer gives a numerical score to each application reviewed. In most instances, the scoring of your entire grant application package is based on a total of 100 points, and typically your grant application needs to score in the high 90s in order to be recommended for the grant award. Explanatory statements on a formal rating form support the numerical score; for each section of the application's review criteria (criteria that was published in the Grants.gov announcement), reviewers describe your application's major strengths and weaknesses.

TIP

Peer reviewers can be fickle about what they like and dislike. Be careful not to deviate from any of the grant application guideline's headings, subheadings, bullets, or specific word-for-word narrative section headings. Read and retype to guide the peer reviewers through their part of the application's evaluation process.

You may wonder what happens if two peer reviewers were to rate you highly (95 points or higher) and the third reviewer rates you below the cutoff score for an award. After each reviewer independently scores your application, all three get together (over the telephone or in person) to discuss and defend their scores. The general rule is that all three reviewers must come within ten points of each other in order for an application to go one way or the other; often, after discussion, application scores change, sometimes in your favor and sometimes not.

Writing your narrative sections

Most government grant application narratives are weighted for a total of 100 possible points. The most comprehensive writing section of any grant application narrative is usually the program design section because this is where you write your goals, measurable objectives, implementation strategies, and timelines; create a logic model; develop the management plan; and comply with any additional information requested by the funding agency. (See the later section, "Incorporating national models in your program implementation strategies," and Chapter 10 of this minibook for more on this important section.)

WARNING

Some government agencies assign more than 100 points to the narrative sections of grant applications. Read every word in the guidelines so you know what to shoot for. You may need to write extra response sections to be considered eligible for the additional review points (see the next section for more details).

In the example that follows in this section, note that the largest point section is the program design, management plan, and evaluation methodologies section, which weighs in at 50 points. Because program design is worth 50 percent of the entire grant application's scoring schematic of 100 points, you want to take more time to research and write this section of your grant application narrative. If the funding agency's formatting instructions tell you that the grant application narrative can't exceed 20 single-spaced pages, you want to earmark 50 percent of the 20 pages (so 10 pages) for the program design and methodologies section.

TIP

When you know the maximum number of pages that you're allowed to write for the entire grant application narrative, you can take the total points (100 points) and divide them by the points for each section. Translate this number into a percentage, and you know how many pages you need to write in each narrative section to fulfill the peer reviewers' expectations.

The following list notes the maximum number of pages you should write in each narrative section based on a 20-page limit. This list also provides you with some of the questions that peer reviewers keep in mind when reading your application. Remember, the total possible peer review score for your grant application is 100 points. (*Note:* The point values included are fairly typical, but the values vary from application to application, as do the section headings.) Here's how it breaks down:

- **Statement of need — 20 points (20 percent of 20 pages equals 4 pages for this section):** Does the application specify those issues that this project will address from the list of issues facing the target population? Overall, is this project likely to successfully address the issues identified? Will the target population be involved in the design and implementation of the project? Does the project meet the objectives of the funding and provide sufficient justification for funding the proposal? (See Chapter 9 of this minibook for more about the statement of need.)
- **Program design, management plan, and evaluation methodologies — 50 points (50 percent of 20 pages equals 10 pages for this section):** What are the goals and measurable objectives for the project? Are they aligned with the purpose of the funding as articulated in the grant announcement? Are the proposed program activities likely to achieve the stated goals and objectives? Is the scope and duration of the program adequate to achieve the proposed outcomes? Have collaborative partners been included in the planning of the program design, and will they remain involved in the project's implementation? Is the appropriate research base used to support the proposed interventions? Is the logic model comprehensive? Does the applicant provide an impact statement? Are the evaluation designs and methodologies adequate to measure the extent to which program indicators and outcomes are being met? Is there evidence of strong and adequate project management, including

key staff and their functions, timelines, accounting procedures, reporting, and collaborative efforts with the partner organizations? (See chapters 10 and 11 of this minibook for details.)

- **Applicant capability — 20 points (20 percent of 20 pages equals 4 pages for this section):** How long has the grant applicant been in operation? Does the grant applicant have sufficient human and financial resources to implement the project successfully? Does the grant applicant have previous experience and expertise in working with the proposed target population and/or delivering similar services? Has the grant applicant managed federal grants previously? What were the outcomes of these previously funded programs (number served, measurable benchmarks achieved, and other statistical indicators demonstrating implementation success)? What is the grant applicant's organizational structure? Is the board of directors hands-on and involved in providing management and financial oversight to administrative staff? Are there clear lines of accountability in the organizational chart?
- **Budget and sustainability — 10 points (10 percent of 20 pages equals 2 pages for this section):** Is there an appropriate amount of money allocated to each key activity/task? Is the total budget allocation adequate to reach project goals? Can the applicant sustain the grant-funded program after the funding period has ended? What percent of the applicant's total project cost is in-kind (noncash) from the applicant? What percent is in-kind from collaborative partners? What percent is cash match from the applicant? What percent is cash match from collaborative partners? (See Chapter 12 of this minibook for more on presenting your budget.)

Earning bonus funding priority points

You can get an edge on the competition by meeting the funding agency's *funding priority* for a specific grant competition. Funders often identify one or more priority target populations, geographic areas, or performance criteria and award a funding preference to applications that document that they meet that preference.

For example, when NASA issues a NOFA for classroom-based space exploration education and summer camps, it may include an opportunity for grant applicants to earn an extra five or ten funding priority (read: bonus) points if their program will be located in the Alaska and Pacific Rim regions. If NASA receives 400 applications and plans to award only 20 grants, the grant applicants who write the best-of-the-best narratives and also meet the funding priority will be at the top of the point list for funding recommendation. Because of funding priority, a normal 100-point application (the best peer review rating possible without the funding opportunity) may be given an extra 10 points, for a total of 110 peer review points — a huge advantage over not-so-competitive grant applications.

Writing to the Peer Review Requirements

Before you start writing, read *all* guidelines for government grant applications and cooperative agreements. Then read them again. Better yet, read them four times, focusing on different aspects with each review:

1. **The first time through the guidelines, concentrate on the list of applicants eligible for funding.**
2. **During your second read, check for due dates, number of awards, and average size of grants.**
3. **The third time, look at the technical requirements.** *Technical requirements* refers to whether the grant competition requires that you submit your grant application to a state agency for preapproval before the final submission due date or that you use a specific font or adhere to line spacing and margin-formatting requirements. Also, pay attention to the maximum pages allowed for the grant narrative sections. Also of importance, submitting your grant application package to Grants.gov requires adhering to the system's permittable file types. The Grants.gov workspace requires PDF uploads. Your grant application package will not make it to the peer review scoring process if you fail to upload it in the requested format.
4. **During the fourth review, read for narrative content requirements.** The following sections walk you through the narrative content requirements for government funding applications (grants and cooperative agreements) so you can understand what you should look for.

REMEMBER

Your government funding request should contain a lot of words and phrases that you glean from the grant application guidelines in the section detailing the *purpose of the grant funding.* Plan to use these terms in almost every section of your grant narrative; doing so shows that you're familiar with the guidelines and that your program is in line with the grant.

Writing a compelling statement of need

One of the major sections in government grant application narratives is the *statement of need,* which is usually an explanation of the problem you hope to address if you receive the grant. Normally, when you're writing a grant or cooperative agreement application, this section is worth at least 20 of the possible 100 points a review committee can grant.

TIP

The statement of need is the place to write about not only your own research findings on the target population, but also facts and figures garnered from regional and national research. (See the later section, "Validating Needs and Implementation Strategies," for details on how to gather all the information you need before you start writing this part of your application.) To win all the points allocated to this section, follow these tips:

- **Be as comprehensive as possible in describing the needs you want to address.** Be sure to address what the problem is, when it started, and how you know it's a problem.
- **Always include results from recent community needs assessments.** Doing so shows the funder that you're basing your statement of need on valid findings about your target population or community.
- **Describe service gaps in the current service delivery system, particularly those that will be addressed with additional funding support.** If your organization has a waiting list of clients who can't be served because of its limited capacity, this is a service gap.
- **Don't talk in generalities.** Use current facts, statistics, quotes, and citations.
- **Cite all your sources and stay current.** Don't use anything older than five years.
- **Show that you know what you're talking about.** You can do so by comparing your problems to similar problems in other communities of your size.

In your statement of need, weave a story about the large black hole of gloom and doom if that's what you see based on the facts. You're not exaggerating with the information you include in this section; you're simply writing to meet the review criteria, and you're addressing each point covered in the program's or agency's goals. (For more on communicating your needs, see Chapter 9 of this minibook.)

Incorporating national models in your program implementation strategies

Another major section in a funding request narrative is what's often referred to as the *program design*. In this section, you lay out your strategy (or your program) for addressing the problem(s) presented in your statement of need. In grant applications and cooperative agreement narratives, this section is usually weighted more heavily than any other section of the narrative (anywhere from 25 to 40 points). To receive the most points possible, the program design must be sound and must contain program elements directly linked to the achievement of project objectives. Therefore, you need to write in a way that uses the language of the government agency's own objectives.

In other words, the program design section includes your proposed project's goals and objectives, which should reflect those of the funder's purpose. Always give back to the reviewers the same language used in the application for grant review criteria.

REMEMBER

Also, always write measurable objectives that state who will be affected (for example, at-risk students), what the change will be (an increase of at least 20 percent), and by when (at the end of one year). Language concerning a time frame is optional in the objectives only when the grant application guidelines ask for a separate timeline section.

The objectives or measurements stated in a grant announcement are like a big finger pointing in the direction you need to write in order to win a grant. The objectives shout out, "Write me, write me!" For more about goals and objectives, head to Chapter 10 of this minibook.

Demonstrating accountability with an evaluation plan

A sound *evaluation plan*, the next major part of your program design narrative, is essential to winning big review points. In some grant applications, the evaluation section is included as a component of the program design section; in others, it's a stand-alone section. Regardless of where it's placed, this section is usually weighted between 5 and 20 points.

Typically, an evaluation plan focuses on two main questions:

- Was the program implemented effectively? (This is the *process evaluation.*)
- Did the program achieve its intended objectives and outcomes? (This is the *outcome evaluation.*)

The evaluation plan should answer the following questions:

- What qualitative and quantitative measures will you collect data on?
- What data collection tools will you use to measure qualitative and quantitative data?
- How frequently will you measure the data?
- How will you use the data collected?
- How often will you implement corrective actions when the data shows that you're falling short of your measurable objectives in any area?

» Who will conduct the evaluation?

» How will the results of your evaluation be shared with stakeholders?

If you brought in a third-party evaluator during the planning stages of your project or service, they are automatically a member of the narrative-writing team. The evaluator can write the entire evaluation plan section because they should be an expert in gleaning a program design and quickly developing research-driven evaluation plans. Head to the later section, "Using Third-Party Evaluators," for more details on working with these folks.

Proving your organization's capability to manage a grant-funded project

The project management and overall organizational capability section of your grant application or cooperative agreement narrative typically carries double-digit peer review points (usually 10 to 20). If you're not capable of carrying out and managing a federal grant award, that inability will show up in this section in one way or another. In a well-constructed *project management statement*, you cite your organization's capability and relevant experience in developing and operating programs that deal with problems similar to those addressed by the proposed project or service. You should also cite the organization's experience in operating programs in cooperation with other community organizations, including collaborative partners.

Also remember to identify your program's executive leaders in the project management section. Briefly describe their involvement in the proposed project or service and provide assurance of their commitment to the successful implementation of that project or service.

TIP

Keep in mind that all key personnel (the people responsible for the project's implementation) should have extensive experience in programs and services like the one you're proposing. You score more points during the review process if you can name actual staff members and show their titles and credentials instead of relying on the standard "yet to be hired" statement. *Note:* Don't forget to identify your third-party evaluator up front; be prepared to include a copy of their full résumé in your appendixes, if requested.

To advance your claims regarding project management, include documentation that briefly summarizes similar projects undertaken by your organization and note the extent to which your objectives were achieved. Also, record and justify the priority this project or service will have within your organization, including the facilities and resources available to carry out your plans. If you have volunteers, mentioning them (how many, what they do, and the value of their contribution to your organization) in this section is helpful. To determine the value of a volunteer hour, go to `https://independentsector.org/volunteer_time`.

REMEMBER

Losing even one or two points in the project management section can hurt you when the total score is tallied.

Developing an expense-driven budget

Your budget forms and detailed narrative must show the grant reviewer that your costs are reasonable, allowable, and worth the result you seek. The budget section is usually worth the remaining review criteria points (five to ten), although not all funders score the budget as part of the review process.

With your budget narrative, most government grants and cooperative agreements ask you to provide a detailed budget worksheet for each year of the project period. You also need to include an explanation of the basis for computation of all costs. (See Chapter 12 of this minibook for more about budget presentation.)

REMEMBER

Add up your budget, and then add it up again. Make sure each expense is directly related to an activity necessary to reach the project's objectives. Don't introduce any costs here that you haven't addressed in your main application narrative.

When you read the guidelines for preparing the budget, look closely for any language about construction costs. Most government grants don't cover new construction, but they do allow program-related renovations.

TIP

When in doubt about the guidelines and how they relate to your budget, call and ask the government agency's grants management officer. Then follow up with an email to create a paper trail for future reference. This contact — even if it seems trivial — can establish a relationship that may be beneficial in getting your grant funded.

Validating Needs and Implementation Strategies

You probably know a lot about the population you want to serve with your hoped-for grant monies. And if you're at the grant-writing stage for a program, you're probably pretty well versed in what you want to accomplish and how you plan to go about putting the program in place. But to write an award-winning application, you need to beef up your facts with even more facts.

Knowing the grant or cooperative agreement's intent or focus sets the direction for the type of research you must do in order to write a high-scoring, competitive grant application. For example, if the monies are intended to fund a new economic development initiative for small businesses in Atlanta, you need to research demographics on the needs of small businesses in the county and city. To get information about small business demographics by state, type keywords into your favorite Internet search engine or use some of the resources available on your state's Small Business Development Center website. Typing "statistics on Atlanta small businesses," for example, garnered links for multiple websites with recent reports on small businesses located in Atlanta.

TIP

Always create an online electronic folder for your research data so you have it at your fingertips when you're not at your computer. Having access to critically needed information from all forms of mobile technology is the best plan when you may take your work home from the office and you need access to files. There are multiple options, including OneDrive, Google Workspace, Dropbox, and others; most if not all have mobile applications that you can download to your smartphone, tablet, and laptop. Remember, when you're on a grant application deadline, all your work may not be done during traditional work hours or in your traditional workspace.

TIP

Google Scholar (`http://scholar.google.com`) is a great resource for finding publications if you're affiliated with a university. In addition, you'll have access to enormous publication databases.

Publications produced by the government agencies that award grants are another good source for facts and figures. You can obtain these valuable resources from each government agency's information clearinghouse. Check out agency websites for links labeled Resources or Publications. You may encounter any of the following publications, which can be of great help:

- **Bulletins:** These documents summarize recent findings from government program initiatives. Designed for use as references, they may contain graphics such as tables, charts, graphs, and photographs. You can re-create some of the most current and relevant graphics in your statement of need or program design.
- **Fact sheets:** Fact sheets highlight, in one to two pages, key points and sources of further information on government programs and initiatives. You can cite the most recent facts (never more than five years old) in your statement of need.
- **Journals:** These publications highlight innovative programs or contain articles on critical issues and trends. You can cite some of the model programs at the beginning of your program design section to show how you're modeling your

project on a successful program. You can also use any critical issues or trends covered in journals in your statement of need.

- **Reports:** These documents contain comprehensive research and evaluation findings; provide detailed descriptions of innovative programs implemented at the national, state, and local levels; and present statistical analysis, trends, or other data on selected topics. Reports may include explanations of case studies, field studies, and other strategies used for assessing program success and replication. Some reports provide training curricula and lesson plans as well.
- **Summaries:** Summaries describe key research and evaluation findings that may affect future policies and practices. Summaries highlight funded programs implemented at the national, state, or local level that may serve as models for other jurisdictions. These publications usually include appendixes, lists of resources, and additional readings.

TIP

You can cite research on evaluation findings in your statement of need. Cite innovative programs considered models in your program design section to build the basis for proposing your own program model.

TIP

Save every research-oriented publication you can get your hands on to your preferred cloud storage space, organized by subject category. As new reports are published, replace the older reports so that you're always working with the most current research findings. Grant writing is so much easier when you have the information you need (and the information you didn't even know you needed) at your fingertips. The Internet makes it easy to bookmark a favorite website.

REMEMBER

With so many ways to save your files, putting everything on your computer's hard drive is not a wise idea. Hard drives fail, and when they do, you're just plain out of luck. You've lost a significant amount of research findings that cannot be easily replaced. Even depending on external drives for your research files can be devastating when your drives are damaged. But it's pretty rare for a cloud drive to disappear. Store your files in a place where they can be retrieved by any type of technology. When you use cloud drives, a locked-up computer won't send you into a frenzy of stress.

Using Third-Party Evaluators

Writing an application for a federal grant or cooperative agreement requires making new friends in your community — not only collaborative partners, but also community specialists such as evaluators. You can always score more review points by using a *third-party evaluator* — basically a person or organization that operates objectively and gives you factual, third-party feedback on your grant-funded goals and objectives.

Even though evaluators are typically paid from grant funds, they will call the situations as they see them when helping grant applicants develop data collection tools, collect and interpret data, and compile comprehensive evaluation reports for funders and other stakeholders. (Chapter 10 of this minibook covers the evaluation process in depth.)

TIP

The following folks make excellent third-party evaluators:

- **Evaluation consultants:** These people normally have years of experience in the field of evaluation. You can often find evaluation consultants by calling your local community foundation. Community foundations often use evaluation consultants to assist in evaluating their own programs.
- **Retired college or university faculty:** Often, these individuals have participated in the grant-writing process and have even helped their college or university development offices design evaluations for government grant applications.
- **Retired government personnel who worked in an administrative capacity in a finance department:** These individuals usually have years' worth of work experience in internal reporting requirements for major organizations or government agencies.

As far as timing's concerned, the best time to bring in an evaluator is when you're sitting down with your staff and your collaborative partners to plan what you'll propose in the grant or cooperative agreement application. Running an online search for third-party evaluators is also helpful, but you may not locate an evaluator close to home. Using an evaluator who doesn't live in your city or town is okay as long as they are familiar with the area, but keep in mind that hiring an evaluator from outside your region may increase the cost of the evaluation if site visits are necessary to plan and conduct the evaluation.

IN THIS CHAPTER

» Knowing how to prepare what a funder requires

» Drafting a cover letter

» Diving into forms

» Creating the abstract and table of contents

Chapter 8

Preparing Preliminary Documents

This chapter covers critical and standard information-gathering forms and other pre-narrative sections you can expect to see in your grant applications. Remember that every type of funding source has different grant proposal formatting and submission requirements. With so many types of funding applications floating around, determining what goes where can be confusing. This chapter explains it all.

Along with a deep dive into general funder requirements, this chapter also discusses cover letters. Cover letters are no longer a standard requirement of grant applications, but some private-sector funders (that is, foundations and corporations) still require that a formal cover letter accompany a paper grant proposal. What do you write in these cover letters? How long should they be, and should they be formal or informal? What do you do if you have to fill out a cover form (something many private-sector and all public-sector grant makers require)? You'll find the answers to all these questions in this chapter.

Complying with Mandatory Application Package Requirements

Not sure what to include in your application? Don't stress. The standard ingredients are broken down for you right here by order of typical appearance and also clarify when each preliminary document is required.

WARNING

Always read each funding agency's guidelines and give the funder exactly what it asks for in the instructions. Never, ever deviate. Also, do not alter any PDF-formatted forms if at all possible. Changing the forms because you need more space on a typing line or changing the font in a form can result in automatic rejection. Make sure that all PDF forms are filled in accurately and uploaded in the funder's required PDF version.

These up-front components (the items that come before the grant application narrative) should be in the following order — although, remember, not every piece applies in every case:

- **Cover letter:** Only for foundation and corporate requests that ask you to include a cover letter.
- **Common grant application form:** Only for foundation and corporate requests when the funder doesn't have its own specific application form or format and instructs you to submit a common grant application form.
- **Application for Federal Assistance:** Always for federal grant applications and sometimes requested by state agencies. Most often referred to as *SF-424* (*SF* stands for Standard Form).
- **Abstract or executive summary:** Appropriate for all types of funders and typically required.
- **Table of contents:** Most often requested in federal and state grant applications. Not every government agency requires a table of contents.

Drafting a Cover Letter (If Requested)

Thanks to the increasing number of funders that now require e-grants (electronic online submissions in the funder's template), you need to only include cover letters for foundation and corporate funders that request one in their published guidelines. (Government funders rarely, if ever, ask for a cover letter anymore.)

If you have to supply a cover letter, make sure it's brief and to the point. When a funder opens your request for assistance, the cover letter provides the first inkling of how well you understand the person you addressed the letter to — the funder. Avoid merely regurgitating the information in your grant request.

TIP

Write the cover letter last, after you've completed the entire funding request and are in a reflective mood. As you consider your great achievement (the finished funding request), let the creative, right side of your brain kick in and connect your feelings of accomplishment to the person who will help make your plans come true.

Follow these handy tips when you write your own cover letters (and check out the cover letter example in Figure 8-1):

- **Use the date that you'll send the complete grant application to the funding source.** You want to create documents that are consistent, so the dates on cover letters and accompanying cover forms should be the same.
- **Open with the contact person's name and title, followed by the funding source name, address, city, state, and ZIP code.** Remember to double-check the contact information with a telephone call or email to the funder. You can also search via the Internet for the correct information.
- **Greet the contact person with "Dear" plus the personal title (as in Mr., Ms., or Mrs.), followed by the last name.** This greeting is your first point of introduction to a potential funder, so you need to use a personal title. Call to make sure the personal title you're using is correct. Bev once used "Ms." for a female program director who preferred to be addressed with "Miss." The request was denied because she didn't do her homework on the person's correct personal title. In addition, some people use gender-neutral titles. When in doubt, call and ask the receptionist for the funder how to address the contact person.
- **Keep the first paragraph short and focused.** Start by introducing your organization (use its legal name). Then introduce yourself and give your job title (executive director, development officer, and so forth). Finally, get to the point. Tell the funder how much money you're requesting and why your organization needs it. Write a sentence or two about what your organization does.
- **Write a second paragraph that's brief and to the point.** Include no more than three sentences stating your organization's corporate structure status and the date it was founded. Then tell the funder your organization's purpose and how it aligns with the funder's mission or funding priority. Validate your existence by adding at least one sentence that includes research-based evidence showing there's a need for what your organization does.

- **Wrap up your cover letter with a summarizing paragraph.** Share a closing thought or reflection about what this funding partnership can mean for the future of your project's target audience.
- Use a creative closing, such as "Awaiting your response," "With great hope," or something else that fits your project's theme/topic area. Sounding both thankful and optimistic as you close your request for funds is important.

Rule
of Thumb

Small Business Book Series

428 Joslyn Castle Drive
Omaha, NE 92203

December 1, 2016

Mrs. Jennifer S. Randall
Trust Administrator
The John B. and Beverly A. Browning Trust
123456 W. Social Security Lane
Medicare, IA 45678

Dear Mrs. Randall:

I am writing on behalf of the Rule Of Thumb for Business (ROTB) based in Omaha, Nebraska. As the Secretary of the Board of Directors, our Executive Committee has authorized me to submit a grant proposal to the Trust requesting $5,000. This generous gift from the Trust will allow us to purchase additional online marketing services to promote our Small Business Book Series. A 2014 report published by the American Small Print Books Association showed that marketing small print books rigorously online (our books are 125 pages or less) can generate 10 times the sales as other non-social media venues. With over one million small businesses (under 500 employees), there is a high demand for our book topics.

Founded in 2012, ROTB is an IRS-recognized 501(c)(3) nonprofit corporation. Our mission is to provide topics of interest and relevance to small businesses to help them to get started and stay in business. When Mrs. Browning started her family's trust, she had already published 39 books. Her 40th book was titled *A Guide to Sustainability for Small Business,* and it targets the same market as ROTB.

In summary, an ongoing partnership with the Trust would indirectly benefit small businesses nationwide. With limited market presence, ROTB has the ability to promote Mrs. Browning's book as well to generate additional income for the Trust.

Awaiting your response,

Bev

Beverly A. Browning
Secretary, ROTB Board of Directors

ATTACHMENTS

FIGURE 8-1: A fully developed cover letter leaves the funder feeling connected to the applicant.

Illustration by Ryan Sneed

» **Sign your first name only; doing so invites an informal, long-term relationship.** Below your signature, type your first name, middle initial, last name, and job title.

REMEMBER

The executive director or board president is the appropriate signatory.

» **At the bottom of the letter, include the note "ATTACHMENTS" or "ENCLOSURES."** This note indicates that a grant proposal is included in the same packet. The capital letters signal that the grant proposal is important.

Shuffling Through Funder Information Requests

No one group of funders uses the same formatting templates or online e-grant text entry forms. So, the following list gives you the most commonly requested information fields that you can expect to see with the majority of funders:

» **Organization name, tax-exempt status, year organization was founded, date of application, address, telephone number, fax number, director, and contact person and title:** These items give the funding source straight information about your eligibility to apply for funds.

» **Grant request:** The funding source wants to know how much money you're asking for before it even reads the full proposal. The amount listed here is the first clue to the funder that you're counting on it to provide a specific percentage of your project support.

REMEMBER

This figure doesn't mean that you're requesting the total amount needed from just one funder; you still send your customized common grant application proposal package to other funders willing to accept this format. Having more than one potential funder lined up increases your chances of receiving the full amount needed.

» **Period grant will cover:** Most foundation and corporate funders award grant monies for only one year. Some fund you for multiple years, but they don't represent the norm among private-sector funders.

» **Type of request:** Typically, the funders want to know whether you're requesting general support (money to pay the day-to-day bills), start-up funds (you're just beginning operations), technical assistance (training, accounting aid, or some other type of specialized consulting), and so on. See Chapter 1 of this minibook for your grant language choices when it comes to the type of funds requested.

- **Project title:** It's a nice touch for every funding request to have a project or program title. A title gives your request personality. Remember to use a consistent title. It should be the same from the cover letter to the cover form to the grant proposal.
- **Total project budget:** The amount you enter here is the total cost to implement your program. Include the value of your in-kind and cash contributions in addition to the amount needed from the funder. (Go to Chapter 12 of this minibook for budget terms and definitions.)
- **Start date of fiscal year:** The date your organization's financial year begins. For example, your fiscal year may begin on January 1, July 1, September 1, or in any month. Check with your financial staff to determine your start date.
- **Total organizational budget:** This amount is your organization's total operating budget for the current fiscal year.
- **Summarize the organization's mission:** The word *summarize* is key here. If you have a long mission statement, give the abbreviated version. *Remember that the entire cover form usually fits on one page.*
- **Summary of project or grant request:** Don't fill out this field until you've written the grant application narrative. Then cut and paste into this section the sentences that most effectively summarize your project. This field typically includes one sentence that provides a brief overview of your project. For example, "The purpose of this project is to provide 2,000 Haitian families displaced by back-to-back hurricanes and tropical storms with temporary housing, food, and medical care."

TIP

Knowing What the Feds Want in a Form (SF-424)

The electronic Application for Federal Assistance Form (also known as SF-424 and available at `www.grants.gov/web/grants/forms.html`) asks for four pages of information. Here, you're walked through the sections you can expect to see when you're filling in the SF-424 online. Better yet, you're shown exactly what the government wants you to include. (Note that mandatory fields are outlined in red in the digital version of this form.)

REMEMBER

Each federal grant-making agency may use a variation of SF-424. Always use the funding agency's link for the specific form.

TIP

If any of the SF-424 instructions use the term *require*, you must enter the requested information. Leaving this section blank will disqualify your grant application from funding consideration.

Here's a glimpse of the form's information fields on the SF-424 (see `https://apply07.grants.gov/apply/forms/readonly/SF424_4_0-V4.0.pdf`):

- **Item 1 – Type of Submission:** Your options are Preapplication, Application, or Changed/Corrected Application.
- **Item 2 – Type of Application:** Here you must select from New, Continuation, or Revision.
- **Items 3, 4, and 5:** Completed by the government.
- **Items 6 and 7:** For state use only.
- **Item 8 – Applicant Information:** Fill in each of the text boxes in this section. You're required to enter the legal name of the applicant that will undertake the assistance activity. This is the organization that has registered with the Central Contractor Registry (CCR). You can get information on registering with CCR from Grants.gov.
- **Item 9 – Type of Applicant:** Click on the drop-down boxes to select your type of applicant. There are three options plus Other.
- **Item 10 – Name of Federal Agency:** This will automatically populate when you are in a specific NOFO. The information will be filled in for you.
- **Item 11 – Catalog of Federal Domestic Assistance Number/Title:** Here you enter the Catalog of Federal Domestic Assistance number and title of the program under which assistance is requested, as found in the program announcement, if applicable.
- **Item 12 – Funding Opportunity Number/Title:** Here you're required to enter the Funding Opportunity Number and title of the opportunity under which assistance is requested, as found in the program announcement.
- **Item 13 – Competition Identification Number/Title:** Here you enter the competition identification number and title of the competition under which assistance is requested, if applicable.
- **Item 14 – Areas Affected by Project:** This data element is intended for use only by programs for which the area(s) affected are likely to be different from the place(s) of performance reported on the SF-424 Project/Performance Site Location(s) Form. Add an attachment to enter additional areas, if needed.

- **Item 15 – Descriptive Title of Applicant's Project:** Here you're required to enter a brief descriptive title of the project. If appropriate, attach a map showing project location (for example, construction or real property projects). For pre-applications, you're required to attach a summary description of the project.
- **Item 16 – Congressional Districts Office:** The actual form abbreviates Office as "Of." Here you're required to enter all district(s) affected by the program or project. Enter this in the following format: two-character state abbreviation, a hyphen, and the three-character district number. For example, CA-005 for the California 5th District, CA-012 for the California 12th District, or NC-103 for the North Carolina 103rd District. If all congressional districts in a state are affected, enter "all" for the district number (for example, MD-all for all congressional districts in Maryland). If nationwide — all districts within all states are affected — enter "US-all." If the program/project is outside the United States, enter 00-000.

  This optional data element is intended for use only by programs for which the area(s) affected are likely to be different than place(s) of performance reported on the SF-424 Project/Performance Site Location(s) Form. Attach an additional list of program/project congressional districts, if needed.
- **Item 17 – Proposed Project Start and End Dates:** Here you're required to enter the proposed start date and end date of the project.
- **Item 18 – Estimated Funding:** Here you're required to enter the amount requested or to be contributed during the first funding/budget period by each contributor. The value of in-kind contributions should be included on appropriate lines, as applicable. If the action will result in a dollar change to an existing award, indicate only the amount of the change. For decreases, enclose the amounts in parentheses.
- **Item 19 – Is Application Subject to Review by State Under Executive Order 12372 Process:** Here, you're required to contact the State Single Point of Contact (SPOC) for Federal Executive Order 12372 to determine whether the application is subject to the state intergovernmental review process. Select the appropriate box. If "a." is selected, enter the date the application was submitted to the state. Use this link to determine if your state has a SPOC: `www.whitehouse.gov/wp-content/uploads/2020/04/SPOC-4-13-20.pdf`.
- **Item 20 – Is the Applicant Delinquent on Any Federal Debit:** Here, you're required to select the appropriate box. This question applies to the applicant organization, not the person who signs as the authorized representative. Categories of federal debt include, but may not be limited to, delinquent audit disallowances, loans, and taxes. If yes, include an explanation in an attachment.

» **Item 21 – Authorized Representative:** This final section is where the authorized representative of your organization must sign and date. You're required to enter the first and last name, prefix, middle name, and suffix. Also, enter the contact person's title, telephone number, email, and fax number. ***Note:*** A copy of the governing body's authorization for you to sign this application as the official representative must be on file in the applicant's office. (Certain federal agencies may require that this authorization be submitted as part of the application.)

Saving the Abstract or Executive Summary Narrative for Last

The *abstract* or *executive summary* is a brief, page-limited overview of what the grant reviewer will find in the full grant application. Brevity is important (this section should be no longer than one page unless the guidelines indicate the need for a two-page summary). Write (or assemble) your abstract or summary *after* you've written the entire grant application narrative because by then you should have all the wordy explanations out of your system. (*Note:* Federal applications often specify a word or line limit for abstracts.)

REMEMBER

Always follow the funder's guidelines regarding word or line limits and the structure of the abstract or executive summary.

If no specific structure is requested, you can create an abstract or executive summary like the one in Figure 8-2 by pulling the most significant sentences from each key writing section in the grant narrative and doing a quick cut-and-paste. Take key sentences from the following areas and keep them in the same order in the abstract or executive summary as they appear in the narrative:

» **Proposed initiative**: Here you enter the name of your project or program and the full name of the funding competition you're applying to for grant consideration.

» **Introduction of target population:** Copy and paste a sentence or two about whom you're planning to target and serve with grant monies.

» **Goals:** Copy and paste your goals from the project design section of your proposal narrative.

» **Program measurements and performance targets (also known as objectives):** Copy and paste your objectives and performance targets from the program design section of your proposal narrative.

» **Plan of action:** Copy and paste the key activities that comprise the program's implementation process.

Abstract

OJJDP FY 2016 Comprehensive Anti-Gang Strategies and Programs
Grant Application – CFDA 16.544
Submitted by: Leadership Training Institute – Hempstead, New York

Proposed Initiative: Long Island Comprehensive Gang Model

Target Population: Comprehensive anti-gang strategies are critically needed in Nassau (pop. 1,357,429)[1] and Suffolk (pop. 1,518,475)[2] Counties (a.k.a. Long Island), New York. The communities of Hempstead, Roosevelt, Freeport, and Westbury/New Castle in Nassau County, and Huntington Station, Wyandanch, Central Islip, and Brentwood in Suffolk Counties are under violent and continuous attack by 5,000 members that reside on Long Island.[3]

Goals: Goal 1 - Provide opportunities to youth at high-risk of gang involvement. Goal 2 - Involve key stakeholders in connecting high-risk youth to community-based social interventions. Goal 3 - Catalyze cross-agency organizational change and development.

Leadership Training Institute (LTI) is adopting OJJDP's Comprehensive Gang Model.

Program Measurements and Performance Targets:
SMART Objective 1a: By the end of the model's implementation period, the number of enrolled youth completing program requirements will increase by 70% or more.
Resulting OJJDP Performance Target
- Percent completed.

SMART Objective 1b: By the end of the model's implementation period, the number of enrolled youth who will have completed an evidence-based program/practice will increase by 70% or more.
Resulting OJJDP Performance Target
- Percent exposed to evidence-based model.

SMART Objective 2a: By the end of the model's implementation period, the number of stakeholders engaged in the Steering Committee/Policy Group (currently known as the Building For Success Partnership) will increase by 60% or more.
Resulting OJJDP Performance Targets
- Number of planning or training events held.
- Percentage of program policies changed and/or rescinded.

SMART Objective 3a: By the end of the model's implementation period, the number of policies changed or rescinded to address local gang problems will increase by 25% or more.
Resulting OJJDP Performance Target
- Number of program policies changed and/or rescinded.

SMART Objective 3b: By the end of the model's implementation period, the number of OJJDP-involved (training and technical assistance recipients) agencies reporting improvements in operations will increase by 25% or more.
Resulting OJJDP Performance Target
- Percentage of organizations reporting improvements in operations based on training and technical assistance.

Plan of Action: The **Long Island Comprehensive Gang Model** will have three strategies. They include:

1. *Opportunities Provision*
2. *Social Intervention*
3. *Organizational Change and Development*

[1] http://quickfacts.census.gov/qfd/states/36/36059.html
[2] http://quickfacts.census.gov/qfd/states/36/36103.html
[3] National Drug Intelligence Center to 2016

Illustration by Ryan Sneed

FIGURE 8-2: The abstract or executive summary draws critical details from different parts of the narrative.

Crafting the Table of Contents When Required

Whether you include a table of contents depends on the grant application guidelines. Rigidly structured guidelines typically call for a table of contents, particularly if the narrative is long (more than ten pages) or if you're asked to provide several attachments or appendixes.

REMEMBER

The table of contents shouldn't include the abstract or executive summary because those parts almost always precede the table of contents. Exceptions to this rule are applications from state or federal agencies that stipulate a format in which the table of contents comes before the abstract or executive summary. Grant guidelines and writing formats vary from one agency to another and even within departments in an agency, so be sure to read the grant application guidelines carefully and follow the format listed in the reviewer's criteria (see chapters 6 and 7 of this minibook for details on review criteria).

Figure 8-3 shows an example of a federal grant application table of contents.

U.S. Department of Justice
Law Enforcement Training – Discretionary Funds – CFDA 12.345

Table of Contents
Submitted by: Grant Writing Training Foundation – Goodyear.

Grant Application Narrative Sections	**Page**
Need for the Project	1–3
Foundation for Implementation	4–8
Quality of the Project Design	9–19
Quality of the Management Plan	20–22
Quality of the SLC Project Evaluation	23–24
Appendices	25–44
Appendix 1: Letters of Commitment	
Appendix 2: Organizational Chart	
Appendix 3: Resumes of Key Personnel	
Appendix 4: Copy of IRS Nonprofit Status	
Appendix 5: Nonprofit Survey	
Mandatory Assurances and Certifications	45–50

Illustration by Ryan Sneed

FIGURE 8-3: A sample table of contents for a federal grant application.

REMEMBER

Keep the following points in mind regarding your application's table of contents:

» The reader expects to see sections and subsections of the grant application listed.

» Appendixes must be listed and numbered.

» Federally mandated or state-mandated forms and attachments or appendixes must be listed as well. (Including mandated forms in your table of contents lets the government know that you included them in the application. If a form disappears during the review process, at least the grant reviewer can affirm that it was included in the original application.)

IN THIS CHAPTER

» Following the funder's instructions

» Demonstrating organizational capability and presenting your current programs

» Presenting validated facts about your target population

» Building in validating statistics

» Creating a compelling narrative to validate your statement of need

Chapter 9

Sharing Your Organizational History and Developing the Narrative

Whether your organization is a first-time grant applicant or a veteran proposal writing machine, you must write current and relevant boilerplate information about the organization in the organization background/history section of the narrative. (A *boilerplate* is information that has minimal changes from year to year.) The section of the grant application narrative that houses this information, whether up front, in the middle, or at the end, communicates who the grant applicant organization is, where it's located, and what services and programs it provides. This section also includes information on your organization's primary community partners — agencies that support your mission, programs, and services by collaborating with you to strengthen your financial, physical, and program-related assets. How much you write for this section depends on each funder and its specific guidelines (content and page or character limitations) for what and how much it wants to see.

In this chapter, you find out how to incorporate your organization's background, programs, and affiliations into compelling introductory paragraphs that introduce the organization to potential funders. These opening sections convince the grant-funding decision makers that your organization is financially and operationally capable to receive and manage grant monies. This chapter also explains how to fill your statement of need with engaging information that helps drive the point home in a way that makes your grant application stand out from the pack.

REMEMBER

A little trivia and a lot of facts create the kind of reader interest every successful grant writer shoots for. The longer you can keep readers' attention, the better your chances are of getting recommended for a grant award.

TIP

Find a full-length sample grant application at `https://www.dummies.com/wp-content/uploads/Grant_Writing_FD_Chapter_13_-_Sample_Grant_Application_for_Reference.pdf`; be sure to check it out before you write.

Adhering to the Funder's Guidelines

In most cases, the funding source's narrative-writing instructions point you in the right direction for what to include in the capability section of the application. Some funders title this section *organizational background* or *history*. Others label it *grant applicant capability* or *organizational capability*. Regardless of what the funder calls this section, when introducing your organization, be sure to divide the information into different parts for easy digestion by the grant reviewer.

For example, you may include these different parts: background (history and accomplishments), programs and activities (current services), constituency demographics (information about your service population), and community affiliations (local, regional, and state partners).

Remember, federal grant application guidelines require extensive, detailed responses; therefore, the writing guidelines are very long as well. Here are some examples of the types of narrative section writing instructions you may see in your application guidelines:

- **Community foundation example:** Organization Background: Provide the history of the organization, its broader purposes, and services to the community.

» **Federal example:** U.S. Department of Labor — Veteran's Employment and Training Service Grant Program: Organizational Capability and Experience — You must describe in your application your organization's ability to manage the operational, administrative, programmatic, and financial reporting requirements specified within this funding announcement. You must describe key staff skills, experience, history, knowledge, qualifications, capabilities, and office locations, and provide an organizational chart.

You must also address your capacity for timely implementation of the program, programmatic reporting, and participant tracking. You must fully describe how the proposed program can or will outlast the federal funding being provided under this grant. You must describe in your application a diverse funding base or illustrate an organizational strategic plan that will lead to the attainment of financial resources beyond those secured through the grant. If you have previously operated a veterans' employment and training program, then you must include the performance outcomes from your last, or most recent (if the grant is active), fourth quarter Technical Performance Report (TPR) and the planned goals for that grant.

If you lack prior experience with implementing these types of grants, you are required to provide program outcomes from other similar programs you have operated. You must describe specific outcomes previously achieved against set targets within these related programs, such as number of enrollments, number of participants who entered employment, cost per placement into employment, benefits secured, and coalitions.

For new grantees that may not have past experience operating an employment and training program, it is important to have detailed information on the specific ability to manage these types of programs.

Creating Organizational Capabilities as a Grant Applicant

When writing the organizational capability section of your application, you need to give the grant reader just enough information about your organization's experience and accomplishments to pique their interest and keep them reading word for word. Remember that you're just introducing yourself — this isn't the place to discuss the money you need or the problems you have. In a federal grant application, you'll lose peer review points if you don't respond to every mandatory requirement for each section of the narrative and budget. Chapter 7 of this minibook explains the federal peer review process and how to write to the requirements for what peer reviewers want to read.

TIP

Although you're shooting for clarity and precision, in order to get your grant application funded, you must be able to make the mundane interesting to the grant reader. Your narrative must be compelling to all who read it, from your community partners to potential funders. Telling and *selling* your organization's story is critical when funders are at the point of making a decision to fund or not to fund. You must write to hit them where their hearts and their minds are!

The first two sections that follow describe how to write the organizational capability section for private-sector funders. The last section explains how to write the same section for public-sector funders.

Stating the history, mission, values, and geographic logistics

The grant reader wants to see the following in the first few sentences:

- The full legal name of your organization.
- The year the organization was founded, by whom, and for what purpose.

TIP

If you don't know the appropriate answers, ask a longtime employee or board member. Sometimes, you can also find the history of an organization in its annual report or in an anniversary issue of its newsletter. Keep researching and asking others until you strike gold.

- The location of the organization's headquarters and any other operating sites (name, city, county, state).
- The mission statement (what the grant applicant's organization is now) and the vision statement (what the organization will become).

In the following example, the text is inviting because there's a face on the organization's history:

- The Grant Writing Training Foundation was founded in 2007 by Dr. Beverly A. Browning in Buckeye (Maricopa County), Arizona. Dr. Browning's vision for this 501(c)(3) foundation emerged when she was managing a for-profit consulting business that wanted to offer more affordable training for nonprofits and units of government. Her vision unfolded in the mission statement of the Foundation: Provide affordable and relevant training in grant seeking, proposal writing, and nonprofit and financial capacity building. The Foundation's vision is to leave a legacy of teaching and reaching those who desire to elevate their proposal writing skills. Dr. Browning has over 45 years of experience in the nonprofit sector. The most important achievements for the Grant Writing Training Foundation include the following:

- Donated 20 percent or more of annual proceeds to training-site hosts and other charitable causes.
- Provided new computers or grant-related textbooks at venues to at least one of the attendees annually since 2007.
- Facilitated low-cost training to over 1,000 nonprofit site hosts since its founding.

Presenting key milestones in organizational development

Complete the organizational capability section by writing about important milestones in the organization's history that relate to the activities covered in the grant application. Write a brief introductory paragraph before you begin listing the milestones.

WARNING

Even though your organization may have dozens of milestones, don't include every last miscellaneous award and achievement. If you're seeking grant funds for a new after-school program, for example, don't mention unrelated accomplishments, such as the school football team's winning record or the cabinet full of medals from the swim team. Taking the grant reader down a dead-end road with unrelated information is a fatal flaw, and it can result in your application not being read or funded.

TIP

Use bulleted, abbreviated statements to share the top milestones. Use a casual voice to make the list more inviting. Your organization's milestones narrative may look something like this:

» The Grant Writing Training Foundation currently offers a full menu of grant-related and small business capacity-building training programs to nonprofits throughout the United States, including foundations, community service organizations, colleges and universities, and government agencies. Current training programs include but are not limited to:

- Grant Writing Boot Camp (2007 to current: 400 sessions)
- Grant Writing Boot Camp Express (2010 to current: 150 sessions)
- Nonprofit Board of Directors Boot Camp (2012 to current: 150 sessions)
- Small Biz Boot Camp (2012 to current: 50 sessions)

When writing the organizational capabilities section, consider using customized bullets to draw attention to the grant applicant's attributes. For example, you can use a dollar sign or a red heart to point to the Grant Writing Training Foundation's accomplishments.

REMEMBER

If your organization is new (just starting up), list the background of the founders and your governing board members along with the planned milestones from your strategic plan. Chapter 2 of this minibook gives you more information on the strategic plan.

Shifting gears for government grants

Strong, emotional writing works best with foundation and corporate grant applications, but you need to adopt a different writing style for government applications. When you describe your organization's history in a government grant application, follow these tips to rack up the review points (see chapters 6 and 7 of this minibook for more on review points):

- Use a compelling but concise writing style; remember to only write what's asked for — no more, no less.
- Stick with the cold, hard facts.
- Don't write the history and accomplishments section in the first person (using pronouns such as *I, our,* and *my*). Instead, use the third-person writing approach. When you write in third person, you're writing as if you're on the outside of the grant applicant organization and looking in with a third-party perspective. Your reference to your organization must be from a formal and straightforward approach. Here are two examples that allow you to compare first- and third-person writing styles:
  - **First person:** Our organization was founded in 2007 and is located in Arizona's Sonoran Desert (Phoenix MSA), Arizona. Last year, we provided more than 100 capacity-building training programs for nonprofits throughout the world.
  - **Third person:** The Grant Writing Training Foundation, founded in 2007, is located in Goodyear (Maricopa County), Arizona. Last year, its founder and director provided over 100 virtual training programs for nonprofit organizations and NGOs throughout the United States, Canada, and Europe.

Sorting Out Relevant Programs and Activities

Use the program section of your opening narrative to write about the day-to-day happenings at your organization. Describe the programs that you currently provide to your constituency (also called the *target population*), not what you plan to provide when your grant request is funded. (You can read more about target populations in the next section.)

If you work for a smaller organization, you probably have only one or two programs. However, keep in mind that having fewer programs doesn't decrease your chances of winning a grant award. Grants are available for organizations of all sizes and shapes. Remember, it's all in the writing.

REMEMBER

In the program section, the grant reader is looking for you to briefly

- Give the name of the program and state how long it has existed (focus on long-lasting and successful programs).
- Tell whom the program serves (youth, adults, women, seniors, veterans, people with physical or cognitive disabilities, or whomever).
- Describe how the target population benefits from the program.

Following is a comprehensive list of current programs for a human services nonprofit organization. This is taken from an actual grant application that was funded by a federal agency:

- Behavioral Heath Outreach Program:
  - Family violence services
  - Family support services
  - Therapeutic visitation services
  - Children currently in state custody
  - Children transitioning home from foster care and their families
  - Youth with juvenile court involvement
  - Parents who are seeking reunification with their children
  - Parents in need of parenting assessment, parent education, and marriage and/or couples

- Counseling
- Children and parents in need of signs of abuse education or anger management/conflict resolution skills
- Sex abuse education, child abuse education
- Youth needing positive role models through mentoring services

» Mid-Cumberland Relative Caregiver Program:

- Grandparents and relatives caring for minor children
- Children and teen social skills groups
- Youth needing positive role models through mentoring services
- Parenting education groups

» Community Prevention Initiative Program:

- Youth needing positive role models through mentoring services
- Youth with juvenile court involvement
- Children and teen social skills groups
- Tennessee Commission on Children and Youth
- Social skills groups for high-risk youth

» Lottery for education and after-school programs:

- Middle-school students in need of academic enrichment and tutoring

» 21st-Century Community Learning Center Program:

- Adult and youth therapeutic groups

» Metro Government of Nashville Juvenile Court Program:

- High-risk youth with juvenile court involvement
- Therapeutic groups for youth suspected of alcohol, drug, and tobacco use

WARNING

Don't make the mistake of pulling the language for this section from a previously written grant (such as last year's failed attempt). Always use fresh, up-to-date programs and activities information. Grant readers are very intuitive and can pick up on outdated, out-of-place information.

Presenting and Validating Your Target Population for Services

The target population section is the place to write about the people you serve. If you're serving certain organizations, you write about the organizations. If you're writing a grant for an animal shelter, you write about the animals.

Give just enough detail to aid the reader in understanding whom your operating dollars benefit — community members who are poor, adults who are unemployed, youths who have dropped out of high school, people who are homeless, or those with a terminal illness, for example. To make this section as accurate as possible, do your homework. Pull old evaluation reports from previously funded grants and review reports given to your board members — both types of documents should detail exactly who benefits from your organization's services.

REMEMBER

In the target population section, the grant reader wants to see

- Characteristics of your target population (age range, gender, ethnicity, education level, and income level). Clearly define your target population. You must convey to funders that you're serving a constituency that falls within their funding parameters. Also, be sure to cite the source of your demographics.
- Numbers served by each program (make a table that covers the past five years).
- Changes in the target population that may relate to why you're asking for grant funds.

TIP

When you write the target population section, use words describing the population that tell your story with accuracy and emotion.

The following example from a Federal Mentoring Children of Prisoners' grant application introduces the grant reviewer to a faith-based nonprofit organization serving inner-city residents. Because you want the reader to understand the importance of the funding request, use italics to make phrases stick in the reviewer's mind.

TIP

Usually, it isn't recommended to refrain from putting any language from the statement of need in the section of the proposal narrative that contains a description of the organization. However, we break this rule when we're writing about projects serving children — specifically, a target population under the age of 18. For children's services programs, drop hints of need every chance you can. This strategy helps reach out and touch the hearts of the grant readers, whether foundation, corporate, state, or federal.

» *Conditions and Characteristics of Youth and Families Affected:* According to a 2020 needs assessment conducted by Prison Families of New York, Inc., children of prisoners:

- *Blame themselves for their parent's incarceration* (one in five children witnessed their mother's arrest)
- *Are embarrassed about their peers finding out about their parent's incarceration*
- *Have difficulty dealing with the loss of a parent* to the prison system
- *Fail to address their emotional hurt* and *often act out*
- *Lack anyone who encourages them to achieve life success*
- Are *deeply negatively impacted by the separation* (demonstrated in lower self-esteem and loss of personal and cultural identity)
- Are *in critical need of an adult mentor who can help them express their feelings* about the incarcerated parent

Almost 58 percent of mothers and almost 59 percent of fathers in state prisons report never having a visit with their children since they entered prison. African American children are 7.5 times more likely to have a parent in prison than white children. Latino children are 2.5 times more likely than white children to have an incarcerated parent. The incarceration of a primary caretaker is traumatic and disruptive for children. Children of incarcerated mothers often move at least once and live with at least two different caretakers while their mothers are in prison. When a parent is incarcerated, children may face dramatically changed family conditions, particularly if the incarcerated parent was the sole or primary caregiver.

Validating Your Statement of Need with a Compelling Narrative

Your *statement of need* (also referred to as a *problem statement* or *needs statement*) tells the grant reviewer that you know what you're talking about. It oozes gloom, doom, drama, and trauma. You use your statement of need to get your point across in the most effective, attention-drawing, memorable way you can. How do you do that? By writing from your heart (where your emotional center lies) and by telling the story of how bad things really are for your target population. Transport the grant reviewer into the setting of the problem so they can make positive decisions about funding your grant proposal or application.

REMEMBER

Gather the facts, read them, feel them in your heart, and formulate them in your mind. Then think about how you'd feel if you were reading those compelling or startling statistics, events, life stories, situations, and so forth about yourself, your family, or your close friends. Keep those feelings fresh, and you're ready to write a compelling statement of need!

TIP

You may find this section particularly helpful if you've been casting your line into the grant-writing competition pool and receiving multiple rejection notices. Odds are your grant requests have been flat, to the point, and significantly lacking in tables and charts. Even if you're submitting mostly e-grant applications, you can still beef up your content with a compelling format for your statement of need. When you use a storytelling approach, you increase the chances of what you write getting funded. The magic is in the storytelling. (And in the visuals, if you can swing them, although we don't get into those details here. When it comes to graphics, think of ways to visually represent the numbers that back up your story; don't include an image just for the sake of having an image. Make sure it serves a purpose and helps to tell the story.)

When you're writing your statement of need for grant funding, remember this: Grant writing has progressed from rote and boring to individual/personality-packed/engrossing/exciting. Like all great stories, your presentation of what's wrong with this picture must be compelling, magnetizing, tear-jerking, and believable. But it must also be supported with facts. The next sections show you how to build your case and then how to tug on the grant reviewer's heartstrings — because they are the one deciding whether your request gets approved or rejected for funding.

Researching recent and relevant information

REMEMBER

Every good statement of need is like a well-written story. And every well-written story is filled with compelling details that bring the narrative to life in the reader's mind. To write your story, you need to gather all the available data from your organization's previous grant evaluations, which may show gaps that still existed when the grant funds were expended.

You may have to play detective to find copies of old grant applications. Whether these applications were funded or not, they still contain critical statistics and other statement of need information.

WARNING

Only look at applications written in the last two to three years; anything older is too outdated for your current funding request.

Start off by looking for current demographics (numbers to support your statement of need) on your services, programs, and *target population* (the folks or animals that your grant, when funded, will impact). Get permission to look at case management files; these files can provide rich details and even quotations regarding clients' needs and service barriers when they came to you for help. Also, look at minutes from board of directors meetings and annual reports (usually gathered by the program staff and presented to the board in the first quarter of your organization's fiscal year).

After you review your organization's materials, conduct an Internet search in hopes of finding the following problem-related information:

- Local and state-level data on the scope (size, demographics, and so on) of the problem. The websites of city-, county-, and state-level human service; public health; police and corrections departments; area universities; research and policy think tanks; and advocacy coalitions are excellent sources for this type of information. Look for congressional testimonies related to your subject area, research findings by experts and graduate students, and newly issued press releases from government agencies or government watchdogs.
- Similar problem area trends in other communities with characteristics like yours (rural or urban, increases or declines in population).
- Solutions to the issue (even though you don't present solutions in the statement of need section of your proposal).

TIP

To find up-to-date and relevant information, run a general Internet search. A general search results in hundreds of local, regional, and national government website links. This approach is much easier than trying to find the Internet address for a specific information site. For example, if your organization works with local businesses to help them expand their facilities and relocate to your new state-of-the-art industrial park, you can enter the phrase "economic development statistics for [your state or county]" in your favorite search engine. You can also use the U.S. Census, Bureau of Labor Statistics, Department of Agriculture, and major research foundations like the Robert Wood Johnson Foundation's County Rankings or the Annie E. Casey Foundation's Kids Count data.

TIP

When you're working on your statements of need, it helps to have a cloud-based storage folder with files of current problem-related information in front of you for review. Look at information provided by the grant application organization and study your own Internet research findings. Sort all this information by topic (for example, rural development, community development, economic development, trends in industrial parks, or business growth trends). To expedite locating or validating the information used after the grant application has been submitted, it's a good idea to then store all website addresses in your Favorites folder under the project's or client's name (in addition to whichever cloud-based storage service you use).

REMEMBER

The more information you have on your topic, the more easily you can write a winning statement of need. With the right preparation, you aren't grasping for straws or generalizing; instead, you're able to give the grant reader true, hard, grant-getting facts. And by including recent (no more than five years old) citations for data sources and names of noteworthy researchers, you show the grant reader that your information is accurate and reputable. Finally, establish a six-month project timeline to gather all the data. Your process must be systematic and seriously undertaken — and certainly not left until the applications are nearing their due dates.

Incorporating real-life information about your target population

The grant reviewer reads your statement of need with the following questions in mind:

- How and when did you identify the problem?
- Do you have a thorough understanding of the problem at the local, regional, and national levels?
- Do you cite statistics and research conducted by your organization and others that support the statement of need? Is this information current? (See the preceding section for guidance on finding up-to-date data.)

In a foundation or corporate funding request, your statement of need should be one typed, single-spaced page unless the funder requests a specific page count/limit or has character/space limitations for each section of the grant proposal narrative. In a government grant or cooperative request, the statement of need can be anywhere from two to ten typed single-spaced or double-spaced pages, depending on the number of pages allowed for this section of the grant application narrative.

TIP

For government grant applications, try using a pages-to-points formula. Here's an example using a 20-page maximum page-limit scenario: If the total pages you can write in the narrative is 20 pages (100 percent of the total point or percentage value for the peer reviewers) and the peer review points for the statement of need is 15 points (or 15 percent), you multiply 15 percent × 20 pages and your result is

3 pages. This means that your statement of need should be exactly — on point — three pages. Some grant applications will have more than 100 percent for a total weight; adjust your calculations accordingly.

REMEMBER

Write each paragraph in your statement of need so that it builds on the paragraph before it. Making your ideas connect and flow is important because each new paragraph is a step forward. Each new paragraph adds excitement and urgency, just like a good fiction or nonfiction story line. If these steps sound like those used to write a bestselling story, you're right on target. You write your winning grant proposal the same way you would write a bestseller!

In your statements of need, consider using words and phrases that carry a lot of weight, such as *economically distressed, orphaned, abandoned, socially isolated, politically disenfranchised, disconnected from the community, underemployed or unemployed, chronically homeless, taken for granted, throwaways,* and *disrespected.* Are you getting a picture of the problem? Do you have your tissues out because your eyes are full of tears? This type of writing works well in both public- and private-sector grant narratives.

TIP

Don't hide key words or phrases in ordinary text. Elevate your grant writing by using bold type and italics (minimally but effectively, and only when allowed by the funder's format) to make a word or phrase stand out. *Personally, we like to call attention to important text with italics.* When you use italics in the right places to emphasize the right words, it's as if you're talking one-on-one with the grant reader. Using this approach to tug at one's heartstrings may result in your application landing in the funded pile.

Building a strong case study

If you're lucky enough to have access to actual client files or case management staff, you can survey them for information about a specific client or member of the target population that sought services from your organization. Being able to incorporate a compelling story about a real client who was in need and came to your agency or organization can put the icing on the storytelling cake.

TIP

Opening your statement of need with an engaging story is guaranteed to keep the grant reader on the edge of their seat and interested in reading more.

Your case study should include information that addresses the following topics:

- Details of the applicant and the problem's background
- Information about the people being served and how those services are rendered

- The environment in which the organization operates, the number of people served, and who they are
- How dire the problem is (supported by a cited reference)

What follows is a grant-winning statement of need that shows how to make this section walk, talk, tell, and sell the case for grant funding; it builds on the case statement above. This example incorporates a compelling case study:

- **Detail of the applicant and the problem's background:** Josiah was only six years old when one of our street outreach workers found him shivering next to a dumpster in the alley behind our facility. His hair was matted and lice-infested. Josiah was only able to tell us his first name. When Mary Jane, our senior social worker, cleaned him up and applied lice removal shampoo to his hair, he was able to talk a bit more about his separation from his family. Josiah's mom died after he was born. His father was left with eight children to care for in a one-bedroom apartment. One night, Josiah's father did not come home. After several days of trying to survive, the children had to fend for themselves for food and discarded clothing found in curbside trash bags. We knew that we had to call Children's Protective Services (CPS) and the police department. Protocol was rigid, even though we are an adoption agency. One of our mental health counselors, Sarah, was also a licensed foster parent and had 10 years of experience in taking in abandoned children. After Josiah was questioned about his father by the police, CPS came to pick him up. Sarah intervened and asked if she and Jake (her husband) could be Josiah's foster parents.
- CPS agreed because before Sarah joined our agency, she was Director of Social Services for CPS. Everyone knew her and marveled at the fact that Sarah and Jake had taken in over 100 abandoned children throughout the years. It was settled; Josiah would go home with Sarah. Well, it's been 12 years since that day and here's an update on Josiah. When he was 12 years old, Sarah and Jake adopted Josiah as their son. He is now 18 years old and will graduate from high school with honors next month. Along the way, our agency was able to provide supportive youth development programs for Josiah. He learned about positive peer relationships, as well as how to use the ChildFind system to locate his siblings, who he has visited in their foster families. He was also able to find out that his dad died of a heart attack while riding on the bus to his second job. He was buried in an unknown pauper's grave. Josiah's story is not unique or the worst tear-jerker we have to share. There are many more children like Josiah who did not have happy endings. Now that we've introduced you to Josiah, you should know the meaning of his name, *God has healed.*

» **Information about the people being served and how those services are rendered:** Josiah's story is not unique, and it's not the first one we've heard that highlights a child's traumatic experiences. Since our doors have opened, we have processed more than 5,000 abandoned children's cases. Not all of them are as lucky as Josiah. Over 2,500 remained in foster care until they aged out. The other half were adopted, either by their foster parents or by couples on the waiting list for a baby that gave up and took an older child home to raise as their own. We've handled 50 multi-sibling adoptions. The problem of abandoned children is not new. Parents abandon their children at the rate of 20 percent of live births in the United States. More than 7,000 children are abandoned each year (United Nations, 2021).The foster care system is in overload. Child Protective Services is understaffed and overwhelmed. Our agency is the only free adoption nonprofit in a 500-mile radius. People who complete the foster parents training program and meet home inspection requirements are not entering into the world of a get rich quick scheme. The state meagerly compensates these families. Our agency provides the bells and whistles (toys, field trips, youth development programs, and one-on-one mentoring). We also work with our foster parents planning to adopt to help them meet the qualifications of non-kin adoption policies. Without our services, these kids would be shuttled from one foster home to another. This is not our plan!

» **The environment in which the organization operates and who they are:** The Southwest Children's Place operates in Maricopa County, located in central Arizona. At one time or another, each member of our staff has either worked for CPS, a private fee-based adoption agency, or in family court. Our agency contracts with over 20 local and regional youth-serving agencies to provide camping and field trip experiences to children placed into one of our foster care homes. Our services are made possible by 20 dedicated licensed counselors (social workers and mental health professionals) who specialize in trauma-informed care for adolescents and licensed foster parents.

» **How dire the problem really is:** Without your support, our general operating funds will quickly be used to serve a waitlist of 200 abandoned children still living out-of-sight on the predator-laden streets throughout the Pacific Southwest. Their safety and physical and mental health is threatened daily. Here's what our extensive research has revealed, by age group, about the children we cannot serve:

- **Infancy and toddlerhood:** Children in this stage of development understand little, if anything, about abandonment. However, they are aware of the emotional climate of the family. For the remaining parent, it is important to cuddle and care for the infant or toddler warmly, frequently, and consistently. The parent-child relationship continues to be central to the child's sense of security and independence. When both parents are missing, at this early state of their child's development, physical and mental health issues begin to emerge.

- **Preschool-age:** Preschoolers tend to have a limited and mistaken perception of abandonment. They are highly self-centered with a strict sense of right and wrong. So, when bad things happen to them, they usually blame themselves by assuming they did something wrong. Children this age often interpret the departure of a parent as a personal rejection. Youngsters are likely to deny the reality of the abandonment and wish intently for the parent to return. They can also regress to behaviors such as thumb sucking, bed wetting, temper tantrums, and clinging to a favorite blanket or toy. They also fear abandonment by the other parent. They generally become afraid of the dark and of being alone.
- **School age:** By the time children reach the early school years, ages 6 to 9, they can no longer deny the reality of the abandonment. They are extremely aware of the pervasive pain and sadness. Boys, especially, mourn the loss of their fathers, and their anger is frequently directed at their mothers. Crying, daydreaming, and problems with friends and in school are common abandonment behaviors in children of this age.

  In the age group of 9 to 12, adolescents usually react to abandonment with anger. They may also resent the additional household duties expected of them. There is also a significant disruption in the child's ability to learn. Anxiety, restlessness, inability to concentrate, and intrusive thoughts about the abandonment take a toll and can lead to a drop in school performance and difficulties with classmates.

  Feelings of sadness, loneliness, guilt, lack of self-worth, and self-blame are common in 9- to 12-year-olds. They also tend to have concerns about family life, worry about finances, and feel they are a drain on the remaining parent's resources.

  In children ages 13 to 18, the feelings are usually the same as with the younger groups except more pronounced. They become concerned about their own futures. Truancy is high, school performance is low, and they have a distorted view of themselves. In this population there is a high incidence of drug and alcohol abuse and aggressive behavior.

We cannot change the parents who abandoned their children; however, we can get these children off of our streets and placed into a loving and caring foster home. Our adoption rate for children who have been fostered by individuals and families trained and supported by our organization is 90 percent. The children still out there and barely hanging on need our help, and we need your help to change the future for abandoned children in the Pacific Southwest.

You know you've written a convincing and compelling statement of need when you get out your hanky to dab away a few tears after rereading your masterpiece!

TIP

If you have a summary of a needs survey or letters from organizations documenting that the demands for your services are greater than your resources to deliver the services, attach these documents to your application. Always reference such attachments in the narrative so grant readers can refer to them and get their full effect while reading the statement of need. These supporting documents allow a grant reader to verify the actual need for grant funding. (See Chapter 13 of this minibook for guidance on how to organize your attachments.)

IN THIS CHAPTER

- » Reminding funders why they're reading your application
- » Writing your goals and SMART objectives
- » Creating accountability that links throughout the rest of your narrative
- » Developing a logic model to connect the dots
- » Proving accountability with an evaluation plan

Chapter 10

Incorporating Best Practices to Build the Program Design Narrative

The program design section of the grant application is by far the most important narrative section in your grant proposal. It's the section that divides the "I don't have a clue" grant writers from the "I have this in the bag" grant writers. The coaching and examples in this chapter show you how to write an award-winning program design section that's all about your vision — as in the positive changes you'll bring about when your proposal wins that grant award!

Reviewing the Components of a Good Program Design Section

In the *program design* section, you roll out all the promising details about what will happen when the bucks are in place to actually create, implement, and evaluate your grant-funded program. The program design narrative shows funders that you have a well-documented project implementation and evaluation plan.

REMEMBER

To write a successful program design section, you need to be optimistic yet realistic and include the following main ingredients in this order:

- **A purpose statement:** A one-sentence, direct explanation of why you're seeking funds.
- **Goals:** Where your program or constituency aims to be when the grant funds are used up. There are two types of goals: outcome-focused and SMART. You'll find examples of both later in this chapter.
- **SMART objectives: S**pecific, **m**easurable, **a**ttainable, **r**ealistic, and **t**ime-bound benchmarks or specific steps that lead to the accomplishment of your goals. (SMART objectives are described in the later section, "Plotting Goals and SMART Objectives.")
- **An implementation plan with process objectives and timelines:** A plan listing the activities (*process objectives*) required to meet and exceed your measurable objectives and when they'll be implemented.
- **A logic model with an impact objective:** Your logic model lays out a graphic roadmap with inputs, strategies, outputs, and outcomes. Adding an *impact objective* reflects the long-term benefit (seven to ten years) you believe your program will have on your target population and/or community.
- **Evaluation:** Shows how you'll track the progress of the project's objectives, what data collection tools you'll use to gather information about the project, and who will conduct the evaluation. This section screams accountability!

  Some grant applications may ask you to include evaluation plans separately, in a section following the program design or even in an attachment. However, many public- and private-sector funders are realizing the importance of having you, the grant applicant, integrate your evaluation plan into the program design.

Your entire program design must give the grant reviewers a detailed explanation of the big picture. In other words, you must lay out each section as though you were placing the pieces into a large puzzle. The large puzzle is your program design, and the pieces are each of the elements in the preceding list.

Starting with a Purpose Statement

As the first part of your program design narrative, the *purpose statement* tells the grant reader why you're asking for grant monies. You have two types of purpose statements to choose from: direct and indirect.

A *direct purpose statement* includes the amount of the requested grant award. Remember that even when you mention a dollar amount, the purpose statement shouldn't exceed one sentence. Get to the point and tell the grant reader the purpose of the grant request and the amount of funds needed. Use the following example as a guide for writing your own direct purpose statement:

> The Grant Writing Training Foundation is seeking your initial and ongoing financial support in the amount of $40,000 for its five-day public health-focused Grant Writing Boot Camp in Johannesburg, South Africa.

An *indirect purpose statement* simply tells the reader the purpose of the grant request — a program or project in need of funding. The following example shows you how an indirect purpose statement should read:

> The purpose of this request is to seek grant funding to conduct a five-day Johannesburg NIH campus-based residential grant-writing training program for Ministers of Public Health from 23 African countries.

TIP

A direct purpose statement in foundation and corporate funding requests more efficiently gets to the point for the reader who will make the final funding decisions. However, using the indirect purpose statement for government grant proposals is a better choice because government grant peer reviewers don't make those same final decisions; an agency staff person with authority over the grant-making initiative does. Therefore, no actual amount of monies requested should appear in the purpose statement of government funding requests.

Plotting Goals and SMART Objectives

The first road-mapping tools in your program design narrative are goals (intent) and objectives (what, how much, when, for whom, and how your measurements will be proven). Your program's goals address the big-picture success of your program, and the objectives are the measurable ways (or *benchmarks*) you plan to reach those goals. Book 1, Chapter 3 introduces goals and objectives in the context of planning your organization's overall strategy. You should already have those in place. Here, we're discussing goals in the context of showing quantifiable outcomes because funding agencies view measurable steps as signs of accountability — showing how their money will make an impact on the problem and your organization's capability to solve the problem.

REMEMBER

Always provide objectives for each goal and each year for which you're requesting funds for an activity.

The following sections help you differentiate between goals and objectives, craft goals worthy of funding, and design objectives that fit within the three classic types. Whether you're new to grant writing or you've submitted a few grant applications in your day, we strongly suggest you review the first of these sections. After multiple year-long stints as a grant application peer reviewer, Bev rated applications from school districts, colleges and universities, and nonprofit organizations that had received grant awards for years, and they all were very weak in the goals and objectives section. Most important, grant reviewers rarely recommend applications for funding that have weak goals and objectives. Write smartly to score well.

Understanding the difference between types of goals and objectives

To keep the terms *goal* and *objective* straight, think of *goal* first and remember that it's the thing(s) you're attempting to accomplish. A goal is where you are when you're done implementing the activities associated with your measurable objectives. Grant application narratives must have goals to show the funder that you have a vision for solving the problem.

REMEMBER

A lot of things have changed since the first edition of *Grant Writing For Dummies* was published in 2001 (the seventh edition of that book is what this minibook is based on). Back then, it was standard practice to teach people in grant-writing classes that goals are never measurable. However, over the past two decades, there has been a shift among some public-sector (government) and private-sector (foundation and corporation) funders. Some of these grant makers are now asking for *measurable goals.* It's a bit confusing to all grant writers. To alleviate any confusion, this chapter provides definitions and examples of a traditional goal and a SMART goal. Recall that SMART stands for specific, measurable, attainable, realistic, and time-bound.

Okay, so what about an objective? An *objective* is simply a major milestone or checkpoint or benchmark on your route to reaching a goal. It's a place where you can say (and report to a funder, if necessary), "We've come this far, and we have this far remaining before we reach the goal." Award-winning objectives are specific, measurable, attainable, realistic, and time-bound (SMART); they also serve to keep goals realistic.

TIP

When writing a government grant request, develop your goals by using the funder's goals for the funding initiative. Always follow the funders' directions as to what type of goal they want to see in grant applications — nonmeasurable or measurable. Then create measurable objectives to track all the funding initiative's intended outcomes (also known as *performance measures*). Everything you need to cue you on how many goals and how many objectives to write is there in the grant application guidelines. On the other end of the spectrum, when you're writing a proposal to a foundation or corporation, you have nothing to tip you off to what the funder wants to see or fund in terms of funder goals and objectives. In those cases, keep it light and usually write one or two nonmeasurable goals. Each goal should always have one or two measurable or SMART objectives.

That said, there's no magic number for goals and objectives. Just be sure your organization's goals are based on the vision of where you want the program or target population to be when the grant period is over.

REMEMBER

Your goals need to align with the goals of the funding. This verbiage will be provided on the funder's website or in its grant application guidelines.

Following the funder's directions to write the right types of goals

There are two types of goals: nonmeasurable and measurable. Always read the funder's guidelines carefully and write the types of goals that it asks for. When you're in the process of writing any type of goal, be sure to write clear, concise, one-sentence statements. Nonmeasurable goals should be action-oriented and full of verbs. Measurable goals are written much like SMART objectives.

TIP

Always start your nonmeasurable goals with the word *provide* until you get into a rhythm. After you have the magic nonmeasurable goal-language machine going, you can venture out and use other starting action words such as *develop, plan, educate, create, build, empower, engage,* and so forth. Nonmeasurable goals truly mirror SMART objectives.

To be sure you've written effective and well-constructed goal statements of any type, ask yourself the following questions:

- Did I follow the funder's guidelines for writing the *right* type of goal (nonmeasurable or measurable)?
- Did I use one sentence?
- Is the sentence clear and concise?

- Do my goals align with the funder's priority areas and program-specific goals for awarding grants?
- Does the grant reader know who the target population is and where the monies are needed (geographic impact area)?

Following are examples of both types of goals (nonmeasurable and measurable). It's best to use only one goal-writing format in your grant application. In other words, don't mix nonmeasurable and measurable goals. Write one or the other — depending on the funder's specific guidelines for what it wants to see in your narrative.

Here are some examples of nonmeasurable goals:

- **Goal:** Provide elderly disabled residents with supervised physical fitness activities offered inside of their gated community.
- **Goal:** Develop an obesity awareness campaign targeting Latino families residing in Denver, Colorado.
- **Goal:** Create a women's business center incubator in Goodyear, Arizona, to train recent parolees from the state prison system in micro-enterprise entrepreneurship.

Here are some examples of SMART (specific, measurable, attainable, realistic, and time-bound) goals:

- **SMART Goal:** By the second quarter of Year 1, elderly disabled residents will increase their levels of physical activity in multilevel community-based exercise sessions by 25 percent as measured by pre- and post-declining health indicators.
- **SMART Goal:** By the third quarter of Year 1, create and carry out 13 weekly obesity awareness campaigns targeting 50 percent or more of Latino families residing in Denver, Colorado, as measured by the number of broadcast media PSAs in Spanish.
- **SMART Goal:** By the end of Year 1, complete 100 percent of the women's business center incubator in Goodyear, Arizona, to facilitate micro-enterprise entrepreneurship training programs targeting recent parolees from the state prison system as measured by the number of building inspections passed, the number of months to complete the facility, and the number of post-parole agreements with regional correctional facilities.

WARNING

If the funding decision maker can't look at your goals and figure out from them what your entire program is about, you've failed to write clearly stated goals — measurable or nonmeasurable.

TIP

When you start writing your program design, remember to incorporate key words and phrases from the grant announcement's purpose of funding statement. During the grant review process, this strategy helps peer reviewers make a clear connection between the purpose of the grant and your statement of need and program design — which should fit like a soft leather glove to the announcement language. This approach of parroting the funding agency's own words results in receiving high review points — starting you down the road to getting a funding award! Just make sure your target population fits the one described in the purpose of funding statement.

Recognizing and writing types of objectives requested by funders

Successful grant writing requires you to understand the three types of objectives (also known as *milestones* or *benchmarks*) and to know when to use them:

- **SMART objectives:** Measurable steps or benchmarks to reach a stated goal
- **Process objectives:** Activities or tasks
- **Impact objectives:** Benefits to end users that continue after the grant funding has ended

Using the right objective at the right time can help you rack up peer review points, which can also help you win big bucks for your program. (See Chapter 7 of this minibook for further insight on the review process.)

WARNING

SMART goals (explained earlier in this chapter) do not mix with SMART objectives. Why? When funders require SMART goals, they simply want goals written like SMART objectives. There will be a measurement term, like *increased* or *decreased*, without any time-bound or time-frame language. These types of measurable objectives are merely performance indicators. You'll see some examples later in this chapter.

TIP

Although you should definitely provide at least one objective for each goal and year of your funding request, some program designs have more than one objective for each goal. If this setup is the case with your design, make sure that you number and alphabetize the objectives (for example, 1a, 1b, 1c, and so on) to eliminate confusion for the reviewer.

Creating SMART objectives

A *SMART objective* is an objective that shows how the goal will be accomplished. Always create SMART objectives for your programs or projects. They're the most common type of objectives funders ask for in their grant application guidelines.

When writing your own SMART objectives, use phrases that imply some sort of measurable change, such as *to increase* or *to decrease*. For example, you can write about an increase of 50 percent in the number of organizations receiving project services by the end of Year 1.

TIP

The easiest way to write measurable objectives is to use the SMART acronym:

- **S:** Is the objective *s*pecific rather than abstract? The objective must point out who will benefit (students, patients, clients, or whatever applies) and specify what will be measured (behavior, participation, and so forth).
- **M:** Is the objective *m*easurable? Can it be tracked easily with valid measurement tools, such as surveys, pre- and post-needs assessments, and more? Use measure-indicating words such as *increase, decrease, reduce, improve, lower,* or *raise.* Also include a percentage benchmark. You can't write, "By the end of Year 1, hire 10 teachers," because that doesn't specifically illustrate a measurable benefit to your target population.
- **A:** Is the objective *a*ttainable? Can your organization really pull off the objective within the time frame of the grant award?
- **R:** Is the objective *r*ealistic? Can the measurement actually be reached for the target population in the given time frame?
- **T:** Is the objective *t*ime-bound? Can your organization accomplish all the required tasks to achieve the objective in the given time frame? Make sure your objective contains a time-bound phrase, such as *by the end of Year 1,* or *the first semester, the second quarter, the grant-funding period,* or whatever time segment your project will occur in.

The following are some sample SMART objectives for Goal 1, a nonmeasurable goal, in the examples in the earlier section, "Following the funder's directions to write the right types of goals" ("Provide elderly disabled residents with supervised physical fitness activities offered inside of their gated community"):

> **SMART Objective 1a:** By the end of Year 1, increase the number of residents inquiring about fitness events in the community room by 25 percent or more as demonstrated by pre-grant and post-grant award comparisons of incidences of interest among the target population.

SMART Objective 1b: By the end of Year 1, increase the number of residents participating in one or more fitness activities by 25 percent or more as demonstrated by pre-grant and post-grant event attendance records.

SMART Objective 1c: By the end of Year 2, increase the number of residents participating in two or more fitness activities by 50 percent or more over Year 1 as demonstrated by a comparison of Year 1 and Year 2 event attendance records.

TIP

In order to accurately measure any percentage increases for your target population (like measurements built into the example objectives), you need to know the baseline numbers (the starting point) for each type of measurement. For example, if the home has 300 elderly residents, how many are participating in fitness activities at the time you're writing the grant request? You need a starting point in order to establish a reasonable (attainable) measurement. If you don't have baseline data, write that in the program design narrative. Explain to the funder that your data collection will include a pre- and post-assessment of the high-risk indicators to demonstrate that your intervention/implementation strategies will/did work.

If the program you're requesting funding for is new, you may not have baseline data to help guide the development of SMART objective targets. In this case, be sure to build baseline assessments into the program enrollment process whenever possible.

REMEMBER

Including the term *or more* in your SMART objective statements is a good idea because, if you meet or exceed conservative objectives, you'll look like a superhero in the eyes of the funder. On the other hand, if you set overly ambitious objectives and fail to meet them, you'll look like someone who didn't know how to collect baseline numbers or indicators for each SMART objective, and you probably won't be re-funded by that funder.

Producing process objectives

Process objectives are the implementation-related activities or tasks needed to reach your goals and meet or exceed your SMART objectives for your grant-funded program. For effective process objectives, write about the actual, chronological activities that need to occur from the time you receive grant funding until the monies have been spent.

The best way to present your process objectives is in a table format. Make sure to follow the funder's guidelines when setting up your timeline segments (explained in the later section, "Providing a Comprehensive Implementation Plan"). You can use quarters if you like, but some funders ask for monthly timelines for all activities.

TIP

When writing process objectives, quantify your activities in numbers rather than percentages or words.

Following are two sample process objectives:

» **Process Objective 1:** Marketing outreach to 300 elderly residents.

» **Process Objective 2:** Enroll 75 elderly residents in one or more fitness activities.

Identifying impact objectives

Impact objectives demonstrate the achievement of the goal of the project or program when you or anyone else steps into the future and then looks back at what was accomplished and the differences that were made. In other words, what will the grant's impact on your target population be in three to five years?

TIP

If you come across a grant application in which the funding agency asks you to write about *benefits to participants,* respond by using impact objectives. Benefits to participants are really presumptions of how the funded program's intervention will change your participants. For example, you can write about changes in the target population's attitude about learning and achieving.

Impact objectives are easy to identify because they're written in past tense. They're futuristic glimpses into the past, your vision for what the program's future impact may be. Unlike process objectives, you don't have any common words to cue your writing. The funder is just looking for signs of significant change — change brought on by the interventions that the funder made possible.

Here is an example of an effective impact objective:

Impact Objective: Residents who participated in Year 1 of the fitness activities have reported lower incidence of hypertension and a reduction in chronic disease progression.

Providing a Comprehensive Implementation Plan

A *timeline* or *Gantt chart* tells the grant reader when major project milestones will begin and end during the grant's funding period (which is usually a 12-month period). The timeline also includes information about who's accountable for each activity and how you'll evaluate the program's accomplishments during that period.

When you develop a project timeline, keep in mind that the grant reader wants to see answers to the following questions:

» What are the key tasks or activities that will be carried out to implement the program successfully?

» Did the grant applicant include all tasks, from the day funding is announced or awarded to the last day of the project's funding time frame?

» Can each task realistically begin and end in the proposed time frame?

» Are evaluation activities included in the timeline chart?

» Who is responsible for seeing that each activity is implemented and completed?

REMEMBER

You can use your word-processing software to create a simple timeline chart. Just be sure not to overdo it with color; use no more than four shading selections (and don't use red or black shading unless you change the font color to white).

Disruptions and malfunctions can be unpredictable when you're implementing a grant-funded program; for this reason, it can be helpful to set up your activity start and stop dates in quarterly increments. However, if you have total control over the activities, you can use monthly increments to show when they begin and end.

The sample activity timeline chart in Figure 10-1 clearly shows what the program plans to accomplish, when it plans to accomplish it, and who is responsible for seeing the activities (process objectives) through the completion phase.

TIP

For programs that request funding for multiple years, you need to include extra timelines in the grant application showing each year's activities and the quarterly time frames for each activity. You can either create a multiyear timeline chart on one page that breaks down the four quarters for each year (do so in landscape format to make room for all the information) or create a separate timeline chart for each year. Figure 10-1 shows Year 1 for the fitness program. Years 2 and 3 would take another two pages of table charts. Whether you choose to set up a multiyear landscape table chart or individual year charts that take up two or more pages depends on the funder's page limitations.

Brentwood Highlands Fitness Program Timeline Chart, Year 1					
Activities/Milestones	**Year 1 July 1 – June 30**				**Key Person/Group Responsible**
	1st Qtr.	**2nd Qtr.**	**3rd Qtr.**	**4th Qtr.**	
Community Association governing body for Brentwood Highlands formally accepts the grant award by resolution adoption	🚲				Community Association Board of Directors
Creation of fitness activity preference survey	🚲				Activity Director
Distribution of fitness interest and past activity involvement survey via delivery to every occupied mobile home in the park's six block sections	🚲				Block section captains
Free-of-charge community cookout to collect surveys and tour the new fitness facility	🚲				Community volunteers Activity Director
Use survey data to identify fitness activity leaders from within and outside of the community	🚲				Activity Director
Meet with interested fitness activity leaders to discuss their day/time/interest preferences	🚲				Activity Director
Use survey data to develop list of indoor and outdoor classes and events to be offered weekly	🚲				Activity Director
Email blast activity schedule to all residents (those residing in the park and winter visitors who arrive by October 1 annually)	🚲				Activity Director e-Newsletter Coordinator
Classes and other activities begin		🚲			Activity Director
Develop retention incentives for all fitness activities	🚲				Activity Director
Develop evaluation forms for residents to rate instructors and activities (type, time, day, intensity)	🚲				Grand Canyon University Evaluation Intern
Administer evaluation forms halfway through each class and again at the end		🚲	🚲	🚲	Activity Director
Monitor class enrollment records to track residents in more than one class		🚲	🚲	🚲	Activity Director
Ongoing process and outcome monitoring and correction actions as needed		🚲	🚲	🚲	Grand Canyon University Evaluation Intern
Winter visitor season-end fitness awards (most inches lost, most weight lost, most classes taken, and most health risk indicators reduced)				🚲	Activity Director
Final reports to stakeholders (funders, Community Association Board, and park residents)				🚲	Activity Director
Grant close-out				🚲	Activity Director

FIGURE 10-1: An example of a timeline of activities.

Illustration by Ryan Sneed

Confirming Narrative Content Connectivity in Your Logic Model

The *logic model* is a graphic blueprint of the key elements of a proposed program. It looks at inputs, activities, outputs, outcomes, and impacts. If you live and work in the world of grants, avoiding the logic model is difficult. Just about every type of funder seems to want you to include a logic model in the program design of your grant application narrative.

Here's what the columns of your logic model graphic should contain:

- **Inputs:** These are the human, financial, and physical resources dedicated to your grant-funded program. These resources include money, staff and staff time, volunteers and volunteer time, facilities, equipment, supplies, and community partners. (See Chapter 11 of this minibook for information on personnel and organization resources.)
- **Strategies:** These are what your program uses to organize the inputs. Using effective strategies helps the program to fulfill its mission. Basically, the funder wants a recap of your goals; copy and paste the goals you wrote in the program design into this column of the logic model. Simplify your SMART goal (if that type of goal is required by the funder) and take out any measurement language.
- **Outputs:** These are the direct results of your program's implementation activities. They're actually written as indicators of productivity. Outputs usually start with the phrase *number of* and reflect how you'll quantitatively track your program activities. You can extract output language from your objectives narrative (found earlier in your program design) and from your evaluation narrative as well.
- **Short-, intermediate-, and long-term outcomes:** These are the benchmarks or measurements for your target population during and after program activities. For the outcomes, you can simply reuse your SMART objectives or SMART goals — extracting the measurements language only (see the earlier section, "Plotting Goals and SMART Objectives"). Some funders want to see short-term outcomes (3-month SMART objective measurements), and others want to see intermediate outcomes (6-month SMART objective measurements). All funders want to see long-term outcomes (12 months or longer SMART objective measurements).
- **Long-term impact or impact statement:** Funders want to know what long-term outcomes or impact (changes in systems and processes after the funding is expended) you anticipate for your target population.

Figure 10-2 shows the basic structure for the logic model with intermediate and long-term SMART objectives. Keep in mind, though, that this is only one example of how funders may instruct you to prepare your logic model form.

REMEMBER

If you have a multiple-year program, you need to have multiple-year logic models. Each year's model should show a set of inputs, activities, outputs, outcomes, and impacts on its own page. Also, if the funder has its own logic model format, forms, or different components, follow those.

Brentwood Highlands Fitness Program Logic Model				
			Outcomes	
Inputs	Strategies	Outputs	Intermediate-Term (6 Months)	Long-Term (12 Months)
*Grant funding *Grant applicant in-kind match *Facilities (indoor fitness room and outdoor aquatic and trail walking area) *Collaborative partner(s) -Association Board -Volunteers -Staff *Equipment *Materials and supplies	Goal: Provide elderly disabled Brentwood Highland residents with supervised physical fitness activities offered inside of their gated community.	# of surveys distributed # of surveys returned # of residents touring the new facility # of activity leaders identified # of classes offered (inside and outside) # of days classes offered # of residents enrolling in one class # of residents enrolling in more than one class # of residents completing activity leader evaluation forms # of residents retained (halfway and at the end) # of residents receiving awards (by type of award) # of residents indicating interest in Year 2 Fitness Program	Increase the number of residents inquiring about community room fitness events by 12.5% or more as demonstrated by pre-grant and post-grant award comparisons of incidences of interest among the target population. Increase the number of residents participating in one or more fitness activities by 12.5% or more as demonstrated by pre-grant and post-grant event attendance records.	Increase the number of residents inquiring about community room fitness events by 25% or more as demonstrated by pre-grant and post-grant award comparisons of incidences of interest among the target population. Increase the number of residents participating in one or more fitness activities by 25% or more as demonstrated by pre-grant and post-grant event attendance records.
Impact Statement	***Brentwood Highland residents who participated in Year 1 of the fitness activities have reported lower incidences of hypertension and reduction in chronic disease progression.***			

Illustration by Ryan Sneed

FIGURE 10-2: The logic model depicts your organization's planned work and intended results for a given project.

TIP

The logic model isn't a process you can pick up overnight. But reviewing the online materials at the W. K. Kellogg website (`www.wkkf.org`) can help with the learning curve. Search the Internet for "logic model development guide" and download the *W. K. Kellogg Foundation Logic Model Development Guide* from the Show All Results menu. Print out a copy and use it as a desktop reference.

Creating the Evaluation Plan for Your Program Design

The most important part of grant writing is the initial step of deciding which grants to pursue, but evaluating your project after it has been funded is a close second. The *evaluation plan* in the program design section of the grant narrative explains to the potential funder how you plan to evaluate the success of your project.

The evaluation plan includes

- A review of your program's objectives and how you'll know whether you met them
- The type of information you'll collect to use in the evaluation
- How often you will collect the information
- Who will collect the information
- Who will analyze the information and report the results

To introduce you to the evaluation process, the following sections explain evaluation terms and the types of evaluations your organization can perform. You'll also learn how to put together an evaluation plan for your program design and how to write a dissemination plan.

TIP

The W. K. Kellogg Foundation has published a handbook describing how to actually go about conducting an evaluation. You can view or download the handbook on the foundation's website (`www.wkkf.org`) by searching for evaluation handbook.

Making sense of evaluation plan terminology

Before you can write an evaluation plan, you need to have a basic understanding of the commonly used terms. The terms in the following sections are ones you should be familiar with and use when writing your evaluation plan for the program design.

Data collection and analysis

You collect data in order to find out whether you're achieving the objectives you describe in the project design section of your grant narrative. You analyze the data to determine whether you met your goals. Both the data collection and analysis processes must be objective, no matter what the findings reveal.

Data is the information about your project gathered using measurement tools. *Measurement tools* can include surveys, pre- and post-questionnaires or tests, and oral interviews.

Data analysis occurs when you examine the information that you collect with the measurement tools. What you're looking for is whether the data produces information relevant to determining the progress of your project. If it isn't, you need to go back and design new measurement tools.

Evaluators

The *evaluator* or *evaluation team* is the individual or group of people you select to determine whether your project succeeded or failed in meeting its goals.

UNDERSTANDING EVALUATION STANDARDS

Evaluation standards are acceptable ways to measure various components of your project. The American National Standards Institute approved the following four nationally used standards in the 1990s. The entire evaluation process should incorporate these standards if you want funders and others in your field to accept your findings as valid:

- **Accuracy standards** are how you plan to show that your evaluation will reveal and convey technically adequate or sufficient information about your project.
- **Feasibility standards** are how you plan to ensure that your evaluation procedures will be realistic, prudent, diplomatic, and frugal.
- **Propriety standards** are how you plan to show that your evaluation will be conducted legally, ethically, and with due regard for the welfare of those involved in the evaluation as well as those affected by its results.
- **Utility standards** are how you plan to evaluate the information needs of the project's participants or end users.

Even if your project failed miserably (for example, your objectives said that, on average, 75 percent of the participants would gain one full grade point, but only 25 percent did so), you and your stakeholders, including the funders, need to know what went wrong and how the outcome could be reversed. Sometimes in this failed scenario, your funding source will actually give you a second grant to fix the problem, which equates to another chance to succeed. But you get the second chance only if your evaluation team is objective and accurate.

A *third-party evaluator* is an individual or company outside your program that designs and conducts your project's evaluation. (See the later section, "Taking the third-party evaluation route," for more information.) Remember to include an expense line in your project's budget to compensate the third-party evaluator for its services. The standard amount to set aside for evaluation is 15 percent of your total project budget. (See Chapter 12 of this minibook for more about budgets.)

An *internal evaluation* occurs when you decide not to hire an outsider to conduct your evaluation and instead choose to gather stakeholders to assess the effectiveness of your program (see the later section, "Keeping the evaluation process in-house").

WARNING

You shouldn't evaluate your own project. You can be a part of the evaluation team if you decide to conduct an internal evaluation. However, refrain from coaching or coercing other evaluation team members (your co-workers, board members, volunteers, community members, or project participants). Everyone on the evaluation team needs to be able to talk openly about their perceptions of the data findings. Focus on being impartial.

Types of evaluations

There are two basic types of evaluations — *formative* and *summative*. This section discusses both.

A *formative evaluation* occurs when you sit down with the project's stakeholders (community members, participants, and staff) and develop a list of questions the funders may ask about your project when determining whether the funding was well placed and used. Looking at several aspects of the project design (goals, objectives, and activities), stakeholders generate questions about how the project can become more effective or efficient. The formative process continues from the time you receive grant funding to the completion of the grant time frame. In light of this ongoing process, you should set a frequency for when the data will be collected to answer the questions you have posed.

Some funders give you due dates for evaluation and financial reports. Others leave the reporting frequency up to the grant applicant or grantee. If the latter is the case, give quarterly reports — at a minimum — to all your funders. When you report quarterly, you find flaws or weaknesses in your program's implementation strategies quickly and have time to correct them — well within the funding period.

TIP

Always have progress reports or *raw data* (information collected but not compiled into summary form or typed in a formal report) on hand for funder queries or visits.

WARNING

If you can't make improvements to your project (for example, if your students just aren't improving their grade-point averages as quickly as you anticipated in your program design narrative), a formative evaluation may not be the right approach to measure the success of your project; instead, focus on using a summative evaluation.

The *summative evaluation* (also called an *outcome evaluation*) occurs near or at the end of the period for which you were funded. This type of evaluation should answer the following questions in a narrative format:

- What did you accomplish?
- How many participants were impacted and in what ways?
- What overall difference did your project make?
- Is this project worth funding again?

Qualitative versus quantitative

Qualitative evaluation describes the approach you take when you want to understand the quality of your project's implementation process. You can use surveys and focus groups to determine the quality of the service delivery process, staff development training, partnership involvement, and other components of your program.

Quantitative evaluation (tracking the numbers) describes the approach you take to measure the progress of your SMART objectives. Did you reach your short-, intermediate-, and long-term outcomes as presented in the logic model (see the earlier related section)?

TIP

Collect data on both qualitative and quantitative approaches in order to analyze the progress and impact of the implementation process.

Keeping the evaluation process in-house

When you plan to conduct an internal evaluation — meaning you aren't hiring an outsider to assist with or conduct the evaluation of your project — the best option is to propose a stakeholder's evaluation in the evaluation plan of your program design. In a *stakeholder's evaluation*, you don't need to identify the evaluators until you know your project is funded. You can then identify select stakeholders from your target population, board of directors, and community partners to sit on the evaluation team.

The easiest way to identify your project's stakeholders is to ask yourself the following question: "Who has a vested interest in our project and will be impacted by the project's success?" The outcome of the project definitely matters to your board of directors, if you have one, as well as to the staff assigned to work on the project. However, it matters most to the project's target population, which is why you should seriously consider inviting some of them onto the evaluation team.

TIP

A clue as to when you may need to propose a stakeholder's evaluation can be found in the grant application's budget instructions. If the budget instructions for the grant or cooperative agreement don't include a specific line item for evaluation or contracted services, and if your program implementation costs will require all the available grant funding, consider a stakeholder's evaluation. It's less costly and keeps the entire evaluation process local and manageable. For example, suppose your organization proposes to operate a homeless shelter for veterans returning from overseas combat. The grantor requires that all proposed homeless prevention plans originate from the feedback collected at public meetings. At your public meetings, have a sign-in sheet that captures each attendee's name, mailing address, telephone number, and email address, as well as whether the person is a veteran or has a family member who's a veteran or on active duty. Each and every citizen who attends your public meeting and provides input on the need for housing for homeless veterans is a potential candidate for the evaluation team.

Be creative and bring together people who have different perspectives. Sometimes, opposing views bring out additional needs that weren't identified during the public meetings. Having one or two devil's advocates on any team, including the evaluation team, can be good for flushing out the real needs and forcing team members to rethink their positions. The number of people you have on your stakeholder's evaluation team doesn't matter as long as everyone's point of view is welcomed, considered, and incorporated into your final intervention or prevention methodology for serving the target population.

TIP

Do you have board members who have wanted to work with your organization in a more hands-on way but who you're afraid will try to micromanage the program? Placing them on the evaluation team is an ideal way to divert their energy. They can really help shape the outcome of your grant-funded program — a program that may very well be the most important part of your organization.

REMEMBER

When it comes to an internal evaluation team, you're not looking for groupthink. You want independent-minded people who can bring objective ideas to the table, giving you a credible evaluation process for your funded project. Also, remember that if you use your staff for the evaluation, they'll need time to oversee the data collection, interpretation, and reporting processes. In other words, the evaluation process will cost money and/or time whether you decide to use internal or external evaluators.

Taking the third-party evaluation route

If you decide to bring in an outsider to conduct your evaluation, that person is referred to as a *third-party evaluator* in the grant narrative. Even though outside evaluators are costly (some need up to 15 percent of your total project budget to conduct the evaluation), the right outside evaluator can bring credibility and visibility to your project, which in turn attracts continued funding.

TIP

The grant application's budget instructions often provide clues that you need an outside evaluator. If the budget instructions discuss evaluation costs and ask you to provide information on third-party evaluators, plan to bring in an outside evaluator.

To find a qualified evaluator, first ask other organizations in your community that provide programs similar to yours about evaluators they've used. Their evaluator may have been a university research department, a college faculty member, or a retired government employee with expertise in the project area. However, be aware that you may have to look outside your home area for an evaluator.

You must choose an individual or organization that has experience in developing evaluation plans, creating monitoring guidelines that track the progress of a project's objectives, and conducting both simple and complex evaluations in the project's focus area.

During your telephone conversation or meeting with the prospective evaluator, work through a list of prepared questions and write down the evaluator's answers. You may have to decide from among several possible candidates, and having the answers on paper will help you review and make your decision. Keep in mind that the evaluator will need sufficient information about the program's design to respond intelligently to your questions.

Start off with the following questions:

- What methodology will you use to understand the day-to-day operations of my project?

» How much time will the work take, and how much will it cost?

» How many on-site days can you provide in order to meet with project personnel and talk to representatives from the target population?

» Are you willing to meet with my board of directors to provide progress reports on the evaluation?

» At what points will you give me written evaluation reports?

Brainstorm with your staff to come up with even more questions. Selecting an evaluator is an important part of your project, and falling short in writing this part of the narrative can result in being denied funding.

TIP

After you select an evaluator, see whether that organization or person can help you write the evaluation plan for the grant narrative. Of course, you may have to pay a fee for the evaluator's time, but the money is well spent if you're going after a multimillion-dollar, multiyear grant with heavy competition. (When fewer than ten grants will be awarded nationwide in a major grant competition, that's *heavy*.) And make sure you write this same evaluator into your budget to bring that person or group back for the full evaluation process when you have a funding award. (See Chapter 12 of this minibook for more on how to incorporate the cost for post-grant award evaluation into your project budget.)

Writing the evaluation plan

After you decide whether to conduct an internal stakeholder or external third-party evaluation, the next step is to start writing or incorporating your evaluation plan into the program design section of the grant application narrative. The evaluation plan goes at the end of the program design narrative if it's not a stand-alone section. The funder's formatting guidelines usually determine the length of each narrative section in the grant proposal. The program design is usually the largest section, so write succinctly but include sufficient details for the funder to see you have a comprehensive evaluation plan.

Your evaluation plan must always be written to address the funding agency's guidelines. A comprehensive evaluation plan includes a narrative on how the program will be evaluated (qualitatively, quantitatively, or both). It also tells the funder what type of data will be collected; who will be collecting, analyzing, and interpreting the data; and the frequency for the data collection process. Don't forget to add detail about each target population included in the evaluation process and tell how information or data will be collected from them (by way of survey, questionnaire, visual observation, and more).

REMEMBER

Most importantly, make sure all data to be collected is connected to determining your progress toward achieving your measurable objectives, which are presented earlier in the project design section of your application. And remember that your evaluation plan must be specific to your program goals and objectives.

TIP

Examples of evaluation plans abound online. If you do an Internet search for "sample evaluation plan" you find that just about every type of funder (foundation and government) has posted outlines and full narrative sections of its best or preferred type of evaluation plans. Don't forget to use the Kellogg Foundation's website to search for and use its Logic Model Development Process information.

The evaluation plan also needs to include information about how you'll share your evaluation findings with other organizations interested in replicating a successful model program. This sharing process is called *dissemination.* The dissemination plan, which is usually a paragraph or two, is written at the end of the evaluation plan.

Worried about giving away too many secrets? Don't be. When you receive a grant award, the funders expect you to share your findings with other organizations and associations. With government grants, everything you do — information and program activities — is subject to public access. Foundation and corporate funders want to maximize their investments, which means you're obligated to disseminate your evaluation findings. Practically all funders ask for your dissemination plans in their grant application guidelines.

When you write your dissemination narrative, include information on what you'll share and how you'll share it. List conferences, forums, website postings, and printed documents mailed out (and to whom they'll be mailed).

WARNING

When you're writing your grant applications, always, *always* follow the guidelines provided for preparing your narrative sections. In foundation funding requests, the dissemination plan can be short and to the point. However, in government funding requests, you may be instructed to write multiple pages on the dissemination process. Carefully reading and following the funding agency's guidelines can be the difference between a funded project and a rejected one.

IN THIS CHAPTER

- » Presenting your grant project's management team
- » Using staff with high-level credentials and/or experience
- » Including overall management capability information
- » Demonstrating federal compliance in the personnel section
- » Incorporating the sustainability plan

Chapter 11

Preparing Project Management Plans and Sustainability Narratives

After you tell the funding organization why you need its financial booster shot in your statement of need (see Chapter 9 of this minibook) and your project's implementation plan (see Chapter 10 of this minibook), you need to explain who's going to manage the grant-funded program and how the grant applicant organizations intend to sustain activities funded by the grant award. This chapter shows you how to write about existing and incoming staff in a way that convinces funders that you have the right personnel to manage their awarded monies.

This chapter also shows you how to put together winning project-management profiles, an additional organizational resources narrative, and a federally guided approach to selecting diverse project personnel. Finally, you're guided on how to craft the sustainability plan. Hint: You are not the creator of this plan.

REMEMBER

You gain credibility when you outline the key personnel, organizational resources, and your equity process in hiring. Some funders call this section of the narrative *key personnel, adequacy of resources,* or *equal employment opportunity statement.* Regardless of the name, this narrative can range in length from one page to several pages. Developing narrative language that meets the requirements laid out in the funding source's grant application guidelines is important. Otherwise, the funder will likely reject your application for grant funding. Also, no funder wants to think that their significant investment in your organization will end when the grant money runs out. You need to be able to write about Plan B.

Presenting the Project Management Team's Credentials

Just for a moment, pretend that you're the grant reviewer. You've already read the key opening sections to your application narrative, and now you're *almost* convinced that the organization in question is worthy of the funding agency's award allocation. At this point, you just need to be taken to the finish line. In other words, before you can make a confident decision (fund this or reject this), you need to know who's in charge of the organization and the proposed project and who's going to carry out the day-to-day direct services. From a funder's perspective, you want written validation that competent administrators will manage the grant monies and highly qualified staff and/or contractors will manage the actual project's implementation, evaluation, and final reporting processes.

REMEMBER

Grant-funded personnel are selected and assigned in one of two ways: by reassigning an existing staff person to the grant-funded project or by hiring someone after the project is funded. When you're writing about to-be-hired personnel, you don't know the specific qualifications of each individual, but you should know and be able to write about the minimum job specifications of those who will carry certain responsibilities.

Whatever specifics you include about your project management team, you'll be held accountable by the funder. For example, if the funder's minimum qualifications for the project director or coordinator is a master's degree and your organization hires an individual with only a bachelor's degree, you aren't fulfilling the written promise that you made in your funding request. You must be conscientious about the qualifications required and the project team members selected or hired to fill the positions.

No matter how you assign project personnel, selecting individuals with project-specific qualifications can help you win a big grant award. And when you've identified qualified personnel for your project, your project's personnel profiles are a lot easier to write.

WARNING

As a regular grant peer reviewer, Bev can tell you that even if the rest of your grant narrative is perfect, you can easily lose peer review points if your project personnel aren't up to snuff. On a point scale of 100, projects scoring in the mid- to high 90s are recommended for grant awards, so losing even a few points can be fatal. Ninety-point projects just don't cut it anymore! (See Chapter 7 of this minibook for more about the point system and review criteria.)

Before you start writing about staffing, resources, and equity in hiring, sit down with existing staff members or your human resources director and go over the project narrative you've already written. Look at your program design narrative and the implementation chart (see Chapter 10 of this minibook) to see what personnel you've committed to carry out the proposed activities. Highlight the job titles and any other information that gives you a clue as to how many staff members you need to implement the grant-funded project.

When compiling information for the project's personnel profile section, be sure to identify the following:

- **A project administrator (or project manager):** This individual provides management oversight. In some organizations, this is the executive director or deputy director. This person should be able to allocate up to five hours per week of their work time to making sure the project meets its grant-funded conditions. The project administrator (along with the project director — see the next point) usually attends meetings with the project's community partners. (Chapter 9 of this minibook covers establishing partnerships with other organizations in your community.)
- **The personnel necessary to carry out the project on a day-to-day basis:** This entry usually means selecting a *project director* or *coordinator* who's responsible for the program's implementation and coordination. This individual reports directly to the project administrator. Identify a project director who has relevant and extensive experience in the same area as the project. In addition, for research projects, another day-to-day individual is the *principal investigator* (PI). This individual is responsible for the management and integrity of the program design as well as the direction and oversight of compliance, financial, and collaborative partnerships.

- **All remaining personnel who will be paid from the project's grant-funded budget:** Work with your financial or business manager to review the project design and determine 100 percent of the staffing necessary to implement the project if funded. List all other personnel who will be hired for or assigned to the project in the adequacy of resources or management plan narrative of your grant application. This section of the narrative connects directly to your project budget. You'll either have direct costs or indirect costs. (More about the budget in Chapter 12 of this minibook.)

REMEMBER

Each project differs when it comes to the personnel needed to carry out activities, so spend some time with your human resources department to determine how much part-time/full-time equivalency should be dedicated to each staff role. See the later section, "The basic profile," for more on full-time equivalency.

WARNING

The process of choosing personnel isn't the time to do a favor for your out-of-work, unqualified friend or relative! Not only do they have the potential to drag your project down, but they also drag down your funding request because decision-making readers shudder when they see unqualified personnel on a project they're considering funding.

Articulating Qualifications

After you choose your staff, you can begin writing your personnel narrative. The grant reviewer looks for the key personnel narrative to answer the following questions:

- What are the project administrator's qualifications? Is the time allocated sufficient? Who will report to the administrator? Is the line of accountability clear?
- What are the project director's or coordinator's qualifications? Is the time allocated sufficient? Who will report to the project director or coordinator? Is the line of accountability clear?
- Which project personnel will carry out the day-to-day activities? Is the time allocated sufficient for each position? Who will project personnel report to? Is the line of accountability clear?
- Do the personnel members have extensive experience in the project's focus area? What percentage of personnel have extensive experience?
- What percentage of each position will be charged to the grant budget?

» What percentage — if any — of all personnel costs will be *cash match* (cash that you have on hand and available to match the grant award for grants that require matching funds in order to receive the award) on the part of the grant applicant? (See Chapter 12 of this minibook for further clarification on cash match and other budget-related terms.)

REMEMBER

Keep in mind that you absolutely must follow the funding agency's guidelines when it comes to writing about your project personnel. Your actual key personnel narrative may look entirely different from the examples in the following sections.

The basic profile

For a basic personnel profile, write about what makes each person qualified for their proposed position. Give information on relevant work background, awards, acknowledgments, and special recognitions. Follow this text with educational information. End with a final sentence to blow the readers away — impress them with one more fact that qualifies the individual for the proposed position. If individuals filling some or all of the budgeted positions have yet to be hired, write a short description of the desired qualifications.

REMEMBER

Unless the funding agency has page limitations for this section of the funding request, write one paragraph for each budgeted personnel position. (Refer to the next section, "The profile with page limitations," to determine what to do when you have to watch how much you write.) This recommendation remains the same whether personnel costs will be charged to the grant or whether they'll be covered by your organization's cash match.

The following example presents the narrative language on the proposed director. Notice that boldface is used to highlight the individual's name, position, and expertise and that it's written in future tense. This plants the idea that this funding *will* be awarded and the proposed staffing-related tasks *will* occur. The designation *FTE* stands for *full-time equivalent* (40 hours per week). (An individual assigned to a project at 0.5 FTE works on it 20 hours per week; 0.10 is 4 hours per week, and so on.) Typically, you won't need to include an explanation of FTE, but you should spell out the abbreviation the first time you use it.

Key Personnel

Project Administrator (0.05 FTE cash match): Dr. Anne Mitchell will be responsible for administering the grant-funded project. Dr. Mitchell is the founder and executive director of the Ready for the World Foundation and has functioned in this position since 2007. She was the visionary who believed there was a need for a forward-thinking nonprofit in a historically static (little change in decades) community environment. Dr. Mitchell has 43 years of corporate management experience

Preparing Project Management Plans and Sustainability Narratives and 10 years of nonprofit management experience. She founded and managed the Women's Business Incubator in Burton, Michigan, for which she was awarded the Clairol Corporation's Entrepreneur of the Year award. She will report directly to the organization's board of directors. Dr. Mitchell is a bright ray of sunshine; everything she's involved in blossoms quickly and fully AND is sustaining.

Sometimes the expertise is in the team as a whole. However, in this example, Dr. Mitchell has the necessary qualities to fulfill this position all by herself.

The profile with page limitations

If your funding request has page limitations and you can't write at least one full paragraph on all project staff members, you can include a brief list of key personnel, including volunteers, in the grant application narrative and note their responsibilities. Also, feel free to attach to the narrative more detailed information about your key personnel if the funder's guidelines allow attachments.

The following is an example of how to develop a list of key personnel:

Project Director (1.0 FTE grant-funded): The organization will conduct a nationwide search for a project director who can lead this project to a successful conclusion. The individual hired will be qualified to carry out the following responsibilities:

- Assist the board of directors in fulfilling the organization's mission
- Have knowledge of the organization's target population
- Effectively carry out the grant-funded project's implementation plan
- Establish an annual program events calendar
- Identify qualified additional staff
- Secure new community partners
- Promote the programs via public forums
- Evaluate the effectiveness of community outreach and program services

This position will report to the project administrator.

Volunteer Coordinator (1.0 FTE cash match): One full-time volunteer coordinator will be assigned to this grant-funded project. Discretionary funds have been awarded from the organization's Regional Bank Association account to pay the salary and fringe benefits for this position. The volunteer coordinator will be responsible for recruiting, screening, training, and supervising adult mentors for our clients. This position requires ten years of volunteer coordination experience in either a paid or volunteer setting. The person assigned to this position must have a positive disposition, exhibit excellent analytical abilities, and demonstrate management-level skills. The Volunteer Coordinator will report directly to the Project Director.

The profile for personnel paid by cash match

When you can provide personnel at no cost to the grant, you look *great* in the eyes of the grant reviewer. And when you look great, you score more points. For example, you may include the project director's salary in the grant proposal budget, but the project administrator's time will be cash match, so it won't be charged to the grant proposal budget. This setup shows the funder that you're focusing on the best use of grant funds and that you want to put the money toward providing services to the target population.

REMEMBER

Grant reviewers are looking for answers to some hard-and-fast questions critical to the success of your project. Even if you aren't asking for grant funds to cover personnel, you still include a brief paragraph on the key personnel and include the résumé of the project director in the application's attachments.

When you have a volunteer advisory council, write a paragraph about the volunteers' individual commitments and how often the council will meet. In other words, you want to show that they have a vested interest in seeing your project succeed!

INCLUDING THE PRINCIPAL INVESTIGATOR IN SCIENTIFIC OR RESEARCH GRANTS

In federal grant applications for scientific or research requests, you're asked to provide a biographical sketch for the principal investigator. In some cases, the *principal investigator* is similar to the project director (see the section "The profile for personnel paid by cash match") but usually holds a doctorate degree in the project's specialty field. The form for a biographical sketch can change from agency to agency. The most common information fields found on the form are

- **Name:** Type in the first, middle, and last name of your principal investigator.
- **Position title:** Type in the project-assigned position title.

(continued)

(continued)

- **User name:** If you already have an agency log-in for the online e-grant portal entry, type it in this box.
- **Education/training:** List the colleges attended and locations, beginning with the baccalaureate degree. Fill in the degree column, the year earned or awarded, and the field of study for each institution of higher education attended.
- **Personal statement:** Write about the purpose of the proposed research and how it relates to the principal investigator's experience.
- **Positions and honors:** List, in chronological order, previous work or job positions, ending with the present position. List any honors, including present membership on any federal government public advisory committees.
- **Selected peer-reviewed publications (in chronological order):** List any publications in which work has been published and read or reviewed by professional peers.
- **Research support:** List all ongoing or completed (past three years) research projects (both federally and non-federally supported).

Typically, biographical sketches range from five to seven pages, including its finished length after you add all the requested information. Government grant applications are often formatted for you to insert a page number at the bottom of the page, and the biographical sketch is no different. When you see the cue at the bottom of a form page, read and reread the funding guidelines to see whether your narrative and all accompanying forms must be numbered in sequential order.

Connecting Accountability and Responsibility to the Implementation Process

In addition to knowing who will be working on the project you're seeking funds for, the granting agency wants to know who reports to whom for your project. The funder wants to make sure that you understand the responsibility inherent in accepting the grant monies. You acknowledge these facts in the management plan and the statement of fiscal agency responsibility.

REMEMBER

If you're writing to foundations and corporations, some funders may ask for a separate narrative section on the management plan. If they don't, you can include it in the section for key personnel. However, state and federal funders usually ask for a qualification of key personnel section and a management plan; these sections are to be written separately and labeled clearly.

Writing the management plan

The *management plan* tells the grant reviewer who's accountable to whom. It clearly shows where the buck stops when questions arise from the funder. You can integrate the management plan into the key personnel descriptions (see the personnel list earlier in this chapter), or you can develop a separate graphic like the one shown in Figure 11-1.

FIGURE 11-1: A sample management plan table.

The Ready for the World Future Forward Initiative			
Position (# of personnel)	**FTE**	**Reports To**	**Funded By**
Program administrator (1)	0.05	Board of directors	Cash match
Program director (1)	1.0	Program administrator	Grant
Volunteer coordinator (1)	1.0	Program director	Cash match

Illustration by Ryan Sneed

Show the management plan in black and white — no color graphics except a lightly shaded title row. The funder wants to see the position name, FTE allocation (explained earlier in the chapter), line of accountability (who reports to whom), and how the position will be funded (grant budget, cash match from funding applicant, or in-kind contribution). List the project personnel in order of ranking, beginning with the highest administrative position and ending with volunteers, if any.

In your plan, the number in parentheses behind each position title indicates the number of individuals hired for each title position. For example, in Figure 11-1, the (1) behind each listed position tells you that The Ready for the World Future Forward Initiative will have one program administrator, one program director, and one volunteer coordinator.

When the funder's management plan guidelines call for something that's not applicable or necessary to your project, write a response to indicate why that particular something isn't attached or discussed further in your application.

TIP

Unless it isn't possible due to formatting guidelines, always include a project organizational chart in the management plan — space permitting. A chart amplifies your key personnel narrative section and gives the grant peer reviewer a visual break from reading line after line of typed text. If the grant application's guidelines limit the number of pages you can write in the narrative and don't specifically request an organizational chart, leave it out; the organizational chart doesn't adequately capture position responsibilities or qualifications to serve as the entire management plan section on its own.

Acknowledging your fiscal responsibility

The management plan should also include a *statement of fiscal agency responsibility.* This concise, one-paragraph written statement by the chief financial officer (CFO) of the applicant organization attests to the fact that the agency will take on the responsibility of accepting the grant award, managing the grant award monies, and preparing and submitting financial and evaluation reports. Basically, it's just one more affirmation to the funder of the grant applicant's internal accountability.

The statement of fiscal agency responsibility is presented depending on the type of funder:

- **For foundation and corporate funding requests:** Written on the grant applicant agency's letterhead, signed by the CFO, and attached to the application and/or in the body of the grant application narrative in the grant applicant capability section. Read Chapter 9 of this minibook for more on this section of the narrative.
- **For government grant requests:** Included at the end of the management plan.

REMEMBER

Make sure to include the following accountability information in your statement of fiscal agency responsibility:

- Legal name and corporate structures.
- The year in which your organization was founded and whether it has any special recognitions, such as an award from the mayor's office or a certificate of recognition from a state agency or another nonprofit organization.
- Whether your organization will be the fiscal agent. (If not, provide information on the fiscal agent and tell the funder why you're using another organization to act as your fiscal agent.)
- Who will monitor your fiscal activities.
- A generic statement about your finances being managed prudently and effectively. (This statement sounds good, and it works to convince funders that you have a solid financial grip on handling all incoming revenues.)
- Who conducts your financial audits and the frequency of those audits.
- The amounts and sources of funds you've received from grant awards.

The following example shows you how a good statement of fiscal agency responsibility reads:

The Ready for the World Future Forward Initiative (RWFFI), founded in 2007, is a public nonprofit charitable organization under IRS subsection 501(c)(3). RWFFI is the grant applicant and fiscal agent for this funding request. Finances are managed prudently and cost-effectively. Fiscal activities are monitored monthly by a CPA and reported to the board of directors within 30 days of receipt of accounting summary records. All financials are audited annually by CPAs, and audits to date have revealed no unfavorable findings. RWFFI has reported an income growth of 125 percent annually since its founding. Total revenues in 2020 were $2,257,000.

Demonstrating Federal Compliance in the Personnel Selection

Equity is created when you manage a program in such a way that no one is excluded. All the individuals hired with grant funds and all the members of the *target population* (those people the grant funds will help) must be given equal access to program opportunities — to be participants (target population) and to be hired (your project staff) without discrimination.

You show equity by opening your project to all who apply, providing they meet objective eligibility criteria. Funders want assurances that you won't violate federal or state antidiscrimination laws.

TIP

Federal and state funders mandate a grant application section on equity. Foundations and corporations usually don't have anything on equity in their guidelines, but including a paragraph on the subject to show your awareness of the issue doesn't hurt.

When evaluating the statement of equity, the grant reader asks the following key questions:

- Does the grant applicant propose to assign or hire project personnel who reflect the demographics of the community and target population to be served under the grant funding?
- Does the grant applicant embrace a sense of fairness to all human beings?

TIP

Here are some tips for writing the equity section without stress:

- **Ask human resources for help.** Some grant application guidelines require that your equity statement actually cite the federal and state legislation that your organization adheres to in its hiring practices. Your human resources department can give you information on the acts you need to cite.

- **Address equitable access for everyone.** The equity statement should include personnel (including the selection of volunteers for the project) and project participants.
- **Be straightforward and make a statement.** Writing that discrimination will not be tolerated is important. Cite the federal and state antidiscrimination laws to which your organization will adhere.

The following example received high peer review points (see Chapter 7 of this minibook for more on the peer review). Notice how the example addresses the makeup of program personnel and how the personnel will be recruited as well as makes a statement regarding discrimination and fair employment practices:

> The Ready for the World Future Forward Initiative will assign and/or hire staffing for the grant-funded project. All staff and volunteers having direct contact with clients will reflect the target population's demographics, culture, and have a demonstrated cultural competency of the individuals served. All staff and volunteers will complete a 16-hour cultural diversity training provided by Model State University. Following the training, staff will participate in role-plays, trading the roles of mentee and mentor. The role-plays will be observed and videotaped for affirmation of cultural competency.
>
> It is the policy of the Ready for the World Future Forward Initiative not to engage in discrimination or harassment against any person irrespective of gender, race, color, disability, political opinion, sexual orientation, age, religion, or social or ethnic origin. The center will comply with all federal and state nondiscrimination, equal opportunity, and affirmative action laws, orders, and regulations.

The federal government requires that all nondiscrimination forms be signed in the application submission package. Frankly, as a matter of best practices, all businesses (nonprofit and for-profit) should have these policies whether they apply for grants or not.

Writing the Sustainability Statement

A *sustainability plan* is a roadmap for achieving long-term goals. It documents strategies to continue your programs, activities, and partnerships beyond the grant award-funding cycle. Remember, the federal government only awards funding that supplements, not supplants. This means that as the grant applicant organization, you must have some existing and planned resources to keep the doors open and keep programs up and running, in part or total.

Sustainability is an important component to address early in your organization's strategic planning and program development stages. The statement you are asked to write in grant proposals must come organically from your governing board's sustainability plan.

Using the board's sustainability plan

First, and foremost, the grant writer cannot create the language in the sustainability statement from a vacuum. The burden falls on the board of directors to create a sustainability plan (`www.ruralhealthinfo.org/sustainability`). The board's plan must address the following organizational factors:

- Adaptability of your programs
- Coalitions and partnerships that will contribute to your organization's sustainability
- Specific communication approaches to brand your plan for longevity
- Funding and financial support (this is what the funder wants to hear about in your grant request)
- Organizational capacity when funding falls short
- Program evaluation (how will the rigorous monitoring and tracking procedures put into place when grants are awarded remain in place when the grant funds have been depleted)
- Political support (federal grant applications will not be awarded year after year without strong political support)
- Strategic planning (the sustainability plan must be incorporated into the grant applicant organization's strategic plan)

Crafting a sustainability statement

As the grant writer, you will undoubtedly be faced with the task of writing a sustainability statement in most grant applications. The sustainability statement spells out how your project will survive in the long term. It assures the funder that resources spent on the grant-funded project will be the foundation for continuing grant-funded programs with other resources — internal and external.

Here is an example of how a funder will request information about your sustainability plan:

> Applicants are required to submit a program sustainability plan that will describe how the grant-funded program will be continued after the grant funding has ended.

This is what we write in proposals for funding to address the sustainability plan:

> On completion of the grant funding, the Grant Writing Training Foundation will follow the steps in the board-developed sustainability plan. These steps include:
>
> - Continuing to seek new financial stakeholders starting in month six of the funding cycle
> - Working with finance staff to develop a reduced services model that can operate successfully under our next fiscal year's anticipated revenues
> - Developing a scaling-down plan that enables our organization to continue providing services to a smaller target population
> - Using the interest on the endowment fund our board established in 2007 to prevent the cessation of services funded with your grant award

You don't need to attach or write the entire sustainability plan document. You simply need to show potential funders that a plan is in place and explain how the program will continue after their grant award has been expended.

IN THIS CHAPTER

» Defining the basics in your budget request

» Eyeballing your budget from a funder's perspective

» Plotting expenses for multiple-year funding requests

» Opting to use a fiscal sponsor

Chapter 12

Creating a Budget That Includes All the Funding You Need

Many grant applicants create the budget section first, but it's actually one of the last sections you should tackle. After all, you can't develop an accurate budget for your grant request until you know all the costs involved in the funded project's implementation. Where do these cost clues come from? The program design narrative (see Chapter 10 of this minibook for more about that).

It's extremely beneficial if you can develop your budget information in tandem instead of tackling it when your proposal narrative is complete. If you're working hand-in-hand with your finance staff, board treasurer, or program administrator, you can work together to create a budget during the narrative writing process. And, of course, budgeting plays an important part when you're building a fundraising plan (as discussed in Book 2, Chapter 2).

REMEMBER

Your budget is connected directly to your project's goals, objectives, and implementation activities. In order to achieve the goals and objectives, a series of implementation activities (also known as *process objectives*) must occur. The line items in your budget are the costs of carrying out the activities that lead to the achievement of your goals and objectives; these costs can include salaries, fringe benefits, travel, equipment, contracted services, construction, supplies, and more. Translation: Dollars are linked to activities and their resulting costs. (See Book 4 for best practices regarding bookkeeping and accounting activities for nonprofit organizations.)

This chapter walks you through the budget preparation process for grant applications. It also tells you what the funder's expectations are when it comes to reading (or scrutinizing) your budget section.

Understanding Budget Section Basics

Most of the terms associated with the budget section of grant applications and cooperative agreements are everyday terms — no big deal. But when you thoroughly understand each section of the budget, you transform from the "I'm not so sure" grant writer to the "I know how to do this" grant writer who's ready to tackle the backside of the grant-writing mountain. As you start the final climb down, don't forget your enthusiasm (and don't forget to breathe)!

Your budget section contains two main parts, allocation and budget detail narrative:

- **Allocation:** This is the dollar amount you assign to each line item. The *budget summary* is the short listing of each line-item expense category and the sum total for the category. At the bottom of it are the total expenses for all the line items listed in the summary. When a funder asks for a budget summary, it wants to see only a graphic table (created by you) or a completed short form (provided by the funder) with your main budget line-item categories and the total amounts for each category. Funders usually don't want to see narrative detail within a budget summary.

  For example, if you're requesting funding for a staff position only, the two columns in your graphic table are Line Item (left-hand column) and Cost (right-hand column). The first line item is Personnel, and the second line item is Fringe Benefits. These two line items are flush left in the left-hand column. The total project budget, also flush left in the last row of the right-hand column, is the sum of these Personnel and Fringe Benefits columns.

- **Budget detail narrative:** Funders require a detailed written explanation or narrative of how you plan to spend their monies if they choose to fund your project. So they typically request your *budget detail narrative* (also referred to as your *budget justification* or just *budget narrative*). In the budget detail narrative, you explain and justify the assumptions or calculations you used to arrive at the figures in your budget summary. The budget detail narrative section isn't the place to spring surprises on the funder. You should have already discussed anything that shows up here in the program design section of the grant application. (See Chapter 10 of this minibook for guidance on crafting an award-winning program design section.) Of course, always read the funder's guidelines and explanations for what should be included in each line-item explanation.

REMEMBER

As far as the order of your budget documents goes, the *budget detail narrative* section (the paragraphs that explain the details behind each expense) usually follows the *budget summary* (the overview of each line-item category and the total expense). Before you start working on the budget detail narrative, however, you need to research the funding source's preference for developing this section of your grant application. Some funders want only the budget summary; others require the summary and detail narrative.

The organization written about in the later budget detail narrative example (which is used throughout this section) is a unit of municipal government — the City of Oz — that has existed since the late 1800s. The city needs additional money to create an energy-efficiency initiative that will save on utility expenses at city hall.

REMEMBER

Don't forget to keep a copy of your proposal documents for your own files! For easy access, move all your grant-related backup files from your computer's hard drive to cloud-based storage.

Personnel

The personnel portion of the budget summary and budget detail narrative is where you indicate the costs of project staff and fringe benefits that will be paid from the grant funds and from your other resources. If your organization plans to assign existing staff to the grant-funded project but not draw the staff salaries from the grant monies, you need to create an in-kind contribution column to show the funder how you plan to support the costs of the project's personnel.

Funding for your project's personnel will either be requested from the funding agency or come as a cash match from your organization (the grant applicant):

- **Cash match** refers to paid human resources or paid ongoing expenses for your organization allocated to the grant-funded program but not paid with monies from the grant funder. A cash match for personnel means that your organization isn't planning to request the salary and fringe benefit expenses from the funder; your organization's operating budget will continue to pay for these expenses or one of your partnering agencies will plan to provide the funding needed to cover some of your implementation costs.

- **In-kind contributions** refer to the donation or allocation of equipment, materials, and labor allocated to the grant-funded program but not requested from the funder.
- **Requested** refers to the funds you need to obtain from outside your organization — from the funding agency.

Use *FTE* (which stands for Full Time Equivalent) throughout your budget forms. FTE is based on a full-time work schedule of 30 to 40 hours per week, depending on how an organization defines *full time*. For the following budget detail narrative example, 40 hours per week is used for a full-time employee: A 1.0 FTE is 40 hours per week; a 0.75 FTE is 30 hours per week; a 0.5 FTE is 20 hours per week; and a 0.25 FTE is 10 hours per week.

TIP

The federal government has published this definition for full-time employment: If an employee works an average of 30 hours a week or 130 hours a month or more, that employee is considered full-time.

REMEMBER

Because fringe benefits vary from organization to organization and from state to state, you need to check with your human resources department to find out your organization's fringe benefit calculation. This figure is always a double-digit percentage multiplied by the total salaries for the grant-funded and in-kind personnel.

Following is an example of the personnel budget detail narrative from the City of Oz's grant application:

Personnel Budget Detail Narrative

Personnel: One 0.5 FTE facilities manager will be assigned to the grant-management duties and project oversight tasks. The operation manager's full-time salary is $90,000 annually. 0.5 FTE equals $45,000.

Total Personnel Expenses: $45,000
Cash Match: $45,000

In-Kind Contributions: $0

Requested: $0

Fringe Benefits Budget Detail Narrative

Fringe benefits are calculated at 40 percent of total salaries; fringe benefits include medical, dental, vision, short-term disability, worker's compensation insurance, unemployment insurance, and employer's FICA match for each salaried position.

Total Fringe Benefit Expenses: $45,000 × 40 percent equals $18,000

Cash Match: $18,000

In-Kind Contributions: $0

Requested: $0

WARNING

You shouldn't include cash-match or in-kind dollar amounts in the *Requested* line item of the budget summary or in the *Requested* line-item detail narrative. Your cash-match and in-kind items should appear in a separate column. Figure 12-1 shows an example from the City of Oz Project.

City of Oz Energy Efficiency Initiative Budget Summary for Personnel and Fringe Benefit Expenses				
Line Item	**Requested**	**Cash Match**	**In-Kind Contributions**	**Total Line-Item Expenses**
Salaries	$0	$45,000	$0	$45,000
Fringe Benefits	$0	$18,000	$0	$18,000
Totals	**$0**	**$63,000**	**$0**	**$63,000**

FIGURE 12-1: The personnel section of a budget summary.

Illustration by Ryan Sneed

Travel

If you plan to reimburse project personnel for local travel, traditionally referred to as *mileage reimbursement*, include this expense in the travel line item of the budget summary and in the budget detail narrative. Be sure to use the current Internal Revenue Service mileage reimbursement rate in your calculations. Also, if you plan to send project personnel to out-of-town or out-of-state training or conferences during the course of the project, you need to ask for nonlocal travel expenses.

Your travel explanation in the budget detail narrative needs to include the number of trips planned and the number of persons for each trip as well as the conference or training program name, location, purpose, and cost. Don't forget to include the cost of lodging, meals, transportation to the events, and ground travel.

When reviewing the budget-related portions of the grant guidelines, you're likely to come across the term *per diem*. In this context, *per diem* refers to the daily allowance your organization gives employees to spend on meals and incidentals during their travel. Federal grant applications may have per diem limits, such as $105 per day.

REMEMBER

Setting a per diem amount may backfire when you or another employee travels to an area such as Hawaii, the East Coast, or the West Coast, with a higher cost of living than the norm. Before you finalize your budget line items, contact the funding agency to see whether you can use higher per diem amounts for higher-cost locales.

TIP

If you want to set a per diem for your project but aren't sure what a reasonable amount is, you can check the federal per diem rates for your state at the General Services Administration website at `https://www.gsa.gov`. Click Per Diem Lookup, then enter the current year, state, city, and ZIP code in the information input boxes to find hotel and other per diem amounts for the area.

Here's a portion of the travel budget detail narrative from the City of Oz's grant application. Notice that the purpose of the travel is clearly explained for the funder. The funds requested are clearly not for "luxurious" travel amenities:

> **Travel Budget Detail Narrative**
>
> **Travel (Out of State):** Grant funding will enable our facilities manager to travel to six metropolitan southwest cities to meet with their facility environment directors and financial staff to determine the most cost-effective fiscal and management process to start this initiative. The following cities will be polled for their processes: Phoenix and Tucson (AZ), Albuquerque and Las Cruces (NM), Salt Lake City (UT), and Palm Springs (CA). Airfare from OZ (commuter airport) to each city is $600 (coach fare) times six flights. Each trip will be a one-day turnaround site visit. No money for meals or ground transportation will be needed.
>
> **Total Travel Expenses:** $3,600
>
> **Cash Match:** $0
>
> **In-Kind Contributions:** $0
>
> **Requested:** $3,600

Figure 12-2 shows you one way of graphically presenting the budget information for the City of Oz Project example.

City of Oz Energy Efficiency Initiative Budget Summary for Travel Expenses

Line Item	Requested	Cash Match	In-Kind Contributions	Total Line-Item Expenses
Travel	$3,600	$0	$0	$3,600
Totals	**$3,600**	**$0**	**$0**	**$3,600**

FIGURE 12-2: The travel section of a budget summary.

Illustration by Ryan Sneed

WARNING

Be conservative yet accurate in calculating travel expenses. No funder wants to see its money pay for junkets or extended vacations. Looking for conferences in exotic places raises a red flag that can get your proposal tossed out during the review stages. (See the later section, "Plotting Ethical Expenses," for more info about the right dollar amounts to include.)

Equipment

The equipment line item of the budget summary and budget detail narrative is where you ask for grant monies to purchase a major piece of equipment, such as a computer, printer, or other critically needed operational equipment.

You can use government funds to purchase equipment when current equipment either doesn't exist or is unable to perform the necessary tasks required by the grant. Equipment purchased with government grant funds must be used 100 percent of the time for the grant-funded project.

TIP

Do your homework before requesting grant monies to cover capital (big-ticket) equipment. Sometimes, you're better off asking a local retailer or wholesaler to donate a big-ticket piece of equipment rather than bogging down the grant budget by adding it to your line items. Also, think about leasing capital equipment. Funders who don't allow you to use grant funds to purchase equipment may allow you to lease it instead. At the end of the lease, you have the option to purchase the equipment. Of course, you also need the funds to do so. Luckily, a lot of vendors have end-of-lease buyouts for $1.

Here's an example of the equipment budget detail narrative for the City of Oz Project:

> **Equipment Budget Detail Narrative**
>
> **Equipment:** The City of Oz will purchase heating and cooling leak-detection equipment. This equipment is highly specialized and comes with user training. The facility manager's staff will use the equipment in teams to check for heating and cooling leaks throughout city hall.
>
> **Total Equipment Expenses:** $80,000
>
> **Cash Match:** $0
>
> **In-Kind Contributions:** $0
>
> **Requested:** $80,000

Figure 12-3 shows you how to graphically represent your equipment expenses in an equipment budget summary. The table contains information from the City of Oz Project.

FIGURE 12-3: The equipment section of a budget summary.

City of Oz Energy Efficiency Initiative Budget Summary for Equipment Expenses				
Line Item	**Requested**	**Cash Match**	**In-Kind Contributions**	**Total Line-Item Expenses**
Equipment	$80,000	$0	$0	$80,000
Totals	**$80,000**	**$0**	**$0**	**$80,000**

Illustration by Ryan Sneed

Supplies

The materials and supplies needed for the daily implementation of the project go on the supplies line of the budget summary and in the budget detail narrative. Examples include office supplies, program supplies, maintenance supplies, training supplies, operational supplies, and so forth.

The following is an example of the supplies budget detail narrative for the City of Oz Project:

Supplies Budget Detail Narrative

Supplies: Grant funds will purchase weather stripping, sealant, plastic sheeting, and other energy-saving supplies for all city hall windows and doors. City hall has 130 windows and 16 doors. The anticipated cost of these supplies is $97,000. The city has an additional $60,000 worth of these types of supplies already in inventory and will use these items first before initiating a purchase.

Total Supplies Expenses: $157,000

Cash Match: $0

In-Kind Contributions: $60,000

Requested: $97,000

Figure 12-4 shows a budget summary for the City of Oz Project. It shows the funds needed from the grantor or funding agency, the cash match (which is $0), in-kind contributions (which are $60,000 for this example because the city has supplies on hand), and the total line item for supplies.

FIGURE 12-4: The supplies section of a budget summary.

City of Oz Energy Efficiency Initiative Budget Summary for Supplies Expenses				
Line Item	**Requested**	**Cash Match**	**In-Kind Contributions**	**Total Line-Item Expenses**
Supplies	$97,000	$0	$60,000	$157,000
Totals	**$97,000**	**$0**	**$60,000**	**$157,000**

Illustration by Ryan Sneed

Contractual

The contractual line of the budget summary and budget detail narrative is where you list the money needed to hire anyone for the project who isn't a member of the staff (staff expenses are listed under the personnel section of the budget covered earlier in this chapter). For example, you may plan to hire a construction contractor to build or renovate a room or building; an evaluation specialist to work on that portion of the application; or a trainer to work with your staff, clients, or board members.

WARNING

In some smaller nonprofit organizations, personnel hired with grant funds are considered contracted services because the term of employment is dependent on continued grant funding. The pro side of categorizing personnel as contractual is that doing so eliminates having project personnel file for unemployment compensation when they have to leave because the funding is up. The con side is that some really qualified individuals may want more of a commitment and may not remain with your project for the duration of the grant period. Also, constantly changing personnel can be a problem when it comes to the evaluation process. (Chapter 10 of this minibook covers evaluation responsibilities.)

Here's an example of the contractual budget detail narrative for the City of Oz Project:

Contractual Budget Detail Narrative

Contractual: The City of Oz will create a "request for bid" document to identify a solar energy vendor. The city council has requested that 100 percent of city hall be heated and cooled with solar panels. The city has collected several estimates for this work. The most cost-effective bid specifications are $542,000 for 50 panels. This price includes installation and a 10-year warranty with guaranteed replacement at no additional charge to the city.

Total Contractual Expenses: $542,000

Cash Match: $0

In-Kind Contributions: $0

Requested: $542,000

To see a contractual budget summary for the City of Oz Project, check out Figure 12-5.

FIGURE 12-5: The contractual line of a budget summary.

City of Oz Energy Efficiency Initiative Budget Summary for Contractual Expenses				
Line Item	Requested	Cash Match	In-Kind Contributions	Total Line-Item Expenses
Contractual	$542,000	$0	$0	$542,000
Totals	**$542,000**	**$0**	**$0**	**$542,000**

Illustration by Ryan Sneed

Construction

When you write a grant that's *exclusively* seeking funds for construction (also known as *building funds*), you don't need to bother with a budget summary and a budget detail narrative. Just insert a copy of the *bid*, which is the written document submitted to you by the construction company that lists all the costs involved in the project. Shortcuts are nice!

Other

You may need to include this section in your budget summary and in the budget detail narrative if you have items that don't fit into any of the other categories. List items by major type and show, in the budget detail narrative, how you arrived at the total sum requested. Typical expenses that fall under the Other category are as follows:

- Internet
- Janitorial services
- Rent
- Reproduction (printing)
- Security services
- Stipends or honorariums for speakers or special project participants
- Telephone
- Testing fees (for evaluations and other outcomes testing)
- Utilities

ACCOUNTING FOR VOLUNTEERS' TIME

For decades, volunteers have rolled up their sleeves and stepped in to serve their communities. Volunteers are most often used where staffing shortages or gaps occur due to funding shortfalls. Nonprofits and for-profits that use volunteers in their organizations treat those volunteers as personnel; they have scheduled hours, they sign in and out of shifts, and they have job descriptions on file in personnel or human resources departments. Volunteers don't receive paychecks or contracted services fees for their volunteer work commitment; however, they're considered workforce or workplace contributors.

For federal and out-of-state foundation and corporate requests, use the national hourly rate to calculate the total value of volunteer hours. The national hourly rate is the number of volunteers on your project multiplied by their average hours each, annually. For state funding agencies as well as foundations and corporations in your state, use the hourly amount listed for your state to calculate the value of your project's volunteers.

Visit `https://independentsector.org/value-of-volunteer-time-2021/` to access a state-by-state list of the dollar value for volunteer hours. Note that this is updated from time to time (in terms of years), so you may have to search for "value of volunteer time" if this link is no longer working.

» Vehicles

» Volunteers (check out the nearby sidebar for help calculating the value of volunteer hours)

For the City of Oz Project, there are no additional expenses for the Other line item.

Distinguishing between direct and indirect costs

Direct costs are expenses for most of the services and products mentioned in the previous sections — everything from the budget categories you've already listed.

REMEMBER

Direct costs and the category's corresponding line item are typically only allowed in government grants or contracts where you actually see direct costs (and indirect costs) in the application guidelines and on the preprinted budget forms.

Indirect costs — often called *overhead* — cover services and products essential to your overall organization that are consumed in some small degree by the project. Some indirect costs include things such as the telephone bill, rent payments, maintenance costs, and insurance premiums.

Indirect costs are usually calculated as a percentage of total direct costs. They can range from as little as 5 percent for a small nonprofit organization to as much as 66 percent for a major university. Your agency may already have an approved indirect cost rate from a state or federal agency, in which case the information is probably on file in the business manager's office. If your agency's business manager doesn't have that information, contact the U.S. Office of Management and Budget or your state's fiscal agency. (Note that to recover indirect costs related to federal awards, you likely have to negotiate an *indirect cost rate,* or ICR, with the federal agency providing the majority of the funding. When this ICR is approved, it's referred to as a *negotiated indirect cost rate agreement*, or NICRA.)

Another option that is much easier than applying for an indirect cost rate from the feds is to use the *De Minimis* rate. This is a flat 10 percent indirect cost rate that you may elect to use in federal grant applications. For more on the De Minimis Indirect Cost Rate, visit `https://fawiki.fws.gov/pages/viewpage.action?pageId=21268677`.

On another note, federal grant applications can be written with 50 percent indirect cost rates built in. This scenario means that if the application is funded and the direct costs total $500,000, another $250,000 gets tacked on for indirect costs. (Those are your taxes at work!) Additionally, many government grants limit or cap the indirect rate that can be charged for the project. Make sure to read the budget guidance carefully so that you adhere to any restrictions.

TIP

If you apply for a government grant and your organization has an indirect cost rate of 20 percent, you can choose not to ask for the entire 20 percent from the funding agency. Instead, because you want to look good and capable of managing a grant, you can ask for 10 percent from the funding agency and make up the other 10 percent as an in-kind contribution.

The following is an example of an indirect costs narrative. Note that the $86,712 requested for indirect costs covers project-related expenses for existing window and door energy-efficiency-related maintenance and repairs, utilities, office space for the facilities staff, and custodial costs:

The City of Oz has been approved for an indirect cost rate of 12 percent by the U.S. Office of Management and Budget. This approval was granted in 2017 when we applied for and received our first U.S. Department of Energy grant to study the use of a wind-driven energy system. Indirect charges are calculated for the total government funds requested or \$722,600 – \$542,000 [contractual expenses] = \$180,600 × 12 percent, or \$21,672.

The reason you would subtract contractual expenses from the indirect cost calculations is because when you contract with outside consultants, your organization (the grant applicant) does not have indirect costs related to other entities' businesses.

REMEMBER

Federal government guidelines don't allow a grant applicant to include the cost of contractual expenses in the indirect cost rate calculations.

Entire budget summary

REMEMBER

When you tally up the total amount of federal funds requested, you add the total direct costs to the total indirect costs. Then you calculate in your matching funds, which results in the total project budget:

Total Direct Costs (Federal Request): \$722,600

Total Eligible Indirect Costs: \$21,672

Total Federal Request: \$744,272

Cash Match: \$63,000

In-Kind Contributions: \$60,000

Total Project Budget: \$867,272

Figure 12-6 shows you how the entire budget summary for the City of Oz Project example looks when it's pulled together.

View Burden Statement

BUDGET INFORMATION - Non-Construction Programs

OMB Number: 4040-0006
Expiration Date: 01/31/2023

SECTION A - BUDGET SUMMARY

	Grant Program Function or Activity (a)	Catalog of Federal Domestic Assistance Number (b)	Estimated Unobligated Funds		New or Revised Budget		
			Federal (c)	Non-Federal (d)	Federal (e)	Non-Federal (f)	Total (g)
1.	Corporation for National and Community Services - Capacity Building Initiatives for Nonprofit Organizations	53.444	$	$	$ 744,272.00	$ 123,000.00	$ 867,272.00
2.							
3.							
4.							
5.	Totals		$	$	$ 744,272.00	$ 123,000.00	$ 867,272.00

Standard Form 424A (Rev. 7-97)
Prescribed by OMB (Circular A-102) Page 1

FIGURE 12-6: The City of Oz Project's entire federal grant application budget summary.

Plotting Ethical Expenses

Completing a project budget can be an individual effort or a team effort. Either way you go about it, however, developing thorough and accurate project budgets to present to funders involves more than just putting numbers down in a line and adding them together. Many factors affect how much you ask for in grant funding.

REMEMBER

When a grant is awarded, it's awarded in good faith and based on both your budget request and the funding source's grant-making capacity. So, your first goal in developing the budget section of your application narrative is to fine-tune your budget request to reflect the actual costs of your program needs. Your second goal is to get your program funded in full, of course!

Gathering accurate cost figures

Not sure what kind of budget numbers to put down? Can't figure out how much you'll have to pay a program director? Unclear how much you'll have to spend on a copy machine? Here's an easy solution: Use your telephone. Call the United Way in your area, for example, to find out its salary ranges for program directors, program coordinators, clerical support, accounting clerks, and other staff positions. Call vendors for specification sheets on equipment. It's amazing how quickly you can find answers by asking people in the know!

The Internet has a wealth of information on nonprofit organizations, including salary surveys. Run a quick Internet search, using your favorite search engine, for nonprofit salary surveys.

TIP

Network with other organizations in your community to locate purchasing cooperatives. With these co-ops, multiple agencies get together to place orders for like items in bulk, thus receiving a bulk purchase discount. All the members of the cooperative benefit by reducing their overall operating costs. Take notes and create a cooperative purchasing information file so you know whom to call or email for future cost-sharing opportunities.

WARNING

Funders often call applicants to get more information on a line item. So be prepared!

Including all possible program income

If you anticipate having any program income at all, you must list a projected amount at the end of your budget summary table and subtract it from the total project costs; doing so means you need less money in grant funds. Examples of possible program income include the following:

- **Interest:** You may earn interest on endowment funds you're allowed to use annually to assist with program costs.
- **Membership or program fees:** A public library has late fees that add to its overall program income, for example. Likewise, a program may charge participants a small fee to enroll in program classes or services.
- **Special events revenue:** You may be planning to hold a fundraising auction or raffle to collect additional monies for field trips, equipment, or other items or activities in the project's design.
- **Ticket sales for planned events:** You may work within a performing arts organization that puts on three plays at the local community theater, and patrons purchase tickets to see your troupe perform.
- **Tuition:** You may receive payment or reimbursement from a state or local agency for aiding a specific population. Your grant request may be for monies to develop additional programs, but you must account for the monies you already take in.

REMEMBER

Not reporting your income is unethical. Just think about the dozens, hundreds, or thousands of proposals a funder receives daily, weekly, and monthly. Ninety percent of the time, the funding source must send out letters to grant seekers regretfully stating that not enough funds are available to fund all the requests received. If you choose to omit the fact that you expect program income and greedily ask for the whole ball of wax, you're taking thousands of dollars out of the funder's annual grant-making budget. Your excess could have funded another grant, perhaps for a struggling start-up agency with no other resources. From an ethical standpoint, asking for grant funds means taking a private oath never to ask for more than you actually need.

Managing expenditures to the penny

Asking for too much isn't looked upon favorably by any funding source. In fact, giving leftover money back at the end of the grant period may mean you can't go back to that funder, ever. No funder wants money back. Why? The funder has already worked the grant award or allocation into its annual giving budgets. Returned money is a hassle, from accounting to reallocation, if the funder has a specific amount of grant funds it awards annually.

To top it off, giving grant award money back may send one or more of these signals to funders:

» Your organization (the grant applicant) didn't submit an accurate budget request — you overshot some of the line items and now you have more money than you know what to do with!

» You aren't creative enough to find a way to use the leftover monies in your project to better serve the target population.

» You failed to carry out all the proposed activities and had leftover monies.

Meet with your board of directors or project advisory council to brainstorm how you can (legally) spend the monies on project-related needs.

REMEMBER

Funders are often willing to work with you if you truly have a legitimate or unavoidable reason for not spending the grant funds as planned. Contacting the program officer as soon as possible when such issues arise is much better than having to send a check back at the end.

Projecting Multiyear Expenses for Grant-Funded Programs

When you're planning to construct a building or purchase specific items of equipment, engineers or vendors can usually give you bids that are very close to the actual cost of the construction or equipment you'll need. However, when you're seeking funding for personnel or line items with prices that fluctuate, take care to account for inflation when preparing your budget.

REMEMBER

In a multiyear request, your line items should increase by at least 5 percent annually.

Here's how to create an award-winning multiyear budget summary table:

» **Column 1:** Type your line-item categories (listed at the beginning of this chapter).

» **Column 2:** Type your Year 1 in-kind contributions by category.

» **Column 3:** Type your Year 1 cash contributions by category.

» **Column 4:** Type your Year 1 amounts requested from the funder by category.

» **Column 5:** Type your Year 2 in-kind contributions by category.

» **Column 6:** Type your Year 2 cash contributions by category.

» **Column 7:** Type your Year 2 amounts requested from the funder by category.

Continue this sequence for all remaining years in your multiyear budget support request. Only run your total at the bottom of each column, vertically. Don't run horizontal totals (at the end of rows); it's too confusing for the funder to nail down the actual costs and requests for any specific year. Search the Internet to find examples of multiple-year budgets.

Building Credibility When You're a New Nonprofit

If your organization is a new nonprofit, you can increase your chances of winning a grant award by applying through a fiscal sponsor. A *fiscal sponsor* is usually a veteran agency with a long and successful track record in winning and managing grants; of course, the sponsor must have 501(c)(3) nonprofit status awarded by the IRS.

The role of a fiscal sponsor is to act as an umbrella organization for newer non-profit organizations that have little or no experience in winning and managing grant awards. Your new organization is the grant applicant, and the established agency is the fiscal sponsor. It acts as the fiduciary (financial) agent for your grant monies. In other words, your fiscal sponsor is responsible for depositing the monies in a separate account and for creating procedures for your organization to access the grant monies.

Why would you use a fiscal sponsor instead of applying directly for grant funds yourself? Because some foundations and corporate givers don't award grant monies to nonprofit organizations that haven't completed the IRS advanced ruling period — typically a 36-month time frame during which the IRS is monitoring your nonprofit-related activities and finances to make sure you're fulfilling the mission, purpose, and activities stated on your nonprofit status application (Form 1023). No funder wants to award substantial grant monies (more than $10,000) to a nonprofit in the advanced ruling period. ***Note:*** Government agencies don't have advanced ruling period–related requirements.

When selecting a fiscal sponsor, try the following avenues:

- Find a well-established nonprofit organization with a successful track record in financial management.
- Ask your local banker to make a recommendation for a suitable fiscal sponsor.

» Look for community-based foundations set up to act as umbrella management structures for new and struggling nonprofit organizations.
» Choose a sponsor you're on good terms with and one you have open lines of communication with. Otherwise, your grant monies may be slow in trickling down.

REMEMBER

Creating a written agreement between you and your fiscal sponsor regarding how you'll use and access the money is essential to prevent any misunderstandings.

When it comes to your relationship with your fiscal sponsor, keep the following points in mind:

» The fiscal sponsor is responsible if your organization mismanages the money.
» The fiscal sponsor is responsible if the fiscal sponsor mismanages the money.
» If an audit for financial expenditures is in order, the funding source can audit the fiscal sponsor, and the fiscal sponsor can audit your organization.

Sometimes a fiscal sponsor wants you to include expenses for accounting services or grant management in the Other section of your budget summary and in the budget detail narrative. This practice is acceptable to funding sources.

TIP

If your fiscal sponsor indicates that it will provide the fiscal management services at no cost, mention this point at the end of your budget detail narrative. Also present the fact up front, in the grant applicant credibility section of the narrative (see Chapter 9 of this minibook for more details).

The following is an example introduction of an organization that plans to use a fiscal sponsor:

> The Finding Evidence of Extinct Ocean Species Initiative (FEEOSI) will use the Ocean Exploration Institute Foundation as its fiscal sponsor. Although our organization is a recognized nonprofit organization in the state of Maine and approved by the IRS for nonprofit tax-exempt status, the FEEOSI has never managed a grant in excess of $1,000,000. Our board's executive committee has met with the financial manager at the Ocean Exploration Institute Foundation and has obtained a written fiscal agent agreement. For this request, the grant applicant is FEEOSI; however, the fiscal agent will be the Ocean Exploration Institute Foundation. We have attached a profile of the foundation as well as its signed fiscal agent agreement. IRS letters of nonprofit determination for both organizations are attached.

IN THIS CHAPTER

» Confirming the contents of your grant application package

» Assembling the mandatory attachments

» Submitting your funding request in a timely manner

Chapter 13 Checking Off the Mandatory Requirements for Compliance

Before you can call your application a done deal, you need to look at what goes into finalizing your grant application package. Putting on the finishing touches is so important because if you fail to adhere to the funder's packaging (meaning how it wants to receive your grant application) and formatting guidelines, you may lose technical review points. (Read about this peer review in Chapter 7 of this minibook.) And if you lose sacred review points, your grant application may be eliminated before it starts the race for a competitive monetary award. This chapter shares the final steps you must take before submitting your grant application for funding consideration.

Triple-Checking All Required Components

Practically all government grant applications and even a few foundations and corporations are now using an application package or online upload checklist — a list of everything you need to prepare and submit a complete application package. Use this checklist to make sure you include each section of the grant application the funder expects to find when its program staff opens your submission. Some funders even ask you to include the checklist in the funding application package. Read carefully for instructions on where to place the checklist in the final application package.

Not all private-sector funders (foundations and corporations) have these easy-to-follow checklists. If you're working on a project for a funder that doesn't provide a handy checklist, you can create your own. Based on what you read in the funder's instructions, type your own list showing the order of the application materials. In other words, what's the first document the funder needs to read when opening your funding package? Continue the list until you have a completed listing for the forms, narrative sections, and attachments. (Be sure to hash out the recommended length for each section or for the entire narrative.) Creating your own checklist gives you peace of mind and cues you as to when the funding package is complete and ready for submission to the funder. While you may have gone over your checklist at least twice to make sure you have not missed any mandatory components, take the time to review the checklist one more time. Yes, that's a total of three eyeball scrolls on your checklist!

The following sections outline the information peer reviewers expect to find in your application.

REMEMBER

Make sure you follow the order that the funder presents in the checklist, which may not be the same as the order presented here.

Cover materials

The cover materials are the first things grant reviewers see when they pick up your application, so make sure each part listed here is finished, well done, and in its proper place.

- A **cover letter,** if required, typed on the grant applicant organization's letterhead and signed by the president of the board or the executive director. (See Chapter 8 of this minibook.)

- All pre-narrative forms in place, with empty information fields filled in with the requested information. Examples of pre-narrative forms include cover page fill-in-the-blank forms and federal grant application cover forms (SF-424A and SF-424B). (See Chapter 4 of this minibook.)
- The abstract or executive summary, which typically has page or word limits, appears on a separate page. This section is an overview of the application's contents and should be placed before the grant proposal narrative. (See Chapter 8 of this minibook.)

REMEMBER

An executive summary is the same as an abstract; it just has a different title. The executive summary or abstract is frequently used in government grant applications, and some regional grant-making forums have designed applications that call for an executive summary. Private-sector funders usually ask for an executive summary.

- The table of contents, which is required by most federal and state grant applications. (See Chapter 8 of this minibook.)

Organization history and capability

The section about your organization's history and capability, which is part of your grant application narrative, introduces the funding agency to your organization and what it does. This section is a formal "this is who we are" type of written introduction (go to Chapter 9 of this minibook for more about building your organization's credibility as a grant applicant). Double-check what you've written in this section, making sure you address the following points:

- **History of the organization:** Why it was founded and how long it has been around. Mention the organization's purpose and mission statement as well.
- **Major accomplishments relevant to the proposed grant-funded project:** Successful capital campaigns, major grant awards, award-winning programs, and successful outcomes for your target populations.
- **Current programs and activities relevant to the proposed grant-funded project:** A simple list of what you do in chronological order with the newest programs and activities listed first and the oldest ones listed last.
- **Target population demographics that mirror the types of populations the funder wants to support in its current funding cycle:** A brief look at your service population over the past five years.
- **Collaborations with local, regional, and statewide nonprofit and for-profit partners:** The who's who in your stakeholder group.

TIP

If you refer to any attachments in the introduction, keep a running list of attached documents so you can double-check that they're in place before submitting the application.

Statement of need

Make sure your statement of need touches on the following topics:

- Evidence of the problem within the community in critical need of grant funding
- How the problem looks from national, regional, and local perspectives
- The current national and local research that proves the existence of the problem
- The gloom, doom, drama, and trauma that justify the need for grant funds

Check out Chapter 9 of this minibook for the scoop on how to create a compelling statement of need.

TIP

Take another look at the first two narrative sections in your funding request. If you didn't include at least one or two graphics, go back and look for key pieces of information you can present in a table or chart; even a simple map of your location helps give the grant reviewer's eyes a visual break.

REMEMBER

For funders with e-grant portals that require online text box entries, you will not be able to use graphics, bullets, bold, underlining, or italics. Make every word count!

Program design

The *program design* is the real meat of your grant application, so making sure you've hit all the right points in it is crucial. Check that your program design contains the following (and refer to Chapter 10 of this minibook for more details on this section):

- **One concise statement expressing the purpose of the program:** What the program will do for your target population.
- **Goals that shadow the funder's specific funding goals:** Nonmeasurable or measurable statements that create the vision for what the funding will do for your target population.

- **SMART or outcome objectives written in quantifiable terms:** Specific, measurable, attainable, realistic, and time-bound commitments to show the steps to achieving your goals.
- **Process objectives:** A list of activities (tasks) that will occur when the grant funding is awarded (timelines).
- **Impact objectives expressed in terms of their benefits to end recipients:** The "step away for five years and look back" statements.
- **The logic model graphic, which helps the grant reader connect the dots between goals and objectives:** The roadmap for lazy readers that is included in the narrative or as an attachment and is a "one page tells the story" document with input, strategy, output, and outcome columns.
- **The time frame for starting and ending all proposed grant-funded activities:** The timeline table that connects the process objectives to when they will start and end during the grant-funding time frame.
- **Integration of the evaluation plan into the overall program design or plan of operation:** Accountability language to demonstrate your process for tracking the SMART or outcome objectives and to show funders that all your performance measurements will be monitored and reported.
- **A dissemination plan:** How you'll get the news out about how your grant-funded program succeeded and share your success with other grant seekers and organizational stakeholders.
- **A sustainability plan:** How your organization will keep all or a portion of the grant-funded program running when the grant-funding cycle has ended.

REMEMBER

Did you refer the reader to any attachments or appendixes? If so, remember to add them to your running list so you can check them later.

Evaluation and dissemination

If the funder requires you to submit a separate evaluation section with your application, make sure yours addresses the following information points:

- **The methods your organization will use to evaluate the progress of your objectives:** Surveys, pre- and post-documentation, observation, and more. See Chapter 10 of this minibook for more about the evaluation process, which is a part of the plan of action.
- **How you plan to share (or disseminate) your findings with others:** Funders expect their grantees to share the outcomes of grant-funded programs with the public-at-large. Have a plan and write it down in concise, action-focused sentences.

REMEMBER

If you refer the reader to any attachments, add them to your attachments checklist for double-checking later.

Management plan, assets, and your equity statement

In this portion of your application, make sure you provide details on the following elements of your program:

- **Key personnel, including each person's qualifications and the amount of time they will allocate to the project:** Experience and education should match position assigned in the grant-funded project. Make sure you include who each person reports to and thereby demonstrate accountability at every level in your management plan.
- **Resources that your organization and its partners bring to the program:** Technical assistance, financial, facilities, executives on loan, and more.
- **A demonstration of equity (fairness/equal opportunity for all) in hiring staff and recruiting program participants:** Proving you can find qualified personnel and follow federal and state equal opportunity legislation.

REMEMBER

If you refer to any attachments, don't forget to add them to the attachment checklist.

Head to Chapter 11 of this minibook for more on how to present your fiscal, human, and physical assets and show fairness.

Sustainability plan

Remember, funders do not want to see your organization's entire multipage plan as an attachment or in the appendixes. You need to be familiar enough with the plan so that you can break down the most important goals for sustainability and include a believable paragraph to convince peer reviewers or program officers that sustainability will happen at the end of their funding award.

Acknowledge that a plan exists; that it was created and approved by the board of directors. Summarize the plan in fewer than five sentences. That's it!

Budget summary and narrative detail

The budget portion of your application is where you must be as accurate as possible. After all, money's a pretty serious thing — especially to the funder handing it over! Be sure to do the following:

- **Double-check your budget summary totals and make sure your formatting follows the guidelines.** Are you supposed to round to the nearest dollar? Are you supposed to omit decimal points?
- **Write a detailed narrative to support the budget summary's line-item amounts.** You need to defend every line item. For further information on connecting the information in your budget to the plan of action, refer to Chapter 12 of this minibook.

REMEMBER

As you've done for the other sections of your application, note references to any attachments so you can ensure that the attachments are in place.

Assembling the Proper Attachments in the Right Order

The attachments to your grant narrative go in a specific order. For most government grant applications, the attachments are compiled in the same order you refer to them in the narrative. So, read through the narrative from beginning to end and put your attachments in that order. Each attachment should be numbered in the narrative — attachment 1, attachment 2, and so on. Make sure you type the attachment number on each attachment (for example, in the upper-right corner).

WARNING

Only include additional information in attachments if the funder permits them; otherwise, you've wasted your time because the additional material won't be read or considered. Some funders may even disqualify your application for unrequested attachments.

The types of attachments you may need to include generally fall into two categories: capability-related documents and financial documents. However, you may also need to provide supporting documentation. The next sections help you figure it all out.

Capability-related documents

A funding agency may request lengthy information on your organization's structure and administration processes. If you don't have sufficient space in your grant application narrative, you can refer the grant reader to the attachments.

REMEMBER

Make sure to follow the funder's guidelines for what should be included in the attachments. See Chapter 11 of this minibook for the personnel information that can be expanded on in the attachments:

- **What are the responsibilities of the board, staff, volunteers, and (if a membership organization) the members?** Write a brief paragraph giving the reader a one- or two-sentence description of each group's responsibilities. Sometimes for a new nonprofit organization, you can insert a copy of the bylaws to fulfill this attachment requirement.
- **How are these groups (the board, the staff, and so on) representative of the communities with which you work?** What are the general demographics of the organization? You can usually provide a board roster that includes each board member's name, address, occupation, gender, ethnicity, and term on the board. Perhaps also attach a list of key staff members and give gender and ethnicity information for each individual. Your board and staff should be reflective of the target population served by your organization.
- **Who will be involved in carrying out the plans outlined in this request?** Include a brief paragraph summarizing the qualifications of key individuals involved. For this attachment requirement, simply put in one-page résumés for each key staff person.
- **How will the project be organized?** Include an organizational chart showing the decision-making structure. Make sure the chart is up to date and includes a box for volunteers (if your organization uses any). Titles are more important than names, especially given that the staff may change over the duration of the grant's funding period.

Financial documents

The attachments in the finance section should cover or include specifically what the funder is asking for in the grant application guidelines. Here are some typical financial-related attachments:

- **The organization's current annual operating budget:** Show your current and next fiscal year's operating budget; detail the line-item expenses for the grant reader.

- **The current project budget:** Be realistic here. Develop a budget that clearly shows you've budgeted adequately to achieve the program goals and objectives.
- **A list of other funding sources for this request (foundations ask for this information):** Include the name of each funder, the amount requested, the date you sent the grant proposal, and the status of your request (whether the request has been funded or rejected or is pending). A four-column table presents this information in an easy-to-read format. See Figure 13-1 for an example.
- **The financial statement for the most recent complete year (expenses, revenue, and balance sheet):** Use the audited version, if available. If your organization has one of those 20-pound financial reports, pull out the comments and breakout budgets for each department and just attach the overall organizational expenses and revenue along with the balance sheet.
- **A copy of your IRS 501(c)(3) letter:** If you don't have 501(c)(3) status, check with the funder to see whether it's willing to fund through your fiscal sponsor (you can read about fiscal sponsors in Chapter 12 of this minibook). You may need to submit additional information and add information on your fiscal sponsor to the portion of your grant narrative that introduces your organization. Another possibility is that the funder may be willing to exercise expenditure responsibility.

Funding Sources Receiving This Request

Potential Funder	Amount Requested	Date Request Sent	Status
US Environmental Protection Agency	$50,000	April 2016	Pending
Green Building Foundation	$100,000	January 2016	Pending
US Department of Agriculture	$250,000	November 2016	Funded
Save a Tree Foundation	$50,000	December 2016	Funded

FIGURE 13-1: A table neatly lists other funding sources, amounts, dates sent, and request statuses.

Illustration by Ryan Sneed

Refer to Chapter 12 of this minibook for details on the budget information that goes directly into grant applications.

Supporting documentation

Other miscellaneous materials funders may request include letters of commitment (up to three). Having some handwritten letters of commitment from your constituency is okay; handwritten letters have a lot of impact on the reader. And don't correct spelling or grammar errors; they make the letters more authentic.

Additional relevant materials include your most recent annual report (an original, not a photocopy), recent newsletters sent out by your organization, newspaper clippings about your programs (make sure they're dated), and previous evaluations or reviews (up to three). Don't go into overkill with too many nonrelevant attachments. When in doubt, call and ask the funder!

Finally, this section is the one where you put the supporting documentation you've referenced throughout the grant application narrative that doesn't fit in any of the other attachment sections. *As always, only include items the funder requests.*

Meeting Submission Requirements

You have likely labored for upward of 20 hours or more on your grant application narrative, the forms, and the other mandatory attachments. Don't exhale yet! It's time to get ready to submit your prize funding-request package. Read the submission requirements two or three times and highlight any technical requirements such as special packaging, the date and time the application is due, and the number of copies needed if you're mailing your application to the funding agency.

Paying attention to submission protocol

These days, most government agencies prefer to receive grant applications digitally. What does that mean for you? That you must upload all your documents, likely in PDF format, via a federal e-portal such as Grants.gov. Most word-processing programs have an option to save a document as a PDF; look in the File menu and look for a Save As or Download As option.

TIP

Make sure your Adobe Reader PDF software is compatible with the federal government's version by logging onto the e-portal website and looking for frequently asked questions or submission guidelines.

If you're applying to one of the few government agencies that still accepts hard-copy submissions, review the government grant application guidelines for guidance on how to secure and submit your final grant application package (the cover forms, assurances, certifications, budget forms, narrative, and required attachments). Usually, you're instructed not to staple or spiral bind the finished document. Practically all government funding agencies need numerous copies for the peer review process, and it's easier to make copies of a document that hasn't been stapled together or bound. Even if an agency's grant guidelines tell you to send one original and two copies, the funder will still make additional copies for the review process.

TIP

For hard-copy submissions, anything other than a simple black metal binder clip looks (and is) wasteful. Unless instructed otherwise, stick with what's unobtrusive and effective. Also, don't create fancy graphics-filled covers; no one asks for them and no one looks at them!

Targeting private-sector funders? The split is about 80-20, with the majority preferring e-grant submissions via e-grant application portals and others requiring paper copies submitted by regular mail services.

Uploading applications on time

REMEMBER

If a foundation or corporate funding source sets a deadline, your application must reach the funding source by that time. Similarly, government agencies make no exceptions for late grant applications. If the grant application is due on a specific date, you should be uploading on Grants.gov at least 72 hours before the due date and time (be on alert for the time zone listed in the grant application guidelines). All the pleading, whining, and cajoling in the world, including calls to the funder from your congressional representatives, won't make a difference if your application is late. Only a natural disaster is a valid excuse.

Clicking Submit without panicking

The Grants.gov website is the main gateway for federal e-grants — and one of the most comprehensive e-grants systems. Chapter 4 of this minibook covers Grants.gov in detail, but this section guides you through uploading your completed application to the site right here.

Grants.gov has upgraded their e-grant submission portal's name to a workspace. Review the provided application summary that pops up after you click the button to confirm that your application will be submitted to the program you want to apply for.

An application can be submitted through the workspace by clicking the Sign and Submit button on the Manage Workspace page, under the Forms tab. This action will submit your application to the federal grant-making agency if completed successfully.

The Sign and Submit button can be found in the Workspace Actions box. The button will be visible and activated for Workspace Participants with the Authorized Organization Representative (AOR) role (authorized individual to submit a grant application on behalf of a grant applicant) under the following circumstances:

- The application package is not closed.
- The workspace does not have an alert message highlighting a submission issue.
- The forms selected for submission are in the Passed status.
- The workspace has an active System Award Management (SAM) registration.
- The application package's Open Date is today or in the past.

REMEMBER

If one of these circumstances is not met, then the Sign and Submit button will be inactive.

If there are no locked forms, or you clicked the Continue button to override locked forms, you will see the Sign and Submit confirmation pop-up window.

You are asked the question, "Is this a changed/corrected application?" and you have the option to select Yes or No. If an application is being resubmitted using the same workspace, the Yes option will be selected by default and the grant tracking number from the previous submission will be listed.

Answering Yes to the question will associate the new submission with the previous grant tracking number. Answering No will not associate the submission with any other application. For more on related submissions, read the "Related Submissions" help article at `www.grants.gov/help/html/help/Applicants/CheckApplicationStatus/RelatedSubmissions.htm`.

To continue to submit the application package, click the Sign and Submit button to complete the process. Otherwise, click the Cancel button. ***Note:*** If you receive an error during the submission process or the PDF confirmation page fails to open in your Internet browser, see the "Resolving Problems and Errors" help article at `www.grants.gov/help/html/help/ManageWorkspaces/ResolvingProblemsAndErrors.htm`.

TIP

Retain the Grants.gov application tracking number that you receive in the application submission confirmation screen. This tracking number is also emailed to you upon submission. If the agency assigns an agency-specific tracking number, you may receive an email with a second tracking number from the agency that is offering the grant.

The Track My Application section (found on the Applicants tab of the homepage) of the site lets you log into Grants.gov to determine whether you've registered successfully with Grants.gov, check the status of your grant application submissions, and manage your applicant profile. Visit `www.grants.gov/applicants/track-my-application.html`.

IN THIS CHAPTER

» Moving to cloud-based storage for 24/7 accessibility on your devices

» Remembering to share documents and information with stakeholders

» Tracking the status of your application

» Communicating with funders post-submission

» Handling multiple grant awards

» Turning funding rejections into future opportunities

Chapter 14

Waiting on the Grant Maker's Decision

You clicked the Submit button, but you're not done yet. Now you have to face a number of cleanup questions: How can you store these documents where you will have access 24 hours a day, seven days a week, in the event a problem arises and you need to view the submitted application document and submit a clarification or a missing attachment?

Have you heard the saying, "It ain't over 'til it's over?" Well in the world of grant seeking, it's not over until you know the fate of your grant request and have carried out the post-notification tasks. Many grant writers, administrators, and boards of directors drop the ball after finding out that a request for funding was rejected. If you fail, you understandably might want to have a major meltdown and just cry, but there is no time for a pity party or speeding through a box of tissues. Grant writers must decide on (or at least have a thorough process for) a *win* or *lose* communications plan.

This chapter shows you how to deal with all the housekeeping issues you need to take care of after you submit a grant application and guides you through the steps you should take — win or lose.

Keeping Accessible Copies of Electronic Files

You have multiple options for storing your electronic files. Using cloud-based storage services is more secure than printing out your notes and other documents and putting them in a file for later reference. Cloud-based services are encrypted and easy to access from any of your mobile devices. Some are free up to a maximum storage level; after that, there's a small fee, which varies from provider to provider. All of these cloud-based storage options for electronic files are compatible with both PCs and Macs:

- **Dropbox (`www.dropbox.com`):** Pros include its folder-sharing options and a feature that allows you to see when someone is accessing a shared project folder to retrieve or deposit information. A small window pops up on the lower-right corner of your computer screen to give you the heads-up on any actions in the folder.
- **Google Drive (`http://drive.google.com`):** This service has file storage and synchronization capabilities. Documents can be shared, and Google Drive has collaborative editing options. You need a Google account to use this service, but signing up is free.
- **Onehub (`www.onehub.com`):** After you subscribe to this collaborative file-sharing cloud-based storage service, you can add Onehub Sync to your desktop and keep all your files handy. There is also a mobile application to add and view files away from your office or home.
- **Microsoft OneDrive (`http://onedrive.live.com`):** A great service to use on Windows-equipped computers. It works the same as Dropbox and Google Drive.

Note: New cloud-based storage services are emerging on a regular basis, so keep checking to see what's out there and what best fits your needs.

Staying Connected and Providing Updates to Your Stakeholders

Remember, before you write a grant request, you should convene your staff, volunteers, community partners, and other interested parties to help your organization develop the plan of action (covered in Chapter 10 of this minibook) and provide the information for the statement of need (see Chapter 9 of this minibook). After you turn in your grant request, you need to bring the stakeholders back together for a debriefing in which you pass on the key information in the following sections.

A few days after the grant application deadline, send thank-you notes electronically or on paper to your key partners. Concurrently, schedule a debriefing conference call or face-to-face meeting online or in your office with your program-level staff, board members, community partners, and any advisory board members who were involved in the planning process of developing the grant application's focus. Follow these debriefing steps:

1. **Review the group's efforts and explain how the information they contributed in the grant-planning meetings was included in the final grant application.**
2. **Give each person or agency a complete electronic and/or paper copy of the final grant request.**

   REMEMBER

   Redact any personnel salaries before distributing. This can be done easily within Adobe Acrobat Pro, which you should have installed for grant work anyway.
3. **Answer questions and propose some what-if questions to find out whether the stakeholders understand their roles and responsibilities if and when the grant application is funded.**

   Consider asking the following questions, in addition to others appropriate for your project:

   - What if we're funded for less than we ask for?
   - What if we're not funded at all?
   - What if the needs of our constituents change before we're funded?
4. **Provide a general overview of the process from here and when the funder will make a decision.**

REMEMBER

Even though you may have worked as a group when putting together the narrative information, people present at the debriefing meeting may not have been present at the meeting for the document's final draft review, where your stakeholders were given a chance to critique and/or approve the final document for submission to funders. Some feelings may be hurt when a writing contributor sees massive changes in the final document. Remind anyone who seems upset of the ultimate goal: to get funded and help a segment of the community.

Tracking the Status of Your Submitted Application

You submitted your grant application. You know the funder received it, but you don't know whether anyone has actually looked at it yet or how to find that out. This section gives you the post-submission protocol of when and whom to call to check on your application's status and when to just chill out and wait for notification. The rules are different based on the type of funding source, so the next sections look at each type individually. Remember, if you are a freelance grant writer, the tracking process is the client's responsibility.

THE WAITING IS THE HARDEST PART

How much patience do you need to have when you're waiting for communication from a funding source? It depends on the funding source:

- **Federal:** Expect to wait three to eight months from the date you turn in the request. The length of time between when you submit the grant application and when the funder decides on funding varies from agency to agency. If you submitted your application in the spring, expect it to be funded no later than September 30 (the end of the federal fiscal year).
- **State:** Expect to wait up to nine months from the date of submission. Some state agencies have rather quick turnarounds on decision making, while others take much longer.
- **Foundation:** Expect to wait a minimum of three to six months and as long as 18 months from the date of submission.
- **Corporate:** Expect to wait a minimum of three to six months from the date the request was submitted.

Requesting that elected officials track your application's progress

As soon as you send your grant application off to a state funding agency or upload it via a federal e-grant portal, start the tracking process.

REMEMBER

Now's the time to use those great political contacts you've made in your state's capital and in Washington, DC. Because the money you're requesting comes from public funds, keep these political do's and don'ts in mind:

- **Do** email a copy of the abstract or executive summary along with the Form 424-A and the Grants.gov application control center number to your elected officials.
- **Do** email the funding agency head (state or federal) any letters of support from elected officials that were written too late to submit with your grant application. Often, your elected officials' offices will email their letters of support directly to the secretary of the federal funding agency (a cabinet appointee appointed by the president and approved by Congress).
- **Do** email or call your senators' or representative's local and Washington, DC, offices to remind them that you need their assistance in tracking the grant application.
- **Don't** scream at or threaten elected officials. You really need their influence to help you get this and future grants funded.
- **Don't** count on getting your grant funded just because you ask your elected officials to get involved in the tracking process. Using the elected official tracking process helps, but it does not guarantee a grant award!

You get a grant award notification

At the state level, you receive a funding award letter or email when your project is selected for funding. Monies are transferred electronically into your organization's bank account. Some monies are awarded and transferred in advance; other monies are released on a reimbursement basis.

At the federal level, you may receive a telephone call or email from one of your elected officials in Washington, DC, who notifies you of your funding award and issues the official press release to your local newspaper. If your official doesn't contact you, you can expect to receive an email from the Office of Management and Budget, known as the OMB. In some instances, the press release from elected officials is published before the grant applicant organization has been notified by the feds.

REMEMBER

If you agree to a lesser amount, you need to rewrite your goals, objectives, and timelines to match the reduced funding: If you're going to receive less grant money, your promised program design (goals, objectives, and timelines) shouldn't remain at the same level as a fully funded program. Reduce your promises by serving fewer members of the target population. Decrease your objectives to take the heat off of having to hit 80 percent or higher. Do less with less — that's the rule! (See Chapter 10 of this minibook for details on setting up goals, objectives, and timelines.)

You receive a standard form rejection email or letter

At both the state and federal levels, you receive a rejection letter when your project is denied funding. No call, no advance warning, just a cold, very disappointing rejection letter or email.

REMEMBER

If you're not funded, request a copy of the peer reviewers' comments using the language of the Freedom of Information Act, the law that entitles you to such public information. Some federal agencies send you the peer review results automatically. In other instances, you may have to call a federal program officer to request the peer review comments. If you don't receive these comments within 90 days of receiving your rejection notice, use the Freedom of Information Act to request them. (For full details and advice on how to make a Freedom of Information Act request, visit `www.foia.gov`.)

Following up on foundation and corporate grant requests

Some foundation and corporate funders use their websites to post information on procedures for grant proposal awards and declines. If you can't locate the funder's guidelines, it's okay to email or call the funder for more information on your funding application's status. However, wait three to six months after your submission date to make this call or to send an email, because the board of directors for these private-sector funders often don't meet monthly and often have a lot on the agenda to cover when they do meet. This meeting schedule often delays the grant-funding announcements.

REMEMBER

These funders want you to be involved in the process that eventually leads to either your success or your failure. Communicating with funders is a key to getting your project or program funded — and if not this project, the next one!

You can expect major (large) foundation and corporate funders to notify you that

- The status of your request is pending.
- Your request has been rejected for funding.
- Your request has been awarded funding.

Note: Of all funding sources, corporate funders and smaller foundations (fewer than five on the staff) are the most likely to fail to notify you when your grant request is rejected. Fifty percent of the time, communication from a corporate funder or small foundation means you have a check in the mail.

Round one: Determining whether your request is under review

When you submit a foundation or corporate grant application, you may soon receive an email letting you know your application has been received. For example, you may receive something that sounds like the following:

> We recently received your request for funding. Our board of trustees meets four times per year. Our next meeting for your area is scheduled for June. If we need additional information, someone from our office will contact you via email or telephone. After we have had the opportunity to fully review your proposal, you will be advised of the board's decision.

A response like this one means you're in the running for the money. Don't call this funder; someone will let you know when it has made a decision.

The least-desired communication from a funder tells you that your grant application was received and that the funder isn't considering it for a grant or other type of funding award. Here's an example:

> Your recently submitted grant proposal was reviewed by our program staff and then forwarded to our board of directors. The board met on December 1 and reviewed over 200 grant proposals seeking foundation funding. Regretfully, your grant proposal was not selected by the board for funding consideration. There simply was not enough money to fund every great funding request.

REMEMBER

Sometimes, a rejection letter comes with a further stipulation that you not submit another grant request for at least one year. This is a standard funder policy. Most corporate and foundation rejection letters are sent to you within 90 to 120 days of the funder's receipt of your grant request.

Round two: Finding out whether you're funded

After your first positive communication from the funder indicating that your request is under review, expect a letter within several months (some come in 90 days; other funders can take up to 18 months) that tells you the outcome of the funder's review. The most desired letter from a funder includes information on the amount of your funding award and how to begin the process of transferring funds. Consider this example:

> The board of directors for the Maybe Foundation met on October 31 to review your grant proposal. I'm pleased to notify you that the board is awarding $15,000 to your Youth Development Leadership Camp. We ask that the money be spent exclusively to ensure that the goals and objectives of your project will be achieved. The grant will be paid to you in one lump-sum payment and processing will begin as soon as the grant agreement is signed and returned to us. On behalf of the board, I wish you every success.

REMEMBER

Many foundation and corporate funders, as well as state and federal funders, require that *grant agreements* (contracts signed by the grantee and the grantor indicating that you'll spend the money as promised in your funding request) be in place before the funder releases the money. This step is standard procedure. Failing to sign a grant agreement means no grant. However, always have your legal department or attorney examine the language before you sign on the dotted line as a precaution. Call the funder if you have questions.

The least-desired letter is a rejection letter stating that although your proposal was recommended for funding, no funds are available in this fiscal year to fund your project. The preceding section shows an example of a typical rejection letter (for an application that wasn't even considered for funding). Read on to find out how to proceed after you've been rejected.

Round three: Following up after a rejection

When your project is denied funding by a foundation or corporate funder, your options for what to do next are similar to your options when dealing with a state or federal funding agency (see the earlier section, "You receive a standard form rejection email or letter").

First, contact the funder to determine why your grant proposal was rejected. Then ask for a face-to-face meeting if the funder is located within driving distance. If meeting in person isn't a viable option, ask for the best time to discuss the weaknesses in your funding request with a program officer over the phone. This step gives you the opportunity to learn from the experience and to evaluate whether to attempt another submission the following year.

REMEMBER

When you consider the time spent researching and writing your grant proposal, you owe it to yourself to find out why you failed. You can't correct narrative weaknesses based on the feedback from a standard form rejection letter or notice — you have to talk to a real person.

WARNING

Never become argumentative with a foundation or corporate funder about your grant proposal's rejection. After all, you may want to submit another grant proposal to the funder in the future. Remember to say thank you for all feedback.

Handling Funding Status Communications from Grant Makers

When the word finally reaches you that your grant proposal has been selected for funding, shout, do a happy dance, call colleagues and community partners, and plan a celebration! But then get ready to hunker down and begin the post-award process. First and foremost, your governing body needs to know so they can enter a resolution to accept the grant award. Next, you need to let the granting agency know that you accept the monies. Most important, you need to know how to report the windfall to your external stakeholders and set up a process for managing the money if you don't already have one in place.

Drafting a resolution

Any agency with a board of directors (such as a nonprofit, school district, or hospital) or trustees, or any government agency with a decision-making body (such as a city council, town board, or county board of supervisors) may be required to adopt *resolutions* to apply for and accept grant funds after an official letter has been received announcing a forthcoming award. Even if the funding source includes a check with the award announcement letter (foundations and corporations occasionally do this), government organizations need a formal resolution before the check is deposited. Make sure to check with the funding agency and your governing body to see if any of these resolutions are required, if they are on file, and if they must be attached to your grant application or signed grant agreement.

The resolution should include the name of the agency receiving the grant funds, the name of the funding agency, the amount of the funding awarded, and the intended use of the funding. Here's an example:

> The Lively Minds Institute hereby resolves to accept $100,000 from the International Association of Advanced Brainiacs for the 2021–2025 Five-Year Institutional Support Initiative. These funds shall be used exclusively for this

project. Approved unanimously by the What Do You Know Institute's board of directors on 11/30/2020.

Signed by Billy Bravo, Founder and Executive Director, Lively Minds Institute

REMEMBER

The funder absolutely needs to see the original signature on the resolution, so either mail the *original* resolution or email a scan of the original resolution to the funding source. Be sure to keep a copy for your own files as well.

Accepting the award

During the post-award process, you must inform the funding source that you accept its offer of funding before you can share the good news with the world. The following steps secure your role as the grant recipient:

1. **Notify all your administrators, including the chief financial officer (CFO), of the award.**
2. **Add the item "Accept grant funds" to the agenda of your board of directors' next meeting.**
3. **Prepare an overview of the grant request document for board review prior to the meeting.** In the overview, include the purpose, objectives, timelines for program implementation, project budget, and a copy of the official award letter from the funding source.
4. **Prepare a brief oral presentation to give to the board and draft the resolution language.** The resolution is to accept the grant award. See the next section for more on drafting resolutions.
5. **If grant agreement forms need to be signed, have these documents ready for the board.**
6. **Prepare a press release (provided the funder doesn't want anonymity) for board approval.** Your senator or representative may take care of the press release if your grant is government funded. Before you make any in-house press release public, verify whether the funder (specifically, foundations and corporations) requires prior approval. Many funders stipulate that they must approve grantee press releases before a release is officially issued.
7. **Create or purchase a certificate of appreciation for foundation and corporate funders and get it signed by your board officers.** Your CEO or board president can also write a formal letter of thanks. Skip this step if you're dealing with government agencies.
8. **Meet with the CFO to discuss fiscal accountability, including creating a clear or single audit trail.** See the later section, "Reviewing post-award guidelines for help with financial reporting," for more on these audits.

Tackling the grant-management process

What is *grant management?* First, it's making sure you keep all the promises you wrote in the program design narrative of your grant application (see Chapter 10 of this minibook for details on the program design section). Second, it's handling all the funder's reporting requirements. Sometimes the grant writer assumes this responsibility; other times, these tasks are divvied up between the grant program manager or project director and the person who makes the financial decisions for your organization (the CFO or business manager). In smaller organizations, the CFO may be a bookkeeper working in concert with an executive director. In larger organizations, entire departments may handle the finances, including fiscal reporting.

The *grant program manager* or *project director* is the person responsible for overseeing the implementation of the grant-funded activities. This person brings the program design narrative in the grant proposal to life. They are responsible for ensuring that all the tasks (process objectives) outlined in the program design's timeline table are accomplished on time.

Other tasks for the grant program manager or grant project director include the following:

- Meeting with collaborative partners to let them know the grant request was funded and working with them to plot out the action steps needed from partners
- Meeting with the human resources department to start the recruitment, screening, and hiring or reassigning of the grant-funded project's staff
- Meeting with the third-party evaluator (if applicable) to begin strategizing the monitoring and evaluating process for the SMART and promised outcomes (covered in Chapter 10 of this minibook)
- Orienting project staff to the purpose of the grant-funded project and giving them a copy of the program design narrative so that they can see how the project should unfold during the implementation process
- Sharing the evaluation process with the project staff and the collaborative partners so that everyone knows what will be monitored, how the data will be collected and reported, and the role of each stakeholder in the feedback process
- Making sure that staff adheres to all task/activity timelines, and developing a corrective action plan to ensure that the SMART or outcome objectives will be met before the end of the grant-funding period if the timelines go off-track

» Working with the CFO or business manager to compile interim and final financial reports for the funder (see the next section)

» Preparing an end-of-project report for all stakeholders, including the board of directors and collaborative partners

Reviewing post-award guidelines for help with financial reporting

In federal grants, the Office of Management and Budget (OMB) works cooperatively with funding agencies to establish government-wide grant-management policies and guidelines. These guidelines are published in circulars and common rules. At the federal level, these documents are first introduced in the *Federal Register* (www.federalregister.gov), the daily journal of the United States Government.

Table 14-1 lists the most commonly used federal grant-management OMB circulars. The circular numbers are the keys to locating the document on the OMB website. To explore the circulars yourself, visit www.whitehouse.gov/omb/circulars.

TABLE 14-1 Office of Management and Budget Circulars

Circular Number	Applicable Agencies
Cost Principles	
A-21	Education institutions
A-87	State, local, and Native American tribal governments
A-122	Nonprofit organizations
Administrative Requirements	
A-102	State and local governments
A-110	Institutions of higher education, hospitals, and other nonprofit organizations
Audit Requirements	
A-133	State and local governments and nonprofit organizations

At the state funding level, the funding agency provides you with the funding stipulations, including the regulations for accessing, spending, reporting, and closing out grant funds.

Foundation and corporate funders give you their funding stipulations and/or regulations, if any, when the funds are awarded. Other than asking you to sign a *grant agreement* (a contract indicating that you'll use the awarded funds as promised in your grant application), most private-sector funders don't have a ton of regulations and usually spell out any stipulations in the grant agreement.

As you read the circulars and guidelines, you may come across some unfamiliar terms. *Fiscal accountability* is the obligation to ensure that the funds granted are used correctly. Fiscal accountability lies with the entity responsible for managing the grant funds — usually, that's the grant applicant, but in some instances it's the fiscal sponsor. (Chapter 12 of this minibook explores what it means to be a fiscal sponsor for a nonprofit organization.)

Fiscal accountability means establishing an audit trail. A *clear* or *single audit trail* is an arrangement that allows any auditor, whether internal or from the funding source, to track the grant monies from the money-in stage to the money-out stage without finding that grant funds have been commingled with other organizational funds.

REMEMBER

Review the grant agreement from the funder. Many require that any grant funds received should be deposited into a separate account and tracked individually by using accounting practices that enable tracking by date, by expenditure, and by line-item allocation against the approved project budget (which is the budget that was approved by the funding source). However, not all funders require separate accounting.

Handling Multiple Grant Awards

Suppose you've applied for grants with 20 potential funding sources. One of the 20 funding sources funds you in full. The money has been deposited, and your project is up and running. But more mail comes in, and guess what? Your project has received two more grants, totaling an amount equal to the full funding request. You must have written one fabulous narrative!

If your project is overfunded, here's what to do:

- Immediately contact each funder and explain your predicament.
- Ask the funders' permission to keep the funds and expand your project's design.
- Ask the funders' permission to carry grant monies over into another fiscal year.

The worst-case scenario is that all funding sources except for the first funder ask you to return the additional funding. The best-case scenario is that you're allowed to keep the funding and create a bigger and better project or program.

REMEMBER

The best way to avoid the predicament of having too much money is to write a letter to each outstanding funding source (sources that haven't communicated with you on their decisions to fund your grant requests) immediately after you know that you have full funding. Be honest and quick. It's the right and ethical thing to do — even though having too much money *sounds* like a good thing. (Chapter 12 of this minibook talks more about the ethical approach to grant seeking.)

Failing to Get a Grant Award

Failed efforts in the grant-writing field are upsetting, but remember that they don't signal the end of your grant-writing career. After all, just because a grant proposal isn't funded doesn't mean it doesn't have some salvageable parts. This section helps you look at why your application failed and then plan how to fix it.

Requesting peer review comments when your government application is rejected

If your grant application was rejected by a state or federal funding agency, you're entitled to review the grant reviewer's comments under the Freedom of Information Act (FOIA). Unfortunately, if you're rejected by a foundation or corporate giving entity, you probably won't receive any reviewer's comments, and you can't use the FOIA to get them.

Government agencies, especially federal ones, typically send a summary sheet with the section scores and an overview of strengths and weaknesses of each application section. If you receive a rejection notice from a state or federal funding agency that doesn't include such a summary, or if the summary doesn't give you enough information, write a letter requesting the peer reviewers' comments (each federal grant application usually has three peer reviewers). When you use the FOIA, you receive the federal peer reviewers' actual written comments and scores (the points they bestowed on each narrative section in your grant application). (For more information on the federal peer review process, head to Chapter 7 of this minibook.)

TIP

In order to invoke the FOIA, your letter should include the following information, at a minimum, to assist the funding agency in locating your requested documents:

- **The name of the federal funding agency from which you're seeking the information:** This name must be in the address section of the letter and on your envelope. You can also email your letter to the granting agency's contact person. You can usually find the contact person's email address in the grant application announcement or on the funding agency's website.
- **The application identification code:** At the federal level, when your application is uploaded to the Grants.gov system, you'll receive an email notice that it has been received by the agency. This notice contains an identifying number for tracking your grant application. If you don't receive this notice or lose the email, you can log in to Grants.gov and click the Applicants tab to see the drop-down list. Click How to Apply for Grants and then choose the Track Application option. When you click this link, you see the information shown in Figure 14-1.

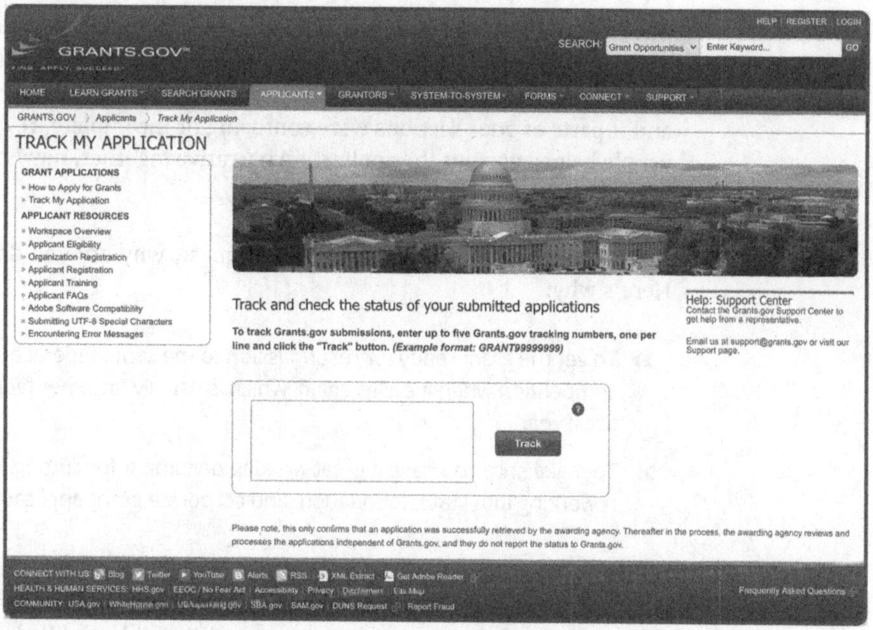

FIGURE 14-1: The Track My Application Package on Grants.gov.

Source: *www.grants.gov/web/grants/applicants/track-my-application.html*

Address your letter to the funding agency program officer listed as the contact person in the grant application guidelines. On the envelope and at the top of your FOIA letter or in the subject line of your email message, write "Freedom of

Information Act Request." Save a copy of your request; you may need it in the event of an appeal or if your original request isn't answered.

Federal agencies are required to answer your request for information within ten working days of receipt. If you don't receive a reply by the end of that time frame (including mailing time, if applicable), you may write a follow-up email attaching your FOIA letter again and reminding them of the date on the letter or call the agency to ask about the delay. Other government agencies have their own set time frames for replies. Calling and asking before writing your letter is the best way to find out how long you should wait for a reply.

REMEMBER

You can try to contact the funding agency's program officer to request written feedback on your failed grant application. However, if you don't receive your feedback in 90 days or less via email or mail, begin to formulate your FOIA letter.

Acting fast to reuse a failed government request

After you receive the peer review comments for a rejected public-sector grant application (see the preceding section), use them to find out what your peers found wrong with the application's narrative sections. Correct the weaknesses, and if parts of your sections were confusing or incomplete, rewrite them. If other people helped you put the application narrative together, now's the time to reconvene the grant-writing team.

If you're stuck holding a failed grant request, why are you doing all this work? Here's why:

- To get the grant ready for resubmission to the same federal or state grant competition when it cycles again, which is usually once per federal or state fiscal year
- To make sure you have a great working document for cutting, pasting, and reworking into state, foundation, and corporate grant application formats

However, face the facts. You went to the feds or the state government because you needed mega monies for your project. No other single funding source can fill the gap that a federal or state grant award would have filled. Consequently, you need to scale down your project design and project budget when you take your request to private-sector funding sources. Base your adjustments on each funding source's limitations, which you uncover through research.

For example, say you asked for $850,000 to clean up contaminated soil near a city playground in your government grant request. Of the $850,000, $150,000 is needed for soil sampling and preparation to decrease surface level contaminants. Look at all your line items. Which ones can be stand-alone line items? Can the project be started in phases? If yes, then target funders to fund each specific phase. Although this will be a much slower start-to-finish process, at least the project will be completed and eventually benefit an entire community.

Chapter 3 of this minibook shows you how to find state- and federal-level grant opportunities. Chapter 5 of this minibook covers how to find out about foundation and corporate funding sources.

Dealing with failed foundation or corporate funding requests

Program officers from local foundations are usually more than willing to discuss the reasons a proposal was denied. However, some foundations and corporations that fund throughout the nation explicitly state that due to the volume of grant applications anticipated, they won't provide feedback on declined applications.

Never, ever throw a rejected foundation or corporate grant request into your files, walk away, and give up. Instead, do the following:

- Go back and do another funding search to identify a new list of foundation and corporate funders you can approach with your grant request (see Chapter 5 of this minibook for more about private-sector funds).
- Convene your stakeholders' planning team to discuss the failed attempt with the first funder or funders. Sometimes, other people in the community have funding leads to share with you. After all, they want to see your project funded as much as you do.
- Beef up your original foundation or corporate proposal to meet the requirements of state or federal funding opportunities. This means writing more narrative and adding more research to support your statement of need. You also need a new project budget based on federal or state funding limitations.

REMEMBER

Foundations or corporate giving entities probably won't provide reviewers' comments; the Freedom of Information Act applies only to grant applications submitted to local, county, state, and federal government agencies.

4

Being Smart about Nonprofit Bookkeeping and Accounting

Contents at a Glance

IN THIS CHAPTER

» Going over basic bookkeeping and accounting terminology

» Understanding your choices of accounting methods

» Assessing your assets

» Taking steps to protect against employee theft

Chapter 1

Starting with Basic Bookkeeping and Accounting

Have you ever talked to computer support people about problems you're having with your computer, and they started using words like API, ISP, BYOD, and other acronyms about which you don't have a clue? If you're like us, when people talk over your head, your brain shuts down. Every profession has its jargon, and accounting is no different. But the good news is that the jargon doesn't have to be an impenetrable wall separating you from the bookkeeping and accounting tasks you need to master.

This chapter introduces you to accounting (including basic terms) and explains why you need to understand it and how it works. You also get started with managing your nonprofit's books, selecting the most appropriate accounting methods for your organization, safeguarding against tax audits, and protecting your nonprofit's physical and financial assets from employee wrongdoing.

Understanding Accounting and Bookkeeping

Whether you're chief executive officer of a multibillion dollar corporation or the manager of your household, you use *accounting* every day. To account is to record and report a quantity of money or objects. Accounting is counting, recording, classifying, and summarizing transactions and events — and then interpreting the results. If you look inside your wallet and count your money, you have accounted for your cash on hand.

Bookkeeping, on the other hand, is the process of accumulating, organizing, and storing information about transactions on a day-to-day basis. When you write a check and record it in your checkbook register, you engage in bookkeeping.

Accounting and bookkeeping have several things in common, but the most basic is transactions. A *transaction* is an exchange of value between two or more parties. For example, you walk into a local store and purchase a pack of gum, handing the cashier a $5 bill. When you get your change back, you count it to verify that it's correct. That purchase is a transaction.

What's the difference between accounting and bookkeeping?

Bookkeeping is the starting point of the accounting process. A bookkeeper is a paraprofessional who records the daily transactions in the accounting cycle such as bill paying, reconciling purchase orders to deliveries, and balancing the checkbook. As part of this process, bookkeepers maintain the following documents:

- Copies of invoices and receipts
- Copies of checks and bank statements
- All other paperwork required for accounting purposes

Bookkeepers perform daily tasks of recording, including:

- Dates of transactions
- Amounts of transactions
- Sources of donations
- Expenses and loss transactions

Accounting summarizes the day-to-day activities recorded by a bookkeeper. Based on this information, an accountant prepares financial reports used to make decisions. An accountant uses *double-entry accounting* to record every transaction because every transaction affects a minimum of two accounts. For example, if you write a check to purchase a printer for $200, your bookkeeper will record it in the check register as cash disbursed to purchase office equipment. Your accountant realizes that writing a check increases your assets (office equipment) for $200 and reduces your cash for the same amount. That's two accounting entries happening with one transaction.

REMEMBER

Accountants evaluate the overall results of economic activity by identifying, measuring, recording, interpreting, and communicating every transaction according to set rules and guidelines. They end the process by preparing financial statements that drive decision making within an organization.

Defining some common financial terms

Accounting is the language for business. As with all professions, it's the jargon that complicates things. In the following sections, we define the most common accounting and bookkeeping terms. (As you read through the minibook, you'll encounter many more accounting terms, which are defined as you need to know them.)

Grasping assets, liabilities, and equity

You've probably heard the terms "asset," "liability," and "equity" before, especially if you've made any major purchases, like a house.

- *Assets* are what you own and include things like cars, buildings, savings, and other items of value. A house is considered an asset, even when you don't yet own it outright.
- *Liabilities* are what you owe, usually in the form of loan payments. Most people who say they're homeowners really aren't; as long as you're paying on a mortgage, the payment is a liability due every month.
- *Equity* (also known as net assets) is the difference between what you owe and what you own. In the case of a house, the equity is the value of the home minus the amount you still owe on the mortgage. In other words, assets minus liabilities equals equity.

Eyeing donation revenues, expenses, and nonprofit income

Revenue is the inflow of assets received in exchange for goods and services, or from donations, investments, and other miscellaneous sources. Donations will probably be your primary source of revenue. *Donations* come from individuals, corporations, foundations, and government entities to help you fulfill your mission. Cash, grants, time, and services are examples of donations.

Expenses are the cost for goods or services. Your nonprofit encounters the same expenses as most for-profit corporations, except for income taxes. You have to account for overhead expenses (rent, utilities, and so on), program management expenses (salaries, fringe benefits, and office supplies), and other incidentals.

Some people have a misconception that nonprofits shouldn't make a profit or generate income, but no organization can operate without income. In the nonprofit arena, *net income* (revenues greater than expenses) increases net assets. Thinking of a nonprofit in terms of *break-even point analysis,* in which revenues equal expenses, is one way to understand the idea of a nonprofit acquiring income, and may motivate people to give to the organization.

Identifying cash flows and operating budgets

To stay afloat, you must identify new streams of cash flow to sustain your organization. *Cash flow* is the amount of money received in and paid out during the same period. In the private sector, corporations are always looking for new ways to increase their cash flow, usually through new or improved products or services. (Think of how often the menu changes at fast-food restaurants!) As a nonprofit manager, you too must continuously look for new ways to appeal to your constituents and tap into new streams of cash inflow. What you did last year may not appeal to them this year.

An *operating budget* is a financial plan for current operations that includes estimating cash inflows from all sources and the related cash outflows you need to operate. When preparing an operating budget, most nonprofits estimate cash inflows first and budget expenses accordingly. Some nonprofits may opt to estimate expenses first and come up with a plan for revenue based on the amount needed to cover those expenses.

Getting a hold on debits and credits

Debits and *credits* are what's done to accounts to record transactions. To get a grasp on debits and credits, you must first know the normal balances of a few accounts. The *normal balance* is what it takes to increase an account.

Think of this as an equation that has two sides, a right side and a left side. What is done on the right must be balanced by recording the same amount on the left. For example, to debit an account is to charge the left side or left column of your journal or ledger. (A *journal* is a book of original entry where transactions are recorded in the order they occur; a *ledger* contains the transactions according to the account they belong to. Check out Chapter 3 of this minibook for more info.)

Asset and expense accounts are increased by debits. On the other hand, to credit an account is always done to the right side or right column of your journal or ledger. Revenue, liability, and equity accounts are increased by credits.

Asset accounts normally have a debit balance, so if you debit an asset account, you increase it. This transaction is placed on the left side of the journal or ledger. If you credit an asset account, you decrease it. Credits are shown on the right side of a journal or ledger.

Assets

Debit side	*Credit* side
shows *increases*	shows *decreases*

REMEMBER

Asset accounts can be current or long term and include the following accounts: cash, grants, accounts receivable, inventory, supplies, prepaid rent, prepaid insurance, land, buildings, equipment, and accumulated depreciation.

Liability accounts normally have a credit balance, so if you credit a liability account, you increase it. If you debit a liability account, you decrease it. As with assets, debits are recorded on the left side or column of the journal or ledger, and credits are recorded on the right side or column. In fact, this holds true for all accounting processes.

Liabilities

Debit side	*Credit* side
shows *decreases*	shows *increases*

REMEMBER

To decrease an account, you need to do the opposite of what is done to increase it.

Equity is handled the same as liability accounts. If you credit equity, you increase it. If you debit equity, you decrease it.

Equity

Debit side	*Credit* side
shows *decreases*	shows *increases*

Adhering to GAAP

Before you can play a new game, you read the instructions, right? Well, before you can fully understand bookkeeping and accounting for your nonprofit, you have to familiarize yourself with the ground rules. The ground rules of the accounting profession can be attributed to *generally accepted accounting principles* (GAAP).

GAAP are the standards that accountants follow when making decisions about how to handle accounting issues. Call them the rules of the profession. See Chapter 6 of this minibook for more on GAAP.

Choosing Your Accounting Method

The two main accounting methods are cash and accrual. Before starting to keep track of things, you need to decide which of the two methods you'll use to account for your activities. You'll also decide if you need to use *fund accounting,* which means you further organize your accounting transactions by purpose.

When you choose the *cash basis,* transactions are recorded only when cash changes hands, not when a purchase is made or when someone pledges a donation. That is, if you pay for something or receive a donation via cash, check, or a credit card, the transaction shows up in your books immediately.

REMEMBER

When you present a check for payment, you are affirming enough cash is in your checking account for the check to clear. The same rational holds true for credit card payments. You are responsible for paying your credit card company once the charge goes through. Thus, both modes of payment are treated like cash.

For example, you run to your nearest office supply store to stock up on pencils, paper, staples, sticky notes, and whatever other fun items you run across. You pay for these goodies at point of purchase by cash, check, or credit card. Under the cash basis you record the transaction immediately. Alternatively, you may have a store account and decide to have the goods charged to that account, which you will pay later. If you decide to charge the same supplies to your account, under the cash basis, you don't record the transaction until the bill is paid.

If you're using the *accrual basis* of accounting, purchases are recorded when they occur, regardless of when they are paid. So if you buy those nifty office supplies on store credit on June 1 and pay the bill four weeks later on July 1, the transaction is recorded on June 1 when you bought the supplies.

In most instances you can choose to keep your accounting records on the cash or accrual basis. Many small nonprofits use the cash basis. Medium and larger nonprofits usually use the accrual basis. The major difference between cash basis and accrual basis has to do with when you record the transactions.

TIP

The cash basis is often used when there is little difference in the bottom line under cash or accrual basis, or if the nonprofit spends all revenue it received in the same year and doesn't have any large unpaid bills or uncollected income left over at year-end.

Keeping track of the cash

Cash is a medium of exchange. Cash is currency, and in accounting, cash is a current asset. Cash equivalents are instruments that can be immediately converted into cash and include

- Petty cash, usually kept to make small office purchases
- Checking account balances
- Certificates of deposits (CDs)
- Savings account balances

Recording transactions using the cash method means that you record revenues only when cash is received and record expenses only when they're paid. This is the easiest method to use because if you make a purchase on account, and the bill doesn't come out until next month, you don't record the transaction until you pay the bill.

TIP

When preparing your organization's financial statements, a certified public accountant (CPA) can easily convert your cash basis accounting information into GAAP-required accrual basis information.

Accrual basis of accounting

To *accrue* means to accumulate or increase. Under the accrual basis, revenues and expenses are recognized when a transaction takes place, whether cash exchanges hands or not.

For example, if you buy office supplies on account, you record the transaction in your accounting books when you make the purchase and again when the bill is paid. To record such a transaction, you initially debit supplies (a current asset account) and credit accounts payable (a current liability account) for the cost of the office supplies. Then, when you pay the bill, you debit accounts payable and credit cash.

REMEMBER

The accrual basis gives you a more accurate account of your nonprofit's bottom line because expenses are reported in the same accounting period as the associated revenue. It also requires end-of-the-period adjustments for salaries and other expenses. Keep in mind, your accounting period may close, but you may have some expenses, such as prepaid subscriptions, prepaid insurance, or salaries, that cross more than one period. The accrual basis of accounting charges expenses to the period they are used.

Introducing fund accounting

Depending on the mission and size of your nonprofit, you may want to incorporate fund accounting into your record keeping. *Fund accounting* means that you track assets, liabilities, revenue, and expenses by their type or "fund."

Two biggies in the world of fund accounting are general and restricted funds. A *general fund* refers to any money you receive or use that has no conditions to its use that you must abide by. On the flip side, a *restricted* fund is just that — money you receive that has been earmarked by the donor to be used only for a specific purpose. For example, if you run a nonprofit child wellness center, the donor may specify their contribution be used only for child education.

TIP

If you decide to use fund accounting, primarily the accrual method of accounting applies (although in some instances, you can use the cash method) using the guidance about the two detailed earlier in this chapter. You record using cash or accrual and then divvy up those transactions into your different funds.

Running Numbers on Your Assets

When you buy items such as printers, computers, cars, or other things that last more than a year, you need to place these items on your books as *assets.* To record an asset, you record it in your books at the price you paid for it.

Because some assets, such as computers, may last for several years, you need to write off the cost (*depreciate*) over the item's life span. For example, if a computer is expected to last three years, you'll need to depreciate it over three years. *Depreciable assets* are commonly referred to as *plant, property, or equipment* (*PPE*). The following sections explain how to put a number to your assets and how to depreciate them.

REMEMBER

When writing off the cost of assets, you never depreciate the cost of land. You need to depreciate the costs of all other assets classified as PPE that last longer than a year.

Evaluating assets by original cost or fair market value

Prices fluctuate just like the wind. You may pay $1,000 for something on Tuesday and then discover that it went on sale the next day for $500. When this happens, how much is the item worth? What amount should you record in your books?

The answers to these questions are simple. The *historic cost* principle states that all assets should record at their original cost. *Original cost* is generally what you paid to acquire the asset. It's an approach that keeps assets on the books at their purchase price with no regard for inflation or the economy.

REMEMBER

Original cost includes sales tax, shipping, and any costs associated with placing the asset in service, such as installation.

Presently, GAAP requires depreciable assets to be recorded at historic value. Depreciation is used to reduce an asset's value due to the asset's use over time. You can't take any additional adjustments for estimated changes in the asset's market value because market values for depreciable assets are only estimates. Estimating a higher or lower market value of an asset isn't done to avoid the possibility of someone using the information to manipulate reported financial results.

In contrast to historical cost, *fair market value* is the price that an interested buyer would be willing to pay and an interested seller would be willing to accept for a particular asset. If you had to liquidate all of your assets tomorrow, then fair market value would be very important to you.

It is allowed under GAAP to record some investments at fair market value and adjust for changes in their value. An example of this is *trading securities,* which are purchased to sell in the short term for profit. Trading securities are recorded initially at cost. Then, as their value goes up and down, you make an adjustment to record them at fair market value, recording the unrealized gain or loss on your income statement. In this instance, market values aren't estimates; they're readily determined, and so there is no room to manipulate financial results.

Grasping depreciation methods

To *depreciate* means to write off the expense of an item over its expected useful life, less any *salvage value* (the amount that can be recovered after an asset's service life). When you purchase equipment or a building, you pay a set amount. As time passes, these assets are assumed to lose some of their value through use.

Therefore, you write off a portion of the cost by depreciating it as an expense. For example, suppose you buy a computer for $1,450, and the computer is expected to be useful to you for three years, at which time its salvage value will be $50. You have $1,400 ($1,450 – $50) of depreciation expense to write off for the computer over those three years.

You get to choose which method you use to write off the cost of the computer. The amount of depreciation expense you get to write off in any year depends on which depreciation method you choose. Because depreciation is an expense that's subtracted from revenue, it directly affects your bottom line.

The executive director and board, with the advice of an accountant, decide which depreciation method to use. You can use a different method for different assets. The most important thing to remember here is that you want to reflect the most accurate value of all of your assets. It's important for you to know the value of the assets you own.

In all that you do, you want to fairly present your financial information in the most accurate way. Some financial types have started discussing how assets are valued on the books compared to their market value. Some organizations have assets that are overvalued on their books, and then when those assets are evaluated, the previous value that has been indicated on the organization's statement of financial position isn't correct.

Choosing declining balance depreciation

Declining balance depreciation is an accelerated method of depreciation. That means there is a larger depreciation expense in the early years of an asset's life and smaller amounts in the later years. Declining balance depreciation can be used on any item classified as *plant, property, or equipment (PPE)*.

When to use this type of depreciation method depends on many different factors. Two to consider are the use and life of the asset. Assets with shorter lives (less than ten years) usually lose most of their value in their earlier years, so declining depreciation methods are warranted. Longer-lived assets tend to lose their value evenly over time, and straight-line depreciation is adequate for these assets (see the next section). Although the IRS and GAAP offer some guidance, use your professional judgment, or solicit the advice of an accountant or CPA.

For tax purposes, the IRS provides useful lives for classes of assets and tables of depreciation percentages for various depreciation methods and asset lives. Office equipment has a useful life of five years; so do most automobiles. Office furniture and fixtures have useful lives of seven years. The IRS system doesn't take salvage value into account, but the tables are useful and can be applied to amounts adjusted for salvage value. IRS Publication 946, How to Depreciate Property, is a good source of information about depreciation methods. You can find the publication online at `https://www.irs.gov/publications/p946`.

Going with straight-line

The easiest method of depreciation is the straight-line method. The *straight-line depreciation method* allocates the same amount of depreciation for each year over the expected life of an asset.

TIP

When in doubt about which method to use, choose the straight-line method because it's the most conservative approach. The equation for the straight-line depreciation method is

(Cost – Residual value) ÷ Useful life

REMEMBER

Residual value is the same as salvage value. It's the value placed on an asset after it's fully depreciated. For example, suppose you expect to use your computer system for three years, and you pay $30,000 with an expected salvage value of $3,000. Plug these numbers into the equation, and your depreciation expense using the straight-line method is $9,000 per year.

$27,000 ($30,000 – $3,000) ÷ 3 years = $9,000 depreciation per year for 3 years

Selecting double-declining balance

In a nutshell, the *double-declining balance depreciation method* is twice the rate of straight-line. The major difference between the double-declining balance and the straight-line method of depreciation is the amount of depreciation in each year of an asset's useful life. With double-declining balance, as opposed to straight-line, more depreciation is expensed in an asset's early years, and less is expensed in its later years.

To calculate the double-declining balance method, you must first compute the rate of depreciation for the straight-line method. Then double this rate. You don't deduct the salvage value from the original cost of the asset when computing the asset's depreciable base. However, you stop taking depreciation expense when the asset's *net book value* (original cost less accumulated depreciation) reaches the asset's salvage value. GAAP doesn't allow a depreciable asset's net book value to be less than its salvage value.

Returning to the example from the previous section, suppose your computer system has a total cost of $30,000, a salvage value of $3,000, and is expected to last three years. Figure 1-1 shows a comparison of the straight-line and double-declining balance depreciation methods.

FIGURE 1-1: A comparison of the straight-line and double-declining depreciation methods.

Straight-Line Depreciation Method	
(Cost - Salvage Value) divided by useful life	
$27,000 ($30,000 - $3,000)/3 years = $9,000	
2021 Depreciation	$9,000
2022 Depreciation	$9,000
2023 Depreciation	$9,000
Total Depreciation	$27,000

Double-Declining Balance Method	
Straight-line rate is 1/3 or 33.33% per year	
Double-Declining Balance Method = 66.66% (33.33% x 2)	
2021 Deprecation $30,000 x 66.66%	$19,998
2022 Depreciation $30,000 - $19,998 = $10,002	
$10,002 x 66.66%	$6,666
2023 Depreciation Limited to $27,000	$336
Total Depreciation	$27,000

Keeping an Eye on Your Assets

It's virtually impossible to know whether an employee will steal. You can do a background check on potential employees and give them assessment exams to find out what type of people they really are. Some major retailers ask a series of questions that gives them a good indication of a person's moral character. You can order or design a similar test for your staff. Also, you can install security cameras in your building that record everything that takes place.

In addition to implementing protective procedures regarding whom your nonprofit organization hires, you can institute internal controls that directly monitor your organization's financial holdings. A good system of internal controls puts some checks and balances in place to protect against employee theft. The following sections give you some ideas about how to keep your assets safe.

TIP

Before you hire an employee, perform a background check on them. Often this can be done through your state's attorney general's office or other law enforcement agencies.

Protecting your nonprofit's physical assets

Tracking and keeping up with inventory is a must to protect your nonprofit's assets. Portable equipment like a laptop computer is so easy to walk away with. To safeguard your valuables, require all equipment to be checked out before leaving the building. Furthermore, some organizations have their employees sign statements agreeing to have their final paychecks withheld until all equipment is returned in good condition.

TIP

Limiting access to certain areas of interest can protect your assets. Consider installing security cameras and key access cards, as well as keeping your petty cash drawer locked and a book handy to record all transactions with receipts to support them.

Setting internal controls

Internal controls are procedures and policies that you establish to limit the possibility of accounting errors, fraud, theft, or *embezzlement* (taking something of value from someone who trusts you).

Keeping some office doors locked and areas off limits is just one kind of internal control to protect important records and data from manipulation. Other internal controls are less obvious than locked doors.

Establishing checks and balances

The founding fathers of the United States knew that human nature is subject to error, and they established the system of checks and balances to provide constant oversight and accountability within the federal government. You can apply a similar system of internal control by which you have checkpoints to balance your books. For example, some organizations do a physical count of all inventories to see if anything is missing or unaccounted for.

Checks and balances in your organization not only can help you avoid a negative audit finding, but also can protect your assets. Start with the following checks and balances and then expand on them for protections that are even more specific to your organization and its operations:

- Require two signatures on all checks over a set amount (usually more than a typical payroll tax deposit amount)
- Separate duties between your record keeper and the person handling cash
- Record employees' hours on timesheets on a daily basis
- Require all invoices for payment to be reviewed and authorized

TIP

Your nonprofit's policies and procedures manual should present and explain your organization's checks and balances in such a way that all the steps are clearly defined. Most nonprofits have written policies about personnel, travel, and purchasing procedures. Put steps in writing about how to deal with personnel matters. Include the limits on travel pay for mileage, lodging, and so forth. Also, create rules to deal with large purchases of, say, more than $500. You need to have a plan for how these types of situations should be handled to bring structure to your organization.

Separating employees duties

You can place some roadblocks in your accounting system that prevent employees from stealing from your nonprofit (or at the very least, make it really hard). You can establish segregation of duties, which is a type of internal control. *Segregation of duties* assigns different steps of a process to different people. So, for example, you don't allow the same person who opens the mail to be responsible for making deposits. Think about how easy it would be for the person opening the mail to borrow cash payments.

Following are some examples of segregation of duties that you can apply to your nonprofit:

- **Accounts payable and receivable:** The person approving payments shouldn't be authorized to make purchases without some oversight by a second party. If yours is a large organization, your accounts payable office should be a separate entity from the accounts receivable unit.
- **Business mail and check deposits:** One person can open business mail and log in each check that's received, but someone else should be responsible for making deposits into your bank account.

Insuring or bonding nonprofit employees

Checks and balances and segregation of duties establish some internal controls (refer to the preceding sections), but you can take your internal protections a step further with risk-management strategies. Insuring or bonding your nonprofit employees ensures that your nonprofit organization faces minimal risk of loss in case of mistakes or malfeasance by the people who manage your organization.

A *bond* is a debt security that guarantees to pay you for acts committed by board members or employees, and it protects you from employee or board theft. A bond is actually paid to you by the bonding company, but the person bonded reimburses the bonding company. Any reputable bonding entity will share some helpful tips about bonding your employees.

You determine the type and degree of insurance and bonded protections your nonprofit needs based on an assessment of your organization. First, you need to evaluate the potential risk and think about how much money is being handled. What is the value of what you own? How much equity do you have in your organization? How much money do you have in your savings and checking accounts? These are some of the questions you'll need to answer to determine how much insurance is needed. For example, your donors list is a valuable asset that you must safeguard (turn to Chapter 4 of this minibook for an explanation of donors lists). You can protect your donors list by respecting those individuals who don't want to be disclosed to the general public. Your donors list should never be sold to another organization to solicit funds.

Do some research by consulting with a few insurance companies and comparing rates. Your board of directors is responsible for finding an insurance company and approving the purchase of bonding insurance. As with most things concerning the management of your nonprofit, your board is responsible for making key decisions.

IN THIS CHAPTER

» Organizing a chart of accounts

» Understanding assets, liabilities, net assets, revenues, and expenses

» Setting up accounting codes

Chapter 2

Setting Up the Chart of Accounts for Nonprofits

To easily keep track of where money is coming from and going to in your nonprofit, you use a chart of accounts. The *chart of accounts* is a list of each account that the accounting system tracks; it captures the information you need to keep track of and use to make good financial decisions.

The chart of accounts is like a big reference card that contains numbers, or codes, and names of accounts; no transactions or specific financial information is recorded on the chart of accounts. An account code from the chart of accounts is recorded into the financial records, and from there into financial reports. So, for example, when you receive a donation, you code it with one account number. When you owe a vendor, you code it with another account number.

This chapter runs down the different accounts in a typical chart, how you can personalize your nonprofit's chart of accounts, and what you need to do to code funds coming in and going out of your nonprofit.

Identifying and Naming Your Nonprofit's Main Types of Accounts

When we talk about naming accounts, we don't mean choosing monikers like Sally, Sam, or Susie, so you can put away the book of baby names. Choosing names for your nonprofit accounts depends on the type of products or services you provide. Your chart of accounts consists of accounts found on your financial statements. Knowing which accounts go with which statements helps you to identify the main types of accounts. For example, the statement of financial position has assets, liabilities, and net assets (see Chapter 10 of this minibook for more on this statement). The statement of activities has revenues, expenses, and increases or decreases in net assets (see Chapter 9 of this minibook for more on this statement).

A typical chart of accounts is divided into five categories: assets, liabilities, net assets (fund balances), revenues, and expenses. Each account is assigned a unique identifying number for use within your accounting system. We explain these five categories in the following sections.

Figure 2-1 shows a sample chart of accounts for nonprofit organizations. Your nonprofit organizations might have most of the following accounts plus others as well.

Keep in mind that you name and chart your accounts based on their function. For example, Federal Grants is definitely revenue to your nonprofit. Assign revenue an identifying number starting with 4. The "Coding the Charges: Assigning Numbers to the Accounts" section at the end of this chapter gives a full-blown numbering guide.

REMEMBER

Aside from certain conventions regarding numbering and the order in which information is presented, you can tailor your chart of accounts to your organization's specific needs. Your chart of accounts belongs to you. It's an internal system used by you to keep track of where things go. It classifies accounts by giving them a name and number, and it's the first thing any bookkeeper needs to keep your books in order. It arranges all similar accounts to clarify what's what. If you run out of numbers, you can assign new numbers. The example chart of accounts in Figure 2-1 is merely a suggestion of how you can set up your chart. You must decide what's best for you.

Accounting for assets

The first grouping of accounts in a chart of accounts is assets. *Assets* are the items an organization has as resources, including cash, accounts receivable, equipment, and property. Basically, assets provide economic benefit to your organization. The following are the main types of assets:

- **Current assets:** An asset that will be sold or depleted in the near future (within one year) or a business cycle. An example of a current asset is cash.
- **Fixed assets:** A fixed asset is a long-term tangible asset that your nonprofit uses that will mature or be used up more than 12 months after the date of the statement of financial position. Example of fixed assets are computer equipment or office furniture and fixtures.
- **Other assets:** This is a statement of financial position classification that covers miscellaneous assets. Prepaid expenses is a good example of other assets and one that you'll probably have for your nonprofit.

Assets

Current assets:

1110 Cash

1111 Cash in checking account

1112 Cash in savings account

1113 Cash on hand (petty cash)

1120 Notes receivable

1130 Grants receivable

1140 Accounts receivable

1150 Inventory

1160 Prepaid rent

1170 Prepaid insurance

Long-Term Assets

1210 Land

1220 Building

1221 Accumulated depreciation: building

1230 Equipment

1231 Accumulated depreciation: equipment

Liabilities

Current liabilities

2110 Notes payable

2120 Accounts payable

2130 Salaries payable

Long-Term Liabilities

2210 Mortgage payable

2220 Bonds payable

Nonprofit Equity

3110 Net assets

Revenue

4110 Federal grants

4200 Corporate grants

4300 State grants

4400 Program fees

4500 Interest income

4600 Fundraising

4700 Individual donors

Expenses

5110 Fundraising

5200 Salaries expense

5300 Depreciation expense

5400 Rent expense

5500 Interest expense

5600 Office supplies

FIGURE 2-1: A typical chart of accounts.

All assets start with the number 1 in the chart of accounts (refer to Figure 2-1). Assets are usually listed in descending order of liquidity. This means that cash and other assets that are easily converted to cash are listed first. Receivables and inventory are typically not as liquid as cash, so they normally list after cash accounts, followed by long-term assets.

The following are asset accounts:

- **Checking account:** Here's where you record cash on deposit in a checking account with a bank.
- **Petty cash, change funds, undeposited receipts, cash on hand:** This account includes cash used by the nonprofit organization for revolving funds, change funds (cash used to supply change to customers and others; can also be used to cash payroll checks), petty cash funds, and undeposited receipts at year-end.
- **Savings accounts, money market accounts, certificates of deposit:** This category records funds on deposit with banks and other financial institutions and are usually interest-bearing.
- **Contributions receivable:** When people give you pledges, you record them here, even if the donor restricts the pledged contribution to use in a future period. However, if the pledge won't be paid until a future period, it should be classified as a noncurrent asset.
- **Land:** This account records the amount paid for the land itself, costs incidental to the acquisition of land, and expenditures incurred in preparing the land for use.
- **Buildings and improvements:** This account records the cost of relatively permanent structures used to house people or property. It also includes fixtures that are permanently attached to buildings and can't be removed without cutting into walls, ceilings, or floors, or without in some way damaging the building.
- **Furniture and equipment:** This account records the cost of furniture and equipment, such as office desks, chairs, computer tables, copy machines, large printers, and the like.
- **Data processing equipment:** Here's where you record the cost of data processing equipment used by your nonprofit, such as flat-screen monitors, desktop computers, hard drives, and such.
- **Leasehold improvements:** These costs usually include improvements made to facilities or property leased by your organization.
- **Accumulated depreciation:** This account records depreciation that has accumulated over time by periodic adjustments for annual depreciation. When an asset is sold, depreciation recorded for the item is removed from the records.

Labeling liabilities

Liabilities are obligations due to creditors; in other words, they are bills your non-profit owes and thus indicate how much debt the nonprofit is obligated to pay. Liabilities are either current or long term:

- **Current liabilities:** These are obligations that are due within one year or within the business cycle. An example is accounts payable.
- **Long-term liabilities:** These are liabilities that aren't due within one year or within the current business cycle. A long-term notes payable is an example of a long-term liability.

Like assets, current liabilities list first followed by long-term liabilities. All liabilities start with the number 2 in the chart of accounts (refer to Figure 2-1). In this example, the current liabilities second digit is a 1. The long-term liabilities second digit is a 2. (Check out the section "Coding the Charges: Assigning Numbers to the Accounts" at the end of this chapter for more info about numbering.)

The following are liabilities:

- **Accounts payable:** This account records current liabilities, which represent debts that must be paid within a relatively short period, usually within 30–90 days of the statement date.
- **Salary and wages payable:** Here's where you record the liabilities for salaries, wages, and employee benefits the employee has earned but payday might not be for another week or two.
- **Accrued payroll:** This account records the liability for payrolls accrued at year-end. The accrual should include all salaries and wages earned by employees; thus, this entry would include all time worked by employees up to the end of the year.
- **Payroll taxes payable:** These accounts record liabilities for various payroll taxes payable to governments arising from salaries and wages and payroll withholdings.
- **Unearned revenue:** This account records amounts that have been received by your nonprofit, but the earning process hasn't been completed. For example, if your nonprofit offers subscriptions for one year to your inside newsletter and people pay for them annually, you may have revenue that has been received but not yet earned. That is, if you have only issued four in the series of ten newsletters, you still owe the subscribers six issues.

- **Notes payable:** You use this account to record the outstanding principle due within the next year on notes owed by your organization. As the amount of the payable is due with one year, classify it as short term.
- **Mortgage payable:** This is just what it sounds like. You record the outstanding principle due within the next year on mortgages. As the amount of the payable is due with one year, classify it as short term.
- **Accrued interest payable:** This account records interest due on notes, capital leases, and mortgages at the end of the accounting period.
- **Grants payable:** If you owe outstanding grant awards to outside organizations, you record it here. The figure represents amounts earned but not paid at year-end.
- **Long-term debt:** This account records noncurrent liabilities, which represent debts that must be paid in a future period that is at least one year or more after the current fiscal period. This includes the balance on any note or mortgage payable that is due beyond 12 months of the statement date.

Net assets: What you're worth

Net assets (your nonprofit's equity) show the financial worth of the organization. It represents the balance remaining after liabilities are subtracted from an organization's assets. (Accounting software designed with for-profits in mind may report net assets under the heading *equity.*) Net asset accounts begin with the number 3. (Check out the section "Coding the Charges: Assigning Numbers to the Accounts" at the end of this chapter for more info about numbering.) They are classified as:

- **Net assets without donor restrictions:** This account records net assets that can be used at the discretion of the nonprofit board. It includes revenues that were derived from providing services, producing, and delivering goods, receiving unrestricted contributions, and receiving dividends or interest from investing in income-producing assets, less expenses incurred in fulfilling any of those tasks.
- **Net assets with donor restrictions:** This account combines temporarily restricted and permanently restricted net assets.

  Donors' temporary restrictions may require that resources be used in a later period or after a specified date (time restrictions), or that resources be used for a specified purpose (use of purpose restrictions), or both.

  Permanently restricted assets have donor-imposed restrictions that don't expire with time or with the completion of activities that fulfill a purpose.

REMEMBER

Only people and organizations outside your nonprofit can place restrictions on grants and gifts. Your board of directors may designate a gift for a specific use, but it can turn around and undesignate it. Your nonprofit can't place restrictions on gifts. Restrictions are only enforceable when imposed by outside entities.

Revenue: What you earn

Revenue accounts measure gross increases in assets, gross decreases in liabilities, or a combination of both when your nonprofit delivers or produces goods, renders services, or earns income in other ways during an accounting period. Keeping different sources of revenue (donations and income) separate is important because you may have to account for what you did with the income.

For example, you'll account separately for government grant revenue, which can be set apart using your chart of accounts. You may have to account for gifts received with restrictions on them. So assign account numbers that clearly identify all revenue sources because this will serve as documentation for you during an audit.

Your chart of accounts helps you keep track of revenue sources through the assignment of unique account numbers. Revenue accounts start with the number 4 and are further classified by subaccounts such as federal grants, private gifts, and investment income. (See the section "Coding the Charges: Assigning Numbers to the Accounts" at the end of this chapter for more info about numbering.)

Here are common nonprofit revenue accounts:

- **Federal grants:** This account records revenues earned for grants from federal agencies. Generally, revenues are earned for operating grant programs and by incurring qualifying expenses. Establish a subaccount for each federal grant.
- **State grants:** This account shows revenue earned from grants from one or more states. The revenue/expense relationship is similar to that of federal grants. Establish a subaccount for grants from different states.
- **Private gifts and grants (contributions):** Here's where you record revenues from private gifts and grants, including corporate gifts, grants from private foundations, and contributions from individuals. This account can also be used for pledges that aren't contingent on future events. Set up a subaccount for each corporation (unless anonymity is requested).
- **Fees from special events:** When you collect membership fees and funds raised through special events, you record them in this account. Subaccounts should be established for each type of fee collected.

- **Special events (net revenue):** This account records the net proceeds (gross collections less expenses) from special events. Establish subaccounts to record receipts and expenses.
- **Investment income:** This account records income from investments. The balance of these accounts should include investment income received during the year, as well as accrued investment income earned but not received by year-end.

Your nonprofit may also receive donations and contributions of nonfinancial assets, also known as *in-kind contributions*. These include donated goods, buildings, below-market rent, and pro bono legal and professional services.

TIP

Wondering how your nonprofit accounts for in-kind contributions? Well, there is an FASB for that! Financial Accounting Standards Board (FASB) Accounting Standards Update (ASU) No 2020-07 is effective for all financial statements with a June 30, 2022, year-end and after. See Chapter 6 of this minibook for more about FASB ASU No 2020-07.

Nonprofit expense: What you spend

You can't make money without spending money. *Expenses* are expired costs, the using up of assets, or incurrence of liabilities from operations. Examples include personnel costs, costs of supplies, and the costs associated with accounts payable. If you're using the accrual method (see Chapter 1 of this minibook for an explanation of the accrual method and its counterpart, the cash method), expenses should be recognized when they are incurred, and revenues should be recognized in your accounting books when they are earned. Expense accounts start with the number 5. (See the section "Coding the Charges: Assigning Numbers to the Accounts" at the end of this chapter for more info about numbering).

Here are some common expense accounts:

- **Salary and wages:** Here's where you record the cost of salary and wages paid to employees of your nonprofit. This account includes both full- and part-time personnel costs.
- **Payroll tax expense:** This account records the employer's share of Social Security and Medicare taxes based on the amount of salary and wages paid to employees.
- **Unemployment insurance contribution:** This account records the employer's contribution for employees' costs of the state unemployment insurance program.

- **Workers compensation:** Here you record the cost of workers compensation insurance premiums for your nonprofit.
- **Board member compensation/stipends:** When you pay stipends to board members, you record them here.
- **Accounting and tax services:** This account records accounting and tax services for bookkeeping services, payroll, and preparation of tax returns.
- **Legal services:** This account is used to record legal services either for specific services or retainers.
- **Temporary services:** If you use temporary services (like temporary clerical or secretarial personnel) from workforce agencies, you record the expense in this account.
- **Management services:** This account records the costs of management services acquired by the organization; for example, consulting services.
- **Honorariums:** When you pay honorariums (a sum paid to a professional for speaking engagements or other services for which no fee is set), you record the amount in this category.
- **Supplies and materials:** This account records the cost of supplies and materials used in the daily operations of your organization.
- **Travel:** Here you record the costs of employee travel, including food, lodging, and transportation.
- **Communication:** This account records the costs of landlines, cellphones, high-speed Internet, and postage.
- **Utilities:** This account records costs for things such as electricity, water and sewer, and gas.
- **Printing and binding:** This account records the cost of printing, binding, and copying documents used or distributed by the nonprofit.
- **Repair and maintenance:** This account covers the costs of routine repairs and maintenance, including service contracts.
- **Employee training:** Here you record the cost of employee training, including tuition, conference registration, and training materials.
- **Advertising and promotion:** This account records the cost of advertising program services, solicitation of bids, obtaining qualified applicants, or advertising fundraising events.
- **Board member expense:** Here's where you record the cost of board member travel and per diem expenses.
- **Office rent:** This account records the cost of office rent.

- **Furniture and equipment rental:** This account records the cost of furniture or equipment rental. Lease-purchase agreements that meet the criteria of a financing lease (a lease recorded as an asset accompanied by borrowing of funds) should be recorded as capital outlays (a liability intended to benefit future periods).
- **Vehicle rental:** You record the cost of vehicle rental in this account. Lease-purchase agreements that meet the criteria of a capital lease should be recorded as capital outlays.
- **Dues and subscriptions:** Record the costs of professional fees for organizations your nonprofit is a member of in this account.
- **Insurance and bonding:** This account records the costs of insurance on facilities and liability insurance.
- **Depreciation:** This account records the estimated periodic charge against asset values for use, deterioration, or obsolescence.
- **Contracts, grants, and stipends:** This account records contracts, grants, or stipends with outside organizations or individuals.
- **Other expenses:** This account records any other expenses not classified above.

Net income/increase – decrease in net assets

The statement of activities reports the change in net assets as either a positive (increase) or negative (decrease) figure and is comparable to net income. Generally, you record revenue as increases in net assets and expenses as decreases in net assets. For example, if January 2023 revenue is $100,000 and expenses are $75,000, the change in net assets is $25,000 ($100,000 – $75,000).

Next, calculate ending net assets by taking the January 2023 change in net assets and add it to or subtract it from your beginning net assets. For example, if beginning net assets on January 1, 2023 is $45,000 and current period change in net assets is $25,000, the ending balance in net assets on January 31, 2023 is $70,000 ($45,000 + $25,000).

TIP

The statement of activities reports revenues, expenses, and a change in net assets. The statement of financial position reports assets, liabilities, and net assets. Chapters 9 and 10 of this minibook provide more information about both statements.

Coding the Charges: Assigning Numbers to the Accounts

Your chart of accounts is a list of all accounts used in the five categories we discuss in the previous section. The chart of accounts assigns specific account names and numbers to each account found on your statement of activities and statement of financial position.

REMEMBER

You recognize account types by looking at the first digit or leading number. To number your accounts, remember this basic numbering system:

- Asset accounts begin with the number 1, so 1110 to 1999 are assigned to asset accounts.
- Liability accounts begin with the number 2, so 2110 to 2999 are assigned to liability accounts.
- Equity accounts (net assets) begin with the number 3, so 3110 to 3999 are assigned to equity accounts.
- Revenue accounts begin with the number 4, so 4110 to 4999 are assigned to revenue accounts.
- Expense accounts begin with the number 5, so 5110 to 5999 are assigned to expense accounts.

Within each category of accounts, the second digit identifies the subclassification. For example:

- Within 1110 to 1231 of asset accounts, you could have
  - 1111 to 1170 as current assets.
  - 1210 to 1231 as long-term assets.
- Within 2110 to 2220 of liability accounts, you could have
  - 2110 to 2130 as current liabilities.
  - 2210 to 2220 as long-term liabilities.

You use your chart of accounts to code accounting transactions. This chart can help you locate accounts in your ledger. Furthermore, you need to follow a systematic approach of assigning numbers to your accounts. Having a systematic method to identify your accounts helps when errors are made while preparing your trial balance. For more about your ledger and trial balance, see Chapter 3 of this minibook.

IN THIS CHAPTER

» Getting an overview of the accounting process

» Making entries in the journal

» Transferring information to the general ledger

» Making sure everything balances

» Finding and fixing errors

Chapter 3
Recording Transactions and Journal Entries

Just like a coin has two sides (a head and a tail), an account has two sides (a debit and a credit). When your nonprofit makes a transaction, you have to record it in two or more accounts: the *debit* (the left side of an account) and the *credit* (the right side of an account). When you record the transaction in your accounting books, you're making a *journal entry*.

This chapter touches on the basics, including the different types of accounting and an overview of the accounting process. With this information you can make journal entries, prepare a worksheet, make adjusting entries, and find errors in your books.

Choosing Your Basis of Accounting

Your nonprofit's *basis of accounting* is the method by which you account for things. Most organizations can choose between two bases of accounting to track their transactions: cash or accrual. Depending on the basis you choose, you account for things when they happen or you wait until later. The method you choose affects when you make journal entries about transactions. They're centered on how and when you recognize revenues and expenses.

You need to choose between the two following methods:

- **Cash-basis accounting:** The cash-basis method is simple to use because you recognize that a transaction has taken place only when you receive or distribute cash.
- **Accrual-basis accounting:** The accrual-based system recognizes revenues when a promise or pledge is given and when revenues are earned, while expenses are recognized when they're incurred and not when they're paid.

Your donors aren't concerned with which method you use to account for your finances. They're more concerned that you effectively manage the funding and use it for its intended purpose. Check out Chapter 1 of this minibook for more on the ins and outs of these two types of accounting methods.

TIP

Using the accrual method of accounting may be your best choice. All audited financial statements must be prepared according to generally accepted accounting principles (GAAP), which usually uses the accrual method. To keep things simple, go with the accrual basis to stay in compliance with GAAP.

If you're running a small nonprofit and you're keeping your own books or you have a part-time bookkeeper doing the work, you may want to account for your transactions on the cash basis and pass the books on to your accountant or CPA firm at the end of the year to compile your financial statements. Your CPA can convert your cash-basis books to accrual basis.

Navigating the Accounting Process

Although accounting can be quite maddening at times, it does follow a clear logic. As you try to get a firm grasp of the accounting process, start with the end in mind first. In the end you provide financial statements. Your donors care that your financial statements fairly represent your true financial position for a given time period as of a certain date. So your goal is to keep adequate records that enable you to account for every transaction. The following sections highlight the nuts and bolts of the accounting process and what the general recording process looks like.

Eyeing the specifics of the process

To fully understand how to record and track your nonprofit's financial transactions, you need to understand the ins and outs of the process. You also need to know what the different accounts are and how putting them together creates your nonprofit's bottom line.

REMEMBER

So how does the process work? It starts when your organization receives a donation. You enter the donation into a journal and post it to the general ledger (check out the later sections in this chapter for the specific how-to info). Once a month or when the accounting period is over, you (or your bookkeeping and accounting staff) prepare a trial balance. A *trial balance* is a listing of all accounts and their balances. If the total of the accounts debit balances equals the total of the accounts credit balances, then your accounts are in balance (refer to the later section, "Reaching the Trial Balance," for specifics).

At the end of the month or year, you take your *unadjusted trial balance* (a trial balance prepared before adjustments; it's the account balances from your ledger) and make adjusting entries. *Adjusting entries* are made to your accounts to bring them to their actual balance. For example, adjustments are made for prepaid accounts and for expenses incurred but not yet paid. You make adjustments to the following:

- Accrued revenue (earned revenue that hasn't been recorded because payment hasn't been received)
- Accrued salaries that are unpaid and unrecorded
- Depreciation (allocating the cost and usage of assets as expense)
- Prepaid expenses, such as insurance
- Office supplies used
- Unearned revenue (payments received in advance)

After you finish adjusting the entries and everything balances, you're ready to do an *adjusted trial balance*. Your adjusted trial balance verifies that things are in balance. If your entries are out of balance, then you must find and correct your errors. For help with this, see the later section, "Correcting errors." Figure 3-1 provides a snapshot of the accounting process.

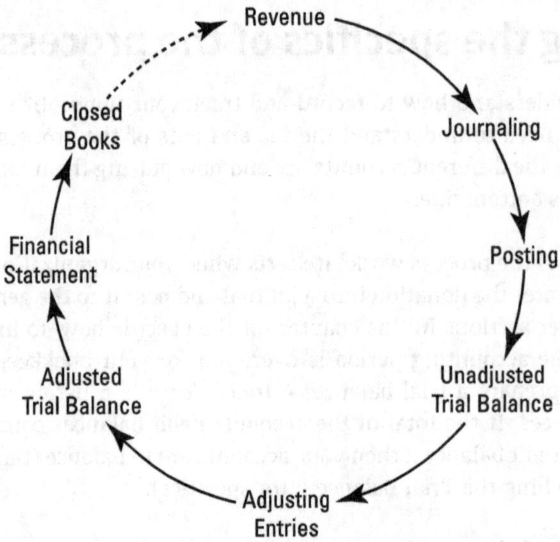

FIGURE 3-1: The accounting process.

Looking at the two sides of an account

Before you begin recording transactions and making journal entries, you need to understand debits and credits. You even need to record purchases made with cash in your books. Why? When you disburse cash, it reduces the amount you have available. You make a journal entry to decrease cash, or a credit. And if the purchase adds something of value, such as an asset, you increase what you have, so you debit. When you fully understand debits and credits, you'll be able to do journal entries like a pro. Knowing this information is important because it's the building blocks for your record-keeping transactions. If you make a mistake at the beginning of the accounting cycle, finding it later is more difficult and can throw your books out of balance.

For example, you purchase $100 of office supplies. You must credit your cash, which means your cash decreases by $100. You enter this transaction on the right. You also debit your office supplies, which increases your assets. You enter this transaction on the left.

REMEMBER

To understand journal entries, you need to know the mechanics of accounting. You should remember the following.

- Revenue, liability, and equity accounts are increased by credits.
- Asset and expense accounts are increased by debits.

TIP

Think of accounts as having two sides. The debit side is on the left, and the credit side is on the right. And because credits increase revenue, liability, and equity accounts, debits decrease them. Think of your journal page like a capital "T." Any transaction you enter on the left is a debit; anything you enter on the right is a credit. If you hear someone talk about "T" accounts, this is what they mean.

Consider the debit and credit outline in Table 3-1. This table shows you how normal balances affect accounts on the statement of financial position and statement of activities. *Normal balances* indicate what you do to increase the accounts. To decrease the accounts, you do the opposite. For example, because a debit increases an expense account, to decrease an expense, you credit the account.

TABLE 3-1 Understanding Normal Balances of Accounts

Balance Sheet Accounts	Normal Balance
Assets	Debit
Liabilities	Credit
Equity	Credit Income
Income Statement Accounts	**Normal Balance**
Revenue	Credit
Expense	Debit

Recording Journal Entries

Many people write in a personal journal to reflect on the events of their daily life. In accounting, you use a *journal* to record transactions in the order that they occur. A journal is often referred to as the *book of original entry* because it's the first place where you record transactions in the accounts.

TIP

Your journal doesn't have to be a physical book. Calling it a book doesn't mean you need to purchase a notebook to write down your transaction. You can do it on your computer. Or if you choose, you can use columnar paper and three-ring binders.

REMEMBER

Journaling is recording transactions in a journal. Each account has a title or name, such as "cash," and you record monetary increases and decreases for each one. Your journal entries indicate the transaction date, the names of the accounts involved, the amount of each debit and credit, and an explanation of the transaction. At the time you record journal entries, you don't need to make any specific reference; just make sure you get the info recorded. See Chapter 2 of this minibook for more about making the entries to the right accounts.

Every transaction is recorded in at least two accounts with equal debits and credits to keep your accounting books in balance. For example, if you pay the cost of your monthly radio ads for $300 on December 2, 2022, you record the transaction in two accounts. First you need to debit advertising expense for $300 and then credit cash for $300.

TIP

Transactions are first memorialized in your journal, then you record them in the general ledger, which you find out about later in this chapter in the "Posting to the General Ledger" section.

Figure 3-2 shows a sample journal entry. (Flip to Chapter 1 of this minibook for explanations of double-entry bookkeeping.) The following sections dive in to recording the actual journal entries in three easy steps.

General Journal — Page 1

Date	Account Titles and Explanation	Debit	Credit
20XX			
Dec.	2 Advertising Expense	300	
	Cash		300
	To pay for monthly radio ads		
	3 Computer Repair Expense	75	
	Cash		75
	To pay computer technician		
	5 Cash	500	
	Donation Revenue		500
	To record donation from United Way		
	6 Salaries Expense	400	
	Cash		400
	To pay receptionist salary		

FIGURE 3-2: A sample journal entry.

Step one: Write the transaction date

The first step you take when making journal entries is to record the transaction date. This information includes the year in small figures, the month on the first line, and the day. You need to know the dates that transactions took place to help keep your books up to date. You record journal entries in the order of their occurrence.

So, for example, you receive a check for $1,000 from a donor on Oct. 8, 2022. Besides putting a smile on your face for receiving the money, you also need to deposit the check. You create the journal entry following these four steps:

Date	*Debit*	*Credit*
20XX Oct. 8		

In this journal entry, you increase your cash by $1,000 by debiting cash. And you increase your donations by $1,000 by crediting donations. Cash is an asset account. Donations are revenue accounts.

TIP

When recording journal entries and ledger postings, don't use dollar signs because the only thing you can debit and credit to accounts is money. Everyone knows you're talking about money.

Step two: Write the account names

The second step of recording your journal entries includes writing the names of the accounts to be debited and credited. You write the name of the account to be debited first, and write the name of the account to be credited indented about one inch. Doing so helps readers identify quickly which accounts have been debited and which have been credited. Placing the account to be debited first is important so other bookkeepers can follow your flow.

For example, to record the $1,000 donation you received, you may write the account names as such:

Date		*Debit*	*Credit*
20XX			
Oct. 8	Cash		
	Donation Revenue		

Step three: Write the amount of each debit and credit

In the third step, you write the debit amount in the debit column opposite the name of the account to be debited, and write the credit amount in the credit column opposite the account to be credited. So, if doing one thing to one side of an account increases the account, then the opposite happens when you record the entry on the opposite side. Asset and expense accounts are increased by debits; to decrease them, you credit them.

For example, for the $1,000 donation, record the amount as such:

Date		*Debit*	*Credit*
20XX			
Oct. 8	Cash	1,000	
	Donation Revenue		1,000

Step four: Write an explanation or reason for the transaction

Each transaction has an explanation. The last step to recording a journal entry is to state the reason for the transaction. Write the explanation on the next line, indented about ½ inch. Keep this explanation short and to the point, but be sure to include enough information to explain the transaction.

For example, in the case of the $1,000 donation, you record the following:

Date		*Debit*	*Credit*
20XX			
Oct. 8	Cash	1,000	
	Donation Revenue		1,000
	To record $1,000 individual donation from Jasmine Bentham, check #1299.		

TIP

Leave some space between journal entries to set them apart. This space keeps entries from running together and makes it easier for you or someone else to read later.

When you're making journal entries, usually no posting references or numbers are listed, but when you get ready to post to your general ledger, you'll enter account numbers of the ledger accounts to which the debits and credit are copied. See the next section on posting to your general ledger.

Posting to the General Ledger

With bookkeeping and accounting, you want to keep track of any changes to the different accounts in the chart of accounts (for more info about the chart of accounts, see Chapter 2 of this minibook). You keep track of the changes by posting journal entries to your general ledger. The *general ledger* shows all the accounts in your chart of accounts ordered by account number and reflects all transactions affecting each account. Assets, liabilities, and net assets, which are statement of financial position accounts, are placed first. Next are revenues and expenses, which are statement of activities accounts.

Here's an example of how usual accounts in the general ledger are arranged:

- **Cash:** This includes coins, currency, checks, money orders, checking and savings accounts, and short-term CDs.
- **Donation receivables:** These are promises and pledges to give.
- **Prepaid insurance:** Here is what you've paid in advance for insurance coverage that expires as the days go by.
- **Inventory:** This account records the price paid for any product sitting on your shelves that you plan to sell.
- **Land:** This account includes land purchased or owned by your organization. Although a valuable asset, land should not be depreciated (see Chapter 1 of this minibook for more on depreciation).
- **Buildings:** This includes your office building if you're buying or already own it. Buildings usually have a depreciable span of 39 to 40 years.
- **Equipment:** This account records the purchase of copy machines, computers, vehicles, office furniture, file cabinets, and similar items. Equipment usually has a useful life span of three to seven years.
- **Accumulated depreciation:** This account shows how much depreciation has occurred on assets so far. The flip side of accumulated depreciation is depreciation expense. (You learn more about expenses in Chapter 9 of this minibook.)
- **Accounts payable:** These are short-term liabilities usually paid within a month or two. They're considered a current liability.
- **Salaries payable:** These are usually recorded on the statement of financial position because employees have earned salaries but have not yet been paid.
- **Notes payable:** These are liabilities or promises to pay a certain amount on a certain date.

- **Mortgage payable:** This is a long-term liability to a creditor for a large purchase of land or buildings.
- **Bonds payable:** This is a long-term liability between the issuer and lender. Some organizations borrow large sums of money to finance large purchases, equipment, and other assets. The money is obtained by issuing bonds. Bonds are paid back, and usually you have a bonds payable and interest payable account to account for bonds payable.
- **Revenue:** These accounts are established for all sources of income: donations, grants, fees from services rendered, and interest income. For most nonprofits, donations from individuals, corporations, foundations, and state and federal grants are each recorded in a separate account.
- **Expenses:** These are usually the last group of general ledger accounts. You name your expense accounts according to their purpose. Typical expenses are rent expense, supplies expense, insurance expense, salaries expense, and so on.

Keep in mind the accounts in the general ledger vary from one organization to another. Which accounts you set up depend on

- The nature of your organization
- The way you operate
- The size of your nonprofit
- The amount of detail required by your board
- State and local laws
- Requirements by federal programs

When transferring entries from your journals to your general ledger, you post information following these steps:

1. **Find the account name and number in your ledger.**
2. **Copy the date of the transaction as written in the journal to your ledger.**
3. **Enter a description of the transaction.**
4. **Enter the posting reference, letter G (general journal).**
5. **Write the amount as shown in the journal in your ledger as either a debit or credit following the guidance given earlier in this chapter in the "Looking at the two sides of an account" section.**
6. **Enter the new balance after making the entry in your ledger.**

Referencing Figure 3-2, check out Figure 3-3 for an example of what the Cash in checking account general ledger page looks like after you've posted transactions from that general journal to the general ledger.

TIP

Depending on the magnitude of your accounting transactions, posting journal entries from the journal to the ledger is usually done near the end of the day. Everything entered in your journal for that day should be posted to your ledger.

General Ledger

Account Name: Cash in checking account				Account #: 1111	
Date	Description	Post Ref.	Debit	Credit	Balance
1-Dec-22					645.00
2-Dec-22	Advertising Expense	G		300.00	345.00
3-Dec-22	Computer Repair	G		75.00	270.00
5-Dec-22	Donation Revenue	G	500.00		770.00
6-Dec-22	Salaries Expense	G		400.00	370.00

FIGURE 3-3: A sample general ledger page.

Reaching the Trial Balance

After you post the last entries to your general ledger, it's time to prepare a trial balance. Your *trial balance* lists all the balances of the general ledger accounts and totals all accounts having a debit balance and all accounts having a credit balance. The total debit and credit balances of each account in the general ledger are transferred to the trial balance. The sum of the debits in the trial balance must equal the sum of the credits.

The following sections walk you through creating a trial balance, help you adjust as needed to come up with the final balance, and address what to do when you find errors.

Preparing the trial balance: The how-to

Your trial balance is a test to see if your debits equal your credits and to provide evidence of accuracy in the accounts. This allows you to verify that your numbers are correct before you prepare your financial statements. Most organizations prepare a trial balance at the end of the month. Most accounting software on the market today doesn't allow you to enter accounts that are out of balance. They'll send a warning message when debits and credits don't balance.

TIP

To prepare a trial balance, you write down all your account titles from your general ledger and the debit or credit balances in each. Each time you've posted to your ledger, you've balanced it, so now all you need is to make a list by writing down those account titles and their balances. That's it!

Understanding which accounts require adjustments

Two accounting principles dictate adjusting. *Adjustments* are journal entries of changes in accounts. For example, adjustments are made to correct, to depreciate, or to make any changes required by an auditor.

Generally accepted accounting principles (GAAP) require you assign revenues to the period in which they're earned (the realization principle). Expenses incurred are reported in the same period as the revenues earned (the matching principle). For example, if it's time to close your month or year and you have salaries that have been earned but not paid, you need to make adjusting entries to record that salary expense.

For example, adjusting entries are as follows:

Date		***Debit***	***Credit***
20XX			
Dec. 31	Salaries Expense	105	
	Salaries Payable		105
	To record the accrued wages.		
20XX			
Dec. 31	Unearned Daycare Fees	125	
	Day Care Fees Earned		125
	Earned day care fees that were received in advance.		

REMEMBER

If you are preparing financial statements using the accrual basis of accounting, revenues should reflect the accounting period in which they're earned. Expenses should also be charged to the accounting period in which they're incurred. Sometimes this requires making adjustments.

You may need to prepare adjustments for the following accounts:

» **Prepaid expenses** include payments in advance of use. A prepaid expense is considered an asset until it's consumed in the operation of your business. An example of a prepaid expense is paying an insurance premium for twelve months and you are only five months into the policy period. The remaining seven months is considered prepaid insurance.

- **Accrued expenses** are expenses incurred but not yet paid. For example, at the close of your accounting period some expenses may be unrecorded because the payment is not yet due. Examples of accrued expenses are utilities, telephone bills, and unpaid wages.
- **Unearned revenues** include payments prior to delivery of the product or service; for example, the sale of tickets for a benefit dinner or golf tournament. You may collect money weeks in advance of the event.
- **Depreciation** is an allocation of the purchase price of an asset based on its useful life. Assets are expensed over their useful life through depreciation. As they lose their value, a portion is written off as an expense.

Check out the later section, "Correcting errors," to see how adjustments are made to these accounts.

Finding errors

No matter how meticulous you are with your accounting, you're going to make mistakes. There's no way to avoid it. If you find an error in your trial balance, don't despair. It happens to everyone. You know you have an error when your figures don't add up when you total all debits and all credits.

TIP

If you know you have an error because the figures don't add up, organize all of your records and then take a short break before coming back to the problem. Walking away from the numbers for a few minutes can give you a fresh outlook and help you solve the problem faster. Count to ten, take a restroom break, grab something to eat, and then come back to the problem.

What if you've re-added the numbers, gone over your paperwork, and checked the figures, but you still aren't sure where the error is occurring? Spend some time looking over the following areas.

Ferreting out basic errors

Your general ledger is only as accurate as your journal. If you entered incorrect data while journaling, you probably transferred the same incorrect information to the general ledger. Go back to the beginning and compare journal entries to general ledger entries. If you still can't find the error, go back over each transaction, and look at receipts, invoices, checks, and bills. Carefully review each item to ensure that you recorded the correct information in your journal and in your ledger.

TIP

If you find that your trial balance is still out of balance and the difference is evenly divisible by 9, you've made a transposition error. A *transposition error* occurs when you switch the order of the digits; for example, you write 428 instead of 482 (see Chapter 4 of this minibook for more on detecting these mistakes).

Even if your accounting system is computerized, you or one of your staff members has to enter the numbers. Occasionally, the person entering the information makes a mistake that throws things off. One of the objectives of an audit is to find errors that have a material effect on an organization's financial statements. Do the following to locate errors:

- Refer to your journal and check the posting and totals.
- Check the posting and balances in your general ledger accounts.
- Check all balances in the trial balance.

Being aware of hidden errors

Keep in mind that some errors can't be detected. For example, if you forget to record a transaction, or if you copy the incorrect debit amount and credit amount in accounts, it's highly unlikely these would be found.

Some errors cancel each other out. If you make a $1,000 error twice, the two may cancel each other out. Or you may make an error by debiting the wrong account within the same account group. For example, if you charge something to Vehicle Expense that should have been charged to Office Supplies, you might not detect this error. However, your auditor will detect material amounts. He'll also define for you what's considered material for your nonprofit.

TIP

One way to reduce the chance of errors like these is to create a monthly trial balance. Tracking your accounts by creating a monthly trial balance can save you lots of time and energy. If you keep everything in balance month by month, you'll breeze through the final process at the end of the year. (See Chapter 13 of this minibook for more on closing the year-end books.)

Correcting errors

So after hunting through your transactions, you find your error. Although some errors are easier to find than others, most are easily correctible. Errors made in calculations and balancing, posting to the wrong side of an account, entering the wrong amounts, or simply forgetting to enter a transaction can be easily corrected. The trial balance shows these errors quickly. How you correct the error depends on whether it's in the journal and the general ledger or in your journal only.

Making a journal correction

Depending on where and when you find an error in the journal affects how you correct it. Usually you can correct it by drawing a line through the error and writing the correct amount or title above the error. If the data has been journalized and not posted to the general ledger, that's all you have to do.

For example, say you see the following entry in your journal:

Date		*Debit*	*Credit*
20XX			
Oct. 8	Office Furniture and Fixtures	75	
	Cash		75
	To record the purchase of office supplies.		

If you made the previous entry when you purchased office supplies on October 8, then the following entry is needed to correct the error.

Date		*Debit*	*Credit*
20XX			
Oct. 8	Office Supplies	75	
	Office Furniture and Fixtures		75
	To correct entry of Oct 8 when the Office Furniture and Fixtures account was debited in error instead of Office Supplies.		

The debit to Office Supplies records the purchase in the right account and the credit to Office Furniture and Fixtures cancels out the error of the first entry. There's no need to bother with cash because it was handled properly.

If the incorrect information from the journal has already been recorded in the ledger, you have to take a few more steps to make everything right. The next section shows you how.

Making a ledger correction

If you find a mistake after it's been posted to the general ledger, you need to correct both the journal entry and the general ledger to fix the problem. Using the Office Furniture and Fixtures/Office Supplies example from the previous section

"Making a journal correction," there are two steps to carry that correction to the general ledger:

1. Post the $75 adjustment to the Office Supplies general ledger account following the same steps as in the earlier section "Posting to the General Ledger," using Figure 3-3 as a guide.
2. Draw a line through the erroneous posting to the Office Furniture and Fixtures, hand-write in a brief explanation, and adjust the balance. In this case you decrease the Office Furniture and Fixtures ending balance by $75.

IN THIS CHAPTER

» Understanding the checkbook register

» Taking in and tracking donations

» Paying bills and recording expenses

» Reconciling your checkbook register

» Ferreting out and fixing errors

Chapter 4
Balancing the Checkbook: Donations and Expenses

The center of every transaction in nonprofit organizations starts and ends in the checkbook register. In fact, you can find the keys that unlock your nonprofit's financial position in the checkbook register and bank statements. Having more money than you thought you had in your checking account is okay, but having less money can cost you if a check bounces.

The bank records every donation deposited and expense paid out of your checking account and sends you a monthly statement showing this activity. All deposits are considered *credits* (additions) to your account, and all withdrawals are considered *debits* (subtractions). The difference between credits and debits equals your checking account *balance*.

Having a checking account saves you time and energy. For example, driving to each utility to pay your bill in cash would take a lot of time away from bigger duties — serving your community. It makes it easier for bookkeeping and record keeping if you pay bills out of a checking account instead of using cash. That's why organization is a must. Having a plan to track all donations and expenses is essential; if you don't have a plan, you'll inevitably run into major problems because you won't know whether you have enough money to cover your expenses and pay your bills.

Writing a check creates a paper trail between your checkbook, the bank, and the vendor or bill you're paying. It's easier to trace your steps when you have a bank that provides a bank statement. This paper trail comes in handy during your nonprofit's audit.

This chapter focuses on how to use the checkbook register to balance your nonprofit's checking account and shows you how to record and log transactions when they occur.

WARNING

If you just opened a checking account, balancing the account in your head may seem like a practical approach when only a few transactions are taking place. Don't rely on this system as an adequate method. You'll regret it later. Not balancing your checkbook can cost you returned check fees and overdraft fees, and cause you to lose your credibility.

Getting the Lowdown on Your Checkbook Register

Before you can balance your nonprofit's checkbook register, you first need to know what the register is. You're probably familiar with your personal checking account register; it's where you record the payment and deposit details to keep track of your money. With your nonprofit's checking account, the checkbook register holds valuable information, too.

You use a *checkbook register* to record the following:

- Each check when written
- Each deposit when made
- Each withdrawal either from an ATM or at a teller window
- All bank service charges

Figure 4-1 shows you an example of a checkbook register for a fictional nonprofit organization. In this figure you can see entries for the transactions that take place in the checking account. The rest of this chapter discusses how you record information in your register to balance your nonprofit's checkbook.

TIP

Duplicate checks can be a lifesaver when it comes to recording information in your checkbook register. *Duplicate checks* create a copy of a check as you fill it out, so you have all the details of the check after you hand it over to pay for something. These nifty copies help you stay on top of your account balance because you can look at the copies and transfer the transaction information to your register.

Date	Check #	Payee/ Description of Transaction	Withdrawal Debit	Deposit Credit	Balance
Beg Bal					$1,000.00
10/1/2022		Donations received		500.00	1,500.00
10/5/2022		ATM Withdrawal	50.00		1,450.00
10/8/2022	255	George Rembert Supplies	100.00		1,350.00
10/8/2022		Bank Charges	8.00		1,342.00
10/8/2022		Fundraiser		750.00	2,092.00
10/9/2022	256	Web Design	25.00		2,067.00
10/10/2022	257	Salaries Paid	925.00		1,142.00
10/13/2022		Donations received		300.00	1,442.00
Balances			1,108.00	1,550.00	$1,442.00

FIGURE 4-1: A nonprofit's checkbook register.

TIP

Another lifesaver to keeping your register balanced is online banking. You can see an updated and current balance in your account when you access your account online. Online banking gives you a heads-up. But even with online banking, you still need a paper trail because one day you may be audited, and you'll need to have all deposits and withdrawals from your checking account recorded in the check register. Even if you're not a number cruncher, you still need to keep a checkbook register because you need to stay on top of your finances.

Adding and Tracking Nonprofit Donations

To have a complete picture of how much money your nonprofit has on hand, you need to keep an accurate picture of the money coming in. Most of what comes in is in the form of *private donations* (charitable contributions that individuals as well as organizations give to your nonprofit) or *grants* (funds received from foundations and government agencies that are generally secured via an application process).

Your nonprofit may have other sources of income (check out the nearby sidebar, "Identifying other potential income sources," for more info). However, you should deposit all donations and other sources of income into your nonprofit checking account.

Most of your donations may come in the form of checks written by donors, foundations, and corporations. Keeping track of those donations and depositing them into your checking account is important because you want to make deposits in a timely fashion, so the money is available to support your organization. If you don't deposit a donor's check right away, it may bounce. It's best to deposit all checks right away so they can clear the donor's account, allowing your nonprofit to avoid unnecessary bank fees.

The following sections focus on how to log monetary donations into your checking account, the diverse types of donations you may encounter, and why you need to differentiate between them.

Logging donations in your register

As your nonprofit receives donations, you need to make sure you write them down (or *log* them) in your checkbook register as soon as you deposit them. Keeping your checkbook register current is necessary to avoid *overdraft fees* (fees the bank charges you when you write a check for more money than you have in your account) and to stay on top of your organization's income and expenses.

IDENTIFYING OTHER POTENTIAL INCOME SOURCES

Your nonprofit can generate revenue from numerous sources. The most common include contributions, corporate and foundation grants, government grants, government contracts, membership dues, interest on savings and temporary cash investments, dividends and interest from marketable securities, rental income, gains or losses on the sale of investments, and holding special events.

WARNING

All nonprofits must have a mission statement. The Internal Revenue Service (IRS) has strict rules regarding business income unrelated to your mission statement. Earning too much money by means outside the scope of your purpose may trigger federal income taxes in the form of Unrelated Business Income Tax (UBIT). Reporting UBIT is done via Form 990-T. For more about unrelated business income, see Chapter 8 of this minibook.

For example, if you don't record a deposit, you may put off making an important purchase because you think you don't have the money (when in fact you do). Or if you incorrectly record a deposit, such as writing $2,850 when the deposit was actually $285, you may end up being charged an overdraft fee if you write a check for more money than you have in your account.

TIP

To record your deposits in your checkbook register, you enter the date, the source of the deposit, and the amount of the transaction in the corresponding columns. In the sample checkbook register shown in Figure 4-1, there are three deposits. The first deposit of $500 was made on October 1, 2022; the second deposit for $750 was made on October 8; and the third deposit for $300 was made on October 13. The total of the deposits is $1,550.

Recording cash, checks, and other donations

People can write checks, hand you cash, or pay by credit card when they donate money to your organization. Larger groups, such as the United Way, may give you a grant to finance your mission. No matter what form the donations take, you need to know the type of donation they are before you can record them in your checkbook register. This section takes a closer look at the diverse types of donations that you need to record as deposits.

REMEMBER

In addition to tracking donations, you need to keep a list of donors. The donors list should include donors' names and addresses, and the amount donated. You'll need this list for information purposes and to track your donations. Your auditor will use your donors list to randomly verify donations received.

Cash donations

The best way to handle the rare event of receiving a cash donation is to give the donor a receipt if the donation is made in your office. In the unlikely event of receiving cash in the mail, you should send the donor a receipt. You don't want to turn down cash just because it requires taking action to leave a paper trail, but your nonprofit should have some checks and balances in place to properly account for cash donations. (See Chapter 1 of this minibook for more on setting up checks and balances.)

SEARCHING FOR THE RIGHT BANK

Shopping for and finding a bank that addresses your nonprofit's needs is especially important. You want a bank that will honor your status as a nonprofit organization by waiving checking account fees. In today's market, banks are competitive, so if you do your research, you can find one that will benefit your nonprofit the most.

So what should you look for in a bank? Ask yourself what's important for your nonprofit. One important factor to consider is how much activity you transact within a given month. Pay attention to banks that offer free services up to a minimum number of transactions, and then charge $1 per transaction thereafter. However, if you make lots of deposits and use your bank card daily, you may end up paying your bank too much. Some banks don't charge service fees or fees for online banking.

Many banks offer overdraft protection — where the bank will pay the check if you overdraw your account. This can save you some embarrassment and some money, not to mention overdraft fees from the merchant and the bank. Talk with your banker about overdraft protection.

Online banking is an excellent way to keep an eye on your bank account. You need to keep an eye on your checking account because banks make mistakes, too. Find out if online banking is free before you sign up for it.

For example, what if someone walks into your organization and gives a $1,000 cash donation to your receptionist? What procedures do you have in place to ensure that the money is reported? Although you hope everyone in your office is honest, you also know people face hardships in life, and sometimes the temptation to pocket the money is too great. If the receptionist is in the office alone, what happens if she decides to borrow it until payday? When payday comes, the receptionist decides to wait until the next payday. What started out as a mere loan has turned into a pile of debt, and no one knows about it but the receptionist.

Donations made by check

Most of your donations will come in the form of a check. Although these are more secure than cash donations, they can be tedious to process. (See the later section, "Handling and recording the donations," for more about depositing donations.)

WARNING

Watch out for bad checks. Be prepared because occasionally donors will write you checks that they don't have enough funds in their checking accounts to cover. The best way to know whether you've received a bad check is to review your account online. Even then it may take a few days before you know whether a check has cleared. It may appear that you have a good working balance in your checkbook register because people have been giving and you've recorded the donations as deposits. But don't count your chicks before they hatch. Until those checks clear your bank, don't count them as available cash.

TIP

If you can afford it, purchase a *check-swiping system*, such as TeleCheck, to speed up the check-clearing process. These systems are connected directly to banks and reject a check if the money isn't in the account. This is the best way to avoid delays in waiting for checks to clear your bank account. This is the same system used by some of the large retail stores. Not many people write checks at stores these days, but some stores have used these machines; the clerk swipes the check from a customer through the machine and hands it back to the customer. You can do the same for checks written to your agency. The cost of the terminal and printer varies based on the vendor and factors unique to your nonprofit. You'll also have transaction fees and monthly customer service fees. For more about TeleCheck quick check-clearing processing, visit `https://getassistance.telecheck.com`.

Credit card donations

Credit card donations are another popular way you receive donations. However, when reporting these donations, you need to know that when someone donates $1,000 on their credit card, you don't receive $1,000. So you can't record credit card donations for the total amount donated. The major credit card companies — American Express, Discover Card, MasterCard, and Visa — all charge a user fee or percentage for processing the payment. When a donor contributes to your organization by swiping their credit card, you're not going to get the total amount.

For example, when you swipe a donor's credit card, the bank takes 1 to 5 percent of the amount donated as its processing fee. If a donor uses their credit card to give you a $100 donation and the bank charges a 2 percent fee, you only receive $98 in your bank account. The donor has given a $100 donation, but you have to pay a $2 bank fee.

WARNING

Don't count credit card donations until they are deposited into your account. The credit card company may reject the payment and cause you to overdraw your checking account. The amount of time it takes for credit card transactions to hit your bank account depends on the bank, the credit card company, and the day of the week. Usually it takes up to three business days. You can always call your bank to check the status of credit card donations.

Direct bank draft donations

Direct bank draft donations allow people to donate a hefty sum of money broken into smaller amounts over a longer period of time. Each month the employer takes the designated amount out of an employee's paycheck as a payroll deduction and sends the money to the nonprofit. These types of donations are a win-win; the donor can make small donations that add up over time without feeling a big difference in take-home pay, and the nonprofit receives a donation that's often larger than a one-time donation would be. Many nonprofits do direct bank drafts from employees' pay.

This method results in the deposit going directly into the nonprofit bank account around the same day of each month. You need to pay attention to the timing of these deposits so you can record them in your checkbook register on the right day.

REMEMBER

Banks may not record deposits on weekends or holidays. Keeping this in mind can help you with the timing differences and help to keep everything in balance. When the deposit date falls on a nonbusiness day, the bank will make the deposit according to its policy, which usually is the next business day.

Grants

A *grant* affords your organization large sums of money that you don't have to pay back. Some foundations and corporations donate grant money in the form of a check, while some government grants reimburse you by direct deposit after the money is spent. No matter how you receive the grant money, remember that a good steward manages grant money by tracking and monitoring how the money is used.

All contributions received from the grant should be deposited into your bank account and recorded in your checkbook register. Make a copy of the check before you deposit it; don't just cash it. Some people open a new account just to manage the grant, but this is up to you. Whether to open a separate account depends on how much money the grant is for and how likely it is that you'll have problems keeping transactions separate.

Handling and recording the donations

When you receive donations, you need to properly track and record them. You want to ensure that you create a paper trail that leads back to the donors list for auditing purposes. You want to get those donations in your bank account and write your donor a thank-you letter. Make sure you do the following:

1. **At the end of the day, add all the donations you received during the day.** Record the amounts on a bank deposit slip. If the money came from a new donor, add the person to your donors list. If the donation came from an established donor, open the donor's account, and record the new donation.

2. **Make copies of the checks and deposit slip before you deposit the checks.** Because banks make mistakes every day, it's important for you to keep track of every deposit made to your account. Keep copies of the deposited checks and deposit slips in a safe place so when the bank sends the monthly bank statement, you have proof of deposit. This is very important if you make deposits after banking hours through night depositories.
3. **Write down the deposit in your checkbook register.** Although forgetting to write down a deposit is not as bad as forgetting to write down a written check, not writing down a deposit can throw your checking account out of whack.
4. **Take the checks and the deposit slip to the bank and make the deposit.** If you have a high volume of checks coming in for large amounts, you don't want to keep them at your office any longer than necessary. You open yourself up to possible robbery or some other unforeseen event. Your bank has a night deposit box that you can use to make your deposits after hours. This requires a trip the next day to pick up the deposit slip and bank bag, but it may be worth the trouble.

At the end of the month, you can compare your records against the bank's records. You'll receive a bank statement that lists all the transactions made on your account. This statement makes it easier for bookkeepers to track the transactions that the bank received and serves as a checkpoint. Just eyeballing this statement isn't enough; you should use the statement to balance your checkbook register (see the later section, "Tie It Together: Balancing the Checkbook").

WARNING

To stay in IRS compliance, you must send a written acknowledgment substantiating a charitable contribution that is more than $249. Check out the following to see what information must be contained in the acknowledgment: `https://www.irs.gov/charities-non-profits/charitable-organizations/charitable-contributions-written-acknowledgments`.

Subtracting Your Expenses

To balance your checkbook, not only do you need to record and add all donations (as the previous section explains), but you also need to record and subtract all expenses. Every check you write to pay a bill is an expense; if you don't carefully record all these expenses, your checking account balance won't be accurate, and you may end up overdrawing your account.

The following sections take a closer look at the types of expenses you need to subtract from your checkbook register and how to record the transactions in your register. By paying close attention to this information, you can get a clearer picture of how much money is in your checking account.

Making the necessary deductions in your checkbook register

Like death and taxes, bills are inevitable. When you receive them, you can't ignore them. You have to pay them and record them in your checkbook register right away. If you forget to record just one transaction, you can throw your account out of balance and end up paying unnecessary bank fees.

For example, you have $1,840 in your checking account, and you have to write checks to cover your utilities for $300, your rent for $1,000, and your insurance for $300. You subtract each check from your total; now you know you have $240 left in your account. If you don't write down one of these expenses, such as the insurance bill, you'll think you have $540 in your account, which may cause you to write a check for $500 to cover your car payment. Doing so results in an overdraft and potential costly overdraft fees.

TIP

After you pay the expenses, make sure you log them in your checkbook register. Doing so keeps your checkbook register current.

To record your expenses in your checkbook register, you simply log them in as you write the checks. For example, Figure 4-1 shows that check 255 was written for $100 to George Rembert to purchase supplies; check 256 was for $25 to pay the web designer; and check 257 was for $925 for salaries paid. You list each piece of information for the transaction in its own column: date, check number, payee/description of transaction, and withdrawal. For each amount, you subtract it from the running balance in the last column labeled "Balance."

Now, suppose you had to pay your $1,500 insurance bill, but you forgot to log in the $100 check written to George Rembert. Your account balance would show $1,542, and you'd think you had just enough money to pay your insurance. As you can see from the account balance, you only have $1,442 in your account. If you forget to log in a check for even $100, it can put your account into overdraft.

REMEMBER

In addition to keeping track of checks you've written, you need to keep track of expenses associated with the use of a check or debit card. Most of the time when you open a checking account, the bank sends you a check card. Because they look like credit cards, these cards can cause you to forget to track expenses associated with their use. The bank card can be used as a credit card or a debit card. A fee may be charged to your account for using it as a debit card, so you need to know the fees associated with each type of use. Don't forget to write down these fees to keep your balance current.

Identifying common expenses

As much as you may want to, you can't avoid the dreaded cycle of paying your nonprofit's bills. In fact, it may seem like every time you open your mailbox, you have at least one bill rearing its ugly head.

You need to have a clear grasp of the types of bills your nonprofit may receive so you know what needs to be deducted from your check register. Some common expenses paid out of your checkbook include the following:

- **Rent:** This is an expense for your office space or building that you're leasing.
- **Utilities:** These include telephone, fax, electricity, water, and garbage.
- **Payroll/wages:** These are expenses in paying those who provide a service.
- **Payroll taxes (federal, state, Medicare, Social Security taxes):** These are expenses that are reported, deducted, and must be paid, if applicable, to federal and state governments.
- **Contract labor:** This expense is used when additional help is needed, and a contract is issued and signed for a specific time period to complete the task.
- **Travel expenses:** These expenses occur from going to and from different destinations. They include transportation and lodging, as well as meals.
- **Licenses and permits:** These are expenses for your nonprofit licenses and permits that allow you to operate and be recognized as a nonprofit organization in your state, county, and city municipalities.
- **Insurance:** This expense is a necessary component to protect you, your clients, your board, and your organization from potential hazards that could be disastrous to your nonprofit.
- **Office expenses and supplies:** These include paper, pens, and other small-ticket items, including postage and printing-related supplies.
- **Office furniture:** This is usually for desks, chairs, tables, and other office furniture.
- **Computer hardware and software:** This category includes computers and software you use to run your nonprofit.
- **Internet website expenses:** These expenses may include web page design, domain name fee, the maintenance and updates of your web page, and the storing and processing of web page data.

- **Bank service fees:** Banks are competitive, and most allow you to have a free checking account because you're a nonprofit organization. This doesn't mean you get your checks for free, but you won't be charged a fee for the account. Pay attention to the hidden banking fees. Other types of bank fees include the following:
  - **Credit card processing:** These fees may be charged by your banking institute for handling monies deposited and withdrawn with credit cards.
  - **Transaction fees:** These are fees for using a check card or debit card rather than writing checks to make purchases.
  - **Non-sufficient funds (NSF) fees:** Your bank charges these fees for processing a check or credit card transaction when the money wasn't available in your account. This is commonly referred to as a bounced check.
  - **Fee per transaction:** These fees may be charged if you go over the amount of transactions designated by your bank. Some banks offer free checking with a maximum of 25 transactions. With the 26th transaction, you may be charged $1 per transaction thereafter.
  - **ATM user fees:** If you use an ATM owned by a different bank, you may be charged. These expenses can range from $1 to $3 per transaction.
- **Electronic payment fees:** Receiving and paying bills electronically is part of the going-green concept. It not only offers convenience, but it also saves the environment when you receive your bills in your email account versus in the mailbox. Electronic billing is faster than traditional mail and saves time and energy.

  If you choose to pay your bills electronically, either directly through the vendor or through your bank, watch out for any bills that go up and down each billing period. Not having a consistent amount drafted from your checking account month to month requires some oversight.

  REMEMBER

  As a general rule, most people don't keep a lot of extra money in their checking account. If your utility costs are up and down, you must keep an adequate amount in your account to cover the differences.
- **Building security expenses:** These expenses may include security cameras and security guards, as well as security alarm system installation and monthly access fees.
- **Miscellaneous expenses:** Any fee not listed in the preceding categories that only occurs occasionally or is incidental may be classified as a miscellaneous expense. For example, this may be the tip you give for prompt delivery of your new computer system or some other small, nonessential expense.

WARNING

Be careful with bills that aren't a fixed amount each month. For example, if the price of natural gas is up, you may want to opt for the budget plan for the gas bill. The *budget plan* (or estimated payment plan) means you pay the same amount for gas year-round, eliminating high or low bills throughout the year, and settle any underage or overage cost at the end of the year.

REMEMBER

Any payment made for an item that could be considered an asset is technically a cost rather than an expense. The payment is still deducted from your checking account balance but does not show up as an expense until it is depreciated. See Chapter 1 of this minibook for more information about assets and depreciation.

Relying on direct or automatic bank drafts

To prevent potential errors, you can set up automatic or direct bank drafts with your checking account. Automatic or direct bank drafts are bills that are paid directly out of your checking account on the same date every month. You should consider direct drafts for bills that are the same amount each month, because bills that fluctuate in balance can do a number on your checking account.

Using automatic bank drafts has a few advantages and disadvantages. Some of the advantages are:

- You save time by not having to write a check.
- You save money by not having to buy stamps.
- You save time and money by not going to the post office.
- You save time by not having to remember to pay the bill.

Because direct drafts are automatic, they pose the following disadvantages:

- You may forget to record and deduct the draft in your checkbook register.
- You may forget to make sure you have enough money in your account to cover the payment.
- If you don't have enough money to cover the draft, you may be hit with an overdraft fee on your account.

WARNING

Doing a direct draft for bills that vary considerably may not be advisable. A good example of this is your utility bill, which may fluctuate based on the time of year and how much you are running your heat or air conditioning.

TIP

It's a good idea to subtract direct drafts on your check register at the beginning of the month. If you're really organized, you can make a note to record the draft when the payment is scheduled to be made directly from your account. Forgetting to log in these expenses can put your organization's finances in a whirlwind.

Tie It Together: Balancing the Checkbook

Most nonprofits hire a bookkeeper to handle the day-to-day finances of the organization and a part-time accountant to tie it all together. Bookkeepers and accountants perform different duties. A good bookkeeper captures everything needed for the accountant to put together your financial reports.

Whether you're doing the bookkeeping yourself or you have someone else do it, this section provides information to help you keep a balanced set of books and track and record income and expenses. Staying on top of this saves you time later when filing reports to the IRS (see Chapter 8 of this minibook), your nonprofit's board of directors, and auditors.

Balancing your nonprofit's checking account each month is a must. Catching an out-of-balance checking account gives you a timely warning that you may have entered a transaction incorrectly in either your manually kept accounting records (see Chapter 3 of this minibook) or your accounting software package such as QuickBooks (discussed later in this chapter). It also alerts you to the fact that you may have forgotten to enter a transaction.

REMEMBER

Don't allow a lot of time to pass without reconciling your checkbook register to your bank statement. Waiting too long can cause you to bounce a check because you were unaware of a deduction on the bank statement that was either not entered or was entered incorrectly.

TIP

To help you reconcile your account, order duplicate checks or choose a bank that sends copies of each check. The more records you have as documentation, the easier it is to get everything to balance.

Using the bank statement

At the end of the month, your bank issues a bank statement — either by a paper mailing or online, if you have set up online banking with your bank account. Either way, it contains a list of deposits and withdrawals (withdrawals include cash you've taken out, checks you've written, and miscellaneous bank fees) that have cleared your account.

If your bank statement comes in the mail, you can use the handy worksheet on the back of the statement to balance your checkbook. It has a grid and instructions (like those presented below) to walk you through the process.

To make sure you know the true balance of your nonprofit's bank account, compare the balance you have in your checkbook register with the balance on the bank statement. Because these two figures probably won't be the same, you reconcile your checking account to the bank statement.

Reconciling your checking account involves accounting for the differences between the bank statement and your checkbook register. Follow these steps to reconcile:

1. **Compare your bank statement to your checkbook register to figure out which checks have cleared your account and which haven't. Put a check mark next to the checks that have cleared.**

   A check has cleared when the money has been moved from your account to the payee's account.

2. **Repeat Step 1 for your deposits.**
3. **Repeat Step 1 for withdrawals and debit card purchases.**

   If the bank shows something that isn't listed in your checkbook register, check your records to make sure you made the transaction. If you did make the purchase and forgot to record it, write it in now. If you didn't make the transaction, call your bank and ask for more information about it.

4. **Repeat Step 1 for any bank fees or interest the account may have paid or earned.**
5. **List the outstanding checks on a separate piece of paper. Also list any outstanding withdrawals and debit card purchases. Add the numbers.**

   When a check or other transaction is outstanding, it hasn't cleared the bank yet. The transactions that are outstanding are those you didn't put a check mark next to in steps 1–3.

6. **List any outstanding deposits. Total the outstanding deposits.**
7. **Write down the ending balance shown on your bank statement.**
8. **Subtract the amount of outstanding checks and withdrawals that you came up with in Step 5 from the ending balance you wrote down in Step 7.**
9. **Add the total of outstanding deposits you came up with in Step 6.**

   After completing steps 8 and 9, your total should match the balance in your checkbook register.

10. If the number you came up with in Step 9 doesn't match the number in your checkbook register, you have some sleuthing to do.

Double-check your math in your checkbook register; make sure you've accounted for all checks, deposits, withdrawals, and fees in your checkbook register; and then go through steps 1–9 again to make sure you didn't leave anything out or do the math incorrectly.

REMEMBER

When reconciling your account, you should rely more heavily on your own records than the bank's. The bank statement only covers a set time period; your records are up to date because you have been tracking every transaction. The following transactions can make it difficult to balance your checkbook:

- Checks written but not yet cleared (see the section "Considering outstanding checks" at the end of this chapter).
- Online bill-pay transaction fees. Sometimes utility companies charge a fee to process online payments. It's easy to forget to record these in your register.
- ATM/debit card transactions and fees. You may have recent transactions that occurred between the time the statement was printed and now.
- Deposits made or recorded after the statement date.
- Bank fees and earned interest not recorded in the checkbook.

Entering the information with a software program

Small nonprofits, especially when first starting out, may opt to keep accounting records manually. If your nonprofit is among that group, make sure you check out Chapter 3 of this minibook for a manual accounting tutorial. However, medium and large nonprofits (and even some small ones if you're a techie kind of person) should consider using a software program. QuickBooks is one that can help you with payroll, check writing, accepting credit card payments, and accurately completing and demonstrating financial accountability. It also can help you balance your nonprofit's checkbook.

With QuickBooks you can skip all the manual steps taken to track and manage your nonprofit's finances. For more information about QuickBooks and which version might be right for your nonprofit, go to `https://quickbooks.intuit.com/oa/get-quickbooks`.

TIP

Financial software company Intuit develops both QuickBooks and Turbo Tax, making it easy to convert your day-to-day bookkeeping and accounting records to financial statements and IRS reports.

Smoothing Out and Avoiding Errors

As careful as you are when recording your donations and expenses, and reconciling your checkbook to bank statements, sometimes errors will happen. A few simple tricks can help you lower the chances of having errors. The following sections explain what to do if you encounter an error and offer some suggestions about how to lower the odds of errors.

Finding and addressing errors

Errors made when writing down numbers are called transposition errors. These errors can drive you crazy because it looks like the numbers are adding up correctly, but they aren't. You add the numbers once and get one amount ($859.89), but when you add them again to double-check the math, you get a different amount ($859.98). See how tricky those two numbers are? Somewhere along the line you may have written down the digits you're adding in the wrong order (or entered them in the wrong order if you're using a calculator or adding machine).

TIP

To figure out whether an error is caused by transposing digits and not incorrect math, find the difference of the two sums. If it's evenly divisible by 9, you know you have a transposition error. So when you subtract $859.98 and $859.89, you get $0.09. Because that amount is evenly divisible by 9, you know you've got a transposition error within the numbers you added to reach the total.

To avoid these kinds of errors, take your time when writing down and adding numbers. A 10-key adding machine can be useful when checking your math. It gives you a tape of what you keyed in. You can also use a computer spreadsheet to check figures. The old pencil-and-paper method is still a good one to use.

If you've checked and can't find the difference, consider the following suggestions:

- **Ask someone else to look at the numbers.** A fresh set of eyes may be able to find the problem.
- **Call your bank and ask for help.** Because the management values you as a customer, someone will help you.

Considering outstanding checks

You can also prevent errors in your nonprofit's check register by being aware of outstanding checks — checks you've written that haven't yet cleared the bank. Your bank records only the checks that have been paid out of your account. Your bank doesn't know about the checks you've written but it hasn't received yet. These checks haven't made it to your bank, so they aren't reflected in the bank's balance of your account.

To keep outstanding checks from being a problem, make sure you keep up with your own balance and check your records against the bank's every month. It's your responsibility to manage your money and account for all expenses as accurately as possible. Overlooking outstanding checks can put you in a financial bind. Talk with your banker about overdraft protection to alleviate the fees associated with a bounced check.

WARNING

Some organizations hold on to checks for long periods of time before depositing them. If you're not keeping track of your own account, when these checks hit your account, checks could start bouncing.

Some banks have time restraints on how long a check can be held before cashing. Some are only good for 90 days, but you should find out from your bank how long it will honor payments on checks. You may want to consider printing "Void after six months" on your checks to avoid problems with old outstanding checks. Some banks cash checks without even looking at the date. Regardless of when the check is cashed, you owed someone something, and that's the reason the check was written.

When considering outstanding checks, you also need to account for the timing difference in available funds. For example, when you deposit money, it may not be available for a day or two, but when you write a check, the money could be gone within a day, if not instantly. Make sure that when you pay bills you have enough money to cover them. Make a note of when you expect the check to clear and pay close attention to see when it does clear.

IN THIS CHAPTER

» Understanding why you need a budget

» Outlining your nonprofit's goals

» Projecting and comparing revenues and expenses

» Sticking to your plan

Chapter 5
Balancing Cash Flow: Creating an Operating Budget

Your organization needs to know where it's going, whether you put it in writing or not. However, to spend money without thinking or planning indicates a lack of control and responsibility. A budget helps you manage your money and prioritize your spending, and also serves as a checkpoint to impulsive buying. It shows projected revenues and the amount set aside for planned expenses. To keep track of your money, you need a budget to keep cash flow in balance.

Basically, your budget is your organization's financial plan. Without a detailed budget, your nonprofit's risk of failure increases significantly. Not to worry, though. This chapter explains why your nonprofit needs a budget, what you need to do to create a budget, and how to create, track, manage, and evaluate your financial plan.

Understanding the Importance of Having a Budget in the Nonprofit World

For your nonprofit to survive and thrive financially, you must create and follow a budget. In fact, it really can be life or death for your organization. A *budget* is an itemized list of what income you expect to receive and what you expect to pay out during a given time period, whether a month, quarter, or year. It expresses in monetary terms what your objectives are. Knowing when you've reached your target goal is nearly impossible if you don't know what you need.

REMEMBER

Without a budget, you're on a cross-country road trip without a map. If you start out on a trip with no planned destination, who knows where you'll end up. Your nonprofit is too important to allow things to just happen to it. You need to control as much about your finances as you can. A budget can tell you

- The amount of revenue you're expecting to receive from grants, fundraisers, contributions, and investment income or gains
- An estimate of program expenses, fundraising expenses, and losses
- How much you need to cover management and general expenses

Operating on a budget is important at all times, not just when money is tight. Following your budget means you're planning for income and expenses and controlling your money. Your budget is a prediction or forecast (not the kind you get from a crystal ball) based on prior events and expected future events. Not only does a budget include projections, but also, after time expires, you have the reality of what actually happened.

You can use your budget to cut costs and run your organization more efficiently. It's smart management to look at your income and expenses to determine how you can reduce your overhead expenses. For example, if a program grant is discontinued, you need to know the impact on your organization. Without a budget, you won't know how much the loss of that revenue is going to hurt you. And without a budget you won't have a clue about any steps you need to take. For example, you may need to decrease expenses to cope with the effects of the unanticipated grant closure.

REMEMBER

Many people feel that having a budget limits their spending ability. But contrary to popular belief, a budget means you're aware of and in control of your money.

Large corporations monitor and control their spending. They're always assessing and re-assessing how they manufacture products and how they can reduce expenses to keep profits up. Although you're not in your field for the money, your organization can't be successful without money. Therefore, it's important that you have a financial plan or budget.

INNOVATIVE SHORT-TERM WAYS TO REDUCE EXPENSES

As a nonprofit, you're always looking for ways to reduce expenses, so you may want to consider some short-term approaches. For example, you may cut overtime or pay increases, freeze hiring, stop all travel, and downsize your expense accounts. You can also focus on reducing your electricity bill by setting the thermostat higher during the summer and lower during the winter. You may even have the thermostat set to come on one hour after arriving to work and to shut down automatically one hour before closing.

Getting Off to a Good Start: Preparing to Create an Operating Budget

Before you can put together your nonprofit's operating budget, you have to make the necessary preparations. If you were planning a month-long trip to Europe, you wouldn't wake up on the morning of your flight and run to the airport with only a carry-on bag and no planning. Weeks in advance you have to book your flight and hotels, pack accordingly, and have a general idea of where you're going.

Your budget is your resource allocation instrument. Creating an operating budget for your nonprofit follows the same lines. You have to prepare by determining guidelines, setting your priorities and goals, and keeping everything organized. By creating your operating budget, you'll know how much money you have, how much you plan to receive, how much you need, and what you can plan to achieve. You can use your operating budget to plan for future purchases. You can also use your budget to determine how much you need to secure in contributions to sustain your nonprofit.

Your financial statements indicate what has already happened (check out chapters 9 through 13 of this minibook for putting together your nonprofit's financial statements). You prepare these statements after the fiscal year ends. You can use your financial statements as a tool to help you predict your budget for the upcoming fiscal year. Use your financial statements to figure out why things happened and then analyze the figures to come up with your new operating budget to offset some of the occurrences that occurred (and may occur again). Creating an operating budget gives you another chance to plan and control what happens in the upcoming year.

TIP

Start your budget process by forming a team that includes your executive director, chief financial officer, and finance committee or budget task group. Make sure to have a copy of your mission statement handy. The team assigned to draft your budget will use your mission statement to come up with the guidelines, priorities, and goals needed for the budgeting process.

The following sections walk you through the different steps your organization needs to take before creating your nonprofit's budget.

Setting clear guidelines

Start your budgeting process by looking at your organization's vision and purpose, as defined in your mission statement. Your budget guidelines are centered on your mission and what it takes to accomplish your organization's goals. They guide your nonprofit in developing a budget that shows how your funding priorities support your strategic plan. Most strategic plans cover three to five years, defining steps to achieve goals with charts that direct the process. Your strategic plan should be in writing so you can look at it and see whether you're on track. (For help in establishing your strategic plan, check out Book 1, Chapter 3.)

Budget guidelines allow you to review and evaluate budget requests and submit recommendations to your board of directors. These guidelines help you make measurable progress toward your goals. All budget items should be tied to performance indicators so you can measure their outcomes.

Your guidelines define how you plan to improve the effectiveness of your current system. Some of the items included in budget guidelines are

- Guidelines for salary increases
- Budget for operations
- Line item transfers
- Guidelines for adjustments
- Annual fundraising goals and priorities

Remember that these budget guidelines are just that — guidelines — and they're not written in stone! You may have to make adjustments as your fiscal year progresses.

REMEMBER

Having clear guidelines helps you recognize the importance of budget maintenance for your organization. Your budget allows you to focus on items and issues that are relevant to your board's fiscal priorities.

Identifying your nonprofit's objectives

As you're creating your budget and setting and following your guidelines, it's important for you to establish and know the importance of your objectives. These objectives are what your organization wants to achieve — in other words, your organization's priorities. You need to identify your objectives and put them on paper so you can track your progress and see what needs your immediate attention.

With so much to do every day and so many distractions, having clear goals and objectives for your organization and for each program is important. What may be a priority for you may not be for the next person. Knowing your priorities makes day-to-day decisions easier. Planning and strategizing aren't just for the for-profit industry. As a nonprofit, you need a plan for your future. A five-year plan with set priorities is an excellent roadmap.

Commonly stated budget priorities include the following:

- Maintain financial stability of the organization.
- Maintain commitment to target population.
- Assess and ensure quality of program delivery.
- Improve and expand capital campaign.

To identify your priorities, do the following:

1. **Write down the activities that are most important and rank them in order.** Ask yourself what your organization's most important activities are.
2. **Make a list of current and future activities that you plan to achieve.** Ask yourself what the benefits of the activities are. Determine the purpose and goals, and rank your list according to the greatest benefit to the groups that will be helped.

TIP

Many organizations assign a score for priorities within each program. For example, you can assign a number to each priority on your list indicating its importance.

Setting and prioritizing goals

Without a vision, organizations perish. Your nonprofit's goals are visionary statements that motivate you and others to do something. Goals are end results that you desire to obtain, and you can't obtain them without the right budget in place. So, before you can put together your operating budget, you need to know what your organization's goals are. (Don't forget to factor in evaluating your progress toward goals, which is covered in Book 1, Chapter 4.)

REMEMBER

Defining clear goals and having a plan in place to reach them can save you from going into financial crisis mode. You're in financial crisis mode when you operate day to day with no definite plan for sustainability. To avoid operating in crisis mode, set clear, concise goals for your organization as a whole, as well as for each of your programs.

To obtain your goals, you must have objectives that are tied to the goals. Activity makes goals happen. But if you do nothing but think about it and take no action, nothing is going to happen.

Ideally, your goal statement starts broadly by first identifying the overall goals for the organization and then indicating on a program-by-program basis what the major actions should be for the upcoming budget year. Start with goals for the entire organization and then look at goals for each program.

Organizational goals

Your nonprofit's goals are the big picture of success for your organization. They may include growth in personnel, effectiveness in the sphere of influence, the ability to partner with other organizations, and so on.

TIP

You, as the director of your nonprofit, and your board need to set your organization's goals. To do so, take the following steps:

1. **Decide what you want the end results to be.**
2. **Set a measurable way to indicate performance.**
3. **Assign a number by which you can gauge whether you've met your goals.**

   This number serves as a checkpoint of sorts. You need to decide and set realistic measurable performance numbers, such as 10 percent more people will be served in the upcoming year.

After you set your organization's goals, you have to prioritize them. Some people assign numbers to their goals based on priority. To prioritize, you need to rank in order the steps needed to accomplish your goals. Whatever the first step is to reach your goal can be assigned number one. Your top priority is the first step toward reaching your goals. Just work your list by moving on to step two and so on.

REMEMBER

Setting goals alone doesn't yield results. You have to do something to bring your goals to reality.

You can't accomplish your organization's goals without a clear funding plan. Your funding plan defines how much money you need to raise from all sources to operate. You need the following to organize a funding plan:

» Mission statement defining your purpose or vision
» Funding goals
» Funding objectives
» List of potential funders
» Action plan

TIP

To create a funding plan, simply write down the five preceding items on a sheet of paper or on your computer. Your funding plan contains information about where you plan to get the money (list of potential funders) to fund your programs. We suggest you do your budget first, so you can identify what your goals, objectives, and needs are, and then do your funding plan.

Individual program goals

You also need individual program goals to keep you and your staff motivated. These program goals are performance levels of what you see as the end result of a particular program. The only difference between organizational goals and program goals is that organizational goals include program goals, whereas program goals are only for one particular program. For example, if your program is a mentoring project, then your goal may be that 5 percent more children will be mentored this year than last year.

Program goals require much of the same thought process as setting organizational goals. You need to have clearly defined goals, a well-written plan in place to keep programs up and running, and innovative ideas to attract funders. You can then use these goals to help you establish a program budget.

TIP

Creating a separate budget for each program shows good fiscal management. Separate program budgets allow you to see what programs are sustaining themselves and which ones are experiencing cash shortages. Tailored budgets also help when a program needs to be cut or budget items have to be reduced. You create a budget for a program the same way you create a budget for your organization, except you may have different categories. (Check out the later section, "Coming Up with an Operating Budget," for more on how to develop your program budgets.)

TIP

After you set a goal, begin working toward achieving it right away. Every activity you do should lead to accomplishing your goal. A good way to reach your goals is to break them down into smaller steps. So if you have a fundraising goal for the year of $15,000, you may want to see how much you've raised after each quarter. When you get to each quarter, you can check to see whether you've achieved one-quarter, half, and three-quarters of what you plan to achieve. If you haven't, then you can make adjustments to the budget or look for ways to increase funding.

As you reach your goals, cross them off the list. If you reached your goal of raising $15,000 at the midway point, you can cross that goal off the list, because you've achieved it.

TIP

Your program goals don't have to stay the same year after year. As your organization changes, you have to re-evaluate your goals and priorities.

Staying organized

In order to achieve your goals for your organization and programs, you can't let important details slip through the cracks. Staying organized is key to meeting your goals and staying on budget. Planning and getting organized not only helps with your goals and budget, but also with your stress levels. Being organized allows you to find things, so it saves you money. Remember the old saying, "Time equals money, and money equals time." If you spend less time looking for things, you'll be more productive and focused on operating your organization.

Staying organized requires paying attention to details, time frames, and deadlines. It's a process that takes time, energy, and motivation. The following tips can help you stay organized.

Use a detailed calendar with time frames and deadlines

For staying organized, calendars on which you note time frames and deadlines are essential. You handle many tasks within your organization that have beginnings and endings. Knowing these dates allows you to schedule time to work on them so you don't miss important deadlines.

Your budget and work plan should be scheduled so everyone involved is on the same page. Developing a budget calendar with a time line can help your board, finance committee, budget task group, and treasurer stay on track. You can use helpful tools such as planners and address books, smartphones, and client databases to keep calendars updated.

You want to schedule the time line for creating next year's budget based on your fiscal year. Most people allow at least three months from preliminary to approval. So if your fiscal year starts in May, you'd start working on the new budget no later than February 1. Some larger tasks can be broken down into smaller tasks, and the due dates for those incremental steps should be noted and shared with everyone.

File all paperwork in a timely manner

You evaluate your budget and monitor your progress throughout the year. Therefore, you need to create a set of files to keep up with the changes so you can easily access the information. Organizing your papers helps organize your thoughts. You can purchase a file cabinet, a file box, and some hanging file folders and manila folders to sort the papers. You can label files by month. Filing the paperwork month by month saves time and reduces your stress levels. Make sure you keep up with receipts for major purchases and supplies, as well as documents related to payroll taxes.

Throw away what you don't need

As your board meets to discuss changes needed to the budget and new programs that need to be implemented, you may find yourself swimming in paperwork. It may not be a good idea to hold on to the paperwork from the first budget meeting 15 years ago. At some point, you need to clear out the old and make room for the new. Throw away anything more than five years old. De-clutter your storage files and cabinets. Consider throwing away or donating items you don't need. Manage your mail. Pick up a magazine rack and throw away magazines more than a month old.

Outline your tasks

When you outline tasks, you create a systematic way to know when to start and complete something. You can make a to-do list and prioritize which tasks need to be done and when. For example, creating a daily to-do list can help you to organize your work and time. Even if you don't finish everything on the list, at least your priorities are already organized for the next day. When you complete a task, you can cross it off your list and then manage the remaining tasks to know which ones you can realistically expect to complete.

As you set your goals, you establish an outline of tasks to ensure that you reach the goal. As you accomplish a goal, cross it off the list and start on another one.

To complete your tasks, you use a bit of time and money. If you know how much of each is needed, assign that portion so you can get an overall idea about what is needed financially to accomplish each task and ultimately reach your goals.

Your spending plan is your budget. To outline your spending plans for the coming year, you want to review the following tasks:

- Developing new programs
- Expanding existing programs

» Creating fundraising recommendations

» Securing funding for new projects through grants

» Developing a dedicated website for donations

» Developing an application to accept donations

» Enabling online donations through services such as PayPal, Venmo, or Zelle

» Locating in-kind funding to match grants

TIP

Some people like to group tasks into phases. Phase one is usually the planning phase. Phase two may be securing funding for a project. Phase three is implementation of a project.

Coming Up with an Operating Budget

After you make the necessary preparations by establishing guidelines, identifying your priorities, and setting goals, you're ready to put everything down on paper in the form of a budget. You want to look at what your expenses are and how much money it takes to cover them. Also, consider new programs that are needed and think about how you might fund them. With these points in mind, you're ready to create your organization's operating budget (see Figure 5-1).

The following sections explain the simple steps of how to put together an operating budget, including details on what to include.

REMEMBER

You may wonder how your operating budget differs from the financial statements you're required to prepare. Your budget shows what you expect to happen financially; it's based on predictions. Your financial statements show how much you collected and how much you spent; they're based on the reality of what happened.

Walking through the steps to the budget

Creating a budget isn't complicated. Start with a blank piece of paper in hand and follow the steps in this section.

Step 1: Prioritize and determine the need

Look at last year's budget and compare it to every new item to be added to this year's budget. Ask yourself the following questions:

20XX Operating Budget

	Year to Date			
	Actual	Budget	Variance	
Income:				
Private Donations	50,000	45,000	5,000	F
Public Donations	75,000	71,000	4,000	F
Special Events	6,000	7,000	(1,000)	U
Investment income	5,000	4,500	500	F
Total income	$136,000	$127,500	8,500	F
Expenses:				
Management and General	23,500	22,300	1,200	U
Travel	2,000	3,500	(1,500)	F
Supplies	6,000	5,300	700	U
Rent	12,000	12,000	-	
Fundraising	13,000	9,500	3,500	U
Telephone	600	700	(100)	F
Salaries	67,500	67,500	-	
Payroll Taxes	5,200	5,200	-	
Total Expenses	129,800	126,000	3,800	U
Excess of income over expenses	6,200	1,500	4,700	F

U = Unfavorable
F = Favorable

FIGURE 5-1: A sample operating budget.

- Is there a need for this activity?
- How important is it that we do it?
- Are there ways we can reduce the cost of running a program?
- How much does it really cost us?

This process is time consuming and one of the reasons many organizations don't create a budget. However, by not taking this step, you miss things that need attention, like how you fund your activities and whether there's a way to provide more services for the same or less amount of money. You then refer to the results of these questions as you start talking numbers.

Step 2: Make a list of everything coming in and going out

Write down your actual revenue amounts and their sources — the grants and donations you already have — followed by your actual expenses and their amounts. Refer to Figure 5-1 for an example.

You have two types of expenses to consider:

- **Variable expenses:** These are amounts you pay that change from month to month. An example is the cost of utilities.
- **Fixed expenses:** The cost of these expenses is the same from month to month. A rent payment is generally considered a fixed expense.

TIP

To make more expenses fixed, such as utilities, see if the provider offers a budget plan (also called an estimated payment plan). The budget plan takes an average of a year's worth of utility costs and charges you the average amount each month. It stops fluctuations in bills. Going on a budget plan can help you stay in balance with your expense projections.

If you're not sure how much to budget for, take a look at your budget and receipts from last month, last quarter, and last year. Use these documents to make realistic predictions about what will happen next month, next quarter, and next year.

Step 3: Separate actual income versus projected income

Your budget is an estimate of your expected cash flow. Based on prior periods, you can gauge what will happen in the future. When creating a budget, you focus on these two items:

- **Actual amounts:** Your actual amount is what you have already received or a fixed amount. (Fixed amounts are those things that are preset and not subject to change, such as money you already have on reserve, and existing grants and contracts.)
- **Projected amounts:** Your projected amount is what you expect to receive, such as a large donation. Your projected income includes your actual income plus your expected income.

One of three things is going to happen: You'll get what you expect (project), or you'll get more or less. Yet, forecasting your expectations is crucial to your organization's budgetary process.

So when separating actual and projected income, do the following:

1. **Take realistic projections.** Begin with amounts you feel somewhat sure about, like grants and contracts you've received in the last year. Make sure these amounts are realistic projections, not merely a wish list, because what you plan to purchase and how you plan to pay your employees are contingent on you being realistic.

2. **After the time period expires, list what actually happened.** You can do so at the end of the month, quarter, or year. Just make sure you compare what you projected with what you received. Keep a close eye on your budget as time passes, so you can be prepared to adjust it as needed. You want to know how well you've planned things to help you plan better the next time.
3. **Evaluate the difference between what you projected and what actually took place.** Subtract what happened from what you expected to happen and look at the results. Sometimes you may get more than you expect, which is good. Other times you may have less. So plan an alternative way to raise the money, which may be another fundraiser or loan. It's a decision that you and your board need to discuss.

Step 4: Compare income to expenses and make adjustments as necessary

After you know what your expenses are likely to be and how much money you expect to bring in, you can figure out your projected bottom line for the period. In other words, you can subtract your projected expenses from your projected revenues and see whether you'll have a net increase or decrease in assets (refer to Figure 5-1).

If your budget shows a positive number, you've got a net increase in assets, meaning you have some money left over. You can increase your spending in one of the expense categories, or you can plan to save the additional revenue in case something unexpected happens — the economy takes a nosedive, you have to replace the heating and cooling system, you lose grant funding, or some other unfortunate event takes place.

If your budget shows a negative number, you have a net decrease in assets, meaning your expenses are larger than your revenues. You can handle this a couple of ways:

- Look at your expenses and see where you can cut some costs.
- Look at your revenues and determine how to increase the amount of funding you're bringing in.

Getting your budget approved

Your organization's finance committee should have a budget time line for preparing, reviewing, and getting board approval of your budget in an organized and timely fashion. Most nonprofits have a calendar with a time line of budget meetings that covers a two- to eight-week period. As things happen or change, you can make adjustments to your budget. Your annual budget may require your board's approval, but you can evaluate your budget as new grant programs are funded, as old grant programs expire, and any other time something happens in your organization that directly affects your revenues and expenses.

If you're the executive director, you and the finance committee discuss and assess the organization's priorities and present the budget to your board of directors. Your board of directors reviews and evaluates your operating budget to assess how it aligns with your budget priorities, mission, and strategic plan. Your board of directors adopts your annual budget through recommendations and an approval process.

Now, your board and executive staff can compare the expected amounts to the actual results. Seldom do things go as planned, but nevertheless you must plan. Your board and management staff carefully evaluate the gap between actual and budget performance and use it as a tool for future endeavors.

IN THIS CHAPTER

» Understanding the importance of compliance

» Obeying federal and state guidelines

» Conforming to the FASB, GAAP, and SOX

Chapter 6

Staying in Nonprofit Compliance

Knowing the rules of engagement for your nonprofit is similar to following the laws to drive your car. If you understand and obey traffic laws, register your vehicle, and renew your driver's license, you keep your driving privileges. The same is true for operating your nonprofit. As long as you comply with federal and state laws, you keep your nonprofit status. You need to know exactly what the IRS expects of you and what your state officials require of you. The core requirements of maintaining nonprofit status come from the IRS. Then you have to comply with the state statutes regarding your nonprofit's operation.

A preponderance of nonprofits keep their books under the accrual method of accounting, preparing their financial statements using generally accepted accounting principles (GAAP), which are accounting standards set by the Financial Accounting Standards Board (FASB). Tax return preparation follows the Internal Revenue Code (IRC), which varies from GAAP.

If you don't keep up with accounting standards and rules, complying with federal and state laws can cause you some grief. However, if you have a firm grasp of federal and state laws and the accounting standards, you can sort through the red tape and know what you need to do to stay in compliance. This chapter helps you determine how to comply with federal and state laws and accounting rules to keep your nonprofit in good standing.

Understanding Why Being Compliant Is Important for Your Nonprofit

The IRS has the authority to give and take away your nonprofit status. So, the bottom line is you want to keep the IRS happy and also stay in compliance with the appropriate federal and state laws and accounting rules. You need to stay in compliance for two main reasons:

- **To keep your nonprofit status active:** Failure to comply with federal laws can cause you to lose your federal tax-free status. Because you're managing other people's money and you've been given a tax waiver from the IRS, you should follow the rules to keep your status active.
- **To keep your reputation of being a good steward:** Following the do's and don'ts keeps everything in good standing.

As long as you continue to provide the services you promised, stay within the purpose of organizing your nonprofit, and submit paperwork to the government in a timely fashion, you'll be okay. This chapter delves into these rules and explains in further detail what you should and shouldn't do.

In addition to federal rules, you need to comply with your state laws. These laws vary from state to state. Check out the later section, "Register with the proper state authority," for more about what your state requires of you.

Staying in Compliance: The How-To

Knowing the federal and state laws governing your nonprofit isn't enough to stay in compliance. You and your staff have to take the necessary steps to make sure nothing slips between the cracks. Although keeping track and staying within those specifications can be stressful at times, your organization's nonprofit status depends on it. It may not be a fun job, but someone has to do it! The following sections address the four main components your nonprofit must adhere to in order to stay in good standing. Keep reading for specific hands-on advice you can follow so your agency doesn't lose its nonprofit status.

Register with the proper state authority

The first step to ensure that your nonprofit stays compliant is to register it with the appropriate state authority. Each state has its own guidelines about how you should register, manage, and maintain nonprofit organizations. Some states require nonprofits to register with the secretary of state's office, state department of revenue, and/or state attorney general's office. Some states offer benefits similar to the IRS by granting a sales tax exemption. To find your state laws, visit `501c3.org/state-nonprofit-guide`, or call your state attorney general's office or secretary of state to get more information about your state's requirements.

Account for nonprofit activities

If your nonprofit requires an independent auditor's report, compliance generally means you need to present your nonprofit's financial activities in accordance with the standards established by the Financial Accounting Standards Board (FASB). As of July 1, 2009, the FASB Accounting Standards Codification (ASC) became the single source of non-governmental authoritative generally accepted accounting principles (GAAP) in the United States. Introduced in Chapter 1 of this minibook, GAAP offer guidance and a list of rules about how to account for nonprofit activities.

TIP

At present, GAAP is the same for public, nonpublic, and nonprofit organizations.

You may be wondering if the Securities and Exchange Commission (SEC) has nonprofit rules you must follow. The SEC has the statutory authority to set accounting standards for publicly held companies, but historically has relied on private-sector bodies to set those standards.

TECHNICAL STUFF

A *publicly held company's* shares are freely traded on a public stock exchange. Although it may seem counterintuitive that a nonprofit could trade its net assets, accounting standards for public entities apply to a nonprofit if the nonprofit qualifies as a public entity. This is an advanced financial accounting topic that probably will not apply to smaller or new nonprofits. However, it's a great topic to add to your questions for your accountant or CPA.

Because presenting this how-to information is quite involved, more detail is included in the later section, "Following Accounting Standards."

Hire professional help

At the end of your accounting year, it may be necessary to have an independent audit of your financial statements to stay compliant with grant and other contributor requirements. As a result, you need to hire an independent certified public accountant (CPA) to perform this audit. The CPA has an involved set of procedures set by generally accepted auditing standards (GAAS) for evaluating your financial records to verify whether they comply with GAAP and properly reflect your activities. At the end of the audit, the CPA will issue an opinion as to whether your financial statements are materially correct.

REMEMBER

You can hire a bookkeeper, accountant, or internal auditor for day-to-day bookkeeping, accounting, and internal controls, but only an external CPA or CPA firm can perform an independent audit of your financial statements. You can keep a CPA on retainer, so you stay abreast of new rules governing your nonprofit. See the later section, "Selecting an audit committee to hire an independent CPA," for more about choosing an independent CPA. Also, check out Chapter 1 of this minibook for more specific information you can follow when hiring professional help.

Abide by IRS statutes

Another important process to follow to ensure that your nonprofit stays in compliance is to adhere to IRS statutes. To do so, you need to file an annual report to the IRS about your nonprofit's activities. Individuals and for-profit corporations pay federal income taxes by filing an annual income tax return, but nonprofits file an informational, generally tax-free form. Nonprofits file one of the forms in the IRS 990 series, Return of Organization Exempt From Income Tax. (Chapter 8 of this minibook has step-by-step instructions for filing Form 990.)

WARNING

The IRS requires financial information about all organizations given tax-exempt status to make sure the nonprofit is in compliance with its mission statement and doesn't have excessive unrelated business taxable income. If you file your annual return late, you may have to pay a penalty. And, if you forget to file your annual return for three years in a row, you can lose your nonprofit status. To reinstate your tax-exempt status with the IRS, you'll have to file the necessary paperwork and pay a fee. So make sure you don't make that mistake. For more information, go to `irs.gov/charities-and-nonprofits`.

Following Accounting Standards

Your nonprofit must have relevant, reliable, and meaningful financial data to ensure that accounting books and records are materially correct. External financial reports issued by your nonprofit should be prepared following guidance from the Financial Accounting Standards Board (FASB), generally accepted accounting principles (GAAP), and, depending on the circumstances, the Sarbanes-Oxley Act (SOX) as well. Did someone spill a can of alphabet soup?

So what do all these letters mean? The FASB is the authoritative body of accounting and reporting standards. GAAP provides the specific rules dictating how financial accountants must organize the information on the financial statements. If these standards weren't enough, the Sarbanes–Oxley Act of 2002 was enacted as federal law mandating certain practices in financial record keeping and reporting that apply to all U.S. publicly traded companies, their boards, management, and public accounting firms.

The rest of this chapter takes a closer look at these three sets of regulations and what you need to do to ensure that your nonprofit is in compliance with them.

The fascinating FASB

The FASB sets financial accounting and reporting standards for your nonprofit via the adoption of the FASB Accounting Standards Codification (ASC) in 2009. However, keep in mind the ASC didn't change GAAP by rewriting all the accounting rules and reporting standards. Instead, the ASC organizes GAAP in a more user-friendly fashion and placed a consistent format across the board for all GAAP topics. This section focuses on ASC sections that are common to all nonprofits, large and small.

TIP

The FASB allows free, limited access to the ASC. To check it out, go to `https://asc.fasb.org/Login`. Click on "Access the Basic View." Accept the terms and conditions to be taken to the codification basic view page. If you access the left-hand menu bar, you can select "Industry" and go to section 958 for Nonprofits.

ASC 958-205-05, Not-for-Profit Entities: Presentation of Financial Statements

This ASC addresses the following financial statements required to be prepared by all nonprofits (see chapters 9–12 of this minibook).

- **Statement of financial position:** This statement sums up your organization's overall financial picture.
- **Statement of activities:** This document shows how your nonprofit's net assets have increased or decreased.
- **Statement of cash flows:** This form shows how your nonprofit's cash position has changed.
- **Statement of functional expense:** This statement is required for all nonprofits. Your statement of functional expense reports expenses by their function and nature. Your statement of functional expense can be its own financial statement, or you can include the information on your statement of activities or in the notes to the financial statements.

ASC 958-205-55, Not-for-Profit Entities: Implementation Guidance and Illustration

This ASC provides handy examples for how the statement of financial position, statement of activities, and statement of cash flows should be prepared. It also provides examples of notes to the financial statements and addresses the two groups of net assets: net assets without donor restrictions, which are not subject to donor restrictions; and net assets with donor restrictions, which are subject to donor restrictions.

TIP

If the nonprofit board votes to restrict an asset, that asset is also classified as net assets subject to donor restrictions.

ASC 958-605-25-5A, Not-for-Profit Entities: Revenue Recognition – Contributions

This ASC provides guidance for classifying assets as either with or without donor restrictions. For the nonprofit to deem an asset as having donor-imposed restrictions, both of the following conditions must be satisfied:

1. **The donor-imposed condition must have one or more barriers to overcome before the recipient is entitled to the asset transferred or promised.**
2. **There must exist a right of return to the contributor or a right of release of the promisor from its obligation to contribute the asset.**

ASC 958-360-35, Not-for-Profit Entities: Depreciation

This ASC requires all nonprofits to recognize depreciation in the financial statements and to disclose the depreciation expense, the balances of major classes of depreciable assets, the accumulated depreciation at balance sheet date, and a description of the depreciation method used.

The world according to GAAP

The generally accepted accounting principles (GAAP) lay the ground rules for accounting and reporting standards. All financial accountants use GAAP when accounting for, preparing, and presenting financial information. Think of GAAP as a uniform way to examine and record financial activities.

The principles allow you to fairly evaluate and compare numbers. These guidelines create a level playing field, so all nonprofits play by the same rules. That means the way you present your financial position is the same way another similar nonprofit using GAAP evaluates its position.

REMEMBER

Most GAAP-based financial statements are presented using the accrual basis of accounting, which deals with the recognition of transactions. For example, all transactions are recorded on the books when they occur, no matter when cash actually exchanges hands. (See Chapter 1 of this minibook for more information about the accrual basis of accounting.)

To ensure that you stay in compliance and protect your nonprofit's status, make sure you adhere to the GAAP principles covered in the following sections.

Cost principle

The *cost principle* requires assets to be recorded in the books at their cost. This is the price paid in exchange for the asset. This cost is commonly referred to as the historical cost because it doesn't change. It doesn't matter if the asset's current value goes up (appreciates) or goes down (depreciates); the value recorded on the statement of financial position remains the same, according to the cost principle.

Business entity concern

The *business entity concern* deals with the separate legal entity concept, which means that if you incorporate, your nonprofit is a separate legal entity from you and/or the owners. The biggest advantage to incorporating is to protect your board and staff from personal legal liabilities, such as lawsuits. If the nonprofit is separate from you, then it, not you, is generally responsible for its debts and any charges of misconduct.

WARNING

Of course, being a separate business entity doesn't mean that you can't be sued. Anyone can file a lawsuit, so the ultimate protection is to acquire board of directors, management, and officers' insurance.

Objective principle

The *objective principle* states that you determine and verify the value of all donated items as objectively as possible. All donated items go on your financial statements as assets either with or without donor restrictions. To fairly represent your true financial condition, you have to give them an objective value.

TIP

When valuing assets donated to your organization, you should seek an objective opinion or outside help to evaluate their value. Asking a qualified unrelated third party who has no interest in the outcome gives an objective view. To determine a donated asset's value, check the following sources:

- Sticker price or purchase invoice
- Sales invoice
- Property deeds
- Transfer of title
- Kelley Blue Book value
- Banker or creditor

WARNING

Don't value the donated assets you receive by simply asking the donor and reporting the amount they say. You still need to verify the item's worth by asking an independent third party who has no financial interest in the outcome to give you a value.

Matching principle

The *matching principle* requires donations and revenues received and expenses incurred to be recorded in the same period you receive or incur them. In other words, you should recognize expenses in the period you incur the expense. For example, if you pay your employees in January for work done in December, when you complete your financial statements, you should record the liability in December.

You should match contributions received with expenses incurred in the same time period on the statement of activities. If someone makes a $50 donation to pay a volunteer, you should match that donation with the volunteer expense in the same time period, unless there are restrictions.

Revenue-recognition principle

The *revenue-recognition principle* requires that when you receive donations, you must recognize them as revenue when they become unconditional. For more information about restricted and conditional contributions, see Chapter 10 of this minibook.

Conditional contributions and restricted contributions are often confused because restrictions can be conditions. But not all conditions are restrictions. Let's say a donor offers you a potential gift of $10,000, but they won't give it to you unless your organization can raise X dollars or meet some criteria. If you meet the condition, you get the money with no strings attached; it's recognized as an unrestricted contribution. However, the donor may say you can have $10,000 for your capital campaign to be spent to purchase a building if you raise *X* dollars. If you raise the money, the gift becomes unconditional, but it's restricted to being spent only to purchase a building, and so recorded as a restricted contribution. When spent on bricks and mortar, the restriction is met, and it becomes unrestricted.

Expense-recognition principle

The *expense-recognition principle* deals with the timing of when expenses are recognized. Expenses are reported as decreases to unrestricted net assets on the statement of activities. A classic example of recognizing expenses occurs at the end of the year when employees have worked, but won't get paid until January. You need to account for this expense in the period you incur the expense. A lot of places pay you only after you've worked, and you may have a couple of weeks in the hole. When the paychecks are cut in January, they are for work completed in December. You should account for this on your statement of financial position and statement of activities ending December 31.

Full-disclosure principle

The *full-disclosure principle* states that changes made to accounting methods, inventory valuation, and pending lawsuits must be disclosed in the notes to the financial statements. Follow the FASB guidance for required disclosures, keeping in mind that any event out of the ordinary or material to your financial condition should be noted or disclosed in the financial statements. Materiality is another great topic to add to your list of questions for your accountant or CPA.

Comparability principle

The *comparability principle* means the financial information is prepared in such a way that it can be weighed against similar nonprofits or past financial statements for the same nonprofit.

Consistency principle

The *consistency principle* dictates that the same accounting events are handled in a similar fashion. Changing it up midstream causes old financial statements to be skewed when comparing them to current statements.

Sorting out the Sarbanes-Oxley Act (SOX)

In response to public outcry after Enron, Global Crossing, and WorldCom, Inc. (and the subsequent billions of dollars of investor losses), Maryland Senator Paul

Sarbanes and Ohio Representative Michael Oxley worked together on protective measures to stop the fraudulent practices of accounting firms and their clients across the nation. These protective measures resulted in the *Sarbanes-Oxley Act of 2002*, commonly referred to as *SOX*.

SOX isn't exactly light reading, and it only applies to publicly traded companies — those registered with the SEC. However, many nonprofits have adopted provisions of SOX that help improve the management and financial reporting of their organization. In light of the 2002 United Way of the National Capital Area scandal — where a former CEO defrauded the nonprofit to the tune of $497,000 — nonprofits are striving to become more transparent and accountable to their constituents.

Following are two SOX sections your nonprofit may be interested in adopting.

Selecting an audit committee to hire an independent CPA

SOX Section 301 – Public Company Audit Committees mandates audit committees be directly responsible for the oversight of the engagement of the company's independent auditor, and ensure that auditors are independent of their audit clients. An *audit committee* is responsible for board financial and accounting oversight. The committee, which consists of at least three independent members of your board, with at least one being a financial expert, oversees the work of both the internal and external auditors. Individual board members aren't part of the organization's management team or paid management consultants; their only compensation is for being a board member.

REMEMBER

The terms "independent auditor" and "independent CPA" are interchangeable.

Internal auditors, who are employees of the nonprofit, are tasked with setting up strategic processes to ensure that the objectives of the board are fulfilled by the nonprofit. *External auditors* are independent CPAs required to report to the audit committee prior to and during the audit of the financial statements.

External auditors must be independent in fact and appearance, have adequate training and experience, and exercise due diligence during all phases of the audit. *Due diligence* means the external auditor plans and adequately supervises any professional activities for which the external auditor is responsible.

The *general standards on auditor independence* outline what your audit committee should consider when choosing whether to enter into a relationship with or service provided by an auditor. You should make sure the external auditor is independent, objective, doesn't perform certain non-auditing services, and is prohibited from forming certain relationships with your nonprofit.

Being *independent* means the external auditor has no special relationship with or financial interest in your nonprofit that would cause them to disregard evidence and facts. *Objectivity* means the external auditor is impartial, honest, and avoids any conflicts of interest with your nonprofit.

The external auditor is prohibited from providing the following non-audit services to an audit client, including its affiliates:

- Bookkeeping
- Designing and implementing financial information systems
- Appraisal or valuation services, fairness opinions, or contribution-in-kind reports
- Actuarial services
- Internal audit outsourcing services
- Management functions of human resources
- Broker-dealer, investment advisor, or investment banking services
- Legal services and expert services unrelated to the audit

REMEMBER

The purpose for all of these guidelines is to make sure your financial statements fairly represent your financial position. To avoid a biased opinion, it's important that your auditor is totally independent and has no other deals with you that may possibly sway his professional opinion of your organization.

Prohibited relationships are also an important point to remember under SOX. They're relationships between you and/or your nonprofit and the firm, CPA, or auditor who will offer an opinion about your financial statements.

The following are general rules about prohibited relationships deemed to affect independence and should be addressed by the CPA in their engagement letter. An *engagement letter* solidifies the audit arrangement by detailing the duties and obligations for both the nonprofit client and the CPA. In addition, every state in which the CPA is licensed will have numerous and perhaps unique ethical and code of conduct rules by which the CPA must abide.

- **Employment relationships:** Usually a one-year cooling-off period is required before you can hire certain individuals who were formerly employed by your auditor in a financial reporting oversight role. The audit committee should consider whether hiring someone who is or was employed by the audit firm will affect the audit firm's independence.

- **Contingent fees:** Audit committees must not approve engagements that pay an independent auditor based on the outcome of the audit results. In other words, your external auditor gives a professional opinion based on your records and reports, not on how much or how you pay them. The fee for the audit is always included in the engagement letter.
- **Direct or material indirect business relationships:** Auditors and their firms can't form direct or material indirect relationships with the nonprofit, its officers, directors, or major donors. *Direct business relationships* refer to relationships where something tangible or of value (such as an investment) is involved between you and the auditor. For example, a relationship where the auditor has an investment in your organization would not be good. *Material indirect business relationships* are relationships where you may have some other business dealings with a family member or affiliate of the CPA firm or auditor, whereby ownership is more than 5 percent.
- **Certain financial relationships:** Your audit committee should be aware that certain financial relationships between your nonprofit and the independent auditor are prohibited. These include creditor/debtor relationships, banking, broker-dealer, insurance products, and interests in investment companies.

REMEMBER

To avoid any potential problems, set up an audit committee, be cautious when selecting an auditing firm, and disclose all accounting policies and practices to your audit committee. Above all, make sure your auditor is independent. While the auditor has an exhaustive checklist they run through before accepting a nonprofit as a client, the onus is on the nonprofit to honestly answer questions while the CPA firm is researching your fitness to be taken on as a new client.

Requiring a signed financial statement

SOX Section 302 – Corporate Responsibility for Financial Reports shifts the responsibility for the financial statements to the chief executive officer (CEO) and chief financial officer (CFO). It requires that they review all financial reports. They must report any deficiencies in internal control, report fraud committed by the management of the audit committee, and indicate any material changes. This means the CEO and CFO certify that the financial report does not contain any misrepresentations and the information in the financial report is fairly presented. Although signing off on a nonprofit's financial statements isn't legally required, doing so indicates management takes responsibility for the statements.

TIP

For more information about SOX that is updated through 2022, go to `sarbanes-oxley-101.com`.

IN THIS CHAPTER

» Creating payroll accounts for employees

» Calculating federal, state, and local taxes

» Paying quarterly payroll taxes

» Submitting IRS payroll requirements

» Reporting info about contract employees

Chapter 7

Accounting for Payroll and Payroll Taxes

You're the executive director or manager at a small- to medium-sized nonprofit, so you may assume that because of your organization's nonprofit status, you don't have to pay any taxes. After all, your status does mean your organization generally owes no corporate income taxes. However, you're still responsible for paying federal payroll taxes for your employees.

The good news is that you can account for payroll and payroll taxes for nonprofit employees similarly to how for-profit organizations do so. As an employer, you're required to withhold and/or pay state and federal payroll taxes on behalf of your employees.

You can easily set up your organization's payroll accounting yourself. Or if you prefer, you can hire part-time help or buy prepackaged software for nonprofits. Regardless of the method you choose, you're responsible for accounting for payroll, taking out the right amount of taxes, and submitting taxes with the required paperwork on time.

Not to worry, though. This chapter shows you how to account for your payroll taxes and all other deductions for the federal, state, and local governments. After reading this chapter, you'll know how to file the necessary paperwork, where to send forms, and when to file forms so you stay current with your paperwork — not to mention keep your nonprofit status.

REMEMBER

As an employer, you need to concern yourself with establishing and paying a fair rate of pay and submitting payroll tax payments on time. Some issues, such as minimum wage, have already been decided for you.

TIP

Go to `https://www.irs.gov/forms-instructions` to access all of the forms mentioned in this chapter. You'll also find instructions for using those forms and other helpful information.

Setting Up Payroll Accounts for Nonprofit Employees

Before you can pay federal and state payroll taxes for your employees, you need to make sure you have the proper records and documentation. To do so, establish payroll accounts for your employees by creating a file for each employee. These files can be either electronic or hard copies, depending on your preference. If you use computer software to set up your payroll, your computer walks you through this process. Only your personnel clerk, bookkeeper, accountant, supervisor, and executive director should have access to payroll files. You should keep these files under lock and key because of the private information they contain.

Federal law requires all employers to keep records of total wages and hours worked by employees, but it doesn't specify how to keep these records. A great place to keep track of hours and wages is in your employee personnel files, which you can create on an employee's first day. Set up a file for each employee with the following information:

- Employee's name, Social Security number, home address, job title, gender, and birth date
- Workweek hours and dates
- Total hours worked each workday
- Total daily or weekly regular time earnings
- Regular hourly pay rate

- Total overtime pay for the workweek
- Deductions from wages
- Additions to wages
- Pay date and pay period

Make sure you include Form W-4, Employee's Withholding Allowance Certificate, in the paperwork you give your new employees to fill out on their first day of work. Form W-4 indicates filing status, exemptions, and any extra taxes to be taken out of an employee's salary. The purpose of Form W-4 is to tell you how much federal income tax to withhold from your employee's paycheck.

Federal law requires that every U.S. employer complete Form I-9, Employment Eligibility Verification. This form helps you verify your employee's identity and employment authorization. For more information about your I-9 filing requirements, forms, and instructions, visit `https://www.uscis.gov/i-9-central`.

TIP

Retaining employee timesheets can help you justify why you paid what to whom to assure both the government and your employees that you're adhering to federal employer-employee guidelines. The Department of Labor oversees these federal guidelines concerning employer and employee relationships. The Department of Labor enforces laws established by the Fair Labor Standards Act, which ensures that employees receive fair wages and overtime pay. The act also requires employers to allocate and pay payroll deductions in a timely manner.

Deducting the Right Amount of Taxes

Before you start calculating how much to deduct from your employees' paychecks for payroll taxes, you need to know how much to deduct for federal and state income taxes. Don't worry. You don't have to be a math whiz to do so. The IRS and state governments offer you tax tables to tell you how much to deduct for federal and state taxes.

You calculate the amount of federal income tax to withhold from each employee based on a federal income tax table, which considers the information your employees put on the Form W-4 they fill out on their first day of work. This information includes how many dependents they want to claim, what their filing status is (single, married, and so on), and if they want extra money taken out of their paychecks.

REMEMBER

Don't forget to get the current tax tables for the year in which you're filing. The laws change constantly, so the tables that you used last year aren't valid this year. To find out where you can get copies of these tax tables and all other tax forms, go to `https://www.irs.gov/pub/irs-access/p2053a.pdf`. Contact your state department of revenue for state information.

When figuring out how much to pay in federal payroll taxes for each employee, salary is an important factor to consider. However, it's not the only one. This section highlights the areas you need to consider when determining how much to pay in federal payroll taxes.

Salaries and wages

Before you determine how much to pay in federal payroll taxes for your employees, you need to know the IRS's two main classifications of employees. These classifications significantly impact when and how much you pay in taxes. The two types of employees are

- **Exempt:** These employees are paid a set salary and don't qualify for overtime pay.
- **Nonexempt:** These employees are paid an hourly rate and do qualify for overtime pay.

REMEMBER

According to federal law, nonexempt workers are entitled to a minimum wage of at least $7.25 per hour. Many states also have minimum wage laws. If an employee is subject to both the state and federal minimum wage laws, the employee is entitled to the higher of the two minimum wages.

Overtime and cash advances

When calculating how much tax to deduct from your employees' paychecks, you need to consider two important areas other than salary: overtime and cash advances. *Overtime* is the amount of time an employee works beyond normal working hours. According to federal law, employers must pay workers overtime pay at a rate of at least one and a half times their regular pay rate when the workers work more than 40 hours in a given workweek.

For example, if an employee works 48 hours in a workweek and is paid $15.00 per hour, the employee is entitled to $22.50 per hour for each hour of overtime ($15.00 × 1.5). The employee's regular pay for 40 hours is $600. For 8 hours of overtime, the pay rate is $22.50 × 8, which equals $180. This employee is entitled to $600 plus $180 for a total of $780.

AN AUTOMATIC WAY TO GIVE AND RECEIVE

Some donors give organizations contributions via authorized payroll deductions, which are deductions right from their paychecks. They're like money in your bank account because you receive the money in a systematic way around the same time after each pay period. Donors choose which paychecks you receive donations from. For example, some donors allow you to take deductions out of their second checks if they're paid twice a month.

Larger nonprofits have been using authorized payroll deductions for years. For example, United Way takes authorized payroll deductions right out of its donors' payroll checks. Doing so works well for both the people giving and the organization receiving because it spreads the donations out over longer periods of time for the donors, and gives the recipient — United Way, in this example — a solid projection of expected revenues.

You figure out how much you need to withhold in federal payroll taxes by multiplying the salary amount by the federal payroll tax rates, which are established by law. You can find payroll tax rules, rates, withholding tables, and reporting instructions in IRS Publication 15, Employer's Tax Guide, also known as Circular E. You can find Publication 15 and other IRS publications at `www.irs.gov/publications/p15`.

TIP

For questions about overtime pay, call the Wage and Hour Division of the Department of Labor at 866-4-US-WAGE (866-487-9243).

Your nonprofit may periodically allow an employee's request for a cash advance. *Cash advances* are loans that the employer gives to an employee that will be repaid from the employee's future pay. Giving cash advances to your nonprofit employees is a subject for board discussion and approval.

If you do decide to give cash advances, don't confuse advances and wages. Advances aren't taxed; they're loans. The employee's wages are taxed. The employer withholds the amount advanced to an employee from the employee's gross pay as repayment of the advance. Before you decide to give cash advances, be sure to check with your board of directors and CPA.

FRINGE BENEFITS AND THE IRS

The IRS doesn't concern itself with regulating what fringe benefits employers provide to employees. You are generally not obligated to provide fringe benefits to your employees under federal law. However, check with your CPA, because you may need to familiarize yourself with state laws that do affect these benefits.

Common fringe benefits include the following:

- Paid sick and vacation leave
- Holiday pay
- Providing on-site day-care services
- Health insurance
- Company cars and employee personal use of a company car
- Retirement plans
- Immediate payment of final wages to terminated employees rather than waiting for the normal payroll cycle

The IRS's only concern is that you properly remit any taxes due on the fringe benefits. For example, employee personal use of a company car is usually added to the employee's gross wages and subject to payroll tax. Paid sick, vacation, and holiday pay are included in the employee's gross wages in the applicable payroll cycle, and subject to tax the same as regular wages. This is a good topic to discuss with your CPA when setting up your nonprofit.

Calculating Specific FICA Payroll Taxes and Deductions

Before you start calculating payroll taxes and posting them in the books, you need to know the details about each employee's withholding allowances or exemptions. After you've pulled this information from each employee's Form W-4, you need to compute each employee's gross pay for the pay period. After doing so, you're ready to calculate payroll taxes and deductions.

The Federal Insurance Contributions Act (FICA) is a federal payroll tax that both employees and employers have to pay. The funds collected from FICA are used to fund Social Security and Medicare retirement benefits and to provide for disabled workers and children of deceased workers.

The FICA rate was 15.30 percent for many years, but in recent years it did fluctuate. As of this writing, it is back to 15.30 percent. This is important information you should check at the beginning of each year in the Circular E. Of that 15.30 percent, you withhold 7.65 percent of employee's gross wage (subject to threshold limits) for FICA. As the employer you must match this by paying the same 7.65 percent.

Now what about that threshold limit we mention above? To understand the threshold limit, you also have to understand how the 15.30 percent is allocated. Of the 15.30 percent, 12.4 percent (6.2 percent each for the employee and employer) funds Social Security, with the remaining 2.9 percent (1.45 percent each for the employee and employer) funding Medicare.

As of this writing, the Social Security threshold is $160,200. That means that when your employee is paid over $160,200 in the calendar year, you no longer deduct or match the 6.20 percent. Medicare has no threshold. Both you and the employee are responsible for the 1.45 percent regardless of how much the employee makes.

Running through a basic payroll FICA tax calculation, let's say you have an employee who grosses $500 during the pay period and their total year to date is under the $160,200 threshold. You — as the employer — have to pay $38.25 (7.65% × $500) for FICA taxes. Your employee has the same $38.25 withheld from their gross wages.

The IRS calculates FICA taxes at the same rate on regular pay, overtime pay, and bonus pay. When you have to remit payroll taxes to the IRS depends on the amount of payroll taxes your nonprofit collects; that is, how much money you are obligated to remit to the IRS in the form of payroll taxes in a given week, month, or quarter.

The current guidelines for when to remit payroll taxes to the IRS are found in section 11 of Publication 15. Smaller nonprofits normally deposit on a monthly schedule. Medium and larger nonprofits should add when to deposit payroll taxes to the list of questions they have for their accountant.

On a monthly schedule you must remit payroll taxes by the 15th of the following month. So, if your payroll tax liability on August 31 is $1,500, the $1,500 must be remitted to the IRS by September 15. See the following section, "Paying Quarterly Payroll Taxes with Form 941 and Electronic Funds Transfer," for more information about making payroll tax deposits for FICA and federal withholding tax.

CHURCHES MAY NOT HAVE TO PAY

Because they are protected by the First Amendment of the Constitution, churches and religious organizations are generally exempt from paying income taxes. However, certain income they generate may be subject to tax; for example, unrelated business taxable income (UBTI). See Chapter 8 for more on filing UBTI. For a well-organized IRS tax guide for churches and religious organizations that's written in plain language, go to www.irs.gov/pub/irs-pdf/p1828.pdf.

Members of religious groups who meet certain criteria can apply to be exempt from participating in the Social Security program. If you are employed by a group granted exemption and you make more than $100 per year, you're considered self-employed. This means you pay your own FICA tax at the 15.30 percent rate. This is done via Schedule SE, which you file with your Form 1040. If you are new to the self-employment/Schedule SE game, it is highly recommended you talk about this with a tax specialist to get the correct information about your depositing and filing requirements.

REMEMBER

Here's some good news regarding paying taxes on federal unemployment benefits under the Federal Unemployment Tax Act (FUTA). You don't pay FUTA tax if your organization holds an IRC Section 501(c)(3) exemption status under IRC Section 501. To verify your exemption, take a look at your letter of determination from the IRS to find out how the IRS classified your nonprofit status and under which code it established your nonprofit status.

Paying Quarterly Payroll Taxes with Form 941 and Electronic Funds Transfer

Quarterly payroll taxes are taxes that your nonprofit owes to the IRS for that which you have withheld from your employee's gross pay and your matching portion of FICA. As an employer, you're responsible for matching the employee's FICA which is generally 7.65 percent of gross wages (don't forget about the Social Security threshold we discuss earlier in this chapter).

The employee portion of the payroll taxes is called the *trust fund portion*. The trust fund portion is not an expense to your nonprofit. You are merely safeguarding the trust fund portion until it's time to make your payroll tax deposit.

WARNING

It's very important to make your payments to the federal government on time. The IRS takes this very seriously. There is nothing more certain to lead to hefty IRS late payment penalties than failing to timely deposit your payroll taxes.

There is a whole section later in this chapter walking you through how to make your payroll tax deposits electronically. For now, let's discuss the payroll tax form you must file quarterly.

You file Form 941, Employer's Quarterly Federal Tax Return, to report your quarterly wages and payroll taxes to the IRS. Total taxes on Form 941 should generally reconcile to your electronic tax deposits. See the later section, "Accessing the EFTPS to make tax deposits," for more information about electronic funds transfer.

Form 941 includes the following information:

- Wages you've paid
- Tips your employees received
- Federal income taxes you've withheld
- Employer's and employee's shares of Social Security and Medicare taxes
- Advance earned income tax credit (EITC) payments
- Adjustments for prior quarterly payroll taxes

WARNING

We can't stress enough how important paying these quarterly taxes is. If you fall behind, catching up can be extremely difficult. If you do fall behind on payroll taxes, talk with your tax accountant about what steps to take. You may want to go to your local bank and borrow the money. The penalties and interest on IRS outstanding debts is quite possibly higher than any credit card on the market. The following sections walk you through Form 941 and electronic funds transfer. You'll also find out how to file the forms and where to send them and your payment.

TIP

Create a file with copies of all the forms, checks, and everything else you send to the IRS. Sometimes the IRS makes mistakes. Plus, you need to keep up with what you've paid.

Completing Form 941

As an employer, you withhold federal taxes from your employees for the federal government. Form 941 is your explanation to the IRS of how much you've deducted from your employees' paychecks and held for the federal government in federal income taxes, Social Security, and Medicare taxes. According to the IRS, preparing, copying, assembling, and sending Form 941 takes just two hours of your time every three months.

TIP

To save time, you can save a copy of the online form on your computer so that each quarter you need to fill in only the information that has changed since the last quarter.

Over the years this form has morphed from a simple two-page form to the current six-page version — some of which is reserved for future use. As some of the six pages will not be applicable to your nonprofit, the following discusses the commonly filled out portions, starting with page one of six:

1. **Fill in the top portion of the form.** Fill in your EIN (employer identification number), the name of your organization, your business address, and the reporting quarter.
2. **Complete Part 1, Page 1.** Part 1 is the meat of the form. Answer the questions about how many employees you have, how much they've earned, how much federal income tax you've withheld, taxable Social Security and Medicare, and tax due. If working through this part by yourself is difficult, consider contracting out your payroll services to a bookkeeper, accountant, or payroll service.
3. **Complete Part 1, Page 2.** Page 2 determines your tax liability for the quarter, asks for the deposited amount, and calculates if there is a balance due, overpayment, or if total tax due is the same as deposits.
4. **Complete Part 2.** Line 16 spells out if you have to list your tax liability for each of the three months in the quarter. If so, using this info, the IRS determines if you made timely deposits each month and will send you a penalty/interest statement if you did not deposit on time. If you need help, you may want to hire an accountant.
5. **Complete Part 3.** Part 3 asks specific questions about your business, which you leave blank if non-applicable.
6. **Complete Part 4.** Part 4 asks whether you authorize someone else to discuss your taxes with the IRS.
7. **Complete Part 5.** Provide your signature, printed name, date, daytime phone number. If you hired an accountant to prepare the form for the nonprofit, have them supply this information as well.
8. **If you have a balance due, detach and fill out Form 941-V.** Prepare a check for the balance due. Include Form 941-V and payment when you mail Form 941.

Filing Form 941

After you complete Form 941, you need to file it with the IRS, and if you haven't made tax deposits or still have a balance due, you need to make a tax payment with the 941. Because Form 941 is only a report, you need to submit a payment voucher — Form 941-V — if you're submitting a payment with your quarterly report.

If you're a new nonprofit with no previous tax payment history, you are generally required to deposit monthly via the Electronic Federal Tax Payment System®. Monthly deposits are due by the 15th of the following month. For example, you have to deposit taxes from paydays taking place during December by January 15. After you've established a payment history, the IRS can project what your future payments are likely to be. Based on this projection, the IRS will notify the nonprofit if there is a change in depositing frequency. Larger nonprofits may have to deposit more frequently on a weekly or semiweekly schedule.

If your nonprofit owes less than $2,500 in payroll taxes, you may be able to pay the payroll taxes quarterly with a timely filed Form 941, enclosing your check and payment voucher 941-V. To make sure your nonprofit meets that criteria, read the instructions on Form 941, Page 5, and discuss any questions with your accountant.

TIP

You may be able to bypass the quarterly Form 941 and report yearly using Form 944, Employer's ANNUAL Federal Tax Return. You can do this only if the IRS notifies you in writing that it's okay to do so. Go to `www.irs.gov/newsroom/employers-should-you-file-form-944-or-941` for more information about switching from Form 941 to Form 944.

Refer to Table 7-1 to find out when your quarterly Form 941 is due.

TABLE 7-1 Due Dates for Quarterly Filing of Form 941

For the Quarter	Quarter Ends	Form 941 Due Date
January, February, March	March 31	April 30
April, May, June	June 30	July 31
July, August, September	September 30	October 31
October, November, December	December 31	January 31

WARNING

Don't wait to send a payment with Form 941 unless you're certain you qualify for the quarterly payment schedule. If you owe more than $2,500 and wait to pay it when you file your Form 941 at the end of the quarterly reporting period, you'll have made a late payment and may have to pay a penalty.

When paying your payroll taxes with Form 941, write a check or money order payable to the "United States Treasury." Where you send your payment and Form 941 depends on where you live and if you are mailing the form with or without a payment. Go to `https://www.irs.gov/filing/where-to-file-your-taxes-for-form-941` for mailing information.

Accessing the EFTPS to make tax deposits

The IRS has made paying your payroll taxes a fairly easy task through the Electronic Federal Tax Payment System® (EFTPS). The EFTPS is free, easy to sign up for, and once you get started it's a breeze to make your payroll tax deposit. Plus, you can use the EFTPS to deposit any federal taxes — not just payroll.

WARNING

It's old news but worth repeating: In the past, many businesses used the 8109 coupon to make a tax deposit at their bank. This form has been obsolete since January 2011.

To get started with the EFTPS, have your Employer Identification Number (EIN) and banking information available. Go to `www.eftps.gov` and select "Enrollment" on the menu at the top of the page. Check to see whether you have already received a pre-enrollment PIN in the mail. Then, just follow the enrollment steps on the screens. After submitting your information you receive a PIN in the mail in about a week.

After receipt of your PIN, go back into the EFTPS website, select "Log In" on the menu at the top of the page, fill in the fields, and then click "Need a Password." Follow the instructions to create your new Internet password, and you'll be all set to make your payroll tax deposit at the "Payments" menu option.

If you don't want to use the EFTPS, ask your bank if it's possible to make your deposits using ACH Credit or same-day wire payments. Another option is using the EFTPS voice response system at 800-555-3453 to make payments.

Completing End-of-Year Forms

At the end of the year, you'll need to fill out Forms W-2 and W-3. This section gives you an overview of these two forms and what you have to do with each one.

Filling out the W-2

Form W-2 is the Wage and Tax Statement for a given year. Employees usually receive three copies. The employee files one copy with the federal return (Copy B) and one copy with the state return (Copy 2). The employee keeps the third copy (Copy C) in their personal records. The W-2 Wage and Tax Statement summarizes all tax deductions for a given year.

You find the following information on a W-2 Wage and Tax Statement:

- Employer's federal identification number
- Employer's name, address, and ZIP code
- Employee's Social Security number
- Employee's name, address, and ZIP code
- Taxable wages, tips, and other compensation
- Federal income tax withheld
- Social Security wages and tips
- Social Security tax withheld
- Medicare wages and tips
- Medicare tax withheld
- Name of state of employment
- Employer's state identification number
- State wages, tips, and other compensation
- State income tax withheld

Form W-2 Wage and Tax Statement consists of the following copies:

- **Copy A:** Sent by employer to Social Security Administration.
- **Copy 1:** Sent by employer to state, city, or local tax department if required.
- **Copy B:** Filed by employee with employee's federal tax return.
- **Copy C:** Kept by employee in employee's records.
- **Copy 2:** Filed by employee with employee's state, city, or local income taxes.
- **Copy D:** Kept by employer in employer's records.

As an employer, you need to fill out a W-2 for each employee. After you've completed all of your W-2s, you need to fill out a Form W-3, too. See the next section for more about Form W-3.

Filling out the W-3

Form W-3 is the Transmittal of Wage and Tax Statements, which the employer has to submit to the Social Security Administration. The Wage and Tax Statements are your W-2s; the W-3 transmits them. Your W-3 totals and reports the amounts for all the W-2s it transmits, so both the W-3 and W-2s are filed with Social Security.

REMEMBER

Form W-3 provides a complete summary of all W-2s attached. Do not cut, fold, or staple forms in the W-3/W-2 package.

WARNING

The Social Security Administration is very picky about the physical state of Form W-3 when it arrives via the mail. Social Security only accepts the original red/white form. So if you download and try to submit the online version, you may be charged a $50 penalty if the IRS can't scan your form.

Where to send the W-2s and W-3s

After you complete these two forms, be sure to send Copy A (red/white) of all Form W-2s along with the red/white Form W-3 by regular mail to the Social Security Administration by the due date (the last day of January of the following year) to the following address:

Social Security Administration

Data Operations Center

Wilkes-Barre, PA 18769-0001

You can also file these forms electronically at the Social Security Administration's Employer W-2 Filing Instructions and Information web page at `https://www.ssa.gov/employer`. You can also create versions of W-2/W-3 at this web page that can be filed with Social Security and printed for your employees and your records.

The due dates may change from year to year by a day or two allowing for weekends and holidays. For any tax year, you have to file Copy A of Form W-2 and Form W-3 with the Social Security Administration by January 31 for the previous year. The correct due date for each year is printed on Form W-3.

REMEMBER

Be sure to distribute the W-2s to your employees. You may also have to mail forms to your state tax department.

TIP

Keeping up with your paperwork is important because the IRS matches the amounts reported on your quarterly payroll taxes (Forms 941) with the W-2 amounts totaled on Form W-3. If you do make a mistake when figuring your taxes, you can amend your forms and make corrections by using Form 941-X. For more information about making corrections on Form 941-X, go to `https://www.irs.gov/forms-pubs/about-form-941-x`.

To find out more about ordering official IRS Form W-2 and Form W-3, go to the IRS Online Ordering For Information Returns and Employer Returns at `www.irs.gov/businesses/online-ordering-for-information-returns-and-employer-returns`. If you have no questions about the process, you can go directly to ordering at `https://apps.irs.gov/app/taxmat/information-employer-returns`.

IN THIS CHAPTER

» Selecting the right form

» Avoiding unnecessary penalties

» Filing according to standards

Chapter 8

Doing the Accounting for Tax Form 990

Your nonprofit organization is tax-exempt, so you're probably wondering why we've included a chapter on filing a tax report. You may be surprised to find out that even though you generally don't have to pay federal income taxes, your organization does have to file a return. IRS Form 990, Return of Organization Exempt from Income Tax, is an annual information return that most tax-exempt organizations must file. Although this is a topic most people may prefer to ignore, failure to accurately complete this form leads to repercussions none of us want. The information a tax-exempt organization provides on this form serves as the primary source of information for the public about that particular organization. Therefore, the information you provide on this form becomes the basis for how the public and the government perceive your organization.

Which version of this form your organization needs to complete depends on your organization's gross receipts and total assets. Before getting too worried about this form, read this chapter to find out the steps you need to follow to prepare your information form for the IRS. Wouldn't it be great if you could spend all your time running the programs that benefit our communities? But there's a time for everything. And right now, it's tax time!

REMEMBER

Be prepared for that first phone call or email from a concerned citizen requesting your Form 990. Your Form 990 is considered public record and must be made available to the public upon request. You have to give your Form 990 to whoever requests it with only a minimal charge equal to the cost of copying the form. To save paper and time, you can post your Form 990 on your website. When someone requests a copy, you can simply tell that person how to locate the form on your website.

TIP

Go to `https://www.irs.gov/forms-instructions` to access all of the forms mentioned in this chapter. You'll also find instructions for using those forms and other helpful information.

Choosing the Right Form: Which One Do You Need?

Your gross receipts and total assets from grants, donations, contracts, and so on determine which version of Form 990 your organization must file with the IRS. Your organization may be exempt from income tax, but you have to file one of the following three forms:

- **Form 990-N:** Form 990-N, e-Postcard, is for small nonprofits.
- **Form 990-EZ:** Form 990-EZ, Short Form Return of Organization Exempt from Income Tax, is for medium-sized nonprofits.
- **Form 990:** Form 990, Return of Organization Exempt from Income Tax, is for large nonprofits.

TIP

The thresholds and limits that determine which version of Form 990 your organization files are subject to change, so make sure you check the IRS's website, `https://www.irs.gov/charities-non-profits/annual-filing-and-forms`, for the most up-to-date information.

See Table 8-1 for tax thresholds and limits in place for the last few years through to the publication date of this book.

TIP

Total assets is not relevant for Form 990-N (e-Postcard) as it is not one of the eight items for which you fill in information.

TABLE 8-1 Tax Thresholds for Form 990

Form to File	Gross Receipts Threshold	Total Assets Limit
990-N (e-Postcard)	Normally less than or equal to $50,000	Total assets information is not a criterion for using this form
990-EZ	Less than $200,000	Less than $500,000
990	Less than or equal to $200,000	Less than or equal to $500,000

Knowing What Happens If You Don't File Form 990

If you don't file your personal income taxes, you know Uncle Sam gets upset. The same is true for your organization. Although your nonprofit isn't required to pay federal taxes, you still need to file Form 990. If you don't file, you put yourself and your organization on Uncle Sam's bad side. Make sure you file Form 990 to avoid any repercussions and dire consequences for your nonprofit.

WARNING

If your nonprofit is filing a Form 990 for a tax year beginning after July 1, 2019, or later, you probably have to file electronically. See the later section, "Submitting Form 990." This is nothing new for the Form 990-N. This form has always been submitted electronically.

What happens when you don't file Form 990, or you send in an incomplete form? You pay the following penalties:

- The IRS charges smaller organizations a penalty of $20 a day, not to exceed the lesser of $10,500 or 5 percent of the gross receipts of the organization for the year, when you file a return late, unless you can show that the late filing was the result of a reasonable cause. Organizations with annual gross receipts exceeding $1,094,500 are subject to a penalty of $105 for each day they fail to file (with a maximum penalty of $54,500 for any one return). The penalty begins on the due date. Additionally, the organization can lose its exempt status.
- If your organization doesn't file a complete return or doesn't furnish correct information, the IRS sends the organization a letter that includes a fixed time period during which you can resubmit the form. After that period expires, the IRS charges the person who fails to comply a penalty of $10 a day, with a maximum penalty of $5,000 for any one return.

OTHERS WILL PLAY FINANCE DETECTIVE

With the availability of Form 990 on the Internet, donors can easily investigate whether your organization has been a good steward of donor investments. They can look up your IRS Form 990 to see how much money you brought in, what you did with the money, and how much you paid in management expense. Many donors are skeptical about giving to charitable organizations because some aren't doing the right thing. Donors want to know that they're giving to a reputable organization; they don't want to worry about misuse of their money.

Donors may decide whether to donate to your organization based on the financial picture they glean from reviewing this form. Your Form 990 reveals the same information found on financial statements; the form just makes it easier for the government and public to analyze your numbers.

You can find Form 990s online at Charity Navigator (`https://www.charitynavigator.org`), GuideStar (`https://www.guidestar.org`), and Candid (`https://candid.org/?fcref=lr`).

REMEMBER

You only have to provide information about your nonprofit; you don't have to include a check with this return.

TIP

The IRS has free Stay Exempt Training courses and other very helpful information to assist with nonprofit tax compliance at `https://www.irs.gov/charities-non-profits/annual-electronic-filing-requirement-for-small-exempt-organizations-form-990-n-e-postcard`.

Understanding the Minimal Requirements: Form 990-N (e-Postcard)

The IRS created Form 990-N specifically for small, tax-exempt nonprofit organizations that gross less than $50,000 a year. Refer to Table 8-1 in the section "Choosing the Right Form: Which One Do You Need?" earlier in this chapter for more information on the gross receipts you need to use this form. Form 990-N is an electronic notice and very easy to complete, which is why it's also called the e-Postcard. You need to file this form every year by the 15th day of the fifth month after the end of an exempt organization's tax year. For a calendar year, the deadline is May 15.

For many years, the IRS didn't require small nonprofits that made less than $25,000 a year to submit any paperwork, but things have changed. Don't fret, though. Filling out Form 990-N is quick and simple. Here's what you must provide:

- Organization's employer identification number (EIN)
- Organization's legal name and mailing address
- Any other names your organization uses
- Organization's website address (if applicable)
- Name and address of a principal officer of your organization (usually the executive director)
- Organization's annual tax period
- A confirmation that your organization's annual gross receipts are $50,000 or less

If applicable, indicate whether your organization is going out of business. The IRS needs to know if your nonprofit is no longer operating because it regulates nonprofits.

REMEMBER

The IRS requires that Form 990-N be filed electronically. No paper form is available. To file Form 990-N, you must have access to the Internet, but you don't have to download any software. If your nonprofit doesn't have a computer, you can fill out Form 990-N using the computer of a friend, a relative, or your public library.

WARNING

If you don't file Form 990-N on time, the IRS sends you a reminder notice, but the IRS won't assess a penalty for filing it late. However, an organization that fails to file the required Form 990-N (or Form 990 or 990-EZ, for that matter) for three consecutive years automatically loses its tax-exempt status. The revocation for the organization's tax-exempt status doesn't take place until the filing due date of the third year.

Filling Out Form 990-EZ

Form 990-EZ, Short Form Return of Organization Exempt from Income Tax, is the annual information return that many organizations exempt from income taxes have to file with the IRS. To find out if your organization can file Form 990-EZ rather than Form 990, refer to Table 8-1 in the section "Choosing the Right Form: Which One Do You Need?" earlier in this chapter. As its name implies, Form 990-EZ is a less detailed version of Form 990.

All filing organizations must complete the top portion of the form and Parts I through V. The top portion of the form is self-explanatory with simple questions that identify you by name and EIN. Just fill in the blanks.

Parts I through V require information about the organization's exempt and other activities, finances, compliance with certain federal tax filings and requirements, and compensation paid to certain people. These five parts, along with the information you need to include in each part, are as follows:

- **Part I — Revenue, Expenses, and Changes in Net Assets or Fund Balances:** This part is basically your nonprofit organization's statement of activities. Part I is logically divided into revenues, expenses, and net assets.
- **Part II — Balance Sheets:** This part provides your organization with a simplified version of its statement of financial position (see Chapter 10 of this minibook for more information on this statement). You can use the numbers from your statement of financial position to fill in some of the info in this part.
- **Part III — Statement of Program Service Accomplishments:** Here you get to showcase your major accomplishments during the year. In this part, you report organizational and financial accomplishments that relate to your nonprofit's core program areas. Your responses to the questions in this part highlight your accomplishments.
- **Part IV — List of Officers, Directors, Trustees, and Key Employees:** In this part, you report the income for your organization's most highly compensated employees. If your organization provides no compensation, you should list the top three officers, such as president or executive director, treasurer, and secretary.
- **Part V — Other Information:** In this part, you answer a series of questions according to each question's specific instructions. Understanding all these questions is important because they disclose information about unrelated business income, the person who takes care of your books, and any new activities not reported in the prior year.

Only Section 501(c)(3) organizations have to complete Part VI. The questions in Part VI ask about your political activities, changes to your bylaws, unrelated business income, and so on. Because these questions are fairly basic, you can answer them rather easily. For example, one question asks you for a list of officers, directors, trustees, and key employees. All the questions in Part VI are straightforward.

Furthermore, you may need to complete additional schedules depending on the type of your organization and its activities. A *schedule* is a supplemental form with questions pertaining to a specific subject or topic that the IRS requires you to fill out, depending on your responses on other tax forms. Form 990-EZ requests information regarding specific activities on two schedules:

- **Schedule A:** If you are a section 501(c)(3) organization (or organization treated as such) filing Form 990-EZ, you must also complete and file Schedule A. Schedule A requests information regarding your reason for public charity status, information about your public support, and investment income.
- **Schedule B:** As of April 2022, some states have lifted the requirement to file Schedule B. However, the IRS still requires Schedule B if you receive large gifts falling under specific guidelines. The guidelines are subject to change, so you should check the Schedule B instructions each year. At present, the guidelines cover contributions of the greater of $5,000 or more than 2 percent of revenues you receive from any one contributor.

See the later section, "Submitting Form 990," for details on what to do with the form after you complete it.

Filling Out Form 990

Form 990 is the primary reporting mechanism for all organizations that are exempt from federal income tax. Every exempt organization that doesn't meet the requirements for the shorter Form 990-N or Form 990-EZ has to file Form 990 and must complete the top portion of the form and Parts I through XI. See Table 8-1 in the section "Choosing the Right Form: Which One Do You Need?" earlier in this chapter for the requirements of the three versions of Form 990.

The next sections help you understand how to complete Form 990 and how to submit it.

Walking through Form 990

Form 990 isn't an overly complex form to complete. You can find a lot of the information you need on your nonprofit's financial statements. First, you have to fill out the top portion of the form by following the directions and reporting general information about your organization, such as its name, address, EIN, and so on. The specific parts of Form 990 are as follows:

- **Part I — Summary:** This part basically asks you to summarize your organization. It requests details regarding your organization's activities and governance, revenue, expenses, and net assets.

- **Part II — Signature Block:** This part requires your signature to verify that the information on this form is correct to the best of your knowledge.
- **Part III — Statement of Program Service Accomplishments:** Simply put, this part is where the organization describes its accomplishments in the services it provides. It requests the amount of grant money and allocations your organization received for the services provided, along with all expenses related to the programs.
- **Part IV — Checklist of Required Schedules:** This part determines whether you need to complete any schedules in addition to Form 990 itself.
- **Part V — Statements Regarding Other IRS Filings and Tax Compliance:** This part alerts your organization to other potential federal tax compliance and filing obligations it has.
- **Part VI — Governance, Management, and Disclosure:** This part contains three sections: governing body and management, policies, and disclosure. These sections pose questions concerning the organization's conflict of interest policies and monitoring system. This part also asks about the review of Form 990 by voting members of the organization's governing board.
- **Part VII — Compensation of Officers, Directors, Trustees, Key Employees, Highest Compensated Employees, and Independent Contractors:** This part requires the organization to report the calendar-year amounts paid to compensate employees and independent contractors, taken from W-2 (see Chapter 7 of this minibook) and 1099 forms.
- **Part VIII — Statement of Revenue:** Just as its title states, this part is where you state all your organization's sources of revenue, including contributions such as grants and gifts, program service revenue, and fundraising revenue.
- **Part IX — Statement of Functional Expenses:** This part requires you to list your organization's expenses by category. The expense categories include program service, management, and fundraising.
- **Part X — Balance Sheet:** This part requires you to fill in the information found on your statement of financial position. Refer to your own statement to help you fill out this part (see Chapter 10 of this minibook for more information on statements of financial position).
- **Part XI — Reconciliation of Net Assets:** This part requires you to fill in the information found on your statement of activities. Refer to your own statement to help you fill out this part (see Chapter 9 of this minibook for more information on the statement of activities).
- **Part XII — Financial Statements and Reporting:** This part asks questions regarding the organization's accounting methods, and financial statement reporting and preparation.

TIP

If you answer "Yes" to Form 990, Part IV, line 1, you must complete and file Schedule A with your Form 990. The guidelines for if you need to file Schedule B with Form 990 are the same as that for Form 990-EZ and are outlined in the section "Filling Out Form 990-EZ" earlier in this chapter.

Submitting Form 990

Whew! The worst is over. You've completed Form 990 and Schedule A, and Schedule B if required. Now all you have to do is turn it in on time to avoid late fees. Don't get those postage stamps out just yet! While there are exceptions, effective for tax years beginning after July 1, 2019, you must file Form 990 electronically. If you're a Form 990-EZ filer, for tax years ending July 31, 2021 and later, you must file Form 990-EZ electronically as well.

To see if your nonprofit meets the exception criteria, every year review the updated instructions for whichever Form 990 you file. For more information about your e-filing requirements, check out the IRS December 13, 2019 news release at `www.irs.gov/newsroom/irs-recent-legislation-requires-tax-exempt-organizations-to-e-file-forms`.

REMEMBER

Form 990-N has always been submitted electronically. Form 990 is due by the 15th day of the fifth month after your organization's taxable year ends. If you fail to turn it in on time, you generally have to pay a penalty of $20 a day which is capped at $10,500 or 5 percent of your organization's gross receipts, depending on which amount is lower. Be sure to review the form for any omitted information so you don't have to pay the fee for incomplete returns (a fee of $10 a day up to $5,000).

Completing Form 990-T (Reporting Unrelated Business Income)

Your nonprofit may be subject to corporate income taxes if you engage in for-profit business enterprises in which you gain unrelated business income. Unrelated business income is any income generated by a business that is *regularly* carried on and *unrelated* to the exempt function of your nonprofit.

The IRS rule states that all nonprofits that have $1,000 or more in gross receipts from an unrelated business transaction must file Form 990-T, Exempt Organization Business Income Tax Return. You have to file Form 990-T to provide the IRS the following information about your nonprofit:

» **Unrelated business taxable income (UBTI):** If your nonprofit conducts a trade or business that produces income by selling merchandise or providing a service that isn't related to the cause or purpose of your organization, the income generated is considered unrelated business income if the trade or business activity takes place on a regular basis.

» **Unrelated business income tax liability:** This tax liability is the amount over $500 that your nonprofit owes for unrelated business transactions. This includes all gross income less deductions directly connected with producing the income.

» **Proxy tax liability:** This deals with notice requirements of nondeductible lobbying and political campaigning activities engaged in by certain membership associations that hold a tax-exempt status such as, 501(c)4, 501(c)(5), and 501(c)(6).

TIP

You can find information, instructions, and Form 990-T online at `https://www.irs.gov/forms-pubs/about-form-990-t`.

WARNING

Be careful with activities outside the scope of tax-exempt purpose. These unrelated business transactions can come back to bite you in the butt. Engaging in excessive unrelated business transactions can change the status of your organization from a nonprofit to a for-profit, which means you lose your exempt status. As long as you stay within the scope of the tax-exempt purpose of your nonprofit, though, you don't have anything to worry about. This is another great topic to add to the list of questions you have for your accountant or tax return preparer.

IN THIS CHAPTER

» **Knowing what's reported on the statement of activities**

» **Comparing current revenues and expenses to prior periods and other nonprofits**

Chapter **9**

Analyzing the Statement of Activities

Rarely do financial disasters happen overnight. Often, when a nonprofit has to close its doors due to lack of funding, the situation probably could have been avoided with proper financial oversight. Usually, the statement of activities contains signs that, if properly evaluated, reveal the likelihood of trouble and ways to avoid disaster. Good financial managers use their statement of activities as planning tools and indicators of future events.

The Financial Accounting Standards Board (FASB) requires nonprofits to report information about all expenses in one location. This can be on the statement of activities, as a note to the financial statements, or on a separate financial statement. See Chapter 6 of this minibook for more information about the FASB.

Information found on a statement of activities provides

» **A summary of transactions, events, and circumstances that change an organization's net assets:** This ties in both revenue and expenses.

» **Information about the relationship between transactions and events:** This assists in an important nonprofit control relating to program cost identification and classification.

» **Information on how revenues are used to provide program services:** Revenue must be spent in a way that is consistent with donor restrictions, limitations, and any regulations by which the nonprofit must abide.

By evaluating your statement of activities on a frequent basis, you know where your resources come from, how and when they flow, and how to set your course. Knowing how you're doing compared to what you've planned can help you make necessary changes. This chapter explains how to come up with the numbers on your statement of activities and how to use those numbers to strategically plan, carefully forecast and track your donations and expenses, and ensure that your nonprofit is compliant with any restrictions or regulatory requirements.

Understanding the True Meaning of the Statement of Activities

Your *statement of activities*, also referred to as *income statements*, is a summary of all the income you've earned and every expense you've incurred for a particular time period. It also shows whether your net assets or equity have increased or decreased over that time period.

Large corporations evaluate their expenses and make conscious efforts to downsize; you may need to consider doing the same thing when operating your nonprofit. Choosing what to cut and what to keep requires careful evaluation of your revenue sources, restrictions on those resources, and your expenses. In addition, you can compare planned expenses, just like you compare revenues, to keep your spending on track.

In a nutshell, your statement of activities (see Figure 9-1) indicates whether your nonprofit had a surplus or is operating in a deficit position (a *deficit* is a negative amount that means you've used all of your revenues and then some, and could signal that you're in financial trouble). It also identifies whether you've made any out of the ordinary large purchases or had unexpected revenue. Basically, the statement of activities indicates whether you've had a good year (ending in the black) or a bad year (ending in the red).

The sample statement of activities in Figure 9-1 also reflects the FASB requirement that all income and expenses be allocated either *without donor restrictions* or *with donor restrictions*.

OASIS, Inc.
Statement of Activities
For Year Ended December 31, 20XX

	Without Donor Restrictions	With Donor Restrictions	Total
Revenue, gains and other support:			
Contributions	$ 20,743	$ 12,500	$ 33,243
Event Income	31,774		31,774
Investment return, net	550		550
Gain on sale of asset	175		175
Other	36		36
Net assets released from restrictions:			
Satisfaction of program restrictions	3,500	(3,500)	
Expiration of time restrictions	7,000	(7,000)	-
Total net assets released from restrictions	10,500	(10,500)	-
Total revenue, gains, and other support	63,778	2,000	65,778
Expenses and losses:			-
Program A	15,600		15,600
Program B	8,400		8,400
Management and general	7,300		7,300
Fundraising	25,000		25,000
Total expenses	56,300		56,300
Fire loss on furniture and fixtures	80		80
Total expenses and losses	56,380		56,380
Change in net assets	7,398	2,000	9,398
Net assets January 1, 20XX	102,992	65,493	168,485
Net assets December 31, 20XX	$ 110,390	$ 67,493	$ 177,883

FIGURE 9-1: A sample statement of activities.

You can use your statement of activities to evaluate ways to downsize or cut expenses and increase revenue streams. When created on a monthly or quarterly basis, your statement of activities can be used to

- Focus on peak periods when contributions are up.
- Plan for the downtimes when contributions come in slowly.

Knowing your peak periods and slow periods can help you plan to sustain your nonprofit during the slow periods.

REMEMBER

Tracking your revenues and expenses on a monthly, quarterly, and annual basis helps you make better decisions about what expenses to keep and what to give up. When revenues decrease, most organizations look for ways to reduce expenses. As a general rule, most nonprofits try to keep administrative costs down to have more funds available for programs.

TIP

Going back to Chapter 2 of this minibook, you need your chart of accounts to set up your statement of activities because the chart of accounts lists your ledger account names and numbers in the same order that they appear in your financial statements.

Before you can fully use this important statement, you need a firm grasp of what the statement of activities shows. The following sections reveal what information is found on this statement.

Revenues

You have two types of donations to account for on the statement of activities:

- **Without Donor Restrictions:** This money can be used for anything. For example, a donor gives $10,000 to your nonprofit and doesn't specify how you can spend the money.
- **With Donor Restrictions:** These donations have strings attached or imposed sanctions. When your nonprofit receives restricted gifts, you have a legal obligation to comply with the donor's restrictions.

If your board of directors designates a portion of revenue without donor restrictions for a specific purpose, it may be called an *appropriation* or *board-designated support*. Board-designated funds (see Chapter 1 of this minibook for more information about fund accounting) aren't restricted in the same way as donor-restricted support.

A board can change its mind and remove this self-imposed limit on some resources, but it can't change the limitation placed on resources contributed from an outside donor. Remember, boards are inside the nonprofits and they designate; donors are outside your nonprofit and they have the ability to restrict.

To classify revenues on your statement of activities, you should list the totals from all accounts from your general ledger beginning with the number 4. These will include individual contributions, grant support, special events, ticket revenue, unrelated business income, in-kind contributions, and all other sources of income earned by your nonprofit, which must be further broken out between those without or with donor restrictions.

Make sure to follow through Figure 9-1's revenue section to see how to report all revenue accounts, and especially net assets released from restrictions and the subsequent effect on total revenues, gains, and other support.

Expenses

Your nonprofit incurs program expenses and overhead expenses. Depending on your establishment, you may have program, management and general, and fund-raising expenses. You won't forget to include your expenses if you refer to your chart of accounts and your general ledger.

You generally report all expenses on the statement of activities in the Without Donor Restrictions column. After you add up all of your expenses, subtract the total from Without Donor Restrictions revenues. As a reminder, expenses show up in your chart of accounts coded to the 5 series of accounts. See Chapter 2 of this minibook for more information about the chart of accounts.

Gains and losses

Gains and losses come from activities that are incidental to an organization's central activities or from events and circumstances beyond the organization's control. Gains are reported in the revenue section and losses are reported in the expense section of the statement of activities. Gains increase net assets and losses decrease net assets. There are two types of gains or losses:

- **Realized gains and losses essentially come from transactions or events that have occurred.** The economic impact has happened and can be felt. A transaction example is the gain or loss from the sale or disposition of an organization's investments or some other asset it owns. You have a gain when you receive more than the asset's cost and a loss when you receive less than its cost. An event example is a loss from a fire where the fire caused a decrease in value of an asset.
- **Unrealized gains and losses come from the change in fair market value of trading securities that an organization holds.** The nonprofit hasn't sold the trading securities, so there is no realized gain or loss. However, there has been a gain or loss in their value; it just hasn't been realized or felt because the asset hasn't been sold. Therefore, the gain or loss is reported on the statement as unrealized. For more information about trading securities, go the Chapter 1 of this minibook.

Make sure to follow through Figure 9-1 to see how to report expenses and losses, through the change in net assets and finishing up with the reconciliation from beginning to ending net assets.

What this statement doesn't show

There are a few limitations to the statement of activities. You may have some things of value that you can't accurately measure or report on the statement. These include the following:

- **Uncollectible accounts and pledges receivable:** They are assets and potential liabilities, and they're reported on the statement of financial position. We discuss the statement of financial position in Chapter 10 of this minibook. Changes in the estimate of the amount of uncollectible receivables changes revenue in the statement of activities, but the total value of the estimate is reported on the statement of financial position.
- **Accumulated depreciation:** Although you report the depreciation expense for any year on the statement of activities, you report the depreciation expense that has accumulated over the years on the statement of financial position as accumulated depreciation. Accumulated depreciation holds the write-off amount to keep the current value of a fixed asset accurately stated on the books. It reduces the carrying value of the fixed asset. (See Chapter 1 of this minibook for more about depreciation.)
- **People's loyalty and devotion to your organization:** Even if someone tried to measure these attributes, it would be difficult to put a number on them.

Evaluating the Data

You can use your statement of activities to analyze more than just the total revenues earned and expenses incurred for a given period. For example, you can compare the following:

- Current month revenues and expenses to prior months
- Current quarterly revenues and expenses to prior quarters
- Current annual revenue and expenses to prior years

Depending on your scope of services, you can also use your statement of activities to

- Compare your data to similar organizations
- Track how economic conditions affect your contributions
- Evaluate changes in giving trends
- Position yourself to better focus on organization and program efficiency
- Identify programs or areas that need your immediate attention

You can also use information found on the statement of activities to figure out what percentage of your revenues come from the following:

- Individual donors (private)
- Foundations
- Corporate sponsors
- Fundraising
- Grants
- Fees for program goods and services provided

See Chapter 12 of this minibook for ratio analysis instructions.

REMEMBER

Knowing where your resources come from can help you to assess your capability of generating future revenues. The following sections cover all of these topics.

Analyzing revenues and expenses

The numbers alone on your nonprofit's statement of activities don't have much meaning. You want to analyze and determine the relationship of its parts and how the results affect your nonprofit.

To analyze the numbers on a statement of activities, you need to convert the numbers to percentages, which gives you a better idea of what percentage of revenues come from which sources and which categories of expenses are too high. When the dollar amounts are converted into percentages, it shows how significant the components of your income statement are. Then when you compare revenues and expenses, you can better understand the relationship between the two. Reducing numbers to a simpler form helps you discover the true relationship of the parts of the statement of activities to the whole.

Take a look at the following example, which shows how much money a hypothetical nonprofit collected.

Revenues Collected for 2009

Individual donors	$45,000
Corporate sponsors	$25,000
Foundation grants	$85,000
Government grants	$300,000
Fee for services	$45,000
Total revenues collected	*$500,000*

By converting these figures into percentages, you can evaluate the revenues much easier. See Chapter 12 of this minibook for more information about percentages and ratio analysis.

TIP

To calculate the percentage for each revenue collected, divide the amount by the total revenues collected. For example, take the $45,000 collected from individual donors and divide it by $500,000, which is the total amount of revenues collected ($45,000 ÷ $500,000 = 0.09 or 9%). This means that $45,000 is 9 percent of $500,000, so you know that 9 percent of the revenues came from individuals.

TIP

Be sure to double-check your math by adding up the percentages. Your total should equal 100 percent.

The result of converting the revenues from each source into a percentage is shown in the following table.

Percentage of Revenues from Sources

Individual donors	9%
Corporate sponsors	5%
Foundation grants	17%
Government grants	60%
Fees for services	9%
Total revenues collected	*100%*

Based on these percentages, this organization is relying heavily on grants, to the tune of 77 percent of its revenues (17 percent from foundation grants plus 60 percent from government grants).

Although we wouldn't attempt to operate a nonprofit organization without grants because they're important to a nonprofit's funding, having this much money coming from grants can be a good or bad thing. If an aggressive grant-writing campaign is ongoing, then it may be okay. But if the nonprofit isn't aggressively seeking new grants, then it's putting itself in a precarious position because grants aren't permanent sources of income. The nonprofit could be in danger of running low on revenues when the grants end. (Book 3 covers grants in detail.)

Evaluating your expenses gives you a better indication of how much money is going to administrative, program, and overhead expenses. For more information about administrative expenses, see Chapter 12 of this minibook.

Determining change in net assets

A complete statement of activities indicates whether you've increased or decreased your net assets over a given period. Subtracting total expenses from revenues equals either a positive number or a negative number.

- A positive number means you've taken in more revenues than you have expenses. This is excess income — a *surplus* — and you're "in the black."
- A negative number means your expenses are higher than your revenues. A negative number equals a loss — a *deficit* — which means you're "in the red."

For example, if your total revenues are $100,000 and your total expenses are $95,000, then your change in net assets is a surplus of $5,000. But if your total revenues are $100,000 and your total expenses are $105,000, then your change in net assets is a $5,000 loss.

Revenues – Expenses = Change in net assets

REMEMBER

In the private sector, stockholders benefit from a positive difference between revenues and expenses by collecting dividends paid from the company's profits. In the nonprofit sector, stakeholders are the beneficiaries (your donors, as well as the people you help), and the money that's left after you've paid your expenses is reinvested in the nonprofit. When all revenues are collected and all expenses are paid, you need to have a surplus to stay afloat. Just because you're a nonprofit doesn't mean you don't need a positive difference between revenues and expenses.

Using the statement to make comparisons

As the world changes, so do your nonprofit's finances. Revenues go up and down; expenses go up (and sometimes down). You can use the data on the statement of activities to compare

- Current and historical amounts for your nonprofit
- Your nonprofit's finances to other nonprofits in the industry

Seeing how the numbers compare over time

You can compare numbers on your statement of activities on a monthly, quarterly, or annual basis. Looking back at previous time frames helps you gauge how well you're doing in the current period.

Comparing your current-year data to prior years shows trends and can help your nonprofit focus on important contributors (start with your donors list to see how much was given by whom) and high expenses. Of course, some expenses are probably up because of the changes in the economy, and there may be little that you can do to change that, but you may be able to offset other expenses. Take a look at Table 9-1, which compares current year revenues and expenses to prior years.

TABLE 9-1 Comparing Prior Year Data to Current Year

	2022	2021	2020	2019	2018
Revenues	$500,000	$475,000	$450,000	$425,000	$400,000
Expenses	$450,000	$450,000	$425,000	$400,000	$390,000
Change in Net Assets	$50,000	$25,000	$25,000	$25,000	$10,000

Table 9-1 shows a comparative list covering five years of revenues and expenses and the change in net assets. If you take what's happening in 2022 and compare it to any other year, it gives you a bit more than just looking at the numbers. For example, consider revenues starting with 2018 and look at what was reported in 2022. If you divided the revenues from any year into 2022, it gives you a percentage of change. The same is true for the expenses. By dividing the numbers, you can see that the trend of revenues increased faster than expenses. It appears that expenses plateau from 2021 to 2022; you'd need to investigate why to see if this is the start of a trend or a single occurrence.

Comparing your nonprofit to other nonprofits

Not a day goes by that the meteorologist doesn't compare today's temperature with last year's temperature, or even last week's for that matter. A comparison of your nonprofit's finances to other nonprofits gives you something by which to measure and test your progress.

Just as people can find your nonprofit's Form 990, Return of Organization Exempt From Income Tax, on the Internet, you can take a gander at other nonprofits' Form 990s. You can look up your favorite charities and other nonprofits with operating budgets and programs similar to yours. To do so, go to the GuideStar website at `https://www.guidestar.org`.

REMEMBER

When comparing your nonprofit to others in the industry, you want to compare apples to apples and oranges to oranges; therefore, try to find a nonprofit that is of similar size and with similar programs in your city. That way you're both subject to the same economic conditions and environment. Of course, you first have to be around for a few years before these types of assessments and analysis can be compared.

TIP

Another factor to consider when comparing your statement of activities to another agency's statement is the accounting method used by the other organization. For example, if the other nonprofit uses the cash method and you're using the accrual basis, then it's not a good comparison. The primary difference in the two methods is timing recognition of revenues and expenses. For more information about these two accounting methods, see Chapter 1 of this minibook.

IN THIS CHAPTER

» Knowing what the statement of financial position reveals

» Classifying assets and liabilities

» Using the numbers to analyze your position

Chapter 10
Reporting Financial Condition on a Statement of Financial Position

Some experts feel that out of all the financial statements, the statement of financial position is the most important. The statement of financial position provides a quantitative report of your organization's financial health. It demonstrates responsibility and accountability. It also monitors the progress of your organization and its financial condition.

This chapter walks you through this important financial statement and shows you how to use the numbers on your statement of financial position to analyze your nonprofit's financial health.

Grasping What the Statement Says about Your Nonprofit

The *statement of financial position* (also known as the *balance sheet*) reveals what your nonprofit owns (the assets) and what it owes (the liabilities) as of a particular date. The difference between your nonprofit's total assets and total liabilities equals your nonprofit's net assets:

Assets – Liabilities = Net assets

REMEMBER

A statement of financial position reveals the overall value of your organization at a point in time. It shows your organization's *solvency* (its ability to pay its bills) and *liquidity* (how quickly assets can be converted into cash) at a particular point in time.

Internal users (such as board members, accountants, and managers) use the statement of financial position to get information about

- **Your nonprofit's ability to meet its obligations.** This is revealed by the amount of your current assets, which are used to meet your current liabilities. If your current liabilities are greater than the current assets, then people will wonder whether you're having cash flow problems, making it difficult to pay your debts.
- **Your organization's net assets (the difference between what is owned and what is owed).** You can find this information at the bottom of the statement of financial position. Net assets represent the net cumulative results of your nonprofit's changes in net assets over the years. You report the change in net assets for any year on the statement of activities; you report the ending net assets on the statement of activities on the statement of financial position.

  Net assets are the accumulation of surpluses and deficits over your nonprofit's history and help explain how you acquired some of your assets. You acquire assets by either borrowing money to buy them (liabilities) or by spending your own surplus funds (this amount is represented by net assets).
- **Your agency's progress and ability to continue to provide services.** Simply compare changes in balances from prior periods to the current period.
- **The need for external financing.** You're in this situation when your current assets won't cover current debts, or if your long-term assets can't be converted into cash in time to pay current liabilities.

» **The results of economic activity.** This is revealed by the overall financial results as displayed on the statement of financial position as of a certain date.

You can tell a lot about an organization by viewing how its finances are managed. External users (such as bankers, creditors, and private and public donors) use the statement of financial position to evaluate whether your nonprofit's financial position is stable enough to secure a loan or whether your nonprofit is worthy of their investments. These folks may also take an interest in the same information your internal users look at. Additionally, many grant proposals require you to include a copy of all financial statements, including the statement of financial position, with the proposal.

REMEMBER

Although a statement of financial position may only be prepared quarterly or annually, it represents a single point in time. It is subject to change overnight. So if you're having a board meeting and your financial condition has improved or declined significantly due to a large donation or an unexpected large expense, you'll definitely want to reveal the good or bad news by giving your board members copies of the updated statement of financial position.

Creating and Reading a Statement of Financial Position

The statement tells a story about your position and condition; it's an X-ray of your financial health. It's based on what you own (current and long-term assets), what you owe (current and long-term liabilities), and the difference between the two (net assets).

Creating your statement of financial position is simple. You can use your chart of accounts to help you identify which accounts should be included. (If you're not sure about your chart of accounts, see Chapter 2 of this minibook.)

Before you can create and read your nonprofit's statement of financial position, you need to know what the different numbers mean. Figure 10-1 shows a sample statement. As you read this section, follow along in this figure to see what the different numbers mean.

OASIS, Inc.
Statement of Financial Position
December 31, 2022

		Without Donor Restrictions	With Donor Restrictions	Total
Assets				
Current Assets				
Cash:				
Operating account		69,000		69,000
Money market account		22,193		22,193
Total cash		91,193		91,193
Other Assets				
Investments		1,500	65,000	66,500
Grants receivable		5,500		5,500
Total current assets		98,193	65,000	163,193
Long-term assets				
Fixed assets:				
Office equipment	25,000			25,000
Less accumulated depreciation	(21,000)			(21,000)
Total fixed assets		4,000		4,000
Total Assets		**102,193**	**65,000**	**167,193**
Liabilities and Net Assets				
Current Liabilities:				
Accounts payable		2,900		2,900
Unearned revenue		37,100		37,100
Total current liabilities		40,000		40,000
Net Assets:				
Without donor restrictions		62,193		62,193
With donor restrictions			65,000	65,000
Total Net Assets		62,193	65,000	127,193
Total Liabilities and Net Assets		**102,193**	**65,000**	**167,193**

FIGURE 10-1: A classified statement of financial position.

Understanding the statement's structure

The top of your statement of financial position should include the name of your nonprofit, the name of the statement (statement of financial position), and the date of the balances reported on the statement.

The statement of financial position is like a scale with two sides. It has a top half and a bottom half. The top half shows assets, and the bottom half shows liabilities and net assets; the two halves have to balance, which is why this statement is sometimes called a balance sheet.

Figure 10-1 is a classified statement of financial position, which categorizes assets and liabilities as either current or long term. This is done so you have a more in-depth example of this statement to work through. It makes the analysis in the later section, "Evaluating the Numbers," easier to piece together.

Most statements of financial position included as part of an independent auditor's report will be *unclassified,* which means assets and liabilities will list in order of liquidity with no current or long-term subtotals. Additionally, fixed assets/accumulated depreciation are netted. Figure 10-2 shows the asset section only for an unclassified statement of financial position.

OASIS, Inc.
Statement of Financial Position
December 31, 2022

	Without Donor Restrictions	With Donor Restrictions	Total
Assets			
Cash and cash equivalents	91,193		91,193
Investments	1,500	65,000	66,500
Grants receivable	5,500		5,500
Property and equipment (net)	4,000		4,000
Total Assets	**102,193**	**65,000**	**167,193**

FIGURE 10-2: Asset section of an unclassified statement of financial position.

Every balance sheet has two main parts:

- **Assets:** Assets are always shown first on the statement of financial position. Adding all current assets to your fixed assets and other long-term assets gives your total assets. When you've reached your total assets, you've finished half of the statement.
- **Liabilities and net assets:** In this area on your statement of financial position, you add your current liabilities to your long-term liabilities to get your total liabilities. Notice in Figure 10-1 that this nonprofit only has current liabilities.

REMEMBER

Net assets equals all assets minus all liabilities. Don't confuse assets with net assets. In Figure 10-1 the net assets are $127,193.

Underneath net assets, you find net assets without donor restrictions and net assets with donor restrictions. *With donor restrictions* simply means donors have imposed limitations or conditions on gifts that will be met at some future time, while *without donor restrictions* means there were no limits or restrictions on the resources, and you're free to use them however you'd like.

OASIS, Inc.'s statement of financial position in Figure 10-1 shows total net assets of $127,193. The organization's net assets come from $62,193 without donor restrictions and $65,000 with donor restrictions.

To finish the bottom half of the statement of financial position, you add your total liabilities of $40,000 to your total net assets of $127,193 to get your total liabilities and net assets of $167,193. Notice how this is the same amount of total assets at the top half of the OASIS, Inc. statement of financial position. This is how total assets equals total liabilities plus net assets. You've just completed your statement of financial position. You're done!

TIP

A good checkpoint to remember is that total assets will always equal liabilities plus net assets.

REMEMBER

Your statement of financial position is unique, and it shows what you own and what you owe. No two organizations will have the exact same statement of financial position. So don't worry if you don't have every line item listed on the statement shown in Figure 10-1.

Here we've covered the basics of the statement of financial position and how it has to always stay in balance. The following sections explain the different parts of the statement of financial position and what information to include in the different fields. Here you can see how to create your nonprofit's statement of financial position. When you're preparing your own statement, just relax and don't let the numbers throw you off.

Classifying assets

Assets are classified on the statement of financial position in the order of their *liquidity*, which means how quickly assets can be converted to cash. This section presents asset categories in the order they should appear on a statement of financial position.

TIP

To come up with the figures for each category, you simply add up all the items under each category of assets and take that sum and place it on your statement of financial position.

Current assets

Current assets are those items that can be converted into cash within a year of the date of the statement. Current assets are usually listed in the following order — which generally follows ease of liquidity:

- **Cash:** Checking and savings account balances (cash is the most liquid asset, so it's listed first) and petty cash.
- **Marketable securities:** U.S. Treasury bills, certificates of deposit, stocks, and bonds.
- **Grants and accounts receivables:** Assets expected to be collected within the year.

  REMEMBER

  Grants and accounts receivables list under long-term assets, if the money will be received more than 12 months after the date of the statement.
- **Prepaid expenses:** Prepaid rent, prepaid insurance, and supplies on hand.

Long-term assets

Long-term assets are also referred to as noncurrent assets. Long-term assets are items that you anticipate holding more than 12 months from the date of the statement. Long-term assets consist of the following:

- **Investments:** Bonds, stocks, and real estate that you don't intend to sell within a year.
- **Tangible assets:** Any assets you acquire to fulfill your mission purpose and that have a useful life of more than one year from the date of the statement. Common examples are property, plant, and equipment (PP&E) such as land, buildings, equipment, office furniture, and fixtures. Tangible assets are also called fixed assets.
- **Intangibles assets**: Copyrights, patents, trademarks, trade names, customer lists, and other assets that you own. They're called intangible because they don't have a physical presence.
- **Other assets:** Anything that's not classified in the other areas.

Net fixed assets

Net fixed assets equals the cost of an asset minus the accumulated depreciation. Accumulated depreciation is the total depreciation expense charged to assets over the years. (See Chapter 1 of this minibook for more information about depreciation.)

REMEMBER

Assets are recorded on the statement of financial position at their original cost less depreciation. Your depreciation expense is listed on your statement of activities (see Chapter 9 of this minibook), but to show the office equipment at its book value on the statement of financial position, you have to subtract the accumulated depreciation amount from the cost. Figure 10-1 shows office equipment purchased at a price of $25,000 less $21,000 (accumulated depreciation) for a book value of $4,000.

Total assets

Total assets are your current assets plus long-term and net fixed assets. Your total assets include cash in your bank accounts, CDs (certificates of deposit), accounts receivables, and the value of all equipment and any other long-term assets you have. It's important that you know how much readily available cash you have on hand in order to meet your current obligations on time.

To calculate your total assets, add all current assets to all long-term and net fixed assets. For the balance sheet in Figure 10-1, the total assets are $167,193. The total current assets are $163,193, and the net fixed assets are $4,000.

Classifying liabilities and net assets

Knowing your nonprofit's liabilities is important because you need to have assets available to pay your obligations. Have you ever heard someone say, "We're not broke, but our assets are tied up"? This means the organization doesn't have anything it can quickly and easily convert to cash to cover what it owes. You need to have current assets to meet your current liabilities such as accounts payable or salaries payable. Not having current assets available to pay the bills can cause serious cash flow problems for your nonprofit.

Furthermore, by identifying your nonprofit's net assets, you can see pretty quickly how stable your organization is. The difference between your total assets and total liabilities gives a snapshot of your nonprofit's sustainability. Net assets are the same as net worth for a person, and the two are calculated the same way (total assets minus total liabilities).

TIP

In the notes to your financial statements, you should disclose information about the maturity of assets and liabilities and all restrictions on their usage. (See Chapter 13 of this minibook for more info.)

Current liabilities

Current liabilities represent items that are due within 12 months of the statement date. Your nonprofit should have sufficient current assets to pay the current liabilities as they become due. Some common current liabilities include the following:

- **Accounts payable:** These include credit card payments or purchases from vendors on credit.
- **Salaries payable:** This category is for salary expenses incurred but not yet paid at the end of the period.
- **Payroll taxes:** These are payable for state and federal taxes owed on salaries.
- **Bank loan payable for money borrowed for working capital:** Working capital loans are short-term loans taken to pay immediate items such as salaries payable. Normally, the collateral for working capital loans are accounts or grants receivable expected to be collected in the very near future. Check out the later section, "Calculating working capital," to see how to figure your nonprofit's working capital.

TIP

To identify your current liabilities, just take a look at your chart of accounts. Of course, the specific financial information can be found in your ledger. Just add the totals to get your total current liabilities.

In Figure 10-1, there are two current liabilities, accounts payable and unearned revenue, which total $40,000. Unearned revenue are payments received in advance before a service or product is earned; for example, a membership fee is paid for a year and only four months have elapsed. The eight months remaining on the membership is unearned revenue.

Long-term liabilities

Having too much debt can be risky business. To determine how much of this risky debt your nonprofit has on its books, look at long-term liabilities on the balance sheet. Long-term liabilities represent obligations due after 12 months from the date of the statement. Some common long-term liabilities are

- Notes payable for mortgages and land payments.
- Equipment payable for vehicles and heavy-duty copy machines.

TIP

To come up with long-term liabilities, add up the amounts for all obligations that you owe that aren't due or payable within a year. These consist of long-term debts, such as mortgages, vehicles, heavy machinery, and so on. In Figure 10-1, OASIS, Inc. has no long-term debts.

Net assets

Net assets represent the difference between your total assets and your total liabilities. Net assets are classified as without donor restrictions or with donor restrictions. If donors choose to restrict their gifts, they set the terms and length of the restrictions.

REMEMBER

Include any information about the nature and amount of donor restrictions as either a part of the statement of financial position or in the notes to the financial statements, which we cover in Chapter 13 of this minibook.

TIP

In the for-profit world, retained earnings represent the net difference between liabilities and assets on the balance sheet. In the nonprofit world, we have net assets.

REMEMBER

Asset accounts (statement of financial position accounts) aren't closed at the end of the accounting year. Statement of financial position accounts are considered real or permanent accounts. The only accounts that are closed are revenue, expense, gains, losses, and income summary accounts, which are referred to as temporary accounts.

When preparing financial statements, you always prepare the statement of activities first, because you close the end results of revenues and gains minus expenses to net assets.

There is a direct relationship between what happens on the statement of activities and the statement of financial position. Your end results from the statement of activities accounts (revenues – expenses = increases or decreases in net assets) is transferred to your statement of financial position. This is why the statement of activities is the first financial statement prepared. You can't prepare the statement of financial position until after you have the difference between revenues and expenses. (See Chapter 9 of this minibook for more about the statement of activities.)

You need to report your net assets on your statement of financial position. They help keep the statement of financial position (balance sheet) in balance. You calculate and report the beginning net asset balances, the change in those balances, and the ending net asset balances on the statement of activities. These ending net asset balances also appear underneath liabilities on the statement of financial position.

In the OASIS, Inc. statement of financial position in Figure 10-1, you see net assets without donor restrictions of $62,193 and net assets with donor restrictions of $65,000, for total net assets of $127,193.

TIP

You can double-check yourself when calculating your net assets by thinking of net assets as the difference between total assets (listed on the top of the balance sheet) and total liabilities. The total assets are $167,193, and the total liabilities are $40,000. Therefore, OASIS, Inc.'s total net assets must be $127,193 ($167,193 – $40,000 = $127,193). Also double-check that the net asset balances on the statement of activities agree with the balances on the statement of financial position.

Restricted net assets

Sometimes donors make contributions but place some restrictions on how and/or when the money may be used. These contributions are called net assets with donor restrictions. Donors include contributors and makers of certain grants to your nonprofit. These donors may restrict the money for a wide variety of functions, including to buy a new building, start a new program, or build an endowment. Your donors will tell you if a gift is restricted when they give it to you. It's your responsibility to honor the terms of the gift and to keep accurate records of how you manage the gift.

You need to report on the statement of financial position or in the notes to the financial statements whether donors have imposed restrictions on contributions.

Your donors list is a good starting point to find these nest eggs. In the statement of financial position in Figure 10-1, you can see that OASIS, Inc. has $65,000 in net assets with donor restrictions.

WARNING

Borrowing from restricted assets can cause you to lose the entire contribution.

Unrestricted net assets

Net assets without donor restrictions arise from gifts and other revenue that have no restrictions on their use, or from restricted gifts whose restrictions have been met. Unrestricted income is like gold. It has no pre-imposed terms and generally can be used immediately for anything you want.

In the OASIS, Inc. statement of financial position in Figure 10-1, you see net assets without donor restrictions for $62,193.

WARNING

If your nonprofit receives donated gifts with donor-imposed restrictions that limit their usage to long term, you can't classify them with cash or other assets that are unrestricted. It's important that you separately classify available assets and those intended for future use and not mix the two. Information about the donor-imposed restrictions should be disclosed in the notes to the financial statements (see Chapter 13 of this minibook), so that users of your nonprofit statement of financial position know what's available to you with no restrictions and what's not.

Total liabilities and net assets

To complete the statement, add together the total liabilities and the total net assets. This number should match the number of the total assets line on the top half of your statement of financial position.

In Figure 10-1, OASIS, Inc. has liabilities of $40,000 and net assets of $127,193. When you add the two figures together, you get $167,193, the exact same amount as the total assets. Success!

Evaluating the Numbers

There is more to your statement of financial position than just the numbers or total amount of assets, liabilities, and net assets. Accountants take the numbers from this statement to evaluate how well you're doing. You can do the same: Think of this evaluation of your nonprofit's statement of financial position as a financial checkup.

TIP

You can get a sense of whether your organization is in good financial shape just by looking at the lines for total assets and total liabilities and net assets.

If the number on the top half (total assets) of the statement is less than the total liabilities number on the bottom half, you have a problem. How long your problem lasts, or if it worsens, depends on your nonprofit's plans for the future. Some problems are only temporary. For example, you may have experienced unbudgeted increases in expenses. Maybe a water pipe burst, causing you to slip into a different position.

REMEMBER

The statement of financial position date shows the nonprofit's results from the first day of operation to the date on that statement. Going back to Figure 10-1, let's say OASIS, Inc. opened its nonprofit doors on March 1, 2019. Figure 10-1's statement of financial position shows OASIS's results from March 1, 2019, to December 31, 2022. Contrast this to the statement of activities, which only shows how your nonprofit is performing for the time frame listed on the top of the report; for example, "for the year ending December 31, 2022" or "for the quarter ending March 31, 2023."

The statement of financial position reveals your organization's ability to pay its bills. It also plays a part in determining what interest rate your lender will charge for credit like working capital or long-term loans. By analyzing current assets and current liabilities, you can figure out how much cash is on hand to pay liabilities. You can study your nonprofit's financial position and get a crystal-clear picture of how your nonprofit is doing by using the statement of financial position to compute working capital and analyze your debt-paying ability.

Internal and external users of your balance sheet are interested in evaluating your financial health. Bankers, vendors, investors, donors, board members, constituents, accountants, and executive directors can easily evaluate your financial position by making a few simple computations. They look at your working capital and debt-to-equity ratio to determine whether to lend you money, issue credit cards, or charge higher interest rates.

The following sections show you how to analyze your financial position and compute debt-paying ability and working capital.

Calculating working capital

Working capital is the difference between current assets and current liabilities. Working capital indicates how much money you have available after paying your current liabilities and your ability to cover other obligations that may arise in the future. Creditors use working capital to determine interest rates.

TIP

To figure out your nonprofit's working capital, you subtract the total current liabilities from the total current assets.

Take a look at Figure 10-1. The total current liabilities for the year are $40,000, and the total current assets are $163,193. Subtracting the total current liabilities from the total current assets gives you a working capital of $123,193 ($163,193 − $40,000 = $123,193).

REMEMBER

Working capital is the amount you have left after you've paid your bills. If you have excess working capital, it means you can cover your current liabilities and have cash left over for other needs. Some may call working capital excess cash. Excess cash is like spare change.

Calculating a debt-to-equity ratio

Creditors use the numbers on your statement of financial position to determine what percentage of your total assets is used to pay your liabilities. One of the most commonly used ratios is the debt-to-equity ratio. A *debt-to-equity ratio* is total debts (liabilities) divided by total liabilities and net assets. This ratio gives the users of the statement an idea of how the nonprofit is financed — through debt or through equity. A high number signals that your nonprofit may have wild fluctuations in income or grant/accounts receivable collections and not be able to pay its bills when they're due. The higher the number, the more highly you are leveraged.

Looking at Figure 10-1, OASIS, Inc. has a total of $167,193 in total liabilities and net assets and a total of $40,000 in liabilities. To calculate the organization's debt-to-equity ratio, you divide the total liabilities by the total liabilities and net assets. The math comes out to 24 percent ($40,000 ÷ $167,193 = 0.24). This is a low debt-to-equity ratio and to be expected, as OASIS, Inc. has no long-term debt related to a mortgage or financed equipment purchases.

REMEMBER

Having a low debt-to-equity ratio is a good thing. Anything over 50 percent is considered risky.

IN THIS CHAPTER

» Understanding what's shown on the statement of cash flows

» Creating and using a statement of cash flows

» Using cash flow ratios to flag potential problems

Chapter 11 Eyeing the Statement of Cash Flows

The statement of cash flows is one of the major financial statements required by generally accepted accounting principles (GAAP). This statement reports the inflow of cash to an organization and the outflow of cash from an organization. Cash inflows are cash receipts that come from operating, financing, and investing activities. Cash outflows are cash payments for operating, financing, and investing activities.

The information found on the statement of cash flows gives users an idea about your organization's ability to generate positive future cash flows, its ability to pay debts, and a summary of sources (inflows) and uses (outflows) of cash. The statement of cash flows is a better indicator of this than the statement of activities because the statement of activities can report transactions on the accrual basis, not the cash basis. (See Chapter 9 of this minibook for more about statements of activities.) This chapter explains the importance of the statement of cash flows, how it indicates a nonprofit's ability to pay its debts, and how you can create it and use it to make decisions based on your need for available cash.

What the Statement of Cash Flows Can Tell You about Your Nonprofit

The *statement of cash flows*, also called the *cash flow statement*, provides important information about your nonprofit. This statement answers questions about your nonprofit with information not found on other financial statements. It reveals how your organization's growth and expansion were financed. It also identifies cash amounts from operations, selling and acquiring securities, purchasing, selling capital assets, and financing activities with creditors. Your statement of cash flows can cover your monthly, quarterly, and annual cash inflows and outflows.

Cash includes balances in your checking and savings accounts, as well as currency and coins. Cash equivalents include short-term investments that are quickly and easily turned into a known amount of cash and are so near to maturity that changes in interest rates won't affect their value. Examples of these types of investments are treasury bills, commercial paper, and money market mutual funds.

TIP

You can improve your cash flow by keeping cash in an interest-bearing account or buying certificates of deposit.

Using the statement to see the big picture

The statement of cash flows summarizes where your cash came from and where it went during the period. Donations of cash, checks, credit card contributions, money collected from fundraising, and grants received from all sources are considered cash inflows. Cash outflows are all purchases made with cash, payments for salaries and payroll taxes, and outlays paid with cash during the period.

To have a positive cash flow means that your inflow exceeds your outflow. One major problem most organizations have is the timing of the cash flow. Unfortunately, cash inflows (revenues) tend to lag behind outflows (expenses), creating a shortage of cash or a negative cash flow.

REMEMBER

Your nonprofit may use a working capital loan to bridge the gap between collecting on receivables and urgent outflows such as salaries and wages. (We discuss working capital loans in Chapter 10 of this minibook.)

This statement also shows cash flow divided into categories. This is helpful to board members and other users because it breaks down cash inflows and outflows for the differing types of transactions. The statement of cash flows enables users to

- Understand how an organization obtains and uses cash.
- Analyze the short-term viability of an organization; it reveals an organization's liquidity or solvency.
- Evaluate changes in statement of financial position accounts (assets, liabilities, and net assets; see Chapter 10 of this minibook for more on these).
- Compare current information to prior statements.
- More accurately predict amounts and timing of future cash flows.

WARNING

The statement of cash flows does have some limitations. It doesn't tell the full story of your organization's financial condition; it only explains how your cash balance has changed.

REMEMBER

The statement of cash flows differs from an accrual basis statement of financial position and statement of activities because it shows the cash flow of activities during the reporting period. Another difference is that the statement uses the cash basis of accounting, meaning that transactions are recorded when cash is received or paid. Other financial statements may reflect the accrual basis of accounting, whereby revenues are matched with expenses in the period earned or incurred, not when cash changes hands. (See Chapter 1 of this minibook for more information about these two accounting methods.)

Making decisions based on the statement

You should use the statement of cash flows along with the statement of financial position and statement of activities when making long-term financial decisions for your nonprofit. This is because you can have a stellar asset balance on your statement of financial position and have no available cash to pay your current liabilities, a fact that will be abundantly clear from review of the statement of cash flows. The statement of activities may include restricted gifts that are outstanding, such as pledges to give. All financial statements indicate performance, and the statement of cash flows is sometimes overlooked because many people don't know how to use it.

Proper use of a statement of cash flows can help you determine the following:

- If you need to borrow money
- When you can make major purchases
- When you need to consider downsizing

You know what happens when an organization can't pay its debts: It defaults on creditors, borrows money, files for bankruptcy protection, or a combination of all three. You can use cash flow ratios to get an early warning about potential cash flow problems in your organization. We explain two important ratios in the later section, "Analyzing Cash Flow Indicators."

Understanding How to Create and Use a Statement of Cash Flows

The statement of cash flows is closely related to what happens in your organization's checkbook. To fully understand the statement of cash flows, you must know the extent to which your organization relies on the cash it generates and the extent to which it relies on investments. You should view the statement of cash flows alongside your nonprofit's other financial statements (see chapters 9, 10, 12, and 13 of this minibook for the statements to have) to get the total picture of your nonprofit's financial standing.

The following sections identify the different parts of this statement and explain how to read it so you can fully understand your organization's cash flow status. If you're interested in creating your own statement of cash flows, here's some hands-on direction to get you started.

Getting the statement started

Before you can begin creating your organization's statement of cash flows, you need to have a battle plan. How do you plan to prepare the statement? You have two methods to choose from: direct or indirect. Both methods classify and report cash receipts and payments from three activities: operating, investing, and financing activities. Both methods report cash flows from investing and financing activities in exactly the same manner, but they differ in how they report cash flows from operating activities.

- The *direct method* reports operating cash receipts and disbursements, such as cash received from donors or from providing services, and cash paid to employees or vendors. Cash receipts are what you have coming in; disbursements are what you have going out. The net total of these operating receipts and disbursements is net cash flow from operating activities. This method focuses on operating cash receipts and payments.

Many people believe that knowing the sources of operating cash receipts and the reasons for making operating cash payments is more useful than just knowing the organization's change in net assets. They also believe knowing operating cash receipts and disbursements from prior periods can help predict future operating cash flows. But the statement of cash flows is hard to prepare using this method if your books are kept on a running accrual basis. If you keep your books on the cash basis all year long and post accrual adjustments at the end of the year, using this method shouldn't be too difficult. But books with transactions recorded on the accrual basis have to be adjusted to be reported on the cash basis. Your other choice of methods, the indirect method, adjusts accrual basis records to the cash basis.

» The *indirect method* begins with the change in net assets (net income, see Chapter 10 of this minibook) and makes accrual to cash adjustments for revenues and expenses that didn't arise from the receipt or payment of cash during the reporting period. This method focuses on the differences between changes in net assets (net income) and net cash flow from operating activities.

Many users believe that the change in net assets, when adjusted to net cash flow from operating activities, is a more useful predictor of future cash flow than operating cash receipts and payments.

REMEMBER

As of this writing, the FASB (Financial Accounting Standards Board) allows nonprofits to use either the direct or indirect method. Additionally, nonprofits are no longer required to prepare an additional disclosure reconciling the change in net assets to net cash flows from operating activities if using the direct method. The FASB eliminated the additional disclosure to encourage use of the direct over indirect method. In practice, many nonprofits use the indirect method as it can be easier to prepare.

Identifying the parts of the statement

To completely grasp the statement of cash flows and what it can tell you about your organization, you need to be able to identify its parts. The statement has three sections (see Figure 11-1):

» **Cash flows from operating activities** includes operating revenues received and operating expenses paid in cash. If it isn't an investing or financing activity, it's an operating activity.

» **Cash flows from investing activities** includes cash paid for acquiring and cash received from selling securities and/or assets.

» **Cash flows from financing activities** includes obtaining cash from creditors, repaying creditors, and receiving donations with long-term donor restrictions.

OASIS, Inc.
Statement of Cash Flows
Indirect Method

Cash flows from operating activities:	
Change in net assets	$ 66,423
Adjustments to reconcile change in net assets to net cash used:	
Depreciation	2,580
Increase in contributions receivable	(5,000)
Increase in accounts payable	3,000
Net cash from operating activities	**$ 67,003**
Cash flows from investing activities:	
Purchase of fixed assets	(2,363)
Proceeds from sale of investment	5,000
Net cash flows from investing activities	**2,637**
Cash flows from financing activities:	
Proceeds from restricted contributions	12,506
Payments on long-term debt	(8,716)
	3,790
Cash and cash equivalents beginning of year	43,656
Cash and cash equivalents end of year	**73,430**

FIGURE 11-1: An example of a statement of cash flows using the indirect method.

Doing the math

As Figure 11-1 shows, you use the cash flow amounts from three categories to determine your organization's cash flow. You add the totals for each section to determine your organization's increase or decrease in cash for that period. Here your organization has net cash from operating activities of $67,003, net cash from investing activities of $2,637, and net cash from financing activities of $3,790 to give you a net increase in cash of $73,430. Remember: Parentheses and dashes are negative numbers.

You also have a beginning cash balance from the previous period that you can use to see how your cash flow has changed over a longer period of time (the beginning cash balance for a period is actually the ending cash balance for the previous period). The difference between the beginning cash balance from the previous period and ending cash balance from the current period is the net increase or decrease in cash between the two periods.

Figure 11-2 is an example of how the same information you use to prepare an indirect statement of cash flows shows up on a statement of cash flows prepared using the direct method. Note that net cash balances in each of the three parts and beginning and ending cash are the same regardless of which method you use.

OASIS, Inc.
Statement of Cash Flows
Direct Method

Cash flows from operating activities:	
Contributions received	146,398
Other Income received	8,055
Cash disbursements	(87,450)
Net cash received from operating activities	**$ 67,003**
Cash flows from investing activities:	
Purchase of fixed assets	(2,363)
Proceeds from sale of investment	5,000
Net cash flows from investing activities	**2,637**
Cash flows from financing activities:	
Proceeds from restricted contributions	12,506
Payments on long-term debt	(8,716)
	3,790
Cash and cash equivalents beginning of year	43,656
Cash and cash equivalents end of year	**73,430**

FIGURE 11-2: An example of a statement of cash flows using the direct method.

REMEMBER

The statement of cash flows gathers your organization's change in cash from operating, investing, and financing activities, then adds the change in cash to the organization's cash balance at the beginning of the year (last year's ending cash balance) to arrive at this year's ending cash balance. This year's ending cash balance on the statement of cash flows should equal the cash balance in the current asset section of the organization's statement of financial position. This is because the balances on the statement of financial position are end-of-year balances, so end-of-year cash on the statement of financial position should equal end-of-year cash on the statement of cash flows.

The following sections break down these three parts and explain how you can use these numbers to your advantage.

Operating activities

The operating section of the statement of cash flows reports how much money was received and disbursed from operating activities. Remember, if it isn't an investing or financing activity, then it's an operating activity. Nonprofits depend on gifts and contributions from individuals, corporations, foundations, and government entities. Some may generate revenue by charging a small fee for the services they provided, but for the most part, they rely heavily on fundraising activities to raise the necessary funds for operations.

Check out the operating activities part of the Figure 11-1 indirect method statement of cash flows. You begin with change in net assets, which is comparable to for profit net income. Then, all of the activity here is reported on the cash basis. Thus, depreciation expense is added back since depreciation expense is not a cash transaction, but is included as accumulated depreciation in the change in net assets. See Chapter 1 of this minibook for more information about depreciation.

REMEMBER

Your cash receipts and cash disbursements (payments) are recorded in your checkbook register. That means your checkbook register serves as a cash disbursements journal and a summary cash receipts journal recording only the cash deposited into the bank.

Many nonprofits keep the detail for cash deposits in other registers called journals. Accounting journals are day-to-day records of events such as receiving cash in or paying cash out. You can have a cash receipts journal for any kind of cash income; for example, contributions, special events, investment income, and grant proceeds received. When you receive the payment, you first enter it into the cash receipts journal by entering the date and description of the cash receipt. Then in the left-hand column (debit) enter the amount received, and in the right-hand column (credit) enter the related income account.

TIP

If you're using accounting software, the program keeps these journals and does the posting for you. See Chapter 4 of this minibook for information about QuickBooks for nonprofits.

REMEMBER

At the end of each month, you should post the totals from your cash receipts and cash payments journals to all affected accounts in the general ledger. Summarize the journals by adding the columns, and then use that summary to develop entries to post to your general ledger.

Investing activities

The investment section of the statement of cash flows reveals amounts used to sell or buy securities and to sell or buy property or equipment. Take a look at the cash flow from investing activities in Figure 11-1 (keeping in mind that the investing activities and financing activities sections are the same whether you use the indirect or direct method).

Reflected in this section are the proceeds from an investment you sold and your purchase of fixed assets. In our example, you sold $5,000 of investments and used $2,363 to purchase fixed assets, yielding $2,637 of net cash used by investing activities. Remember, you get this detailed information from the cash receipts and cash disbursements journals that make up the total amounts posted to the cash account in the general ledger.

The cash disbursements journal (also known as a cash payment journal) records any payment your nonprofit makes using a form of cash, such as writing a check. When you make a cash payment, you first enter it into the cash disbursements journal by entering the date and description of the cash payment. If paying by check, enter the check number and the payee. Then, in the left-hand (debit) column, enter the amount paid, and in the right-hand (credit) column, enter the related cash account.

Financing activities

Financing activities are essentially borrowing money, repaying the debt, and receiving gifts with long-term donor-imposed restrictions. Typical long-term credit instruments are mortgages and notes payable. Typical gifts with long-term restrictions are contributions for long-term endowment funds.

You find these amounts in your activity posted to your debt accounts in the general ledger. These numbers were first recorded in either your cash receipts or cash disbursements journal, and then posted to the affected accounts in the general ledger.

Check out the financing activities section in Figure 11-1. The amounts in this section of the statement of cash flows reflect principal payments on the organization's mortgage and the total received from donors' restricted contributions. In this example the organization repaid $8,716 of principal on its mortgage (long-term debt), and received gifts restricted for endowment of $12,506, resulting in net cash provided by financing activities of $3,790. If you had borrowed some money, you would have reported the amount of cash received here as well.

REMEMBER

Significant noncash investing and financing activity must be disclosed in your financial statement notes (see Chapter 13 of this minibook) or as a supplementary schedule accompanying the statement of cash flows.

Analyzing Cash Flow Indicators

Cash flow ratios are used to evaluate an organization's ability to pay its current liabilities given its current assets. Knowing this number tells you how likely it is that your organization can continue to support itself.

TIP

If you're experiencing problems meeting your current obligations, you need to call an emergency board meeting. Your board can help you remedy this problem. Some cash flow problems are temporary and can be resolved with a short-term loan. If you think your cash flow problems are more significant, you may want to hire a CPA to help you foresee future cash flow problems.

Although you can calculate several ratios from the statement of cash flows, this discussion focuses on two of the most important indicators: operating cash flow ratio and free cash flow. The following sections take a closer look at each.

REMEMBER

Financial ratios are only meaningful if a reference point is used, such as comparing ratios to historical values and similar organizations. Ratios should be viewed as indicators, and some are limited by different accounting methods.

Calculating the operating cash flow ratio

The operating cash flow (OCF) ratio evaluates whether an organization is generating enough cash to meet its short-term obligations. To calculate the OCF ratio, grab your statement of financial position (see Chapter 10 of this minibook) to get the total current liabilities at the end of the period. Then divide the net cash flow from operating activities (taken from your statement of cash flows) by the current liabilities. Here's the equation:

Operating cash flow ratio = Net cash flow from operating activities ÷ Current liabilities

For example, Figure 11-1 shows net cash flow from operating activities of $67,003; the total current liabilities are $40,000 (taken from Figure 10-1 in Chapter 10 of this minibook). Dividing $67,003 by $40,000 equals 1.68. This number is the operating cash flow ratio for OASIS, Inc.

REMEMBER

When you calculate a ratio, you measure performance. This result indicates whether an organization can sustain itself. As a general rule, a ratio below 1.0 indicates potential problems with paying short-term debt. It signals a need to hold a fundraiser, sell some stock, slow down on spending, tap into your reserves, or borrow money. Any ratio above 1.00 is considered safe for most organizations.

Determining free cash flow

Free cash flow (FCF) tells you how much money you have after paying your bills, including paying for investments in capital assets — you can consider FCF spare change.

TIP

To calculate free cash flow, you need to grab your statement of cash flows (see Figure 11-1). Subtract cash used for purchases of fixed assets (it's in the investing activities section) from net cash flow from operating activities (in the operating activities section). Here's the equation:

> Free cash flow = Net cash flow from operating activities - cash used for purchases of fixed assets

For example, net cash flow from operating activities is $67,003 and cash used for purchases of fixed assets is $2,363. Subtracting $2,363 from $67,003 equals $64,640.

Many organizations include debt payments made for loans that were taken out to buy fixed assets. If you do this with this example, you also subtract the cash used by principal payments on mortgage (it's in the financing activities section of the statement of cash flows). This is the amount of cash you have after paying all of your operating expenses and your payments for fixed assets. This cash is available for paying other debt and any other investments or expenditures the organization wishes to make.

So, for this example, you subtract $2,363 and $8,716 from $67,003, which equals $55,924. This number is excellent. Based on the information provided, OASIS, Inc. is stable and has sufficient funds to meet its financial obligations as of the end of the year.

The lower your amount of free cash flow, the less money you have to pay for other debts and other nonoperating activities. If it's zero or negative, you might have cash flow problems! Free cash flow indicates amounts of cash available for expansion of programs, facilities, or endowments. Obviously, more is better.

IN THIS CHAPTER

» Allocating expenses by function and nature

» Analyzing spending and efficiency

Chapter 12

Organizing the Statement of Functional Expense

Your statement of functional expense reports expenses by their function and nature. First, expenses are classified by their function, which includes program costs, management and general expenses, and fundraising expense. Next, expenses are separated into their "natural" classification, such as salaries, rent, utilities, supplies, and depreciation.

All nonprofits have the option to report expenses by nature and function in one of three ways: in the notes to the financial statements, in the statement of activities (see Chapter 9 of this minibook) or in the statement of functional expense, the topic of this chapter. Nonprofits that have more than one function usually opt for the statement of functional expense.

Prior to 2017, only voluntary health and welfare group organizations were required to include a statement of functional expense. However, the Financial Accounting Standards Board (FASB) issued Accounting Standards Update (ASU) 2016-14, which requires all nonprofits to report the functional and natural relationship between expense categories for fiscal years beginning after December 15, 2017. See Chapter 6 of this minibook for more information about the FASB.

This chapter looks at how expenses are divided by function and nature and how to use the numbers to measure efficiency.

Classifying Functional Expense

Your challenges as a nonprofit executive director or manager are to address the needs of your constituents, pay your organization staff, and keep administrative costs down, all while running effective programs. To do so, you can rely on the statement of functional expense. To fully use this statement, you need to know how to classify your organization's expenses.

The functional classification of an expense determines what category the expense belongs in (program services or supporting services). You classify expenses according to function to measure how well you're doing. In other words, you track how much of the donors' money is used to run programs versus being spent on supporting services.

There are two steps to break out your expenses by function and nature:

1. **Understand the difference between program services and supporting services.** *Program services* are what you provide in the way of goods or services that fulfills your nonprofit's mission. *Supporting services* are your management and general, fundraising, and membership development activities.
2. **Have an allocation policy in place for your nonprofit.** *The allocation policy* is your methodology for apportioning expenses to functional classifications and can use methods such as employee timesheets or analysis of square footage. Using your allocation policy, the second step is to go over your natural expenses categories and record the allocated expense to the correct fund.

TIP

While classifying and allocating may seem simple enough, putting this into action the first time can be laborious. For example, to allocate an expense into program services, you have to make sure the expense is directly related to program activities and further allocated to the program that receives that direct benefit. Any expense that is of benefit to the nonprofit as a whole goes to supporting services. This is true even if it appears to relate to a specific program, such as collecting donations.

After you have done all the background work classifying and allocating your expenses, it's time to report the results. Figure 12-1 is a sample statement of functional expense.

OASIS, Inc.
Statement of Functional Expense
Year Ending December 31, 20XX

	Salaries, Employee Benefits, and Taxes	Professional Fees and Other Expenses	Travel and Staff Development	Grants and Awards	Rent, Telephone, Postage, and Supplies	Depreciation and Amortization	Total Expenses
Program services							
Mentoring	$ 102,000	$ 1,450	$ 8,800	$ 10,400	$ 31,000	$ 350	$ 154,000
Tutoring	57,000	1,450	5,700	9,500	18,500	350	92,500
Total program services	159,000	2,900	14,500	19,900	49,500	700	246,500
Supporting services							
Managerial and general	24,600	28,285	500		965	650	55,000
Fundraising	10,800	250	700		1,450	300	13,500
Total supporting services	35,400	28,535	1,200	-	2,415	950	68,500
Total expenses	$ 194,400	$ 31,435	$ 15,700	$ 19,900	$ 51,915	$ 1,650	$ 315,000

FIGURE 12-1: Sample statement of functional expense.

REMEMBER

Functional expense classification determines to which category the expense relates. The natural expense classification shows how the funds were spent. For example, a nonprofit will have a "bucket" such as mentoring program (functional expense) and a "sub-classification" (natural expense) for salaries directly related to the mission of the mentoring program.

Keeping track of time

Allocating time and matching it with the correct programs aren't mere suggestions when it comes to federal grant programs. It's required that all employees who are paid from grant funds document their time and attendance. If your nonprofit receives any grant money, you're required to use this statement to record in detail your time expense.

The best method to capture this information is by employees preparing time and attendance (T&A) reports that indicate which program to charge. Time and attendance reports are also called timesheets. Timesheets indicate how an employee spends their time. They also reflect which program or supporting service may be charged to the employee's salary.

One way to track and allocate employee expense among the categories is by keeping track of how much time is spent doing what. If you make a habit of writing down how you spend your time every day, it removes the guesswork.

If you're like most nonprofits, your agency has three types of workers:

- Employees who are ineligible for overtime pay (paid on salary)
- Employees eligible for overtime pay (paid hourly)
- Unpaid volunteers

TIP

You should ask each employee to keep a log of how they spend each hour of their workday. They should also record time off for holidays, weekends, sick days, and vacation time. The time and attendance report should be filled out to coincide with your nonprofit's pay period, signed, and dated by the employee. Then you or the employee's supervisor should review, sign, and date the report as verification of the employee's time. This report can be used to allocate the employee's personnel expenses to the various functional categories.

Keeping time and attendance reports yields the following benefits:

- Helps settle disputes about an employee's pay
- Creates a paper trail for auditors
- Verifies how federal dollars are spent
- Provides a way for management to keep up with employee costs
- Provides a basis for allocating personnel costs to functional categories

REMEMBER

Time and attendance reports are mandatory for employees paid out of federal grants. Federal grants program managers require these reports because they give accountability and add credibility to how the money has been used. Plus, signed time and attendance reports provide documentation for audit use.

TIP

Keep completed time and attendance reports with your grant files. Program managers may ask to see them during a monitoring visit or audit. The timesheet in Figure 12-2 displays how to document and track your time and your employees' time.

TIP

You can also ask volunteers to fill out a time and attendance report. If a volunteer donates professional services (such as legal or accounting services) that your nonprofit would otherwise have to pay for, you may be able to account for the volunteer's time as an in-kind donation. This is a great topic to add to your questions for your accountant or CPA.

SSN: **000-00-0000** NAME: **Mary Smith** PERIOD ENDING: **1/15/23**

DIVISION: Executive Division EMPLOYEE BASE: Montgomery, AL

Month											COMP	
January	1	2	3	4	5	8	9	10	11	12	TIME	TOTAL
Tutoring		2.00	1.00	2.00	3.00	2.00	3.00					**13.00**
Mentoring		2.00	2.00	1.00	1.00	2.00	3.00					**11.00**
Fundrasing		3.00	2.00	1.00	1.00	2.00	1.00					**10.00**
General		1.00	3.00	4.00	3.00	2.00	1.00	8.00	8.00	8.00		**38.00**
TOTAL DIRECT HOURS		**8.00**	**8.00**	**8.00**	**8.00**	**8.00**	**8.00**	**8.00**	**8.00**	**8.00**	**0.00**	**72.00**
ANNUAL LEAVE												**0.00**
SICK LEAVE												**0.00**
HOLIDAY LEAVE	8.00											**8.00**
PERSONAL LEAVE												**0.00**
MILITARY LEAVE												**0.00**
COMP LEAVE												**0.00**
OTHER												**0.00**
DAILY	**8.00**	**8.00**	**8.00**	**8.00**	**8.00**	**8.00**	**8.00**	**8.00**	**8.00**	**8.00**	**0.00**	**80.00**

Mary Smith 1/15/23 *James Oliver* 1/15/23

EMPLOYEE DATE SUPERVISOR DATE

FIGURE 12-2: A simple timesheet helps you track employees' hours.

Allocating expenses

The expenses listing on your statement of functional expense relates to program services and supporting services, which are ordinary, day-to-day expenses including, but not limited to, salaries, employee benefits, professional fees, travel, scholarships and awards, rent, telephone, supplies, and depreciation. Any of the many expenses your nonprofit incurs may be charged to program costs or supporting services such as management and general costs and/or fundraising costs. You just need to make that determination by identifying the expense by program and then segregating by the expense's natural classification using your allocation methodology.

REMEMBER

Your allocation methodology must be included as a note to your financial statements.

TIP

Some high-tech devices, such as copiers or printers, can allocate expenses based on actual usage. For example, you can have your copier or printer set up to assign codes to each program and person. Then, each time something is photocopied or printed, the copier or printer matches the expense to the program or person. So when you're making copies of a fundraising event flyer, your copier can assign the cost of printing to fundraising expense.

The following sections break down the types of program services and supporting services expenses to help you differentiate between them, so you know how to classify them on your statement of functional expense.

Program expenses

Your programs are used to implement your mission. Program expenses are the costs of goods and services used to fulfill your purpose and to operate your projects. Some common programs are

- Food pantries and soup kitchens
- Mentoring programs
- Tutoring programs
- Support groups

Of course, many programs benefit people, so these are just a few examples. Program expenses are costs directly related to a program. Common program expenses are

- Supplies
- Wages of people working solely or directly for a program
- Personnel costs related to the program's direct employees

TIP

The total program expense on the statement of functional expense should equal the program expense reported on the statement of activities. The totals for managerial and general expense and fundraising expense should also agree with those amounts reported on the statement of activities.

If an expense is incurred by two or more programs, you divide it using your allocation methodology (see the "Classifying Functional Expense" section earlier in this chapter). For example, consider the cost of labor (salaries, payroll taxes, and fringe benefits). This is usually a high expense for nonprofits. By using time and attendance reports, you can divide the expense by the hours spent working on each program (see the section "Keeping track of time" earlier in the chapter).

Management and general expenses

The second classification of expenses on the statement of functional expense is supporting services, which includes management and general (M&G) expenses, also referred to as general and administrative expenses. These costs aren't identifiable to any program or fundraising activity. That is, they aren't directly related to an activity nor are they reasonably allocable to an activity. These expenses represent costs that are shared by all activities and are necessary for the organization's operation. They provide an indirect benefit to your organization as a whole, and you incur them whether you run one or more programs.

Management and general activities include

- Accounting staff
- Business management
- Insurance
- Legal expenses
- Payroll taxes
- Rent/mortgage
- Salaries
- Travel
- Utilities
- Administrative activities of the organization as a whole

For example, you use a postage machine in your office for day-to-day business. You wouldn't go out and buy a new postage machine just to operate a new program and to keep expenses separate. You use the postage machine as needed for the new program, and you allocate a portion of the phone bill to all programs that benefit from its use. This could be accomplished through meter setup or programming.

Your T&A reports are the best way to allocate expenses for salaries and fringe benefits to the right category. Finally, your operating budget separates program costs from M&G and fundraising costs. See Chapter 5 of this minibook for more about operating budgets.

TIP

If you can't identify the cost as a program or fundraising cost, then it's automatically an M&G cost. Make sure the total M&G on the statement of functional expense matches the M&G amount on the statement of activities.

Fundraising expenses

Supporting services also includes fundraising expenses. You're fully aware of how important fundraising is to your organization. You seek philanthropists who will donate money, goods, services, time, and effort to support your cause with no quid pro quo. Keeping track of the expenses related to fundraising is important to help you determine whether your efforts at raising money are working and whether you're spending money in the right areas.

Fundraising activities include

- Advertising and direct mail campaigns
- Maintaining donor mailing lists
- Conducting fundraising events, including dinners and dances, concerts and fashion shows, sporting competitions, and auctions
- Preparing and handing out fundraising materials
- Conducting other activities involved with soliciting contributions from individuals, organizations, foundations, corporations, and government entities

The cost of all activities that create support for your nonprofit in the form of gifts, grants, contributions, and services are considered fundraising expenses. Some fundraising expenses stand out. For example, the cost of a direct mail campaign is easy to allocate to fundraising expenses because you know how much postage was used, how many envelopes were mailed, and how many copies you printed.

WARNING

Some fundraising activities held by some nonprofits may not be considered fundraising events by the IRS. Instead, the IRS could consider them unrelated to your nonprofit's exempt purpose and if deemed such, the revenue would be taxable unrelated business income. (See Chapter 8 of this minibook for more information about unrelated business income.)

The following activities can trigger unrelated business income recognition:

- Sales of gifts or goods or services unless they're of nominal value (nominal value is less than real or market value)
- Sweepstakes, lotteries, or raffles where the names of contributors or other respondents are entered in a drawing for prizes
- Raffles or lotteries where prizes have only nominal value
- Solicitation campaigns that generate only contributions

If need be, check with your accountant to verify you're classifying the expenses correctly.

TECHNICAL STUFF

A new method is emerging to conduct fundraising campaigns over the Internet. This new wave is called *ePhilanthropy,* and it allows you to solicit funds from your website, even while you're sleeping.

Using the Statement of Functional Expense to Calculate Ratios

Potential donors typically like to give money to organizations where they know their money is being spent wisely. They sometimes calculate how much of your total expenses are used for programs versus how much is used for management and general expenses. Let's face it, no one wants to give to an organization and have their gift squandered. You can use the statement of functional expense to show your donors exactly how your nonprofit is spending its money and that you're using your donations to help the people you're trying to reach.

To show how you use your funding, you can calculate different ratios that provide insight into your organization's operating performance and financial position. You calculate ratios to measure your nonprofit's organizational efficiency. The total expenses alone don't give a clear picture of your efficiency, but calculating ratios gives the numbers more meaning. (To calculate a ratio, you divide one number by another number. Ratios indicate the relationship of one thing to another.)

REMEMBER

Ratios are only as good as the numbers used to calculate them, so make sure the figures on your statement of functional expense are accurate.

As a general rule, you want to keep your administrative and fundraising costs down and spend donations on their intended purpose of running programs. By figuring the ratios in the following sections, you can show that your donors' contributions aren't being used to pay high salaries and other extravagant expenses. You can ideally advertise that your nonprofit has low administrative and fundraising costs.

Program expense ratio

The program spending ratio tells you what percentage of your total spending goes toward programs. Having your program expenses broken down by percentages gives the statement of functional expense more meaning. It allows people to get a quick overview of how much of their donations support programs.

To calculate the program spending ratio, you divide total program expenses by total expenses. Refer to Figure 12-1 to see the two types of program services, mentoring and tutoring, for this example.

The total allocated to the mentoring program is $154,000. The total program expense for the tutoring program is $92,500. The total program expense is $246,500.

The total expenses for the year are $315,000. The program spending ratio is 78 percent ($246,500 ÷ $315,000 = 0.78). This means that 78 percent of your total expenses are used to run programs.

Overall you're better off with a high program spending ratio because donors want to fund programs, not the administrative and fundraising costs to operate your nonprofit. If the percentages in this example were the other way around, you probably wouldn't get too many donations if only 22 percent of the total expenses supported programs. Of course, sometimes there's room for exceptions. If you're renovating or upgrading your building, for example, you'll have something to show for the disparity.

Fundraising efficiency ratio

The fundraising efficiency ratio tells what percentage of dollars were spent to raise another dollar. Nonprofit managers have a challenging job to raise capital while keeping costs down. This ratio is important because donors like their money to go directly to the programs they're supporting.

You divide fundraising costs by total contributions to get your fundraising efficiency ratio. (You need to refer to your statement of activities to get the total contributions for the year; see Chapter 9 of this minibook for more on the statement of activities.) To calculate the fundraising efficiency ratio, consider the following hypothetical scenario.

If you received $425,000 in contributions and your fundraising costs were $13,500, your fundraising efficiency ratio is 3 percent ($13,500 ÷ $425,000 = 0.03). It only costs 3 cents to raise a dollar.

A 3 percent fundraising efficiency ratio is considered a good ratio because it shows that you're keeping fundraising costs down. A bad ratio depends on what your board and stakeholders expect from you. Larger organizations can have a higher ratio, but small nonprofits should strive to keep this number as low as possible.

IN THIS CHAPTER

» Knowing why you need to close the books

» Completing year-end entries

» Including notes with your financial statements

Chapter 13

Closing the Nonprofit Books

As you come to the end of your accounting year, you need to wrap up your books for previous 12 months and start the books for the next year. Your fiscal year may be on a calendar year from January to December or some other fiscal 12-month period. No matter when your accounting year ends, you need to close your books and start a new accounting cycle or year. To do so, you have to make some closing entries to certain accounts. Closing your books is an important process because you need to transfer the balance from statement of activities accounts to another account, so that only statement of financial position accounts remains open.

When you close your books, you need to make sure all of your temporary accounts, such as your revenue and expense accounts, have zero balances so revenues and expenses in the next accounting cycle can be properly recorded and closed.

This chapter discusses closing the temporary accounts (revenue, expense, gain and loss), making some of the necessary notes to your financial statements, preparing adjusting and reversing entries, and preparing your books for the next accounting period.

REMEMBER

If you're using a manual system, closing the books may turn out to be a little more work than if you were using accounting software because computerized systems close the accounts for you (see Chapter 4 of this minibook for information about using QuickBooks computerized accounting software). No matter which system you use, you need to understand the procedures to end one accounting period and begin another.

Understanding the Need to Close Your Nonprofit's Books

During the course of the year, you've had money coming in (revenues) and money going out (expenses). This is a continuous cycle taking place in your organization. At the end of your accounting year you need to close your books.

REMEMBER

You close the books to move your nonprofit's bottom line from the statement of activities (see Chapter 9 in this minibook) to the statement of financial position (see Chapter 10 of this minibook). Your accounting period had a beginning and ending date. If you operate on a calendar year, your beginning date is January 1, 20XX and your ending date is December 31, 20XX. If you don't close your books, you have no ending to your accounting period and no new beginning.

You can't prepare accurate financial statements until your books are adjusted. Start by reviewing your unadjusted trial balance to determine what accounts require adjusting journal entries. After making all adjusting journal entries, prepare the adjusted trial balance and then your financial statements. At this point you can close your books and start a new accounting cycle. After your financial statements are done, you can turn your information over to a CPA if your nonprofit is required to secure an independent audit.

To understand how to close the books, you have to know the difference between temporary and permanent accounts:

- **Temporary accounts:** Revenue, expense, gain, and loss accounts are considered temporary accounts and are the accounts you close out at the end of the accounting cycle. Temporary accounts report on the statement of activities (also called the income statement; see Chapter 9 of this minibook for more about this statement). The closing process resets these accounts to zero so that only current accounting period transactions are accumulated in the accounts.
- **Permanent accounts:** These accounts report on the statement of financial position (also called the balance sheet; see Chapter 10 of this minibook for

more about this statement). They carry over from year to year, so you normally do not close these accounts. However, it is necessary to close your temporary accounts to a permanent account, which we discuss later in this chapter in the section "Closing entries: A 1-2-3 step."

When you close the books, you transfer the balances of your temporary accounts to the income summary account. The income summary account records the net effect of closing all temporary accounts for a given period. This will be 12 months if you are closing the books at the end of the calendar or fiscal year. A *fiscal year* ends on the last day of any month other than December.

REMEMBER

The balances for all your accounts — revenues, expenses, gains, losses, assets, liabilities, and equity — are in your general ledger.

Think of the income summary account as a bucket holding the net effect of the difference between total revenues/gains and total expenses/losses. That net effect results in either an increase or decrease in net assets, which then is closed to the statement of financial position. The net assets at the beginning of the year is added to the current period net asset increase (decrease), resulting in the total net assets at end of year.

REMEMBER

All net assets must be allocated between those without donor restrictions and those with donor restrictions (see Chapter 9 of this minibook for more information).

Closing entries accomplishes two things:

- **It causes all revenue, expense, gain, and loss accounts to begin the new accounting period with zero balances.** Each accounting period shows performances taking place only during that period. Thus, revenue, expense, gain, and loss accounts are only used temporarily to store current period accounting activities. After the accounting period ends, you transfer the results of everything that transpired during that period to the income summary account.
- **It transfers the net effect of the past period's revenue and expense transactions to an equity account.** During your accounting cycle you made purchases, received support and revenue, and paid bills. Now that this accounting period has expired, you only need to reflect the net effect of the activities that happened in it. So by closing revenue, expense, gain, and loss accounts to the income summary, the income summary reflects the net effects of those accounts. This net effect is transferred to an equity account by closing the income summary to net assets.

The following section explains the steps in adjusting and closing the books and explains when reversing journal entries may come into play.

Adjusting, Closing, and Reversing Entries

During your year-end closing process, you'll probably need to adjust some of your accounts to correct some balances and make cash to accrual adjustments. After you make your adjusting entries, you can prepare an adjusted trial balance, which you use to prepare your financial statements. Then you need to make closing entries to close your temporary accounts to the income summary account, and close the income summary account to net assets. Finally, at the beginning of the next accounting period, you may want to reverse some of the cash to accrual adjustments you made at the end of the previous accounting period.

The following sections walk you through the actual closing process, including when you may have to reverse and adjust some entries at year-end.

Adjusting entries: Year-end

Adjusting journal entries gives you more accurate financial statements. For example, under the accrual method of accounting, when a transaction begins in one accounting period and ends in a later one, an adjusting entry matching expense to the revenue for the same reporting period is required. Adjusting entries are used to make corrections due to transposition and other errors made during the year. These types of adjusting entries are also called correcting entries.

Record adjusting entries in the general journal, posting in chronological order. The general journal is where you post various entries for events that affect accounts but aren't part of the normal transaction process or are somehow special or unusual. Examples are closing entries, correcting entries, and other adjusting entries.

Certain accounts require adjustments at the end of your accounting period due to their nature, like prepaid expenses. *Prepaid expenses* are assets until they're used in the operation of your organization. Examples of prepaid expenses are the unused portion of subscriptions to journals and magazines, or insurance that was paid in full for a year and only four months of the policy period have elapsed.

You may also have adjustments relating to the basis of accounting and time-period concepts. Using different bases of accounting may require adjustments if you've kept your books on the cash basis throughout the year and your financial statements must be presented on the accrual basis according to generally accepted accounting principles (GAAP).

The cash basis reports revenues and expenses when they're received or paid. GAAP require assigning revenues to the periods in which they're earned and expenses to the period in which they're incurred. You use adjusting entries to make cash to accrual adjustments. (Chapter 1 of this minibook walks you through the differences between the cash and accrual methods of accounting.)

Adjusting journal entries are required when accounts like payroll overlap accounting periods. The entire adjustment process is based on revenues being recognized in the accounting period in which they are earned, and expenses recognized in the period they were incurred.

Say the mortgage payable balance in your general ledger is $4,900 and your interest expense is $900. However, your notice from the bank says your mortgage balance is $5,000 and the interest you paid for the year was $1,000. After you verify that the notice from the bank is correct, you make the following entry to correct (adjust) the balances in your general ledger (to increase an expense you debit it and to increase a liability you credit it):

Date		*Debit*	*Credit*
20XX			
Dec 31	Interest expense	100	
	Mortgage payable		100

To adjust mortgage payable and interest expense to bank's records.

Or suppose you get paid every two weeks, but the end of the year falls right in the middle of the two-week period. Wages for the first week were $2,000. Accrual accounting requires you to recognize the payroll expense when it was incurred, not when it is paid. So to post an adjustment:

Date		*Debit*	*Credit*
20XX			
Dec 31	Wages expense	2,000	
	Wages payable		2,000

To accrue the last week's wages for 20XX.

Here's an example for a cash to accrual adjustment. Assume there is a zero balance in accounts payable at the end of the year. However, in early January, you receive a $50 telephone bill for the month of December, which you pay in January. The expense was incurred in December, so the accrual basis of accounting requires

Closing the Nonprofit Books

you to recognize the expense in December, not January. To do this you post the following entry:

Date		Debit	Credit
20XX			
Dec 31	Telephone expense	50	
	Accounts payable		50

To post accounts payable at 12/31/XX

When you record the payment in January, you either debit accounts payable in your cash disbursements journal or debit telephone expense if you reversed the cash to accrual adjustment at the beginning of the year. We discuss reversing entries later in this chapter.

To make the adjustments at the end of each accounting period, prepare a worksheet called a Working Trial Balance (see Figure 13-1). This worksheet allows you to see what will appear on your financial statements. Follow these steps:

1. **Begin with your unadjusted trial balance (Figure 13-1, Part A).** The unadjusted trial balance is the listing of your account balances in the general ledger before you post any required adjustments to these accounts.
2. **List all your adjustments to the accounts (Figure 13-1, Part B).**
3. **Post the adjustments, which gives you the adjusted trial balance (Figure 13-1, Part C).**
4. **Figure 13-1, parts 4 and 5** allocate the adjusted trial balance between income statement and balance sheet accounts.

REMEMBER

The Statement of Activities (Chapter 9 of this minibook) is comparable to the income statement, and the Statement of Financial Position (Chapter 10 of this minibook) is comparable to the balance sheet in the Figure 13-1 worksheet examples.

TIP

After you have posted your adjustments to the general ledger, the account balances in your adjusted trial balance should equal the balances in the general ledger.

When your adjusted trial balance is balanced, you can complete your financial statements. Just move the information from your worksheet (Figure 13-1, parts 4 and 5) into the correct categories on your financial statements. Check out chapters 9–12 of this minibook to help you put together the different financial statements you need. Now all you have to do to finish closing out your year is to post your closing entries.

Saltwell Community School Work Sheet for Month Ended December 31, 20XX										
	A) Unadjusted Trial Balance		B) Adjustments		C) Adjusted Trial Balance		4) Income Statement		5) Balance Sheet	
Account Titles	Dr.	Cr	Dr.	Cr.	Dr.	Cr	Dr.	Cr.	Dr.	Cr.
Cash	325				325				325	
Prepaid Insurance	1200			50	1150				1150	
Office Supplies	60			23	37				37	
School Library	1440				1440				1440	
Office Equipment	3440				3440				3440	
Account Payable		380				380				380
Unearned Day Care Fees		1500	125			1375				1375
Net Assets		3950				3950				3950
Day Care Fees Earned		1950		125 100		2175		2175		
Rent Expense	500				500		500			
Salaries expense	700		105		805		805			
Utilities Expense	115				115		115			
Insurance Expense			50		50		50			
Office Supplies Expense			23		23		22.5			
Depreciation Exp Sch Bks			40		40		40			
Accum Depre Sch Books				40		40				40
Depreciation Ofc Eqp			63		63		62.5			
Accum Depre Ofc Eqp				63		63				63
Salaries Payable				105		105				105
Account Receivables			100		100				100	
TOTALS	7780	7780	505	505	8088	8088	1595	2175	6492	5913
Net Income							580			579
							2175	**2175**	**6492**	**6492**

FIGURE 13-1: Working Trial Balance worksheet.

Closing entries: A 1-2-3 step

To close out your accounting period, you need to make three important closing entries: one for expenses, one for revenues, and a final one for the income summary. Here are the steps:

1. **Close expense accounts.** Your expense accounts are found in your general ledger; each one has to be reset to zero. To close an expense account, you need to decrease it or zero it out by doing a credit. (Remember: Expense accounts have a normal balance of a debit.) Expense accounts are closed by credits equal to the total account's debit balance.

   To close, you write a closing entry in the general journal listing all the expense accounts such as this:

Date		***Debit***	***Credit***
20XX			
Dec 31	Income summary	WW	
	Telephone expense		XX
	Supplies expense		YY
	(Keep listing expenses)		ZZ
	To close expense accounts to the income summary.		

Note in this example the total of all the credits to the expense accounts equals the debit to the income summary. So for this example, XX + YY + ZZ = WW. Closing the expense accounts transfers the total of expenses to the income summary.

2. **Close revenue accounts.** Your revenue accounts are also found in the general ledger, and you have to reset each one of them to zero. To close a revenue account, you need to decrease it or zero it out by doing a debit. Revenue accounts have a normal balance of a credit, so you close them out by making a debit equal to the account's credit balance. To close a revenue account, follow this example:

Date		***Debit***	***Credit***
20XX			
Dec 31	Contributions	WW	
	Program fee income	XX	
	(Keep listing revenues)	YY	
	Income summary		ZZ
	To close expense accounts to the income summary.		

In this example, the total of all the debits to the revenue accounts equals the credit to the income summary. So for this example, WW + XX + YY = ZZ. Closing the revenue accounts transfers the total of revenues to the income summary.

3. **Close the income summary account.** Your income summary account is a temporary account in the general ledger set up to close the revenue and expense accounts. The balance in the income summary equals the total expenses (debits) posted to the account in Step 1 netted against the total revenues (credits) posted to the account in Step 2. If the income summary has a credit balance, then you had a surplus (increase in net assets) for the year. If it has a debit balance, then you had a deficit (decrease in net assets) for the year. So the last step is to transfer the balance from the income summary to net assets by closing the income summary to net assets. The entry looks something like this:

Date		***Debit***	***Credit***
20XX			
Dec 31	Income summary	XX	
	Net assets		XX
	To close the income summary.		

Notice in this example there was a surplus for the year because we had to debit the income summary to close it. There would then be a credit balance in the income summary, which means revenues exceeded expenses. In this scenario, if the debits had exceeded the credits, a deficit would have resulted, showing that expenses were more than revenues.

The income summary account is closed to your net assets account on your statement of financial position.

Reversing entries to close temporary accounts

If you keep your books on the cash basis during the year and make cash to accrual adjustments at the end of the year for your financial statements, you need to reverse those cash to accrual adjustments at the beginning of the next year. If you don't, then you'll count the revenue or expenses twice: once in the period you made the cash to accrual adjustment, and again in the next period when you receive the accrued revenue or pay the accrued expenses. Reversing the accrual entry subtracts the revenue or expense that was accrued and recognized in the previous period, and it eliminates the amount accrued to the related asset or liability account on your statement of financial position.

Record reversing entries in the general journal. To prepare a reversing entry, you debit what was credited, and you credit what was debited in your year-end cash to accrual adjustment. Remember the example for an adjusting entry for December's $50 telephone bill received and paid for in January? We moved the expense from January into December by making the following adjusting entry:

Date		***Debit***	***Credit***
20XX			
Dec 31	Telephone expense	50	
	Accounts payable		50
	To post accounts payable at 12/31/XX		

If you continue keeping your books on the cash basis and don't make reversing entries at the beginning of the next year, you will recognize the $50 of telephone expense twice, once in December and again in January. You'll also still show $50 in accounts payable even though the bill has been paid. That's because accounts payable is found on the statement of financial position and is a permanent account; it is not reset to zero at year-end. So to prevent all this from happening, you post a reversing entry:

Date		***Debit***	***Credit***
20XX			
Jan 1	Accounts payable	50	
	Telephone expense		50
	To reverse previous year's telephone accrual		

Looking at the two journal entries above, December 31 shows an increase to accounts payable by crediting it for $50 and an increase to telephone expense by debiting it for $50. The effect of the December 31 journal is completely reversed with the January 1 journal entry by debiting accounts payable and crediting telephone expense. You would then proceed to reverse all of the previous year-end's cash to accrual adjustments in a similar fashion.

WARNING

It may not be necessary to reverse all your adjusting journal entries. Some adjustments correct balances and should not be reversed. Some expenses, like depreciation, aren't paid with cash, and so those entries wouldn't be reversed. But entries that move income or expenses from one period to another need to be reversed if you keep your books on the cash basis and make year-end accrual adjustments for financial statement purposes.

Completing the Notes to the Financial Statements

The notes (also referred to as footnotes) to your financial statements provide additional valuable information about your financial picture that can influence the overall judgment about your organization's future. According to generally acceptable accounting practices (GAAP), all financial statements should contain notes of disclosure (see Figure 13-2 for an example).

The following sections give you a better idea of what to include in the notes to your nonprofit's financial statements. Some examples are organization and operation, significant accounting policies, liquidity information, and explaining your allocation methodology (see Chapter 12 of this minibook for more information about allocation).

REMEMBER

Folks inside and outside your nonprofit review your financial statements to figure out how well your organization has done and is doing. However, many consider the notes to financial statements just as important as the financial statements themselves because the notes explain things that the numbers can't. Think of your notes as the written story behind the numbers.

Explaining changes in accounting methods

The note outlining the various accounting methods (also known as significant accounting policies) you use to prepare your financial records is usually contained in the first or second note written to your financial statements. Important disclosures for nonprofits are the method of accounting, classification of net assets, and any change in accounting methods.

OASIS, Inc.
Notes to Financial Statements
December 31, 20XX

NOTE 1 — Organization and Operation

OASIS, Inc. is a nonprofit organization under Section 501(C) (3) of the Internal Revenue Code. OASIS's purpose is to mentor and tutor middle school children by providing a positive adult role model, and is conducted through programs within the public school system.

NOTE 2 — Summary of Significant Accounting Policies

Basis of Presentation

The accompanying financial statements are presented on the accrual basis of accounting in accordance with accounting principles generally accepted in the United States of America.

Net assets and revenue, expenses, gains, and losses are classified based on the existence or absence of donor-imposed restrictions. Accordingly, net assets are classified as follows:

Net Assets with Donor Restriction — subject to donor restrictions that may be or will be met by actions taken by OASIS in the passage of time.

Net Assets without Donor Restrictions — available resources other than donor-restricted contributions.

Contributions

Classified as either conditional or unconditional. Conditional contributions are recognized when donor imposed hurdles are satisfied. Unconditional contributions are recognized as revenue and receivable at commitment.

Cash and Cash Equivalents

OASIS considers all cash on hand, checking accounts, and short-term highly liquid investments available for current use with a maturity of three months or less when acquired to be cash and cash equivalents.

Liquidity Information

Assets list by nearness of cash conversion and liabilities list by nearness to resulting use of cash.

NOTE 3 — Contingencies

OASIS participates in grant programs assisted by various governmental agencies. These programs are subject to financial and compliance audits by the grantors or their representatives. Management does not deem any liability arising from such to be material.

FIGURE 13-2: A sample notes of disclosure.

The method of accounting is normally accrual in accordance with accounting principles generally accepted in the United States. The discussion about net assets explains the fact that net assets and changes therein are classified between net assets with donor restrictions and net assets without donor restrictions.

Occasionally, your nonprofit may have a changing accounting method that might bear a significant effect on your reported income or skew results when doing year-over-year trend analysis. Thus, any changes must be disclosed. Some common accounting methods disclosed in your notes are

- **Inventory methods chosen to record value and cost:** Your chosen inventory method sets the price you use to value your inventory. You may have recorded it at the cost you paid for it, or its current market value. The inventory valuation method you use should be indicated in the notes to the financial statement. Also, you should disclose in the notes when you make changes, a topic that should always be discussed with your CPA.
- **Depreciation method or writing off of assets:** Depreciation is the writing off as an expense the cost of an asset over its useful life. Because depreciation reduces net assets, changing your depreciation method affects your net income. Likewise, discuss a change in depreciation methods with your CPA.

If last year's statements were prepared using a different method, they will most likely not be comparable with the current year's statements. Financial managers like to compare apples to apples and oranges to oranges, and changes to accounting methods will probably necessitate comparing apples to oranges. Even though they're both fruits, they're pretty different. You need to disclose any changes in your accounting methods and the financial impact of those changes in your footnotes.

For example, think of the relationship between your statement of activities and your statement of financial position. Your statement of activities records all revenue, expense, gain, and loss. Your statement of financial position records all assets, liabilities, and equity. The difference between revenues, expenses, gains, and losses are closed out to the statement of financial position as an increase or decrease in net assets. So if you change the accounting method for any account tied to an expense, the change in method makes a difference in your net assets.

Two principles shed some light on changes in accounting methods:

- **The Full Disclosure Principle:** This principle states that investors and creditors have every right to information relevant to the user's decision making.
- **The Consistency Principle:** This principle states that consistency should be used with the same accounting events period after period.

Noting all lawsuits

Because lawsuits may have an adverse effect on your nonprofit's finances, you need to both disclose any lawsuit and fully describe the nature of the lawsuit in the notes of your financial statements. Why do you need to include this information? Your stakeholders need to know who may potentially want to sue you and why because they have a vested interest in your nonprofit's livelihood.

Generally accepted accounting principles (GAAP) requires this information at least via a footnote. Based on the circumstances, you may have to prepare a journal entry to show the effect of the lawsuit as an actual part of the financial statements. See the next section, "Including all contingent liabilities," to learn the two criteria for reporting lawsuits as a part of the financial statements.

Wondering how a nonprofit might be a party in a lawsuit? A disgruntled employee may want to sue the nonprofit, seeking damages for injury or workers compensation, or someone may want to take you to court for wrongful death or negligence of someone entrusted in your care. For example, if you operate a nonprofit daycare facility and one of your employees leaves a child in a van, you could face a lawsuit from a disgruntled parent.

Although you can't prevent lawsuits, you can protect your organization by purchasing liability insurance to offset the effects of someone winning a case against your organization.

Including all contingent liabilities

Based on the facts and circumstances of the contingent liability, you may have to report the effect of contingent liabilities on your financial statements. A *contingent liability* is a noncurrent liability that exists when your nonprofit has an existing circumstance as of the date of the financial statements that may cause a future loss, depending on events that have not yet happened (and indeed may never happen).

Examples of events that could be considered contingencies are

- Pending litigation, which means the nonprofit is actively involved in a lawsuit that is not yet settled, such as an ex-employee's lawsuit for lost wages or wrongful termination
- Not filing Form 990 and forgetting to file an extension that results in penalties

If a loss due to a contingent liability meets the following two criteria, it should be accrued and reported in the nonprofit's financial statements:

1. **The chance of the loss event happening is probable, which means that the future event will likely occur.**
2. **The amount of the loss can be reasonably estimated, which means you can come up with a highly accurate loss dollar amount.** For example, if the nonprofit finds out it has to pay damages in a lawsuit, the cost is fixed and determinable.

Refer to Figure 13-2 for how the wording appears for contingent liabilities in the notes.

Noting conditions on assets and liabilities

Sometimes donors impose restriction on the assets they give your nonprofit, and these restrictions need to be included in the notes to your financial statements. Also, if you have pledged assets as collateral for loans, you should include this in the notes. If you have long-term liabilities, you should disclose the effective interest rate, maturity dates, repayment terms, and so on.

Putting Last Year Behind You and Looking Forward

After you've closed the books, you can prepare your financial statements. When all of that number crunching is finished, make sure to store the journals, general ledger, and any supporting documentation someplace safe. You never know when you're going to need that info, and you definitely don't want to mix the old records with the new ones.

You also need to start a new set of books for the new fiscal year. Start with journaling, maintain good records throughout the year, and end with polished audited financial statements. When you end the year, you'll find yourself going over the same procedures for the next. Think about how good you'll feel when it's over!

5

Speaking on Behalf of Your Nonprofit

Contents at a Glance

IN THIS CHAPTER

» Grasping the basics of public speaking

» Tuning in to your body language

» Knowing the importance of breath

» Learning to practice

» Giving a successful speech

Chapter 1
Getting Started with Public Speaking

If you're the director of a nonprofit organization, or otherwise involved in the nonprofit sector, you may need to give a speech at some point. And, if you're like the vast majority of people, you may not have a lot of experience doing that, which may make you anxious.

When you give a speech or presentation, remember that it's all about your message to the audience; it isn't really about *you*. This is especially true when you're involved with a nonprofit organization, and you want to spread information about your good cause. Some of the smartest and the most accomplished people tend to forget about the message and focus all their anxiety on themselves as speakers. "Should I have cut my hair? What if I forget the most important point?" Although you certainly want to look your best during a speech, and you want to deliver the main point, hyperfocusing on these points can take your focus from living in the present. And when you're speaking, the present means delivering your message to the audience.

Dealing with Issues That Stand in Your Way

Whether or not you have a good idea of what your specific problem with public speaking may be, many issues can arise while preparing for and during your speech. It's important to have a good sense of them. You may be afraid, your body language may be making you feel less than confident, you could have a vocal problem, you could be running out of breath and not getting to the ends of your sentences. There are many possible reasons for these things.

REMEMBER

Here are a few things to remember:

- Performing requires effort — but you don't want the audience to see that effort.
- A powerful speaker is relaxed and comfortable.
- Your public speaking voice should be the same one you use when talking to your family, friends, and colleagues. (A male politician told a friend he was working with a pubic speaking coach. "Whatever you do," his friend said, "don't turn into one of those fake-sounding politicians." You need to have your own style and sound like yourself.)

You may just need little tweaks — or you may need more work.

Fighting the fight, flight, or freeze response

You've probably heard the statistics. People rate public speaking up there with *dying* on the all-time fears list. It should be no surprise then that during public speaking, the automatic response that we usually see when facing a life-threatening situation kicks in: It's sometimes called the *fight, flight, or freeze* response. This was first described by physiologist Walter Bradford Cannon in his book *The Wisdom of the Body* in 1932. It's a physiological response to fear that traces back to prehistoric days. A Cro-Magnon was always on guard, looking out for danger — because danger was real back then, and it came from everywhere. We aren't cavepersons anymore, despite how you may feel some days behind the lectern, *but we still feel the fear.* It's built in to us.

Let's get something straight right off the bat: It's okay to be nervous, because that shows that you care. When you're presenting, adrenaline (often triggered by fear) courses through your body. That's a good thing. That adrenaline is doing you good — it's giving you an extra boost during an extraordinary time. When your body is stressed for a long time, as when a prehistoric ancestor was fighting off a herd of saber-toothed cats, the stress hormone cortisol is also secreted. And that's when we have problems. When you're scared, your voice reflects it. You may sound shaky, or you speed up, or you speak so quietly that you can't be heard, or you blank and can't think of what to say next.

TIP

Here's something you're going to read often in this chapter of this minibook: The best solution to conquering fear and anxiety is proper breathing technique. Breathing slowly — as opposed to the short little breaths you take when anxious — stimulates your brain to activate the calming rest and digest parasympathetic nervous system. Basically, proper slow breathing shuts off the tap that's supplying you with stress. By adopting a positive attitude, changing your body language, and saying yes instead of no, you can actually change the way you feel about yourself. And that translates into better public speaking.

Affirming your worth with affirmations

Do you say no before you say yes? People are hard-wired to say *no* first, thanks to our ancestors the aforementioned cave dwellers. Is your own mind getting in the way of success? You can get positive about presenting by adopting a better attitude.

That all starts with affirmations. *Affirmations* help to kick-start belief in yourself. "I am a great speaker," "My message rocks!" and "I am the expert!" Say these things to yourself and before you know it, you'll start believing them — and believing in yourself.

One of Stephen Covey's *Habits for Highly Effective People* is to begin with the end in mind. What do you want to happen *after* the speech? What do you want the audience to *do*? Put your focus on the audience and the message you want to impart on them. See Chapter 5 of this minibook for more about this.

Creating reality with visualization

Most people are very good at imagining themselves doing something negative. Why not turn that around and visualize a great presentation? Picture the audience nodding in approval. Your mind plays tricks on you all the time through negative thinking. Well, two can play at that game. The brain is flexible. You can consciously change it to think more positively.

External visualization is where you're looking at yourself as if you're in a movie, and *internal visualization* is where you see yourself actually performing the task from your point of view. Elite athletes use both kinds and find them very beneficial.

If you're using external imagery, you can watch yourself sitting in the audience, rising when the host calls your name, calmly striding up to the lectern, taking three breaths, and beginning your speech — which will be great. The audience is giving you appreciative nonverbal reactions. Your visual aids are all in place. You end your speech to genuine applause.

With internal imagery, you simulate giving the speech in your own body. When you go through your speech, how are you feeling? What are you seeing and hearing?

Getting rid of tension

We all need some amount of tension in our bodies. If we didn't have tension, we wouldn't be able to sit or stand. So, it's not tension in general that we need to think about and get rid of, but rather, *misplaced* tension.

Proper alignment is the first step in relieving unnecessary tension. The spine, as you know, is crucial to alignment. It's the mast of your ship. If you have unnecessary tension, it starts with your spine. And that makes it harder on your muscles to just keep you standing. Then everything else gets out of whack. Your breath will be impeded, your shoulders and neck may be tight, and your vocal energy may be low. The audience mirrors you, so if you're feeling tense, they will too.

So what can you do about it? You have to get physical. Working out relieves tension. Go for a walk or run, dust off your bike, hit the pool, or practice some yoga.

Progressive relaxation is a tension and release exercise that was developed by American physician Edmond Jacobson in 1908 to help patients overcome their anxiety. This is an exercise where you tense all body parts individually and then release to feel the difference. You start by lying on the floor in a quiet place. You learn to tense and release all parts of your body. Then if you feel tense before or during a presentation, you can tense a part of your body, like your toes, and release.

Improving Your Body Language

Body language can be even more important than your voice in delivering your message to the audience. Body language is crucial in exuding confidence in yourself and showing trust in your audience.

TIP

Believe it or not, changing your posture can actually change your mood and, ultimately, how you perform.

First things first. You need to stand up straight — not like you're waiting for the sergeant to inspect your barracks, but in an *up and out* position. You feel your bones stacked up on top of each other, your head is directly over your shoulders and on top of your neck, your chin is neither tucked in nor jutting forward, your chest is out, your feet are planted, and you have energy surging through your body past the crown of your head and up into the sky.

The opposite is the *down and in* position. When you slouch and gaze at the floor, it doesn't show confidence in you or your audience. Averting your eyes and looking down send the message to the audience that you'd rather be anywhere else. If you're not properly aligned, down and in also impedes your breath. You won't be able to drop your breath deep into your body like you should.

Here are some other body language tips:

- **Handshakes are part of body language, too.** Give a firm one if you want to make a good impression. Don't be a limp rag, but don't squeeze and hang on for dear life. That may make a lasting impression, but not a good one.
- **Stand up and sit up straight.** If you'll be presenting sitting down, such as in a boardroom, have both feet firmly planted on the floor and don't slouch into your chair.
- **Be mindful of crossing your arms or legs.** Crossing your arms while talking to colleagues at the water cooler may feel natural for you, but what impression does it give to your listeners? Defensiveness, that's what. Crossing your legs may feel comfortable, but to some it looks like you are in a closed-off position. Crossing your arms and your legs doesn't make you look very approachable.

Gesturing

You don't know what to do with your hands? Try moving them. Practice doing that and see how comfortable it becomes and how it activates your parasympathetic nervous system.

The autonomic nervous system consists of three parts:

- The *enteric* system controls the stomach and intestines.
- The *sympathetic* nervous system activates the "fight or flight" response.
- The *parasympathetic* nervous system, or the "rest and digest" system.

In Mark Bowden's book *Winning Body Language* (McGraw-Hill Education, 2010), the author states that moving your hands in a horizontal plane extending out from your navel has a calming effect and activates the parasympathetic nervous system. He calls this the *truth plane* because you look and feel more genuine when your hands are in this position.

TIP

When you're giving your presentation seated at a boardroom table, gesture away. Just make sure to keep your hands up where everyone can see them. If you drop them under the table, no one knows what is going on down there.

Moving

Some speakers just want to stay put and stand motionless behind the lectern. That may be fine (unless they're gripping the thing with white knuckles). Others feel the need to move constantly. Both are individual choices and are up to you.

TIP

When you do move, make sure you move with a purpose. Choreograph where you want to move and when. The movement should make sense in combination with what you're talking about. Through practice, movement will soon become second nature.

WARNING

Swaying side to side or back and forth is fine for rocking a baby. When you're speaking, though, you want the focus to be on what you have to say. Plant those feet and imagine roots growing down from them into the earth.

Making eye contact

The audience is your friend, and they want you to succeed. Believe it or not, they're not planning to throw rotten fruit at you the moment you falter.

TIP

Find someone in the audience who is giving you nonverbal cues that they are listening and is interested in what you're saying. Look that person directly in the eye for about five or six seconds. Then move on to someone else. Look at the same person for too long, and they'll start to feel uncomfortable. And the rest of the audience may start wondering why that one person is getting a solo performance.

TIP

If you're really that scared when you speak, find that friendly face and look at that person. Sometimes you may feel that it's easier to look above and over the audience's heads. That way, you don't have to connect with them. But the audience can tell that you're not looking at them. If your eyes are the windows to your soul, the audience is never going to get to know you if they can't engage with you and your message. Practice when the stakes are low — look your colleagues in the eye, the delivery guy, your kid's basketball coach.

Adjusting Your Pace: Perfecting the Pause

One of the most common problems speakers have is speeding up their speeches as they progress through them. It's obvious they want to get their speech over with as soon as possible.

If you find yourself speeding up, but you don't feel particularly scared, maybe you've practiced it so much that you're just going through the motions. Think of the way you absentmindedly murmured the Pledge of Allegiance as a kid, or the Lord's Prayer. Congrats on being prepared — but you're doing it wrong.

REMEMBER

When you deliver your speech, that's the first time the audience will hear it. A speech is a performance. When you watch a play, the actors don't do everything faster than they did on opening night just because they know their lines better. Be clear and slow down so that the audience has time to register what you just said. Practice saying one sentence slowly. Then take a breath.

What is that little dot at the end of a sentence? Right, it's a period and it represents the end of a thought. Use it to pause and take a breath. When speakers pause, it shows that they are confident and that they have control of their presentation.

A pause can also create suspense for the audience. What is the speaker going to say next? As a speaker, you may feel as if your pause is soooo long. Actually, you're really just taking a breath. The audience doesn't see it as taking a long time.

REMEMBER

When you pause to take a breath or allow a thought to land and take hold of them, it shows the audience you're confident. You've got this under control.

WARNING

Often, people use *filler words* in place of breath pauses, like *um* and *ah*. Some people feel as if they must constantly keep talking. Don't do this. Yes, it may give you time to gather your thoughts for your next sentence, but you're taking away the opportunity for the audience to do the same.

When you tell a joke or a humorous story or even say a line that the audience laughs at, pause and wait for the laugh to subside. Otherwise, they'll miss what you say next.

Supporting Your Breath

TIP

If you take away only one thing from this chapter, let it be *the importance of breath*. Breath is your fuel. It's the stuff that runs your speech. Breathing deep and slow helps you relax, and when you feel relaxed, you're less stressed. It's a perfect feedback loop.

Your *diaphragm* is a cone-shaped muscle attached to the lower edges of your rib-cage. When you breathe in, the abdominal and pelvic muscles relax, the diaphragm flattens, the ribs expand up and out, and the breath enters the lungs. When you breathe, visualize your breath dropping deep into your lower abdomen.

TIP

To find out if you're breathing correctly, put one hand on your upper chest and the other on your lower abdomen and inhale. Pay attention to which hand moves first. If it's your hand on your upper chest, then you are not taking full breaths. Imagine filling your lungs up like a balloon. Balloons fill up starting at the bottom. When you exhale, your balloon deflates, and your navel is pressed toward your spine.

WARNING

Taking the time to breathe deeply will help you sustain your breath to the end of your sentence. If you run out of breath before the sentence is over, you tend to drop your volume and mumble your way through the end of the sentence. When you do that, the audience can't hear what you said. You lose your impact, and your message is lost.

WARNING

If you hold your breath because you missed something in your speech or you look out at that audience gripped with fear, your brain won't get the oxygen it needs — and you may blank. So keep breathing!

EXERCISE: SAYING DIFFERENT SENTENCES, TAKING DIFFERENT BREATHS

This exercise can improve your lung capacity and how much breath you need for each sentence.

Different sentences require different amounts of breath. Speak each of the following lines on one breath:

- I read *For Dummies* books. (breathe)
- I read *For Dummies* books because they give me so much information. (breathe)
- I read *For Dummies* books because they give me so much information that I can use every day. (breathe)

Each sentence requires more breath. Your breath should sound as free and easy on the last sentence as on the first. For each, try to take in only as much breath as you need. Try not to lift your shoulders when you breathe in.

Boosting Confidence through Preparation and Training

You've been asked to present and you're thinking, *Why me? I'm not worthy!* Sure, you may look snazzy and dressed up, but inside you're screaming, *I'm an imposter!*

TIP

Get rid of self-defeating thoughts. Let them go. You *are* good, or you wouldn't have been asked to speak. Perfection doesn't exist. And if it did, it would be boring. You don't want to strive to be perfect. How about striving for excellence instead? Be the best you can be. That is what the audience wants — to see your authentic self, flaws and all.

Think of your presentation as a learning experience. Maybe your dad told you that all the time through school. You didn't listen? Well, listen now. Analyze how you did afterward. Have a checklist of things you did that you felt good about and things that you could improve. The more you present, the more your list of improvements will shrink.

Do you try to wing a speech? How did that go? Winging an important presentation doesn't work for most people. Even if you manage to fill up the allotted time, you may have missed important facts. You probably rambled on because you had no idea where your speech was going. You were grasping for what to say next, what you wanted to remember, what you were forgetting. Recall that the audience mimics what they see — if you look and feel befuddled, so will they.

TIP

It all comes down to practice, practice, practice. It takes years to go from amateur to master in any field of endeavor. The thing about learning a new skill is that you just don't learn it and forget about it. What makes people great at anything is that they always learn it more from doing it over and over. Even if you give the same presentation 20 times, each time will be different. So take the mistakes and learn from them to get better.

TIP

Never look in the mirror when practicing your presentation. You look in a mirror to make sure that your shirt is tucked in, that your hair is parted correctly, or that the piece of spinach is off your teeth. And these are the things you're doing when you look in the mirror while practicing. You're not in the moment. It's much better to record yourself on video — or record your voice on your phone or other device to hear how you sound. See Chapter 4 of this minibook for more about this.

Breathing (your own) life into speeches

For writers, it's all about finding your voice. It's the first step to becoming confident in your work. The same can be said for writing a speech. It doesn't matter what your speech is about — fractions or septic systems or deodorant sales — get some personality into your speech.

A speech is a great opportunity to give the audience a real treat. You want to show the world that you're an intelligent human being when you present. You're not writing a technical manual — you're allowing your audience to look deep into you.

TIP

After you've written your speech, practice it out loud. Did you write it in your own voice? You'll discover what words fit for you and the audience. More on this in Chapter 2 of this minibook.

Planning your speech

As you write your speech, ask yourself:

- What do you want to say?
- What does the audience need to hear?
- Why are you speaking to them?

In the public speaking world, speeches have three main purposes:

- **To entertain:** That's the speech you give at a wedding.
- **To persuade:** That's when you're selling something, an idea, service, or tangible object.
- **To inform:** You're giving information. Think of a college lecture.

You need *all three components* in your speech. Doing that will make your speech a lot more interesting.

How should you begin your presentation? With a rhetorical question that the audience doesn't have to answer but that gets them thinking? A statistic or cool fact? A provocative or inspiring quote? A comment about an event that happened locally, a compliment to the audience, or a personal story?

All of those have the same objective: to get the audience engaged right off the bat. There's more about this in Chapter 2 of this minibook.

Getting ready for the big day

It's the night before your speech. You've gone over your presentation enough times to feel really comfortable with it. What now? Make a list of things you need to be a success. For example, do you have your speech printed out or your cue cards? Do you have your USB stick or any visuals handy? Where's your water bottle? Will the hotel supply you with a water glass? Will they give you some food beforehand? Practice in the clothes you plan to wear, because you never know if that tie is too tight or those heels too high.

On the day of the event, get to the venue early and meet your organizer or the person you've been in contact with. Talk to the technician or the person responsible for your visuals. Walk on the stage if you can — it will help you feel more comfortable when you do it for real. Meet the early birds and have a good chat. That's another good way to feel more comfortable. It's also a good way to feel out the tone of the conference or meeting. Did they just listen to a speaker who told them that they will need two million dollars in the bank to retire? That would be good to know.

TIP

Don't take yourself too seriously. Yes, you need to do well when you present. You want to get your message across. But there's no need to put undue pressure on yourself.

Honing Your Delivery

Warming up is vital if you want to give a great speech. You're a *speech athlete*, and all athletes warm up before they compete. Remember, you are using your body. Speakers, just like athletic competitors, need to warm up physically and vocally.

Articulating

What's that, you say? You might be passionate about your speech, but if you don't open your mouth and pronounce your words clearly, no one will care. *Articulation* helps you communicate your ideas to your audience. That starts with your mouth.

You need to open your mouth to be understood clearly. Many speakers hardly open their mouths. Perhaps they're mirroring other people around them who have shut their traps. Or mumbling is a habit. Or they're scared. Your *articulators* include the tongue, lips, jaw, and the soft palate.

You may feel self-conscious about your accent. By the way, we all have accents — we all sound different depending on region of origin and other factors. If you're from New York, your *accent* or how you pronounce words is probably very different from a Texan's. All you Canadians out there, don't be thinking that the only people with accents are from Quebec and Newfoundland. Every community says words differently. So embrace your accent. You don't need to get rid of it — in fact, you can't. You just need to be clear in your pronunciation.

TIP

If you're told constantly to speak up, you don't have to push your voice. Just make sure you pronounce the endings of the words. Don't think your microphone will be your savior. Yes, a mic will amplify your sound so the audience will hear you at the back of the room. But they'll also hear your vocal problems, too.

Resonating

Your whole body resonates and amplifies your sound. The most important parts are the head, throat, mouth, and chest. Think of yourself as an amplifier. If you hold tension in your body, you won't be able to resonate fully, and your sound won't be as rich and vibrant.

Using the right tone

You express meaning through tone. Yes, *express*. Speakers often have trouble with this because they don't want to exaggerate and look foolish. But if you feel excited that the recent fundraiser exceeded its goals, shouldn't you show it? Yes — make sure you show it.

REMEMBER

When you speak, you need to use vocal variety. The speaker who sits on one note is boring and loses the audience's attention.

TIP

Be mindful of what you're saying and how you're saying it. If you're selling a group of seniors a new retirement package, don't be condescending. Remember your message and what you want the seniors to do. You don't want them to write you off as some young whippersnapper who just wants money.

Adding visuals

Visuals like slide shows *can* help enhance your message. But make sure they really add to your presentation and don't just give you something you think you can hide behind.

You definitely don't need to put a whole bunch of words on slides and proceed to read them. Boring! Your slides or other visuals should only relate to main points or provide context for what you're saying, and your slides should always have as few words on them as possible.

TIP

Answer this question: Do your slides truly complement your speech or did you just stick them in because you felt your words weren't enough? If you took the slides away (which could happen — machinery has a tendency to fail at the worst possible moments), could you still give your speech with full confidence? Your answer should be yes.

TIP

Try using pictures. When we look at a picture, it evokes feelings in us and carries us into our imagination. That's usually more than words on a slide could ever do. Words on a slide just give the audience a visual version of what you're saying already.

Make sure you're consistent with your message. If you are talking about, say, plumbers and their right to make a choice about striking, and your slides are all about stats on how many plumbers are in the union, the audience doesn't know which to focus on. If they read the stats, they miss what you have said. If they listen to you, they miss the stats. If they read the stats fast and you're still talking, they may just zone out completely.

TIP

Be creative. Think outside the box. Try to incorporate other kinds of visuals, such as props. Props can create more impact than a PowerPoint slide. Just make sure to use a prop that's big enough for the whole audience to see. Chapter 3 of this minibook discusses visual aids in detail.

Getting laughs

Getting the audience laughing can be a fantastic technique. But comedy can be tricky to pull off. The audience will smell a phony, so be authentic. Even if you aren't a naturally born jokester, you can tell a joke or a humorous story. You don't need to be a comedian to be funny. The trick is to find your funny bone and add humor to your speech without alienating the audience.

Start by writing what you know. Write about you and your life. Many times we've heard friends talk about funny incidents that have happened to them that they would never share in front of people who aren't their good friends. Well, now's your chance.

Here are some quick tips to being funny up there:

- Focus on what the audience and you have in common.
- Try it out on friends.
- Don't be afraid to be vulnerable and open — audiences love that.
- Don't say, "Have I got a funny joke for you."
- Don't assume they will laugh. Appreciate it when they do.
- Once you start the joke, keep going and stay committed to telling it all the way to the end.
- Use situational humor.
- Talk about what's bugging you.
- Keep it clean.
- Find someone who is funny and ask that person about your story.
- Don't be the first to laugh, but feel free to laugh at yourself if the audience does.

Telling stories

Everyone loves stories. Using narration helps to get your message across in a fun way that engages the audience. A personal anecdote helps the audience get into your world and relate to you. You can use part of a story as a hook and then wrap it up in the conclusion. Chapter 2 of this minibook is devoted to using stories in speeches.

Dealing with the Audience (and Hecklers)

As a speaker, there is nothing worse than saying something and getting a groan from the audience — especially early in your speech. Avoiding groans starts with knowing your audience. It's your job to find out the kind of audience that will be listening to your speech.

Here are a few things to consider:

- Be sensitive if something tragic has happened in the community.
- Use appropriate language and tone. If you're talking to a group of seniors about their retirement plan, don't be condescending and don't alienate them.

WARNING

» If you're telling a joke, don't *ever* be off-color.

» Don't pit part of the audience against the other. "Women, don't you think that men . . ." That might work for the professional comedian, but you want the entire audience to be engaged and on your side.

TIP

Heckling is just an obstacle you may have to address. Don't take it personally. Remember that you're the boss up there and follow these tips to get you through it:

» Keep your cool and keep breathing.

» Address the heckler and ask an open-ended question. "How do you feel about that?" That may lead the heckler to run into a ditch on their own.

» If the heckler persists, tell them that you will address their concerns after the presentation. (If you do talk to the person later, give them a time limit. You have five minutes and then you have to go chat with the organizer.)

» If the heckler keeps going, turn to the audience and say, "I think the audience wants to hear more about what I'm saying."

IN THIS CHAPTER

- » Planning your speech
- » Making your point and hooking the audience
- » Using the PIE method
- » Making your speech sound like you
- » Cuing yourself with punctuation
- » Honing your speech-writing skills with a few exercises

Chapter 2 Crafting a Captivating Speech

Can you remember the last time you were at a conference and a very interesting keynote speaker with presumably a lot to say droned on mindlessly for what seemed (or really was) hours, spewing information in no particular order? Probably not. Those people are weeded out early in the process, and regardless of their merit and worldliness, they don't often get to go onstage and spew words. At least not twice.

REMEMBER

This highlights a very important point you must grasp to get anywhere in public speaking: *Presentation is king.*

Of course, that's not an absolute rule. You must have something to say in order to say it. If you don't know anything about plumbing, and even if you craft the best speech you can about the mechanism below the toilet, it will still probably come out not great. But the opposite phenomenon also happens: You can have all the clout and respect in the world when it comes to a subject, but without the proper words, structure, argument, and, ultimately, presentation behind it, you will sound like a rookie.

Don't believe me? Pull out your phone (or a recorder) and start talking about the subject you know most about. Then pour yourself a healthy glass of wine and listen to yourself. There's probably some repetition in there, and lots of "ums" and "uhs" as well. Where's the narrative? It was all up there in your mind just a second ago. Did it disappear?

This chapter offers guidance on composing the speech of your dreams about any subject you know well.

Planning and Preparing

You may not be the type of person to plan things meticulously. You are, of course, the expert on the subject you are about to talk about. And certainly, in the public speaking world, there *are* those who can wing a perfect speech and deliver it with a punch. But unless you're one of those people (and if you are, you probably don't need this book), in order to present your expertise in a way that engages your audience, you first have to understand the mechanics of what makes a speech effective.

REMEMBER

Giving a speech is a performance. And if your message is going to be received in the way that you want it to be, you have to give a good performance. If you think of any other performance you've seen onstage, you know that it almost certainly followed a specific script.

Maybe the most famous improv troupe in the world is in Chicago: Second City. *Improv* (short for *improvisation*) is an art form that's built on spontaneity, and the best improv appears to be completely made up on the spot. You may think the performers are winging it, and in some ways they are. But even in improv, a very specific set of rules governs the performance. In a typical improv performance, the actors ask the audience for suggestions for a situation. They use the sacred rule "Yes Let's" as a method to continue action. "Yes Let's" means when one actor says something new, proposing a new direction for the action or creating the situation proposed by the audience, the other actors immediately agree to it — they never push back. This way, everything moves forward smoothly. Before they are ever on stage, the performers work tirelessly in the studio to prepare for anything so that when they perform, it looks as if their performance is completely spontaneous.

So, regardless of whether you want your speech to feel like a meticulously scripted piece of drama or a spontaneous piece of improv, you first need to learn the basics about what makes up a speech.

What's Your Point?

The first thing you have to decide when you're planning your speech is your *point*. This is like the punch line of the joke. It's the reason everyone will gather with eager anticipation to hear you reveal the magic bullet of just whatever it is you do or know. "But," you may say, "There is no magic bullet! I've worked years at learning this skill I'm about to talk about, and in no way can I condense it into a five-minute speech!"

This is the case with many who feel overwhelmed by a speech or presentation they have to give. It's *not* their lack of understanding of the material. Often it's the opposite: It's that their understanding is so *vast*. It's a challenge to reduce a body of knowledge down to a small talk that both demonstrates that knowledge and gives the audience what they need to know, *specifically*.

To determine the overall point you want to make in your speech, answer the following questions:

- **What do you want to say?** The answer to this question probably popped into your head immediately after you were asked to give a speech. "Well," you thought, "I'll tell them about X."
- **What does the audience need to hear?** This question gets slightly more complicated, encouraging you to explore the other side. How will *your audience* be better off by hearing about what you, the expert, knows? You may hold the knowledge, but the speech is more about the audience than you.
- **What language should you use?** A psychiatrist speaking to healthcare providers would use different terminology when speaking to patients about the same topic. Pitch your speech to the audience.
- **Why are *you* speaking to them?** What makes *you* the right person to be sharing this idea? What is your particular perspective? What do you have to add to the conversation that only you can add?
- **What do you have to say that's so important people will want to hear it?** Does what you want to talk about matter to your audience? If the answer isn't a strong, immediate *yes,* then can you find a way to make it matter? You don't want your audience to leave at the end of your speech (or, worse, in the middle) wondering, "Okay, so what?" Either find a way to make what you have to say relevant to your audience or find a new topic.
- **Can you say it in one sentence?** The answer to this question is always *yes.* Even the most complicated topic can be summarized in a single sentence. You need to write that sentence down, and that's the hard part.

Hooking Your Audience

Good speakers grab the listeners' attention from the beginning and draw them into the topic. You do this with a *hook*. The hook often comes in the first sentence, but not always.

REMEMBER

The hook is the first idea you give to the audience. It establishes the tone for what's to come and sets up your point.

Here are some proven techniques for creating and delivering your hook:

» **Ask a question.** Asking a question is an easy way to engage an audience. They don't have to answer it, but they will think about the question as you talk. This works to arouse their curiosity about your subject. Be prepared to predict their answer. Don't arouse their curiosity about something you *aren't* going to talk about. Keep it short and sweet; for example, "What if you went to get your morning coffee and there was no water?" or "How did you travel to this conference today?"

» **Begin with a powerful quote.** A quotation from someone the audience respects is a way to both introduce and elevate what you're about to talk about. Use the quote to position you as a fellow admirer of the wisdom imparted by this person. Your audience will find it easier to relate to you as a fellow student than as a "teacher."

WARNING

Don't use a quote in a way that makes you seem to be trying to elevate yourself to the level of the person you're quoting. Audiences are sensitive to that.

For example, in a motivational speech, you might begin with something like, "Amelia Earhart said, 'The most effective way to do it, is to do it.'"

» **Show a visual.** Presenting a visual is a great way to start a speech, especially if you're nervous. It draws the audience's attention away from you, and it briefly makes you a member of the audience too as you turn to look at what they're looking at. Your visual might be a photograph, short video, or graph. If you're talking about something concrete, showing a good picture of it makes a lot of sense.

TIP

If you're stuck, it sometimes works to center your speech around a visual. Here's an exercise that can help: Prepare a two-minute speech on anything. What image could accompany that two minutes that would grab the audience's attention? How about holding up a picture of your dog before you start speaking about finding homes for dogs and cats in shelters? Granted, all the dog lovers in the audience will be immediately hooked, but a picture can grab anyone right away. And they'll want to know more just looking at it.

- **Present a surprising fact or statistic.** A statistic can be a great attention-grabber, especially if it refutes a widely held belief or otherwise surprises the audience. For example, did you know that you're more likely to be killed by a falling coconut than by a shark? That might be perfect for a presentation to convince an audience not to be so afraid of sharks (or, to be more cautious around coconut trees). A statistic can have an emotional impact on your audience and raise your credibility. Perhaps best of all, your audience might just remember it.
- **Compliment the audience.** It may sound corny, but one effective way to get an audience on your side is to compliment them or otherwise convey your respect. You want them to respect *you,* and ultimately respect your opinion enough for them to consider it, so starting by throwing a little respect their way can do wonders.

  For example, you can begin like this, as one speaker did: "It is an honor to be speaking with you today. You are the top sellers in real estate in the city, and I am thrilled to present to this high-achieving group." This speaker had the audience in the palm of their hand.

  WARNING

  Something to consider with this approach: *Be genuine.* The audience can smell "fake" a mile away. Don't just tell them you're happy to be in front of them — show them. Act like you're seeing an old friend for the first time in a while.
- **Be humble.** If you've been chosen to speak among esteemed colleagues, or even people with a higher standing than you, don't pretend to be something you aren't. "It's a great honor to be speaking in front of you here today" establishes that you know your place in their world and helps you sidestep any chip-on-the-shoulder issues, especially if you're about to refute an old status quo idea or propose a new one.
- **Sprinkle in some local flavor.** If you're speaking outside your home turf, mention something that demonstrates you have some familiarity with the area. You might say something about a local sports team, a coffee shop or restaurant you stopped at, a local news story you heard that morning, a popular event that's being held, or some other topic of local interest.

  When comedian Amy Schumer performed on a cold winter night in Edmonton, she commented about the weather — and without missing a beat, mentioned that it was way colder in Calgary. She had the audience's attention immediately because she had learned something about the rivalry between Edmonton and Calgary. The audience may know you're not a local, but they'll be on your side.
- **Tell a story.** Everyone likes a good story, so consider telling a simple (short) story related to the topic you're about to speak about or a story that leads smoothly into that topic. A personal story is best, because it invites the audience to join you in your world.

- **Use sound effects.** Think about how freaky it is to walk into a haunted house around Halloween. Every creak and groan of a floorboard, every witch's cackle can make your spine shiver. You can use sound to build an emotional cue for your audience. You could use music — or not. The clinking of glasses, a door opening, the banging of hammers. What are some sounds related to your subject matter that could grab an audience?

  WARNING

  Be careful when using sound effects. Test your audio beforehand to make sure it works as planned and so you don't blast everyone's ears. If you've picked music from *2001: A Space Odyssey* to start your speech about trekking through the Arctic, make sure the sound is at a comfortable level. You'll find information on using audio — including using copyrighted material — in Chapter 3 of this minibook.

- **Use humor.** Yes, tell a joke! (Just make sure it's a good one, and not off-color.) A good joke softens a crowd and makes them more willing to like you and, just maybe, what you have to say.

  WARNING

  Be careful here, too. The key to using humor is knowing your audience. Nothing's worse than crickets after a punch line, especially when you're using the joke to start your speech. Don't alienate anyone. Be professional. Stay away from jokes that pit one group against another — or you against the audience.

ARE FIRST IMPRESSIONS EVERYTHING? NOT QUITE

You never get a second chance at a first impression, isn't that what they say? Well, let's not subscribe to that belief. Let's say you spilled red wine on your first date's mother's dress. You're toast, right? Maybe, maybe not. It depends on how quickly and gracefully you recover. If you mumble an apology and act awkward the rest of the time, all she has to go on is that you're some kind of wine-spilling buffoon. But suppose, immediately after the spill, you did something memorable and endearing — such as dumping the rest of the glass on yourself and saying something like, "Well, at least we match now." Assuming it struck her as charming, you'd have a fan for life.

Supporting Your Point: The PIE Method

Once you've chosen your main point and hooked your audience, it's time to get down to the nitty-gritty. You have to pack your speech with arguments that back up your main point. Treat an audience that has come to see you as being open to your ideas, but skeptical until convinced otherwise.

Remember writing essays in school? You may have thought that procedure was tedious and pointless at the time, but it did instill in you the basics of building an argument. A speech in which you are trying to persuade someone of your point should operate on some — but not all — of the same principles as an essay.

This section applies mostly to persuasive speeches — those times when you're trying to get the audience to sympathize with one side of an issue. But the advice here can be used in any other kinds of speeches as well.

Enter the PIE method—no, not the dessert. But your argument should be just as enticing. (That's a joke, of course — nothing can compete with pie.) *PIE* is an acronym for focusing on three important components in your speech:

- Point
- Illustration
- Explanation

Now, a persuasive argument will have a main point, of course. But embedded in that is a line of logic that makes a number of smaller points. You have to back all of those up. The PIE method is a good tactic to use for your overall speech, but the following sections show you how to apply it to the minutiae of your argument.

Point

Finding the main point of your speech is discussed earlier in this chapter. Now let's take a look at how to fit your point into your speech effectively.

In an essay, your point, or *thesis*, comes in the first paragraph. It's one of the very first things you should see on the page. But a speech, it turns out, is not an essay.

REMEMBER

A speech is a performance. As such, it requires a certain measure of entertainment — unlike an essay. In a speech, your point doesn't necessarily come first. If you've taken the advice of starting with an anecdote, say, it may be a while before you get around to your point. That's fine. But don't put it off for too long.

TIP

Make your point sooner rather than later. Why? Because it's hard to support an argument before you've made it. (It *can* be done, but it's tricky.)

Let's try a noncontroversial example. The point we'll try to make and support isn't a tough one:

I believe pie is tasty.

To make it a little tougher, suppose the audience is from a horrible island where (shudder) pie doesn't exist. In fact, these poor folks have never even heard of pie before.

Illustration

This part — the *I* in the PIE method — is where we start to get into the argument. You've made your point: *I'm here to tell you, pie is tasty, ladies and gentlemen.* Now it's time to give examples of, or otherwise illustrate, why they should agree that your point is correct.

The illustration step is fairly rudimentary, but it's crucial to the whole of the argument. You'll see that once we get to the explanation portion of the argument.

So, to help illustrate the point, let's add the following:

Some pies are made with berries, and other pies are made with apples.

Now, this isn't going to convince anyone of anything yet. Sure, of course, some pies are made with berries, and some pies are made with apples. That's indisputable. Many of the illustrations you'll make using facts aren't necessarily groundbreaking, even if your argument is (hopefully) a little more nuanced and complex than that one. In fact, choosing illustrations that the audience either knows or can relate to is key here. If you've established a point that can cause others to be skeptical, and your illustration of that point feeds into that same skepticism, your point is lost. Even people who hate pie must concede that it is in fact made with berries or apples some of the time. And the folks on this island are learning something new with this fact, but it's not something they can dispute because it's just a fact.

But you're not done here. One illustration is not going to do it for most audiences. You have to give them enough so that they're going to believe you in the end. That's not all that's in a pie, right? Maybe your next illustration is this:

Pie is usually made with pastry.

Then something else:

Pie sometimes has sugar sprinkled on top.

And another for good measure:

Pie is baked to make it flaky on the outside and soft and warm in the middle.

Explanation

This is where you start bringing in your opinion. You're starting to analyze the facts you illustrated in the last section that few in the audience would dispute. You're beginning to engage in your argument, on the way to finalizing your point.

Here's an example:

Berries and apples taste good.

It's not a fact anymore — it's an opinion that these two fruits taste good. But it's still a pretty easy argument to make. You have to start small, before you get to the big one.

Let's keep going with this:

Pastry is delicious on its own.

And:

Everyone loves a bit of sugar.

Finally:

Flakiness and warmth are the most important attributes a dessert can have.

It's important to choose a more universally accepted position than your main point, which is an original thought that maybe the audience hadn't heard before they saw you onstage. For the folks on this island who have tasted both berries and apples, like sugar, and know about warm, flaky dessert, your assertion that they taste good should make your argument more accessible.

So what?

We've completed PIE, right? Well, sort of. But there's one final step to really hammer home your point, and that's the "So what?" part of the argument. *So what* if what you say is true? How is it significant to the overall message you're trying to get across? Let's continue the pie example:

> *Because berries and apples are tasty, and berries and apples are in pie, then pie must be tasty as well.*

We're bringing it all together here. In this admittedly very simple example, we've successfully explained to the audience why pie is tasty. We took an indisputable fact and applied it to the argument so the audience can both relate to it and, hopefully, believe it.

Conclusion: Ending with a bang

You've subtly checked your watch or the organizer is giving you a cue, and it's now time to wrap up your speech. You're pretty sure you've convinced the audience that you're right about your point. You've got them in your pocket. It's time to make this a *memorable* speech for the audience — not just a persuasive, entertaining, or informative one. How do you do that? It's all in the conclusion.

The *conclusion* is one of the most important parts of your speech. It's the last thing you'll say, and chances are, it's the part of the speech the audience will remember most. So it's important to make the conclusion count. Think of it as another hook. With your first statement, you're trying to grab the audience so they hold on tight during the rest of your speech. The stakes in the conclusion are even higher: You're trying to grab the audience *beyond* the speech — maybe for the rest of their lives, if you've done it correctly. And it all starts by bringing them back to the whole reason they're watching you speak: your point.

As in an essay, when you restate your thesis at the end, it's vitally important to remind people why they've been listening to you for the past several minutes. And as with your hook, it's important to convey your point in a catchy, digestible way that your audience will take away from your speech and use it as kind of a keepsake for the speech as a whole.

TIP

If you start your speech with a story, you may want to wrap it up with one, too — or give the ending of the story you began earlier at the end of your speech. In the same way that you used the story to help the audience relate to an abstract notion, you can use the story to tie back to your point.

TAKE IT FROM POLITICIANS: STAY ON MESSAGE

Politicians are often good at public speaking, and political speeches are worth studying as examples of persuasive argument. A political speech may go on for 20 minutes, an hour, or longer. It may outline all the politician's values, what they think they can do for voters, how they'll do it, and why. It may talk about their humble upbringing and their dogged rise to leadership, and how they did it as a testament to the spirit of the people. Or maybe the speech explains the hardships of people and offers proposals to help them. Whatever it is they're saying, successful political speeches end with a punchy, digestible version of the message, or *takeaway.* In fact, this ability of politicians to never stray too far from their core argument is even called *staying on message* or *staying on point.*

Say someone is running for city council, purely on the "bike lane" ticket. Many residents of the city are fed up with the lack of proper cycling infrastructure. This candidate has stated their *point* that they will represent the long-neglected cyclists in the city and has *illustrated* and *explained* how they're the right person for the job. They need to solidify that in the minds of voters and attach their point to their name when voters fill out their ballot. The candidate could say something like this:

"If elected, ***I will*** *change the bike lane laws,* ***I will*** *construct more bike lanes, and* ***I will*** *make our city a safe place for cyclists."*

Here, they are using the powerful repetition of "I will" to solidify and make memorable the idea that they are the bike lane candidate.

Writing in Your Own Voice

We've gotten out of the habit of writing. Sure, we text that we need milk and bread, we send an email to remind someone of a meeting, and we congratulate our kid on social media for winning a softball game, and . . . that's about it. It wasn't so long ago that people wrote all kinds of elaborate letters all the time. They wrote to loved ones who were traveling or serving in the armed forces. They wrote to friends, foes, newspapers, radio stations, companies, movie and TV stars, sports heroes, and politicians. If you go back and read correspondence from, say, the middle of the last century and earlier, you can really hear the unique voices of the writers.

The same should go for a speech. You want to make your point in your own voice. But because writing is a bit of a lost art these days, speeches can easily end up sounding like they're coming from someone other than the writer.

Keeping it simple

Part of the process of writing in your own words is to consider how the audience is going to react to the information you have to give. Many speeches go off the rails early, using esoteric lingo or jargon or making logical leaps that the audience can't follow because they just don't have the fundamental understanding of the subject that the speaker does. Worse, because speakers are reading off their speech, they can't backtrack even if it becomes evident the audience is lost. They just power through.

In a conversation, when it becomes clear that the person you're talking to is beginning to lose the plot, you can stop, go back, and explain the missing pieces. This is pretty easy to tell in a conversation because the person you're talking to will say something like, "Wait, what do you mean?" Your speech is a conversation between you and the audience, and they will respond with nonverbals, but one element is missing — the audience will be very reluctant to stop you and ask you to go back and clarify something. So when writing your speech, it's important to compensate for that lack of verbal feedback.

There are plenty of reasons somebody might not understand what you're talking about. If you're an expert in a subject, fundamental building blocks of knowledge about it were formed in your mind years ago. This is called the *curse of knowledge.* It refers to a cognitive bias whereby an expert in something simply assumes other people have sufficient background to understand what they're talking about. Chances are, you unconsciously take a lot of what you know for granted when you speak to someone about the bigger picture. There's a line that Denzel Washington says in the movie *Philadelphia* that can help illustrate this phenomenon: "All right, explain this to me like I'm a 2-year-old, okay? Because there's an element to this thing I just cannot get through my thick head." In the movie, he plays a lawyer, and he realizes that in order to represent his client and understand his client's case, he needs to know the whole story as well as his client does.

REMEMBER

Keeping it simple means not taking your audience's background knowledge of your subject for granted. Think of your audience as a blank slate that you're going to fill in with the information that only you provide. It's a fine line, though. Don't assume they know too *little,* either. The audience is smart, not dumb. They just haven't spent as much time on your particular subject as you have.

Writing and reading out loud

Before you put pen to paper, spend some time thinking and talking out loud about what you're going to speak on. Speaking and writing are not the same things. As mentioned earlier, people nowadays may be intimidated by extended, complex writing or out of practice with it.

TIP

Never forget that the medium you will present your ideas in is *speech*, not writing, so it makes sense not to begin explicitly with that other, different medium.

The following activities can help free up ideas for when you actually have to get to your computer and write the thing up:

- **Take a walk and make your points to yourself.** Walking (as well as other activities) can help to free up your headspace to toss around ideas. Forcing yourself to sit down at the computer and try to bang out ideas without thinking about those ideas first might result in you staring at a blank screen. That's horribly frustrating.

  Engaging in an activity can take your mind off the task. And soon you'll find yourself thinking about what you wanted to talk about. Remember, though, it's important to have a general sense of what you want to speak about before you go out on a walk. Once you get home, write it all down.
- **Talk to yourself in the shower.** Ever have an argument with yourself in the shower? Do you always win? Once you've figured out a few ideas in your head, it's time to start verbalizing. And where is it better and more socially acceptable to talk to yourself than in the shower? Crank that faucet, lather up, and, instead of singing your way through Taylor Swift's catalog, vocalize the ideas that are bouncing around in your head. How do they sound to you? If they're lame, no worries — try again, rework them. Sound better? Is there something that sticks? Dry off and write it down.
- **String ideas together out loud.** Once you have a few loose ideas that you've spoken to yourself about, try figuring out where they should go in relation to each other. Talk to yourself when you brush your teeth. Have a conversation with yourself in the car on the way to work. How does this one sound paired with another one? Should you move them around? Maybe an idea doesn't actually fit with the message you're trying to get across. Toss it. It's much easier to tell what works and what doesn't if you can hear it for yourself — out loud. Write down what seems to work and jettison what doesn't.
- **Come up with an ending.** Once you have the general idea of how things are going to go, try thinking about how you're going to end it. It doesn't need to be polished, but is there something in your normal vernacular that will help you end on the right message? The conclusion can be one of the biggest hurdles. Conclusions are difficult because in life, we don't often stop doing something that abruptly. As a result, many people find themselves writing a conclusion using language they would never say in real life and find it grating when they speak it out loud.

Show, Don't Tell: Painting a Picture in the Audience's Mind

We've all heard the advice *Show, don't tell.* It's often given to writers. What it means when it comes to speeches is twofold. First, being extremely technical and strenuously logical about every little bit of information can come across as very boring. And why don't you want to be boring?

REMEMBER

A speech is a performance.

Second, to show and not tell, you must give people room to make leaps in their own heads. You don't have to spell out everything in prose if you can get the audience picturing what you're talking about in a story. People actually like making connections and having surprising thoughts of their own. They, too, bring some energy to your speech. If you can lead them *just* up to the point where they can make the connection you're after on their own, you're going to become an audience favorite. Your speech is supposed to be appreciated, not spoon fed.

In 2017, for the first time in years, there was a total solar eclipse that spanned across the continental United States. The moon, a big round space rock, passed slowly in front of the sun, temporarily casting a huge shadow on the earth.

But if you were to go in front of a group of people and describe the importance of taking part in the event, would you explain it like that? Of course not. You'd paint a picture of the entire scenario: millions of people flooding into the countryside to get a clear view, many of whom have waited years to see something like that.

The stories are endless. Some people dressed in costumes or wore funny hats. There's the couple who coincided their wedding vows with the moment of total eclipse. There's the old man who first saw one over a half century ago and the young girl who will one day tell her children about it — and urge that they see one, too.

TIP

Hooking your audience with a story or anecdote, which is discussed earlier in this chapter, is a great way to employ this principle of showing instead of telling. Yes, you *tell* a story, but what you're really doing, if you spin a tale properly, is offering the audience a screenplay and letting them cast and direct the film in their minds. This is also a great way to give the benefit of the doubt to the audience and trust them to take your story and apply it to the subject of your speech.

The next section talks about the importance of story in greater detail.

HEMINGWAY'S ICEBERG THEORY

The "iceberg theory" was popularized by the American writer Ernest Hemingway. It described his own writing: He would give his readers the tip of the iceberg of the story, just the surface events, and expect them to understand on their own how the events connected underneath it all. Hemingway's prose was quite stark, and it's not recommended that you completely emulate his technique. But you can learn from it.

Allow the audience to come to their own understanding of the events. Allow them to work a little. When you guide people like this and they come to their own conclusions, not only is there a better chance they'll get on board with your ideas, they'll also feel a sense of pride that they figured it out.

Crafting Your Narrative: Story Time

Our culture is literally built on story. In fact, all cultures are. The big three — religion, mythology, and history — are nothing but stories. And sometimes, as storytellers, we get lucky. A perfect story, one with a beginning, middle, and end with just enough conflict falls right onto your lap. All you have to do is tie it up in a neat little bow and present it in whatever medium it needs to be in. But more often, we have to take the raw materials of a story and construct them into something that *looks* as if it fell into your lap.

You're the boss: Acting like a protagonist

Let's face it: On a certain level, your speech is going to be about you. Whether it's about your company and its products, or the effects of climate change on drinking water, or a park that should or shouldn't be built in a certain neighborhood, what brings together that story and your audience is *you.*

The *protagonist* of a story is the hero. That's not necessarily your role in the actual story you're telling. You could be speaking in more of a narrator capacity, with knowledge of the subject but without a hand in the movement of the plot. Or you could be right in there, telling your own story. Or maybe you're telling a story about someone else from your personal point of view — like the character Nick Carraway in *The Great Gatsby.* In any sense, treating yourself like a character in the story is an important step to engaging with the audience. To them, you are their connection to the story, so you want to keep yourself involved in the story as much as you can.

Here are a few tips to keep the *you* in the narrative:

- **Use "I."** This may be the simplest way to keep the story about you: Talk about yourself. This is easy if you're telling a story about something you did, or some experience you went through. It gets a little trickier when you're explaining something that someone else did. Regardless of where the story came from, though, you are the one up on the stage. Using phrases like "I saw" or "I heard" places you in the narrative.
- **Clarify your participation.** There's the one extreme where you are the instigator of the conflict in a story, are the one affected by it, or are the one who bears the consequences. And then there is the story where you're really just an observer, or you're being told the story well after it happened. It's important to establish for your audience where you fit on that spectrum. If you claim to have more influence over the story than you really did, an audience will sense it and be suspicious. Don't be flattered by the stage. Tell the truth. But make sure you don't *downplay* your participation. It might look like you don't deserve the credit, and an audience will question that.
- **Be subjective.** The information in your speech may be extremely dry by its nature. That's not your fault. But if your speech is boring, it is definitely your fault. Perhaps you're being asked to turn a business report into a speech. No one, absolutely no one, is looking for you to just read that damn report. The problem with the report is not that your colleagues are illiterate. How do you take such a dry topic and turn it into something with even a little bit of juice? Again, connect yourself to the story. Be subjective.

  That report may be as factual as the sky is blue, or it could paint a far too rosy picture of your business's future. It doesn't matter where your information falls on that scale — acting as though that information is yours and is coming from you and your perspective allows you to be the conduit for the information, and therefore a conduit for the audience. And — hopefully — not too boring.

Telling the story of your organization

So you have a nonprofit organization. Invariably, that organization has a story. Every organization does. In fact, thanks to the web, the story of an organization has become part of its identity in ways it never could have before the "About Us" tab appeared on websites.

This is both good news and bad news. Here's the bad news first: You won't be breaking any ground by telling your organization's origin story. It's been done to death. But that's also good news, because it has become easier to tell what works and what really doesn't.

Here are a few questions the story of your nonprofit organization must answer:

- **Why does your organization exist?** This seems like an easy question. And it is, once you understand it. What you're looking for here is *what your organization can give to the audience.* If your audience is your potential stakeholder, why does it exist for *them?* How does it help the community as a whole? Your town, city, state, or country?
- **What is your service and how did it come to be?** This question might call for a little more thinking. If it's a common service and you just seem to be providing it, why did you think to do that in the first place? Where did you get the idea that this service would not only be needed, but that you're uniquely positioned to provide it?
- **Who are your stakeholders?** This may be an internal question, and maybe you're giving an internal speech, but regardless, this is important to know. Consider what kind of speech this is. Are you trying to tell the story of your organization, or are you trying to sell the audience on it?

  REMEMBER

  The message must change depending on whom you're talking to.
- **What motivates you?** No matter who the audience is, you're going to have to go into it knowing why you do what you do. If you had the option to do something else but you didn't, why is that? What helps you get up in the morning and provide those services every day?

Getting real: Enhancing your story

Sometimes you need to "get real" with part of your speech. That's not to say that other parts aren't real or true, but getting down into the dirty aspects of why something is the way it is can make the difference between showing and telling (see the earlier section, "Show, Don't Tell: Painting a Picture in the Audience's Mind").

Getting personal

You're probably familiar with the term *TMI*, meaning *too much information.* It's a phrase we tend to hear a lot as children. Few of us are born with the social inhibition needed to get anywhere in society. As kids, we tend to just say whatever pops into our heads until told otherwise, and then we adjust next time (that's the theory, anyway). At some point, we're all told that a certain detail or story we've just mentioned is too much information, and we should have kept that to ourselves. Being wary of TMI is something many of us have internalized. But what if the TMI thing really matters?

Try this. When you're thinking of a speech about yourself, say, and you get to a part that you feel uncomfortable telling, flag it. Go ahead and write it out and highlight it. Try recording yourself giving the speech including that piece of information. Now think: Does it need to be there? Perform both versions for someone you trust. Can they understand the story without that detail? Or is it a true building block for your narrative? Their answer may be your answer.

WARNING

Of course, there's personal, and then there's *personal.* It's not worth a painful dive into your soul if it only makes the audience uncomfortable. We once attended a comedy festival where local celebrities came on the stage and did standup. A well-known personality came up to the mic and talked about why he divorced his wife. And it was messy. Certainly, messy is par for the course in standup comedy. But the messy part also has to be funny, which, in this case, neither the details nor the delivery were. Into the teeth of very little laughter, still he pushed through. The audience just stared at each other and tried to get through it. We truly were a compassionate audience, looking back on it. But it's never good when something like that happens.

Getting dramatic

How do you take a personal tidbit and turn it into something you can use? Drama helps. And not the kind around the lunch table in high school. Not necessarily, anyway. No, getting *dramatic* with your story can enhance the vulnerability of a personal narrative or bring its suspense to the forefront. Drama can best be used to enhance what's already there — a great narrative that just needs a little help. Remember, every speech is a performance, whether you're talking about tires or tutus.

Here are a couple things to keep in mind when looking for that perfect piece of drama:

TIP

- **Draw out the suspense.** Make the audience feel like they *need* that punch line. Many times in speeches, people possess fantastic information that they give away too quickly — or they disclose it in such a way that it comes and goes without giving the audience time to register it.

  If your speech is based on one shocking or wonderful event, let it breathe. Give the idea time to mature in the audience's heads, so that when they hear it, they're totally ready.

- **Study others.** It's important to know how successful speakers really do it. Grab a pen and pad next time and take notes. Watch it once, and just mark all the information you get from it, in double-spaced point form — every bit of the story they're trying to tell.

  On your second viewing (assuming you're watching a video), write how the speakers treat each piece of information below it. Do they get really quiet? Does their voice change? Use such techniques in your own speech and see if it makes a difference.

USING PUNCTUATION (YES, IT MATTERS)

Writers use punctuation, like we're doing in this book, to organize and clarify the message — and as clues to rhythm, pronunciation, pausing, emphasis, and so on. When you read these sentences in your head, note that you are actually hearing them. Reading is a lot like listening. Pay particular attention to what your brain does when it encounters marks of punctuation. How would you read this sentence if. We. Did. This? What happens to the voice in your head when you expect a question mark but none appears. Wrong punctuation can frustrate — the reader and send; the meaning the writer is trying to, get across astray. See?

But preparing a speech isn't the same as writing for the page — it's writing to be *heard*. In fact, many people who write speeches write them in shorthand. They may write them in point form or use punchy keywords to keep them on the right track. Now, I'm *not* advocating for you to read off the page at your next speaking engagement, but it is important to at least map out everything in your speech, especially if you're just starting out. And the way you write it down can affect the way you give the speech.

Punctuation on the page is like markings on a musician's sheet music. For a piano player with sheet music in front of them during a performance, every crescendo, every staccato phrase and dramatic rest can be mapped out on the page ahead of time.

There are two main areas to consider regarding punctuation and speech: emphasis and breathing. New speech writers are generally confident with the knowledge that punctuation is used for emphasis — it's the use of punctuation as markers for breathing that stumps most people. This list offers an overview of how certain punctuation works in speech.

- **Periods (.):** Periods indicate the end of a sentence. What does that mean for a speech? Pretty much the same thing, with a slightly different lingo. You should treat periods in a written speech much the same as you would in any other writing, but you need to be aware of what you're going to use them for. Periods, for your speech, indicate the end of a phrase or statement and a chance to breathe. In writing, it's possible to have a sentence run much longer than you can read aloud — you only have two lungs and limited lung capacity, after all, and some authors' sentences run on for a page or more. Often sentences vary in length. If there's a sentence that you need to say in one breath, make sure you take enough breath to sustain your speech until the end of that sentence.
- **Commas (,):** Commas are used to separate phrases, sometimes to emphasize a certain part of the phrase and sometimes to list things. For speech, we should think of the comma as "period light." You're not going to stop the progression of your

(continued)

phrase, but you're not going to power through it, either. You should use a comma as a signal to slow down. You can also use commas as a chance to breathe, but don't breathe on *every* comma like you do a period. Often when you resume speaking after a comma, you change the pitch of your voice. So, the comma can be used for dramatic purposes and for other reasons of emphasis.

- **Colons (:):** Generally in speech, we use a colon before we get into some sort of list. A colon is a very helpful tool when it comes to pacing. For many speeches that include colons, the phrase leading up to it prepares the audience for the list to come. It's necessary, but it's what's *in* the list that counts. That's why it's good to take longer pauses at a colon as a mental reminder to the audience of something important coming up. Colons can also be employed when used as visual aids (see Chapter 3 of this minibook for more on visual aids).
- **Question marks (?):** You may want to present a rhetorical question to the audience — meaning one you're not really expecting an answer to. It may seem trivial, but it's important to remind yourself of that in your speech. Vocally, a question mark indicates a rise in your pitch at the end of the sentence. Question marks are also a perfect time to slow down your read. Allow yourself a few beats between question and answer, enough time for the audience to realize that you don't know the answer, if that's the case.
- **Quotation marks (". . ."):** Say this sentence aloud to yourself: *He sure seemed like the "best" candidate.* How did you say the word *best?* Chances are, your intonation changed to reflect the quotations around that word. Or maybe you said *quote unquote best* or even did "air quotes" with your fingers. Think about how you would say that sentence to yourself if there were no quotation marks around that word. We often use quotation marks in this way to imply something, and to really emphasize its presence.
- **Exclamation marks (!):** This one's a no-brainer. If you're looking to exclaim, this is your mark. The issue with this one, especially when people first begin to write speeches, is that they're so nervous about expressing any emotion they forget when it's right to exclaim. We do this all the time in real life. "My dog's breath is so smelly!" and "My kid ate all the leftovers!" In real life we're committed to our emotion and show exactly how we feel in how we talk. Your pitch goes higher in your voice, volume increases, and you probably gesture with those hands. So don't feel silly about it: Put that exclamation mark on the page and go for it!
- **Italics and bold font:** We use these to emphasize *key* words, and they **pop** off the page when you're reading. When you write your speech and use italics or bold, you should emphasize them **more** than the other words *when you're speaking.* For example: That speech was incredible! When you put it in italics, it's even more *incredible!* If you use italics and bold, it becomes amazingly ***incredible!***

IN THIS CHAPTER

- » Using slide shows to augment your speech
- » Showing pictures and bullet points effectively
- » Knowing when — and when not — to use audio and video
- » Venturing into other visual aids

Chapter 3
Using Visual Aids

Many people probably still think of slide presentations as all being "PowerPoint" (from Microsoft; https://products.office.com/en-us/powerpoint). It's sort of the Kleenex or Xerox of its field. But there are other presentation software options:

- » Prezi (www.prezi.com)
- » Google Slides (https://gsuite.google.com/products/slides/)
- » LibreOffice Impress (www.libreoffice.org)
- » Apache OpenOffice Impress (www.openoffice.org/product/impress.html)

The variety of options doesn't change the age-old question of presentations: Do you need a visual aid? Generally, the thinking goes like this: Some people feel that just standing in front of an audience and delivering their message is not enough. They need something more to entice and captivate the audience.

Sometimes that's true. It's hard to describe a picture. Plus it's worth a thousand words, right? Why not just show it? But other times, feeling compelled to use a slide show has more to do with anxiety than anything else.

So, when should you use visual aids during your speech — and when shouldn't you? This chapter answers those questions, and more.

Augmenting Your Speech with Slides

Some presenters are afraid that if they don't inundate the audience with information, they run the risk of not looking like they don't know what they're talking about. It's similar to the freshman essay in college. Load the paper with information to impress the teacher. But does that work? No — not likely, anyway. And some presenters may be drawn to using a slide show as a way of distracting the audience from staring at them the whole time.

Without having a *deck* — hip presenter lingo for *slides* — at a meeting, some people believe the audience will think, "What are you here for?" This kind of thinking is common. The slide show *validates* the message and, ultimately, validates *you*. Anyone who's ever put a slide show together knows that validation comes at a price. Spending more time on your slides than on practicing your actual presentation out loud is *not* a good way to go about giving a speech.

So back to the questions: Do you *really* need that visual aid? Do you *really* need PowerPoint? Is it *really* adding to your story — or might it be confusing? Does it *really* help to get your message across — or does it get in the way? In the end, only you can answer these questions.

WARNING

Whatever your answer, don't try to make your slide show the star. *You* are the star. Don't let your slide show take away from what you are saying. And don't get too carried away by those fancy pictures and graphs — they won't take the place of your speech.

The late Steve Jobs was apparently not a fan of PowerPoint. In Walter Isaacson's biography *Steve Jobs* (Simon & Schuster, 2011), he quotes the co-founder of Apple: "People who know what they're talking about don't need PowerPoint." There's something to that sentiment. Still, sometimes a slide show may be able to help you get across your message to an audience. Here are a few general tips:

- You'll get about ten seconds out of a slide. That's all you can expect people to pay attention to it.
- For bullets, only use five or six lines of text, revealing one line at a time, as you speak about it, and no more than five or six words per line.
- Consider carefully whether your information would be presented better with a picture or with text — or neither.
- Less is more when it comes to slides. Don't overwhelm the audience. They can only remember so much. They want to find out about you and your message.
- Don't repeat what's on the slide word for word. The audience can read. Your message is the meat and potatoes. The slide is the side dish.

WRITE FIRST, ADD SLIDES LATER

Often in theater, the *last* thing that was added to the performance is the actors' costumes. If they received costumes first thing in rehearsal, they would have taken precedence over what the actors were saying and who they were as characters. The costume helps create the character, of course. But it can't be allowed to impose upon the character. It should only be used to augment the actor's performance — to add just a bit of reality to it.

Yes, at times women would wear skirts to rehearsal to get used to the feel of wearing a skirt. If a specific piece of clothing was instrumental in how the actor moved or was vital to create their character, they would wear that piece as soon as possible so that it became a part of them and felt like something they would wear every day. And if it was a Shakespearean play, men would wear tights or leggings in rehearsal just so they could get familiar with them, so they became second nature. (Wearing the codpieces must have taken a while to get used to.)

It's the same way with slides. If anything, they are only there to augment your performance, not become your performance. Take away the slides, and you should have the same basic presentation. It's best to add slides *after* you've already written your speech. That way, they aren't building blocks in your presentation, and you won't depend on them.

But just like in theater, there are exceptions. If you know that you have a slide with a picture that you need to write about first, that's fine. And if you're telling the story of your fabulous vacation in Egypt through pictures — sure, in that case write to the pictures. But if the slides contain nothing but words, don't worry about writing the slides after you've written your speech. And don't create too many slides — don't try to have a slide for every sentence. Your slides aren't your speech.

A Picture's Worth a Thousand Words

If your public speaking gig is to lead a workshop, you may consider not using slides at all. Better to come prepared to lead the group in various hands-on exercises than show them a string of slides. If you're asked to give a keynote speech, however, you will often want to use slides — and, as recommended earlier, those slides can be very effective with pictures on them only and no words. Some people shy away from using just pictures. They feel they need some info up there to explain everything to the audience.

Give the audience some credit. Don't spoon-feed them. Let them figure some things out on their own. People feel proud when they connect the dots for themselves. If you're a staunch "info slide" presenter, consider simply using pictures instead and see what results you get from your audiences. You may be surprised.

Knowing when a picture works and when it doesn't

Let's say you're giving a speech on how your dog, Artie, has brightened your life. You could have just two slides. One is of Artie frolicking in a ravine with his buddy, a black lab named Indy. The second slide is the same picture except superimposed on top are these words: *Artie and Indy enjoy playing together.*

Now, think about it. Didn't you get that information from the first slide? You should have. Chapter 2 of this minibook talks about showing, not telling. You can see that there are two dogs and they're having fun. Audience members can take the image and relate it to their own life. *My dog needs a buddy, My dog likes to run and play too,* or *How I really want a dog!* Trust that the picture alone will affect the audience in some way. Remember, always be critical of not just the type of information, but the amount you put on a slide, too.

TIP

Don't worry too much about connecting the dogs — or whatever image you show — with your message directly with every slide. It doesn't all have to be so on the nose. Allow the audience to engage with the slide without being hammered with your message.

Not all pictures are great. Here are some things to avoid:

- **Too small:** If the whole audience can't see the picture, then it's too small. If you're in a boardroom, you know what kind of space that is, and you can be confident everyone in the room will see your picture. The same isn't always true for a larger space. Always test out the equipment and your slide presentation to make sure everybody will be able to see them. Telling the audience "Some of you won't be able to see this, but . . ." is bad. You're alienating those who can't see it.
- **Too much detail:** Some photos are like those *Where's Waldo* books — spot Waldo and you win. But if the audience has to spend time looking for the equivalent of a man with black-rimmed glasses and a red toque, they're going to miss what you're saying. Better to crop such pictures (cropping is covered in the next section).
- **Poor quality:** You've spent the time to write a great presentation, so take the time to find a clear picture. If you have to explain or apologize for a fuzzy photo, you've lost the audience.

Cropping pictures to fit ideas

Cropping pictures has become much easier in the digital age. You used to need actual scissors. Now you stretch a box around a picture in an image editor and click a Crop button. With cropping, you're trying to get rid of some of the less important bits so the audience focuses on what you're trying to showcase. In a slide show, cropping means trying to highlight something in each slide while cropping away noise that may distract.

TIP

A simple rule of thumb is to crop an image so it very clearly shows just one thing. Strive for one main thing per image.

Considering color

Go ahead and add some color to your slides. Maybe your message is colorful. It's your slide show, after all.

TIP

It's a good idea to pick a consistent color scheme that uses just a few colors, and uses them consistently, rather than having the text a different color in each slide, say. This general design principle applies to everything from website design to marketing, advertising, and publishing. Choose one color or a few colors that go well together and stick to that. It makes your presentation look professional and is easy on the audience's eyes.

Be mindful about the different types of feelings in the audience that may be provoked by different colors. The psychology of color is not an exact art, and there's lots of room for different philosophies about which colors are good for which themes. For example, here's how the ancient art of *feng shui*, which at least has a long history behind it, views certain colors:

- **Yellow:** Generates happiness and intellect and stimulates the mind
- **Orange:** Expressive, lively, dynamic
- **Blue:** Serene, peaceful
- **Purple:** Royalty, riches, quietude, knowledge
- **Pink:** Love, joy
- **Brown:** Grounding, being rooted
- **Green:** Harmony, growth, bounty
- **Red:** Hot, courageous, dominant

You may not agree about how these colors make you feel — or even whether colors make you personally feel anything at all. But it's always good to consider these things.

WARNING

Certain colors, when combined, can definitely clash. Hopefully, you know it when you see it. Use common sense.

There's also the issue of color blindness. People with color blindness (or color *deficiency*) have a problem discerning among some combinations of colors. Sometimes they can't distinguish certain colors at all.

The issue of color blindness is perhaps most important to keep in mind when you're using text on a slide. If you use text, make sure the color of the text stands out in contrast to the background image on your slide. Colors can even cause problems with some people who have fine vision. If you have a light background, don't use light color text. And if you use a dark text on a dark background, the audience won't be able to read anything.

MAKE YOUR TEXT EASY TO READ

Back in the day, people used to handwrite everything: letters, essays, the Declaration of Independence. Some handwriting is so poor that deciphering it can be difficult — *many* people have horrible handwriting that is nearly impossible to read.

Luckily, it's easy to add text fresh from a keyboard to your slides in just about any typeface, font, and color you can imagine. But some fonts are harder to read than others. Pick clear, familiar, easy-to-read fonts. Don't use unusual or weird-looking fonts on your slides. Make it easy for the audience or they will be distracted or zone out. The words are there to be easily read and understood. Your message is what's important, and you don't want to mess with that.

Place your text smack in the middle of your slides, or as near to that as you can without interfering with an image. Putting text way up or down in a corner of the slide isn't easy to read. And it should go without saying — size your text big enough so that everyone can read it.

Mastering Essential Slide Show Skills

This section is kind of a hodge-podge of advice we've gathered from years of helping people put together presentations.

- **Let the slide speak for itself.** You may have been to a presentation where the speaker puts the slide up of bullet points and proceeds to read them out loud. Often, you've already scanned the bullets by the time the speaker is done reading the first one. Never forget that the audience is smart. We can read. Reading aloud bullets that all people in the room can see for themselves gives the audience the opportunity to zone out. Some might even mutter, "Why don't you just send us the slide deck and let us go home?"
- **Remember the ten-second rule.** An audience will generally engage in a slide for no more than ten seconds. That means they'd better be able to read everything on the slide in that amount of time. That means you need to limit the amount of text you place on each slide. A good rule of thumb is no more than five or six short lines per slide, with each one being revealed as you talk about it. If you can't make your point with that amount of info, consider breaking the slide into two.

  TIP

  One handy trick is to use the function, available in most slide show software, that makes bullet points appear (and perhaps disappear) as you talk about them. This trick takes advantage of the ten-second rule and gives a little more life to your slide. Speak about each point as it comes up. You can use this function like a cue card.
- **Resist the urge to read the slide.** It bears repeating. The slide, like an old-fashioned cue card for a speech, is a jumping-off point. It's not your script. Let the audience read the slide. You can embellish the point that's on the slide.
- **Don't turn your back on the audience.** It's not that they might stage a sneak attack on you, or at least most audiences won't. It's more a matter of professionalism and presentation. What's more exciting to look at, your back or your face? A good rule, if you need to look at the slide, is to stand at a 45-degree angle from the slide and cock your head to look at it.
- **Use one slide per idea.** Each of your slides should represent one idea. The slide should represent one beat in the overall rhythm and structure of your speech. There is no better place to look at how this can be done successfully than with the presentation style called PechaKucha (see the nearby sidebar).

- **Make sure you can see your notes.** The room is usually dark when you show slides. Unfortunately, that gives the audience an excuse to shut their eyes for a minute because no one will see. Try to make sure the room is just dark enough to see the screen but light enough to see your notes — and for you and the audience to see each other.
- **Stand away from the screen.** You need to choreograph where you're going to stand as you present your slides and be sure you're out of the way. You don't want the graph of the Realtors Association statistics projected on your head, do you? A good rule is to stand at a 45-degree angle from the screen. That way you can refer to your slides while still sort of facing the audience.
- **Back everything up.** This should go without saying. Technologies like the cloud make it easier than ever to back up your data. You may think it'll never happen to you, but every day lots of people learn the hard way that they should have backed up their work. Even if you've sent your slides to the organizer, and even if they've already played them on their end, make sure you always have access to your own copies.
- **Be prepared for your slides to not work.** Never fully rely on your slides. Here's a cautionary tale: Alyson attended a conference with the theme of promoting entrepreneurship and innovation. She was particularly excited to hear one of the speakers who had started a company that makes a spread out of a very unique vegetable. The speaker mounted the stage and, like many before them, appeared nervous. (That's okay. It shows you care.) The speaker began to talk, and a slide came up. Then — horrors! — the same slide stayed up there. It was frozen. And the speaker froze, too. A nightmare scenario. But it didn't have to be. This was a familiar story for the speaker. Speak to the audience as if they're at your dinner table.

  REMEMBER

  The audience doesn't really need the slides — not if you've prepared your speech properly. They need you. Never count on technology to get you through. And never rely on your slides to tell your story.
- **Think outside the box.** You could show a slide with the following information: "According to the National Eye Institute, color blindness affects approximately 1 in 12 boys and 1 in 200 girls in the world. The gene is passed on by the mother." That may be true, but it's boring on a slide.

  What if, instead, you showed a picture of boys and girls playing in a playground with a caption: "8% of boys and .5% of girls are colorblind." In your speech, then, you expand upon those stats.

  TIP

  Stats can be fine to include on slides, but make them succinct. Try to think of new or unusual ways to present them. Don't try to put the abstract of a scientific study on there. Just sum up the results in an interesting way.

PECHAKUCHA: SPEED PRESENTING

PechaKucha ("chit-chat") is a presentation style created in 2003 by Astrid Klein and Mark Dytham of Klein Dytham Architecture in Tokyo. The form aims to speed things along by constraining a presentation to 20 slides with 20 seconds per slide, for a total of 6 minutes and 40 seconds. The slides contain mainly images, with little or no text.

PechaKucha presentations require you to be really precise and to the point. Slides need to do two things to be effective in this form: Impact the audience and transition smoothly to the next slide. PechaKucha forces you to become completely confident with your content. You have to stay on your message because you have so little time. PechaKucha forces you to practice your presentation over and over to nail down the timing. By the time you present, you know the entire thing inside and out.

Presenters using this style often tend to talk really fast to pack everything they want to say into each 20-second time allotment. Again, the constraint encourages being concise — which is a good thing. If you need to cut something, well then, cut it. This form is all about content management.

Here's a pretty typical scenario: The audience looks at the speaker, who's about to give a speech. Up pops the first slide with a whole bunch of bullet points. The speaker starts talking about the downfall of oil and gas in 2016 — but the slides are all about the price of gas in 1980.

Sure, that's probably relevant information somehow. It might tie in later. But right now it's confusing to the viewer. What does the audience do? Read the information on the slide or listen to the speaker? They're confused! Many of them simply shut down. They can't be bothered to think through that stuff. They zone out and don't register anything.

Try listening to your favorite podcast or radio show and reading an article at the same time. Can you do it? When we're reading, we're probably not in sync with speakers even if they're talking about the same thing we're reading. If we read the slides too fast, we may wait around and think of something else while the speaker is speaking. If we're reading the slides and the speaker has finished and is going on to the next slide, we feel frustrated.

TIP

Try this technique: Repeat the bullet point and then expand on that. Once that happens, if the listeners are lost, they can just look back at the slide to figure out where they are.

Above all, it's you and your message that need to resonate with the audience — not your slides. Alyson has a friend who is an English professor at a university. She used to provide her students with the PowerPoint slides she used in class but found that the students relied on them too much. Ultimately, attendance dropped. The students would find the slides online and not go to class. So she stopped giving out the slides online.

The Do's and Don'ts of Audio

Using audio can enhance your presentation as much as slides — but here, too, make sure it doesn't become the star of the production. Running onto the stage to the theme song from *Rocky* could be great. Trying to *speak* over that music? Not so great.

We'll start with the don'ts.

Don't let music play for a long time

We've all heard "Gonna Fly Now" (the *Rocky* theme song) before, and we certainly don't need to hear the entire song again. We get it — in fact, we got it with the first few notes. Plus, you're on a time restraint. Don't waste time. Playing a piece of music for five or six seconds is ample time for the audience to feel the emotion or reaction you're (presumably) going for. Fade the music out when you're about to speak. If you can't do that yourself beforehand in software, if possible have the technician or organizer fade out the song when they see you onstage ready to start.

WARNING

Remember that any music you play, unless you wrote and recorded it yourself, is almost certainly protected under a copyright law, and that needs to be addressed. If you find that you *must* use a copyrighted piece of music in your presentation, give yourself plenty of time (as in weeks, at least) to track down the rights holder (probably the publisher, but not always) and secure written permission. Music copyright laws are well beyond the scope of this book. Many online sites explain copyright law in detail; check out `https://www.copyright.gov/what-is-copyright` for an overview of copyright law, and `https://www.soundstripe.com/blogs/details-about-music-copyright` for information on music copyright law in particular.

WARNING

What you want to avoid at all costs is standing awkwardly onstage waiting for the sound to stop.

Don't play music too loud or soft

Don't damage the audience's ears, please. If it's too loud, they'll be irritated and resistant to your message. Once the music is over, all they'll think about is how loud that bloody song was. On the other hand, if you intend it to be heard, let it be heard. Always test volume levels beforehand if at all possible.

Don't play music during your whole presentation

Think about a yoga class where the instructor plays music. That's normal. But what if it wasn't the calming, set-the-mood music usually used in yoga class? What if the music was rock or other bouncy music? That music makes you want to dance, which isn't very conducive to yoga. It's not easy staying in Downward Dog while listening to Van Morrison's "Brown-Eyed Girl."

The same principle goes for playing music while you're giving your presentation. Music can cause listeners to go into their own worlds — you want them coming to your world.

And now for a couple of do's.

Do have a sound check in the space prior to your speech

This is by far the most important thing you should do regarding the audio component of your speech. If you're lucky there will be a technician on hand, but often it's just the organizer and you. You will need someone at the soundboard for the venue's sound system to raise and lower the volume. A good idea, although it may not be practical, is to bring someone else to your speech who can cue the technician to raise the volume or lower it. You may have to ask the organizer to be your helper. Remember that the room will sound different when it's full of people; bodies tend to absorb and muffle sound.

Do check your equipment

Choose the right equipment for the job, whether it's a laptop, phone, or tablet. If it needs power, make sure you have access to a working electrical outlet. In any case, be sure to fully charge any and all devices before your speech.

PLAYING EXCERPTS FROM OTHER SPEECHES DURING YOUR SPEECH

Maybe you're in the middle of a presentation about achieving your goals and you want to insert Martin Luther King's "I Have a Dream" speech, or something like Kurt Russell's speech as Herb Brooks from the movie *Miracle.* This kind of thing can be tricky. But if you insist, here are some guidelines:

- If you use recording, don't use a bad one. You want the audience to hear it above all, and if it was recorded sometime in the last century, the quality may not be the best. Tread carefully.
- Don't walk around aimlessly while a recording plays, grabbing water or looking at your notes. That gives the audience permission to zone out and check their phones. Rather, be an example: Stand and listen to what is being said so that you're just as affected by it as the audience. Be in awe. Guide the audience in how they should feel.
- Don't play the whole thing. This is *your* speech, remember? Find a short section or a few lines that pertain to your message and recite that. That way, it can be vague enough that it might just have to do with what you're talking about.
- Find and play only the section in the speech that gives the most impact to your message.

Using Video . . . If You Must

If you use video in your speech, which isn't highly recommended, use it to your full advantage, and don't let its many drawbacks harm your speech.

TIP

Make sure the video is vital to your speech. And make sure it's short.

Here's a scenario where you may want to use video. The female CEO of your company is away and can't attend the meeting. Maybe you have a video of her announcing to the audience (who are the employees) that they will indeed receive the Christmas bonus. As a matter of fact, because the shares have doubled, they're getting 30 percent more than last year! It doesn't have to be fancy or elaborate. You could record her with your phone in her office, or anywhere else that makes sense. (Don't shoot her playing golf.)

WARNING

Make sure there's no extraneous noise that could distract from her message — a phone ringing, a copy machine churning out photocopies, somebody laughing down the hall. All of those things would be captured by the mic.

If you can't get video in a situation like this, you could try voiceover. *Voiceover* is when a voice gives a narrative story that plays on the audio. In the case of the CEO, maybe all the audience would see on the screen is her picture displayed while a recording of her plays as the voiceover. And maybe that's the best you could do.

WARNING

Make sure to keep this kind of thing as short as possible — it can be boring to just stare at a picture.

To repeat the recommendation from earlier in the chapter: Use video in speeches only sparingly, if at all. "But," you may say, "a video would be more engaging!" Well, just because it's a video doesn't mean it's more engaging. In fact, video can put people to sleep.

A male high school teacher that Alyson knew covered the history of metals. He created a cool video where he shot drawings of people in the Bronze Age and Iron Age. He added narration in his own voice. On the day he would present the film, the plan was he'd just press the play button and then sit back and watch. But he noticed the students weren't engaged. And, yes, this was high school — they often aren't engaged at the best of times. But these kids were especially drowsy. So the next year he scrapped the video. He showed pictures and talked about them live and in person. And guess what? The kids were much more engaged than they were during his fancy movie.

BEWARE OF ANIMATING SLIDES

So, you want to show an animation of a dancing girl at the corner of your slide as the CEO announces the bonus. Beware! Just like strobe lights can quickly become annoying, so can animation. Here's a good rule to live by: Don't have anything shake or move on-screen for more than five or six seconds. And *don't* use slides that move in and out of focus — they'll make the audience dizzy. Your organizer will not appreciate the cleanup.

Still not convinced? Have you ever been on Facebook or a website and some dumb icon comes up and starts flashing? It's like a mosquito, right? You just want to swat it away. Use animation briefly and sparingly, if at all. And remember your audience: If you're giving a presentation to high school kids and parents on fundraising for the prom, don't think you're cute by showing a couple dancing in the corner of the slide. You *do* want the kids to come to prom, right?

BEWARE OF ANIMATING SLIDES

IN THIS CHAPTER

» Practicing your speech out loud

» Taking video of yourself — and taking notes

» Marking up your speech for emphasis

» Slowing yourself down

Chapter 4
Practicing Your Speech

Your speech is on paper — and it's spectacular. Seriously, it's looking like a longer version of the Gettysburg Address. Even the punctuation is spot on and in all the right places. It's in a font that tickles your eyes, you love it so much. And the paper is that beautiful texture, the expensive kind you get at that really nice stationery store downtown. So what do you do with this glorious document? How do you get from the page to the stage?

Practice.

The old adage says practice makes perfect. Forget that — you're not looking for perfect, you're looking for *human.* You practice so that you can sound like an augmented version of yourself. Still yourself, but a more eloquent, more confident version. Worthy of that speech you've got in your hands. Worthy, if someone were to transcribe it, of the transcription to be on a similar type of paper, with a similar font.

This chapter talks about getting to that level.

Practicing Out Loud

It sounds like an obvious thing, but many would-be speakers have never practiced their speech aloud. Why is that? A speech is absolutely an oral performance. Good speakers look like they didn't even write it, that it's just done on the spot. So why do so many practice public speaking by silently reading to themselves? The reasons for this can include the following:

- They feel silly speaking out loud to themselves.
- They have no place to do it.
- They have no time to do it.
- It never occurred to them that practicing aloud could be important.

REMEMBER

Get it through your head now: You *have* to practice your speech by reading it out loud. Many times. Not only that, you need to also record yourself giving your speech on video, and watch it. If not on video, on audio, and listen to it. Many times. Admittedly, it is a strange experience to hear your own voice played back to you. Some people have problems merely talking to themselves. It may feel like you're marooned on an island, and talking to yourself is the last resort for company.

To repeat: You have to practice what you write. It's the only way to improve. Think of how gymnasts practice a big maneuver: over and over, correcting every little movement, conscious of where every body part is and how every muscle is firing. They may *know* the trick inside and out. They may have seen video of the trick, know how it's supposed to be performed, know every little pitfall of a wrong hand placement. But if they don't feel what it's like to actually *do* it, they will fail. On top of that, if they aren't conscious of how they're supposed to do it, they won't be able to adjust on the fly. Speaking is the same way.

But you're not just practicing over and over like a robot. You do *not* want to sound like a robot. You want to sound like a human being — an ambitious, curious, gem of a person. And to make that adjustment, you need to speak to the audience as if they are speaking back to you.

TIP

Take parts of your speech and practice it when you're driving in the car, in the shower, doing the dishes. The more you practice it, the more you'll embody it.

The rest of this section offers advice for getting you into the idea of having a conversation with the audience.

Hear yourself

This is admittedly a weird one. Your voice that you hear in your head when you speak and your voice that the camera or recorder picks up are two vastly different things. It seems like they're not even related. That whiny, high-pitched squeal or hoarse, muffled mumbling can't be your voice!

Sorry to say, but it is. The reason you hear a different voice from the microphone isn't the microphone's fault. When you feel the need to speak, the brain sends a message to the vocal folds to join together and lightly form a closure across the larynx. Breath travels up from the lungs, and the air pressure builds up until there is so much pressure that your vocal folds open. The sound you hear travels through your skull and eardrum. As the vibrations travel through the bone, the sound spreads out, and the frequency, which is the number of vibrations that the vocal folds move in one second, drops. That's why you think you have a lower and richer voice. You hear your voice vibrating through your neck, skull, and face, *as well as* through the air, which gives it a much richer quality. All the microphone hears is your voice vibrating through the air. And that's what everyone else hears, mic or no mic. That's what you're working with.

The later section, "Recording and Critiquing Yourself," talks about recording yourself in more detail.

REMEMBER

That beautiful, rich timbre you normally hear is an illusion. You have to know what you sound like to a microphone, what your speech sounds like to a microphone and through speakers, because that's how an audience is going to hear it.

Stand up

It seems trivial, and yes, it's harder than lounging on the couch, but you really need to stand up when you say that speech aloud. Sure, it's okay to write sitting down (even though there are standing desks nowadays). But there are a few key reasons why standing while you practice is a must.

First, it signals a shift from writing mode to speaking mode. They are two different things. You've done the writing. Now it's the presentation that matters.

Second, your breath can totally change if you sit in a slumped, down and in position with your head pulled down and neck tensed. Your lungs are squished, and you can't breathe to your full capacity. If you're sitting in an up and out position, with feet flat on the floor and sitting on your "sitting bones," with your body lengthening up to the sky, that is fine and can be just as good as standing. You're way more open, and there is more available lung capacity to hit all those fancy college words you threw in there to impress your boss.

Third — and this is a recurring theme in this chapter — you will be standing when you speak. You might as well get used to it.

There are exceptions. There will be times when you're giving your sales pitch about the new home lottery to a client and you're all sitting around the boardroom table. However, most of the time, you speak standing up.

Prepare those props

Have any sort of props or set pieces? Then you'd better know how you're going to use them. Before actors use props on stage, they improvise without them. They put tape on the stage floor so they know where a table is, or a couch, so they get used to working around (or with) them. Actors first get used to acting by themselves, and then eventually they work with the props. That's so they don't use the props as crutches for the performance.

TIP

Treat your props the same way. If you're speaking about your marathon, and intend to hold up your worn-out shoes, how would you do it? Practice it in your head a few times, and then practice without the shoes, and then pick them up. Once you do, you'll see how you're holding them, and what you're holding them for. And you won't be hiding behind them, either.

Power up those slides

If you're using a slide show, be prepared. Some people dread doing slide shows, and others rely too heavily on them. Chapter 3 of this minibook talks about visual aids. Like it or not, technology is likely going to be part of your speech, especially if you're going to be doing a lot of public speaking.

People who hate technology often hate the variables and the unpredictability involved. They don't understand why something would go wrong and almost panic when something goes awry. Others understand that it's just a computer. It's only doing what it's told. As often as not, the problem turns out to be human-caused.

Because computers only do what they're told to do, that means it's up to you to tell it the right things. So, even if you know the ins and the outs of the program you're using, you must practice with it beforehand. You may know what to do when the program crashes on your desk — but what will you do when it catches you flatfooted onstage? Will you know how to continue without it?

TIP

Be prepared for the very real possibility that, for one reason or another, your slides will just not work. If that happens, be ready to smile, shrug it off, and give your speech.

Maybe the most important thing you need to know is exactly when to go to the next slide. Is it a particular word or picture that should trigger it? Sometimes, slide shows are used as a sort of reveal — like the picture of the new home for the lottery that you are pitching to the client, for example. Maybe you focus a certain portion of your speech around a picture or a word. With the new home, there is a man cave complete with a bar, an ottoman, and signed sports jerseys hanging on the wall. Practice aloud to yourself and find out where your slides best fit which parts of your speech.

REMEMBER

Don't use the slides as a crutch or a fig leaf. Try not to hide from the audience by looking at your slides — or worse yet, reading off them — during your speech. Practice without looking at your slides.

Find an empty room

This could be a room in your home, an empty boardroom at work, a janitor's closet in your child's school. Wherever it is, ideally it has become your own personal bubble where you feel you can scream and no one will hear you. It's a safe place. You need such a spot, where you can totally mess up, where you can video yourself and it's no big deal. This is your practice room — it's the room you prepare yourself in before facing the audience. It's the secondary space. Here is where you practice as if there's an audience.

Do everything you would do onstage. And act like it *is* a stage. Come in from stage left if that's how you're going to do it. (Remember, stage left is the area of the stage to the left of center stage when you're facing the audience.) If you're about to present in a boardroom, get some chairs in there. Can you get some crash test dummies in suits? We're only half-kidding. Act as if this is the real thing, while knowing it's not. It will get you prepared when you have to step out under those lights or in front of those bosses.

Time yourself

This is a concept many often find hard to figure out. Let's say you're given 20 minutes for your talk. How do you translate that into content? Do you even have 20 minutes in your arsenal? When you're onstage, it's often hard to differentiate 15 minutes from 5. When we write, we split everything up into pages or words — those are easy to count. It's important to know how long you're going to speak, and then you can go from there.

One of the first things you have to do once you're finished writing the speech is time yourself reading it. If the organizers say five minutes and your read takes seven minutes, you're going to have to cut. This can be a good thing in that it may force you to get rid of everything except what is essential. Maybe a certain section is just an ancillary point, and can be cut.

TIP

Better to finish with time left over than feel like you have to rush. Get your message out, but slowly and clearly.

Get someone to watch you

It's great to review your own performance, but you should also get some sort of second opinion before hopping up in front of your colleagues and spilling all your great ideas. This is a scary one: recruiting your first bit of audience. That word *bit* is used intentionally, because this person or couple of people will be the smallest audience you're ever going to face.

For anyone working with a speaking coach, it's easy: Their coach is that person. But you'll have to choose someone who's going to help you, not just act as a stand-in. It's important you give that person some guidelines to work with. For example:

- Is my message getting through?
- How is my posture?
- Am I moving aimlessly without purpose?

Things like that are tough to spot on your own.

MIRROR, MIRROR, ON THE WALL

If you've ever been in a dance studio, you'll notice two things. The dancers can contort the human body in ways that seem painfully impossible, and there are floor-to-ceiling mirrors so all the dancers can watch every side of them do that. The mirrors aren't there as just an ego thing. If they didn't have those mirrors, it would be hard to know what they were doing.

The *feeling* of doing something with your body can only go so far. In order to really understand it and be able to correct anything you're doing wrong, you need to be able to see yourself. The following section, "Recording and Critiquing Yourself," outlines how and why you should be recording your voice. It's time to dig a little deeper and put those two things together.

Looking in a mirror isn't really natural for speakers, or for people in general. Dancers in a dancing studio look in mirrors and see things to work on. You might see a rip in your jeans and too much eye shadow. We mostly use mirrors in bathrooms and maybe bedrooms as we dress. And when we look at ourselves in the mirror, we typically begin to criticize everything we see in our appearance.

Luckily, you've got technology on your side, so why not use it to your advantage? Better to record yourself on video and/or audio and critique later — not while trying to give a speech in front of a mirror.

Recording and Critiquing Yourself

This section focuses on using recording technology (instead of the old-fashioned mirror) to help you practice.

Take video of yourself presenting

If you're going to take a video of yourself to help improve your speaking, there are a few things you should know. First of all, if you want to use video as a public tool, either on your website or in social media, get a professional to help you. You want a video like that to be produced professionally. But here are some tips to shoot your own video to help critique yourself:

- **Use a tripod.** If you're recording a video with your phone, a small tripod would be useful. Set it up so you frame yourself in the middle of the shot.
- **Shoot close up.** Be within six feet of the camera — that will make sure you're getting good audio.
- **Use good lighting.** Do it in a quiet, well-lit room. Soft light that comes from a source level with or slightly higher than your face works best. Use the light on the camera while on "auto exposure." Ceiling lights are not flattering and won't give you a good look.
- **Don't use "selfie" mode.** The front-facing camera on most phones will reverse the image (try it when you have writing on a t-shirt). Use the main camera.
- **Pretend there's an audience.** Take the video facing the phone but don't stare into it the whole time. Pretend you're addressing your audience and feel free to move (within the shot). You don't have to be stuck to one place.
- **Wear the clothing you intend to wear during your speech.** That way you can critique your "look" and get comfortable with what you're wearing.

TIP

A recording of your presentation before an actual audience will be invaluable.

You're not done learning or growing just because you made your speech. It may be easy to move on after presenting and never critique or revisit it, but that's no way to improve. Was that the only speech you're ever going to give? Unlikely. If you were compelled to do one, you'll be compelled, at some future date, to do another. So, why not learn from that first one? It may be super weird to watch the video later, but trust me, that's part of getting comfortable with yourself and your performance.

TIP

Find out if the presentation is going to be officially recorded, and whether you'll get a copy or a link online. It's also a good idea to record it yourself. Either set up a camera on a tripod in the back or ask someone sitting toward the front in the audience to record it with their phone. Make sure that person gets a nice tight shot of you and the audio is decent enough to work with.

At home, take a nap. Then look at the video and take notes. What worked for you? How was your breath? Your volume? Did you do any weird things with your hands you didn't expect? The next time you practice for a speech, look over those notes.

Record your voice

It's important to listen to just your voice, in isolation and without seeing your body language and whatever it is you may be doing with your hands (we get to that eventually, too).

Record your voice using your phone or another recording device, but don't hold it in your hand while you're saying your speech. There are a few reasons for this. You may distort the audio if you wave your hands around. It's also a distraction you don't need while you give your speech.

TIP

Put the phone or recorder somewhere high, on something secure, like the top of a dresser, and stand a few feet away from it. Yes, stand — don't sit — because you'll be standing when you speak for real. Later, when you listen back, reflect on a few things:

- Do your words make sense?
- Are you speaking in a monotonous pitch? Is your voice too high or too low?
- Is your volume varied, or is it too loud or quiet?
- Is your tone of voice appropriate for your subject matter?
- Are your energy and passion coming through?
- Does your breathing seem easy and free?
- Do you maintain a conversational tone, and does your voice flow easily from one change of thought to another?

Work on your face and nonverbals

Ever heard communication experts talk about body language? Psychologist Albert Mehrabian's study of nonverbal communication is cited a lot. His findings on how we perceive the meaning of words boils down to 7 percent from the word itself, 38 percent from tone of voice, and 55 percent from body language. Nonverbal communication is a thing, and it's a thing you will need to master to become a public speaking guru. So how do you do that?

TIP

Take a look at your recorded presentation again. Go through the entire thing with the sound off. Look at your hands first. Do they move at all when you speak? Does it look like they're moving naturally and are a part of you?

Try talking to a person in front of you as if you are having an argument. Maybe it's your boss or a coworker. Do you move your hands? In your speech, when your hands are down by your sides, body language specialist Mark Bowden calls this the *grotesque plane* in his book *Winning Body Language* (McGraw-Hill, 2010). It affects many aspects of your body, and not in a good way. Your breath is shallow due to breathing from your upper chest, your neck is jutted forward, and your muscles in your face feel heavy, as does your entire body. Do you know what all that does to your audience? It makes them tired, too.

What you want to do is move your hands in a horizontal plane extending outward from your navel, what Bowden calls the *truth plane*. What happens to your breath when you use your hands this way? You are probably dropping your breath deeper into your lower abdomen. How are you feeling? It should make you feel calmer and in control. The audience will feel it, too.

Next, take a look at your posture. Are you in a closed-off position, or do you look open to the world and to ideas? Notice your face. Are the proper emotions showing through? Is there *any* emotion? Make sure your face matches the content and the emotions you want it to elicit. Don't smile at a drop in stock price, for example.

Mark My Words: Adjusting Your Script for Emphasis

There's a saying in the arts: *A professional writes it down. An amateur says they'll remember.* Have you ever seen the sheet music of a classical violinist? There are pencil marks all over it. How about the manuscript of a famous novelist? Same thing. Notes make this world go round, and nothing is too pretty to annotate.

To turn your speech into a masterpiece on stage or in the boardroom, you're going to want to do what the professionals do: Mark up your work for emphasis. You want to emphasize the part or parts of your speech that you want the audience to really pay attention to, and optimize your language there that you want to carry the farthest.

Here are some things to mark up in your speech for emphasis:

- **Mark for intensity.** Some of your lines probably need a little extra *oomph* to get going. They could use a bit of raw intensity that will separate them from the rest. This means you want to hit a few words with more energy than normal.

  TIP

  You can mark sections for intensity by highlighting certain words or underlining them. Just make sure you mark them in some way that will get your attention and cue you to add some energy in those parts.

- **Mark for volume.** It's okay to raise your volume, but only when appropriate. It's okay to be quieter, too, if that subject matter calls for it. You need variation to avoid boring the audience. You don't want to give your whole speech and use the same volume throughout.

  TIP

  Getting louder and then quieter is a good way to contrast ideas. If you're mad about something, show it! If you're getting into a sad topic, it's okay to lower your voice a bit, as long as the audience can hear you. Mark those sections with your own choice of symbols that mean louder or quieter to you. Maybe it's all caps for louder.

  TIP

  Pair movement with volume. When you're loud, *look* loud. Jump up. Take big steps. Use large, sweeping hand movements. When you're quiet, get smaller. Be more conservative with your steps. Use smaller hand movements.

- **Emphasize the big message.** When you know you have to hit that important point, make sure you know when it's coming. If there's a certain phrase or line you really want to be heard, underline or highlight it. That way, it'll give you an idea in practice of what you're going toward. How you emphasize that is your choice. But be sure you know it's coming.

- **Mark for pitch.** *Pitch* refers to how high or low you're speaking. Pitch is dependent on the frequency of the vocal folds vibrating together. As the number of vibrations increase in time span, the pitch goes higher, and vice versa. The keys on the left side of a piano produce low-pitched notes, and the keys on the right side produce high-pitched notes. The human voice also varies in pitch. Usually that variation is natural — it's something we all learn as we learn to speak. One thing you shouldn't do is just settle in the same pitch range of two or three notes for the whole speech. That would sound monotonous. You don't want to sound like a robot.

TIP

To indicate pitch changes on your speech, use up and down arrows. If you're excited about something and want to get the audience on board, bring your pitch up and put an up arrow beside that line. If you want to sound authoritative, get deep. Write in a couple of down arrows.

- **Mark for inflection.** It's important to know where you're going in terms of inflection before you get to the end of a sentence. *Inflection* is the bend of your voice on a certain syllable or syllables for a certain emphasis. Some of it is built into punctuation already. For example, a question mark tells you to raise your pitch at the end of a sentence. Because question marks come at the end of sentences, though, sometimes it's hard to tell which sentence will be a question or not.

TIP

If you are asking a question, put an indication of that right in that top of that line. Make sure you know that you're asking something before you actually have to ask it. If there is another bit of inflection you want to use, you can use a scooping up or down arrow to indicate that. See the nearby sidebar, "Exercise: Increasing your volume without tension," for more about inflection.

- **Mark for rate of speech.** Sometimes you need to speed things up a bit, and sometimes you need to slow them down. A speech usually contains a mix of speeds. What is for certain is that if you are speaking the same speed for your whole speech, your audience will get bored. There's no two ways about it. The next section talks more about the importance of slowing down.

TIP

In general, slow down during the most important parts. If there's a subordinate phrase, or one that only supports the main idea, make that bit faster than the main ideas. You want to get to the good bits, don't you? Write a big fat *SLOW* or *FAST* on top of bits where you want to regulate the speed. But remember, you still need to be understood, no matter the speed.

- **Mark your pauses.** Sometimes we all need a little silence in our lives and in our speeches. Have you given your audience a lot to digest? Give them a beat to think about it. Put a nice big pause in between ideas. Pausing also lets them know there will be a slight change of topic.

TIP

To indicate pauses in your speech, put a slash (/) right before the word where you want to pause. You can also use pauses in sentences, and before big words for similar effect.

Practicing Your Speech

EXERCISE: INCREASING YOUR VOLUME WITHOUT TENSION

Lie on the floor, breathing in and out. Release your neck, throat, shoulders and chest. Imagine them sinking into the floor. Speak some lines of your speech, quietly, with a voiced sound (don't whisper). Gradually add volume — but try not to raise your pitch. Keep your pitch the same. You can use lots of inflection, but don't keep driving your pitch up.

Now do the same exercise while standing. Repeat the speech conversationally. You can even move around. Feel free to use plenty of inflection, but avoid going too high or low in your pitch. Speak the speech as you would to an audience. Keep your neck free. Check your shoulders. When you feel tension, stop and try to release by giving your body a good shake and think of the steps to releasing.

Slowing Down: Speed Kills

On the highway, speed kills. It's kind of the same for your speech. You won't die if you go too fast, but your message will. Fast speakers tend to rush through so quickly that it sometimes feels as if they weren't up there speaking at all.

Some presenters lament about having to give boring stats, for example. So they barrel through those parts, fast and furious, making the audience dizzy with all the information. Does that sound like you? Slow down — your audience wants to hear what you have to say.

Cutting your speech when your time is cut

Sometimes speakers don't end up having as much time as they thought they would. Maybe things are running late. That's life. It happens.

WARNING

What you shouldn't do is tell the audience, though. It makes them uncomfortable and it looks unprofessional. The show must go on. If you continue professionally, what the audience doesn't know won't hurt them. But if you have less time, *shorten* your speech — don't read it faster. It will be disaster if you think you can just speed up your speech to fit everything in.

TIP

It's a good idea to always have your speech on 3×5 cue cards with the main points in your pocket or purse handy, just in case you need to cut or move around some info.

Resisting the urge to rush

Many presenters are so fearful that they just want to say their speech and get it over with. So they rattle through it. But you might as well hand out a brochure and go home. You have been asked to *speak.* And unless you're speaking to a junior high school audience who, you'll know from experience if you have kids, may well hate you the minute you step onstage, the audience wants you to succeed. The audience came to hear what you have to say.

German psychologist Hermann Ebbinghaus studied memory and coined the term *the forgetting curve*, which refers to how much information we retain over time. According to Ebbinghaus, 20 minutes after hearing a speech for the first time, people retain 58 percent, after one hour it's 44 percent, and after a day only 33 percent is remembered. So you need to go beyond that. You have to give the audience a *feeling. That* they will remember.

Think of reading a story to a child. Take the time to land your thoughts. That gives you time to settle into your speech and breathe, and gives the audience time to register what you are saying. If you speak too fast, the audience won't be able to follow and will lose interest. Record yourself speaking for at least five minutes. Are you tired of keeping up with yourself? So is the audience.

EXERCISES IN SPEED

- **Decreasing your need for speed:** Find an object like a computer (with the screen turned off) and sit in front of it. Look down at your first sentence in your speech. Look up and take a good look at the object. Really take that object in. Then say the sentence to the object just like you would to a real audience. Then wait, as if to check that the sentence has registered with the audience. Then look down and start the process again with the next sentence.
- **Reading lists:** Take a line like "Thank you to the sponsors, teachers, and parents who have made this event possible." If you race through that, those people aren't going to get the credit they deserve. For this exercise, find a spot on the floor. You're going to move with the list, a bit like a dance. "Thank you to sponsors (move left), teachers (move right), and parents (move to the center)." This will slow you down because it takes time to move. Think of that when you're speaking. If there are a few important things to say in each sentence, give them all the proper time they need. You don't need to move when you're actually giving the speech, but you can remember how that movement slowed you down.

Making the most of tactical pauses

Pauses in speech can be tricky. To some, they seem like just the absence of something — *dead air*, in radio speak, where nothing is going on even though something really *should* be going on. And in some instances, a dead-air effect is what you want. A perfectly placed pause can do so much for a speech that has the perfect content to support it. Pauses can create suspense and build excitement. Pausing displays control. It allows the audience to reflect on what you just said. It gives you time to breathe.

WARNING

Of course, pauses have pitfalls, too. Too many pauses suggest a hesitancy and insecurity. You might look unprepared, or worse, that you forgot your lines. So what's the right balance? How do you insert perfect pauses in your speech? Here are some examples of when pauses can achieve an effect that words might not:

- **After a comma:** Commas are grammatical cues to pause slightly. It's okay to take a small breath at a comma. Let it linger a bit before getting to the next thing on the list.
- **After a sentence:** In written speech, a period, exclamation point, or question mark at the end of a sentence signifies the end of the thought. Almost always take a pause after that. It doesn't have to be long. But you do need to breathe, remember. A slightly longer pause can be used to allow the audience to think about that sentence and anticipate the next one. Often speakers neglect the poor period and barrel through.
- **Before starting a new paragraph:** A well written speech is organized into paragraphs that separate the main ideas. Know where your paragraphs are, why they are there, and how to pause between them for your audience. Your speech should still flow, but paragraphs are there for a reason. Finish your thought and allow space for a segue.
- **For a visual:** If a visual pops up out of nowhere on the screen behind you, you need to pause to let your audience digest it for a second. Regardless of whether you're talking about it right then, or if you've fired the slide too early, let them see what it is first, and then continue on.
- **For laughter:** Ever been to a really funny movie in a packed theater? You may have to see it twice to hear everything. It's often so hard to hear the full jokes over all that laughter. That's unavoidable for movie stars, but you can prevent it. If you expect that people are going to laugh at a joke you make, give them space to laugh. Pick up once again when it goes down. And if people laugh unexpectedly, let them while you pause. Otherwise they won't catch the next thing you say.

- **For a sip of water:** Always have some water handy during your performance. Better to have it and not need it than need it and not have it. If you don't have water, you'll be sorry if you need it. Water also gives you an opportunity to pause when changing topics. Taking a sip of water lets people ruffle in their seats a little bit, and get comfortable again. Once you put down your bottle, they're ready to go.
- **For a rhetorical question:** When you ask your audience a question, you have to give them time to formulate an answer. They will be frustrated if they can't. It may give them the idea that you think only *you* have that answer.

  The same is true when you ask the audience to visualize something or think about something. Allow them the time to think about it.

TIP

How long should you pause for? As in writing, the comma in the middle of a sentence is a shorter break than the end of the sentence. Each pause should be appropriate to its intended effect. Have fun and vary them. Pause longer than you think. The audience will wait.

Avoiding filler words: Ums and ahs

Have you ever seen a politician who is extremely smart and may be quite charismatic? When this person reads a speech from the page, their intonation is perfect. They use pauses to great effect. And, unlike some people, when they speak to an audience, it sounds as if they are speaking in a conversation. Sometimes the odd "um" sneaks in. But then, after the prepared speech, when they begin to answer questions from the audience, those *ums* and *ahs* explode. They're everywhere, in between sentences, within sentences. Anytime they can't think of an answer, a long *ummm* creeps in. It's difficult to focus on the speaker's message when their sentences are so disrupted.

This takes the speaker from being an authority figure when they read that speech to seeming very unsure of themselves — a babbling mess. Lack of confidence doesn't appeal to voters.

The same is true if you use filler words in a presentation. *Ums* and *ahs* happen when you feel the need to think and speak at the same time. It means you're searching for the right word. You're thinking out loud. But up on that stage, you need to look as if you've already thought about the subject and you're sharing the conclusion you've come to. If you look like you're winging it, you have little credibility.

If you're using filler words, you might not even know you have this affliction. The first thing you really need to do is to determine whether you use filler words. Here are a few tips to finding out if you do, and then getting rid of filler all together:

- **Check your video.** You recorded your speech on video, right? How many filler words did you use? What kind were they? Where did they come? Write notes indicating whether they appeared in the middle of sentences or at the ends, for example. Maybe it was just in a particular sentence. Where they occur can provide clues as to why you're putting in filler words. For example, maybe you don't understand the concept behind a particular section well enough, and you're just saying the words. That's a problem.
- **Get a spotter.** Recite your speech to a colleague. Don't make that person actually *count* the filler words, but let them know that's what you want them to focus on before you recite it to them. After you do your speech, get the person to ask some questions about the subject matter that you will answer. See if you use more filler words. Now it's your turn to ask questions. What did the person notice most about the filler words? Where did they come in most? In connection with a certain topic? When you switched from one idea to the next? That information can give you a better idea of what you need to work on.
- **Position your body.** When people are in a down and in posture, they tend to say more filler words. Try putting your hands in your pockets and watch those *ums* soar! Adopt an up and out body posture and see what happens. You are confidently looking out at the world. This won't cure you, but you will definitely have fewer *ums*.
- **Practice, practice, practice.** Yup. It always comes down to practice. The more you practice, the more you'll know what you're going to say. It's going to cut down on your anxiety, too. Be totally prepared.

Speaking, not reading

We've all listened to speakers who pull out their notes and proceed to read them word for word. They may not even look up to see if the audience is there. If they do, they often look lost or fearful, and then settle back to their notes. Don't do that. It makes you seem as if you don't care about the audience. If you don't care about them, why should they care about you and what you have to say?

REMEMBER

Communication is between you and the audience, not you and your notes. When you don't connect with your audience, you'll get no response from them. It also looks like you don't really know what you're talking about if you need to be engrossed in the page.

There are many other pitfalls to reading word for word. You can stumble over your words. Often you read too fast. It's extremely hard to read in a conversational style. Reading is reading. Reading is not speaking.

REMEMBER

You're communicating your ideas more than your words. The audience doesn't have the luxury of reading your speech. You need to help them out and lift that speech off the page.

You may not always have the luxury of a perfectly prepared speech. You may even get tapped to speak right before it's supposed to happen, and all you have time to do is write up a script. In that case, here are a few do's and don'ts for reading from the stage:

- **Don't memorize — familiarize.** Try to familiarize yourself with the speech as much as you can. It's not always easy to do this, but make it a priority. If you're going to say this speech, you might as well look like you know what you're going to say. Get familiar with it. Try to only look down to find your place in the speech. If you have a general idea of the flow of what you're going for, then use it.

  TIP

  Maybe you've worked on your speech so much (and good for you!) that you have it memorized. But even if you memorize it, you still need spontaneity in delivering your speech. If you practice it *too much* word for word, it can sound stilted. What happens if you miss a word in the actual presentation? To avoid this, consider keeping the same points but varying them slightly in practice.

  TIP

  Always have a copy of your presentation up there. It can be the entire speech or the main points written on index cards. If you lose your focus because a cellphone rings or a baby cries, you can always look down on your page and find your place.

- **Don't look down at embarrassing times.** This happens more often than you might think. Some speakers start off their presentation like this: "Hi everyone, thanks for coming today, my name is . . ." and then they look down. We know they know their name. That's not in dispute. But it sort of *looks* like they need a refresher on that. And that just looks terrible. This can happen with any number of things you should just know. Needless to say, look at the audience when you say your name.

  REMEMBER

  Think of your speech as a conversation between you and the audience. Don't look down at your notes in the middle of a sentence.

- **Pick someone to look at.** When you look up from your page, don't just scan the crowd. It looks like you're not interested in connecting with them. Instead, look at certain people. You don't have to stare into their eyes — just make eye contact for a few seconds. Give people a sense that you're addressing your message to them. When you just sweep your eyes and scan the crowd, people feel like wallpaper.

» **Don't read verbatim.** It's the message you're trying to give people, not the words. If you try to read verbatim, you will mess up eventually. That looks bad. Instead, try to go for a flow. You know what you have to say. It's all right if you don't say the exact words on the page.

REMEMBER

Unless you're the author at your book reading, your speech is not a novel to be read. It's written to be spoken. So, when you're writing it, say it out loud to hear how it sounds.

Breathing just enough

In breathing exercises so far, we've told you to breathe in through your nose, which is a cleansing breath and filters out pollutants in the air and helps achieve the feeling of dropping your breath into your lower abdomen. However, in everyday speech, we keep our mouths open, and that's what you need to do when you give a speech. Inhaling with your mouth closed tight looks odd to the audience and stops the flow of your speech. Also, breathing through your nose takes more time than breathing through your mouth. We shouldn't be aware of you taking a breath in and out. It should be easy.

TIP

Before you begin your speech, take a deep breath. If you have the chance because the MC is introducing you, take a couple of deep breaths. This helps you relax and gives you the breath you need to start speaking.

EXERCISE: FINDING OUT HOW MUCH BREATH YOU NEED

Align yourself with your feet planted, shoulder width apart, and your energy beaming up to the sky. Take a deep breath in through your nose. Count out loud to 5, and exhale all your breath. Try not to collapse in your body when you are breathing out. Count higher up to 20 if you can and avoid any tension. How far can you count on one breath?

Every sentence is different and needs a different amount of breath. Apply this exercise in a sentence with a few words, and then with a longer sentence. For example: "Let's give a special thanks to the sponsors of today's events." That needs more breath than "Special thanks to the sponsors."

EXERCISE: TAKING A WALK

This is an exercise inspired by an exercise called Walking the Sentences from Barbara Houseman that Alyson learned in theater school. Basically, you do what it says. You *walk* your sentences. For each of your sentences, you walk and only stop when you reach the end of your sentence. You will find the best places to breathe within a sentence that won't disrupt the flow of your thought. Your breathing will flow naturally, but you'll also find out how big of a breath you need for each sentence.

Take the first sentence of your speech. As you walk, move with purpose and imagine there's someone a few feet ahead of you that you want to talk to. Say the first sentence, and when it has ended, come to a full stop. Then start the next sentence and change direction. Don't rush your words or your pace. You can change direction every time there is a comma in the sentence as well. You will soon find out how much or little breath you need.

IN THIS CHAPTER

» Remaining loose and reducing tension

» Diagnosing and remedying your slouch

» Battling the fight, flight, or freeze response

» Learning from your mistakes

» Focusing on the audience

Chapter 5
Overcoming Performance Anxiety

If performance anxiety is your problem, do something for yourself. Ready? Here goes: Video yourself presenting a speech for two minutes.

Two minutes may seem too short to figure out problems, and for some things, it is. In two minutes, you may not be able to determine what to work on, emotion or intonation or other things of that nature. But two minutes is all it takes for someone to go from a comfortable stance to an awkward slouch that inhibits breath, tone, and pretty much all the other speech fundamentals you learn in this minibook. You may think whatever's ailing you is in your head, that it's anxiety that's doing you in. And you may be right. But without proper physical form, you won't be giving an effective speech no matter what.

After that two-minute test, next try a little bit of physical activity — just to get limber — and a vocal warmup. Then do the test again. You might find the change remarkable. Now, you're not going to always be able to do jumping jacks before a presentation, but understanding your body's role in your performance is critical.

This chapter covers the importance of releasing your tension and how to fix poor form such as slouching.

Staying Loose: Tension Can Ruin a Speech

Consider athletes. Look at the slow-motion videos of elite runners. They look so relaxed, as if they're floating down the track. Uta Pippig, the first woman to win the Boston Marathon three times, says relaxation is the key to winning. Relaxing your mind helps to relax your body. The opposite is also true: Relaxing your body helps to relax the mind. It's a circle of relaxation. Where you start is up to you.

Runners use every bit of energy available to them to propel themselves forward through the air and — they hope — to the podium. Then there are target shooters, whose outfits are a little less revealing (no need for aerodynamics). If you can watch them in high-definition, you should. They maintain such control over their muscles that they can remain perfectly still. Any movement of their body, even a slight sway or an adjustment from the wind, can ruin their shot. They're trained to squeeze the trigger for maximum control rather than pull it with their arm.

Both kinds of athletes are at the top of their game, and both can control the muscles they need to an almost superhuman degree. But although both are perfect for their particular sport, if these athletes switched sports, they couldn't function in the same capacity.

Then there's a sport that combines both kinds of skills. During a biathlon you cross-country ski as hard as you can toward a target, then stop, release all your tension, and shoot. Biathletes have to slow down their heart rate and release muscle tension so it doesn't affect their shot.

TIP

That's how to think of your presentation. No matter how much stress you have before the speech, be able to release it all once you're up on stage.

Aligning yourself with proper posture

Proper posture is your first step to releasing unwanted tension. It's essentially the same process your car goes through when you have your wheels aligned. It goes something like this: For whatever reason — maybe you hit a speed bump too hard — your wheels shift slightly out of alignment on the axles. Sometimes it's hard to tell that this has happened until you begin to notice little things. Your steering wheel might not point the car straight anymore, for example, and may pull to one side. Alignment affects your entire vehicle.

It's the same thing with your body. If you brought your body to the mechanic and told them it's not steering straight, the first thing they would check is your spine. Yes, your spine is the key to alignment in your body.

EXERCISE: FINDING YOUR NEUTRAL

Stand with your feet shoulder width apart. Roll forward onto the balls of your feet, eventually putting all your weight forward on your toes. How does it feel? Well, it should feel like you're propelling forward in the world, and pushing everything else behind. Think of the scene with Jack and Rose on the bow of *Titanic* (the ending of the movie doesn't apply here).

Return to your normal stance. Then go the opposite way: Roll back onto your heels as far as you can without falling over. When you're standing on your heels it's like you don't want to be a part of the action. You're holding back. Now go to where you can feel your toes, balls of your feet, and heels equally on the ground. You should have a good feeling of where that neutral stance is, and when you're speaking, that's where you want to be, solidly planted.

So what happens when your spine is misaligned? As with a car, your body will try to compensate for it. Muscles that weren't built to carry the load will try to. It will be harder to keep you up straight, and your back may cave in a little bit. Your lungs won't be able to take the full breaths that they would if the spine were aligned correctly. As a result, your vocal energy will be low. Meanwhile, your shoulders and neck may be tense, your knees may hyperextend, and that additional tension will carry through to your voice.

Good posture is what we're looking for, although *posture* sometimes connotes a moral meaning. Like, say, a nun slapping your desktop with a ruler for slouching. And in that same way, whenever you say the word *posture* around people, they seem to straighten up. Try it around your friends. They'll all straighten up for the nun.

Most of us are aware of what good posture looks like — but for all the wrong reasons. "Straightening up" can actually do harm to your alignment if you force the movement. When you stand up straight —the military kind of straight — your knees lock and might even hyperextend, and the rest of your body compensates to keep you from falling.

Try balancing a book on your head: The first thing people do when they try that is stop breathing. Great, look at that, there's a book on your head! But you're not breathing, and you need to do that to speak.

In renowned voice teacher Patsy Rodenburg's book *The Right to Speak* (Routledge, 1993), she says, "The natural way of standing is based on achieving balance, ease, and feeling centered." This natural alignment is from head to toe:

- Your head should sit balanced on top of the spine.
- Your shoulders should be released.
- Your arms should hang down by your sides.
- Your upper chest should be open and not tense.
- Your vertebrae should feel stacked one on top of the other. Your spine is neither slumped forward nor pushed out.
- Your lower abdominal muscles should be released without being pulled in or out.
- Your knees should be unlocked.
- Your feet should be firmly planted.

EXERCISE: FEELING KINESTHETIC LIGHTNESS

Looking to get in touch with your natural alignment? Stand with your feet shoulder width apart. Make sure your feet are flat on the floor and that they're each taking an equal amount of weight. Now imagine roots growing down from the bottom of your feet, going down farther and farther.

In a trance yet? We're about to go deeper. Visualize all the bones in your body. Can you feel them all individually? Your anklebone is growing up into your shinbone. Your shinbone is growing up into your thighbone. Your thighbone is growing up into your pelvis. Your vertebrae are growing out of your pelvis, stacked neatly on top of each other. Your shoulders are spread wide across your chest. Your arms are gently down by your side. Your head is floating on the top of it all, like a bobblehead.

Now, imagine a light coursing through your body, flowing through your legs, stomach, arms, neck, all the way through the crown of your head up to the sky. Does that feel good or what? You should *feel* the light. In fact, this effect has a name: *kinesthetic lightness.* You are feeling support from the ground, which leads you to your natural alignment. You're not stiff or rigid and your muscles are not contracted but expanded. This exercise is a technique actors use, and some people find that it works to get them physically ready for performance.

Identifying the tension

You're starting to get yourself aligned. Once good posture is established, it's much easier to figure out where any remaining tension is coming from that may inhibit your speech performance. If you're a reasonably healthy person — no serious back problems, able to walk around, pretty active — you may be thinking, what tension?

The type of tension caused by public speaking doesn't usually exist in your everyday life. But the mere thought of presenting makes it come out. You start to tense up muscles in areas of your body where you wouldn't if you were doing literally anything else. With some people, the mere mention of a speech or presentation has them gripping their abdominal muscles — something that would never happen to them in, say, the grocery store.

That is the tension we're trying to break here, that tension we hold without even knowing we hold it. In many ways, it's the hardest kind of tension to work on. First, you have to acknowledge that it exists.

EXERCISE: MUSCLING THOSE MUSCLES

Do you know what each muscle in your body does? This exercise can help you get to know your muscles better. You can do this either standing up or lying down. Whatever your position, you should be comfortable and as relaxed as you can be.

Start with your toes. Tense them and feel that sensation. Then release them and feel that sensation. Travel up your body, tensing and then releasing every muscle group you come across. Tense your feet muscles, your calves, your quads, your hamstrings, and every little muscle group in your back. If it's difficult to do this on a particular muscle, try pressing it lightly with your fingertip while you tense. Make a note of how each one feels when you tense it, and if each muscle returns back to normal when you release it. If any release feels tense or doesn't release like you think it should, that could be a sign of some unknown tension there. Try it again and see if you can feel a release: Practice until you become a scholar on the muscle groups in your body so you'll have a good idea if anything's amiss.

Next, read your speech and imagine thousands of people in the audience — a number far outside your comfort zone. Now stop. Do you feel any tension? Are any muscle groups not releasing? If so, that could be a key to where you need to work (keep reading for what you can do about it).

There's a difference between *relaxing* and *releasing*. Generally, when we speak about relaxation, we're referring to the mental side of it, and then of course, the physical side follows. Think about coming home from work after a super busy day and sinking into the couch with a glass of wine. That's pure relaxation. But maybe you carried a heavy box at work and one of your back muscles is tight. It's possible to be in a state where your back muscles are tense and also be relaxed. If you're giving a presentation and you've locked your knees, people can hear it in your voice. Your voice sounds tight and restricted, and that can inhibit your performance, even if you're not mentally tense.

TIP

It's important to focus on *releasing*, not relaxing. You're in a relaxed state just before going to bed. Or maybe with that glass of wine or cup of tea. When your muscles are released, you're not holding any undo tension, and they're ready to fire up at a moment's notice. Sure, it's good to feel relaxed after a long day at work. But that's not what you're going up on stage to do. You want your muscles released, but you also want to be on alert — a cat ready to pounce.

Releasing the tension

You've expertly pinpointed where you hold tension (or you've got a pretty good idea about it). Now, it's all you can feel when you tense that muscle, no matter whether it's during a performance or leading up to it. You squeeze it, and maybe it doesn't release like it should. This section offers some tips and tricks to lose that tension.

"Exercise more." It's almost become a cliché, a sort of panacea that drives people crazy and makes them long for the couch even more. *But it really does help* to be doing some physical activity. If you haven't realized it by now in this chapter, speech is physical. You're not going to excel if you don't have any other physicality in your life.

Regular exercise gives you a better understanding of your muscle groups. That exercise you did earlier, where you tensed and released all your muscles? That will get easier after you get to know what muscles do and how to use them. Another thing physical activity does for you is release *endorphins*, chemicals that make you feel exhilarated and happy and block feelings of pain.

REMEMBER

You don't have to run five miles a day to get to where you need to be. Going for a walk, doing some yoga poses, or even taking the stairs instead of the elevator can help.

EXERCISE: VISUALIZING TO RELEASE STRESS

You can do this exercise sitting or lying down. Close your eyes. Now think of a white, sandy beach. The sun is warm, but not hot. The waves are close enough to hear, but not close enough to swallow you up. You smell the sea. You're lying on that sand feeling great.

Breathe in and out with the waves. All that tension you have, let it go out with the tide. Let every breath sink you deeper into the sand, until your perfect imprint is all that remains. Remember, incorporate every sense of this place that you can: Imagine the sight, smells, sounds, the feeling of the sand, the taste of salt on your lips. Try to feel like you're actually there.

Stay on the beach for 10–20 minutes and explore all your senses in your new world until you feel completely relaxed. Your body is like a limp rag. Go back to the beach any time you feel stressed.

TIP

Is your yoga mat nowhere in sight? Maybe you're sitting at a conference table, waiting to give that PowerPoint presentation you spent all night working on. It would probably be socially awkward (at the very least) to lay yourself across the floor, close your eyes, and begin tensing every muscle. Well, if you've become an expert on your body, you may have a good idea where your tension is coming from or will come from once you start your presentation. If you're subtle, you can tense it and release it right there at the table. No one will know, and you won't have to splay across any dirty floors!

Chin Up and Don't Slouch

He's no slouch is a compliment. You shouldn't be slouching, but often the slouch isn't a physical problem, it's a mental one. Many slouchers are trying to protect themselves, so they start to curl into a ball. When your spine collapses, your lungs can't fill properly with air. That's going to travel to your neck, and then your jaw. You'll end up looking like Shaggy on *Scooby-Doo*. The dreaded slouch is one of the worst postures in speaking, but luckily, it's one of the easiest to remedy.

Breathing as a sloucher

Think back and remember the last time you saw a baby. Can you visualize how they breathe? Babies do this ingenious thing when they breathe: They follow their instinct. When babies breathe, they have very little tension in their abdominal and back muscles, so they can breathe in and out easily and take deep, uninterrupted breaths. Sometime during the stage between baby and now, we adults have learned a lot of great things and nasty things. One of those things is the horrible habit of shallow breathing, as if from the upper chest.

There are a few reasons for this adult style of breathing, but the big one is stress, which, not surprisingly, babies don't have a lot of. Stress causes the muscles to contract tightly around your abdomen, making you take quick, shallow breaths. Now, guess what happens when you slouch? The problem gets much worse. We'll do something about that in the next exercise.

We slouch because it's often the most comfortable position we can find. It's often the path of least resistance. It's a way for all our muscles to become dead weight on top of each other. Aligning yourself for good posture goes against all of that.

REMEMBER

It will take time and it will be uncomfortable for a while until you wean yourself off the slouch. But once it becomes natural, it begins to feel great.

Why feeling bad ends up sounding bad

We don't yet have the ability to separate our bodies from our voices, even though it may seem that way for some narrators. So we're stuck with having our voices be conduits for any maladies our bodies seem to have on that given day — or conduits for something more chronic, like stress. If your body is tight because you're anxious due to an upcoming speech, your voice will reflect that. You're stressed and think you can fake it? That's a tough one. The only way to get rid of that sound is to dig it up from its roots.

EXERCISE: BOWING TO THE SLOUCH

This exercise is meant to prove to you that slouching is a breath killer. Slouching has its time and its place (for example, on the couch during a ball game), but that time and place is *not* during a speech or while preparing for it.

But right now you *are* going to slouch. Ready? One, two, three, slouch. Curve your back. Let your neck scrunch up, like it does when you're binge-watching your favorite show. Now, try to take a deep breath. What? You can't?

Now flip back a few pages and redo the alignment exercise. How do you feel now? Can you feel a huge difference in how you breathe? How your body has positioned itself?

EXERCISE: FINDING YOUR BREATH

Here's another exercise to prove something to you. Let's see "where" you breathe from.

Stand with your feet shoulder width apart and plant those feet like you have roots growing under them, through the foundation of the building your standing in, all the way down into the dirt, and there's a big tree growing out of the crown of your head into the sky. Breathe a few times. Now, put one hand on your upper chest and another on your lower abdomen and breathe again.

Where do you feel the most movement? If it's in that upper chest, try again, this time trying to fill up your lungs with all that air. The belly moves because the diaphragm is expanding fully and the abdominal muscles are released enough to respond fully to this expansion. Take a few more long breaths, in and out, and then pause. Feel where your body is when you take those breaths. That's how you should be positioned when you're performing.

WARNING

Your voice will betray you. That quiver you feel in your gut on the day of the performance will be heard. This is why you need to work on releasing your tension with these exercises.

Here are some common vocal symptoms of an anxious presenter and suggestions for what you can do about them:

» **Quiet speaking into a microphone:** This idea that you must use a microphone to be heard is endemic and in many cases it's just wrong. Let's go ahead and say it: You probably don't need a microphone. *But,* you protest, *what if I'm about to speak at a conference for five thousand people?* Well, then you're going to need a microphone. But generally, for a small crowd size, using a microphone is a crutch and often doesn't end well. When you speak quietly, it's often because your muscles are tense and you can't project your voice.

Why shouldn't you use this technology that's made specifically for the projection of the human voice? One reason is that you probably won't use a microphone when you practice your speech. So, you'll practice the speech and get it perfect with a great projected voice, and then get there and see a microphone in your face and have to suddenly figure out a whole new way to do it. Have you ever heard your voice coming out of speakers? If you haven't, it's best not to try it out during a speech. It's horrifying. Your voice doesn't sound like you. Totally weird. So what you'll do is compensate and speak quieter than you should, and because of that you could potentially lose some power.

- **Speed speaking:** It's amazing how fast people can speak when they're just trying to get through something. Logically, what's the best way to get through a very anxiety-ridden speech? To do it as fast as you can, of course. But that's not going to help you in the long run. It's one of the easiest things the audience will pick out about your speech. And it's one of the biggest problems new speakers experience. Luckily, there's a cure for it: Realize it's going to happen, and slow down.
- **Shaky voice:** Have you ever heard speakers who sound like they're about to cry the whole time? Sometimes that's for effect. Sometimes they *are* going to cry, and it's so completely powerful that the audience cries, too. But sometimes you can tell from the beginning that it's not the type of subject matter to get teary-eyed about. A business plan might be beautifully executed, but the board of directors doesn't expect you to cry about it. Having a shaky voice can get awkward.

  The reason for shaky voice is simple: no breath support. If you've ever played an instrument like a trumpet or saxophone, what happens when you don't blow enough air into the horn? A poor sound. The same idea applies to our vocal folds if there's not enough air going through. The vocal folds don't *approximate* (come together) fully and won't vibrate with ease and efficiency.

  The answer: Breathe deep, as if from down your lower abdomen, not from up in your chest. Take long breaths in, and then out again. Keep your shoulders down and your chest up and out on the inhale. Inhale for a count of four, then exhale on a whispered "ah." Allow the sound to flow freely out of your body. Repeat a few times and then replace the whisper with a spoken "ah." Eventually graduate to a sentence in your presentation.
- **Voice cracking:** Assuming you're not 12 years old, your cracking voice is due to something other than hormones. So, how come you become a preteen throwback every time you go up to speak? The same reason some people get shaky voice. It doesn't happen with everyone. It depends on how deep or high your voice is and the control you have in your voice already. But either way, the cure is proper breathing. Slow down those breaths and bring them in as if from deep in your abdomen. Try to release your abdominal muscles after every sentence. And take a breath after every sentence. This will allow you to fully catch up and also give the audience time to process what they just heard.
- **Dry throat/loss of voice:** This is a physiological response to stress that causes muscles in your body to tighten, and that goes for your throat, vocal folds, and chest as well. This is common enough, as are the remedies, such as hot water with lemon and honey. But what if that doesn't do the trick? If not, it may be that the fight, flight, or freeze response has been activated, and moisture is being diverted elsewhere. So, if you're full to the brim with water and your mouth is still dry as a bone, keep reading for ideas on combatting this sometimes troublesome gift of evolution.

» **Clearing the throat/coughing:** Not a cougher until you're on stage? That seems mighty suspicious, doesn't it? When you're stressed, you often breathe quickly and shallowly from your upper chest, which can cause your throat to dry. It can also be just a nervous habit.

» **Yawning when you're not tired:** Do you constantly yawn before you give that presentation? Physiological responses to threat include increased heart rate and tightening of the muscles. When this occurs, our bodies heat up. Yawning is an unconscious way of cooling your brain down.

» **Trouble putting thoughts into words:** Oh, things may be all fine and dandy when you're just remembering what you wrote. But what if there's an unexpected question period? And you've lost the ability to speak your mother tongue? Breathe deep! And keep reading, because the next section discusses how to fight the fight, flight, or freeze response.

Using Your Body to Battle the Fight, Flight, or Freeze Response

One evolutionary trait that truly doesn't help us when we're getting started in public speaking is the fight, flight, or freeze response. If you remember from science class, this response is the central nervous system responding to protect you from some external terrible thing: a tiger coming through some bushes, a branch cracking above your head, or — nowadays — your name being called to give a speech at your daughter's wedding.

Evolution doesn't know or care, but one of those things is not like the others. If you forget your words to your only daughter's wedding, you're not going to be seriously injured. (Depending on how you raised her.) But that fear on a hair trigger is deeply ingrained, and your body responds in the same way. It perceives a threat, and a cocktail of adrenaline and other hormones gets pumped throughout that tell you to

» Get ready to fight

» Get ready to take flight.

» Freeze.

EXERCISE: ASSUMING THE POSITION

Stand upright in a neutral position. Feel roots growing down to the earth from the bottom of your feet while the rest of your body is growing up to the sky. Now slouch down and droop, like Shaggy from *Scooby Doo*. Try to walk around the room in this position. What happens to your pace? Where's your focus? What are your thoughts? Put one hand on your lower abs and one on your upper chest. Breathe in and out. What hand moves first when you are breathing in?

Give your body a good shake and return to your normal stance. Now stand as tall as you can, with your chest out, and walk around the room again. Notice your pace. Are you moving faster? Is your focus more focused outward, at the world? Where does your breath feel like it's coming in when you inhale? Are you dropping it deeper into your lower abs? What are you thinking about? What are some words that can describe this feeling?

When you hold your head up and stand tall it sends a message to the brain that you are strong and confident, so you actually begin to feel more confident. Before, when you were Shaggy and your body was contracted and slouchy, you were instinctually taking up less room, and your voice sounded smaller and less confident.

None of those, especially that last one, is particularly helpful when called on to say a few words. But you may be surprised to learn that you can use that adrenaline to actually help you. What are some things your body can do to fight back? This section includes exercises that will help you regain control when you step in front of those bright lights.

Here's an exercise Alyson uses in a workshop to explore the difference in the positions called *in and down* (slouched) and *up and out* (tall with head held high) that involves role-play. She has each group pair off and play out a scenario with a problem. For example, it could be a boss reprimanding an employee who always comes late to work.

The pair then decides which one will be in an in and down position and who will be in an up and out position. They tend to conclude that it's more likely the boss would maintain the up and out pose and the lowly employee the down and in. They role-play for a few minutes and then keep the characters and problem but switch their body positions.

What happens is interesting. In an up and out position the boss is confident, can articulate clearly why arriving late is a problem, and comes up with solutions — such as set an alarm clock. When they're in a down and in position, though, they can't make eye contact, have trouble stringing two sentences together, and just want to get the heck out of there.

EXERCISE: STANDING UP WITH LESS EFFORT

Sit in a chair with your feet flat on the floor. Put your hand on the back of your neck. Now try to stand up. Are your neck muscles tightening? Do you feel your neck pull forward? Your neck is just an innocent bystander and it shouldn't be involved when you stand up. The Alexander Technique, created by Frederick Matthais Alexander, is a process of initiating movement with ease. We can move in a more comfortable way with no strain.

So, try it again. Sit in a chair, with your hand on your neck. Start to stand up. When you feel a pull from your neck, just roll your neck slightly forward until you don't feel the pull. Then stand. Doesn't that feel easier? It takes less effort, and your neck will thank you.

When the employee is in the down and in position they feel bad and have little self-esteem, and might even feel that they're going to get fired. When they're in the up and out position, they wonder why there is a problem. They think clearly and come up with answers.

TIP

As you probably know, you don't need to be standing in front of a thousand people to feel anxious. Sitting around a conference table explaining the goings on in your department can do it. So sit up straight! A 2009 study in the *European Journal of Social Psychology* held a test for body posture and self-evaluation. Participants were asked to write down their strengths and weaknesses. When they were slumped in a down and in position, they were not as articulate and had difficulty listing their strengths. Those who sat up straight with their feet flat on the floor in an up and out posture wrote more positive qualities about themselves.

REMEMBER

Changing your posture can also change your mood about things, which may be particularly important when you need to include your input in something. When you're in a slumped position sitting around the boardroom table, you're more likely to be persuaded by others even if you know that your idea is better.

Cutting Yourself Some Slack

Feeling positive? Good, because now it's time to talk about something everyone has a problem with: mistakes. Yup, *everybody* makes mistakes in some form or another. It's not possible to go through life without messing up stuff.

Maybe there are a few really big ones in there for you. Some real tragedies. Or maybe we're talking more small-time flubs. In the world of speaking, all kinds of mistakes are waiting for you to make them. For many, the issue isn't the size of the mistake, it's the worry that *any* mistake will cost you your next shot. And in some cases, that may be true. It's sometimes harder to get a second opportunity after messing up your first.

How you react to making a mistake can make all the difference. Do you dwell on it, looking horrified and making it all the more obvious? Or do you dust yourself off and get ready for the next challenge?

REMEMBER

The way humans learn is to make mistakes and learn from them. That's not new. It's tough to make mistakes in front of peers, your boss, or an audience. But as Frank Sinatra said, "I pick myself up, dust myself off, and start all over again." It's time to learn how to give yourself a break.

Here are a few tips on how to cope with mistakes so that next time you can take the knowledge you learned and move on and do better next time:

- **Take some time alone to think about it.** This has to be the first step. You know you messed up, the other people at the speech know it, the audience knows it. It doesn't matter how big the screw-up was. If you screwed up, you have to give yourself some time to just ponder it. The alone part is crucial to healing and getting over it. In the end, you're the only one who is accountable to you on this. Get your own opinion about the incident before you start to be proactive.
- **Reflect on the whys.** Figure out why it happened — conduct a formal investigation into the incident. Did you totally freeze for 30 seconds and become unable to go on? Why was that? Did you have a coughing attack? Find your answer, but don't feel the need to solve it just yet. Just pinpoint the reason as best you can.

  TIP

  Talk to someone else who has given a presentation that went awry. *Everyone* who speaks publicly regularly has had a speech go totally off the rails. It happens! Find someone who didn't watch your flub. You're looking for fraternity, not sympathy. Find out what that person did, but also what they did to get over it. Maybe they jumped back in the ring right away. Maybe they gave it some time. Bond over your shared experience.
- **Find what worked.** Did your entire speech suck? Probably not. Take a sheet of paper and write down three things that *worked* on the night of your speech. Even if it was a total disaster, maybe you looked especially good that evening. That's a plus. Did you make it there on time? Great. These things don't have to be huge, and they don't have to outweigh the mistake you made. You're not trying to change history here. But give yourself some props.

- **Consider how you will improve next time.** Take that dissection you did earlier — those whys — and do some research. If it was obviously a certain section you had trouble with, then work on that bit. You had a coughing fit and couldn't continue? You're not allergic to the stage, so maybe it was that you had no water? Or you were sick? Whatever it is, put in the time and figure out how to root that behavior out of your presentation. Work on it for the next speech.
- **Laugh at yourself and be kind.** You've figured it all out, and it's never going to happen again. It's a learning experience! Now it's time to let it go. When you went to that person who also made some mistake in his presentation, did they laugh about it? Probably. It's likely a great story now after all this time. Make *your* story, so that when you've done this a bunch, someone can come to *you* and bond. It's okay to find the funny side of it. It doesn't diminish how serious you're working to undo it. And be kind in your retelling.
- **Do more work if necessary.** Hopefully you've figured it out by your next presentation, but maybe you didn't. Are you cursed? Doubtful. But there may be a more persistent problem than a one-off issue. That's okay! It's common. But it's going to take more work.
- **Forgive yourself.** Remember, everything is temporary, even this feeling. Emotions about stuff like what happened don't last forever. So look forward to that. Then forgive yourself. Surely everyone else has forgiven you. Even if others haven't, make sure *you* have a benchmark for yourself so you're not feeling guilty forever. Are you doing your due diligence so this doesn't happen again? Are you jumping back into that ring? Then cut yourself some slack.

Shifting Your Focus to the Audience

The speech may be about your life — your struggles, your travels, your family, or your career. But even that speech isn't about *you*, meaning it's not *for* you. It's for your *audience*.

Sure, it's created by you, experienced by you, and delivered by you. Maybe your speech is a part of your job, or perhaps you're getting paid. Maybe you're trying to establish a greater presence in the community. There is some incentive for you to be doing this — but your incentive ends there. The *content* is the reason the audience is listening. So make sure you give them what they want.

There are three main purposes for public speaking:

- **To inform:** A college lecture is the perfect example of this type of presentation. You're telling people — who are hopefully open to information — something they don't know, that you're an expert on.
- **To persuade:** Political speeches are a great example. You're trying to convince someone of something. It doesn't have to be political, of course. There are plenty of persuasive speeches made in the business world and the academic world and elsewhere.
- **To entertain:** A wedding speech is a good example. You're telling stories and getting laughs. You're sharing memories. You're trying to get the message across that the person you know is a great person, and you're trying to keep the mood of the party intact. People have their leisure hats on, and you're following the tone of the gathering. But entertainment can also happen in different settings. Some of the best keynotes are completely about entertaining the crowd.

TIP

Here's the key: A persuasive speech can also be entertaining, an informative speech can also be persuasive. In fact, a speech does much better if it does all three things at once.

Few people want to sit in a lecture hall and listen to scientific facts about, say, some specific animal found somewhere in the world without a little bit of spice added to the conversation. Remember these three purposes of speeches as you read on and learn how to use them to your and your audience's advantage.

Beginning with the end in mind

This idea is inspired by one of Steven Covey's habits in his book *The 7 Habits of Highly Effective People* (Free Press, 1989). Let's say you have a message you want to get across, and you know whom you want to get it across to. That's pretty good so far. But a serious question must still be asked — one that involves the audience *after* you've left the stage: What exactly do you want the audience to do with that message?

For some types of presentations, that's simple. A politician has a *stump speech* — a standard presentation touching on the issues the politician finds important, given over and over in the same way — and they want you to vote for them. A college professor has a standard lecture they give every semester, and they want you to study and learn.

But it's not always so obvious. And the question of what the audience is supposed to do with your speech may get harder when you take yourself out of the equation and start asking what the audience wants.

The next few sections ask some questions to ask yourself before you face the audience.

What is the audience expecting to learn?

The audience is there waiting for you. Maybe it's a boardroom, maybe it's a parent teacher meeting, maybe it's a convocation speech at your alma mater. They are expecting something out of you, either from the description of the event or potentially from your reputation.

Are you going to give them what they expect? Now, the audience isn't always right about a speaker. Your perception of what they're looking for should not necessarily be the golden light you are walking toward. But it should guide you. If you think they're going to get something on your specialty — say, marine wildlife — there should be some talk of marine wildlife in your speech. A room full of your marine biologist peers would be disappointed in a lecture on the chemical properties of popcorn.

That doesn't mean, though, that that's *all* you have to give. Maybe you could begin with an on-land analogy. Maybe you throw some jokes in there. You can change it up with a number of devices to go from a pure, fact-based speech to a more exciting talk that gives the same message in a more persuasive and entertaining way. But you can only figure out how to do that if you have a good guess about what the audience is expecting to hear.

What are your audience's demographics?

Knowing what your audience is expecting or thinks requires that you understand who they are. You're not going to want to do a whole lecture on professional wrestling if you have elderly New York socialites sitting in front of you.

Start by supposing you're in your home country (or state, or city) and you have a pretty good understanding of the kind of people who would attend this sort of meeting (We get to foreign engagements in a moment).

The first and easiest thing to look at is age. Age is the biggest indicator of how people are going to perceive humor, emotion, and a message in general. If you're speaking to a retirement community, and then you give the same speech on a college campus the next day, how are you going to change the speech while keeping the integrity of the message? What kind of bias does one group have that doesn't really appear in the other?

The same kinds of things can be asked about a number of different types of social groups: socioeconomic, racial, religious, education level, and others. It's so important to recognize whom you're giving the message to and how it will be best received.

WARNING

Don't outright *pander* — unless it's in a humorous way. It may be okay to throw out a few dad jokes to teens, like, "Hey, I'm old and you're young, ha ha." But walk away from that after the initial joke. People of any demographic can see right through it. It's okay that you're different from the audience. It may be why they came to see you in the first place. But don't use it as a wedge.

When you're speaking in a different country, knowing demographics is harder. It doesn't matter if you're going to another English-speaking country, the norms and traditions will be different. It's certainly best to figure those out before you get there. Research online, find and talk to someone from that country, or better yet, have a coffee with the organizer before the event. Ask if there are any strange quirks about the audience you may not be aware of, being from a different country. If that person gives you a strange look, that's probably good. You may be in the clear.

What level of knowledge on the topic does the audience have?

You must base your presentation on the level of knowledge your audience has on the subject. You're not intending to teach graduate-level meteorology students about the ROY G. BIV method of ordering the colors of the rainbow, are you? Don't explain what the audience already knows. First, it wastes time and may insult them. The audience doesn't want to feel like you think they're dumb. If you're explaining a project you're working on to a bunch of your bosses, you probably don't need to explain the fundamentals.

The same thinking has to work in the opposite way, of course. Don't go over the audience's head. They might start to feel self-conscious, that they should already know this stuff if you've assumed they do. Or they might just get totally bored. You can't lose your audience.

How big is the audience?

This is something you should know as soon as you're asked to speak. If you're told it's just going to be a handful of colleagues, it would be quite a shock to be ushered into a large auditorium full of hundreds of people. A large audience presents a wider range of knowledge, demographics, desires, and goals.

REMEMBER

Your focus has to be much wider when speaking to a large, unknown audience. It's a lot easier to assume people know more about what you're speaking about at a small conference of your peers. Even if the audience is large, make sure your eye contact includes the entire group. It is a great idea to break your audience into three parts: Find someone in the center to speak to, then look over and find someone on the left side, and then the other side.

Why is the topic important to the audience?

This is the big one, and that's why it's last. In other places in this minibook, you're asked to consider "What is the point?" of your speech. Now, if you haven't already done so, it's time to pay close attention to that question when it comes to the audience.

Why are *they* the ones who are listening? Why are *you* the one giving it to them? And what are you hoping they're going to *do* with the information? Look at your speech and be totally honest with yourself. Are they going to do what you intend them to do? If you end by asking that they throw themselves in front of whaling ships, unless you have some sort of hypnotic, cult-like powers, you're not going to get them to do that. You have to manage your expectations. If you're talking about the glorious work of blood donation, and then — surprise! — there's a place to donate blood in the lobby, that's more manageable.

REMEMBER

Be honest with yourself about the practicality of your ask and of your ability to ask.

Addressing one person in the audience

Now it's time to talk about the techniques you can use regarding where you should look while speaking, or whom you should look at. Of course, there's the classic: *Imagine everyone in their underwear.* There's one Alyson likes to call the Pacifist: Stare right over the heads of the people in the audience. After all, it's tough to see exactly where a speaker's eyes are pointing. Even at close range, it's often hard to tell whether someone is looking at your eyes, your nose, or even your ears.

It's good to think of giving your speech as having a conversation, and the best way to do that is to humanize your audience as best as you can. That doesn't mean giving each audience member equal stare-into-their-eyes time. (Engaging with someone for five or six seconds is enough.) But you should act as if you know them, or are giving them a speech personally.

Here are a few tips to get you on your way to a one-on-one experience:

- **Actually meet people in the audience.** Remember to get to the event early. After you've checked everything and you're ready to go, when people start milling about, go mill about with them. They're going to want to talk to you. You're the speaker, after all.

  TIP

  Try to meet three of them. Get to know their names, what they do for a living, and why they're there to see you. Then, when it's time to speak, find them in the audience and speak directly to them. Give them extra attention. It's easier to talk to a friendly face.

- **Read your audience.** Ever hear someone say something totally inappropriate somewhere, maybe at a Christmas party, and then someone whispers, "Read the room, dude"? You don't want that to happen to you during your speech. Always understand what's going on with the audience before you put your foot in your mouth. If you think of it as a conversation, instead of you being alone up there, you should be in good shape.

- **Don't worry if everyone isn't engaged.** You're not going to win over everybody, so get over that idea. It's a bummer to look out there and see some folks looking at their phone, face lit up, texting or playing some stupid game. Don't assume they're not listening. They might just be terrific at multitasking.

  TIP

  Sure, you can ignore them — but you could also work a little harder to convince those people to listen. It may not work, but try speaking to the doofuses for a minute. But don't forget to appreciate everyone else who is paying attention. Those are the people you want to give your message to.

Knowing when not to apologize

Apologizing is the death of the public speaker. If you're feeling sorry, that's going to affect the audience. They're in turn going to feel sorry, or awkward, or something like that.

Everything looks bad when you apologize. You're supposed to be a strong, confident authority on your subject, yet your body language looks as if you'd rather be anywhere else. Your voice loses that timbre of someone who knows what they're talking about. Sometimes the first thing speakers say is that they're sorry — sorry for coughing, sorry for being late, sorry for having to be the one to give you this talk, blah, blah, blah. It takes the wind out of the audience's sail.

The show must go on. When you apologize *without good reason*, you can lose credibility. It's not easy, but you need to have a good idea of what's an acceptable level for apology to an audience. How about this: Be humble. But never forget, you're the authority up there. Act like it.

Here are some examples of apologies and how to avoid them:

- **"I'm sorry, I'm out of time."** The problem here is no one knows that but you and the organizer. Unless a school bell rings, if you have the audience totally rapt, finish up. Don't allow the red light coming on over their heads to become a reason to blame yourself or anyone else for it. They don't know your script. Finish up with some final thoughts and thank them. They'll be none the wiser.
- **"I have the flu and I just found out that I was giving the speech today. I'm sorry you won't be hearing a good speech."** Unless you've got a serious illness that will hinder your performance (sore throat, inability to stand), don't even mention it. The audience probably can't tell, and any mention of being sick may erode not only your credibility, but the credibility of the institution that threw you to the fire. And even if they can tell, they will respect you for pressing on without using it as an excuse.
- **"Sorry for keeping you so long. I know it was supposed to finish at eight."** The end of your speech is not the time to apologize, so don't do it. All that great stuff you just said? All those ideas you want them to keep in their mind? You just undercut all of that, and the audience will leave remembering that you apologized for it all. Give them the old Warner Brothers treatment: *That's all, folks!*
- **"Sorry about the projector, everyone."** Don't be sorry about the projector. Don't be sorry about anything outside of your control. It's not your fault the back fan is really loud, or that the traffic noise is loud in the room. Just soldier on and don't mention those things.
- **"Sorry, but I can't answer that question."** If there's a Q&A, people are going to ask you questions you don't know. Not just in your speech, but literally everywhere. You're not a wizard. You don't know everything. People know that. They're not expecting a wizard. If you don't know something, let them know you'll get back to them. Find out the information they want afterward and let them know after the presentation.

6 Spreading the Word through Social Media Marketing

Contents at a Glance

IN THIS CHAPTER

» Learning what social media is

» Discovering the key components of a good SMM campaign

» Constructing an SMM roadmap

» Understanding the rules for successful SMM

» Keeping people engaged and measuring your success

» Responding to criticism

Chapter 1
Launching SMM Campaigns

Launching a social media marketing campaign is, in some ways, similar to launching any other marketing campaign. But at the same time, you need to approach certain aspects of it very differently to maximize the results.

In this chapter, we discuss the components of a successful SMM campaign and how you can make it work in harmony with other marketing efforts. We also discuss how best to respond to criticism, how to turn a crisis to your advantage, and, finally, some tactics for turning the campaign into a long-term marketing asset.

Defining Social Media Marketing

Social media marketing (*SMM*) is a technique that employs *social media* (content created by everyday people using highly accessible and scalable technologies such as social networks, blogs, micro-blogs, message boards, podcasts, social bookmarks, communities, wikis, and vlogs).

Social media (which has probably been one of the most hyped buzz terms of the last decade) refers to content created and consumed by regular people for each other. It includes the comments a person adds at the end of an article on a website, the family photographs they upload to a photo-sharing service, the conversations they have with friends in a social network, and the blog posts they publish or comment on. That's all social media, and it's making everyone in the world a content publisher and arbitrator of content. It's democratizing the web.

Facebook (`facebook.com`) is the most popular social network. It allows you to connect with friends and share information in a matter of minutes. Facebook has 2.41 billion monthly active users around the world.

Discovering the Types of SMM Campaigns

At this point, it's important to talk about the different types of campaigns. After that, we discuss the rules and guidelines that make SMM campaigns successful. In the realm of social media marketing, how you implement a campaign is nearly as important as what you implement.

REMEMBER

Before you launch your SMM campaign, make sure that you've done an inventory of all the other major campaigns going on at the same time that target your stakeholders or are within your nonprofit niche. The last thing you want is to launch a campaign in which you're asking your stakeholders to do basically the same thing that they may have just done for another nonprofit organization.

WARNING

In 2017, the FTC (Federal Trade Commission) imposed guidelines on how pharmaceutical companies can market using the social web. Those regulations cover the promotion of FDA-regulated products. More information can be found on this FDA website: `www.fda.gov/AboutFDA/CentersOffices/OfficeofMedicalProductsandTobacco/CDER/ucm397791.htm`. If you're operating in a regulated space, be sure to check with your lawyers about what you're allowed and not allowed to do before launching an SMM campaign.

UGC contests

Contests in all their various forms have always been a big hit in the marketing campaign arena. But now contests structured around user-generated content (UGC) are all the rage. And with good reason: They are invariably extremely popular, engaging, and fun. With *user-generated content* (*UGC*), you structure a contest built on participants who contribute something in return for rewards. This can be something as simple as crowdsourcing a TV advertisement, as General Motors did in the early days of social media with its Tahoe campaign in 2006, to asking users to contribute video clips of their funniest moment with a product. The best clip (by the predetermined criteria) gets a prize, with all the other participants getting some sort of recognition.

As *Wired* magazine reported, in the case of the Tahoe campaign, the microsite attracted 629,000 visitors, with each user spending more than nine minutes on the site and a third of them going on to visit the main Chevy.com website. Sales took off from that point, even though environmentalists tried to sabotage the UGC campaign by creating video clips that highlighted their views on the impact the vehicles had on the environment.

Another successful contest was run by the restaurant chain Applebee's in the summer of 2014. Applebee's asked its customers to snap pics of their meals or themselves chowing down. The best photos were then published by Applebee's on its Instagram feed using the hashtag #fantographer and were cross-promoted on Facebook and Twitter with posts and ads. When the campaign ended in the fall of 2014, engagement had risen 25 percent and tweets tagged with #fantographer appeared in 78 million users' timelines (users would submit their photos to Applebee's via Twitter and used the hashtag when doing so).

Podcasting

A *podcast* is a digital audio file that is made available via web syndication technologies such as RSS. Although it's not, strictly speaking, social media, it's often classified as such because it allows anybody to easily syndicate their own audio content. You can use podcasts as a way to share information with your audiences. Often, podcasts take the shape of celebrity interviews or discussions about an entity's product, services, or brand.

A successful example of a podcast is the Butterball Turkey Talk podcast. It's a seasonal podcast including stories from Turkey Talk hotline workers. You can subscribe to it via iTunes and other online podcast directories.

REMEMBER

Podcasts typically don't form a whole SMM campaign in and of themselves but work well with other parts of a campaign and are a great way to get the word out about your good cause.

Recognizing What Makes a Good SMM Campaign

A *social media marketing campaign* is one that specifically allows for social influence to take place digitally. A few years ago, marketing through social media was a niche activity, and the notion of targeting influencers was an obscure one. The closest comparison was word-of-mouth campaigns conducted in the offline world to build brand awareness for a product by incentivizing people to talk about it among themselves. Digital campaigns, for the most part, were about *display advertising* (banner ads that appear at the top and side of a website) across large magazine and newspaper websites, complemented with paid search campaigns and maybe email campaigns. These campaigns were used to drive prospects to a *microsite* (a site devoted to that particular campaign) or a website, where they were encouraged to make purchases or engage with the brand.

REMEMBER

With an SMM campaign, you mustn't drag people away from the social platform on which they're communicating and interacting with each other. They don't want to be distracted, and you'll probably only waste precious marketing dollars trying to lure them to your website. Instead, it's more important to execute the campaign on those very platforms where your potential stakeholders are in conversation. You have to engage your stakeholders where *they* want to participate, not where you want them to be. And unlike in a digital marketing campaign of yesteryear, the stakeholders of an SMM campaign ignore you unless your SMM campaign is aligned with their objectives and behavior patterns on those social platforms. In the following sections, we outline specific guidelines that you should follow when launching an SMM campaign.

MEET USERS WHERE THEY ARE

A good example of a failed "build it and they will come" attempt was Bud.TV by Budweiser. They tried to create an entertainment destination bypassing YouTube. The effort failed miserably because Budweiser had to spend valuable advertising dollars to encourage consumers to do something that they had no interest in doing — moving away from YouTube, where they had the most entertaining content (and all their friends), to a corporate-sponsored website. What's more, the fact that users couldn't embed the video clips elsewhere (including YouTube) hurt the effort. Bud.TV launched in January 2007 and was shut down early in 2009. Fast forward to 2019, and you'll notice that very few advertisers launch social media marketing campaigns where they try to pull customers to their websites to engage with them (granted, pulling customers to a website to make a purchase is different and appropriate if done with sensitivity).

Creating Your SMM Roadmap

As with any other good marketing campaign, you need to construct a roadmap that shows you where you're going and how you'll get there. In this section, we discuss seven steps that you can take to bulletproof your campaign structure:

- Define your objectives.
- Develop a powerful story/experience.
- Create an action plan.
- Craft the content path.
- Execute for influence.
- Create partnerships.
- Track the results.

Define your objectives

This may seem obvious, but it is amazing how many of us forget about articulating the objectives when it comes to an SMM campaign. Your objectives need to be tightly defined, and they must be practical and actionable, too. The objectives must be specific to the stage of the marketing funnel that you're playing in as well. Saying that the objective of the campaign is simply to take a TV advertisement and make it *go viral* is definitely not enough.

TIP

The objectives must also specify *where* you're planning to run the campaign, *whom* you're targeting (which stakeholders and which influencers), the *duration* of the campaign, and *how it synchronizes* with other digital and offline marketing efforts. It's easy to forget that no SMM campaign happens in isolation. How you participate on the various social platforms is always a mirror of what you do and think in the physical world. If you ignore that fact, you'll lose your stakeholders and supporters even before you've had a chance to meaningfully engage with them.

Develop a powerful story/experience

People's expectations about how they will learn about your organization and services have changed completely. Because the Back button on the browser is ever-present, waiting to take users away from your website, you have a very short window to engage and educate. You have to work to communicate the intrinsic value of each service you offer and who benefits from those services.

Also, because people want to know whom they are dealing with, you need to inject the *why* into your nonprofit's story. You need to let them know why you started your organization and what you care about. The social aspect must be visible. The following are stories you should consider telling during your campaign:

- **Why you're running this campaign:** Yes, you want to provide services and/or raise money, we understand that. But what's the larger picture? Who's benefiting from your services? What problem are you solving? How are communities at large benefiting from your services? Are you providing a service that doesn't currently exist? You have to be specific.
- **What value the stakeholder will get from participating:** Stakeholders want social proof that others you have dealt with have had a great experience. You need to gather testimonial stories to share. If you can provide video of people speaking whom you've previously helped, you have a way to demonstrate authenticity. You also need to show how your organization will either specifically improve stakeholders' lives or contribute to their sense of worth in relation to their friends and family (otherwise they won't share your content).
- **People who are impacted:** Provide visuals that tell a story. Well-known screenwriter Robert McKee has said that stories "unite an idea with an emotion." Make sure that yours does. And with so much of social media being visually driven today, using rich, evocative photography has become all the more important.
- **Who the hero is:** Have a story about the person or thing that is leading this effort. It can be a service that works, a founder on a mission, and so on. Show that hurdles have been overcome. To borrow an example from the business world, the late Steve Jobs was a visionary who figured heavily in the promotion of Apple products because he was the heart and soul of the business.
- **How internal staff feels about what they do:** Borrowing once again from the world of business, a commercial by General Electric showed children talking about what their parents do at GE. The message comes through loud and clear: Not only are the employees proud of what they produce, but their children are, too. Who among your staff or volunteer pool would love to show what their organization means to them? Why do they want to be a part of your story?

Create an action plan

Obviously, the actions you take are dictated by the length and complexity of the campaign. Every campaign has special features and highlights that need showcasing. However, here are some things that are common to most SMM campaigns you'll want to consider creating:

- **A clear call to action:** Decide what action you want the user to take, and make sure that everything you do supports that. If the user has to sign up for something, display the sign-up process front and center at all times.
- **Hashtags and other tools:** Most SMM campaigns create a hashtag for Twitter and Instagram so that people can follow the conversation. A hashtag has the pound sign (#) and a word or phrase related to the project.

  For example, a 2011 campaign to feed people on Thanksgiving was started by Pepto-Bismol with the hashtag #HelpPeptoFeedAmerica. Whenever someone retweeted the message with that hashtag, the makers of Pepto-Bismol donated money to hunger relief. Dyson, the vacuum cleaner brand, uses several hashtags when it posts to Instagram but chooses them carefully so that it doesn't come across as heavy-handed. Here's an example of the hashtags used in a single post on June 4th, 2019: #dyson #dysonhome #insidedyson #vacuum #instatech. Most organizations limit themselves by only using one or two hashtags.
- **A venue for crowdsourcing:** Are you going to create your own web page for people to share and submit their comments, or will you use the current platforms? Decide whether you want to create a Facebook page, or a community on your own website or another third-party one such as Tumblr. There are pluses and minuses to each choice. If it's important to own the content, by all means create your own. Just remember that getting people to participate is easier where they normally hang out. A new venue could be an impediment.
- **Content that can be shared:** The key to every great SMM campaign is the content you create to get attention. If you're a small or new nonprofit and can't afford to create something splashy, you can still do a video and create PDF posters, contests, and graphics. Look at all the content you have already created, and see what you can repurpose. Have your stakeholders create content, if doing so makes sense, and pick a winner.

Craft the content path

When creating SMM campaigns, people often forget to map where their actual touchpoints will be and how they will look. It's not enough to say, "We'll send a tweet with a link." You need to be specific about it. You need to document that you will send three tweets a day at 9 a.m., 5 p.m., and 9 p.m., say, with certain text and a link.

As a handy way to document your campaign, you can map each of your channels and the content that will go into it. One of the best ways to do this is to create a mind map that shows you the big picture of your campaign and all the moving parts on one sheet of paper. Mind maps start with a circle in the middle and radiate ideas that relate to it. For example, you can put your campaign name in the center circle and then radiate circles of the different platforms you are using. From each platform circle, you can note the content that will be sent. From those mind maps, you can then create specific content calendars that help you manage the content production process.

REMEMBER

Your preplanned content is only the first part of what you will be doing. You have to also organically create messages that respond to the ongoing campaign to make it real. When people post something about your campaign on Facebook or Twitter, make sure to respond to it in a reasonable amount of time, which should typically be no more than 12 hours later at the very most. The preplanned items are just the starting point. Social marketing means reacting to real-time events.

Execute for influence

Traditionally, most campaigns have focused on getting a potential stakeholder (or donor) to take a specific action or to view a specific message. The focus has always been on that individual engaging with the nonprofit in some form. However, with an SMM campaign, you need to design for sharing, influencing, reciprocity, and social currency.

Unlike most other campaigns, an SMM campaign needs to accomplish two objectives concurrently:

- **It needs to engage the individual who's being targeted via the campaign.** This is similar to any other type of digital marketing campaign. You want to engage with your target audience in a specific fashion and solicit a specific response.
- **You need to design the campaign so that the target person shares or discusses it with someone else.** Sharing is the social currency element. The person should feel that by sharing the campaign with someone else, they derive greater value from it. This greater value could be something as tangible as a free gift (say, a coffee mug or tote bag) or something as intangible as status among their peers. The point is that the more people the person shares the campaign with (or discusses it with), the more value they generate from it. In this sense, the campaign takes on a network effect, with its value growing each time someone participates.

Create partnerships

Few SMM campaigns are successful in isolation. A more traditional digital campaign, which is based on display and search advertising, comes together through a series of partnerships between the agency, the advertiser, and the publisher, and the same is true of an SMM campaign. However, in this case, the participants vary slightly. Rather than have a regular publisher, you have the social platform to contend with. Your campaign must be in compliance with that platform's policies; otherwise, you can't run on that platform. For example, Facebook (`facebook.com/terms.php`) and YouTube (`youtube.com/static?template=terms`) have strict terms of service regarding the type of advertising that can appear on their platforms.

REMEMBER

The platform players aren't the only things you have to consider. With most large brands, for example, ad hoc user groups that have a sense of ownership over the brand or product category spring up on the social platform where you're planning to run the campaign.

For example, on Facebook, if you were to search for "Ford," you'd find not just the Ford Motor Company page (`facebook.com/ford`), but literally hundreds of pages created by and for people interested in the Ford Motor Company. If you're a marketer at Ford, when you're planning an SMM campaign on Facebook, it's not enough to talk to Facebook and your own agency about the campaign. For it to be a truly successful SMM campaign, you must engage with these ad hoc groups when the campaign is starting. They can be your biggest marketers, helping the campaign succeed. On the other hand, if you upset them, they can turn into saboteurs.

Irrespective of the social platform you're running an SMM campaign on, the ad hoc user groups might already be there. Find them and be sure to engage with them. An SMM campaign means new players and new partnerships that need to be forged early on for it to be a success. Finding and engaging with those communities of people becomes critical.

Track the results

There's a saying in the world of social media that only successful SMM campaigns can be measured; failures can't be. The point is that marketers often say that SMM can't be measured if in their heart of hearts they know that their campaign has failed. If the campaign is a success, you bet they'll be telling you about it and explaining exactly why it was a success.

You can measure an SMM campaign in a lot of different ways. The best method depends on the objectives, the targeted audience, and the social platform on which the campaign is running. But you must determine what you're going to measure and how *before* you run the campaign. Otherwise, you're never going to know whether it's a success. SMM campaigns often spiral out of control, and the law of unintended consequences starts applying.

That's not a bad thing, but it doesn't take away from the fact that the campaign you're running is being run for a purpose — and you'll know whether you've achieved that purpose only if you're measuring the results. It's also important to measure a baseline of online activity before you begin the SMM engagement and decide what to measure. The baseline helps you determine how successful your campaign is relative to the level of conversations and online activity before running it.

Getting into measurement is outside the scope of this book, but for now it's sufficient to say that you must measure not just how many people you reach or who is aware of your campaign, but also the following: the influence generated; the *brand lifts* (increased awareness of the brand — that is, your nonprofit organization — across key brand attributes); and, most important, whether any of this effort led to people signing up for services, promising to make a donation, or requesting information about becoming a volunteer. With the measurement tools in the marketplace (many of which are free or close to free), you can easily track your SMM campaign to the point where the user completes the action you wanted them to take. The measurement tools that exist on the social platforms are getting stronger and stronger by the day, too. Don't hesitate in trying to measure this.

Participating: Four Rules of the Game

Many different factors can make or break an SMM campaign, and sometimes it's even just a matter of luck. But four rules matter above all else when it comes to SMM campaigns. These rules don't always apply to other forms of marketing. Pay attention to them, and make sure that your SMM campaign abides by these.

Be authentic

Authenticity is a tricky word, because it's overused in the context of social media. Everybody talks about being authentic when marketing in the social media realm, but what that means is rarely explained. To spell it out, authenticity is being honest, transparent, and true to the values of the brand: It's as simple as that.

Here are some examples:

- **When you set up a blog as part of your campaign, make sure that you're using your own voice.** Don't outsource the publishing of content to a third party. If you have to, make sure that writers accurately identify themselves as contributing on your behalf.

  George Colony's blog The Counterintuitive CEO is a great example. The blog (`http://blogs.forrester.com/ceo_colony`) is written in the first person by Forrester's chief executive officer, George Colony. There's no doubt that he is the writer.

- **When you're publishing your thoughts and opinions or simply sharing information, don't do so anonymously.** In the world of social media, your stakeholders don't relate to or care about organizations as much as they care about the people behind them. People build relationships with each other, not with anonymous entities. Let your stakeholders know who is behind the voice blogging, tweeting, or running the contest on Facebook. You're not authentic if your customers don't know who you are. Worse still, don't ever use a pseudonym the way the Whole Foods CEO did when responding to critical comments in a discussion forum about his company in 2007. Fortunately, companies learned from his mistake; fast forward to 2023 and it's rare for someone to use a pseudonym to defend their company or organization.

- **Learn from the community and respond to its feedback.** A key part of being authentic is telling your stakeholders the way it really is, hearing their feedback (both positive and negative), and being willing to respond to it. It's no use participating in the social realm if you don't respond to commentary or feedback. If you're worried about not having the time to respond, consider not participating at all.

- **Be humane in your approach.** It's easy to forget that for every comment and every unique visitor, there's an actual person somewhere in the world. Make sure that you participate with consideration and with the same respect that you'd reserve for someone you're talking to face to face.

For more information on authenticity as it applies to word-of-mouth marketing and social media marketing, visit the Association of National Advertisers (ANA) at `https://www.ana.net`. Through their acquisition of the Word of Mouth Marketing Association in 2018, they have amassed a rich repository of research around word-of-mouth marketing that you can find at `https://www.ana.net/content/show/id/womma`.

Remember quid pro quo

For all the altruism associated with the social web, it's easy to forget that it operates on the premise of quid pro quo. We're all good human beings, but most people expect something in return if they're giving you their time. As you develop an SMM campaign in which you'll be demanding your stakeholders' attention (and often a lot more than that), think about the possible quid pro quo. Are you giving enough back in exchange? If you're not giving something back, your stakeholders won't participate. They'll simply ignore you. The social web is littered with marketing campaign failures. These campaigns assumed that just by putting a banner advertisement in front of stakeholders, they would achieve their objectives.

Much better is the example of an SMM campaign that provided a strong quid pro quo for its audiences and was highlighted by Ad Age. Target ran a marketing campaign in the summer of 2014, through which it donated millions of dollars to the Kids In Need Foundation by contributing money for each Up & Up school supply purchased during a specific time period in the summer. The campaign was launched and promoted extensively through social media, which served as the anchor to the entire marketing campaign. This was an SMM campaign that encouraged the consumer to purchase a particular product by tying the purchase to a cause and then motivated them to share their experience and encourage others to participate in that fashion. Success of the campaign was defined as much by the amount of money raised as it was through any traditional measure.

In a similar fashion, Shiv's company Eargo, which offers a high-end hearing loss solution, ran a 2019 summer campaign in which for every hearing aid sold, it donated a hearing aid to a person in need via charity. With the hearing aids costing approximately $2,750, this was a major cause marketing effort tying the purchase to people's belief that giving back is important. Customers were encouraged to share their purchase on social media and encourage others to purchase as well given the altruistic dimensions to the campaign.

Give participants equal status

Many marketing campaigns are designed to make the stakeholder feel special — more special than everyone else around them. That's a good thing. They feel special, and they end up having favorable feelings for your product and go out and buy it. Apple and Harley-Davidson are two brands that personify this philosophy: They make their customers feel special and different from everyone else.

That's wonderful, but it doesn't apply to the SMM realm in the same way. People across the social web like to believe that they're as special and as unique as the next person, as they should. If someone is doing something special, others want to do that as well. If a person does something interesting, others want access to it as well. That's human nature, and the social web encourages behavior through the voyeurism it allows for.

Let go of the campaign

By virtue of starting the campaign, you probably feel that it is your responsibility to moderate and shape it. That doesn't have to be the case. Successful SMM campaigns are the ones in which the organization's advocates take the campaign in new directions. As you develop the campaign, think of yourself as a participant and not just the owner of the campaign. You make better decisions regarding its evolution that way, and by letting go, you allow others to take it in new and amplified directions. As always, remember that your stakeholders will be in control of the campaign. That's what makes social media marketing different. However, you will always be in control of your own response to the audience's participation, and that always presents exciting opportunities.

Keeping Your Supporters Engaged

You're probably used to thinking of campaigns as having a start date and an end date. And they usually need that. You have a finite marketing budget; the campaign is geared around a series of events (like end-of-year celebrations or fundraising dinners and auctions); new services might join existing ones throughout a year; and all of that forces you to end campaigns and launch new ones. However, SMM campaigns are unique in that after they start, they may not stop when you want them to. It's like turning off the lights midway through a dinner party. If you have a conversation going and have brought a community of people together around your organization, service, or campaign, the last thing you want to do is to suddenly disown those people. It's very important that you plan for migrating that community of people to a broader purpose or goal.

Here are four ways to move people onward successfully:

» **Give participants new reasons to engage with you.** Your original SMM campaign has a set purpose and objectives. After those objectives are accomplished, don't turn off the lights. Instead, think of the next campaign that you have planned and how you can customize it to this community of people.

In fact, try to weave the campaigns together into a program that benefits these people. As you do this, remember the four rules of participation that we outlined previously: authenticity, quid pro quo, equal status, and letting go of the campaign.

- **Encourage participants to coalesce into communities.** Often, the people who participate in your SMM campaign all share something in common. This may not always be the case, but depending on the campaign type, they may indeed be interested in forming a community. If you believe that to be the case, encourage people to coalesce into self-supporting communities. It only helps you in the long run and gives new life to the campaign. Campaigns that have generated goodwill transform into stakeholder communities that you can tap into for future marketing and fundraising efforts, or when you need more volunteers.
- **Treat participants like existing community members.** People who have participated in your SMM campaign may not have used your services (or donated to your cause), but they have given you their time and probably have shared a bit of themselves with you in the process. This may have taken the form of commenting on a blog post, participating in a contest, or sharing your viral video clip with friends. Because they have done more than someone who experienced a traditional marketing campaign, you owe them more.

  Treat them like existing members of the community, whether that means sending them special offers or inviting them to participate in focus groups. But always remember that when you send your stakeholders a special offer, it must be on an opt-in basis. Don't spam them if you don't have their permission to communicate with them.
- **Extend the campaign to the website.** Many an SMM campaign has failed because it was kept separate from the company website. The campaign is traditionally built on a microsite with display advertising promoting the campaign. When the campaign has run its course, the microsite is shut down and the advertising is stopped. In the case of an SMM campaign, don't shut down the microsite. Instead, promote the SMM campaign on the nonprofit's website, and when the campaign winds down, find a place on the nonprofit's website for it. That way, your stakeholders can always find it, and if they coalesced into communities during the course of the campaign, they always have a place to return to. In fact, it may be best to launch the campaign on the nonprofit's website itself and move away from developing discrete microsites.

TIP

Often, your participants may know better than you how to create greater meaning from the SMM campaign in the form of a community. Ask them what you should be doing, if anything at all. You'll definitely get strong advice from the people who care the most.

Monitoring Conversations

It's no use running an SMM campaign if you can't measure it. You should always measure your SMM campaigns. Depending on the SMM campaign, different measurements may matter more than others. Brand and conversation monitoring tools help you measure the success of your SMM campaign and your ROI (return on investment). But they do a lot more than that. These tools also help you plan and design your SMM campaigns. They give you a peek into actual user behavior on social platforms, telling you what people are discussing, whether those conversations are positive or negative, and where they're taking place.

Any time you're planning to launch an SMM campaign, you must begin by knowing what your target audiences are doing across the social web. These tools help you do that. They can be classified into three groups:

- **Low-end tools** that primarily focus on the volume of the conversation over a period of time and cover only positive and negative sentiment. Many of these tools are free or dirt cheap. Included in this category are HootSuite and Social Mention.
- **Middle-of-the-road tools** that do some analysis but don't always have the breadth of sources or the depth of analysis that the high-end tools have. Tools in this category are Salesforce Radian6 and Sysomos. Cision, through its Viral Heat acquisition, is another player that straddles the high and low ends with different service levels and capabilities.
- **High-end tools and services** that use linguistic analysis and deep data mining to provide insights into the conversations, who is having them, and where. These tools can cost anywhere from $5,000 a month to $50,000 a month, based mostly on the number of topics mined and the frequency. Included in this category are Sysomis, NetBase, and Crimson Hexagon (since merged with Brandwatch).

When choosing which tool to use, keep the following factors in mind:

- **Your audience:** If you don't know your audience and aren't sure what their motivations are, where they are participating, and how, you want one of the high-end tools.
- **The length of your SMM campaign:** If you're running a short campaign targeting a small population of users, you probably don't need to use one of the high-end tools. It won't be worth the money.

- **The size of the campaign:** If your campaign touches lots of people, you need a higher-end tool that can help you track the activity as well as manage responses.
- **Influencer identification:** If you're planning to focus on influencers rather than the mass population, choose a tool that's strongest at *influencer identification* (the ability to assist you in identifying people who influence customers about your brand). Not all tools do this equally well.
- **Regulatory considerations:** If you work in a highly regulated industry, you want a tool that lets you view commentary and glean insights anonymously. Higher- and mid-level tools have this capability.
- **Dashboard functionality:** Some marketers require interactive dashboards through which they can view the conversation in real time. If you're one of them, be sure to look for a tool that allows for that.

REMEMBER

Lots of free tools for conversation monitoring are out there. Regardless of the complexity of your SMM campaign and tracking needs, there's never any harm in beginning with the free tools. It'll cost you only the time in setting up the domain names. Keep in mind that these tools are valuable to departments like public relations and customer research, too. They may be willing to share the costs of the tool or service with you.

Responding to Criticism

No SMM campaign is a complete success. It never is. Although you may reach many more people than you could have ever imagined, more likely than not, you're still bound to upset some people and even potentially spark an inflammatory response among a few others. From the outset, before you launch your SMM campaign, you need to plan for the potential criticism that may come your way. There's no perfect way to respond, and the answer usually depends on the type of criticism, how widespread it is, and where it is coming from. Your PR department, if you have one, is usually more versed in responding to criticism (and more broadly, crisis management) than anyone else, so be sure to bring that department into the process early.

Regardless, here are some guidelines to keep in mind as you launch your campaign and prepare for the criticism that may come your way:

- **Respond early and often.** There's no greater insult to people criticizing your SMM campaign than to be ignored. Ignoring criticism results in greater anger and more vitriolic responses that can snowball into a full-fledged crisis as the anger percolates across the social web. Before you know it, the board — or maybe *The New York Times* — is calling your desk, so respond quickly.

- **Respond honestly and clearly.** Be sure to use your own name when you respond. Just as you have to be authentic with your campaign, so you have to be with your response. Be clear about your rationale for why the campaign is designed the way it is, admit mistakes when the fault is yours, and be inclusive in your responses.
- **Be prepared to change based on the feedback.** It's easier to be stubborn and not to change your SMM campaign. But if criticism about the campaign is valid, whether it's of the structure, the creative aspect, or the rules regarding the type of conversation, you should incorporate the feedback and make the appropriate changes. You'll win back trust quickly.
- **Don't hesitate to bring humor to the situation.** Some of the best responses have been those that included a touch of self-effacing humor. Organizations aren't above people, and neither is yours. Humor goes a long way in the social web, and sometimes the response becomes the new SMM campaign.
- **Use the same channels for the response.** This may seem obvious, but it really isn't. Respond to people in the way they've criticized you. Don't go on national television to respond to a YouTube outburst. You'll become the laughingstock of the social web.

IN THIS CHAPTER

» Understanding why you need to have an SMM voice

» Differentiating between SMM voices and brand voices

» Building your voice in the social web

» Choosing the owner of your company's SMM voice

» Crowdsourcing SMM voices

Chapter 2
Developing Your SMM Voice

A social media marketing (SMM) campaign, program, or strategic approach won't be successful if no observable people are behind it. Consumers want to know who the people behind the message are. Being a trusted organization is not enough. Putting your director's name on the About Us page of your website isn't, either. When people engage across the social web, they want to engage with real people who have personalities and opinions. In other words, the people representing the nonprofit organization need to be SMM voices whom people can search on Google or Bing to find out more. That means that the stake-holder should be able to search the person representing the organization and see, via the search results, that the organization has put forth a real person to talk on its behalf. That's why you need an SMM voice.

Having voices that can be found through the search engines is instrumental to establishing credibility and being authentic. This chapter discusses why you need an SMM voice, how it differs from a brand voice or personality, where it is mani-fested, who can play that role, and how the two can come together over time. We then discuss using that person's relationships to help with *crowdsourcing* (asking people in a community to provide their content for a specific purpose).

Figuring Out Why You Need an SMM Voice

As we write this chapter, the United States, and indeed the entire world, is suffering from a breakdown in trust. Practically every major corporation is dealing with a trust issue. In this environment, does it make sense to introduce a new type of voice into your organization with potentially overlapping responsibilities confusing stakeholders? On the surface, it may not appear so, but it's actually more important than ever. If the last economic downturn has taught us one thing, it's that consumers are tired of engaging with large, impersonal brands and often turn against them on the social web, trusting them less and less. They simply do not trust big brands as much as they once did. In fact, half of the respondents to a survey conducted by *The Economist* magazine said that the last economic crisis intensified their distrust of big business. The magazine went on to say that the downturn accelerated the use of social media because people began placing more value on the recommendations of their friends than they did in big business. According to the 2019 Edelman Trust Barometer, trust in business increased to 54 percent from 48 percent the previous year, showing that while trust in business is stabilizing, it's still quite low, with nearly half of the American population not trusting big business. This is just another point on how trust in big business has not bounced back significantly from the downturn. The stock market gyrations in markets around the world should indicate to everyone that people are scared and confused.

If you run a business or a nonprofit organization that tries to reach consumers in the social web, this distrust presents a problem. Those users don't want to listen to you as much. They'd much rather listen to their friends. This means that they're not paying attention to all the advertising that you're pushing at them and certainly aren't making product-purchasing or donation decisions based on it. In fact, many users aren't even watching TV the way they once did. Compared to the past, they are either fast-forwarding through most of the advertising or are watching their favorite shows online via subscription services that may not support advertising. This means that you have to change your marketing strategy, and because you're reading this chapter, you've probably already realized that you need to.

It also means that if your stakeholders trust their friends more than big organizations, you have to behave more like their friends to earn their trust. And at the heart of becoming more like their friends is developing an SMM (social media marketing) voice that's associated with a single person in your organization through whom you reach out to those consumers. It can't just be your nonprofit name, your logo, or your witty copy that does it. It has to be a *real* person within your organization who's reaching out to your stakeholders. And that real person can't be the director, either — unless, of course, that person can truly invest the time to talk to consumers directly.

TIP Sometimes the best way to discover whether you need an SMM voice is by scanning the conversations about your organization across the social web. You'll probably find people talking about you or your services, at the very least. That can give you a sense of how important it is, and the volume of conversations may serve as a guide to how quickly you need to establish your SMM voice.

Defining SMM Voice Characteristics

The SMM voice is fundamentally the voice through which you engage with your consumers in the social web. Every conversation touchpoint on any social platform from YouTube (`www.youtube.com`) and Facebook (`www.facebook.com`) to Twitter (`www.twitter.com`) and Instagram (`www.instagram.com`) and your own discussion forums needs to be in the SMM voice. This strategy can take the form of one voice, or it can be several employees who work closely together. But all SMM voices share certain characteristics that are in contrast to a traditional brand voice (which can also be the voice of a nonprofit organization). In the next few sections, we look at some of those key characteristics.

Multiple and authentic

Most companies have multiple, authentic SMM voices. The reason is obvious. They are generally too large to have one person representing them digitally in all the conversations. Multiple people focus on different conversation areas, whether it's customer support, industry insights, product information, or awareness building.

In some cases, each person represents the company on different social environments. Each person talks in their own voice and loosely follows centralized guidelines. Zappos (`https://www.zappos.com/beyondthebox`) is a good example of a company with multiple SMM voices. The company is proud of its multiple SMM voices and trusts those employees to represent the brand effectively without losing their own authenticity. Another example is the Virgin Atlantic blog called "Ruby" (`https://blog.virginatlantic.com`), which uses multiple social media marketing voices that still conforms to general tone and voice guidelines while being deeply engaging.

Transparent and easy to find

Your SMM voices can't be anonymous voices. They have to be real people who are traceable; otherwise, they won't be taken seriously. Now, this may seem to be a bad strategy because so much is invested in the one person or very small group who's playing the role of the SMM voice, but it's necessary. When making these decisions, think about celebrity endorsements. People recognize that a celebrity may not be the permanent SMM voice, but people would much rather be talking to someone with whom they can form a relationship and relate to, even if it's only for a finite period, than to an anonymous brand voice. For an SMM voice to be real, it has to be someone people can find through Google. There's no question about that.

Engaging and conversational

Some people know how to have a conversation, and some *really* know how to. Your SMM voice, whoever that is, needs to be truly conversational. They need to be a person who can start a conversation, build trust, and be responsive. The person needs to have more of a customer service mentality than an on-message marketing or public relations mindset. This is not about marketing or PR, but about more genuine, deeper conversations. The person or people who carry responsibility for the SMM voice can come out of PR, but they need to keep in mind that this isn't about PR.

Social web savvy

Your SMM voice needs to be someone who knows the social web intimately: the rules, social norms, acronyms, culture, and best practices of participating in the social web. This person ideally should have individual credibility that extends beyond the organization that they work for and must be easily accessible on all the major social platforms. Keep in mind that your SMM voices will make mistakes, and they will probably get flamed (insulted) at times, too. You have to allow for that to happen. It's all part of the learning process.

Unique to the person

In contrast to a brand voice, this SMM voice must be unique to the person and not unique to the company. This is incredibly important for the trust to develop. Otherwise, the whole effort is a waste of time. Furthermore, this voice should be irreplaceable. When the person goes on vacation, the voice cannot continue to participate and be responsive to customer queries. Someone else has to take over and introduce themselves first. Think of it like a news anchor on a major television channel who takes the night off. The replacement is a different person, and that's not hidden from the viewer.

Distinguishing between SMM Voices and Brand Voices

At this point, you're probably thinking that your SMM voice is similar to your brand voice or personality. You're probably already thinking of people in your organization — maybe representatives from public relations, community management, or marketing — who can be your SMM voice. Before you jump into this decision too quickly, check out Table 2-1, which compares brand and SMM voices. Use this table to explain to team members why the two voices are different and why this effort may not be best relegated to the public relations department.

TABLE 2-1 Brand versus SMM Voice

Brand Voice	SMM Voice
Singular, anonymous company voice	Multiple, authentic individual voices
Reflects the brand personality and attributes perfectly	Transparent, easy to identify online, and only loosely on brand
Strictly followed by everybody	Engaging, conversational, and responsive
Designed to appear across all brand touchpoints	Mostly relevant only where the conversations are
Usually unique to the company	Usually unique to the person
Sometimes manifested in a person, but not always	Always manifested in a real person or many people
Used everywhere from signage to ad copy	Used only in real conversations by real people

REMEMBER

An SMM voice is very different from a brand voice. Someone who's spent a lifetime representing your organization and keeping everyone else around on brand message is probably not the best person to be the SMM voice.

As you compare the two voices, ask yourself whether you have an SMM voice and, if so, how it relates to your brand voice. It can be closely associated with your brand voice, but it doesn't have to be. What matters most is that the SMM voice is driven by an individual or several individuals and is truly authentic.

REMEMBER

Establishing an SMM voice may appear in conflict with a nonprofit's overall brand and community management objectives. The best way to avoid this conflict is to include your marketers and your PR team in the early conversations about your SMM voices. It will prevent an adversarial relationship from developing because they will truly understand why you're creating it. They will also have a lot of valuable advice for you based on their experiences in dealing with the mainstream press and customers through other channels. It's worth noting that you can have multiple SMM voices, some of whom can be people who currently are your marketers and PR representatives. Their success, however, may require a change in how they're used to talking to the outside world, but that can be discovered only in time.

TIP

Over the last few years, some brands have been able to evolve their SMM voices into brand voices. This is where the brand voice and the SMM voice have become so similar that they can be combined. That's fine as long as the voice continues to be authentic, personally identifiable, conversational, and in tune with the ethos of the social web. It's important that the voice be personally identifiable because there will always be cases in which conversations with stakeholders in social media may need to be taken offline. In those cases, it helps for the stakeholder to know that the person they are talking to via phone is the same person who responded online. The Virgin Atlantic blog mentioned earlier is one example where the brand voice and the SMM voices are coming together.

Outlining SMM Voice Objectives

When you're defining your SMM voice, you need to consider what you'll be using the SMM voice for. Knowing the objectives that it serves and how it supports your marketing and business efforts more broadly is instrumental. If you haven't defined the objectives for the SMM voice, don't take up valuable time (and potentially resources, too) in identifying that voice and putting a program around it.

Some of the more common objectives served by having an SMM voice include the following:

- **Providing industry and organization insights to all stakeholders:** A lot of people are probably talking about your organization on the social web. Many of them are probably forming strong opinions about your industry, your organization, and your brand, too. Some of these people may be very influential. They could be key influencer bloggers, shareholders, customers, competitors, or market analysts. An important objective for having an SMM voice is to share your organization's own take on issues with the broader world and negate any false or unfairly biased perspectives.
- **Building awareness for your programs and services:** Every month there appears to be a new social platform on which you need to have a presence. This may be Facebook, Tumblr (www.tumblr.com), Pinterest (www.pinterest.com), Snapchat (www.snapchat.com), CafeMom (www.cafemom.com),

LiveJournal (www.livejournal.com), or Twitter (www.twitter.com). Your customers may be gravitating to that service and could be discussing your brand and forming opinions about your product there. Your SMM voice is needed to simply build awareness of your products and services, communicate accurately about the products, and dispel any myths about them on these social platforms.

- **Forging deeper, more trusted relationships with your stakeholders:** Sometimes your SMM voice is important to simply deepen your relationships with your stakeholders. It may be focused on giving them advice, sharing tips and tricks related to your programs, and helping them through decisions regarding services or volunteer and donation opportunities. In other instances, it may be about simply participating in conversations and being a helpful representative of your organization in ways that enhance your stakeholders' lifestyles or their sense of who they are.
- **Responding to customer service and complaints:** When customers are struggling with products, they often complain about them in conversations with their peers or other people who are facing similar challenges. The same is true of anyone receiving services your organization provides or otherwise interacting with your nonprofit. You have a huge opportunity to listen in on these conversations, hear those concerns, provide support where you can, and learn from those complaints.

  Some of the most dynamic examples of companies embracing the social web successfully have been from companies hearing complaints on platforms such as Twitter, responding to them in real time, and providing superior customer service. The ROI (return on investment) of this strategy is easily measurable. The shoe company Zappos (www.zappos.com), acquired by Amazon in 2009, conducts this customer interaction successfully.

Choosing the Owner of Your Organization's SMM Voice

There's no question that you need an SMM voice for the social web. It's instrumental to forging relationships with donors, volunteers, and expert, positional, and referential influencers in addition to the industry at large. But setting your objectives up front is as important as knowing the difference between your SMM voice and your brand voice. It's no use participating if you do so in a manner that's in conflict with the fundamental ethos of the social web. You invariably do more damage to your organization and credibility than you may realize. Remember that whatever mistake you make in the social web gets quickly amplified, so set your objectives carefully, recognize how different your SMM voice is from your brand, and choose the right people to play the roles.

REMEMBER

If you're a small organization, either the director or a staff member with marketing experience should always be your SMM voice or at least one of your SMM voices. Even Zappos, a mammoth shoe company, uses its CEO, Tony Hsieh, as its key SMM voice even after its acquisition by Amazon. The strategy works well, and given that it's building and establishing the brand primarily through social media marketing, the question of how the SMM voice conflicts with its brand voice doesn't really arise. The brand and SMM voices are perfectly aligned. That may not be the case for you, so as you wade into the social web, think carefully about your SMM voice and whether you're even comfortable having one before participating. It's also worth pointing out that there are inherent risks in having a person who isn't a trained marketing or communications professional as your SMM voice. Where possible, if you're going down that route, be sure to get the person basic media training first.

Richard Branson, chairman of the Virgin Group, has his own presence on Twitter (with more than 13 million followers) and represents himself and his company (`www.twitter.com/richardbranson`). The airline Virgin America (which is part of the Virgin Group) also has its own Twitter presence (`twitter.com/virginamerica`) that is used to interact with passengers, share special offers, and announce travel advisories. With 800,000 followers, arguably the Twitter activity makes a difference.

In the case of Marriot Hotels, its company blog "Marriot on the Move" (`https://www.blogs.marriott.com`) is written from the firsthand perspective of its CEO, Bill Marriot. His posts are a mix of business success tips, information, celebrations of how Marriot is doing, and stories from his personal life. What's most powerful about the blog is that it's easy to tell that Bill Marriot blogs from the heart in a very personal and authentic way.

Now that you know what an SMM voice is, how it differs from your brand voice, and what business objectives may drive the need for this voice, the only remaining question to answer is "Who exactly in your organization should serve in this role?" The next few sections look at the most common types of people who serve as the SMM voice and what they're typically best at doing.

Director

A director can be an SMM voice. In many cases, that person is already close to being an SMM voice anyway. They are representative of the nonprofit but are recognized and noticed as an individual personality with independent opinions that happen to drive the organization's direction. This person is best used as an SMM voice providing industry and organization insights. After all, they have the credibility and experience to do so. In many cases, you can use the director SMM voice to forge deeper relationships with stakeholders — especially donors — as well.

In a corporation, the CEO could be the SMM voice. For example, the CEO of Forrester, George Colony, is actively blogging (`http://blogs.forrester.com/ceo_colony`), and you can tell that it's really him. The CEO participating in the social web and sharing his insights (and responding to blog comments) has done an immeasurable amount for the Forrester brand. If your director does not have time to truly commit to the online community, whether Twitter or a blog, do not ask them to. It's better that they have no presence than an abandoned one.

WARNING

Never let your director, or for that matter any staff member or volunteer, comment about your organization on discussion forums anonymously. Although this may seem obvious, the CEO of Whole Foods Market, John Mackey, was caught commenting on an investor forum about his competitors. He got into trouble for trying to influence the stock price of his competitors.

WARNING

When choosing SMM voices, be mindful of the PR disaster experienced by Domino's Pizza when two young employees at a franchise put up what they thought was a funny YouTube video about sanitation behind the scenes. The video went viral, and the CEO had to issue a major apology. The fallout was definitely not funny. Although more junior staff may know the social platforms the best, they probably also require greater supervision and education. This is because they may not know the culture of the company that they represent or be familiar with what's good practice versus bad practice when representing a company to its customers. This is why the SMM guidelines are so important. Those are discussed later in the chapter.

Social media lead

The social media lead is becoming a more common role within many large organizations. This person coordinates all social media activities across the organization between all the different departments and to stakeholders as well. They are, of course, the most natural choice to be an SMM voice or one of the key SMM voices. This person knows the social web well, often has independent credibility within it, and understands how to strike the right balance between representing the organization and speaking authentically as an individual. They can accomplish practically any of the objectives with the exception of industry insights, which, to carry credibility, may need to come from the director, a member of the board, or a marketing executive. (In some organizations, this person might have the title of community manager, social media manager, community evangelist, or outreach coordinator.)

PR manager

The PR manager typically manages relationships with the mainstream press. Arguably, managing mainstream press relationships and being a brand voice can and does conflict with the SMM voice, but that doesn't mean that an enterprising PR manager can't play the role of the SMM voice. They may need to choose to take on the responsibility at the cost of being the brand voice to do this authentically, however. After they do, they, like a social media lead, can accomplish all the major SMM objectives with the exception of the industry and company insights.

Crowdsourcing SMM Voices with Guidelines

For all the strategies that you may put into place to support your SMM voice, you still need to do more. If you're a large organization with hundreds or thousands of staff and volunteers, you can't stop them from participating in the social web. Just as you cannot stop an employee from talking about your organization at a dinner party, you can't prevent them from talking about you online. That's not necessarily bad: The more people who know your organization and talk about it favorably, the more it can help you. But it's important to establish some guidelines so that everyone knows how to talk about you online.

Employees care about their companies, and obviously this applies to a nonprofit's staff and volunteers. They care about what the organization is doing, and they'll welcome the guidelines to better represent the organization in the public domain — that is, of course, as long as you don't make the guidelines too restrictive and incorporate feedback. If you develop the guidelines in isolation, ignoring how staff and volunteers typically participate online and want to represent your organization, you're sure to face backlash. It is also important to design the guidelines to be adaptable based on how the social web is evolving and how behavior is changing on the different social platforms.

TIP

Before you write the guidelines, be sure to check whether your organization has any existing guidelines and policies that can serve as a starting point.

Here are elements that you can incorporate into your SMM policy:

- **Purpose:** Start with the objectives. You need to explain why the guidelines are being established, what they hope to accomplish, and how they help the staff and volunteers.

- **Declaration of trust:** Just as important, you must establish that the goal of the guidelines isn't to restrict staff and volunteers or to censor them, but to encourage them to be better ambassadors of the organization. Similarly, it's important to establish that no one will monitor them, nor will you ask them to edit or delete posts.
- **Statement of responsibility:** Make clear that staff and volunteers are personally responsible for all the content they publish online, whether it is on a blog, a wiki, YouTube, or any other form of social media. They should do so in a manner befitting their identity as an employee or volunteer of the organization, recognizing that whatever they publish may be attributed to the organization.
- **An identification of themselves as staff or volunteers:** They must know that although they do not have to always identify themselves as employees of a company, they must do so when discussing company or industry matters. In those instances, they should either speak as a representative of the organization or include a disclaimer emphasizing that they are sharing their own personal opinions. Similarly, employees and volunteers should declare any conflicts of interest when discussing professional matters.
- **An SMM voice:** Employees should speak as an SMM voice by being engaging, conversational, and authentic but recognizing that they aren't the official brand voice of the organization. And furthermore, it's important to do so in one's own name and not anonymously. (Remember the CEO of Whole Foods Market who commented on discussion forums about his competitors anonymously? When he was caught, it hurt him and his company.)
- **Engagement principles:** Being a good SMM voice also means following certain engagement principles. These include responding to comments immediately, providing meaningful and respectful comments, being transparent in all social interactions online, and always looking to add value.
- **No unauthorized sharing of business information:** Employees should not share client, partner, or supplier information without express approval from the appropriate owners. When referencing somebody, link back to the source.
- **Respect for the audience:** As with any other form of communication, by virtue of being associated with the organization, the employees and volunteers are ambassadors and SMM voices. They can easily tarnish the brand without meaning to do so and without even realizing it. It is, therefore, important to avoid personal insults, obscenity, or inappropriate behavior that is outside the organization's formal policies. This is especially important because when something is expressed in the social domain, it's easily amplified by others. (Just ask Domino's about the crisis it faced when two employees published repulsive videos online.)

- **Respect for copyright, fair use, and financial disclosure laws:** Regardless of the media being published, employees and volunteers should still respect all local, state, and federal laws, especially in the realms of copyright, fair use, and financial disclosure.
- **What to do when they make a mistake:** Regardless of what an employee or volunteer publishes, at some point they are going to screw up. We're all human, after all. The guidelines must address what to do if someone makes a mistake. That means being up front about the mistakes, correcting the errors immediately, and accepting responsibility.

These guidelines are culled from an analysis of several social media guidelines. SMM guidelines can get long and unwieldy. You may not need every element mentioned in the preceding list. If you're a small organization, these guidelines may fold into broader staff and/or volunteer guidelines and may not need to be a standalone document, but you definitely need them in some form. They provide direction to your employees and volunteers without hampering their enthusiasm for social influence marketing. And with the right excitement around SMM, you may find yourself turning everyone into a marketer who is representing the cause in their own SMM voice, authentically and convincingly. You can't ask for more than that! Invariably, these spontaneous, natural grassroots efforts complement your more formal brand and SMM voices. They don't contradict but rather strengthen each other.

REMEMBER

Be sure to invite employees and volunteers across your organization to provide feedback on the guidelines. It's no use creating and publishing guidelines in isolation. They'll provide you with valuable feedback. And, by being included in the creation process, they're more likely to follow the guidelines.

TIP

Here are two helpful online resources for creating SMM guidelines:

- **Hewlett-Packard Blogging Code of Conduct:** `www.hp.com/hpinfo/blogs/codeofconduct.html`
- **Intel Social Media Guidelines:** `www.intel.com/content/www/us/en/legal/intel-social-media-guidelines.html`

IN THIS CHAPTER

» Choosing the right social media platform

» Understanding your audience's activity

» Evaluating your resources

» Assessing the different social networks

Chapter 3
Finding the Right Platforms

If you have been an Internet user since the mid-1990s, you probably know that the popular social platforms today are not the first to have been launched. Many came before Facebook, Twitter, YouTube, and Instagram. In some cases, those early social networks and online communities were extremely successful, too. For example, back in the mid-1990s, The Well was considered the most influential online community. It wasn't the largest, but it was the most influential.

GeoCities, which rose to fame in the late 1990s and was bought by Yahoo! for a whopping $3.57 billion at its peak, boasted millions of active accounts. Friendster, which was the darling of the social networking world in 2003 and 2004, fizzled when its technical infrastructure and lack of new features pushed people in America away from it. (Approximately 80 percent of its traffic came from Asia in its final years, until it was eventually shut down in June 2015.)

The point is that customarily, social platforms such as online communities, social networks, and loosely connected personal spaces online have periods of immense growth, plateaus, and then slow, painful declines. It appears hard for a social platform to avoid this evolution. We've seen this happen time and again. This poses a difficult challenge for marketers.

Where do you invest your marketing dollars if you don't know whether a specific social platform is going to be around in a year or two? Similarly, how do you know which up-and-coming social platform your users are going to gravitate toward after a major social platform starts fizzling? Knowing which social platform is going to have explosive growth next and where your stakeholders will spend their time is not always easy. Nevertheless, you must try to answer those questions.

This chapter helps you identify the right combination of social platforms on which to launch, sustain, and promote your brand.

REMEMBER

Before marketing on these social platforms, you need to figure out your social media marketing voice. See Chapter 2 of this minibook for more information on how to do that.

Choosing Social Media Platforms

The first step in choosing the best platform for you is to recognize that no *single* social platform is going to be enough for your SMM (social media marketing) activities. It's extremely unlikely that your potential stakeholders use only one of the social platforms exclusively. In fact, research shows that a user is rarely on only one platform. Your stakeholders are far more likely to have profiles on two or three social platforms and to use some of them more than others. Furthermore, you have to assume that your donors and volunteers will invariably gravitate from one social platform to another as time passes. For example, whereas Facebook may have the greatest scale, the sharp rise in usage of Instagram, Pinterest, Snapchat, TikTok, and WhatsApp shows how fickle consumers can be.

You've probably also noticed that marketing on several social platforms isn't that much more expensive than marketing on one, as long as your energies are focused. Choosing a few social platforms versus just one to do your marketing makes sense if you can reach different audiences in different ways at different points in the marketing funnel through each one.

Still, the question of where to focus remains. You can't be marketing on every social platform — Facebook, LinkedIn, YouTube, hi5, Flickr, Twitter, Instagram, Pinterest, Tumblr, WhatsApp, Snapchat, Meetup — all at one time with the same amount of effort. Although SMM is considered relatively cheap, your efforts still take time and money when you're on many social platforms at one time. (You're probably going to confuse stakeholders who are on several of the social platforms, to boot.)

The answer is to put a lot of effort into marketing on a few social platforms where your stakeholders participate the most and to have lighter presences on the other platforms.

To pick the right platforms, you can start by looking at the audiences with which you interact, and at where they are most likely to make their purchasing decisions. For purposes of this discussion, you can break your audiences down into the following three groups:

- **Clients:** Obviously, these are the people you serve, and so this is your main target. You want to connect, interact, and prompt them to engage with you and benefit from your services. You need to understand what services they need, where they need those services, and what influences their decision making.
- **Industry:** These are the people who may be competitors, vendors, governing bodies, and so on. In the social media world, this group helps to support your visibility and influence with media outlets and stakeholders directly.
- **Employees and volunteers:** They can be either your greatest strength or weakness, depending on how you prepare them to participate in social media. If you don't have staff to dedicate to a project, you have a different kind of problem to solve.

Following is a look at how to work through the issues of picking platforms that support each group.

Learning about your clients

Choose where to practice SMM by researching and understanding where your clients are spending most of their time. This doesn't mean identifying where most of your clients have registered profiles, but instead researching where they have the highest levels of engagement. This means

- **Finding out how much time they spend on the social platform, what they specifically do, and how they use it to interact with each other:** Tools such as Quantcast (www.quantcast.com) can help you understand engagement, but you may need to reach out to the social platforms themselves to understand the details of the engagement. Keep in mind that with Quantcast, only if the site has been Quantified (which means that the site owner has added Quantcast code to their site) are the statistics the most accurate. Comscore (www.comscore.com) is a paid solution that can provide more accurate numbers for non-Quantified sites.

TIP

You may also want to survey your clients directly to understand their social media usage. There are several good survey tools, including SurveyMonkey and Zoho Survey.

» **Understanding the user behaviors on the social platform:** Let's say you're a nonprofit organization that provides grant-writing training to other nonprofits. Although your clients use LinkedIn to ask each other for advice when making decisions about which grants to pursue, they spend a lot more time on Facebook. However, LinkedIn may still be a better place to practice SMM, because that's where your clients are making the decisions that matter to you. It doesn't matter if they're spending more cumulative minutes on Facebook.

TIP

In addition, consider monitoring mentions of your organization, other similar nonprofits, program names, or industry keywords to determine how much activity there is across the platforms.

Invariably, you discover that three to four social platforms match your stakeholders' demographics, have high engagement levels for them, and are what we loosely call *locations of influence* as far as your product category is concerned. That's where your clients make their decisions and are influenced by others. These factors together tell you where to practice SMM. And as you do so, recognize that you must also consider two broader aspects:

» **Watching the macro trends of the social platform:** For example, does the platform look like it's emerging, has it settled into a plateau, or is it fizzling? Accordingly, you may want to devote more or fewer dollars and effort to it.

» **Determining whether the social platform is a place where your organization will have permission to participate and one in which you will want to participate:** Participating in some social platforms may hurt you. For example, it wouldn't make sense for a high-end, exclusive brand like Chanel to engage in conversations in a casual, music-oriented social environment such as the relaunched version of Myspace.

REMEMBER

Your clients move between platforms as time passes. As a result, be prepared to adjust your social media marketing campaign significantly. Your clients may not always stay on the platforms that you're targeting them on currently. This potential migration matters, especially to marketers in small nonprofit organizations.

REMEMBER

Each social network has a reputation. Make sure that your organization is in alignment with that reputation. For example, Tumblr is known to be photo-centric and has a reputation for attracting young, creative users. Keep a platform's reputation in mind as you choose where and how to market.

Addressing your industry influence

A look at your industry yields a very long list of potential competitors, partners, vendors, and associations for you to connect with. The SMM goal is to make this group aware of your influence in the marketplace.

Here, we take a brief look at three free tools you can use right away to make a quick assessment of your overall business influence. Obviously, you want to take a much more thorough look, but the following can give you some feeling for your current state of influence:

- **Kred** (`https://www.home.kred`)**:** Kred measures your reach. You can evaluate your organization across such platforms as Twitter, Facebook, and LinkedIn at the same time. If you have an employee who has their own influence on these platforms, you can also check them out separately.
- **Website Grader** (`https://website.grader.com`)**:** This tool evaluates the marketing on your website using HubSpot's tool for grading websites. It looks at a variety of measures, including your traffic rank, indexed pages, and linking domains.
- **Followerwonk** (`www.followerwonk.com`)**:** You can evaluate your Twitter account by using Followerwonk. This tool provides a visual depiction of your Twitter feed according to influence, popularity, engagement, and user habits.

Evaluating Your Resources

It's often said that SMM takes a lot more time than money. This idea is proved false when you begin to factor in the amount of resources needed to implement a full-blown strategy. You can't overlook the fact that either you or your staff will have a variety of tasks to complete even before you start tweeting, blogging, and so on. Consider the following resource issues before you begin:

- **Time:** Determine how much time your resources permit you or your staff to spend on SMM each day. How much staff time can be devoted to actually communicating with stakeholders? This is the goal. You want to make authentic contact. This takes time. To make authentic contact first requires conducting rigorous social listening.
- **Technical skills:** Examine the breadth of technical skills you have in-house. Who will do the technical work involved? Some of the platforms are plug-and-play, but more often than not, integrating them into your own sites can

present problems. For example, if your website uses proprietary software, you might need to have technical staff write new code to connect the two applications without causing problems. This might be a quick fix or a long, involved project. You'll want to know that before you move forward.

- **Design skills:** Understand the design skills needed to create visuals, charts, and so on. The quality of graphics and multimedia online continues to increase. You either need a designer on hand or you have to hire someone to create the graphics to match your own branding on one or several of the SMM platforms.
- **Computing power:** Look at whether you're prepared to handle more traffic and sales. You've heard the warning, "Be careful what you wish for." What if you get more inquiries than you can presently handle — or if your site can't handle the traffic surge? It sounds like a great problem to have, and it is, unless you wind up disappointing potential stakeholders (including donors) who can't reach your site or get support.

  For example, during the 2013 Super Bowl, Coca-Cola found itself in a spot of trouble when its Super Bowl microsite crashed after its advertisement aired on television. Coca-Cola had asked consumers to vote online for which ending to the ad was the best, and the voting made the site first slow down significantly and then crash completely. Coca-Cola had underestimated the amount of traffic the promotion on the Super Bowl would generate.

REMEMBER

Be realistic about the quality of your hosting and stakeholder support. Prepare by evaluating how much traffic you can actually handle, and plan for a bit more than you estimate. That way, you won't look amateurish if your promotions succeed beyond your wildest dreams.

Assessing What Each Social Network Offers You

Now that you've looked at the factors that influence your choice of a platform, you can consider the platforms themselves to determine which ones are a good fit. In this chapter, we look specifically at the user profile for the top four social media platforms. As of 2019, the statistics are as follows:

- **Facebook:** Facebook users are 43 percent women and 88 percent of 18–29 year olds are on Facebook. But Facebook isn't a youth platform alone, as 62 percent of online seniors are on the platform as well. The platform has 2.41 billion monthly active users. Users outside the United States and Canada make up 85 percent of its daily users. The average Facebook user has 155 friends. Users focus primarily on social interaction.

- **Twitter:** There are 330 million monthly active users on Twitter as of September 2019, sending 500 million tweets per day. The gender breakdown on Twitter is roughly 34 percent female to 66 percent male. Eighty percent of the users are mobile, with 79 percent of the accounts being outside the U.S. They focus primarily on world events, television shows, sports, and business-related topics.
- **LinkedIn:** There are 630 million users of LinkedIn around the world and approximately 303 million monthly active users. Seventy percent of the users are located outside the United States. Fifty-seven percent of users are men; the largest demographic on LinkedIn is 30–49 year olds. Eighty-seven million Millennials are on LinkedIn, with 11 million in decision-making positions. Users focus on jobs, marketing themselves, and selling services.
- **YouTube:** This site has 1.9 billion users who log in to the site at least once a month, second only to Facebook. These users watch one billion videos every day, and more than 70 percent of that time is spent on mobile. Businesses are active on YouTube as well, with 62 percent of businesses posting videos to a YouTube channel.

This gives you the broad strokes of the user demographics on these platforms. Next, you'll want to dig deeper.

Using platforms as audience research tools

You can use several tools to analyze demographics. In this section, we discuss the use of two platforms not usually used to do market research — YouTube and Instagram. Mining these platforms can bring you unexpected findings:

- **YouTube:** If you have uploaded videos to YouTube, you can use YouTube Creator Studio to get a variety of analytics. But what about looking at YouTube as a large research lab? By using the homepage search function, you can drill down on an almost unlimited number of topics. By using the Sort By drop-down list, you can determine the following:
  - **Relevance:** This is the default search. It brings you the videos most closely associated with the topic you requested.
  - **Upload Date:** With this, you can see what's most viewed right now as opposed to something older. You can find out what's hot here.

- **View Count:** This shows you the general interest in a topic. With the millions of people on YouTube, you can see what's of interest to a big chunk of them.
- **Rating:** This is an interesting measure. YouTube used to use five-star ratings but found them to be ineffective. Most people would rate everything either a 1 or a 5. This didn't really give the viewer enough feedback. YouTube now relies on likes and dislikes, which gives you a quantitative measure.

» **Instagram:** When marketers look at Instagram, their first instinct is to think about how they can display something — their products, conference photos, or staff pictures. Next, they think about how many people have viewed the photos they've posted. Those are both useful, but are by no means the only way to use Instagram.

WARNING

Be very careful how much you push your products, conference photos, and staff photos on a social media platform like Instagram that's so consumer-centric.

You can also use Instagram as a research tool. For example, if you sell wedding invitations, you can use Instagram's search capability to find wedding photos that may include invitations. The idea is to use it as your doorway into customers' lives. Before the Internet, friends and neighbors would regale each other with stories, using slide carousels in their living rooms. Think of Instagram as a grand view into everyone's living room. If you want to see what kind of shoes people are wearing when they travel or millions of other things, you'll find that here. If you think creatively, you can get an enormous amount of information on Instagram.

Getting niche-savvy

In addition to picking the right major social networking platforms for your business, you should investigate niche platforms your customers may frequent. Convert with Content has a useful listing of niche social networking sites that can be found at `https://convertwithcontent.com/60-niche-social-networks-marketers`.

See if you can find something directly related to your audience. The sites cover the following subjects:

» Books

» Business Networking Professionals

» Family

- Friends
- Hobbies and Interests
- Media
- Music
- Mobile
- Shopping
- Students
- Travel

For example, if you sell eco-friendly baby toys, you may want to check out CafeMom. It's listed in the Family category and can be found at `www.cafemom.com`. Here, you can read about what types of toys moms are looking for and what they're currently buying. If you engage in a low-key, respectful way, you learn a lot without offending anyone. Any kind of "hype-y" sales pitch would not be appropriate here.

IN THIS CHAPTER

» Plugging your website into the social web

» Linking your advertising campaign and website

» Streamlining the user experience on your website

» Enhancing your website's social media potential

Chapter 4
Practicing SMM on Your Website

Corporate websites have gone through many changes since their introduction. When Stephanie began working at AOL in 1994, the companies she worked with to create their AOL websites were initially concerned that having a website might be too big a step, but as they watched some of their adventurous competitors do it, they started to become a bit more comfortable. Remember, there was nary a social media platform in sight at that time. Myspace didn't come into being until the early 2000s.

Companies needed websites to be all things to all people. They had multiple audiences, they sometimes needed to sell the product directly, and they had to create a timeless, stable impression. The corporate site didn't cater just to prospective customers but to existing customers, shareholders, members of the press, business partners, and suppliers as well. The site also needed to carry information and include functionality that met all their needs. What's more, the corporate website needed to reflect the company's brand; the company couldn't change its look and feel based on the whims of a specific campaign.

For this reason, the concept of microsites came to be. Companies built these mini-websites to support display ad campaigns, and the microsites were time-bound and oriented toward specific events or audiences. These events could be Christmas shopping, Father's Day, or back-to-school promotions for teenagers. Creative uses for the display ads directly reflected on the microsite, which would typically contain information about the specific offers. After all, with companies spending so much money on the display ads, they needed to drive visitors who clicked the ads to a site that extended the experience of the ad. This strategy of separating the corporate website from the microsite and treating the microsite as an extension of the display ads worked for a long time. But then the social media revolution came, and it all began to change. Now social media sites co-exist along with microsites.

Currently, savvy website owners realize that "owning" their website is a good way to protect themselves from the whims of social media platforms that could change policies on a dime. Websites have again become the hub of corporate activity, and they serve the same purpose for a nonprofit organization. From this hub, you can do things like hold contests, acquaint stakeholders with your physical locations, and provide them with information they need to make decisions about using your services, donating, or becoming a volunteer. To make sure you understand why websites are still important, consider that websites give you control over your:

- **Message and stories:** On your website, you can take all the time and space you need to tell your story your way. You can sprinkle your message throughout the site and emphasize your changing priorities as they develop.
- **Website data:** You have access to all your data and you can analyze it in any way it makes sense. Of course, you want to analyze data from all the social media sites you are on. But you don't need to worry if a social platform changes its policy about access to their analytics.
- **SEO:** By optimizing your website content for search engine optimization (SEO) you can help your stakeholders find you.
- **Product sales:** Interacting with stakeholders directly from your website gives you total control over how information about programs and services is presented and received.
- **Stakeholder information:** Your mailing list and subsequent stakeholder information are protected by your website controls.

In this chapter, we give you recommendations on how to retool your website to allow for the most effective use of social media marketing (SMM), along with tips for integrating your website to the social web in a meaningful way.

Focusing on the SMM-Integrated Website

Today's users are not as easily impressed as they once were. They want more than an ad campaign; they want a committed, longer-term relationship with your organization to which they give their time and money. And given that you spend money advertising to your stakeholders, it only makes sense to generate more than an impression from your campaign. Yes, users will always want more.

When users click links today, either from advertisements or social networks, they expect to be taken to a website that tells them everything about your services or organization that they're interested in. They want to be able to not only view your offer and make a decision, but also navigate the rest of your website. These users want to be able to view what else you have to offer, learn more about your organization, and share that information with their friends. Everything needs to be integrated.

Today's users visiting your website don't want to just depend on you to tell them whether the message you're pushing at them is special. They want to draw that conclusion themselves with the assistance of their social influencers. So, as you think about social media marketing on your website, first and foremost consider that your users want more than an ad click to a homepage.

Making the Campaign and the Website Work Together

The best way to make the advertising campaign and your website work harmoniously in a social world is to make sure you link the two in every way possible. In the sections that follow, we tell you how you can optimize those links.

Treating your website as a hub, not a destination

The first step in practicing SMM on your website is recognizing that it's a hub that fits into a larger digital ecosystem supporting your organization. This digital ecosystem includes your website; your ads across the Internet; your presence on various social platforms; and the conversations about you on blogs, social platforms, in online communities, and on discussion forums. Your purpose shouldn't only be to bring people to your website and entice them to stay on it as long as possible. That might contradict every traditional marketing principle, but it's true.

REMEMBER

If someone wants to know everything about your company — good, bad, or ugly — they should feel that your website is the best *starting point* for them.

If you design your website as a hub versus a destination, your website will immediately become more valuable to your customers. Even though this may mean that you'll be pointing your consumers to external sites, they may treat yours as a starting point in the future. For example, the Mars corporate brand designed its current website (`https://www.mars.com`) so that you can learn everything about its corporate philosophy, various brands, and work in local communities all in one place.

Linking prominently to your presence on social platforms

As long as customers interact with your organization, it matters little where they're interacting with it. For users, the Internet is the social platform on which they share information, connect with their friends, develop business relationships, and get entertained. They're also interacting with companies and organizations on these social platforms. You must highlight your presence on these social platforms right on your website, too. If your stakeholders want to interact with you on social platforms, help them to do so by showing them how they can. For example, the Content Marketing Institute has links to all its major social platforms on the right side of each page on its website. Check out `https://contentmarketinginstitute.com` to see what we mean.

Depending on your business model and the strength of your brand, how prominently you link to the social platforms may differ. For example, if you're a luxury handbag brand that likes to entice customers by creating a feeling of mystique and exclusiveness, linking extensively to the social platforms may do more harm than good. However, if you're Coca-Cola and are keen to deeply immerse yourself in the pop culture, linking to social platforms where conversations are happening (potentially about events that Coke may sponsor) becomes important.

Promoting campaigns on your website homepage

As we mentioned earlier in the chapter, your website serves many audiences and has many purposes. But that shouldn't stop you from using the featured zone on your homepage to promote something (for example, a conference, an ad, or a new program). That's the first step in linking campaigns with your website. This may be obvious to you, but many don't do this.

WARNING

If you're using featured zones on your homepage to promote campaigns, be sure to update them frequently with new promotions. No one likes to see the same promotions again and again. It implies that the company is neglecting its website.

Encouraging deeper interaction through your website

Users who respond to your campaign want to learn more about the programs or services you're promoting to them, and you can do more than just provide them with that information. Instead of just bringing them the information, you can connect them with other prospective or current staff, clients, donors, and volunteers by pointing them to a discussion area on your website (if you have one) or third-party review sites that discuss your organization. You can also introduce a live-chat feature, whereby they can talk to you in real time.

Asking customers to give you feedback on your content

Users feel they own a bit of a company when they're loyal to that company's products. These fans are typically called *ambassadors* because they will likely tell their friends and family about how much they enjoy a particular product. They become like an external sales team. They want to have the inside scoop on a company, its products, and advertising campaigns, too. The behind-the-scenes assets fuel their interest in the company. This ambassadorship can work for nonprofit organizations as well. Make sure that your TV, print, and digital advertisements are available for your fans to view on your website. Allow them to critique the campaign assets and provide feedback. It serves to build trust, enthusiasm, and ownership among them. Be prepared to accept both positive and negative comments. While you can't control the conversation, you can and should help shape it.

Rethinking Your Website

Practicing SMM philosophies on your website isn't only about approaching campaigns differently and tying them into your website more strategically. You should rethink your whole website experience to enable more direct social influence to take place. Redesigning your website with social influence elements can increase visibility and deepen relationships with your core stakeholders. In the following sections, we give you some recommendations on how to enhance engagement on your website.

User experience

User experience (UX) has become a competitive advantage. Just like consumers can shop around to find the lowest price for most goods, anyone who wants to become involved in a charitable organization has many to choose from. Therefore, differentiation has to be derived from something other than price or breadth of services provided. Marketers realize that a great experience brings people to their site and keeps them there.

Simple design

When companies created their first websites, the tools were not very advanced. It took a long time and a dedicated team to make things happen. Now, you can easily plan and execute a website quickly. The focus should be on navigation and the right content. Everything has to be easy and the design needs to be simple. No one will wait for websites to load. They also won't be willing to search around looking for something. The same answer can probably be found on your competitor's website.

Conversational user interface (CUI)

Technology has now made it possible for users to hold conversations with non-profit sites and social media platforms instead of having to click an icon or type a command. You want to have a two-way conversation with your stakeholders, and chatbots make that possible. Make sure that you use these messaging tools on your website.

Content marketing

According to the CXL Institute (`https://conversionxl.com/blog/first-impressions-matter-the-importance-of-great-visual-design/`), it takes .05 seconds for a user to determine whether they will continue to stay on your website or leave. This means that you need to do everything you can to make your site engaging at first glance.

Content marketing is an integral part of any website marketing strategy. You need to audit your website to analyze the content you currently have and determine what's working. You also need to see what you're missing and how you can reach more of your target audience.

Here are three things you need to review to make your website more powerful:

- **Search engine optimization (SEO):** In order to be found, you still need to write content that accommodates search engines. There are lots of shiny objects to try, but this is not optional.

  What you should do: Identify the keywords your stakeholders use when they search for your topic. There are several good tools that you can use for SEO. For example, you could try Ahrefs (`https://ahrefs.com`) or KWFinder (`https://kwfinder.com`).

- **Video:** Video has become essential. According to HubSpot, 54 percent of users want more video content from brands. You can repurpose any video content you create to use on social media sites.

  What you should do: Jump into video creation if you're holding back. Your users probably want to see you on sites such as Instagram, where InstaStories get a great deal of traffic.

- **Podcasts:** Podcasts are increasingly popular. According to the Edison Research and Triton Digital study, "The Infinite Dial 2019" (`https://www.edisonresearch.com/infinite-dial-2019/`), in the U.S. 50 percent of people over the age of 12 have listened to a podcast. This makes podcasts mainstream. It's likely that some of your audience members fall into this group.

  What you should do: Think about how you could use podcasting to increase your reach. You don't need to create an elaborate thirty-minute podcast. You could create a quick tip podcast that is five minutes long. The idea is to provide content in the most popular formats.

About Us and Contact Us pages

The About Us page of a nonprofit's website has traditionally included management team profiles, board of directors information, the organization's origins and history, contact and address information, the organization's mission and values, and fact sheets. Those sections are extremely important, and you can make them all the more so by injecting social features. For example, include links to the blogs and Twitter profiles of the management team along with the traditional profiles.

The director of your organization may want to include a YouTube clip of themselves sharing their vision for the org and how it can serve stakeholders. The organization's history page can link to external websites that explain more about its history, and the fact sheet can include quotes and factoids from third-party providers and individual experts. On these pages, you can feature expert influencers who endorse the nonprofit and its cause.

The Contact Us page requires special attention. It must not be a page that lists only telephone numbers, email addresses, and locations. In today's world, users assume that *Contact Us* means that they can talk to an employee right away about a problem. Live chat technology on the Contact Us page is especially useful for companies that sell a consumer product. Always link the Contact Us page to your organization's Twitter feed.

TIP

The Twitter feed matters because the user may want to engage in a conversation with someone in your company directly, then and there. What better place than Twitter, where you can invariably make a statement that you're authentic and transparent?

Another potential solution for a Contact Us page is to enable users to suggest program and service ideas to your nonprofit. Call it crowdsourcing, but users often don't mind giving free advice. The Salesforce Trailblazer Community (`https://success.salesforce.com`) solicits feedback from customers and encourages customers to interact with one another. In recent years, it has received thousands of ideas from customers about every part of its business.

On the site, customers can comment on the ideas submitted and rate them, pushing the best ones to the top. The most successful ideas are implemented in some form or the other. It is a win-win situation already. The customers feel empowered to provide constructive feedback, their voices are heard, and the company benefits from the fabulous ideas.

Another great way to get feedback is to use a tool like GetFeedback (`https://www.getfeedback.com`), which surveys customers to get their opinions. The feedback is easily obtained by sending a thank-you email with a link in it.

Tips and Tricks for Website SMM

Follow these tips and tricks to enhance your website's social media potential. Many of them may seem small, but time and again, we've seen them directly impact how a potential stakeholder views a brand on a website. They are easy to remember as the four A's — Aggregate, Amplify, Align, and Apply.

Aggregate information for your customer's journey

Social media has empowered users to form stronger opinions and express them more broadly. More people are blogging, commenting, and rating than ever before.

According to a 2018 article by Orbit Media (`https://www.orbitmedia.com/blog/blogging-statistics/`), the average blog post is 1,151 words (an increase of 42 percent over the last five years).

These contributors provide a rich base of knowledge for others to use while making decisions. Users who tap into these blogs know more about your brand than you probably do. Rather than try to control the message, serve as the hub and the aggregator of all information regarding the organization. Let your website become the amphitheater for the conversation. Even if the conversation is negative, you win over the long term, as Chevy did with its Tahoe campaign. The user-generated advertisement contest resulted in 629,000 visits to the website, and Tahoe sales took off.

Amplify business stories

So, you can't control the message anymore. Your users would rather listen to each other than to you. But you still have messages that you want to disseminate. You can do that by shaping, influencing, and amplifying stories that play to your organization's strengths.

REMEMBER

Just because your users are more interested in talking to each other doesn't mean that you have no voice at all. Publish your favorite stories as widely as possible and direct users to the individuals or groups already predisposed to helping your organization promote its programs and services.

Align your organization into multiple, authentic voices

Social influence marketing is about providing space for users to influence each other during the purchase process, even when the "purchase" is the decision to make a donation or become a volunteer. As a brand, you want users to positively impact each other. Provide the space for them to influence one another by aligning your entire organization into a network of multiple, authentic voices. Don't leave stakeholder interactions solely to the community management and marketing teams. Empower other internal constituents across the organization to serve as ambassadors, maybe via blogs. They'll talk about your brand in their own voices to their own communities. They may not be totally on message, but they'll be authentic — and they'll have a strong, positive influence. Trust them. See Chapter 2 of this minibook for more information on SMM voices.

Apply share buttons

It's incredibly easy to make sure that you provide sharing tools for content on your website. There's no excuse for not using them. Use tools such as Click to Tweet (`https://clicktotweet.com`) or a WordPress plugin for your site (`https://wordpress.org/plugins/better-click-to-tweet/`).

Index

B

C

D

E

F

G

H

I

J

K

L

O

Q

R

S

W

Y

Z

About the Authors

Dr. Beverly A. Browning, MPA, DBA (Dr. Bev) is a nonprofit capacity-building consultant and revenue-generating visionary who uses thought leadership to work with eligible organizations struggling with revenue stream imbalances. Dr. Bev and her team have helped her clients win more than $750 million in grant awards. She has researched grant funding, grant-making trends, and board-related barriers to nonprofit capacity building for more than 47 years. The founder and director of the Grant Writing Training Foundation and Bev Browning LLC, Dr. Bev is the author of 47 grant-writing publications and has created six courses for Ed2go.com, part of Cengage Learning. Her instructor-led online asynchronous courses include A to Z Grant Writing (1 & 2), Advanced Proposal Writing, Becoming a Grant Writing Consultant, Nonprofit Manager, Winning RFP Responses, and Grant Writing ACT. Dr. Bev is an approved strategic planning facilitator and training provider for CFRE International (AFP), the Grant Professionals Association (GPA), and the Grant Professionals Certification Institute (GPCI).

Sharon Farris, president of Farris Accounting & Consulting Training Services (FACT$), is an accountant and grant consultant. A Certified Grants Manager, Sharon has provided training and consultation to more than 100 public and private organizations in fields such as accounting, business writing, grant writing, and proposal development. She has developed and taught training certification programs for Auburn University Montgomery and Alabama State University in Montgomery, Alabama. Sharon's clients have included the U.S. Department of Education; United Way of Alabama; State of Alabama Council for Developmental Disabilities; Montgomery County Board of Education; Montgomery County Sheriff's Office; Council on Aging; Alabama A&M University; 100 Black Men of Montgomery, Alabama; Faith in Action Outreach Ministries; Grace Christian Academy; and the Montgomery County Historical Society.

Maire Loughran is a certified public accountant and small business owner. Her professional experience includes four years of internal auditing for a publicly traded company in the aerospace industry, two years as an auditor in the not-for-profit sector, and even some experience as a U.S. federal agent! Her public accounting experience includes financial reporting and analysis, audits of private corporations, accounting for e-commerce, and forensic accounting. Maire is a full adjunct professor who teaches graduate accounting classes. She is the author of *Auditing For Dummies* and *Intermediate Accounting For Dummies* and a contributing author to *Accounting All-in-One For Dummies* (Wiley, Inc.).

Alyson Connolly, BFA, MFA, is a voice and public speaking coach and an expert in helping people overcome the anxiety of public presentations. She has built her career consulting with some of the top executives in Canada as well as up-and-coming businesspeople trying to build their brand. She offers her Painless Public Speaking Workshops and Elite Presentation Skills Master Classes to organizations and also coaches individuals one-on-one. She brings to her work over 30 years of experience teaching drama, directing plays and musicals, and performing onstage. She is also a keynote speaker, presenting the story of her life through a difficult childhood to overcoming her fear onstage, as well as speaking about public speaking. Her website is www.alysonconnolly.com.

Shiv Singh is a strategic advisor to Fortune 500 companies and early-stage start-ups. Prior to that, he was a Senior Vice President at Visa Inc., where he was responsible for driving the go-to-market strategy for some of the company's most disruptive products and innovations. Earlier in his career, Shiv spent several years at PepsiCo leading digital marketing globally, and before that was at Razorfish Inc. in Europe and North America. His work has been recognized by leading-edge industry and consumer publications such as *Fortune Magazine*, *Adweek*, and *The Harvard Business Review*. Shiv is a member of the Board of Directors at United Rentals Inc., a Fortune 500 company.

Stephanie Diamond is a thought leader and management marketing professional with years of experience building profits in more than 75 different industries. She has worked with solopreneurs, small business owners, and multibillion-dollar corporations. She is passionate about guiding online companies to successfully generate more revenue and use social media to its full advantage. As a strategic thinker, Stephanie uses all the current visual thinking techniques and brain research to help companies get to the essence of their brand. She continues this work today with her proprietary system to help online business owners discover how social media can generate profits. You can read her blog at www.MarketingMessageBlog.com.

Publisher's Acknowledgments

Executive Editor: Steven Hayes
Project Editor: Lynn Northrup
Compilation Editor: Nicole Sholly
Copy Editor: Lynn Northrup
Technical Editor: Maire Loughran
Production Editor: Mohammed Zafar Ali
Cover Image: © Dragana Gordic/Shutterstock